T0318480

Clermont-de-Lodève,
1633–1789

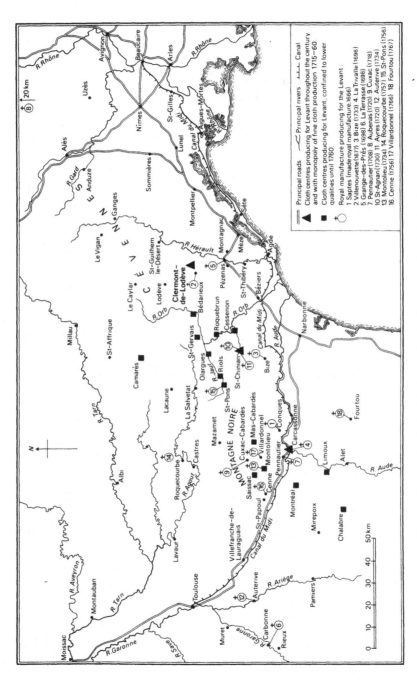

Principal roads ⌒ Principal rivers ⊣⊣ Canal

▲ Cloth centres producing for Levant throughout the century and with monopoly of fine cloth production 1715–60

■ Cloth centres producing for Levant, confined to lower qualities until 1760.

+ ◯ Royal manufacture producing for the Levant:

1 Saptes (made royal manufacture 1666)
2 Villenouvette (1677) 3 Bize (1733) 4 La Trivalle (1696)
5 Villenouvette (1677) 6 La Terrasse (1698)
7 Grange-des-Prés (1698) 8 Aubenas (1720) 9 Cuxac (1718)
7 Pennautier (1708) 8 Aubenas (1720) 9 Cuxac (1718)
10 St-Agnan (1730) 11 Ayres (1720) 12 Auterive (1734)
13 Montolieu (1734) 14 Roquecourbe (1757) 15 St-Pons (1756)
16 Cenne (1756) 17 Villardonnel (1766) 18 Fourtou (1767)

Map 1   Languedoc's cloth industry for the Levant in the eighteenth century

Clermont-de-Lodève
1633–1789

Fluctuations in the prosperity of
a Languedocian
cloth-making town

J. K. J. THOMSON

CAMBRIDGE UNIVERSITY PRESS

Cambridge
London New York New Rochelle
Melbourne Sydney

PUBLISHED BY THE PRESS SYNDICATE OF THE UNIVERSITY OF CAMBRIDGE
The Pitt Building, Trumpington Street, Cambridge, United Kingdom

CAMBRIDGE UNIVERSITY PRESS
The Edinburgh Building, Cambridge CB2 2RU, UK
40 West 20th Street, New York NY 10011–4211, USA
477 Williamstown Road, Port Melbourne, VIC 3207, Australia
Ruiz de Alarcón 13, 28014 Madrid, Spain
Dock House, The Waterfront, Cape Town 8001, South Africa

http://www.cambridge.org

First published 1982
First paperback edition 2003

Library of Congress catalogue card number: 81-12222

A catalogue record for this book is available from the British Library

Thomson, J. K. J.
Clermont-de-Lodève, 1633–1789.
1. Clermont-de-Lodève (France) – Economic conditions – History
I. Title
330.944′84   HC278.C/

ISBN 0 521 23951 6 hardback
ISBN 0 521 54109 3 paperback

Contents

For Magali and Anna

Illustrations

Maps

Tables

Preface

This book is a revised, and substantially enlarged, version of a doctoral thesis which was begun at Reading University in 1970 and completed in 1976.

The research on which it is based was financed between 1970 and 1973 by the Social Science Research Council. Grants towards additional research carried out since 1973 have been provided by the Nuffield Foundation, The Twenty-Seven Foundation of the Institute of Historical Research and the Arts Research Support Fund of the University of Sussex. The carrying out of additional research, and the rewriting of the thesis, were made possible by the grant of two terms of leave from the University of Sussex. The illustrations were generously financed by the Pasold Foundation for Textile History.

I have been assisted by many people during the preparation of this book. In particular I would like to acknowledge the support of Olwen Hufton, who was an inspiring, encouraging and patient supervisor, of Peter Burke, Maurice Hutt and Jordi Nadal, who read the doctoral thesis and offered valuable advice on rewriting, and of Margaret Thompson who, by checking quotations for me and reading through the final manuscript, contributed to eliminating a number of errors. Maurice Hutt, in addition to the specific act of co-operation just mentioned, has helped me in numerous indirect ways. His professionalism, dedication, enthusiasm for history and exceptional knowledge and understanding of the French past have been a constant source of inspiration to me. While I have had little direct contact with French historians I am greatly indebted (as the contents of this book will reveal) to the historical writings of many and in particular to those of E. Appolis, historian of the Lodévois, E. Le Roy Ladurie, historian of Languedoc, F. Braudel, historian of the Mediterranean and of the 'longue durée', P. Deyon, the authority on textile production in 'pre-industrial' France and C. Carrière, historian of Marseilles's commerce. The last of these kindly informed and advised me about the Fonds Roux, held in the Chamber of Commerce of Marseilles.

Jean Maistre, last director of Villeneuvette, kindly allowed me access to his private archives within the former royal manufacture of Villenouvette.[1] Numerous archivists and librarians have been helpful and I would like, in particular, to express my gratitude to Danielle Neirinck, now directeur des archives of the Aude, to J. C. Gigot, former conservateur-en-chef of the archives of the Hérault, and to the rest of the staff of the Archives Départementales of the Hérault for their kind co-operation since I began working there in the Spring of 1971.

Parts of this book have been read as research papers at the following seminars: Olwen Hufton's at Reading, Richard Cobb's at Oxford, Douglas Johnson's at the Institute of Historical Research and the Work in Progress Seminar at Sussex. I am grateful to both the convenors of, and the participants in, these seminars for giving me opportunities for expressing my ideas and providing many constructive criticisms and comments.

Patricia Sinclair has typed various versions of this book for me with great efficiency and good humour. I am most grateful to her. Cambridge University Press has been most co-operative throughout the publishing process and I would like to acknowledge in particular the interest shown, and assistance provided, by Patricia Williams, William Davies and Frances Brown, as well as the encouragement and advice provided by two conscientious, anonymous referees who read the thesis before it was revised.

Most of this book was written under the roof of my parents-in-law, Pilar and Joan Teixidor, and their great hospitality I hereby gratefully acknowledge.

J. K. J. THOMSON,
University of Sussex
Spring 1981

---

1. On variations in spelling of Villenouvette see p. 3, n 7.

Abbreviations used in the notes

ACC	Archives Communales de Clermont
ACCM	Archives de la Chambre de Commerce de Marseille
ADA	Archives Départementales de l'Aude
ADH	Archives Départementales de l'Hérault
ADR	Archives Départementales du Rhône
A. du M.	*Annales du Midi*
Annales	*Annales, Economies, Sociétés, Civilisations*
AN	Archives Nationales
BM	Bibliothèque Municipale
BN	Bibliothèque Nationale
Ec.H.R.	*Economic History Review*
J.E.H.	*Journal of Economic History*
P. & P.	*Past and Present*
R.H.E.S.	*Revue d'Histoire Economique et Sociale*

I

Introduction

This book is largely concerned with the varying fortunes of a medium-sized cloth-making town of Lower Languedoc, Clermont-de-Lodève (renamed Clermont-l'Hérault in 1789) in the seventeenth and eighteenth centuries.[1]

The choice both of subject and of period requires explanation. The decision to work in the field of French economic history was a consequence of studying British economic history as an undergraduate. It was a reading of François Crouzet's celebrated comparative article on English and French economic experiences in the eighteenth century which not only helped me in disentangling the complex question of the causes of Britain's early Industrial Revolution, but also fired my interest in the similar but subtly distinct economic experiences of France in this period.[2] The idea of carrying out research in French economic history was all the more exciting a prospect in that it was evident that the source material was immensely abundant (the regulative system established by Colbert may have made the French economy inflexible but it had also ensured that much of economic significance that had gone unrecorded in Britain was abundantly documented in France) and also in that French economic history (in contrast to British) was little studied – a discontinuity, or what was believed to be a discontinuity, of another type had clearly attracted far more interest than the industrialization process.

Having decided to concentrate on French economic history my next requirement was a well-documented, yet relatively unstudied region or industry. I was fortunate in that both were suggested to me by my supervisor, Olwen Hufton. The Languedocian cloth industry, she

---

1. Also known as 'Clermont-en-Lodévois'. The change in title was to distinguish it from its neighbour, and rival, Lodève. (E. Appolis, *Un pays languedocien au milieu du dix-huitième siècle: le diocèse civil de Lodève*, p. 148.)
2. 'Angleterre et France au XVIIIe siècle: essai d'analyse comparée de deux croissances économiques', *Annales* 21 (1966), 254–91. Translated in R. M. Hartwell (ed.), *Causes of the Industrial Revolution*, pp. 139–74.

informed me, had received little attention from historians since the
publication in 1911 of Léon Dutil's regional study, *L'état économique du
Languedoc à la fin de l'Ancien-Régime*, and yet it had been shown by
recent quantitative work to have been as large and as important an
industry as any in France at the beginning of the eighteenth century.[3] A
reading of Dutil soon convinced me that Languedoc's vast textile industry was, indeed, a good potential subject and particularly interesting, it
appeared, were the experiences of the sector of the industry which had
produced for the Levant market in competition with England's West
Country industry. Languedoc's 'Levant industry' had expanded most
rapidly and brilliantly in the first half of the eighteenth century and then
experienced a painful and protracted decline from the mid 1750s. Both
success and failure had excited a large amount of contemporary comment
and the subject appeared particularly promising in that the discrepancy
between the performance in the two halves of the century was, to all
appearances, representative: a similar pattern had been observed in many
other industrial centres in France and historians (referring to the decline)
had gone so far as to write of a generalized crisis of 'les industries du
passé' in the second half of the eighteenth century.[4]

My choice of region and industry was thus made. A study of
Languedoc's Levant industry seemed to provide the prospect of throwing light on some of the questions in which I was interested. Why then
the narrowing down of the topic to the study of a single cloth-making
town, Clermont-de-Lodève? It might have been thought that my project
was already sufficiently specialized, all the more so in that administrative
restrictions had confined production for the Levant to only three towns,
Carcassonne, Clermont and St-Chinian, for much of the eighteenth
century. But the administrative intervention had had another consequence too: its extent had been such that the amount of documentation
on just these three towns was quite vast and far too large for me to be able
to undertake the detailed study which I planned in the time at my
disposal. The solution was to work on just one of the towns and of the
three it was Carcassonne which was the obvious choice for it had been the
capital of the province's industry in the seventeenth and eighteenth
centuries and as important an industrial centre as any in France at the

3. T. J. Markovitch, 'L'industrie lainière à la fin du règne de Louis XIV et sous la
   Régence', *Cahiers de l'Institut de Science Economique Appliquée* 2 (1968), 1629–30, and
   Histoire des industries françaises, I, *Les industries lainières de Colbert à la Révolution*,
   pp. 205–310; L. Fontvieille, 'Les premières enquêtes industrielles de la France: 1692 et
   1703', *Cahiers de l'Institut de Science Economique Appliquée* 3 (1969), 1109–34, 1270–3.
4. Dutil, *Etat économique*, pp. 279–527; this expression used in F. Braudel and C. E.
   Labrousse (eds), *Histoire économique et sociale de la France*, II, 518–19. Crouzet, likewise,
   refers to a general crisis of the 'vieilles industries textiles' ('Angleterre', p. 269).

end of the reign of Louis XIV.[5] Unfortunately I found that I had been anticipated. Shortly after my arrival in the archives of the old province of Languedoc I was informed that someone else had been at work for many years on a study of Carcassonne's industry.[6] My choice was thus restricted to the industries of either Clermont or St-Chinian. But this concentration could only be justified if the experiences of one of the towns were representative of those of the industry as a whole. The pattern of Clermont's development, most fortunately, seemed to correspond to this requirement – the timing of both the expansion and the decline of its cloth industry conformed to that of the industry as a whole. Its case, therefore, was apparently typical and the choice held an additional advantage – a royal manufacture, Villenouvette,[7] had been founded near the town at a very early stage, 1674, and thus I would be provided with the opportunity of examining the relationship between this privileged concern and the town's industry.

The chronological boundaries of my study emerged more slowly. My primary interest was in the period of crisis and decline in Languedoc's Levant industry which had been much commented on by historians but not satisfactorily explained. Not only did this decadence hold clear significance for the economic decline of the province but an analysis of it might also, it seemed to me, in view of its representativeness, provide some insights into the reasons for the relative economic failure of France in the second half of the century.

A vast and controversial documentation held largely in the intendancy archives at Montpellier soon convinced me that I had indeed focussed on a period which was seen by contemporaries as one both of crisis and of growing industrial inferiority with respect to England.[8] It was clear, too, from nostalgic references to the stability and prosperity enjoyed by the province's industry for the Levant before the 1750s, that the crisis was of recent origin. Explanations for the difficulties were provided too, and in abundance. Unfortunately these were contradictory. Some argued that France's failure was to be explained by her rigid regulative system and

---

5. Markovitch, *Les industries lainières*, p. 271; ADH C2200, Report of Inspector Cauvière, 1694: 'la fabrique du Royaume la plus considérable par le grand nombre de draps quil s'y fait'.
6. One M. Rufas who has since abandoned his project.
7. Another change of name. It was known as Villeneuvette after 1789 (Appolis, *Lodève*, p. 148).
8. The site of Languedoc's intendancy was Montpellier. The intendant had considerable, but not total, authority in economic matters. Final authority lay with the controller-general and Conseil du Commerce in Paris. On economic institutions in Ancien Régime France see A. des Cilleuls, *Histoire et régime de la grande industrie en France aux XVIIe et XVIIIe siècles*, pp. 126–57, and E. Levasseur, *Histoire des classes ouvrières et de l'industrie en France avant 1789*, II, 474–5.

restrictive guilds and that her salvation would come from an adoption of *laissez-faire* principles as applied in England. (Whatever the virtues of this diagnosis it provided evidence that there existed a generalized feeling that England was already more advanced by this period as well as illustrating that a conception existed as to the most suitable economic system for industrial progress.) But for others it was precisely the relaxation in the regulative system since the 1750s, when the physiocratic influence of Vincent de Gournay and others in the Bureau de Commerce had begun to affect policy decisions, which explained French difficulties. The change in 'regime' had been too rapid, it was argued, and some added that the French temperament was not suited for a system of *laissez-faire*. (And again, whatever merit there was in this explanation, it struck me as significant that the French themselves believed in this period that their national characteristics were sufficiently distinct from those of the English to warrant a different administrative framework for economic life.)

So evidence of crisis there was in plenty, and opinions about the cause of the crisis were fully documented too, but the two major explanations were in direct contradiction to each other and it was difficult to establish which of the two, if either, was correct. I had an additional cause for concern and that was that modern French economic historians tended to regard the whole question of the consequences of administrative intervention in French industry as a matter of only marginal significance, maintaining that French economic development was conditioned by more substantial factors, largely related to demand which, in turn, was governed by a combination of the agricultural and demographic situation.[9] If this viewpoint was correct were not these contradictory analyses of the crisis irrelevant as well as confusing and hence of as little value to historians as they appear to have been to contemporary administrative agents who, to little avail, had desperately fluctuated between pro- and anti-regulative policies between the 1750s and 1789? Yet the argument that the nature of the administrative and guild system had *something* to do with the crisis seemed to have truth in it. It was clear that entrepreneurial effort in those towns which had had restrictive guilds and strict regulations had tended in the second half of the eighteenth century to be orientated towards eluding regulations rather than towards more conventional entrepreneurial goals, and it was clear, too, that those towns

---

9. E.g. Crouzet, 'Angleterre', pp. 278–9 and also in his 'Western Europe and Great Britain: "catching up" in the first half of the nineteenth century' in A. J. Youngson (ed.), *Economic Development in the Long Run*, pp. 98–125. But above all the approach is that of C. E. Labrousse, *Esquisse du mouvement des prix et des revenus en France au XVIIIe siècle.* See for instance vol. II, 546–54.

which had escaped guilds and regulations had performed more success-fully in the second half of the century – the depression had not been universal and, of course, cotton, an industry which had appeared after the reaction against regulations, had shown particular dynamism. Nor was the alternative, demand argument totally convincing. There was a slowing down in the expansion of the French Levant trade after the mid-century, certainly, and there was also new competition for Languedocian cloth as an export product – re-exports from the New World and bullion were in demand in Levantine markets – but there was certainly no complete collapse in the demand for cloth, and indeed not only were foreign competitors to Languedoc expanding their cloth exports in the second half of the century but even within Languedoc those towns which had been barred from production until the process of economic liberali-zation allowed them to produce in the 1750s apparently fared far better than the three original centres of the industry, Carcassonne, Clermont and St-Chinian. Bédarieux was one example of a town whose industry developed rapidly in the second half of the century when Clermont's industry was in decline. Besides there were no legal barriers after the 1750s to prevent Clermont's clothiers developing new cloths and pro-ducing for other markets than the Levant (there had been before then). Lucrative alternative markets certainly did exist, and Castres and Mazamet, cloth-making neighbours of Clermont like Bédarieux, were exploiting some of them with great success. A decline in demand from the Levant was therefore not, it seemed to me, a sufficient explanation for the *prolonged* crisis at Clermont, even though it might have contributed to short-term problems whilst the town adapted to producing for elsewhere.[10]

In order to gain historical perspective on these problems I decided to push my research further back. An obvious point at which to begin was the 1670s, the decade in which the royal manufacture of Villenouvette was founded. Now I had assumed, as other historians had assumed, that there was some link between Languedoc's royal manufactures and the province's great industrial success in the first half of the century but I felt that the link was probably of only minor significance. The current orthodoxy amongst historians about Colbertian intervention seemed to be that it was largely ineffective, if not actually counter-productive, and whilst I was involved in my research Charles Carrière published an article about Languedoc's royal manufactures which seemed to show rather conclusively that their role in the province's industrial expansion

---

10. For fuller information on the debate about the decline of Languedoc's Levant industry see chapter eleven.

had been of only marginal importance.[11] So I was not expecting to make
any major discoveries in investigating Villenouvette's role. But I felt that
the history of this superb manufacture, which was held quite justly to be
the most beautiful of the province, and which closed down only in 1954
(after virtually 280 years of continual production), was of interest in
itself, whether its development was linked to Clermont's or not.[12]

Villenouvette's early foundation, before the age of the large inspectorate, had had the consequence that for the first fifty years of its existence
official documentation about its activities was sparse. In the absence of
inspectors' reports I was forced to rely on notarial archives. These for
Clermont were fortunately almost complete for the second half of the
seventeenth century. I began by examining notaries' registers for the
1670s. I had no clear idea of what exactly I would find but I immediately
realized that I was using an extraordinarily complete and exciting source
and it was not long before I found abundant and significant material
relating not only to the royal manufacture but also to Clermont's cloth
industry. The material which I found suggested that Villenouvette's
contribution to the town's industry, contrary to the arguments of
Carrière and others, had been of overwhelming importance. The information which I found about Clermont's cloth industry surprised me yet
more. From both my archival work on the post-1750 period and the
secondary reading which I had done, I had become convinced that
Clermont's industry had known no other structure than that of the large-
scale putting-out system, presided over by rich clothiers or 'marchands-
fabricants'. The notarial registers of the late seventeenth century, however, revealed to me a quite different sort of structure in which the scale of
production was very small, the product of low quality and the clothiers
(who were known as 'marchands-facturiers' or simply as 'facturiers') men
of low status and small resources whose activities were largely of a manual
kind, in sharp contrast to those of the marchands-fabricants of the mid-
eighteenth century which had been above all managerial and commercial.
It thus became clear to me that the industry had experienced significant

11. 'La draperie languedocienne dans la seconde moitié du XVIIe siècle: contribution à
    l'étude de la conjoncture levantine' in *Conjoncture économique, structures sociales:
    hommage à Ernest Labrousse*, pp. 157–72.
12. Described as 'la plus belle de toutes les manufactures de Languedoc' in a 'Mémoire sur
    le commerce du Levant' (c. 1756) held in AN F12 645. On Villenouvette see below
    chapters five to seven and also C. Alberge, 'Villeneuvette: une manufacture en Bas-
    Languedoc', *Etudes sur Pézenas et sa Région* (1970), 17–42, and Appolis, *Lodève*,
    pp. 514–21. On the manufacture in the nineteenth century see H. Baudrillart, *Les
    populations agricoles de la France*, pp. 267–9, A. Audiganne, *Les populations ouvrières et
    les industries de la France: études comparatives*, II, 223–5, and L. Reybaud, *La laine,
    nouvelle série des études sur le régime des manufactures*, pp. 125–31.

structural change between the 1670s and the second half of the eighteenth century and that I had found the roots of the later industry.

Originally I had intended to follow up just a few references to notarial acts but the significance of these two discoveries encouraged me to carry out a thorough survey of all notarial registers for the early years of the town's industrial growth (until about 1710 they provided the only substantial source). I felt that by doing this I would be not only contributing to the solution of questions of local interest but also throwing light on some aspects of France's economic experiences in this period about which (my reading suggested) there existed, still, some uncertainty: the role of royal manufactures and Colbertian policy in France's economic recovery, the timing of the turning-point in French economic fortunes, the origins of emerging entrepreneurial groups, of their labour forces, and of the new industrial techniques of which they made use, the explanation for the general improvement in business techniques and the nature of the relationship between the industrial growth and the recurrent agrarian crises.[13]

But was all this new evidence of relevance to the crisis which it had been my original intention to explain? Elementary logic suggested that the identification of some of the factors which had led to a surprisingly complete Languedocian success against Dutch and English competition in the first half of the century might contribute to diagnosing those competitive qualities which were evidently in default after the 1750s when the industry was in decline. What were these factors? In traditional explanations the success was attributed to three major advantages – official support in the form of bounties on production, a lower wage level, and the locational advantages which Languedoc enjoyed from its closeness both to the Levant market and to Spain, the source of the high-quality, short-staple wools which were used by all three major producers for the Levant.[14] There seemed to me to be grounds for doubting the importance attributed to these advantages, however. The bounties paid on cloth production were in fact small and not sufficient to give a decisive advantage to Languedocian producers. Besides, normal clothiers (in contrast to privileged manufacturing concerns) had only been awarded bounties *after* their cloth's reputation in the Levant had been established. As for the question of wages, these were indeed, local evidence showed, lower than in England in the first half of the eighteenth century but so were they in the second half, and indeed Labrousse's work showed that they were lower in real terms in the second half of the century than in the

13. On this important period see chapter seven and also Braudel and Labrousse, *Histoire économique*, II, 349–50, 359, 363–5, 698.
14. For the debate about the success in the Levant see chapter seven.

first. If low wages had been the decisive variable then how could the decline of the industry be explained if its wage bill was effectively declining in real terms during the century?[15] With respect to the locational advantage too there was obviously continuity between the first and second half of the century for there had been no change in the profitability of different sorts of transport such as that which, it has been argued, contributed originally to the displacement of the Venetians in Levantine markets by the Atlantic powers.[16] Clearly official encouragement in the form of bounties and instruction in new techniques, the lower wages and the geographical advantages would have contributed to success, but even in conjunction these three factors' importance did not strike me as being overwhelming, and offsetting them, in part at least, would have been various disadvantages of a sort encountered by all developing industries – capital shortage, a lack of established mercantile links with the Levant and, hence, on occasions, long delays in obtaining returns on cloth produced, and technical problems involved in achieving a standard of production to rival that of the English and Dutch. In addition, as many studies have shown, the new French trade for the Levant (and all French industrial and commercial activity in the period 1690–1730) was subject to intense fluctuations because of the disturbances in the domestic economy occasioned by harvest failure, warfare, demographic crisis and monetary disorder. Success in production for the new market was by no means assured as numerous bankruptcies amongst clothiers and merchants showed and, indeed, one of the reasons (as will be shown) for the continued administrative tutelage of this growing industry was concern that these repeated crises would lead to its disappearance before it was fully established.

None of the traditional explanations seemed wholly convincing, then. One possibility, however, had never been proposed. This was that Languedocian entrepreneurship, or at least the entrepreneurship of the clothiers in these three Languedocian towns, might have been of exceptional quality. The idea, of course, was in total opposition to a long historical tradition which regarded *poor* entrepreneurship as precisely an invariable characteristic of French industrial activity. Yet my research in the notarial archives had enabled me to identify and to follow the fortunes of a small group of Clermontais clothiers who, despite adverse conditions, had succeeded in greatly expanding the scale of their enterprises and improving the quality of their production during this period. They

15. Labrousse, *Esquisse*, II, 319.
16. F. Braudel, *The Mediterranean and the Mediterranean World in the Age of Philip II*, I, 636–7.

showed definite dynamism and possessed, it seemed to me, exceptional entrepreneurial qualities. These qualities, briefly, consisted in wholesale application to their trade; a mastery of all processes of production (even though, and this was increasingly the case, they employed other workers to carry out some processes for them); the ability to achieve extremely low costs as a consequence of a most economic life-style and the use of their families' as well as their own labour in the production process; the enjoyment of good relationships with their labour force in whose tasks they shared and to whom, in many cases, they were related; and, finally, vast ambition – a great commitment on their own, and their families' parts, to taking advantage of the prospects offered by production for the Levant market to increase their fortunes and statuses.

Now these qualities were clearly not a consequence of either French or Languedocian character traits. They seemed basically to be what might be termed 'artisanal' qualities, typical of small-scale producers and of a type to be found as frequently among peasants as craftsmen. But if these qualities were so conventional, why their importance to the industry which I was studying between 1690 and 1730? The answer is that conditions in Clermont during these years were exceptional. Normally the effects of these relatively universal qualities were restricted by the facts of limited market opportunities and primitive techniques. These restrictions for a number of reasons (and primarily the foundation of Villenouvette and the establishment of contact with the Levant market) had ceased to exist in Clermont during these years. It seemed, then, that Languedoc's clothiers, and Languedoc's cloth industry for the Levant, were beginning a process, a pattern of development, which must have been very similar to that experienced by any small-scale industry permitted by sudden market developments to specialize, improve quality and expand production. All such industries (and this was apparent from other studies) experienced stages of great dynamism during their growth periods.[17] High rates of social mobility ensured, too, that the clothiers' enthusiasm was shared by much of their labour force. A 'young' industry, according to this argument, had considerable advantages over an old one, and above all an 'entrepreneurial' advantage. 'It being granted then, that abundance of Work is to be done, the next thing which I think to be likewise undeniable is, that the more chearfully it is done the better, as well for those that perform it as for the rest of the Society', wrote Bernard Mandeville at the end of his general assessment of the nature of com-

17. E.g. P. Deyon, *Etude sur la société urbaine au XVIIe siècle: Amiens capitale provinciale*, pp. 163–79; E. Coornaert, *Un centre industriel d'autrefois: la draperie sayetterie d'Hondschoote, XIVe–XVIIe siècles*, pp. viii, 375–9, and 'Une capitale de la laine: Leyde', *Annales* 1 (1946), 169–77.

petition in cloth production between nations.[18] Had not the English and
Dutch industries, in their 'youths', successfully supplanted a rigid,
socially divided and lethargic Venetian industry? And there was much
evidence to show that England's West Country industry in this period of
Languedocian dynamism was beginning to suffer from the sorts of problems which characterized 'old industries' – it was plagued by labour
problems and suffering from inefficiency because of the exclusiveness of
'gentlemen-clothiers'. Contemporaries indeed (and notably Josiah
Tucker) tended to attribute this industry's failure in the face of the rise of
Yorkshire's industry to precisely these sorts of factors.[19]

   If this argument was acceptable then the decline at Clermont,
Carcassonne and St-Chinian in the second half of the century was easily
explained. By then these towns had 'old' industries, their entrepreneurs
lacked vitality, their labour forces (now with few prospects of rising
socially because of the acquired positions of the richer clothiers) were
dispirited and estranged. The more favourable performance at Bédarieux
and elsewhere would be explicable in similar terms. These towns, whose
industries had stagnated in the first half of the century, were experiencing
after 1750 the sort of vitality which had characterized Clermont's industry early in the century. There was ample architectural evidence at
Clermont of a change in the life-style of Clermont's clothiers as the
eighteenth century proceeded. Such a changed life-style, it seemed likely,
was incompatible with the sort of control over, and participation in, the
production process which had been the main element in the success of
their artisanal predecessors. To buttress this theory too there were many
contemporary comments on the growing slackness of clothiers in those
Languedocian towns which had prospered during the first half of the
century.

   It seemed to me, then, that I had discovered a cyclical pattern which
not only provided insights into the reasons for the rise and decline of
Languedoc's industry but also was of relevance to the fluctuating fortunes of all great pre-industrial textile centres – a key to the explanation
of the frequently remarked 'fragilité des villes de laine'.[20]

   But the explanation bore little relation to the ways in which con-

---

18. *The Fable of the Bees*, p. 314.
19. On the Dutch and English success: R. T. Rapp, 'The unmaking of the Mediterranean
    trade hegemony: international trade rivalry and the commercial revolution', *J.E.H.* 35
    (1975), 499–525; on the West Country's decline: R. G. Wilson, 'The supremacy of the
    Yorkshire cloth industry in the eighteenth century' in N. B. Harte and K. G. Ponting
    (eds), *Textile History and Economic History*, pp. 235–46, and J. Tucker, *Instructions for
    Travellers*, pp. 24–5.
20. Remark of J. Heers, cited by M. Aymard, 'Production, commerce et consommation des
    draps de laine du XIIe au XVIIe siècle', *Revue Historique* 499 (1971), 6.

temporaries interpreted the crisis. Were questions of regulation and guild restrictions irrelevant, then? That the entrepreneurial decadence should not have been as apparent to contemporaries as it was to me was not surprising. Even the ultimate stage in the cycle which I was able to trace, the retirement of entrepreneurs and the use of years of accumulated industrial profits for the purchase of land, rents or offices, was not apparent from a simple scrutiny of lists of producers: poorer relations, with the same family names as those retiring, continued to produce cloth, giving a false impression of continuity. And memories were short. Few remembered the sorts of entrepreneurial qualities which had characterized the industry's founders.

But contemporaries, I soon found, were not totally wrong in sensing some link between regulation, guilds and the extent and abruptness of the crisis. The 'artisanal' entrepreneurial qualities which Clermont's clothiers possessed at the beginning of the eighteenth century did not remain untainted for long. This was in part a consequence of the working out of that cyclical process just described, but it was due too to contact with those involved in the administration of industry. Soon clothiers realized that an unprecedented public interest was being taken in activities to which they, initially, had attached no more than a personal significance. For them the industry which they were creating was purely and simply a means of amassing wealth and rising socially. But administrators did not think of it in these terms at all. The new industry was important to them in that it would strengthen France economically, by ensuring that manufactured goods rather than specie were exported to the Levant in order to finance necessary return products. A secondary and quite significant virtue of the trade (and again one of only marginal interest to the clothier) was that the rising industrial production was labour-intensive and thus contributed to solving the problem of rural underemployment, improving the tax-paying ability of the local population and decreasing the danger of social unrest.

Had the expansion in the Levant industry proceeded evenly, the disparity between clothiers' and administrators' aims would not have had consequences. As it was, of course, *all* 'pre-industrial' industries were subject to severe fluctuations, and one producing for the Levant more so than most because of the highly speculative nature of the trade, whose prosperity depended on favourable market conditions in two different civilizations. In years both of crisis and of rapid expansion in the trade this disparity between clothiers' and administrators' aims revealed itself. In the former, the clothiers' reaction was to safeguard their investments by reducing or ceasing production. Administrators thus found the achievement of both their aims jeopardized. In the latter, there was a virtually inevitable tendency, in an industry in which the entry costs in terms of fixed capital investment were low, for over-production to occur. This was disquieting to administrators because a rapid expansion in production in a labour-intensive industry, functioning in a type of economy characterized by an inelastic labour supply, could only be achieved at the expense of quality, by decreasing the labour input into each piece of cloth. Such deterioration of quality, administrators believed, threatened the industry's stability. Indeed, in their eyes, the tendency for quality to decline in years of expansion was the fundamental cause for the inevitable eventual decline in demand which followed any boom.

So the administrators' ideal was a stable industry and a production of consistent quality. Now the achievement of such an ideal, should it be practicable, could be of interest to established clothiers too: it would tend to cause prices to remain steady and high and would ensure a regular and certain income from cloth-making, rather than the fluctuating profits to which a speculative trade gave rise; it would ease entrepreneurial tasks, particularly in respect of control of the labour force, and the anticipation of market trends; and in so far as such an ideal inevitably would involve some control over entry into the trade, it would allow them to establish a form of oligopoly. Thus gradually clothiers became aware that they could use the unsolicited administrative interest in their industrial activities to their own ends. This development in itself had the consequence that a part of clothiers' attentions, hitherto so fully focussed on their cloth-making, was shifted to the manipulation of officials: they began to lobby for those types of control on production which, in administrative eyes, would serve to stabilize and guarantee the fortune of the industry and which, they knew, would further their own economic interests. Their requests were in many cases granted, the 'stability ideal' was gradually realized and, as a consequence, an economic environment was created in which their original entrepreneurial skills became less necessary whilst skills of a new kind, the diplomatic qualities necessary for successful negotiation with officials, became increasingly useful.

It seemed to me, therefore, that the intensification of regulation, the enlargement of the inspectoral system and the increasing restrictiveness of guilds (all developments connected with the desire to achieve stability) accelerated the process by which the entrepreneurial qualities apparent at the beginning of the century were eroded. The process would have occurred anyway as it was inherent in the cyclical nature of the fortunes of all important industrial centres before the Industrial Revolution, but administrative intervention intensified and accelerated this cyclical process. And it was not only entrepreneurial qualities that were eroded.

Social mobility within the industry was decreased and the right to produce became the virtual property of those clothiers (and their descendants) who had founded the industry. The growing industry thus became totally dependent on the varying and (according to the cyclical theory) declining entrepreneurial skills of the succeeding generations of these families.

The crisis, of course, had been sudden and prolonged. The nature of the pure cyclical theory might have led one to expect a gradual decline in competitiveness and prosperity. Here again the reinforcing and catalyzing role of administrative intervention can be seen, for it was the suddenness of the reversal in economic policy in the 1750s which seemed to explain both the brusqueness and the extent of the crisis. The reform was undertaken in good faith. Indeed the reformers, and above all Vincent de Gournay, as we shall show, demonstrated most exceptional perception in their analysis of the ills to which excessive regulation and guild restrictions had given rise. But the consequences of reform were disastrous, for the sudden liberalization encouraged a flood of would-be clothiers with no cloth-making experience (they had long been prevented from production by guild restrictions) to start producing and as a consequence there was a massive increase in production of poor-quality cloth. And the effects of the liberalization on established clothiers was yet more damaging to the industry: the step to the taking of which these clothiers' social ambitions had long prompted them, and which their large fortunes now made possible, suddenly became economically desirable too as the industry threatened to become inundated with excess production – they retired from production, and retired *en bloc*.

Thus a natural, cyclical process of rise and decline was much intensified by administrative intervention. The fact that neither 'liberty' nor revived regulation solved Clermont's problems after the mid-1750s was not a sign that they had not contributed to the problems but, on the contrary, a consequence of their having so exacerbated and intensified the crisis that there was no solution, particularly when a near neighbour such as Bédarieux, uncorrupted by administrative intervention, and with a group of entrepreneurs which had qualities similar to Clermont's at the beginning of the century, was now allowed to compete for the first time.

So that was my thesis. And I was convinced that the cyclical pattern, the functioning of which I had observed closely at Clermont, and seen signs of in other Languedocian cloth centres such as St-Chinian, Carcassonne, Lodève, Bédarieux and Mazamet, had relevance to the interpretation both of French economic history and also of the history of the pre-industrial economy of Europe in general, in that, as has often been observed, the pre-industrial economy functioned in a remarkably constant and universal manner.

Some of the relevance of Clermont's early experiences to major issues in French economic history I have already mentioned. In addition, for local Languedocian history an understanding of the industrial collapse at Clermont seems of relevance to the complex and much-discussed question of the province's de-industrialization.[21] With respect to French economic history as a whole in the period 1660–1789 there seem to be several aspects of Clermont's experiences which are of general interest. It strikes me as being significant that the rhythm of the town's industrial rise and decline follows closely that of other French industrial centres. Economic historians often emphasize the predominance of the regional, and the local, in economic life in the pre-industrial period but, though this might hold for isolated areas, there seems to have been an exceptional synchronization in the commerical movement of all centres linked to the international economy. My detailed study of Clermont may, therefore, serve as a case-study of some relevance to the leading sectors of the French economy in the first half of the eighteenth century. (It is clearly of less relevance to growth sectors in the second half of the century but does provide an example of that frequently noted crisis among what were coming to be, but were not previously, 'industries du passé'.) To illustrate the representativeness of the growth pattern of Clermont's industry we can take the example of the timing of the turning-point at the end of the seventeenth century, in the late 1680s and 1690s – this represents an exact coincidence with the turning-point in the destinies of the industries of Amiens and other Norman textile centres. Likewise the crisis in the mid-1750s coincides exactly with that observed at Elbeuf.[22]

So, I hope that the study of growth at Clermont will serve as a microcosm for that of growth in the French economy as a whole in the eighteenth century. And I feel that a particularly important aspect of French development which is in need of illustration, and which Clermont's development illustrates most clearly, is that of the interaction of administrative intervention with economic growth. It was matters such as these which were a major concern of French historians in the nineteenth and early twentieth centuries, but in recent years French economic historians have regarded this preoccupation as having been excessive and have focussed their attentions almost entirely on the excep-

21. On this see chapter twelve.
22. Deyon, *Amiens*, pp. 69, 171–8 and 'La production manufacturière en France au xviie siècle et ses problèmes', *XVIIe Siècle* 70–1 (1966), 55–6; on Elbeuf see J. Kaplow, *Elbeuf during the Revolutionary Period: History and Social Structure*, pp. 44–5; Labrousse, *Esquisse*, II, 549–50.

tionally full quantitative evidence about prices, population and production which has become available as a consequence of a large research effort in the archives. This priority given to the quantitative, and to demand factors, is well illustrated by the devotion of the first sections of the new *Histoire économique et sociale de la France* to agriculture and demography, and in addition the editors of this work proclaim their break with the traditional approach of Levasseur on the first page of their preface.[23] It is not that I feel that the administrative side of French economic development is more important or fundamental than the quantitative. On the contrary I agree (and who could fail to agree?) that administrative intervention, to quote a critic of the traditional approach, was quite incapable of occasioning 'mouvements profonds' in the economy.[24] I do feel, however, that the way in which 'mouvements profonds' interacted with industrial structures which were, at least in part, shaped by administrative intervention, is of significance, and has been a neglected issue. I hope that the evidence which I shall present, about the way Clermont's development, stimulated though it originally was largely by demand factors, was greatly influenced by administrative interaction with this demand, will serve to redress the balance. It is the quality of quantitative evidence for eighteenth-century France which has made the demand approach so effective. As one historian has emphasized, figures for industrial production in France in the first half of the eighteenth century are more complete not only than those for England in this period, but also than those available for France in the nineteenth century. But what this historian and others (unlike Heckscher) have neglected is that the quality of these figures, which gives plausibility to their quantitative approach, is also an excellent illustration of the extent of administrative intervention in the French economy.[25]

Another matter on which the nature of Clermont's development should throw light is that of the role of 'social factors' in influencing French economic performance in the eighteenth and nineteenth centuries. By 'social factors' are generally meant the attitudes and competitiveness of entrepreneurs, and for the eighteenth century and earlier the most marked (damaging) characteristic of French entrepreneurship, it is argued, was the tendency to abandon industrial production for more honourable pursuits once a fortune had been acquired.[26] Such a move

---

23. Braudel and Labrousse, *Histoire économique*, II, vi–vii.
24. C. Carrière in E. Baratier (ed.), *Histoire de Marseille*, p. 210 and, in conjunction with P. Léon, in Braudel and Labrousse, *Histoire économique*, II, 189.
25. Markovitch, *Les industries lainières*, pp. 5–7; E. F. Heckscher, *Mercantilism*, I, 153–73.
26. See Deyon, 'La production manufacturière', p. 63, and R. B. Grassby, 'Social status and commercial enterprise under Louis XIV', *Ec.H.R.* 13 (1960–1), 19–38.

out of industry was made easier, as J. R. Hicks has shown, because of the lack of fixed capital investment in 'pre-industrial' industrial activity and hence the ease with which disinvestment could take place.[27] Now there are various difficulties in linking this supposed repeated process of disinvestment to France's economic failure. Hicks's book is about preindustrial economies in general, and not just the French economy, and, indeed, the phenomenon of disinvestment and abandonment of industrial production was a universal one in the pre-industrial economy. The similarity of the behaviour of English and French entrepreneurs in this connection is emphasized by Crouzet.[28] Another problem is that the fact of the low status of, and movement away from, industry is treated as though it were a permanent characteristic of all French industrial centres *at all times*. But this could not have been the case. It could only have been a characteristic of industrial centres with rich clothiers, near the end of their development cycles. Thus, although all industrial centres producing for the market were at some stage of their growth cycles, near the final stage, ripe for disinvestment, at any particular moment only a minority would be. So, in other words, the explanation of France's economic retardation in terms of the low status given to business activity, and the tendency to early retirement, is not an adequate one. The phenomenon was a universal rather than a French one and at any time it could have affected only a certain number of cloth-making centres. It is, though, highly likely in view of the synchronization apparent in the growth patterns of those French industrial centres linked to the international market that at different stages of French economic growth there were far fewer, or far more, than the average quantity of industrial centres at the mature stage of their developmental cycles. But, again, such a 'synchronization' of economic growth was common to all advanced areas of the European economy and cannot, thus, be regarded as a particularly French characteristic. What might have been unique to France, however, and I would argue that Clermont's case provides evidence for this, would be the administrative intervention which both intensified, and contributed to uniformity in, the developmental cycles of different towns. The universality of the crisis in France's traditional industries in the last years of the Ancien Régime, which were those industries in which there had been intervention, would seem to corroborate this argument.

So the full documentation which I provide in this book on the cycle observable at Clermont and, in particular, on the role of administrative

---

27. *A Theory of Economic History*, pp. 44–5, 142–3. See also on this C. M. Cipolla, *Before the Industrial Revolution: European Society and Economy, 1000–1700*, pp. 95–108.
28. Crouzet, 'Angleterre', 274–6.

intervention in intensifying this cycle, will serve, it is to be hoped, to refine 'social' explanations for possible weaknesses in France's economic performance. It throws light, too, on a question which has often puzzled economic historians, the fact of disparate economic performances by different industrial centres faced with similar cost and demand situations. Clearly the sort of information with which quantitative historians have provided us about demand cannot explain inconsistent performance by different industrial centres. The supply side is clearly relevant. This is a problem with which David Landes grapples in a recent article. It is the inconsistency in the industrial performances of Lille and Roubaix in the nineteenth century which he analyses, and in a talk which he gave in Oxford in 1972 I remember his also mentioning the cases of Mazamet and Castres, Languedocian industrial centres which flourished in the nineteenth century despite the general trend of industrial decline in the regional economy. Landes stresses the importance of the entrepreneurial factor at Roubaix and argues that the town's industrialists were given a particular drive because of their desire to emulate their more privileged and previously industrially more important neighbour, Lille. I am sure that he is right to emphasize the entrepreneurial factor and I wonder too whether both the variation in the timing of the two towns' cyclical development patterns (Roubaix grew after Lille) and also the fact that Lille's industry was subjected to state intervention, while Roubaix's was not, are not factors of relevance. One of the reasons for Roubaix's strong sense of rivalry with Lille would have been awareness that the latter's industry for a long period had been privileged.[29]

A final point concerns the significance of Clermont's experiences in the very long term. The cyclical pattern of industrial development was, I would argue, a universal feature of the pre-industrial economy. It parallels that agrarian cycle, with its repetitive variations in size of land units, the nature of production techniques and the balance between large and small landowners. References which I found to past periods of prosperity in Clermont's industry, and in the industry of other Languedocian centres, convinced me that the eighteenth-century growth in the province's industry was purely a repetition of previous periods of growth and that the cyclical pattern observable so clearly at Clermont was the industrial counterpart of the agricultural cycle whose regular repetition has encouraged historians to regard French society as static between the

29. D. S. Landes, 'Religion and enterprise: the case of the French textile industry', in E. C. Carter, R. Forster and J. N. Moody (eds), *Enterprise and Entrepreneurs in Nineteenth and Twentieth Century France*, pp. 41–86. The talk in Oxford was given at a graduate seminar in economic history held by Peter Mathias in All Souls College on 2 March 1973.

thirteenth and eighteenth centuries.[30] It seems likely that just as the Languedocian peasant reclaiming land in a period of agricultural expansion would have found relics of similar activities by his ancestors in the form of old irrigation schemes, broken tools and collapsed stone terracing so, too, clothiers, in periods of industrial expansion, would have made use of industrial buildings and dye-houses abandoned by previous generations, and when they built or repaired fulling mills they would have found evidence, in the form of old and disused water channels, that they, too, were merely repeating what had been done several times before. These memories, and relics of previous periods of expansion, must have contributed to a cyclical view of human endeavour within an essentially stable structure.

And if the expansion in Languedoc's cloth industry in the eighteenth century was purely a repetition of previous cyclical upturns, then what was its relevance to the debate about French industrialization? The impressive French growth in the eighteenth century, if Languedoc's example was representative, which I believed it was, was not a part of modern economic growth, a movement towards industrialization, but a pre-industrial cycle. The emphasis placed by contemporaries like Young, and by historians like Crouzet and Richet, on the lack of structural change in the French economy in the eighteenth century seemed to me, therefore, to be absolutely correct. The growth, far from generating industrialization, had no self-sustaining potential because of the lack of structural change.[31]

But if it was just a repetition of an oft-repeated cycle, then it was surely the *last* repetition. This seemed to be apparent to contemporaries themselves. As I have already mentioned, there was a growing awareness that something different characterized England's economic expansion of the eighteenth century. That somehow this difference eliminated some of the self-limiting, cyclical characteristics of previous economic expansions and that somehow the French economy, despite its long expansion, had not achieved these qualitative changes. Contemporaries were right. A social revolution as much as an industrial revolution was occurring in Britain, and purely for competitive reasons an industrial cycle on the same basis as previous ones had become an impossibility. The English economy was achieving competitive advantages of a relatively permanent nature in contrast with the temporary ones which, I have argued, went to

---

30. And particularly E. Le Roy Ladurie: see, for example, his 'Les paysans français au XVIe siècle' in *Conjoncture économique, structures sociales: hommage à Ernest Labrousse*, pp. 332–52 and especially p. 343, and 'L'histoire immobile', *Annales* 29 (1974), 673–92.
31. See chapter twelve on this.

an industrial centre in the early stage of a pre-industrial growth cycle. An awareness of backwardness which can be traced quite far back ensured too that all efforts would be made in France to emulate these economic and social advantages emerging in Britain. This, too, made another repetition of the pre-industrial cycle unlikely.

Significantly there is a sharp contrast in the French attitude to their major economic rivals in the seventeenth and eighteenth centuries. Their attitude to the Dutch was one which reflected confidence. The Dutch had achieved their prosperity as a consequence of an unnatural monopoly. This monopoly could be broken and the industrial and commercial techniques necessary for economic success in the seventeenth century could be easily mastered. This confidence was not misplaced. The French expansion in the first half of the eighteenth century was based in great part on the successful copying of the Dutch economic model. The British success, however, was not explicable in such straightforward terms. It was increasingly attributed to a changed economic and social structure which was generating different attitudes and attributes. Indeed it was these social changes which were given greatest prominence in discussions of the relative economic failure rather than the question of the growing French technological backwardness. This was for reasons of a fairly self-evident kind – it was believed that while technological backwardness could easily be overcome by means of government intervention (a misplaced belief J. R. Harris's researches suggest),[32] 'social backwardness', being deeply entrenched, could not. Arguably, indeed, these social attitudes and attributes were never fully imitated in France. And this might be a part of the explanation for the different nature of the industrialization process there. The eighteenth century expansion had strengthened, not weakened, some of the traditional characteristics of French society, and the Revolution, though in part caused by the instability to which growth within traditional structures had given rise, in fact served to strengthen and consolidate the power of those whose prosperity had originated from, and continued to depend on, these traditional structures. In power these groups could ensure, at least in part, that the transformation from one type of economy to another should be a gradual process.[33]

32. *Industry and Technology in the Eighteenth Century: Britain and France* and 'Skills, coal and British industry in the eighteenth century', *History* 61 (1976), 167–82. W. W. Rostow adopts a similar approach in *How It All Began*, pp. 177–81.
33. This interpretation is similar to that of D. S. Landes, 'French entrepreneurship and industrial growth in the nineteenth century', *J.E.H.* 9 (1949), 45–61, and J. E. Sawyer, 'Strains in the social structure of modern France' in E. M. Earle (ed.) *Modern France, Problems of the Third and Fourth Republics*, pp. 293–312.

The book is arranged in the following manner. The second chapter is devoted to a general description of the province of Languedoc and the third to one of Clermont-de-Lodève, which is shown to be very much a representative Languedocian town. In the fourth chapter Clermont's economic performance in the seventeenth century is assessed. The town shared in the general French economic decline, it will be shown, and an interpretation of the form which the decline took is offered. In the fifth chapter the Colbertian reaction to the local Languedocian crisis is described and explained. One instrument of Colbertian intervention, the royal manufacture, has usually been regarded as a clumsy and ineffective one. The veracity of this view is tested in chapters six and seven in which Villenouvette's experiences during its first forty years of existence are analysed in detail, and the connection between the royal manufacture and the industrial growth which began in Clermont in the 1690s is investigated. In chapter eight we leave the royal manufacture to concentrate on the development of the revitalized Clermontais cloth industry and compare the contribution to the industry's growth made by different social groups in the town. An attempt is made to assess the nature of the entrepreneurial qualities necessary for success in the industry. These entrepreneurial qualities did not remain untainted for long for, to the natural decadence consequent upon the operation of the 'Buddenbrooks effect', was added the corruptive influence of administrative intervention. In the ninth chapter, devoted to the second stage in the industry's development cycle, it is shown that Clermont's cloth industry, despite apparent prosperity, was losing momentum by the mid-century. It was awareness of incipient industrial problems, such as those emerging at Clermont, which was one of the causes, we argue in chapter ten, for the radical reform in French political economy which took place in the 1750s: a liberalization occurred and in this chapter this policy change, and its disastrous short-term consequences for Languedoc's cloth industry, are described. The suddenness of the change in policy was, we argue, a sufficient explanation for a severe short-term adjustment problem in certain Languedocian cloth-making centres. Explaining these centres' prolonged decline is a more complex matter, however, and this is what is undertaken in chapter eleven by means of a detailed analysis of the experiences of the industry's entrepreneurs. In chapter twelve a short description of how the inhabitants of Clermont reacted to the structural crisis in their cloth industry is provided and this is followed by a conclusion in which a return is made to a consideration of some of the issues which have just been raised in this introduction.

2

Languedoc

The public Inns on the great Roads in *France* are generally bad; – bad, I mean, if compared with the Inns in *England*: Those in *Languedoc* are some of the best; and if you ask, What is that owing to? It is, because the Trade of *Languedoc* is more considerable than the Trade of most other Provinces in the Kingdom. (Josiah Tucker, *Instructions for Travellers*, p. 60)

That Languedoc was one of the most prosperous and commercially advanced provinces of France in the eighteenth century tends to surprise the twentieth-century observer. All the more so, perhaps, because the region's largely wine-producing population justifies its present rural existence in terms of the sanction bequeathed by centuries of continuous cultivation of the soil. But in fact discontinuity, rather than continuity, has been the characterizing feature of Languedoc's development. Modernization and industrialization involve regional specialization and Languedoc's role in a modernizing and industrializing France has involved the abandonment of its industrial and commercial traditions for a concentration on agricultural production.

The visitor to the region who disregards the propaganda of the 'viticulteur' rapidly appreciates this essential discontinuity. It is betrayed above all by the region's towns whose size, antiquity and splendour signal a past prosperity and development which clearly could only in small part have been generated by agricultural wealth. This historical rather than modern origin for Languedoc's urbanization has been emphasized by historians and geographers. 'La ville languedocienne', Raymond Dugrand writes, 'ne semble ... pas liée à l'industrie'; it represents 'une localisation du passé'.[1]

It is with this prosperous industrial and commercial past that this chapter will largely be concerned.

Josiah Tucker was not alone among contemporaries to emphasize the

---

1. *Villes et campagnes en Bas-Languedoc: le réseau urbain du Bas-Languedoc méditerranéen*, pp. 1, 79.

province's wealth. Most travellers were struck by it and by the contrast presented with other, poorer regions of France. The Marquise de la Tour du Pin, for example, recorded in her memoirs the vivid impression which the change in environment caused her when as a child she accompanied her uncle, Richard Dillon, Archbishop of Narbonne, on his regular journey from Paris to Montpellier to attend the annual session of the provincial Estates of Languedoc, a body of which he was president:

Après avoir parcouru 160 lieues de chemins détestables et défoncés, après avoir traversé des torrents sans ponts où l'on courait risque de la vie, on entrait, une fois le Rhône franchi, sur une route aussi belle que celle du jardin le mieux entretenu. On passait sur de superbes ponts parfaitement construits; on traversait des villes où florissait l'industrie la plus active, des campagnes bien cultivées.[2]

Even so widely travelled, and well-qualified an observer as the future Joseph II when he visited Languedoc during his European travels found much to admire. The provincial intendant, Jean Emmanuel de Guignard de St-Priest,[3] delighted in describing his favourable, but envious, reaction – 'l'état florissant de cette province, la beauté des chemins, la perfection des établissements publics, avaient excité au plus haut point sa mauvaise humeur', he was reported as saying.[4]

Economic prosperity has its counterpart, and some would argue is dependent on poverty elsewhere. Indeed, in the pre-industrial period, in which there was a lack of technological progress and little capital accumulation, the need to extract surpluses from different regions, or people, was even more marked than in the industrial world. And it is true that travellers' reports on the province were largely conditioned by the favourable impressions registered as a consequence of crossing the exceptionally prosperous plain of Lower Languedoc. But Languedoc, like most Mediterranean regions, was characterized by its mountains as much as by its plain. To the 'brilliant but narrow creations along the coastline', therefore, must be added some consideration of its 'vertical norths', the southern promontories of the Massif Central and Pyrenees. These areas were impoverished because of their harsh climate, barrenness and limited cultivable land space. But they were saved from the worst consequences of these natural disadvantages by the links with the plain. The roads from Lower Languedoc acted as a 'kind of extension of the plain' enabling them to draw part of the grain which their agriculture could not supply from elsewhere and concentrate, in particular, on the

---

2. *Journal d'une femme de cinquante ans, 1778–1815*, I, 53.
3. Intendant of Languedoc, 1751–85.
4. An anecdote of the Marquise de la Tour du Pin, *Journal*, I, 57. On Joseph II's visit see also De Vic and Vaissète, *Histoire générale du Languedoc*, XIII, 1313–15.

production of livestock. And it was these same roads which the mountain-dwellers themselves took, in great numbers, in search of work or, in years of extreme hardship, of alms. The archives of the hospitals of Languedoc and Roussillon record the overwhelming predominance of the Massif Central and Pyrenees as the source of their inmates. There could be no better illustration of the diverging prosperity of mountain and plain than the evidence for this continuous southward movement which contributed to that exceptional human mobility which was a characterizing feature of south-eastern France. As Le Roy Ladurie writes, 'Voici toute une France mobile, migrante', and in sharp contrast to the north-west, 'plus calme, plutôt casanière'.[5] For many of these mountain-dwellers Lower Languedoc was not the final destination. There was a regular, seasonal exodus to Spain undertaken above all to avoid the rigours of the mountain winters. 'The Inhabitants of the Mountains call'd *Upper Gévaudan*', a contemporary reported, 'as well as their Neighbours of *Upper Vivarais* and *Upper Limosin*, use to go into *Spain* every Year before the beginning of the Winter, where they are employ'd in the vilest Services to get a livelyhood: wherefore the *Spaniards* use to call *Gavaches* (from *Gabales* or *Gabali*) the ancient Inhabitants of Gévaudan, all poor, dirty spirited Fellows.'[6] If the mountain areas were saved from the dire consequences of over-population by these migrations the plain of Lower Languedoc, and the provinces of Catalonia and Valencia (the destination in Spain of most French emigrants), benefited too for they were provided not only with cheap labour but also with the means of renewing their human stock which was vulnerable because of the excessive mortality occasioned by both their high level of urbanization and the unhealthy marshy conditions, characteristic of most coastline areas of the Mediterranean. Significantly the migratory movement was one-way, north–south, 'à sens unique'. As such it was a sign of the continued vitality and drawing-power of the Mediterranean economy.[7]

For this was the most fundamental explanation of the province's long record of commercial and industrial prosperity. It was a consequence of the centrality of the Mediterranean in European economic life in the pre-

5. Braudel, *Mediterranean*, I, 25–9, 41, 47; E. Le Roy Ladurie, *Les paysans de Languedoc*, pp. 93–111. An unrivalled description of general characteristics of the province is provided by C. D. H. Jones, 'Poverty, vagrancy and society in the Montpellier region, 1740–1815' (Oxford D. Phil., 1978, shortly to be published), pp. 16–49.
6. Anonymous, *An Account of the Theater of War in France being a Geographical and Historical Description of Languedoc in General; and of the Lower Languedoc, and the Principality of Orange in Particular by a Native of Languedoc*, pp. 30–1.
7. Le Roy Ladurie, *Paysans*, p. 96; Braudel, *Mediterranean*, I, 62–6; J. Nadal, *La población española*, pp. 71–80.

industrial period. Europe's economic centre of gravity was shifting northwards from the seventeenth century, but the rate of structural change was slow, as the persistence of traditional migratory patterns, and Languedoc's apparently healthy commercial and industrial situation in the eighteenth century, suggest.[8]

The towns of Languedoc never dominated the Mediterranean economy in the way that Venice, Barcelona or Genoa did at various stages, but they played an important subsidiary role. The province was a natural centre of communications. The advantages of sea transport in the pre-industrial period, particularly for the pirate-infested and stormy Mediterranean, were not invariably decisive (as Braudel has ably demonstrated) and the quality of Languedoc's roads which the Marquise de la Tour du Pin, and later Arthur Young, admired, was in large part occasioned by the importance of the overland links which the plain of Lower Languedoc provided to the trading centres of the Mediterranean economy.[9] As Gilly, merchant and 'député de commerce' for Montpellier, commented in 1725, 'La Province du Languedoc est celle du Roiaume la mieux située pour trafiquer en Levant, en Italie, en Piedmont, Genève, Suisse et même en Espagne.'[10] And if the advantages of sea- over land-transport were not decisive in the Mediterranean they were even less so with respect to trade between the Mediterranean and northern Europe, and Languedoc, as well as providing the trunk overland routes between Spain and Italy, was also well placed for exploiting the south–north, north–south trades which characterized a European economy dominated by the Mediterranean. The two major routes were via the Rhône valley and via Toulouse and the river Garonne, but, as Louis Dermigny and others have shown, there were subsidiary routes, too, above all through the Cévennes, the name given to the southern promontory of the Massif Central, whose 'seven veins' or river valleys provided natural corridors for communications.[11] The cultural imperialism of the present Occitan movement, which lays claims to towns as far north as Limoges and Clermont-Ferrand, had, thus, an economic reality in the pre-industrial period for these towns were outlying parts of a Mediterranean-dominated economy whose French animators were largely speakers of Occitan or Provençal. The geographical spread of the

---

8. For summaries of Languedoc's eighteenth-century economic experiences see P. Wolff (ed.), *Histoire du Languedoc*, ch. 10, and E. Le Roy Ladurie, *Histoire du Languedoc*, pp. 88–93.
9. Braudel, *Mediterranean*, 1, 284–9; Young, *Travels in France and Italy*, p. 42
10. ADH C5517, 'Observations sur l'état des fabriques du Languedoc'.
11. L. Dermigny, 'De Montpellier à La Rochelle: route du commerce, route de la médecine au XVIIIᵉ siècle', *A. du M.* 67 (1955), 31–58.

Occitan language in this period thus provides a useful guide-line to the extent of Languedoc's commercial influence.[12]

If the province's favourable geographical position with respect to important international trading centres contributed to its prosperity, the quality of its communications and the great variety of its natural resources in terms of climate, soil and terrain contributed to an exceptional local market development too. The proximity of mountain and plain meant that areas little separated by distance differed greatly in natural resources and these abrupt contrasts contributed to a precocious specialization, based on comparative advantage, and to the early growth of a market economy. The intendant of Languedoc at the end of the seventeenth century, Nicolas de Lamoignon de Basville,[13] in a description of the province which he prepared for the Duke of Burgundy, the father of the future Louis XV, emphasized some of these contrasts. Upper Languedoc, with its rich soil and temperate climate, combined with the narrow but fertile plain of Lower Languedoc to generate a large wheat surplus which was consumed in part by the grain-deficient mountainous areas of the province and also sold in other parts of France. The hilly and mountainous areas, in turn, in addition to their specialization in sheep- and cattle-rearing, produced a number of profitable exchange crops such as silkworms, wine, fruit, timber, chestnuts and almonds. Quantitatively it was grain production which was of greatest significance to the province. Toulouse and Narbonne were the major centres of the trade which was calculated by Basville to be of a value of 1,200,000 *livres* a year, between one-eleventh and one-twelfth of the total agricultural production of 14,638,000 *livres*. Despite Colbert's desire for an industrial role for the Canal du Midi or Canal des Deux Mers, which was opened in 1681, grain was to be the major commodity carried. An added advantage of this Mediterranean grain was its high quality and conservability, occasioned by the dry climate of the Midi. This made it particularly suitable for use as seed. There were clients for Languedocian wheat all over Europe.[14]

The highly commercialized state of agriculture, the grain surplus, and the variety of other marketable agricultural products, contributed significantly to the economic vitality of the province. They were the cause of obvious economic advantages such as an exceptional degree of moneti-

12. For an example of the 'imperialism' of contemporary Occitanists see R. Lafont, *Clefs pour l'Occitanie*, pp. 11–36.
13. Intendant, 1685–1718.
14. Description included in H. de Boulainvilliers, *Etat de la France*, II, 511–12, 572. See also P. Boissonnade, 'La production et le commerce des céréales, des vins et des eaux-de-vie en Languedoc dans la seconde moitié du XVIIᵉ siècle', *A. du M.* 17 (1905), 240–2, and Le Roy Ladurie, *Paysans*, pp. 53–76.

zation and the spread of commercial values. They contributed to a
favourable local balance of trade. But, above all, perhaps, it was what the
province *escaped* that was of significance. Studies of French Mediterranean grain prices have shown that they were slightly higher but far
more stable than those recorded in areas of central France. The significance of this? Such price behaviour is symptomatic of an advanced state
of commercialization and of the integration of Languedoc into the international economy. The province enjoyed an 'international' price level for
its wheat, defined by Jean Meuvret as 'niveaux relativement élevés des
prix et fluctuations atténuées', a sign that it was spared the disasters of
either abundance or scarcity which caused the far sharper price fluctuations observable elsewhere.[15] The nature of Languedoc's agricultural
sector contributed also to its being spared the worst effects of another
perennial problem of pre-industrial economies – under-employment.
The variety of different crops contributed to labour demands being
distributed throughout the year.

A region in which 'crises de subsistences' were rare, and employment
was available all the year round – it was not surprising that the inhabitants of the barren mountains of the Gévaudan referred to Languedoc as
'Le bon Pais'.[16] Travellers too benefited from the variety of the region's
products: to the advantages of easy and rapid travel occasioned by the
quality of roads was to be added the gastronomic pleasure provided by its
inns. Morris Birkbeck, travelling between Montpellier and Narbonne in
1814, noted cryptically in his diary, '(Breakfast at Bessenez [Pézenas]:
melon, oysters, turbot, lobster, partridges, figs, peaches, plums.)'[17]

The pre-industrial period is often described as one of 'merchant capitalism'. By this is primarily meant a capitalism characterized by minimal
fixed industrial investment, in which profits were largely accumulated by
merchants. It was a less stable form of capitalism (in the short term) than
the industrial variant above all because of the possibility of rapid disinvestment which the predominance of convertible, circulating capital
allowed, and it left economic and social structures relatively unchanged.
One of its typical, and very much defining, institutions was the fair – an
exceptional and privileged occasion (privileged by the grant both of
official protection and, very often, of fiscal exemptions) on which goods

15. J. Meuvret, 'Les prix des céréales dans la France méditerranéenne au xviie siècle' in his
    Etudes d'histoire économique, 97–104.
16. ADH C2554, Petition of Journaliers, Artisans et Laboureurs of Mende to St-Priest,
    1781.
17. M. Birkbeck, *Notes on a journey through France, from Dieppe through Paris and Lyons, to
    the Pyrenees, and back through Toulouse, in July, August and September, 1814, etc.*, p. 55.

were purchased or sold, debts settled, societies formed, commercial contacts made, prices discussed, the state of the economic climate sensed, ideas, techniques and new styles circulated, bankruptcies discovered, marriages arranged, thefts committed, diseases exchanged and, in general, all that involved movement and communication vastly intensified. But the fair was an impermanent phenomenon, an alternative to the development of specialized shops, banks and meeting-places and thus to complete structural change. In pre-industrial Languedoc there were many fairs. The largest and most significant were held (predictably) along the main artery of trade, the Languedocian plain, at Beaucaire, Nîmes, St-Gilles, Lunel, Montpellier, St-Thibéry, Montagnac, Pézenas and Béziers.[18] But smaller fairs and large markets (which served a similar role to fairs) were held all over the province. An almanac published in Clermont-l'Hérault in 1843 lists eighty fairs held annually in the département of the Hérault alone at this relatively late date,[19] and among the papers of a Lyonnais merchant who operated in the late seventeenth century is to be found a document entitled 'Nottes des foires et marchés quj se tiennent en Gévaudan', the poorest area of the province, in which fifty-three annual fairs are listed.[20] Of all the province's fairs the most famous, and that which illustrated best both its prosperity and the nature and causes of that prosperity, was Beaucaire, which Ernest Labrousse describes as the 'grand événement commercial du Midi, et même de l'Europe'.[21] It was held next to the Rhône and drew traders from all directions by road, river and sea (sea-going boats moored beside barges from Lyons along the banks of the river). The status which Labrousse attributes to it was already enjoyed in the middle ages when it attracted traders from the entire Mediterranean economy – Italians, Germans, Brabantines, Spaniards, Portuguese, Greeks, Berbers and Egyptians.[22] It was still an important international commercial occasion at the end of the eighteenth century. This is illustrated, for example, by the description of an impressed Arthur Young. Travelling through the province in 1787 he chanced upon the preparations for the fair which, he recorded, 'fills the whole country with business and motion'. Evidence of its animating powers he found both during the day – 'meet many carts loaded; and nine diligences going or coming' – and at his hotel in Nîmes in the evening where he found (to his discomfort?) 'most motley companies of French, Italians, Spaniards and Germans, with a Greek and an

18. J. Combes, 'Les foires en Languedoc au moyen âge', *Annales* 13 (1958), 231–40.
19. *Almanach des artisans du grenier poétique de Clermont-l'Hérault pour l'année 1843.*
20. ADR, Fonds Moulins, xxi.
21. Labrousse, *Crise de l'économie française*, I, 111.
22. W. Heyd, *Histoire du commerce de Levant au moyen âge*, II, 17.

Armenian'.[23] A great event, but it was a declining event by Young's time: the lack of any of his compatriots at the fair was not without significance. The very existence of fairs was becoming a sign of economic backwardness.

But the types of commercial links which had brought prosperity to Languedoc for so many centuries are illustrated by Young's description, despite this relative decline. Illustrated too by the long survival of these fairs in the province is the strength of Languedoc's commitment to both the commercial methods and the geographical orientation of a Mediterranean-dominated pre-industrial economy.

If it was Languedoc's advantageous geographical situation which was of primary importance in the establishment and many centuries of vitality of these fairs, a significant contributory factor was the province's importance as an industrial centre. True, agriculture remained, as in all areas in the pre-industrial period, the majority sector but Languedoc's industrial production was exceptional in its variety and size. This aspect of the province's life, like the poverty of its mountain-dwellers, could be missed by the less vigilant visitor who confined his travels to the plain, for the industries were concentrated above all in the foot-hills of the Pyrenees and Massif Central. Those intrepid enough to approach Languedoc through the mountains, however, would have been likely to see signs of the province's industrial activity even before they crossed its frontiers for the many-coloured cloths produced in its textile centres were pegged to the hills to be dried and stretched into shape and thus could be seen from some distance. An inspector in the mid-eighteenth century described vividly this sight which had greeted so many visitors to the province: 'On diroit ... que les Montagnes ne sy sont tapissés [que] de draps Ecarlattes, bleus & autres assortimens variés à l'infini.'[24]

Practised within the province was the whole range of pre-industrial crafts. Languedoc's industrial competence stretched from the most fundamental, coal-mining, to the most delicate and esoteric, the production of playing cards, perfumes and surgical instruments. The majority of the immensely varied range fell approximately into three main categories, however – extractive, chemical and pharmaceutical, and textile. In addition to coal-mining, lead- and iron-mining constituted the first category. The second included perfumes, verdigris, eau-de-vie and a large variety of dye-stuffs and medicines, and in the third was the whole range of textile production apart from that of linen: silks, velvets, fus-

23. *Travels*, pp. 43–4.
24. ADH C5519, Mémoire sur le travail des draps, c.1770, by Inspector Rodier.

Ill. 1. A long industrial tradition which came to an end in the twentieth century: abandoned textile mill south of Lodève

tians, ribbons, lace, stockings, hats, blankets and, above all, woollen cloth. Subsidiary industries, not forming part of these major groupings, included pottery-making, glass manufacture, metallurgy, arms production, soap-making, tanning, parchment and paper manufacture and barrel-making.[25]

Most important of all was the province's textile production. This predominance is no cause for surprise. 'Textiles were the great industry ... giving rise to the unbalanced economic expansion of the period', Braudel and Spooner write of early modern Europe.[26] Languedoc was no exception to this rule. But how great an industry the province possessed was not realized by historians until quite recently. Now the quantitative studies of Markovitch and others have shown that Languedoc had the largest textile industry in France at the beginning of the eighteenth century – 'plus forte que la Normandie, avec ses trois généralités de Rouen, d'Alençon et de Caen, plus forte que la Champagne ou la Picardie'.

25. Dutil, *Etat économique*, pp. 519–59; L. J. Thomas, *Montpellier, ville marchande*, pp. 170–82; P. Boissonnade, 'L'état, l'organisation et la crise de l'industrie languedocienne pendant les soixante premières années du xvııe siècle', *A. du M.* 21 (1909), 169–97.
26. In their chapter on prices in the *Cambridge Economic History of Europe*, iv, 419.

Another historian has compared the place of cloth production in Langue-doc's traditional economy with that occupied by the vine today (Ill. 1).[27]
Markovitch's studies on French textile production are based on the analysis of the first national industrial surveys carried out at the end of the seventeenth century and during the eighteenth. Thanks to these we now have a reasonably full idea of the size, nature and distribution of Langue-doc's cloth industry during the last hundred years of the Ancien Régime. But information for the pre-Colbertian period is far more sparse. So much so that the author of one recent general survey of the European economy in the early modern period was led to conclude that industry in Languedoc 'had been almost non-existent before 1660'.[28] We are in fact far better informed about the province's industry in the mediaeval period as a recent study by Philippe Wolff has demonstrated.[29] This gap would not be of such importance if there had been complete continuity in the type, and geographical distribution, of the industry during this long period but there are signs that this was far from the case, particularly for the industry of Lower Languedoc. It is necessary, however, to establish a rough outline, from the sparse evidence which exists, of the state of Languedoc's cloth industry in the period leading up to the beginnings of active and continuous central intervention in the mid-seventeenth century. We are helped in this by a recent article of R. Descimon which in part fills this large historiographical gap but fills it, above all, for Upper Languedoc. Indeed for our purposes the most important contribution of this article is that it demonstrates the sharp distinction which existed between the cloth industries of the two halves of the province. Whereas the industries of Upper Languedoc were oriented towards continental markets, and generally dependent on large merchant centres such as Toulouse, Albi and Lavaur, those of Lower Languedoc were turned towards the Mediterranean and international markets, producing for the fairs of the plain and for Languedocian or Provençal ports. The dividing line between these two industries was to the west of Carcassonne. 'Le Bas-Languedoc, maritime et "international", dont le centre nerveux, au XVIe siècle, est à Marseille plus que Montpellier, s'oppose au Haut Languedoc toulousain, plus continental et français', Descimon writes.[30]
But if the industries produced for different markets what of their

27. Markovitch, 'L'industrie lainière', pp. 1629–30, and C. Fohlen, 'En Languedoc: vigne contre draperie', *Annales* 4 (1949), 290.
28. H. Kellenbenz, *The Rise of the European Economy: Economic History of Continental Europe, 1500–1750*, p. 209.
29. P. Wolff, 'Esquisse d'une histoire de la draperie en Languedoc du XIIe au début du XVIIe siècle' in *Produzione, commercio e consumo dei panni di lana*, pp. 435–62.
30. R. Descimon, 'Structures d'un marché de draperie dans le Languedoc au milieu du XVIe siècle', *Annales* 30 (1975), 1414–46.

organization of production? Were they distinct too? Descimon provides a comparatively full description of Upper Languedoc's industry. It was apparently static. Two maps which he produces show that the Toulouse cloth market was supplied with cloth of low quality by an almost identical range of local centres in the sixteenth as in the fourteenth century while receiving, in both periods, the higher-quality cloths from northern France. The reasons for this division in the supplying of the market emerge from his analysis of the nature of the organization of production, and of the relationship between clothier and cloth merchant in Upper Languedoc. The scale of production was very small – familial, or 'artisanal' as we shall henceforth call it. Specialization was generally 'imperfect'. In other words artisanal cloth-makers combined their industrial with agricultural activities. The use of family labour, and the availability of agricultural supplements to industrial earnings, were the explanations for the cheapness of product and thus for the monopolization of the bottom end of the cloth market. Most of the profits in the cloth trade were engrossed by the cloth merchants, or 'marchands-drapiers' as they were called, from Toulouse, Lavaur and Albi, above all. It was they who sold wools to the artisanal producer as well as purchasing his finished product at a low price – competition among buyers, in contrast to that among producers, was little, Descimon shows. The marchands-drapiers generally bought the artisanal clothier's cloth 'in the white', before dyeing and finishing, and their actual involvement in the physical side of cloth production was limited to the superintending of these crucial final processes which put the cloth in a condition to be bought by the consumer. Lacking was the marchand-fabricant, the merchant-manufacturer, involved in both the production and the commercialization of cloth – 'A Lavaur les grands drapiers ne sont pas encore des marchands-fabricants', Descimon writes. The lack of this figure, and the engrossment of the majority of profit by those involved in the commercial, rather than the industrial side of cloth-making, was probably the major explanation for the primitive nature of the local industry. Deprived of profit the artisanal producer lacked the capital reserves to increase or improve his production.

Notarial acts recorded by the farmer of a *droit de marque* imposed at Toulouse in the mid-seventeenth century provide an insight into the way these relationships between merchant and artisanal producer functioned. The acts were registered in connection with his discovery in cloth-finishers' workshops of a large number of pieces of cloth on which dues had not been paid. In all cases the cloth belonged already to merchants. One piece of *estamet*, made in Limoux, belonged to a merchant of Bordeaux. It is clear that merchants, having made their cloth purchases at local markets and fairs, had the final production operations carried out in the major merchant centres where there were concentrations of the necessary skilled workers. The nature of both the finish and the dye could be varied by the merchant in accordance with the requirements of the market.[31]

Some, perhaps the majority, of Lower Languedoc's industry functioned in a manner similar to that of the upper province. The artisanal production unit characterized all the more remote cloth-making centres of the Gévaudan, Auvergne and Cévennes and continued to do so until the end of the Ancien Régime. Attempts in the eighteenth century to impose industrial regulations and guild systems on these isolated areas were invariably frustrated because of the poverty and illiteracy of producers (they could neither read regulations nor provide the necessary financial support for inspectors), and also the difficulties of communications. Merchants, as in Upper Languedoc, profited from the large number, and geographical separation, of producers to engross most profits. Quality of production thus remained low and scale small. The output of what was, despite this smallness of scale, a vast industry was in part consumed locally but, above all, was sold at the provincial fairs, particularly at those held at Pézenas and Montagnac (there were five held a year, three at Pézenas and two at Montagnac)[32] and at the great fair of Beaucaire, which took place at the end of July. The centres which effectively dominated these rural producers, as Toulouse, Lavaur and Albi dominated the producers of Upper Languedoc, were, in the mediaeval period, the great trading cities of the Languedocian plain, Montpellier, Béziers and Narbonne, from the beginning of the sixteenth century, Marseilles, and in the seventeenth century, Lyons. Montpellier, Béziers and Narbonne, in addition to being mercantile centres for the cloth trade, were important cloth-making centres in their own right too but, significantly, they contained dyeing and finishing facilities of a volume which was clearly not warranted purely by their own production. Montpellier's dyers' corporation had thirty-seven members in 1340 and the town was particularly famed for its scarlets, and Narbonne, the capital of the region's industry in the thirteenth and fourteenth centuries, had a large concentration of 'pareurs' and 'tondeurs' all living in the same quarter of the town 'pour que la fabrication soit publique et

31. AM Toulouse, HH 48, 7 and 28 July 1640, copies of acts originally registered by the royal notary, Guilhaume Lausy. That this was the conventional arrangement is confirmed by the recent article of G. Bernet, 'Jean Giscard, marchand drapier toulousain sous Louis XIV', *A. du M.* 91 (1979), 53–70.
32. L. Dermigny, 'Les foires de Pézenas et de Montagnac au XVIIIe siècle', *Congrès Régional de la Fédération Historique du Languedoc* 26 (1952), 97–116.

sans secret'.[33] Marseilles's ascension in the sixteenth century was a consequence both of the silting up of the Languedocian ports and of the inclusion of Provence in the French kingdom in 1481; its advantages over its Languedocian rivals as the major French outlet to the Mediterranean were evident and plans to develop Aigues-Mortes into an alternative port for Languedoc were abandoned. At Marseilles, again, we note that the growth of cloth-trading led to the development of cloth-finishing facilities. The complex art of scarlet-dyeing, for example, was imported from Italy. Records of Marseilles's cloth purchases are comparatively full. The main markets supplied were the Italian and Levantine and, as in Upper Languedoc, the source for higher-quality cloth was, largely, northern France and that for the lower and middling qualities (by far the largest quantity) above all Languedoc.[34]

But if the bulk of Lower Languedoc's industry was organized on this basis there were important exceptions, and it would be far from accurate to regard the industries of the two halves of the province as identical twins. A first point concerns the quality of production. Although the lower province rarely produced cloth of the highest quality there was a large production of cloth of middling qualities which were of uniform, and internationally recognized, types and standards. So a part, at least, of Lower Languedoc's industry was clearly integrated into international circuits of exchange. The range of cloths was approximately the same as that produced by the industry of Languedoc's neighbour and competitor, Catalonia.[35]

The production of these middling qualities of cloth which competed sucessfully on international markets was carried out by the larger Languedocian cloth-making centres such as Limoux, Carcassonne, Castres, Clermont-de-Lodève and Lodève and there are signs that the nature of the organization of production in these towns was distinct from that in the rest of the province. There is evidence of a considerable division of labour in the production process as well as of the presence of skilled workers involved in the crucial finishing processes. Above all there are signs of the existence of that important figure, missing from the industry of Upper Languedoc, the marchand-fabricant. And there is evidence, too, that such a form of production – complex, and directed towards the sale of middling qualities of cloth in international markets –

33. A. Germain, *Histoire du commerce de Montpellier antérieurement à l'ouverture du port de Cette*, I, 19–20, 25, and C. Port, *Essai sur l'histoire du commerce maritime de Narbonne*, p. 64.
34. R. Collier and J. Billioud, *Histoire du commerce de Marseille*, III, viii, 130–1, 144, 198, 457–65.
35. P. Vilar, *La Catalogne dans l'Espagne moderne*, I, 588–99.

had been the norm for many centuries in these, and probably other, towns. Limoux's clothiers at the end of the seventeenth century claimed, for example, that there was evidence in the registers of their 'maison de ville' of the existence in the town in the years 1100, 1102 and 1103 of 'quantité de marchands drappiers drappans qui fabriquoient des sarges et estametz Blancs La q*^{lle}* sorte de marchandize avoit grand débit A Tule Bourdeaux Marseille Lion et Italie'.[36] The tradition of cloth-making at Carcassonne was as long, if not longer. It was 'une robe de beau et fin drap de Carcassonne' that the twelfth-century troubadour Raymond de Miraval instructed a juggler to purchase and the origins of the statutes of the various groups of workers involved in cloth production stretch nearly as far back: those of the 'drapiers' to 1317, of the 'pareurs' to 1335, and those of the 'cardeurs' and 'tisserands' to 1507 and 1514–15 respectively.[37] Clearly the division of labour was considerable and the early presence of specialized drapiers who were, to judge from their statutes, effectively marchands-fabricants, as well as that of pareurs, is clearly of great significance. The importance of the role of the pareurs in the production process may have given them a slight edge in economic and social status over the drapiers, at least in the mediaeval period, for members of their profession are to be found among Carcassonne's consuls from 1294 whereas the first record of a drapier consul is for the year 1439. This position of superiority most probably did not endure to judge from statutes registered at Carcassonne at the beginning of the seventeenth century in which it was declared that drapiers, cardeurs and tisserands should have precedence over pareurs.[38] At St-Chinian, however, at the end of the seventeenth century, we find pareurs dominating the town's industry and acting as both cloth-finishers and merchant-manufacturers, and as fullers as well in some cases.[39] Castres, like Carcassonne and Limoux, had a 'vintage' cloth industry. As the local historian Granat writes, 'Dès 1393, les étoffes castraises avaient une grande réputation; elles étaient connues dans tout le Languedoc.' Guild regulations, which not only prescribe cloth qualities but also mention dyeing both 'au

36. ADH C2199, Memoir of 15 August 1685.
37. F. Jaupart, 'L'industrie drapière et le commerce des draps dans le diocèse de Carcassonne au XVIIIe siècle', *Bulletin de la Société d'Etudes Scientifiques de l'Aude* 61 (1960), 187–8; ADH C2801, 'Privilèges des pareurs de Carcassonne' and ADH C2799, 'Articles des statuts des maîtres cardeurs, escardasseurs, et peigneurs de la citté et ville basse de Carcassonne'.
38. ADH C2799, articles of cardeurs: 'comme étant lesd. cardeurs, escardasseurs et peigneurs les premiers ouvriers travaillant de laine, et après eux lesd. tisseurs, et après et dernier les pareurs'.
39. The following acts of St-Chinian notaries, among numerous others, illustrate this: ADH II E 79 102, 2 Jan., 4 March, 25 Oct. 1686; II E 79 103, 2 Feb. 1687, 27 March, 12 April, 14 April 1688.

petit' and 'au grand teint', are traceable to this period.[40] Colours which were obtained by dyeing 'au grand teint' included scarlets, blues and greens and such dyeing was a particularly skilful process. It was introduced to Lodève, which had a large and ancient cloth industry (the first record of its existence is for the year 1100) with the co-operation of the town's Bishop between the years 1161 and 1187.[41] There were specialized dyers working in Clermont-de-Lodève, likewise, at an early date. They are mentioned in a feudal transaction of 1341 between the town and its seigneur although it is not specified whether they practised both 'petit et grand teint'. There is evidence of the existence of an important industry at Clermont even before this date. The town's marchands-fabricants, registering new statutes in 1708, claimed that 'précédans Roys' had granted a special cloth mark (*bouilhe*) to the town with which to distinguish its production – a sign that it was producing cloth of uniform standards on some scale.[42]

This variety of evidence suggests that these towns had, and had at a very early stage, cloth industries of some sophistication. Of particular significance was the existence of the marchand-fabricant which made possible the accumulation of industrial capital and hence improvements, or variations, in both the quantity and the quality of production. The possibility of profit also, of course, made cloth production a possible, and indeed very suitable, avenue for social mobility.

In the mediaeval period these towns, though already large cloth-making centres, were of lesser importance than the cities of the Languedocian plain. Narbonne's status as the capital of the regional industry has already been emphasized and a sign of its dominance was its merchants' appointment of a cloth commissioner at Carcassonne to purchase cloth. Between the fourteenth and fifteenth centuries, however, there was a definite shift in the geographical distribution of Lower Languedoc's industry which favoured these and other towns situated in the foot-hills of the Pyrenees and Massif Central. This shift is noted by Descimon. In contrast to the continuity observable in the areas supplying the Toulousain market between the fourteenth and sixteenth centuries his maps illustrating the supplying of Mediterranean markets between the two periods show significant changes – a decline in the production of the cities of the Languedocian plain as well as an eastward shift, the industries of the Lauraguais and Corbières losing their supremacy to areas

40. O. Granat, 'L'industrie de la draperie à Castres au dix-septième siècle et les "ordonnances" de Colbert', *A. du M.* 30 (1898), 447–9.
41. Appolis, *Lodève*, pp. 456–7.
42. P. Barral, *Considérations sur le régime municipal de Clermont-en-Lodévois aux XIIIᵉ et XIVᵉ siècles*, pp. 63, 87; ADH II E 25 108, 1 Aug. 1708.

situated in the more westerly Pyrenean valleys of the rivers Aude and
Ariège and to a long belt of cloth-making centres, situated along the
south-eastern edge of the Massif Central, stretching from Castres to
Nîmes. Thus prominent among the benefitors from this shift were those
cloth-making centres whose significance has just been highlighted and
Carcassonne had emerged as the indubitable capital of the regional
industry. In addition to this geographical shift there had been a decisive
concentration in the areas of production. A number of smaller cloth-
making centres had lost their independent 'appellations contrôlées' for
their cloth. Descimon offers two possible explanations for this phenomenon – either these centres had abandoned production or they had
been absorbed by larger centres and thus ceased to produce cloth on
their own account. The second explanation (given the multiple evidence
for a considerable industrial expansion rather than contraction in the
sixteenth century) would seem the more plausible. The marchands-
fabricants of the larger cloth-making centres of the Lower Pyrenees and
Cévennes were thus, if this explanation is acceptable, now exercising a
dominance over certain rural, artisanal producers which was similar to
that which had previously been exercised by the marchand-drapier.[43]

What were the causes of this shift and geographical concentration?
Unfortunately there is no evidence available to provide an explanation.
All that can be said is that the circumstances which had contributed to the
great prosperity of the cities of the Languedocian plain altered, that war
and demographic crisis contributed to a prolonged crisis in southern
France in the late fourteenth and fifteenth centuries – 'peu à peu l'activité
commerciale s'éteignit dans tout le Midi', Heyd wrote[44] – and that when
a general European recovery began in the sixteenth century it was the
hill-town cloth-making centres which responded most positively to the
new opportunities. There is fragmentary, but widespread, evidence (to
add to that provided by Descimon's charts) of dynamism in these towns.
It was in this period that St-Chinian emerged as a significant cloth-
making centre – two new fulling mills and a dye-house were constructed
there.[45] Carcassonne's industry was in full expansion and benefited in
various ways from a crisis in the neighbouring Catalan industry which
had been in part precipitated by the invasion of Louis XI. Two refugees
from Tuchan, close to Perpignan (then part of Catalonia), the Saptes
brothers, founded a concentrated industrial concern grouping all the
processes of production, in the château of La Torte, Conques, in the
town's immediate neighbourhood. Their cloth rapidly acquired a high

43. Descimon, 'Structures d'un marché', pp. 1415–16.
44. Heyd, *Histoire du commerce*, ɪɪ, 717.
45. A. Delouvrier, *Histoire de St Chinian-de-la-Corne et de ses environs*, p. 343.

reputation. It was soon reported to be the best of the province, achieving sales 'tant dedans que dehors du royaulme'. A cloth regulation made in Carcassonne in 1511 shows that the town's own clothiers were undertaking types of cloth previously made in Perpignan – 'draps fins meslés à la sorte de Perpignan' are mentioned.[46] Clermont-de-Lodève's production was being sold directly to Greek merchants at the fair of Beaucaire[47] and it is clear that all these cloth-making centres benefited from the rapid expansion in France's trade with the Levant which by 1600 was valued at some thirty million *livres* a year, according to Levasseur, and all the more so in so far that the Italian cloth industry, the main competitor in the Levant, was (with the exception of Venice) disrupted by continuous warfare.[48]

All that can be said in an attempt at an explanation of the apparently diverging industrial performances of the cities of the plain and the hill-towns is firstly that it was the cities which, as the areas most committed to international trade, would have suffered most from the disruptions to distant trades occasioned by the disturbances of the fourteenth and fifteenth centuries. Secondly that the French monarchy's policy of centralization contributed to the creation of new institutions in the large cities of the province and thus to a plethora of new offices which provided opportunities for merchants to disinvest from their commercial undertakings. And thirdly that the rising hill-town cloth-making centres enjoyed very obvious cost advantages in their production because of their access to abundant water supplies (Ill. 2), their (relative) lack of restrictive guilds, their abundant labour supplies and their easy access to raw materials. The abundance of labour was particularly crucial. Attempts in the late seventeenth century to expand cloth production at Marseilles were to be quite fruitless because of the lack of labour, above all for the labour-intensive spinning processes. The town could only support a minute industry of some twenty looms.[49]

A qualification is necessary. The industrial decline of the plain was by no means total. Montpellier abandoned woollen-cloth production but took up blanket and velvet production in its place and remained the most important Languedocian centre for the wool trade. Nîmes was, and remained, an important cloth-making centre although, in the second

46. E. Castel, 'Le château de Saptes. Etude anecdotique et descriptive', *Bulletin de la Société d'Etudes Scientifiques de l'Aude* 38 (1934), 79–85; Mahul, *Cartulaire et archives de l'ancien diocèse de Carcassonne*, II, 20 and ADH C2801, 'Règlement' of May 1511.
47. F. Teisserenc, *L'industrie lainière dans l'Hérault*, p. 46.
48. D. Sella, 'The rise and fall of the Venetian woollen industry' in B. Pullan (ed.), *Crisis and Change in the Venetian Economy*, pp. 106–14.
49. BN FF 8037, Industrial survey of 1708, folio 2, Report of Inspector Cauvière of Marseilles, 9 Nov. 1708.

Ill. 2. Water-power, one advantage enjoyed by Languedoc's hill-towns: ruined
fulling mill on the Hérault

half of the seventeenth century, it was to switch to silk production.[50]
Indubitably, though, it is accurate to write of the emergence in the
sixteenth century of the hill-towns as the major centres of the provincial
cloth industry and thus a pattern was established which endured until the
industry's virtual disappearance in the nineteenth and twentieth centuries. The nature of the division of labour established between hill and
plain was a logical one. Increasingly the role of the cities of the plain was a
commercial and administrative one whereas the natural advantages of the
hill-towns favoured them as industrial producers. Indeed the hill-towns
of Languedoc possessed the sort of advantages which economic historians now consider to be of primary significance in explaining the
location of 'proto-industrialization'.[51]

Although this industry, as we have emphasized, at no stage produced

50. L. Teisseyre, 'L'industrie lainière à Nîmes au xviie siècle: crise conjoncturelle ou
    structurelle?' *A. du M.* 88 (1976), 383–400.
51. J. Thirsk, 'Industries in the countryside' in F. J. Fisher (ed.), *Essays in the Economic
    and Social History of Tudor and Stuart England*, pp. 70–88; E. L. Jones, 'Agricultural
    origins of industry', *P. & P.* 40 (1968), 58–71, and 'Environment, agriculture and
    industrialization in Europe', *Agricultural History* 51 (1977), 491–502; F. F. Mendels,
    'Proto-industrialization: first stage of the industrialization process', *J.E.H.* 32 (1972),
    241–61; J. de Vries, *The Economy of Europe in an Age of Crisis, 1600–1750*, pp. 84–112.

the finest varieties of cloth it was clearly not only a very important industry quantitatively but also an advanced one in that from a very early stage in its development a large part of its product was exported and the skilled and costly finishing processes were carried out locally. The Mediterranean cloth markets remained the largest not only for France but for the European economy as a whole until the eighteenth century.[52] This, and particularly the importance 'disproportionné' of the Levant trade was, as Braudel emphasizes, one of the 'continuities' or structural features in an almost unchanging 'système économique' which functioned in Europe for some five or six centuries before the Industrial Revolution.[53] And it is this half millennium or more in which southern markets predominated which is the major explanation for the age of Languedoc's commercial and industrial traditions.

Many recent studies in French history have emphasized the importance of a knowledge of the economic conjuncture. By this are broadly meant those long, repetitive, rhythmic variations in the level of prosperity of the European economy which are recorded by, among other things, long-term price movements. That there was also a repetitive, rhythmic 'social conjuncture', conditioned ultimately by the economic, is evident too but although signs of its functioning are apparent in various historical studies the exact nature of its mechanism has been subjected to far less scrutiny than its economic counterpart. The two extreme points in such a social conjuncture would be, it is clear, moments of very high social mobility and moments of complete social stability. Upward mobility in the pre-industrial world involved, basically, the use of money obtained by commercial or industrial means to buy status of a non-commercial, feudal or landed nature. As we have already suggested cloth-making was one way of rising socially but, and this should be emphasized if the significance of the idea of a 'social conjuncture' is to be grasped, not all periods were equally favourable to industrial expansion and hence to rising socially through cloth production. Before the Industrial Revolution *all* industrial expansions were followed by economic stagnation and decline, the social representation of which was a lack of social mobility.[54]

Of course it was not the case that commercial and industrial activity provided the exclusive means for rising socially. Agricultural production, combined with a politic choice of heirs and heiresses as marriage

52. R. T. Rapp, 'The unmaking of the Mediterranean trade hegemony: international trade rivalry and the commercial revolution', *J.E.H.* 35 (1975), 502–5.
53. 'Histoire et sciences sociales: la longue durée' in his *Écrits sur l'histoire*, pp. 53–4.
54. L. Stone, 'Social mobility in England, 1500–1700', *P. & P.* 33 (1966), 18–19, 23–6; R. Mousnier, *Les hiérarchies sociales*, pp. 38–9; Deyon, *Amiens*, pp. 244–300.

partners, provided an agricultural route for social promotion, too. But industrial production, as Paul Bairoch has shown, held particular advantages in that it required a far smaller investment than agricultural production – the main difference being that no land had to be purchased – while profits could be far larger.[55] For this reason it is clear that Languedoc's large and exceptionally commercialized industry would have acted as a 'social catalyst', providing unusual opportunities for social mobility, throughout its long history. And, indeed, there is plentiful evidence that this was the case. Many of Languedoc's noble families, if not actually owing their origin to industrial production, had been reinforced at some stage by intermarriage with the children or grandchildren of clothiers. A study by Emile Appolis on the nobility of the diocese of Lodève, which contained the two major cloth centres of Lodève and Clermont, shows most local noble families to have been linked in one of these ways to profits from either cloth production or trading. Apparent too is that in some cases the role of 'seigneur' and that of 'négociant' were combined. It seems highly likely that the extent of commercial development in the province encouraged indulgence about the principle of *dérogeance*. The Fleury family itself, which was to have a controller-general amongst its descendants in the eighteenth century, was linked to important cloth-making families of Lodève.[56] The role of the province's cloth industry as a continuous source for social mobility has long been recognized by historians as it was by contemporaries. As Roschach writes in the *Histoire du Languedoc*: 'On sait que la fabrication des draps et des diverses étoffes de laine était en Languedoc, depuis une époque reculée, l'industrie nationale par excellence. C'était la seule sérieuse ... Presque toute la richesse du pays en venait, & la noblesse également ... la plupart des lignées féodales ayant disparu ...'[57] Similarly a Languedocian merchant, referring to cloth production at Carcassonne, emphasized this long tradition of the industry serving as an avenue for social mobility: 'C'est par Luy que les fabriquans des premiers tems ont fait des fortunes considérables et Donné dans la Longue robbe de Sujets quy ont fait honneur à Divers Parlemens.'[58] Throughout the long history of Languedoc's industry, it would seem, production was looked upon as a means rather than an end, a means whereby the greater security and status of landed income and rent from office could be obtained.

Such attitudes, we are informed, were widespread in France. Langue-

55. 'Agriculture', *Fontana Economic History of Europe*, iii, 496.
56. 'Les seigneurs du diocèse de Lodève', *Cahiers d'histoire et d'archéologie* (1947), 226–7.
57. De Vic and Vaissète, xiii, 166.
58. ADH C2508, 'Refflections ...' of Vallon, inspector, 22 Sept. 1732.

docians, therefore, were not unique in holding them but what was perhaps special was the length of time during which this approach to business affairs had predominated. These attitudes, as a consequence, were probably more deeply entrenched than elsewhere. And, arguably then, it was the many cycles in the 'social conjuncture' during those five hundred years or more that Languedoc occupied a central place in the pre-industrial economy, and the consequent crystallization of a rigid, instrumental approach to economic life, that were the cause of what was regarded by contemporaries as a specifically 'meridional' approach to business affairs.

Basville was one of many who commented on what to him, as an outsider to Languedoc (he had previously been intendant at Poitou), were the special characteristics of the négociants and fabricants of the province: 'la pente naturelle des marchands de Languedoc', he wrote, 'les porte à fabriquer de la mauvaise marchandise, et à s'enrichir s'ils le peuvent, en fort peu de temps, sans se soucier de la réputation de commerce, qu'ils quittent, dès qu'ils ont gagné quelques biens'. To Basville, clearly accustomed to parts of France whose populations were socially and economically more inert, the Languedocians seemed undeferential, anti-intellectual and positively obsessed by their anxiety to make money, by any means, and thus to rise socially:

ils sont ardens pour obtenir ce qu'ils désirent et ne se donnent aucun relâche qu'ils n'y soient parvenus, mais ils oublient communément les moyens qui les en ont mis en possession, c'est ce qui fait qu'ils ne regardent guère la reconnaissance comme un devoir, et qu'ils s'en embarassent assez peu, si ce n'est lors que l'espérance d'un nouveau bienfait les attache; de tous les pays du monde où l'auteur croit que l'intérêt met les peuples en action il prétend qu'aucune ne produit des Hommes si vifs sur cet article que celui-ci, qu'il est ordinaire d'y manquer à des devoirs essentiels pour le moindre profit.[59]

Basville was not the only contemporary to record such opinions of the business attributes of Languedocians. We find an ex-clothier of Clermont-de-Lodève, Mathieu Pradier, who had become an inspector of manufactures, and whose own career, as we shall see, provides an excellent example of these meridional tendencies, expressing similar views in the mid-eighteenth century, though generalizing them to the French nation as a whole which, he believed, was less scrupulous in its approach to business than its English competitors.

La constitution de l'Angleterre n'est pas la nôtre, et autant ses négociants sont affermis dans l'idée de la nécessité de perfectionner leurs fabriques pour soutenir leur commerce, qui fait la ressource plus solide et l'inclination de la nation, autant

59. Boulainvilliers, *Etat*, II, 512, 536.

nos Français sont empressés de pousser leur fortune, sans s'embarrasser jusques à un certain point de la réputation de leurs fabriques, qui forment simplement leurs moyens de gain pour sortir de leur état, et passer à des charges qui en contentant leur amour-propre, satisfont à leur inconstance. Voilà le goût général.[60]

This tendency to neglect the quality of production, and abuse the confidence of customers, was one of the main reasons for the severity of regulations, and the gradual augmentation in the size of the *corps* of inspectors. Regulations were an attempt to repress by legislation the speculative business habits of the pre-industrial period. As Basville wrote in a memoir intended for his successor: 'L'Inclination des fabricans est si grande pour frauder qu'il a falu faire passer les draps par trois mains et les éprouver trois fois avant de les faire embarquer.'[61]

Similar views of the qualities of Languedoc's businessmen were held by their business correspondents in more reputable or conservative commercial centres. This is certainly suggested by some of the correspondence of Raymond Moulins, merchant of Lyons, but native of Clermont-de-Lodève in Languedoc. In the 1690s he was involved in business with 'marchands-droguistes' of Clermont-de-Lodève, Galtié et fils, who had sent a large consignment of hats to Basle, Switzerland, which had been rejected there on the grounds of poor quality. Moulins acted for the Galtiés in the dispute and kept them regularly informed of his progress in the matter. In March 1697 he commented in a letter about the Swiss purchaser's apparently poor opinion of Languedocian business ethics – 'Il ma repondeu Brusquement comme un Suisse quil Est ... quil estoit bien Informé des manières des Languedociens.' The contrast between Swiss and Languedocians extended, to judge from Moulins's correspondence, to the very style of letter-writing and manner of talking business. Moulins's letters to Languedocian friends and collaborators are generally direct, personal and, often, passionate but such an approach was clearly unsuitable for his Swiss correspondents. He had had to adapt his tactics and explained to the Galtiés that 'Il faut estre un peu politique avec ces gens là, & saccomoder de leur humeur pesante et tardive, car sy vous témoignez trop de Chaleur Ils sen prévallent.'[62]

That Languedoc should have contained an undeferential population, prepared to adopt any means to make money, and regarding business activities purely instrumentally, as a manner of achieving social promotion, is to be explained, above all, we would argue, by the high level of commercialization of the region's economy and the many centuries

60. ADH C2520, Letter to secretary of the intendancy, 21 Oct. 1753. On Pradier see below pp. 343–7.
61. ADH C4674, Copy of memoir left by Basville for de Bernage, his successor, April 1718.
62. ADR, Fonds Moulins, XVII, copies of letters of 22 March 1697 and 18 Jan. 1698.

during which the full operation of an economic and social conjuncture had cast and recast the nature of its social structure. As a consequence it was more apparent in Languedoc than in more isolated, landed societies that status was not innate but was consequent on commercial success. A second factor which possibly contributed to these phenomena is the following. As Braudel has emphasized, the appearance of prosperity which the Mediterranean region gave to northerners, and which we have commented on earlier in the chapter, was in some ways a deceptive one, for in no way did its natural resources match those of northern Europe – its soil was poorer, its climate too much one of extremes, its timber rarer and slower growing, its mineral wealth smaller, its rivers less suitable for internal navigation, its sea poorer in fish, its livestock more meagre and its land supply limited. What was exceptional about the Mediterranean area, and what caused its agriculture to be more efficient than that of other parts of Europe, was a combination of two factors: the exceptional quality of communications which permitted agricultural specialization and its inhabitants' remarkable horticultural skills – it was the Mediterranean area which was the source, as Le Roy Ladurie has shown, of most of Europe's agronomical progress. In other words, although the commercialization of the Mediterranean zone was precocious, the actual restrictions on economic growth and prosperity were particularly great and thus nowhere, it seems likely, were business acumen, frugality and an alertness to *any type* of economic opportunity more necessary. And these qualities were essential not only in the achievement of prosperity but also in its conservation. The original *mise en valeur* of Mediterranean resources was a task of great difficulty, but it was also a great problem to maintain yields and soil-fertility. This was a general problem which beset Mediterranean agriculture as a whole. So much so that for some the decisive element in the rise of northern Europe was its greatly superior natural resources. It was also, and this has been less emphasized, an individual problem for large landowners. In the Mediterranean region there were few large stretches of fertile land whose administration was easily managed. Land was patchy, scattered and most varied in quality. It was this, as we have seen, which made possible the cultivation of a wide range of crops whose varying harvest dates caused labour demands to be distributed throughout the year and contributed thus to underemployment's being less of a problem in Languedoc than elsewhere. But the phenomenon, in addition to the low quality of much land, must have increased the complexity of farming and estate administration and, as a consequence, it seems likely that the turnover in the landed elite was more rapid than in areas with land resources which were more easily administered. If this hypothesis is valid, then, an additional contribution to social mobility in the region, to add to that which was caused by the exceptional extent of commercial and industrial development, was occasioned by an exceptionally rapid rate of decay in the province's landed elite. Such a rapid turnover would have been one more reason for not regarding the established order as God-given. In addition the difficulty of administering Mediterranean estates would have given a significant advantage to the owner-occupier or small-scale producer.[63]

An added complexity in the whole question of attitudes and social mobility is the problem of the relationship of the province to a centralizing absolutist monarchy. Languedoc maintained a modicum of independence, with its own much-admired Estates. (They were another object of Joseph II's jealousy. Intendant St-Priest, who clearly 'dined out' on the basis of anecdotes which arose from the future emperor's visit, joked that 'Il avait conçu une jalousie extrême de cette bonne administration des Etats et cherchait avec empressement tout ce que pouvait la déprécier.')[64] But from the mid-seventeenth century real power lay in the hands of the intendant at Montpellier, and institutions directed from Paris. Symbolic of the domination was the rise of French from the late sixteenth century as the administrative language. But this was not the only consequence of the French influence. An additional and important one, which we have already mentioned, was the multiplication in the number of offices conferring nobility which created honourable alternatives to business affairs. Montpellier's transformation from commercial capital of European significance to sleepy provincial city, with an exceptionally expanded part of its population living as 'rentiers', cannot have been entirely unlinked with this development. Germain, in his history of Montpellier's commerce, provides a sensitive and suggestive description of the change which occurred in Montpellier's character between the fourteenth and eighteenth centuries:

Le progrès intellectuel du siècle, de la société française en particulier, sur laquelle allait se lever le soleil de Louis XIV, et l'affluence de plus en plus nombreuse dans nos murs, non seulement de disciples rajeunis d'Hippocrate, professeur ou étudiants, mais de fonctionnaires et de magistrats, chez qui le culte des lettres se mariait fructueusement aux études juridiques, membres du présidial, de la cour des aides, de l'université des lois, officiers royaux de divers noms et de divers degrés, tout cela semblait donner à la vieille metropole du commerce un aspect nouveau. A la foule bariolée des hommes de l'Orient ou des deux péninsules d'Italie et d'Espagne, qui se coudoyait naguère dans nos rues, s'était substituée une population plus homogène et plus nationale, moins entassée, parcequ'elle cherchait davantage ses aises.[65]

63. Braudel, *Mediterranean*, I, 238–46; Le Roy Ladurie, *Paysans*, pp. 54–76.
64. Tour du Pin, *Journal*, I, 57.
65. *Histoire du commerce*, II, 65.

And these new opportunities would have been all the more likely to have had a large effect in view both of the exceptional upward mobility to which the economic modernity of the province continually gave rise and of the strongly entrenched, instrumental view which existed towards trade and industry. The existence of an increasing number of prestigious, safe and royally sanctioned situations and investments may have had another consequence too – it probably led to a certain stabilization in the make-up of the provincial elite.

Another important consequence of the increased integration into the French kingdom was the submission of the province's economic life to administrators who resided in Paris and whose policies were influenced generally by experiences in, and knowledge of, areas whose economic institutions and ways were markedly different from those existing in the south. This factor only became of significance, of course, from the time of Colbert, and the beginning of continuous and systematic economic intervention. Its most striking, and possibly important, example was the extension of the guild system to southern France in the second half of the seventeenth, and the early eighteenth, centuries. Guilds, as E. Coornaert's work has shown, were rare in the Midi before then.[66]

It would seem important that these 'social' factors, and above all the heavily engrained instrumental attitude towards business activity, be borne in mind when we consider the response of the province's merchants and industrialists to the opportunities provided in the eighteenth century both by the exceptional economic expansion and by the increased level of administrative intervention in economic affairs. They would seem relevant also (although it is not in our brief to go into this matter) in explaining the to-all-appearances idiosyncratic, meridional reaction to the new range of opportunities which industrialization provided in the nineteenth and twentieth centuries.[67]

66. *Les corporations en France avant 1789*, p. 26.
67. Commented on by Stendhal, amongst others, in his *Mémoires d'un touriste*, p. 686: 'Le Midi de la France est dans le cas de l'Espagne et de l'Italie. Son *brio* naturel, sa vivacité, l'empêchent de *s'angliser*, comme le nord de la France. Un homme du Midi fait ce qui lui fait plaisir au moment même, et non pas ce qui est *prudent*; cet homme n'est pas fait pour la civilisation qui règne depuis 1830.' Cited by F. Crouzet, 'Les origines du sous-développement économique du sud-ouest', *A. du M.* 71 (1959), 78.

3

Clermont-de-Lodève

Clermont is a representative town of Languedoc. It has experienced the same discontinuity as the province in its economic development. Formerly an important regional, commercial and industrial centre, it now has the status of small market town and is largely dependent for its livelihood on its surrounding countryside. Above all it now depends on the vine. A placard at the entrance to the town advertises its claim to be the regional 'capitale des raisins de table'. Like most of Languedoc's former industrial centres it is now distinguished by its *crus* rather than its cloth, achieving its maximal vitality during the grape harvest in late September.

Clermont's urban lay-out and architectural styles are largely a consequence of its industrial and commercial past. Like so many other Languedocian towns, to use Dugrand's phrase again, it is a 'localisation du passé'.[1] Virtually intact is the town which flourished and harboured (if we are to believe Basville's statements about the character of the inhabitants of Lower Languedoc) a hard-working, thrifty, avaricious, independent, enterprising and undecorous population in the pre-industrial period. This lack of physical change in the town, which is immediately apparent to the eye, has its main explanation in the lack of population growth. Clermont's population in 1968 was little larger than it had been in the eighteenth and seventeenth centuries or, indeed, in the mid-fourteenth century (Table I).[2]

In this chapter, once again, my focus will not be on the process of de-industrialization, whose origins can be traced far back, and which was to be decisively accelerated by the full integration of Languedoc into the French economy in the railway age, but on the characteristics of Clermont's economic and social life before this transformation. An

---

1. *Villes et campagnes*, p. 79.
2. Such demographic stagnation is in conformity with that of the province as a whole. Le Roy Ladurie, *Paysans*, p. 141.

Table 1. *Clermont's population, fourteenth to twentieth centuries*

1347	c.5,000	1740	5,000–6,000	1795	5,360
1380	c.4,950	1761	5,004	1796	5,395
1598	4,000–5,000	1767	c.5,000	1803	5,510
1631	4,400	1769	5,000	1815	5,810
1659	4,400	1783	6,000	1820	5,837
1687	c.4,180	1786	4,000	1837	6,582
1719	5,100	1788	4,500	1962	5,767
c.1730	4,746	1793	4,888	1968	6,375
1734	c.5,000				

Sources: 1347, Combarnous, 'Clermont-l'Hérault', p. 266. 1380, Bobo, 'Une communauté languedocienne', p. 5. 1598, Crémieux, *La vie politique*, p. 69. 1631, ADH G4436, *visite pastorale*. 1659, ADH G1061, *visite pastorale*. 1687, ACC BB1, 26 Aug. 1687 (4,000 'comunians' and 60 Huguenot families – calculating 3 to the family). 1719, ADH 11 E 26 180, 16 March 1719: '1,700 familles'. 1730, J. Expilly, *Dictionnaire géographique, historique et politique des Gaules et de la France*, 11, 371: 791 *feux* – calculating 6 to the *feu*. 1734, ADH G1062, *visite pastorale*. 1740, ADH C2498, inspector's report, 29 Dec. 1740. 1761, ADH C6554. 1767, ACC BB6, 26 July 1767. 1769, ADH C949, Mémoire . . . contre les consuls. 1783, ACC BB8, 9 March 1783. 1786, ACC BB8, 5 Dec. 1786. 1788, BM Montpellier, MS. 48, *Mémoire* of Ballainvilliers, 1, 167. 1793, 1795, 1796, 1803, 1815, 1820, P. Amiel, 'Clermont-l'Hérault pendant la Révolution', *passim*. 1837, Combarnous, 'Clermont l'Hérault', p. 269. 1962, 1968, *Recensement de 1962, 1968: Population de la France*.

attempt will be made to provide what Cipolla would describe as 'a static approximation' of the nature of this town during those four or five centuries before the Industrial Revolution when change was at so slow a pace that generalizations can be made about economic and social life which have some validity for the entire period. This long period during which, to quote Braudel again, there functioned in Europe 'un système économique qui s'inscrit dans quelques lignes et règles générales assez nettes'.[3]

Clermont-de-Lodève was also known before the French Revolution as Clermont-en-Lodévois and it is the Lodévois, corresponding approximately to the diocese of Lodève, the *pays* of Clermont, that it is necessary to describe first if we are to understand the town. In this description we are much aided by the superb detailed study of the area by the local historian, Emile Appolis.

The Lodévois (Map 2) consists essentially of the valley formed by the Lergue, a river some 38 kilometres in length, which has its source at

3. Cipolla, *Before the Industrial Revolution*, p. 1; Braudel, 'La longue durée', p. 53.

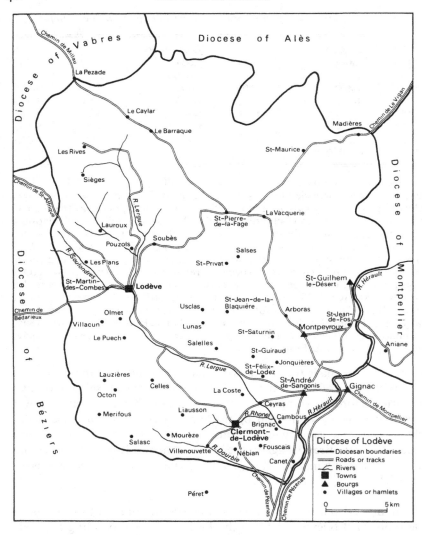

Map 2   Diocese of Lodève

Sièges on the edge of the Larzac, at an altitude of some 700 metres, and joins the river Hérault below Brignac at a mere 30 metres. It is thus a diocese of abrupt geological, geographical and climatic contrasts. North of the town of Lodève it is mountainous, barren, 'un mauvais pays'; between the towns of Lodève and Clermont there is an intermediate zone known as Les Ruffes – arid, formed predominantly of red sandstone, and suitable for a variety of cultivations but giving only poor yields; and to the south of Clermont there lie the beginnings of the plain of the Hérault whose fertility allows, and allowed, a relatively dense and prosperous population.[4]

It is the shortness of distance between areas of such varied climates which contributed, and contributes (as it does in other Mediterranean areas), to the exceptional strength and variability of local winds, and this feature so marked the mentality of the inhabitants of the Lodévois that directions were referred to not in terms of the points of the compass but in those of the provenance of the four major prevailing winds – north, west, south and east were termed 'terral', 'narbonnais', 'marin' and 'aguial' respectively.

Such contrasts, too, contribute and contributed to a great variety in the suitability of different parts of the diocese for different types of agricultural production. In the pre-industrial period, of course, it was often the case that transport difficulties prevented agricultural specialization on the basis of such contrasts but this was not the case in the Lodévois, for the river Lergue and its tributaries provided a natural communications network, roads and tracks following the bed of the river and streams. As a consequence an exceptional degree of agricultural specialization was attained at an early stage in the diocese's development. The information which Basville included about the diocese in his general description of the province demonstrates this: he reported that only a small part of the grain consumed was produced locally, the rest being drawn from the province's surplus areas, but that this deficit by no means signified poverty, for no diocese of the province was more punctual in the payment of its taxes. Clearly, locally produced exchange crops (and the industrial and commercial activities of the diocese which we shall describe) more than made up for the lack of grain. Of prime importance amongst these were the wine, olive oil, almonds and fruit produced in the plain of the Lergue and Hérault, while the more mountainous areas of the diocese provided wool, cheese, timber, chestnuts and livestock.[5]

As well as experiencing the dynamism of the commercial movements to which its own geographical contrasts gave rise the Lodévois benefited from its situation on a major route for those inter-regional trades between the Massif Central and the Languedocian plain which we have described in the previous chapter. A visitor to the Lodévois in the 1760s was a

4. Appolis, *Lodève*, pp. 6–7, 343–4.
5. Boulainvilliers, *Etat*, II, 569. Grain was mainly secured from the dioceses of Béziers, Narbonne, Toulouse and Albi (AN F12 565, 'Etat général . . . de Clermont', 1766).

witness to some of the traffic which the diocese's arbitrating position between mountain and plain generated. During his stay he had seen up to eleven wagons loaded with grain passing daily 'pour porter la vie aux habitans du Rouergue qui estoient dans la disette'. The complementarity of the climates of the two regions, he commented, 'nécessite ... entre elles une correspondance, un mouvement perpetuel d'échanges et de secours'.[6] If the movement of grain was predominantly in a northerly direction, that of livestock tended to be southward. The Mediterranean area as a whole lacked pasture and the one major comparative advantage enjoyed by its mountainous zones lay in the quality of their grazing. The extent of the backward and forward movement of transhumant herds, and of the one-way movement of livestock intended for slaughter and sale in the plain, was so great in the diocese that disputes over the grazing rights of passing herds were continual. Guards often had to be placed in the fields at harvest time to protect crops and one of the specific duties of consuls was that of estimating damage caused to crops by passing herds. Even seigneurial rights were affected. At St-Guilhem-le-Désert, where a bridge over the Hérault occasioned an exceptional concentration of animal traffic, a 'droit de pulvérage', described by a French jurist as 'le dernier raffinement des droits seigneuriaux', was collected in consideration of the environmental damage caused by the dust raised by passing herds.[7]

It was not purely livestock which on occasions threatened the harvest of the inhabitants of the Lodévois for the roads of the diocese were also taken by those impoverished inhabitants of the Massif Central whose migratory habits we have already described. Some of these migrants stayed in the diocese. The demography of the Lodévois, as various studies have shown, was marked by their continuous arrivals.[8] For others the villages and towns of the Lodévois were just stopping-places on their long and regular treks south to the plain of Lower Languedoc or to Spain. Such was the case, for example, of four stone-cutters from Rodez who arrived at Clermont on 11 October 1789, having spent the previous night at Le Caylar, on their way to Spain where they had been annually, they stated, for the last twelve years from St Michael's day until Easter.[9]

If it was the sharp differentials in comparative advantage of mountain

6. ADH C6554, 'Mémoire sur l'état du diocèse de Lodève', by M. Boyer of Alès, undated, *c.* 1768–9.
7. Appolis, *Lodève*, pp. 81, 149. For complaints against passing cattle destroying crops see ACC BB2, 5, 11 March 1708, 7 May 1747.
8. Appolis, *Lodève*, pp. 346–50; J.-P. Bobo, 'Une communauté languedocienne au xviiie siècle, Clermont-l'Hérault', p. 173; R. Laurent, 'Propos sur l'histoire de Lodève', *Congrès Régional de la Fédération Historique du Languedoc* 36 (1963), 123–5.
9. ADH, Ordinaires Clermont, Case 51, 11 Oct. 1789.

and plain which stimulated this continual to-and-fro movement of agricultural products, migrants and livestock in the diocese it was the continued commercial importance of the Mediterranean area, and of overland trade routes, such as those provided by the roads of the diocese of
Lodève, which contributed to the regular movement of another type of
commodity, the more value-intensive drugs, spices, pharmaceutical products and higher-quality textiles which invariably in the pre-industrial
period had primacy in long-distance trade. As Louis Dermigny has
shown, the Lodévois was the base of departure for some of the oldest
and most important overland links between the Mediterranean and the
Atlantic, and its towns and larger villages were 'de véritables pépinières'
of voituriers, marchands-droguistes and marchands who profited from
these trade routes. Four principal routes had a common starting-point in
the Lodévois – one to the Auvergne, whose destination was Clermont-
Ferrand, one to Brittany, which passed through Limoges and Poitiers,
one to the Quercy, Périgord and Saintonge and a fourth to Bordeaux via
the Albigeois. As Dermigny writes, the Lodévois was 'un petit pays mais
aux horizons larges, intimement lié aux grands circuits économiques du
temps'.[10]

Towns, as Braudel writes, 'owed their existence to the control over
physical space they exercised through the network of communications
emanating from them'.[11] In mountainous areas this link between communications and settlements is the more obvious and, in view of the
poverty of most mountainous areas, the more necessary. The harshness
of environment and the steepness of terrain just as they contribute to the
torrential nature of mountain rivers give rise, too, to an exceptional
concentration in human, commercial and animal traffic along the few
passable roads. Mountainous areas support smaller populations than the
plains but the harshness of relief occasions, as it were, a condensation of
these sparse human resources and a precocious density of population in
those (in contrast to the plain) rare places suitably situated to provide the
sites for villages or towns. The importance of roads and communications
to the existence of the villages and towns of the Lodévois was thus
fundamental. This is illustrated, for example, by the nature of the
imposition of the *dixième* and *vingtième* on industry in the diocese in the
mid-eighteenth century. A breakdown of the distribution of the tax
shows that it was supported entirely by areas on, or adjacent to, the main
roads and mule tracks. Short notes added to the different entries, justify-

10. 'De Montpellier à La Rochelle', pp. 32–3, 38.
11. *Mediterranean*, I, 312.

ing the sums imposed, illustrate, too, the centrality of communications in the livelihoods of these towns and villages. Even the smallest of hamlets could draw profit from passing traffic. At La Vacquerie, for example, where the road became impassable for carts, there lived a number of 'voituriers à dos de mulet' for the Auvergne. In Le Caylar, the last substantial village in the diocese before the Auvergne was entered, were situated one of the diocese's seven hospitals (the others were at Lodève, Clermont, Ceyras, Montpeyroux, St-André and St-Jean-de-Fos),[12] used mainly by 'pauvres passants' from the Auvergne, a customs post for oils leaving the province and several inns, blacksmiths and shoemakers whose services were used by passing traders – as was noted, 'ce lieu est très passant pour les voituriers qui vont porter de Montpellier en Auvergne'. Even Les Rives, in the north of the diocese, described as a 'petit village misérable', boasted a 'cabaretier', as it was a 'lieu de passage' for the Rouergue. The inhabitants of the larger villages and towns not only provided the same sort of services as these villages (Lodève was one of the few towns of Languedoc whose inns received honourable mention from Arthur Young, who had high standards)[13] but themselves participated actively in the profitable trading opportunities which the geographical situation of the Lodévois provided. Merchants at St-André traded in agricultural commodities above all – wheat, oil and eau-de-vie, which they processed themselves. Montpeyroux contained a large concentration of marchands-droguistes and voituriers who owned some five hundred mules[14] and serviced a vast area stretching from Rennes in Brittany to the eastern fairs of Champagne and Chalon-sur-Saône. Some of Languedoc's richest merchant dynasties originated in this large village.[15] Brignac, in the south of the diocese, like St-André, was involved in the commercialization of agricultural products, that of wine above all. And both Clermont and Lodève, as we shall see, combined all these varied activities with significant industrial production.[16]

Clermont's geographical position in the Lodévois could hardly be more advantageous. It is situated near the base of the hills, at an altitude of some 90 metres, overlooking panoramically the fertile plain of the

---

12. Appolis, *Lodève*, p. 172.
13. *Travels*, p. 49.
14. Appolis, *Lodève*, p. 450.
15. The Cambon family originated in Montpeyroux, for example. See G. Saumade, 'Cambon et sa famille acquéreurs de biens nationaux, 1791 et 1793', *Annales Historiques de la Révolution Française* 16 (1939), pp. 228–44, 313–38. See also Appolis, *Lodève*, pp. 589–90.
16. ADH C1744, 'Etat concernant les noms des villes, bourgs et villages du diocèse de Lodève compris dans Le Rolle du Dixième de l'industrie pour servir a celluy du vingtième', sent by sub-delegate Bonnafous, 29 Nov. 1750.

Ill. 3. General view of Clermont: château, concentric settlement around the hill of the Pioch, 'cathedral' of St-Paul and suburban development can be seen (see also p. 87)

Hérault (Ill. 3). This position ensures the town an equable and healthy climate, an abundant water supply (from its springs and its small river, the Rhonel), shelter from the harsh northerly winds and, above all, access to those various commercial opportunities which have just been described. As a hill-town Clermont enjoys what Braudel describes as 'the optimum conditions of the Mediterranean habitat, above the unhealthy vapours of the plain, but within the limits between which the *coltora mista* can prosper'.[17] And, indeed, the town has some fame as a health resort, and the waters of its springs are reputed to have medicinal qualities. But clearly the town's development has owed most to its trade. Two of the four major routes which have just been listed intersect at Clermont – that to Bordeaux (also the shortest route between the Rhône and the Garonne) with the road from the Mediterranean (Agde) to central France. The importance (and age) of these old routes is illustrated by the stone sanctuaries, some of which still survive, built at prominent points beside them.[18]

17. *Mediterranean*, I, 56.
18. G. Combarnous, 'Le développement topographique de Clermont-l'Hérault', *A. du M.* 72 (1960) 257–72.

Clermont's merchants, from an early stage, played an important role in the conduct of the trade which was carried along these roads. In 1140 the section of the Rhône–Garonne–Bordeaux route between Montpellier and Clermont was known popularly as 'la voie des marchands de Clermont'.[19] Gradually, it is clear, the town's original defensive function – it was the site of the feudal castle of the Counts of Clermont – developed into a commercial one. And it was a commercial role that was more varied than those of its Lodévois neighbours. This was not only because of the exceptional number and resources of its merchants but also because the town acted as a market centre for those other Lodévois centres themselves. It was thus both regional and local commercial centre.

It was the combination of these functions which gave a particular resonance to Clermont's weekly market. In the seventeeth century this was described as 'sans hyperbole ... parmi les marchés ce que la foire de Beaucaire est parmi les foires du Languedoc'; its importance was caused by the attendance not only of 'un grand nombre de banlieux et petites villes qui sont aux environs' but also of 'tout le Rouergue et l'Auvergne ... qui y conduisent une si grande quantité de bétail gros et menu ... [que] ... Les villes de Nîmes, Montpellier, Pézenas, Agde, Béziers et Narbonne y accourent comme au magasin et la nourrice de tout le pays'.[20] The description is clearly too enthusiastic but that the market did attract traders from some distance is illustrated by another source, the records of the seigneurial court at Clermont: among witnesses to crimes committed on market day we find not only inhabitants of local villages but also four merchants from Provence who attended Clermont's market fortnightly (they declared) to buy sheep, a négociant from Millau, merchants and a shepherd from the Rouergue, a cattle-dealer from Castres and a merchant from Pézenas (Ill. 4).[21] The size of the market and complexity of transactions were such that different types of activity were assigned to different parts of the town. Some street and square names record the position of these specialized markets – 'Rue du Marché à l'Huile', 'Place du Marché aux Boeufs' and 'la Place au Blé' – and there were also separate market sites for the sale of meat, fish, leather, salted products, sheep and coal, and joint sites for pottery, bread, cheese, vegetables and herbs, which were sold around the walls of the parish church of St Paul, and wood, wool, iron and pigs, which were sold in the ditches at the base of the town's fortified walls.[22] Of all these varied items

19. Combarnous, 'Clermont-l'Hérault', pp. 257, 261.
20. *Chronique historique des Guillems*, 1645, cited by Appolis, *Lodève*, p. 592.
21. ADH, Ordinaires Clermont, Cases 192, 134, 317, 176, 236, 176, June 1770, 18 Nov. 1761, 19 Aug. 1767, 4 Dec. 1765, 7 Feb. 1787, 4 Dec. 1765.
22. Combarnous, 'Clermont-l'Hérault', pp. 263–4 and plan (between pp. 264 and 265); Appolis, *Lodève*, p. 594.

Ill. 4. Clermont's Wednesday market still attracts large crowds

it was the sale of livestock which was in greatest volume, and gave greatest regional importance to the market. As another seventeenth-century observer commented, the market resembled a 'foire pour la vente de toutes sortes de bestail dehors la ville'.[23]

Clermont's merchant population can be divided, approximately, between those who operated in gross, or wholesale, and those who were retailers, or 'marchands-détailleurs'. The latter would have possessed or rented stalls, or opened their shops, on market day, as well as selling on a normal

---

23. BM Toulouse, MS 603, Description of Languedoc composed for d'Aguesseau, 1674, folio 360. On the market see also Le Roy Ladurie, *Paysans*, p. 114.

basis throughout the week. The account-book of one such retailer, Marc Jalaguié, who operated at the beginning of the eighteenth century, has survived. This reveals that he had customers in Clermont itself and in fourteen neighbouring villages and that he was selling a wide range of products – cotton, sledge-hammers, salted cod, sardines, iron, pepper, paper, pens, nails, sugar, soap, snails, 'arencades', mustard, candles, rice, wheat, caramel, keys, locks, woad, wax, oil, cloth and cork feature among his sales.[24]

The retail merchant might obtain part of his stock at the regional fairs but he would also purchase some of his requirements from the wholesale merchants who bought in bulk either at the regional fairs or from a normally widespread network of business contacts. These wholesale merchants not only held stock for use in the local distributive trades but were also involved in those regional, intra-regional and even international trades for participation in which Clermont was so well placed. A variety of acts recorded before notaries provide insight into the extent of this large commercial network into which Clermont fitted. For example, two brothers, both 'marchands', Marc and Jacques Germain, divided their business in 1689 after twenty-five years of working in association by giving (quite arbitrarily, it seems) all debts to be collected to Clermont's north – 'despuis la ville de Lodève incluzivement jusques dans les montagnes et pays de Larsac, Rouergue, Auvergne, Limosin et Périgort' – to one, and all those 'despuis Lodève à Clermont dans toutte la plaine diocèze dAgde, Béziers, Montpellier, Nismes et Autres de Languedoc', to the other.[25] Another society, involving two merchants, recorded debts in 1672 in Béziers, Bédarieux, Nîmes, Carcassonne, Bize (in the diocese of Narbonne), St-Chinian and Lyons.[26] The fullest evidence we have of the activities of wholesale merchants is provided by the large correspondence, referred to in the previous chapter, between Jacques Galtié et fils, marchands-droguistes, and the ex-Clermontais, Lyonnais merchant Raymond Moulins. The Galtié family was exceptionally rich, forming part of a small elite among Clermont's merchants, and so it would be wrong to regard the scale of their operations as typical, but the nature of their commercial methods and relationships, and the geographical scope of their trade, do serve to inform us about some of the characteristics of Clermont's commercial life.

The correspondence is not entirely with Raymond Moulins. There are

24. AC Clermont, CC14, 'Premier journal pour servir à la boutique du St. Jalaguié marᵗ de Clermont', begun 4 July 1702. 'Arencades' were a mixture of dried and salted fish, conserved in a barrel with herbs and roquefort cheese (Appolis, *Lodève*, p. 353).
25. ADH 11 E 26 126, 1 May 1689.
26. ADH 11 E 25 89, 5 Jan. 1672.

also letters addressed collectively to a society which Moulins formed on 1 January 1701 consisting of himself, Pierre Fessy, Jacques Galtié (nephew/first cousin of Galtié et fils) and Louis Boschet, who all describe themselves as merchants of Lyons. There are other letters, too, directed to Jean Moulins, nephew of Raymond (oldest son of his brother who had remained in Clermont to look after the family estates) who left Clermont in 1696 for Nîmes, where he worked for a time in association with the frères Bedos, and later resided successively in Aix-en-Provence, Nice, Genoa and Paris. The Moulins and Galtié families were also closely related. Galtié père et fils addressed Jean Moulins as 'cher neveu' or 'cher cousin', and generally wrote in the second person singular, despite the commercial nature of their correspondence. That they had certain reserves about the use of this formula is apparent from a postscript to a letter justifying an unhabitual use of the more formal 'vous': 'Jescris au pluriel pour ne pas donner occazion de parler aux gens fais responce de Mesme.'[27]

Apparent immediately just from the details of those involved in this correspondence is the importance of family links and personal connections in trade. Business correspondents, if not actually related, were known generally as 'amis'. Letters were often intimate and informal, generally including family as well as business news. And indeed both Jacques Galtié père (father, son, and first cousin at Lyons were all called Jacques) and Raymond Moulins as well as co-operating commercially did so too with respect to family affairs. Moulins kept a watchful eye on one of Galtié's younger sons, Jean, who had been apprenticed in Lyons after working two and a half years for the frères Bedos at Nîmes and, similarly, Galtié attended to Moulins's family affairs in Clermont – a godson of Moulins he was employing as clerk in 1696 and he reported regularly on the religious instruction which another of Moulins's nephews (orphaned?) was undergoing at a seminary in Béziers. When this nephew celebrated his first mass in Clermont in 1697 it was Galtié who represented Moulins at the event and who also organized a small celebration afterwards (paid for by Moulins).[28] Clearly, though, the main justification for the correspondence was a commercial one. Essentially there existed between Moulins in Lyons, Moulins neveu in Provence, and the Galtiés in Clermont a tripartite economic relationship. The role of the nephew in Provence lay essentially in purchasing those 'Mediterranean' products which were in demand in central and northern

27. ADR, Fonds Moulins, IV, Galtié fils to Moulins neveu (at Nice), 8 March 1700.
28. ADR, Fonds Moulins, IV, e.g. letters of Galtié père et fils to Moulins of 5 July 1695, 23 July 1695, 22 Jan. 1696, 16 April 1696, 25 Aug. 1696 and Fonds Moulins, XVII, letters of Raymond Moulins to Galtié père et fils, 26 June 1697, 24 Aug. 1697.

France. He dealt at various stages in wines, eau-de-vie, rice, camel hair, anchovies, wools, verdigris, spices, and wheat. Galtié père et fils distributed such products in Clermont's large commercial hinterland and supplied both uncle and nephew with, above all, cloth – bought directly from Clermontais or Lodévois clothiers, or at the fairs of Pézenas and Montagnac where the whole range of Languedocian cloth was sold. They kept Moulins regularly informed in their letters of the state of the cloth market. Moulins at Lyons was largely involved in the reception, distribution and resale of these goods. As a consequence it was he who acted as virtual banker for both the Galtiés and the nephew. They regularly drew letters of exchange on him. Much of the cloth was bought in the white and it was Moulins who arranged for finishing and dyeing to be carried out in Lyonnais workshops. In a small, cloth-bound notebook to be found among his papers, there are detailed lists of the costs of dyeing and finishing all the different types of cloth produced in both Languedoc and northern France.[29] Cloth-trading was the most important element in his trade. The majority of these different Languedocian and Provençal products would have reached Lyons via Rhône barges. This would apply to textiles as well as to more bulky products, it would seem: in a letter of November 1698 Moulins informed Galtié et fils that he had not sent them a length of velvet which they had requested as 'Il nest point descendu de voitturiers par eau à cette foire de St. Martin.'[30]

Clearly Galtié et fils had commercial relationships additional to those which are recorded in their correspondence with the Moulins. For example they did not rely entirely on Moulins's nephew to supply them with the products available in the Languedocian plain. They too, both father and son, travelled for commercial purposes and we find letters written by them to the Moulins while on these travels: from Lodève, Montagnac, Agde, Montpellier, Pézenas, Aix, Marseilles, Beaucaire and Nice. Absences from Clermont were occasionally prolonged. In May 1694 Galtié fils spent three weeks in Provence, a letter reveals, and in June 1697 Galtié père informed Raymond Moulins that he was leaving for Marseilles after the June (Pentecost) fair held at Pézenas and planning to stay there until Beaucaire at the end of July.[31] But though the correspondence informs us about only a part of the Galtiés' affairs it does provide a good impression both of the commercial space in which a Clermontais wholesale merchant operated and of the type of products in which he traded.

29. Fonds Moulins, XXIII.
30. Fonds Moulins, XVII, Moulins to Galtiés, 21 Nov. 1698.
31. Fonds Moulins, IV, Galtié père et fils to Moulins, letters of 11 May 1694, 7 June 1697.

The correspondence also throws light on various other matters relevant to understanding the nature of merchant life at Clermont. One of these is the practice of apprenticeship. It would seem that it was often, though not invariably, a younger son who was apprenticed to another merchant, the oldest generally being employed in the family concern and acting, in general, as a 'second' to the father who enjoyed complete authority in a patriarchal society such as that which existed in Languedoc. It was the oldest, too, who generally inherited the major part of the family patrimony. Languedoc was an area in which there was in fact considerable flexibility in inheritance customs. A part of the father's authority lay in his absolute right to dispose of his (but not his wife's) possessions and property in the way in which he wanted. The conventional practice, though (with the basic purpose of maintaining lands and business intact, and of reasonable size), was to name as 'héritier universel' the oldest son.[32] Thus by apprenticing a second or third son in a superior commercial centre such as Lyons (at some considerable expense, fees being as much as 500 *livres*),[33] the merchant or 'bourgeois' of Clermont hoped to achieve two aims: to rid himself, and his family patrimony, of the burden of supporting a younger son (Moulins, reporting on Jean Galtié's progress, wrote that the boy, having received money to buy clothes, had assured him that 'il ne me demanderoit plus rien, & quil ne vous seroit plus à charge')[34] while providing the son with the possibility of an alternative career and livelihood outside the family. In other words the motives for putting a younger son into apprenticeship were not so dissimilar to those for putting a younger daughter into a nunnery (the fate, incidentally, of one of Moulins's nieces in Clermont) and the parallels might even extend to the need for sexual abstinence for postponement of marriage was mandatory during the apprenticeship, and highly advisable when, the apprenticeship completed, the ex-apprentice would work for a comparatively long period as 'garçon', or paid assistant, to his ex-master or to other merchants before finally putting his many years of experience, and accumulated salary, to use in founding an independent concern. Jean Galtié, as we have noted, was a younger son, and the same, it would seem, was true of Raymond Moulins (his brother in Clermont had inherited family estates, household and documents – usually reserved for the 'heir'). Certainly Raymond Moulins followed exactly the conventional

32. E. Le Roy Ladurie, 'Family structures and inheritance customs in sixteenth century France' in J. Goody, J. Thirsk and E. P. Thompson (eds), *Family and Inheritance in Western Europe, 1700–1800*, pp. 61–2; Appolis, *Lodève*, p. 367.
33. The sum paid by Jean Delpon, apprenticing his son, Jean Jacques Delpon, to Raymond and Estienne of Lyons, 23 June 1691 (ADH II E 26 128).
34. Fonds Moulins, XVII, Moulins to Galtiés, 22 Oct. 1698.

course of a younger son with negligible inheritance – apprenticeship to, and some thirty years working as garçon for, Louis Durand, marchand-drapier, bachelorhood (in 1697 he refused his nephew's request to come and live with him in view of his lack of 'ménage') and many years of preparation, and saving, before beginning to run his own business in the 1690s.[35] Jacques Galtié (cousin), who, as we have seen, entered into partnership with Moulins in January 1701, was less patient and conventional. He was working in the late 1690s as garçon for the merchants Estienne and Birouste, who were both of Clermontais origin, and it was perhaps the beginning of the new century which contributed to his feeling fretful in this limiting situation for he confided to his cousin Jean Moulins, in a letter written in January 1700, that he was anxious to 'quitter la maison'.[36] A letter of Raymond Moulins to Galtié père et fils informs us that by July he had taken this step, against 'le sentiment de tout ses Amys'. Moulins's comments on Jacques Galtié's personality suggest that he had not got the necessary patience to tolerate many years of work in a position of subservience: 'parmy touttes les belles, et bonnes qualitez quil possède Il a se petit deffaut sy on peut lappeller ainsy quil abonde un peu dans son sens, en ne suivant pas ou ne différant pas assez aux Conseils de tous ses Amys'. Moulins was anxious that this opinion should not be divulged to Galtié: 'sil venoit à sa connoissance Il est certain que jaurois en luy un Ennemy'.[37]

Apprenticeships were an important element in a strictly commercially motivated migration from Clermont. Lyons in the seventeenth century was the main destination of this migration. If we include the two different branches of the Galtié family there is evidence for the existence there of no fewer than twenty-two different families of Clermontais origin.[38] But there were other centres, too, in which Clermontais established themselves in this period – Arles, Agde, Perpignan, Bordeaux, Grenoble,

35. See P. Léon (ed.), *Papiers d'industriels et de commerçants lyonnais*, p. 283, and Fonds Moulins, xvii, Moulins to Galtiés, 3 Nov. 1697.
36. Fonds Moulins, vii, letter of 22 Jan. 1700.
37. Fonds Moulins, xvii, Moulins to Galtiés, 18 July 1700.
38. Mentioned in Raymond Moulins's correspondence: Altayrac, Birouste, Estienne Chinion, Desfours, Domergue, Jacques and Jean Galtié, Raymond Moulins. Mentioned in notarial acts: Mathieu Angerly, ADH ii E 26 98, 9 Oct. 1681; Fulcrand Chinion, ii E 26 172, 30 July 1711; Raymond d'Estienne, ii E 25 98, 19 Nov. 1697 (also mentioned frequently by Galtiés and Moulins); Jean Figuière, ii E 26 124, 11 Feb. 1686; Pierre Fraisse, ii E 26 131, 7 Nov. 1694; Fulcrand Grasset, ii E 26 125, 12 Aug. 1688 (also mentioned by Moulins); Jean Liquier, ii E 26 166, 26 March 1702; Jacques Marcelin, ii E 26 124, 28 May 1686; Jean Louis Maysonnade, ii E 26 137, 29 Nov. 1694; Jacques Messier, ii E 25 85, 11 June 1662; Marc Nougaret, ii E 26 123, 11 June 1685; Pierre Nougaret, ii E 26 127, 7 April 1690; Louis Pélissier, ii E 25 105, Aug. 1698; François Tartary, ii E 26 131, 23 May 1694.

Montpellier, Chalon-sur-Saône and Paris.[39] The young Clermontais would thus find on his arrival in Lyons, or elsewhere, as apprentice, a sizeable group of ex-Clermontais, many of them related to his family in some way. Thus the break with the home environment would not be sharp. He would not be alone, he would receive help in integrating himself into his new town, he would receive constant advice, and the same sort of familial, social and cultural pressures would be exerted upon him as in Clermont. There was no question of a romantic, Rousseauesque solitude in a strange city. It was a relation or family friend who would originally help find him a master. It was Moulins whom Galtié fils originally asked to find 'une bonne maizon en vostre ville' for his brother Jean.[40] (It is significant that brother, rather than father, made this request: the heir-apparent assumed family responsibilities even before his accession.) Once a master had been procured it was Moulins, again, who was asked to provide a reference for brother Jean.[41] Finally it was Moulins who was repeatedly urged to keep a watchful eye on Jean Galtié during his apprenticeship by both brother and father. Rarely did either conclude a letter to Moulins without a request for progress reports and for interventions to ensure that the apprentice was applying himself to his tasks: 16 December 1695: 'je vous prie me fere sçavoir sy mon fils contante Mr Cottin [his first Lyonnais master] et sy le jugez quil vailhe un jour quelque choze et ne pas me flater sil vo plaict'; 22 January 1696: 'avoir la bonthé de veilher un peu sur nostre fils sil a bezoin de quelque choze autre que dargent de luy fere bailher sil vous plaict et Lencourager un peu au travailh, me feriez plaizir de me dire sy M^r son maistre en est content'; 5 August 1968 (note accompanying instruction to spend 30 *livres* on his son's clothes): '[but] ne pas y bailher de larg^t attandeu quj pourroit le divertir à quelq aut uzage. Je vous prie Monsieur ne pas vous Rebuter de vos charitables-soings ... à Lencourager à bien fere. Il vous en sera daultant plus redevable.'[42]

This indirect pressure which Galtié et fils exercised on the *cadet* was intended to supplement the direct encouragement which would have

39. At Arles, Pierre Metuel, ADH II E 26 130, 12 Aug. 1693; at Agde, Pierre Bonneville, ACC BB2, 29 Nov. 1703; at Perpignan, Jean Combes and Joseph Metuel, II E 25 108, II E 26 130, 26 Feb. 1708, 12 Aug. 1693; at Bordeaux, Charles Raymond, II E 26 122, 28 May 1683; at Grenoble, the Messier family, II E 25 108, 5 Oct. 1710; at Montpellier, Jacques Desalasc, II E 26 126, 23 Feb. 1689; at Chalon, Jacques Louis Mathieu, II E 25 109, 5 Aug. 1712; at Paris, Jacques Galtié (cousin), Estienne Landier, Jean-Pierre Messier, and Jean Moulins neveu (Léon, *Papiers d'industriels*, p. 285 and Appolis, *Lodève*, pp. 349–50).
40. Fonds Moulins, IV, 5 July 1695.
41. Fonds Moulins, IV, 23 July 1695.
42. Fonds Moulins, IV, letters of these dates.

been included in their own letters to him. Jacques Galtié was, at least on occasions, a tyrannical father and the double dose of advice directed at his son was at times, it is clear, overwhelming. A letter of Raymond Moulins demonstrates this. The *cadet* was having difficulties with his master – 'Mr. Cottin ne luy veut pas rendre Justice' – but these the father clearly attributed to his son's failings and, in consequence, he had written an angry letter to him which, Moulins continued, 'lacablent Entièrement tant Il y est sensible, & cela pourroit estre Capable de le faire tumber Malade. Cest pourquoy sy vous me Croyés vous ne luy ferez plus de plaintes sy fortes. Je lestime destre sy sensible car cest la marque dun bon nature & de bon Coeur.'[43] Despite apprenticeship, the father retained legal authority over his son unless he had 'emancipated' him. There was a special, and formal, emancipation rite celebrated in the Lodévois and it was a necessary legal preliminary before a son could undertake any business transaction on his own account.[44] Thus an act of emancipation usually precedes in the notarial registers that recording a first business transaction. The continuation of paternal authority despite a distant apprenticeship is illustrated by a notarial act registered at Clermont in 1686. Louis Marcelin, bourgeois, 'sachant Sieur Jacques Marcelin son filz marchant drapier avoir resté en la ville de Lion despassé de sept à huit ans et durant led temps y avoir travailhé de sond mestier et maintenant estre assocyé avec Messieurs les frères Etienne aussy marchans drapiers', emancipated him.[45] So Galtié père's evident psychological authority over his son had legal sanction too. Despite the distance between Lyons and Clermont it was customary for the apprenticed son's progress to be monitored, and eventual employment decided, by the head of his family in Clermont.

The problems with Cottin were terminated by Jean Galtié's leaving his employment in 1697. He then worked briefly for a merchant called Périer – a stop-gap solution: 'il pourra rester jusques à ce que jaye trouvé à mieux faire', Moulins wrote. And finally, in May 1698, he was accepted by Estienne and Birouste, and thus not only found himself working with his cousin Jacques, but also for two partners, one of whom was related by marriage to his family (his elder brother Jacques had married Catherine Estienne, daughter of Jean Estienne, bourgeois of Clermont in 1694) and both of whom were of Clermontais origin. This arrangement worked well, another letter of Moulins, written in August 1700, reveals. Despite the precipitate withdrawal of his cousin Jacques, the *cadet* was receiving excellent treatment – 'bien esloigné de sestre apperceu daucune froideur

43. Fonds Moulins, xvii, letter of 24 Aug. 1697.
44. Described by Appolis, *Lodève*, p. 267.
45. ADH ii E 26 124, 28 May 1686.

qu'au contraire Mr Estienne par une faveur singulière lavoit amené à sa grange luy tout seul depuis peu de Jours'. In response to the Galtiés' suggestion that they might establish the *cadet* in Marseilles Moulins gave his considered (and clearly well-informed) opinion on the boy's suitability for such an assignment:

Il ny manque pas dEsprict ny de Vivacité ny des lumières des affaires, mais un gros & pénible travail ne luy conviendroit pas à cause de son tempérament délicat, au surplus Jestime quil sacquittera parfaittement bien de touttes vos Commissions & de celles dautruy, et quil recevra volontiers vos Instructions comme vos réprimandes ayant un Esprit doux & docile enfin Il est du fort bon naturel, cest le Jugement que Jen fais tout autant que je puis le Connoître.

Evidently the *cadet* differed markedly in character from his cousin. Moulins commented on this: 'son génye avec lautre sont fort différents et se ressemblent en rien'. Evident, too, from these letters is the conscientiousness with which Moulins fulfilled his obligations toward the Galtiés as well as the care which was being taken to find the right sort of situation for the *cadet*.[46]

The young apprentice to Lyons was thus, despite his physical absence both from family and from Clermont, strongly influenced by both. The parental authority continued to be exercised and he found himself integrated into a small Clermontais sub-society within Lyons. Among Jean Galtié's close relations at Lyons were not only his cousin, the Moulins and Estiennes but also a branch of his mother's family, the Archimbauds. Jacques Galtié (the cousin) had similarly been surrounded by this world during his time at Lyons and when he returned to Clermont for a time in the 1720s, after a period spent in Paris between 1713 and 1718, he referred to it nostalgically in one of his letters to Moulins. He sent his regards to their 'véritables compatriotes Mrs Estienne, Figuière, Domergue, Birouste et autres' he wrote.[47] Comings and goings between the two towns were continuous and certain merchants clearly served as regular letter-carriers/purveyors of news and information. One such was Jean Altayrac, referred to by one of Moulins's correspondents as 'Laimable Altayrac', the regularity of whose trips between Lyons and Clermont suggests that he was handling a considerable trade between the two areas. Most of Moulins's many Lodévois correspondents recognized his services at some stage.[48]

An understanding of these links with Lyons is important for two

46. Fonds Moulins, xvii, letters of Moulins of 24 Aug. 1697, 5 Oct. 1697, 24 May 1698, 7 Aug. 1700.
47. Fonds Moulins, iv, Jacques Galtié (cousin) to Raymond Moulins, 7 Aug. 1720.
48. E.g. Fonds Moulins, iv, Mathieu to Moulins, 2 Aug. 1718.

reasons. They inform us about the characteristics of, and limits to, commercial life in Clermont, and demonstrate the town's integration into an extra-regional, in part international, economic hierarchy and system. And the manner in which the links were established and regulated provides an insight into the functioning of what was the universal social and economic unit in the period – the paternally dominated family group which operated according to strict, traditional, customary procedures, particularly with respect to the training of sons. Such a system has been referred to as the necessary complement to Absolutism. Certainly the efficient functioning of such a system was a most effective form of social control and there were parallels, it is clear, in the absolute power of kings and fathers, and in the distinct treatment given to different sons in bourgeois as in royal families.

The regularity of contact with other advanced commercial centres acquainted at least the elite of Clermont's merchants with the latest commercial techniques. Galtié père et fils kept regular, double-entry accounts the accuracy of which was boasted of by the son in a letter to his cousin: 'tu sçais de quelle manière je tiens "nos livres". Il ne passe rien dextraord^re jusquici'.[49] Contact was maintained with suppliers and customers by letter-writing and clearly a great part of such merchants' time was spent in a 'bureau', whose walls would be lined with letter- and account-books. Jacques Savary's *Le parfait négociant* would have served as a fundamental text for such merchants, not only providing them with the necessary technical guidance which they required, but also forming and reflecting the moral and philosophic approach to business life of which we have had a glimpse in the Galtiés' correspondence. Savary, like Galtié père et fils and Raymond Moulins, laid great emphasis on the importance of the training of merchants and showed a similar awareness of the dangers of too easy an access to money. The coincidence is no cause for surprise. Savary had worked many years in the wholesale trade, like Galtié and Moulins, before becoming an inspector and writer.[50]

The amount of time spent in the bureau preparing accounts and writing letters was probably the principal distinction between the nature of the occupation of the large wholesale merchant and those of the majority of Clermont's retail merchants, 'trafiquants' and artisans. In other aspects of their occupation there were fewer contrasts. This was particularly true of the need to travel, to visit fairs and to have face-to-face contact with customers and suppliers. We have already recorded

49. Fonds Moulins, IV, 28 Oct. 1697.
50. *Le parfait négociant*, pp. 37–41. Savary retired from commerce in 1660, he informs his readers in his preface.

some instances of the Moulins' and Galtiés' peregrinations but what we have not emphasized is the frequency and regularity of their travelling. It was evidently a crucial element in the occupation of merchant. Among Moulins's records there are details of what seem to be all his commercial travelling on behalf of his employer Louis Durand between 1679 and 1693. During the first years after his apprenticeship in 1671 he would have been employed in relatively menial tasks (the lack of travel suggests) in his master's offices at Lyons. But from 1679 the amount of travelling which he was required to do clearly increased, and for some years voyages must have absorbed most of his time. In 1679 he made three trips to Franche-Comté, in 1681 one to Beaucaire; in 1682, 1686, 1687 and 1689 he visited the cloth-making centres of northern France (as well as those of the Austrian Netherlands and Holland in 1682). In 1687 he visited Grenoble and Chambéry, and regularly, every year, between 1685 and 1693, in addition to the other travelling undertaken in some of these years, he visited Languedoc and Provence attending three or four fairs on each occasion as well as visiting various industrial and commercial centres. These were long and, no doubt, arduous voyages and it was for this reason that they were generally undertaken (it would seem) by younger merchants in their prime. From the late 1690s Moulins visited Languedoc but rarely: by then it was clearly his nephew Jean who was acting as his representative in the province. Moulins kept meticulous accounts of his travel costs and, once he had completed a trip, true merchant that he was, he carefully computed the daily cost of his travel. (There are records of four such calculations, and the cost ranged between 2 *livres* 14 *sous* and 3 *livres* 13 *sous*.)[51] So travel, sometimes for long periods, at times of the year which were dictated by the dates of fairs (whose timing in turn was conditioned by the rhythms of agricultural and industrial life), was an essential activity in any merchant organization, and the predominant occupation of the individual merchant at a certain stage of his career. So regular was such travel that the merchant knew exactly whom he would meet (bar mishap or financial embarrassment) at the fairs and in what inns, for what nights, he would stay. A letter which Moulins wrote in 1711, when he had ceased to travel regularly, shows that inn-bookings were made on a regular basis – 'Je ne sçay pas où les Lionnais logent [à] présent', he wrote with reference to Montagnac, 'de mon tems cestoit au signe et au Cheval blanc.'[52]

That, at least in their commitment to travel, the wholesale merchant shared characteristics with traders of all means and ranks is apparent

51. Fonds Moulins, xxiii, 'carnet de dépenses de voyages'.
52. Fonds Moulins, xvii, Moulins to Rigal of Montpellier, 12 March 1711.

from numerous contracts registered before Clermontais notaries. Some Clermontais merchants would seem to have led almost entirely itinerant existences, dividing their time between their travels and short stays in Clermont, and continuously buying and selling, taking advantage of local and regional price differentials about which – their livelihood depended on this – they were expert. One such, Guillaume Agret, 'marchand', 'estant en estat d'aller fere voiage pour négossier de sa vacation', left the remains of his stock in the hands of his brother-in-law to be sold in his absence. The nature of the stock suggests that Agret was a superior tinker: it was valued at just over 115 *livres* and included stockings, shirts, short lengths of linen and coarse cloth, ribbons, patches of silk and a silver knife and spoon.[53] Other merchants hired 'pedlars' to do the travelling for them. This was the course taken by Antoine Martin who signed two contracts with commercial travellers in the 1690s – one, a native of the diocese of Turin, was promised a salary of 90 *livres* for his efforts as well as free stockings and shoes – most essential extras for the pedlar, there is no doubt, and perhaps a pre-industrial equivalent to the company car – and the other recorded in his contract that he owed his employer 900 *livres* for goods which he had sold in the diocese of Lodève.[54]

These contracts reveal an essential element in Clermont's trade: the distribution and sale of goods in more isolated areas which were without their own retailers. Socially and economically, though, such traders would have been the most humble members of the merchant community. They have their equivalent in Spain in the famed Catalan 'pedlars', who distributed similar products in the backward areas of the Iberian peninsula which, likewise, lacked a commercial, shop-keeping population of their own. Such pedlars shared the wholesale merchant's need to travel but the nature of their role and commercial contacts was at an opposite extreme – the wholesale merchant dealt in bulk, and rarely had contact with the ultimate customer, the pedlar dealt in minute quantities and sold not only to the ultimate customer but to the most humble ultimate customers.

The need to attend fairs was also shared by the generality of Clermont's commercial population. The town must literally have been emptied of the majority of its population five times a year when the fairs of Pézenas and Montagnac were held. It was fairs which made possible the multifarious human contact which provided the links in the vast, and dense, commercial network in which Clermont was involved. There was

53. ADH II E 25 89, 5 Jan. 1672.
54. ADH II E 26 129, 2 March 1692, II E 25 98, 8 Aug. 1695.

a certain specialization between different fairs. If Beaucaire served both as important textile market and as the major centre for Mediterranean and oriental products, the importance of Pézenas and Montagnac lay, above all, in the commercialization of textile production. Merchants involved in trading in skins would travel to Rodez for it was there that 'le grand commerce de cuirs dans cette province se fait',[55] and wool merchants would attend the markets and fairs of Béziers and Narbonne early in the year, before the sheep-shearing in May, to ensure their wool supplies. It is in Narbonne that we find Pierre Flottes in February of 1712 supplying himself with the reputed wools of Roussillon and of the dioceses of Narbonne and Béziers.[56] Then there were smaller, 'general' fairs, likewise attended (there is evidence) by numerous Clermontais, such as those held at Lodève, St-Chinian, Bédarieux and Le Vigan. That a large part of Clermont's population went to these fairs is suggested by a contemporary report which stated that Le Vigan's fair was attended by 'La pluspart de ses [Clermont's] habitants ... tant pour leurs affaires particulières que pour celles de leur commerce'.[57] Even Beaucaire, despite its distance and international fame, attracted a large number of Clermontais of all statuses. There is evidence of the presence there of richer merchants, involved in the wholesale trade, like Pierre Souvier, marchand-droguiste, and Pierre Rouquet, marchand, who formed a society in 1671 'pour l'achapt vente et débit de marchandises des draps serges cadis toilles et toutes autres marchandises dont led sieur Rouquet fils a cognoissance'.[58] And there is also evidence that this great fair provided an outlet for both the economic and the social life of humbler inhabitants of Clermont. Groups of artisans and 'fripiers' (pedlars) came to Beaucaire together and lived five or six to the room for the duration of the fair. Their aims were in part amusement (the enjoyment of a good meal was clearly high on their list of priorities) and in part commercial gain, often on a small scale – two tanners' wives, in 1780, bought a roll of linen at the fair in the belief that they would make a small profit on its resale: 'cette marchandize a du débit à Clermont', they reported.[59]

Thus represented at the great fairs of Languedoc was the whole spectrum of Clermont's commerce, from rich wholesale merchant to humble fripier, and it met there with the wider currents of national and inter-

55. ADH C4924, Letter of de Murat, sub-delegate Carcassonne, 21 May 1724.
56. ADH II E 26 172, 28 Feb. 1712.
57. The presence of merchants at St-Chinian, Le Vigan and Bédarieux is recorded in ACC BB4, 7, 17 Nov. 1735 and 28 Oct. 1775, and ADH, Ordinaires Clermont, Case 780, 23 Oct. 1790.
58. ADH II E 25 89, 11 Dec. 1671.
59. ADH, Ordinaires Clermont, Case 208, 8 Aug. 1780.

national trade. But, as we emphasized in the last chapter, it was the sale of Languedoc's industrial production as much as its exceptional geographical position, communications and variety of agricultural produce which gave these fairs a special importance, and above all the sale of textiles. This primacy we have noted too in the Galtié–Moulins correspondence. And Clermont was an important industrial as well as commercial centre. We have seen in the last chapter that it was one of a chain of hill-town centres which emerged to a dominant position in the regional cloth industry in the sixteenth century. But the town did not produce only cloth. A wide range of other crafts was practised too.

Apart from the feudal transaction already referred to, some of the earliest evidence which we have of the town's industrial life is provided by the statutes of, and clerical reports on, the 'confréries', professional organizations which had a mixed religious, social and economic role.[60] Confréries existed in the seventeenth century for the hatters, shoemakers and tanners, glovers, carpenters, masons and joiners, weavers, 'laboureurs' and merchants.[61] The long industrial tradition of Clermont is illustrated by the invariable claims made in confrérie statutes that the craft in question had been practised 'de tout temps immémorial'.[62] Without confréries were numerous other crafts: linen-weaving, tile-manufacture, pottery, stocking-knitting, soap manufacture, card- and comb-making (for the textile industry), barrel-making, harness-making, blacksmiths' workshops, baking, wheel-making, fulling, dyeing, shearing, carding, spinning etc.[63] Apprenticeships to these various trades were generally registered before notaries and an analysis of all such contracts between the years 1686 and 1700 gives some idea of the size and importance of some of these crafts or professions (Table 2).

Apparent from this analysis is that there were two sides to Clermont's industrial, as there were to its commercial, life. It was both local artisanal production and service centre within the Lodévois and also, in the case of three industries (cloth manufacture, hat-making and tanning), a regional centre of some importance. The same contemporary who extolled the importance of Clermont's market in 1645 emphasized too the importance of these three industries. Clothiers, he reported, were using high-quality Spanish wools to make fine cloth and their industry was of sufficient

60. As in Provence, confréries showed a tendency, until the Colbertian reforms at least, 'à la liberté en matière de travail, mais à l'association en matière de vie sociale et religieuse', a special characteristic of southern France according to M. Agulhon, *La sociabilité méridionale*, I, 140–2.
61. ADH G1060–1061, 'visites pastorales' of May 1649 and 18 May 1659.
62. For instance those of the hatters and weavers, ADH II E 25 43, II E 26 126, 18 Sept. 1633, 8 May 1689.
63. Appolis, *Lodève*, pp. 567–76.

Table 2. *Apprenticeships at Clermont, 1686–1700*

Professions	Apprenticeships
The cloth industry	
Weavers	73
Shearers	9
Clothiers	5
Dyer	1
Other industries and trades	
Hat-makers	37
Shoemakers	19
Card-makers	16
Leather-bleachers, tanners and curriers	8
Merchants	8
Tailors	5
Surgeons	4
Soap-makers	3
Apothecaries	2
Saddlers	2
Joiners	2
Bakers	2
Blacksmith	1
Potter	1
Stocking-maker	1

Source: all the notarial studies for these years: those of Villar (11 E 25 89–97), Pouget (11 E 25 98–103), Azemar (11 E 25 104–9), Pons (11 E 26 89–105, 133–49), Fulcrand Delpon (11 E 26 116–32), Manié (11 E 26 164–8), François Delpon (11 E 26 171–4).

importance to justify the permanent presence in the town of cloth-commissioners from Lyons, Nice and Genoa; Clermont's large hat production was of the highest quality and its leather-workers were selling 'abondance de parchemins, maroquins et autres telles marchandises'.[64] Of these three industries it was undoubtedly cloth production which was the most important and this even before the process of industrial concentration in favour of Languedoc's hill-towns which we have observed in the sixteenth century. The feudal transaction of 1341 specifically mentions the annual appointment of officers to inspect wool and cloth qualities which suggests that Clermont's production was already of some size and importance.[65] Cloth production, to quote the minutes of the

64. Cited by Appolis, *Lodève*, p. 353.
65. Barral, *Régime municipal de Clermont*, p. 63.

discussion of the 'conseil de ville' for 1692, had been for many centuries 'laffaire principalle de lad. Commt^e et quj donne le principal secours au payement des tailles'.[66]

Some of the basic features of Clermont's agricultural life have been briefly mentioned in our description of the *pays* of the Lodévois. Additional information needs to be provided, however, if only to warn against the tendency to regard agricultural life as a separate compartment of the town's economic life for this, as we shall show, was far from being the case.

Each 'communauté' in the Lodévois had attached to it a certain agricultural area, known as its 'terroir', on the agricultural production of which, originally, its inhabitants had lived. With the growth of a large population, living in great part from industrial and commercial earnings, this ceased, of course, to be the case and with multiple land sales and purchases the land ownership of different communautés ceased to be rigorously confined to their terroirs. Still, the majority of the land holdings of Clermont's inhabitants were contained in the town's terroir, and the majority of land in the terroir was owned by Clermontais. (Deyon's study on Amiens shows that there was an understandable preference shown by urban land-purchasers for properties in their immediate vicinity.)[67] The physical characteristics of, and varieties of cultivation on, the 3,249 hectares which composed Clermont's terroir[68] are revealed to us by an immensely painstaking analysis of the seventeenth-century versions of the town's *compoix*[69] by the local historian, Adolphe Crémieux. One particularly striking characteristic disclosed is the extraordinary diversity in the quality of land included in the town's terroir. This was, of course, in major part a consequence of Clermont's geographical position in a zone of climatic and geographic transition, but an exceptional variability in the quality of terrain was also, and continues to be, a general characteristic of southern France and the Mediterranean area. Indeed it is to this exceptional variability that we owe the thoroughness of meridional cadastral surveys: the imposition of tax, to be done fairly, required very exact estimations of the potential yields of different types of land, suited for different types of crop. The most highly taxed category of land in the Clermontais was 'jardins et farregals' (gardens and land used for fodder crops) and the lowest category 'bois de haute futaille, guarritz et autres hermes et campestres' (rough woodland, scrub or low-

66. ACC BB1, 11 Nov. 1692.
67. *Amiens*, p. 326.
68. Appolis, *Lodève*, p. 143.
69. Land register maintained for fiscal purposes.

quality grazing). The best quality of the first category paid 720 times more tax than the lowest quality of the second. Between these two extremes, in descending order of quality, came 'prés', olive groves and the joint category of 'champs et vignes'. Each category was divided into up to seven grades: 'Passe-bon', 'Bon', 'Passe-moins', 'Moins', 'Passe-faible', 'Faible' and 'Faible de Faible'.

The primacy in this hierarchy given to 'jardins', 'farregals' and 'prés' is significant. The high value given to, and obtainable from, such land was a reflection of scarcity. As in most Mediterranean areas, land with soil of sufficient quality and with adequate irrigation facilities to support intensive cultivation or to provide good grazing was in short supply. We are reminded again that only a small part of the Languedocian land surface could support the type of intensive husbandry, with its exotic products, which attracted the eye of the northern traveller. The 'jardins', privileged with respect to the amount of manure which they were allotted, and in the frequency with which they were tilled, and, as agricultural historians have emphasized, the 'laboratories' for agronomical experimentation, were in particularly short supply.[70] Thus the first three, and most highly taxed, types of land only account for a small part of the Clermontais land surface and it was in fact the classic Mediterranean combination of wheat, olives and vines which occupied the majority of Clermont's terroir. Olives and vines were of similar importance – there was no vine monoculture as yet though the opening of the port of Sète in the 1660s and the completion of the Canal du Midi in 1681, by improving the supply situation for grain and facilitating the commercialization of the products of the vine, were encouraging a slow move towards such a monoculture. A calculation made in 1628 showed that approximately 18% of Clermont's terroir was planted with vines, and some 439 hectares (or $13\frac{1}{2}$%) with olives.[71] 'Champs' (Crémieux's calculations show) accounted for slightly less than the combined area planted with olives and vines, or about 30% of the total land surface, and thus (in view of the fact that the quantity of land occupied by 'jardins', 'prés' and 'farregals' was negligible) the lowest category of land, rough grazing and woodland, was also the largest, accounting for about 40% of Clermont's terroir.[72]

Whereas much of the grain production would have been consumed locally, the products of olive and vine were pre-eminently non-

70. J. Meuvret, 'Agronomie et jardinage aux xvie et xviie siècles' in *Eventail de l'histoire: hommage à Lucien Febvre*, 11, 154–6. A. Crémieux's analysis of Clermont's seventeenth-century *compoix* shows that tax was imposed on only slightly over 3 *seterées* of 'jardins' and 6–7 of 'farregals' (*La vie politique et économique à Clermont*, pp. 154–6).
71. Appolis, *Lodève*, pp. 418, 428.
72. Crémieux, *La vie politique*, pp. 101–12.

subsistence, commercial crops. Thus we can make a first correction to the idea of sharp agricultural/commercial/industrial distinctions in the Clermontais – agriculture was highly commercialized, its products were traded in extensively, and the activities of 'ménager' and merchant would thus have had similarities. The quality of Clermont's olive oil was particularly high and this added to its suitability for trading: in 1741 it was described as 'de tout temps . . . la meilleure de ce pays et la plus estimée et la plus recherchée par les voituriers qui en font transport'.[73] The product of the vine was commercialized in various forms: as table grapes, distilled as eau-de-vie, dried, or as wine. The local Clermontais 'muscat' was held in high esteem and had, like the town's olive oil, distant customers: in 1695 we find a voiturier of St-Flour-en-Auvergne contracting with a Clermontais merchant to carry twelve *charges* of wine to Clermont-en-Auvergne, for example.[74]

The category 'champs' was a less definite one then those of 'vignes' or 'olivettes', not only because 'champs' could be used in a variety of different ways, but also because those of lower quality were little superior to 'hermes' or waste land. The great virtue of Le Roy Ladurie's study on Languedoc lies in its demonstration of variations in both the extent and the form of the exploitation of the soil as a consequence of fluctuations in population pressure.[75] These variations mainly affected 'champs' which thus formed a category which grew in times of population expansion and heavy demand for land, and shrank in times of population decline. These fluctuations are revealed in the Clermontais *compoix* – neglected 'champs' might decline to the status of 'hermes' or, in counterpart, 'hermes' might be improved to the extent that they became described as 'champs'. This was a cyclical process. In the mid-eighteenth century, for example, the neglect of much of Clermont's terroir had reached such proportions that a proposition was made by the consuls to oblige all newcomers in the town to cultivate some abandoned land and hence contribute to the payment of taxes, but between 1750 and 1789 it would seem that renewed population pressure led to the reclamation of land which had gone out of cultivation.[76] Both the decline and the rise in the 'champs' category are thus revealed in these cyclical variations experienced in the eighteenth century. But it should be added that the ease with which land might slip into or out of the 'champs' category as well as enhancing this cyclical process illustrates a characteristic of Mediterranean agriculture about which we have already commented – its

73. ACC BB4, 16 Dec. 1741.
74. ADH II E 25 98, 28 Oct. 1695.
75. *Paysans*, p. 8: 'je croyais percevoir l'immense respiration d'une structure sociale'.
76. Appolis, *Lodève*, p. 202 and see p. 439.

relative poverty, with respect to the quality of soil above all, and its dependence on a continuously high labour input for its fertility to be maintained; a season's or two seasons' neglect and land became worthless. The rate of degradation was high and an inheritance composed of degraded land was frequently refused for it would not have generated sufficient income to pay the tax imposed on it. The need for a high labour input to secure a reasonable return from land applied to other types of cultivation too – to the 'jardins' (as we have emphasized), to vineyards (which generally, in this period, occupied poorer-quality land and were often owned by smaller landowners) and to olive groves, above all, which required up to five tillings a year – 'la culture de cet arbuste exige des soins minutieux', Appolis writes.[77]

Most of the other facets of Clermont's agriculture which emerge from the *compoix* are relatively predictable in view of what other studies on the region·have revealed. The 'feudal' system was relatively light, and the extent of fiscal privilege low (Languedoc was an area of 'taille réelle', tax-exemption being attached to particular pieces of land rather than arising from the status of the landowner). Units of land were small for the most part and there were few large concentrated properties. The estates of big landowners were generally composed of a large number of fragments: for instance those of two large landowners cited by Crémieux were formed of forty-two and fifteen different plots of land.[78] The extent of land ownership was widespread: the fact that there were slightly over one thousand property-owners listed in the *compoix*, when the total number of families living in Clermont cannot have been much larger than this number, suggests that there were few Clermontais with no property at all. It would seem that both the nature of terrain and the labour-intensive character of the major crops contributed to denying significant economies of scale to the large-scale farmer and favoured, in contrast, the committed small-scale producer prepared to use his own and his family's labour intensively. Included in the *compoix* were urban buildings as well as agricultural property and, as I have already suggested, there was clearly no sharp demarcation between the two. There is plentiful evidence in the *compoix* to illustrate that Clermont (and this is a typical characteristic of Mediterranean towns) housed a significant agricultural as well as industrial and merchant population. The existence of a confrérie for laboureurs we have already signified but the *compoix* also illustrates that whereas there were very few isolated farms or agricultural buildings *outside* the town, *inside* there were a great number of houses which had

77. *Lodève*, p. 427.
78. *La vie politique*, p. 94, n. 2.

attached to them buildings and facilities designed for agricultural use.[79] This concentration of agricultural activity in the town did not improve its general salubrity. Pigs were slaughtered within the town's precinct and the practice of using interior courtyards (which were described as 'patus') as compost/manure heaps was particularly unhealthy. A doctor visiting Lodève in 1751, where this practice existed too, reported on the nauseating conditions to which 'la malpropreté de leurs manoirs, l'impureté de l'air qu'ils y respirent ... la saleté et les mauvaises odeurs des laines qu'ils y travaillent ... les exhalaisons impures des patus ou cloaques qui sont par malheur si nombreux dans cette ville' gave rise.[80]

Only two sorts of sizeable buildings, or groups of buildings, existed in any abundance outside the town. First, on the hillsides to the north of the town were situated a few large 'bergeries'. The significant investment in such buildings illustrates something which we have already noted in connection with the town's market – the importance of the livestock trade in the Clermontais and Lodévois. Clearly the stabling of large herds of sheep or cattle was not possible within the town. Secondly, scattered throughout the terroir of Clermont was a relatively restricted number of what were known as 'mas' or 'métairies' which consisted generally of a residence, stables, barns, 'colombier' or 'pigeonnier', gardens, farmyards and a small surrounding domain. These collections of buildings had both agricultural and residential functions and have as much social as economic significance for they were the 'country seats', as it were, of the rare noble or more abundant bourgeois families of Clermont. The top echelons of Clermont's society owned both town and country houses.[81]

The possession of a country property by the bourgeois town-dweller or, for that matter, of a town property by the rich country-dweller, was very much a characterizing feature of the social life of Clermont and the Clermontais, as, indeed, it was of the Mediterranean region, and pre-industrial economy as a whole. The existence of the same tradition at Lyons we have already observed – Moulins had mentioned in his reports on Jean Galtié (the apprentice) the singular favour which had been shown to him in his being invited to spend a few days at his master's 'grange', or country house. And the Moulins family itself had both a town and a country property in the Clermontais: while the nephew who had entered the priesthood inhabited the town house another nephew and niece were inhabiting the country house which was close to the neighbouring village of Lieuran.[82] Ownership of a rural property, particularly

79. Crémieux, *La vie politique*, p. 149.
80. Appolis, *Lodève*, pp. 345, 439.
81. Crémieux, *La vie politique*, pp. 132–5.
82. ADR, Fonds Moulins, IV, contains a large batch of letters to Moulins from members of his family in the Clermontais region.

if attached to it was noble land which would justify its owner's referring to it as a 'seigneurie', represented the height of the aspirations of the rising merchant in Clermont.

The 'character of ruling groups ... varied from place to place and reflected the economic, social and political balances within each town', L. A. Hunt concludes at the end of a study in which she illustrates the divergencies in the make-up of the elites of Reims and Troyes.[83] The divergencies extended, of course, to the entire social structure and it would seem relevant, too, to add some consideration of the fact of variations in the make-up of elites over time as a consequence of fluctuations in the 'social conjuncture'. As we have already suggested, the 'social' counterpart of economic expansion was, on the one hand, increased social mobility and, on the other, the development of class-like social divisions, whereas depression tended (to quote Mousnier) to reinforce 'les rapports sociaux traditionnels'.[84]

So commercially involved a town as Clermont experienced fully the long secular swings in the economic and social conjuncture which characterized the European economy in the pre-industrial period and this makes necessary a certain caution in describing its social structure. There were, without doubt, variations in the composition of its elite, and in the extent of social mobility, over time. With this reservation made, however, it does seem justifiable to state that Clermontais society, although not without members from the first and second estates, was exceptionally dominated by its commercial and industrial groups.[85] The clerical presence was relatively reduced. There was no bishopric as at Lodève where bishop, chapter and entourage complicated the town's social structure; nor powerful abbey as at St-Guilhem-le-Désert whose abbot, like the bishop of Lodève, added to his spiritual an important seigneurial role. Nor was there a sub-delegacy, and the consular municipal offices, until the eighteenth century, were elective, temporary and carried only a small stipend. Virtually the only offices which were exercised within Clermont were those connected with the relatively unimportant seigneurial court. These were those of 'viguier', 'juge', 'lieutenant-de-juge', 'procureur juridictionnel' and 'greffier'. The minor significance attached to even the most prestigious of these posts is

83. 'Local élites at the end of the Old Régime: Troyes and Reims, 1780–1789', *French Historical Studies* 9 (1976), 397–8.
84. *Les hiérarchies sociales*, p. 38.
85. And in sharp contrast to social structure in isolated rural areas. See, for example, P. M. Jones, 'The rural bourgeoisie of the southern Massif-Central: a contribution to the study of the social structure of *ancien-régime* France', *Social History* 4 (1979), 65–83.

shown by the fact that it was usually exercised in conjunction with the office of notary.[86] 'Les négossiants ici font noblesse', a military captain, no doubt accustomed to more conventional types of social structure, commented during a visit to Clermont in the 1740s.[87] As we shall see, there were special circumstances contributing to a particularly marked dominance of the town by a commercial/industrial elite in the 1740s but the mere fact that this was a possibility suggests a relative weakness in alternative elite groups. Typical of what was effectively the dominating social group in Clermont were the Galtiés who were large landowners as well as rich wholesale merchants. One of the letters from Galtié père to Raymond Moulins illustrates well their pre-eminent social position within Clermont. The letter was written in connection with the marriage of Jacques, his oldest son, to Catherine, daughter of Jean Estienne, bourgeois (brother of Raymond Estienne, merchant of Lyons). Having drawn up a marriage contract in Jean Estienne's country house, a métairie at Lacoste (a neighbouring village), a gratified Galtié wrote to his Lyonnais correspondent telling him about the proposed marriage but not providing great detail about the Estienne family or their daughter, 'pourquoj [il] vous es cogneu que cest de la plus honneste la plus reglée et la plus comode de nostre ville quant à la personne vous lavez vue à vostre ville chez Monsieur son oncle'.[88]

Having once accepted the idea that Clermont's social structure was exceptionally dominated by commercial wealth it is necessary to consider the question of the relationship of Clermont's elite with other towns for there was not only a social hierarchy within each town but also, as it were, a pecking-order between towns which was of particular significance in its effects on elite behaviour. It was to the superior town that the member of the local elite might go to advance his career or social status, and it was on the behaviour of the superior town's elite that he modelled his own. There were various types of hierarchy – administrative, military, judicial, ecclesiastical and economic being the major ones. In Clermont's case Lodève was its immediate ecclesiastical superior, Toulouse its judicial, and Montpellier its military and administrative capital. The question of the identity of its economic superior, or superiors, is more complex for two reasons. First, in that it, or they, changed over time with the decline in the commercial and industrial importance of Languedoc's traditional provincial commercial centres as a consequence of the province's gradual integration into a national and international economy dominated by a

86. Appolis, *Lodève*, pp. 33–7, 149.
87. ADH C6763, Dampierre, captain in the Bourbonnais regiment, to de la Devèze, commander of the province, 29 May 1749.
88. ADR, Fonds Moulins, IV, 3 Aug. 1694.

series of different merchant centres, and secondly in that economic links, unlike administrative ones, rarely took a simple, symmetrical, pyramidal form but tended to radiate in a variety of directions.

In view of the importance of commercial life in Clermont, and the weakness of other sections of the town's elite, these commercial links were of particular significance. The town's commercial elite was conscious of forming part of an economic hierarchy in which it had a number of superiors, some within the province – Montpellier, Nîmes and Béziers – but others, and increasingly the most important, outside – Lyons, Chalon, Grenoble, Marseilles, Paris, Bordeaux, Genoa, Geneva, Seville, Rome. It was to such centres that the Clermontais merchant was effectively subordinated economically (and thus socially) and it was to them that he apprenticed his son, or moved himself, if he was anxious to improve his family's 'condition'. The continual comings and goings between Lyons and Clermont we have described but what we have not emphasized (it is fairly self-evident) is the respect in which the ex-Clermontais, Lyonnais merchants (such as Moulins or d'Estienne) were held and the consciousness of all correspondents with Lyons that they were in touch with a town superior to Clermont.

It would seem that these strong economic and social links with a variety of commercial centres (foremost of which was Lyons in the seventeenth century and, as we shall see, Marseilles in the eighteenth) marked significantly the social structure of the town. Towns in more isolated, agrarian areas of France, dominated more completely by agricultural, administrative and judicial elites, would have had what one might describe as 'autonomous' social structures. By this is meant that the whole cycle of social mobility could be achieved within the town, a climax being reached with the individual's purchase of land and office. If social or career ambitions could not be satisfied locally, inhabitants of such conventional towns would seek preferment in the regional administrative, judicial, ecclesiastical or economic centres. It is not that Clermont's pattern of social mobility completely ignored such a conventional and symmetrical pattern. There was, invariably, such a self-contained local or regional cycle of social mobility. But the town's integration into these varied and geographically dispersed economic and social circuits would undoubtedly have added to the complexity of the whole process of social mobility. Some of the major consequences would have been likely to be as follows:

1. Awareness of the superior fortunes, and social status, obtainable by merchants in larger commercial centres would have caused Clermontais merchants to:
   (a) be less satisfied by their local commercial success;
   (b) be less impressed by the status of local landed families.

2. Movement of a part of the town's bourgeoisie to other towns would have resulted in there being more 'space' in the town for other Clermontais to develop their fortunes.

3. Contact with more advanced sectors of the European economy would have contributed to the diffusion in Clermont not only of advanced commercial and industrial techniques but also of 'modern' ideas and attitudes.

Not the least ideological and religious consequence of these links was the infiltration into Clermont of the ideas of the Reform movement. The town at the beginning of the seventeenth century contained some two hundred Protestant families and was declared in 1602 a 'place de sûreté' for the Huguenots.[89] Persecution, which was intensified from the 1650s and reached its climax with the Revocation of the Edict of Nantes, caused a gradual dwindling in this number. In 1687 it was declared by the first consul that the town's Catholic population had been boosted by sixty families of 'nouveaux convertis'.[90] A rump of Huguenots continued to practise in the eighteenth century, however.[91] The existence of this large congregation (about one-fifth of the town's population) had been both a sign of Clermont's commercial and hence ideological openness and, in that Protestants married Protestants, and Protestants were, increasingly, excluded from conventional forms of social promotion, a reinforcement to the observed tendency for an important part of Clermont's elite to be integrated into social circuits which were only in part provincial.

It was perhaps the distinctiveness of Clermont's social structure, and the town's exclusion from some more conventional sources of social mobility, that contributed to a sense of rivalry with its more privileged neighbour (from the point of view of administrative offices and clerical appointments), Lodève, and an often-remarked spirit of independence. A significant episode, demonstrating both these characteristics, was the adoption by the town of a new name, Clermont-l'Hérault, in 1789, in place of that of Clermont-de-Lodève, which had implied a position of subordination to the diocesan capital.

Among those who commented on these characteristics was Louis Bazile de Bernage, intendant, who in 1733 expressed his view that in Clermont 'Tous les esprits ... sont ... depuis longtemps, des brouillons'.[92] The sub-delegate at Lodève, Bonnafous, held similar views: he confided in a letter to the intendant in 1729 that in 'Ce pays là [the

89. A. Durand, *Annales de la ville de Clermont-l'Hérault et de ses environs*, p. 35.
90. ACC BB1, 26 Aug. 1687.
91. A survey carried out in 1761 states that there were thirty-two Protestants at Clermont (ADH C6554).
92. Cited by Appolis, *Lodève*, p. 258.

Clermontais] ... l'esprit de cabale et de faction reigne plus que la vérité.'[93] Inspectors, who arrived in the town with the objectivity which is the privilege of the outsider, were struck by the same phenomena. Dominique Tricou, writing to the secretary of the intendancy about industrial problems, blamed the difficulties on the 'impunitté qui est le Dieu tutélaire de ce pais', and added, 'la plus grande partie de ces gens d'icy ils sont grossiers, insolents et sans éducation'.[94] The Chevalier de Quérelles, a rare member of the town's elite whose status came from the holding of office rather than from trade, expressed similar views. As 'lieutenant du roi' for Clermont he was responsible for the maintenance of law and order – no mean task, he was to find. In September 1763 he reported to the commander of the province that he had ordered two 'cavaliers' of the 'maréchaussée' to arrest a persistent trouble-maker and justified his action in terms of the example it would provide 'dans cette ville où le peuple ne connoît d'autre loy que sa volonté et son insolence'. But the example clearly had little effect for a year later we find de Quérelles writing to de Montaran, intendant du commerce, of the difficulty he was having in getting the latter's orders fulfilled and explained that 'ils sont si peu accoutumés à la subordination et à l'obéissance dans ce pays, qu'ils regardent comme quelque chose de méritoire de ne rien faire de ce qui leur vient de la part des magistrats'.[95]

So Clermontais society had (in an extreme form, it would seem) many of those characteristics which, as we argued in the last chapter, were comparatively widespread in Languedoc in the pre-industrial period. The comments of administrators and clerics are of particular interest because they are those of outsiders, who had been formed in different social environments and who were thus acutely sensitive to the original features of local society. The vehemence of their reaction is probably to be explained by their insecurity in a society which was undeferential or, if deferential, attributed as much status to wealth as to rank. Frequently, indeed, their scorn was directed specifically at members of the commercial elite of local towns whose wealth would have been greater than their own. Thus Bishop Souillac of Lodève described Jean Altayrac (the 'aimable Altayrac' of the Moulins correspondence), who had acquired a vast fortune and purchased the mayoralty of Clermont, as 'un personnage qu'il faut humilier pour le contenir', and he held similar views of the rich clothiers of his episcopal town – in a letter to Intendant de Bernage he

---

93. ADH C2498, Bonnafous to de Bernage, 29 July 1729.
94. ADH C2424, Tricou to Le Nain, 7 April 1745.
95. ADH C6764, De Quérelles to Marquis de Moncan, 4 Sept. 1763, 23 Sept. 1764. De Quérelles was a conseiller du roi, auditeur in the Cour des Aides of Montpellier and lieutenant du roi in Clermont.

complained of the 'grossièreté d'esprit et de manières qui fait le caractère de ces gens'.[96]

Appolis's explanation for Clermont's 'spirit of independence' is that it was a consequence of the town's long struggle with its seigneur, the Count of Clermont, in the seventeenth century.[97] But this explanation does not seem satisfactory in that, as we have seen, there is evidence not only for Clermont's relationships' with other towns being marked by independence and a lack of mutual respect but also for a widespread independence, and disrespect for authority, *within* the town. A more complete explanation, which would account for both aspects of this independence, is that it was a social consequence of both the widespread division of property and the exceptional extent of commercial activity in Clermont and resultant high levels of social mobility. The widespread distribution of both land and commercial and industrial capital encouraged a feeling of equality and independence. The recent, commercial origins of the town's elite would (it seems likely) have detracted from the respect in which it was held. The military captain who categorized the members of the town's elite as 'négossiants' blamed Clermont's law and order problem on their lack of authority: 'cette ville, goûterait toutes les dousseurs de la vie dans son genre montagnare', he wrote, 'si les chefs de la police, savoient mettre les mains à leuvre'. As an example of their vacillations the captain cited the action of the mayor who, jointly with consular colleagues, had been responsible for his original summons to the town: terrified of a popular reaction to his participation in the request for outside help in maintaining order the mayor 'assuroit tout Clermont, par les fenêttres qu'il n'avoit jamais donné sa voix pour faire venir les troupes icy ... regétans toute la chose sur le lieut-maire'.[98]

So these were the varied economic and social 'continuities' which shaped and conditioned Clermont's development for many centuries in the pre-industrial period. In the nineteenth century the process of French industrialization disrupted these 'continuities' and Clermont's role decayed to that of purely local market and agricultural centre. The town itself, however, has remained unchanged and is a fascinating monument to these centuries of prosperity. A tour of the town not only informs us about details of its prosperous economic past but can actually provide insights into the various stages of its growth in the pre-industrial period (Map 3).[99]

96. Cited by Appolis, *Lodève*, pp. 159, 494.
97. Appolis, *Lodève*, p. 258.
98. ADH C6763.
99. This last section draws heavily on the article of G. Combarnous, 'Clermont-l'Hérault', pp. 257–72.

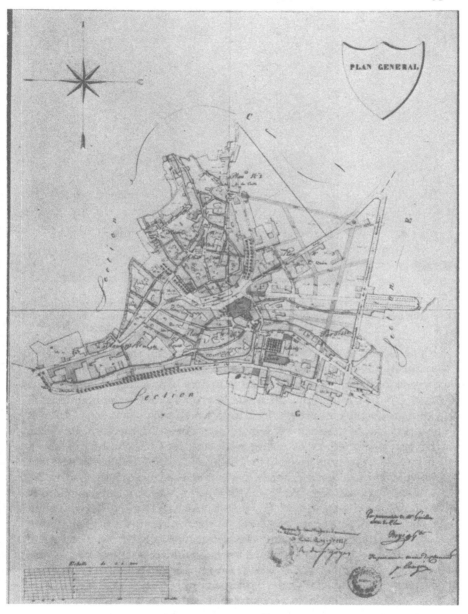

Map 3 Plan of Clermont-de-Lodève (ADH II S 122)

Ill. 5. Priority given to defence in the early mediaeval period: the main entrance to the town, the Pourtal Noou, adjoined the château on the hill of the Pioch

The origins of Clermont were Gallo-Roman but the oldest surviving architectural evidence is its feudal castle, built in the early middle ages on the peak of the hill of 'Le Pioch', 190 metres high, which dominates the town. To the south of this castle, the 'Acropolis' of Clermont as Gaston Combarnous, an enthusiastic local toponymist and poet, describes it, was grouped the first urban settlement for which architectural evidence remains, protected by defensive walls and four towers, one of which survives. The priority given to the castle, and to defence, in this period is shown by the fact that the main entry to the town was from the north side, via the impressive fortified 'Tour du Pourtal Noou', a gateway directly adjoining the château (Ill. 5). Prosperity, peace and a growing population in the twelfth, thirteenth and early fourteenth centuries contributed to a considerable urban growth: the defensive walls of the town were extended; the number of fortified towers doubled; a large, and likewise fortified, cathedral was built outside the ramparts to the town's south and was linked by defensive walls to the main body of the town; market sites formerly outside the walls were absorbed within the growing town; large open spaces, called 'plaines' or 'planols', were maintained between the ramparts and buildings outside the walls. What is known as the 'old town' thus achieved the size and form which it has maintained to this day.

Ill. 6. Interior of the old town: Renaissance façade

Clermont had become a large and well-protected citadel, sufficiently strong to escape occupation or damage during the Hundred Years War and Wars of Religion.

A decline in population pressure, continued military insecurity, and economic depression were the causes, it seems likely, of a lack of further urban growth in the fourteenth and fifteenth centuries. Clermont's richer inhabitants continued to live in the relatively cramped, fortified interior of the town. A few fine Gothic and Renaissance doorways and façades provide elegant memorials to their residence there (Ill. 6). Already in the fourteenth century, however, there had been some expansion outside the ramparts, in the 'faubourgs' of the town. Of primary importance in this expansion were religious foundations, and the advantages which adjacency to the River Rhonel, situated some 500 metres from the defensive walls, provided for certain of Clermont's industrial crafts and, particularly, for its tanners, clothiers, millers, fullers, soap-makers, dyers and potters. The industrial concentration along the Rhonel is recorded by the name of one of the streets adjoining the river, the 'Rue des Calquières' ('calquière' being a local term for tannery).

With the return of more favourable demographic (and economic) conditions and greater internal security in the sixteenth century, it was, it is clear, what became known as the 'new town', outside the walls, which expanded. Already by the seventeenth century about one third of the town's 571 houses[100] were situated outside the walls and in the eighteenth century the new town, it seems, outgrew the old, for the renewed expansion of the cloth industry occasioned a significant amount of building along the Rhonel, and road improvement occasioned an intensification in commercial through-traffic and the establishment of inns, carters, blacksmiths etc., along the far side of the Rhonel in what was named the 'Rue de la Coutellerie'. This suburban development was referred to by Pierre Delagenière, inspector of manufactures,[101] in a memoir which he composed about Clermont in 1740: 'les fauxbourgs sont presque aussi grands que la ville', he wrote, '[et] la plus habitée par des fabricands, dont quelques uns les ont embeli par des maisons de fabrique bien batties, avec leurs teintureries et un grand espace pour placer les Rames et sécher leurs Laines'.[102] Political power, too, shifted in favour of the more commercial 'new town', and its representatives, who began to dominate local politics, insisted on the primacy of their quarter. 'Clermont qui nétoit originairement qu'un pauvre village Bâti sur une Montagne sest étendu dans la plaine; que la Basse ville est aujourdhuy Clermont par le nombre la qualité et les facultés de ceux qui l'habitent', they claimed.[103]

This boast was not entirely justified for it is clear that the preference of some of Clermont's richest inhabitants was for those substantial houses within the fortified 'old town' which overlooked the plaines or planols which, decreasingly required for defence, had been planted with trees and served both as places for promenades and sites for the town's weekly markets (Ill. 7). Here are situated some of the town's finest houses and

100. Crémieux, *La vie politique*, p. 140; Combarnous, 'Clermont-l'Hérault', p. 266, n. 12.
101. On Delagenière, and other inspectors, see Appendix 2, p. 462.
102. ADH C2498, 'Etat contenant la situation présente et le détail de la fabrique de Clermont Lodève', 29 Dec. 1740; Combarnous, 'Clermont-l'Hérault', p. 268.
103. ACC BB6, 13 Feb. 1769.

Ill. 7. 'The preference of some of Clermont's richest inhabitants was for those substantial houses within the fortified "old town" which overlooked the plaines or planols'

recorded in notarial contracts are the special permissions granted by the representative of the Count of Clermont for the wealthy owners of some of these houses to pierce the defensive walls to make doors and windows. But with the exception of this privileged circumference the claim of the 'new town's' representatives holds, for it was increasingly the poorer members of the community who were confined to the old town. Weavers, spinners and other cloth-workers, above all, were crowded in the densely populated, narrow streets immediately adjoining the seigneurial castle. Their long presence there is recorded in the street-name 'Rue de la Filandière'. The workers in the artisanal hat industry were concentrated in the old town too – in the 'Rue de la Poulaillerie', behind the maison de ville which overlooked the planol.

In Clermont, then, as in so many cities, the old, cramped interior of the town was deserted by its richer inhabitants and became a ghetto for the poor. The contrasting fortunes of the two parts of the town are illustrated well by the varying quality of their housing. The buildings of the old town, apart from those adjoining the walls, were (and remain in many cases), to quote Inspector Delagenière, 'basses et mal batties', whereas those of the suburbs are, in the main, tall, well built, and equipped with vaulted 'rez-de-chaussées' (for the stock, animals, workshops of their owners) and stone staircases leading to front doors above the rez-de-chaussées. So common was this architectural feature in Clermont that a street whose slope made such constructions impracticable was previously known as 'Sans-Débasses' ('débas d'oustal' being Occitan for 'rez-de-chaussée'). Nothing illustrates better the nature of the existence of Clermont's population in the pre-industrial period than these rez-de-chaussées which form part of so many of the town's houses. 'Families', which could include, in addition to the conjugal unit, the parents of one of the spouses, domestic servants, apprentices, assistants and compagnons, resided above the workshops, storerooms, offices and stables on which their livelihoods depended. Here were processed, manufactured, refined or merely stored the articles in which the Clermontais traded.[104]

The layout of Clermont, therefore, as well as innumerable details of its architecture, reveals both the stages of its development, stages which (this is not surprising) are in accord with those long, rhythmic movements of expansion and depression on which French historians have rightly laid such emphasis in recent years, and also some of the permanent characteristics of its economy and society before the Industrial Revolution. Food, clothing and building were, as various historians have emphasized, the only substantial consumer goods in the pre-industrial period.[105] But whereas pre-industrial food and clothing have generally perished, examples of pre-industrial buildings survive in abundance. Thus in Clermont, as in so many other historic southern towns, the pretensions of the rich are recorded in numerous elegant doorways, windows, interior courtyards, staircases, examples of elegant ironwork or complete complexes of buildings, just as the lack of resources of the poor is eloquently portrayed by the simplicity and barrenness of the housing in parts of the old town. Clermont (like the polar ice-caps whose apparent white uniformity reveals to the scientist accurate information on the

104. Combarnous, 'Clermont-l'Hérault', p. 266, n. 14.
105. Cipolla, *Before the Industrial Revolution*, pp. 27–43.

Ill. 8. The Rhonel: 'A walk along this dry river-bed provides a melancholy view of Clermont's industrial and commercial decline'

climatic and atmospheric conditions of past millennia), despite the apparent uniformity of its dull orange/rose-coloured tiles and its dreary, greying whitewash, bears the marks of its many centuries of slow evolution and reveals to careful scrutiny the nature of its past economic and social life. From the towers of the castle five hundred years of Clermont's development can be scanned. Visible are the concentric nature of its growth until the fourteenth century as it spread slowly down the hill of the Pioch, the defensive gap between the fortified walls and the suburbs, the impressive, fortified cathedral, the concentration of industrial buildings along the winding Rhonel, and of commercial ones along the main Agde – Bédarieux road, and the greater volume of the new town than the old. From the bed of the Rhonel, now reduced to a trickle, its waters having been diverted to form a reservoir, the clearest impression of the reversal of the town's fortunes is obtained. The houses built along its banks have their accesses to the water, whose abundance and qualities were the original cause of their construction, boarded up. A walk along this dry river-bed provides a melancholy view of Clermont's industrial and commercial decline (Ill. 8).

4

Clermont during the seventeenth century

Some background information of relevance to Clermont's economic life in the seventeenth century has already emerged in previous chapters. As we have seen, the sixteenth century, in contrast to the period 1350–1500, was one of exceptional prosperity for France and Languedoc. The proximity to Spain brought three major advantages – employment for the excess French population, an excellent market for both industrial and agricultural products, and access to the bullion supplies whose European source was Seville. At the same time political circumstances disrupted the industries of Languedoc's major industrial competitors, the Italian and Catalan cloth-making centres, and access was obtained to Europe's most profitable overseas trade, that with the Levant, as a result of new trading arrangements with the Sultan and military disruptions to Venetian trade. The agricultural economy, as all studies have shown, was in expansion too, boosting the domestic demand for industrial goods. These varied stimuli to the Mediterranean economy were clearly to the province of Languedoc's, and thus to Clermont's, economic advantage.

The Wars of Religion brought a halt, but only a temporary halt, to the industrial and commercial expansion resultant on these stimuli. Growth was renewed, once peaceful circumstances returned in the early seventeenth century, and continued until approximately 1650 when a period of depression, and this time a durable depression, began. It was during this long period of expansion, this long 'A' phase, that, as we have seen, the geographical spread and organization of production of Lower Languedoc's industry took the forms which, with minor variations, were to be maintained until the industry's disappearance – the period of expansion favoured those cloth-producing towns situated in the foothills of the Massif Central and Pyrenees at the expense both of the cities of the Languedocian plain and of rural producers, and the characteristic structure of production became that in which the marchand-facturier or -fabricant occupied a dominant position. The industry was significant, and 'modern', not so much on account of the quality of its production (predominantly middling to low) but in that standardized cloths, finished and dyed locally, were being produced for sale in both domestic and foreign markets. It was significant too in that the organization of production was of a nature to allow some industrial accumulation of capital and thus to make the cloth industry a suitable avenue for social mobility.

Clermont, as we have seen, was one of those towns so situated as to benefit from the expansion. The importance of its cloth, tanning and hat-making industries in the sixteenth and seventeenth centuries has already been emphasized and they were representative of a general prosperity from which the town as a whole, like so many other Languedocian communities, benefited. A sign of this prosperity was the need for renewal of the town's *compoix* in 1646: this would have been a consequence of the number of property transactions to which the favourable agricultural conjuncture had contributed.[1] Another sign of prosperity was the large number of butchers operating in Clermont. No fewer than eight in 1628, according to Appolis, in contrast to a mere two who were to be working in the town in the mid-eighteenth century.[2] As both Le Roy Ladurie and Braudel have emphasized, there are few more sensitive indicators of prosperity than the presence, or absence, of butchers. Meat, and above all beef, was a luxury which could be afforded by the generality of people only in good times.[3].

In this chapter I shall provide further information on the experiences of Clermont's cloth industry during the period of renewed expansion in the first half of the seventeenth century as well as following, as closely as the sources permit, the fate of this industry during the general depression of the second half of the century. The focus will be on the cloth industry, but in so far as the fortunes of this major sector of the pre-industrial economy were linked to those of agriculture, and representative of those of other industries, and, in addition, had their reverberations on the nature of social structure, then, clearly, the experiences of this single sector had wide implications. Some of these implications I shall explore.

In the absence of more direct sources, the level of alum imports to the province (alum was then the most important dye-fixative for cloth) provides an approximate gauge of the prosperity of Languedoc's cloth

1. The making of a new *compoix* in 1646 is mentioned in a petition of 1680 by the consuls of Clermont against Villenouvette's being allowed to separate itself from the town's *compoix*. This petition is held in the Archive de la Manufacture. See below, pp. 173–6, on this.
2. Appolis, *Lodève*, pp. 177–9.
3. Le Roy Ladurie, *Paysans*, pp. 179–86; Braudel, *Civilisation matérielle, économie et capitalisme, XVᵉ–XVIIIᵉ siècle*, I, 159–63.

industry. After a long period of steady expansion a decline in this is observable in the 1570s. Imports fell to a low level at which they remained until 1620 when there was a sharp revival to peaks higher even than those registered in the sixteenth century.[4] Additional fragments of information provide support for the accuracy of this rough guide-line. It was in the 1570s that several of Languedoc's cloth centres were ravaged by participants in the Wars of Religion.[5] And, a sign of a renewal of activity, new cloth regulations were registered at the Bourse of Toulouse in 1601, 1611 and 1622. The registration of new regulations was an expensive process, undertaken, generally, when industries were expanding.[6]

The earliest significant evidence which we have about Clermont's industry is provided by three notarial acts registered in 1633 by two confréries, one grouping the 'marchands-drapiers', 'marchands-cardiers', 'fouleurs', 'pareurs' and 'tondeurs des draps', and the other the 'tisserands'. These acts provide some useful insights into the state of the industry.[7]

That the town was emerging, or had emerged, from a period of some difficulty is suggested by the preamble to the act registered by the 'merchant' confrérie. The new statutes were being registered, it was stated, on account of the loss of the previous ones during the plague and civil war which had afflicted the town: the loss of the confrérie's archive was probably one of the least damaging economic consequences of the disruptions. That the industry had revived to a substantial size is shown by the large number of masters present at the drawing up of the acts. In the case of the first confrérie there were no fewer than fifty marchands-drapiers, four marchands-cardiers and eight pareurs present and other masters (it was stated) had failed to attend, and in the case of the second thirty-seven weavers were present.

The large numbers and the variety of professions demonstrate that there was a considerable division of labour in the industry. Significant was the presence of workers involved in the skilled and specialized finishing process. The importance, and status, attached to these trades is demonstrated by their practitioners' inclusion in the 'merchant' confrérie.

---

4. J. Delumeau, *L'alun de Rome, XVe–XIXe siècles*, pp. 13–14, 244–5, 271–4; P. Wolff (ed.), *Histoire du Languedoc*, p. 339.
5. Lodève was captured, and its cloth workshops were pillaged, in 1573 (Teisserenc, *L'industrie lainière*, p. 47).
6. Statutes for Carcassonne's industry were confirmed in 1611, Mahul, *Cartulaire et archives*, VI, 131. Those of 1622 are mentioned in an act recorded by Clermont clothiers in 1655 (ADH II E 25 61, 1 July 1655).
7. ADH II E 25 43, 5, 18 Sept. 1633, Acts registered by weavers' confrérie; act of 29 June 1633 (registered before notary Roubert), a copy of which is contained in ADH C2152.

The weavers' separation into a distinct confrérie, apart from all those of 'merchant' status, would suggest that there were comparatively sharp social and economic distinctions between them and other participants in the industry. The content of the two acts registered by the weavers not only provides proof for this 'suggestion' but also shows that these sharp social and economic divisions were of comparatively recent creation. In their first act the weavers, like the merchants, were registering new statutes. But their explanation for the need for such an act gives rise to some doubts about the genuineness of the merchants' prior justification for the registration of their new statutes. They explained that previously there had been but a single confrérie in the industry, grouping weavers, 'marchands cardeurs pareurs et pinchineurs'. This had existed since 1493 but, despite this long pedigree, the merchants had unilaterally, 'sans permission aulcune', registered new statutes *excluding* weavers. The latter had attempted to get these statutes disallowed but had failed and had therefore been obliged to register new statutes themselves. It would seem, therefore, that although the disruptions of civil war and plague (which had indeed occurred)[8] may have caused a loss of statutes this loss had been used as an excuse by the merchants for an unprecedented measure, the division of what had previously been a single confrérie, and the exclusion of those members of lowest status, the weavers.

This forced separation is an added sign of a dynamism in Clermont's cloth industry in this period. As has been observed in many studies of textile industries, periods of expansion tended to occasion an increase in the economic and social divisions between employers and employees, and a concentration in favour of the large-scale producers capable of achieving economies of scale.[9] The 'egalitarian' statutes of the 'corporations' and confréries of the late middle ages (of which the pre-1633 Clermont confrérie is an example) very often included clauses designed to prevent such concentrations. It is possible, therefore, that the exclusion of weavers was not the only purpose of the merchants' registering of new statutes in Clermont – the previous ones may have included such inhibiting clauses.

The second act registered by the weavers provides further evidence not only of the extent of the economic division between employers and employed but also for the recent origin of these divisions. The act was registered in connection with a dispute over the ownership of the scraps ('pezets et fillets') of wool and cloth which fell from the loom during the process of weaving. These, claimed the weavers, had since time

8. A. Durand, *Annales de la ville de Clermont-l'Hérault*, pp. 35–6.
9. See for example Deyon, *Amiens*, pp. 200–28, and Coornaert, *Hondschoote*, pp. 288–9, 304.

'immémorial' belonged to them but now the 'viziteurs des draps & les prévosts des marchands-drappiers' of the newly created merchants' confrérie were claiming them for the drapiers. To oppose this threat with a united front the weavers declared that no member of their new confrérie should surrender these scraps to his employer under penalty of a fine of thirty *livres* and the sealing of his loom. Why should the ownership of these scraps of wool and cloth have suddenly come into dispute when for so long the custom had been to grant them to the weaver? Why were the newly appointed officials of the merchant confrérie finding it necessary to intervene with the weavers who were now members of a separate confrérie? The act certainly provides added proof of a discontinuity and a possible explanation for this discontinuity would be as follows. The apparent expansion in the industry, and the increased social and economic division to which this expansion had given rise, would have had, it is probable, deleterious effects on labour relations, and it was by the theft and embezzlement of raw materials that industrial tension most frequently expressed itself in the pre-industrial period. The opportunities for theft were multiple, given the lack of direct supervision of the weaver's work. It would seem, then, that the merchants' officials were trying to counteract a tendency towards increased theft which their own separation into a new confrérie had in part encouraged. And this theft of raw materials would have been all the more damaging in view of the fact that the industrial revival in the town would have taken the form not only of an increase in production, but also of an improvement in quality as the concentration on export, rather than domestic, markets increased. We have already noted the description of Clermont made in 1645 which in addition to attesting to the presence of cloth-buyers from Lyons, Nice and Genoa in the town also mentions the use of Spanish wools, for the large production of fine cloth. Spanish wools could be worth up to three or four times as much as coarser, local wools.

It was not only by its exclusion of weavers that the new 1633 merchant confrérie differed from that of 1493. Also absent from the membership of the new organization were the categories 'pinchineurs' and 'cardeurs'. 'Pinchineurs' were the makers of *pinchinats*, a coarse, low-quality broadcloth, designed for local sale. Cardeurs dressed and carded the wool before it was spun by spinners who often worked under their direction. The lack of a group of pinchineurs in the new confrérie is probably to be explained by this title's falling out of use as a consequence of the widening of both the range and quality of the production of Clermont's clothiers. In the case of the cardeurs' non-inclusion there seem to be two possibilities. The exclusion might have been the consequence of a relative decline in status of cardeurs who, in an increasingly concentrated industry, had possibly become dependent on richer marchands-drapiers. Alternatively it could have been a consequence of a change of title and role. Apprenticeship contracts to marchands-drapiers at Clermont suggest that the profession included the carding processes. Masters promised to teach their apprentices the 'métier de drapier et cardeur'. So the lack of cardeurs among the membership of the merchant confrérie in that case would simply have been a consequence of cardeurs' preferring to call themselves 'drapiers'. It is probable that the change was a consequence of a combination of these factors – poorer cardeurs, it is likely, had become dependent on the richer marchands-drapiers and thus were excluded, while richer cardeurs had extended their role from that of purely preparing the wool for spinning to that of controlling the entire production process and had thus adopted the title marchand-drapier.

So both the exclusion of weavers and the disappearance of the categories pinchineurs and cardeurs from the merchant confrérie would seem to have been consequences of an industrial expansion which had encouraged specialization and increased economic and social divisions within the industry. The quality of production was apparently rising and the industry, it would seem, was concentrating on the supply of distant rather than local markets.

How long did this expansion and prosperity continue? An act registered in 1655 by Clermont's 'marchans-drappiers' and 'marchans-facturiers' to record new regulations for the different cloths produced in the town would suggest that it endured until the 1650s at least, for not only does the large attendance at the drawing up of the act (forty-eight clothiers) show that the industry remained large but the list of cloths regulated demonstrates that the town's production remained of a high quality and included a wide range of cloths. Indeed the nature of the range suggests that the often-repeated contention that Languedoc's textile production was invariably confined to low-quality cloths might be in need of revision (Table 3).[10] It is not only the fineness of the first two qualities which is significant but also the fact that there should be included among the repertoire of Clermont's clothiers the new Dutch-style cloth for the propagation of which a royal manufacture had been established by Mazarin at Sedan in 1646. The production of the new Dutch-style cloth involved the use of high-quality Spanish wools, the spinning of a finer and more regular thread (than that produced for normal broad-cloth) with the larger, Dutch-style spinning wheel, particularly close weaving, the batten of the loom being pressed four or five times on the weave, and special attention to the finishing processes. The

10. See Le Roy Ladurie, *Paysans*, pp. 124–6.

Table 3. *Cloth regulated at Clermont by act of the confrérie of marchands-drapiers/-facturiers, 1 July 1655*

Cloth type	Threads to warp	Wool	Width
drap fin façon dollande	3,200	fine	$11\frac{2}{3}$ pans
drap rafin vingthuictain	2,800	fine	$11\frac{1}{2}$ pans
vingtquatrain	2,400	fine	$11\frac{1}{2}$ pans
vingtdeuxain	2,200	fine	$11\frac{1}{3}$ pans
vingtain, façon de Seau	2,000	—	9 pans
seizain	1,600	—	$9\frac{1}{2}$ pans
douzain	1,200	—	$8\frac{1}{2}$ pans

Source: ADH II E 25 61, Act of this day registered by Nègre, notaire.

expansion of the Dutch cloth-industry in the seventeenth century, at Leyden above all, was a consequence of the successful development of new cloths in the production of which these new techniques were used and the importance of the 'Dutch-style' or 'Spanish cloth' as it was also called (it was developed in the Spanish Netherlands too) has been compared by Julia Mann, historian of England's West Country industry, with that of the 'new draperies'. Attempts were being made to introduce it into England in the first half of the seventeenth century and its production at Clermont in this period would suggest that the town's industry was technologically as well as commercially advanced.[11]

The analysis of a number of notarial acts for the period 1650–5 serves to inform us more about this still-significant industry. First, one is impressed by the evidently large numbers involved in cloth production. The act registered in 1655 has already introduced us to forty-eight different clothiers. Additional acts registered during these years record the names of a further eighteen individuals who described themselves as marchands-drapiers or -facturiers. In addition the names of thirteen cloth-shearers and of eight fullers are recorded. The large number of cloth-shearers provided a livelihood for a specialized shear-grinder and there is evidence, too, for the existence of two specialized dyers, neither of

11. On the technological novelty of this cloth see J. de L. Mann, *The Cloth Industry in the West of England from 1640 to 1880*, pp. xiv–xvii, 9–13; for an excellent technical description of how the new cloth was made see H. Freudenberger, *The Waldstein Woollen Mill*, pp. 18–33; on the Leyden industry see C. H. Wilson, 'Cloth production and international competition in the seventeenth century', *Ec.H.R.* 13 (1960), 212–18; Dutch-style cloth-making techniques were introduced at Elbeuf in 1607 (C. Brisson, 'Origines et développement de l'industrie drapière à Elbeuf et à Louviers', *Etudes Normandes* 13 (1952), 25).

them natives of Clermont.[12] Additional evidence of Clermont's contact with the advanced centres of French industry is provided by their presence – one was from the town of Orange and the other was from Tulle in the diocese of Limoges.[13] Clermont's industrial production between 1650 and 1655 was still, it is evident, of a quantity, quality and regularity to provide employment for specialized, skilled workers. The value placed on the skills which these workers possessed is demonstrated by the apprenticeship fees which they charged. Whereas the apprentice to a weaver rather than being charged was rewarded at the end of his years of service and the apprentice to a marchand-drapier paid, generally, a fee of between 30 and 35 *livres*, the apprentice shearer paid 60 *livres* and the apprentice dyer 80.[14]

Not all clothiers' apprentices paid such low fees it would seem. There is one example of considerably more being paid during these years. In 1653 Jean Astruq bourgeois of Clermont paid 180 *livres* to Pierre Cointre, marchand-drapier of Carcassonne, who was to accept his brother Estienne as apprentice. The contract explicitly stated that Cointre should both instruct the apprentice in his 'boutique' and take him 'une fois pour le moings' to 'la foire de pézenas et de montagnac'.[15] It would seem that there were comparatively sharp distinctions in the wealth and status of drapiers and facturiers and that the nature of the profession varied too. Thus richer clothiers might hardly be involved in the physical side of cloth-making, whilst poorer ones might be involved in little else, perhaps not even selling their own products at the fairs. The ambiguity in titles – the same individual might be described as marchand, marchand-drapier or marchand-facturier – would suggest that at the summit of the profession there were merchants who as well as investing in cloth production were involved in the wool and cloth trades and no doubt in other wholesale trades too. There were no restrictive corporative statutes giving a cloth-making monopoly to the full-time facturier and it would seem that the merchant with resources combined cloth-making with other activities.

The compatibility of bourgeois status with participation in cloth production is demonstrated not only by the apprenticeship contract just cited but by another act too, registered in December 1654 – Jacques Chinion, described as bourgeois, received as apprentice in that month the

12. This information is extracted from the following notarial registers held in the departmental archives of the Hérault: 11 E 25 58–62, 11 E 26 46–8, 70–1.
13. On the industry of Tulle see Markovitch, *Les industries lainières*, p. 413.
14. E.g. ADH 11 E 26 70, 22 May 1650, weaver's contract; 11 E 26 70, 20 Oct. 1651, marchand-drapier; 11 E 26 70, 22 June 1651, shearer's; 11 E 25 63, 13 March 1658, dyer's.
15. ADH 11 E 26 48, 20 Sept. 1653.

son of a laboureur who was to be taught 'le mestier de drapier et car-deur'.[16] The mixed nature of the profession, its combining of drapiers or facturiers of most varied resources, receives further illustration from the nature of the signatures added to the act registering new statutes in 1655: these vary from, at one extreme, elegant, refined flourishes to, at the other, a bare capacity to compose an initial or mark. A marriage contract drawn up in 1653 by two members of the richer drapier families gives us a glimpse into the resources, life-style and status of those at the summit of the profession. The bridegroom, his father and brother-in-law, the bride's father and two of her cousins (Jacques Figuière fils, Jacques Figuière père, Fulcrand Randon, Jean Messier, Pierre and Jean Chinion) were all to be among those present two years later at the registration of new regulations and another of the bride's cousins was the Jacques Chinion, bourgeois, referred to at the beginning of this paragraph. So the two families indubitably included among their relations a considerable section of the body of drapiers. The bride's dowry consisted of 1,500 *livres* and two dresses, a 'robe destoffe burat' and a 'robe poudre soye', given by her father and 300 *livres* given by her uncle; the bridegroom's parental donation consisted of 2,400 *livres*. The sums were respectable and the presence of an uncle of Jacques Figuière who was an 'écuyer' at the drawing up of the marriage contract provides added proof of the high social status of these wealthier cloth-making families.[17]

Thus evidence for both the 1630s and the 1650s shows that Clermont's industry was large and prosperous during the first half of the seventeenth century. It attracted merchant investment and there was evidently considerable movement in to and out of the industry. If we compare the list of sixty-six clothiers whose presence in the town between 1650 and 1655 has been noted with that of the drapiers present at the formation of the confrérie in 1633 we find that only sixteen of those producing between 1650 and 1655 had family names which appear in the 1633 list. To these documentary records of industrial vitality can be added both architectural evidence and folk-memory. The building of several new fulling mills has been traced to this period and in 1753 two of the oldest members of the profession assured Vincent de Gournay, visiting the town, that ninety to a hundred years previously there had been eighty clothiers at work in Clermont.[18]

16. ADH II E 25 60, 1 Dec. 1654.
17. ADH II E 25 59, 15 May 1653.
18. On the building of fulling mills see Combarnous, 'Clermont-l'Hérault', p. 268. De Gournay's report on his visit is held in ADH C5552. The prosperity of the industry at some stages of the period 1500–1650 may well have been even greater than that experienced in the eighteenth century. This is the belief of Gaston Combarnous,

The majority of this information about Clermont's industry is cor-
roborated by details that can be drawn from an important document
concerning Carcassonne's cloth-industry in this period. In 1642 a *subvention* was placed on goods produced in Carcassonne and a separate
register was kept 'de toute nature de draps'. The first of these registers,
which was kept from 6 October 1642 until 10 March 1643, has survived.
Recorded in it is all cloth marked by 'Messrs les marchandz de Ceste ville'
– all of Carcassonne's production for these months would thus be
included and also a small part of the production of some neighbouring
cloth-making centres which had their cloth finished in Carcassonne. The
register was well kept and records the name of each producer, his profession or status (in most cases), his town or village of origin and the type
and length of cloths taxed. It provides, thus, an exact record of
Carcassonne's industrial production for these four months. The information is all the more valuable in view of the fact that it was Carcassonne
which, as we have seen, had emerged in the sixteenth century as the
indubitable capital of the regional industry (Table 4).[19] The range of
cloth produced at Carcassonne corresponded approximately with that
listed in the new regulation drawn up by Clermont's clothiers in 1655.
The amount produced was large. Recorded is approximately one-third of
Carcassonne's annual production and so the town's total production
would have been in the region of 10,000 half-pieces. The majority of the
cloth produced was of medium to low quality but it is evident that there
existed the ability to make cloth of higher quality too in a variety of
different styles. Included in the category of very fine broad-cloth were no
fewer than eighteen different varieties: *suprafin façon dollande, suprafin
large escarlatte, suprafin de Sagobie large, suprafin large, raffin large, raffin
large noir, raffin, drap large façon dollande, drap large façon d'Espagne,
drap 28ain large, drap large suprafin, drap large, sagobian large, escarlatte,
drap de Berry, drap façon de Berry, drap de Berry escarlatte* and *drap large
gris*. Some of these different names probably described the same cloth but
it does seem that Carcassonne's cloth industry was capable of producing
the majority of the finest variants of broad-cloth on the market in this
period, even if the bulk of the town's production consisted of medium to
lower qualities.

Responsible for the production of these 3,433 half-pieces of cloth were
approximately 152 individuals. The scale of production varied con-

author of the article just cited. In addition in 1706 Antoine Raissac, clothier, dyer and
shearer, referred in a cancelled notarial act to the fact that whereas there were then six
shearing shops functioning in Clermont, there had been a time when the town had had
thirteen such shops open (ADH 11 E 25 108).

19. ADA 5 C 41. Register of the *droit de subvention* for the 'ville basse & cité . . . de toute
nature de draps y ayant un cayer separé pour les autres marczandizes'.

Table 4. *Cloth recorded in the register of the 'subvention',*
Carcassonne, 6 October 1642–10 March 1643

Cloth-type	Length in cannes and pans (8 pans = 1 canne)	½-pieces of 9 cannes (to nearest piece)
Varieties of very fine broad-cloth	1,272.7	141
Fine/medium (types of *contraints*)	1,790.4	199
Medium (types of *seau*)	13,197.6	1,466
Low-quality (*17ains, 16ains*)	13,852	1,539
Types of *serge*	342.4	38
Cloth from other towns	119.6	13
Miscellaneous short runs	124.2	14
Illegible or unknown cloth types	206	23
TOTAL	30,905.5	3,433

Source: ADA 5 C 41, Register of *droit de subvention* for cloth production.

siderably. At one extreme there are a number of producers who are only credited with the production of half a piece of low-quality cloth during these four months and, at the other, there are some merchants who produced continuously, and in large quantities. For example the merchants Maffre et Castel produced eighteen pieces of the first category of cloth, fourteen pieces of the second, 153 pieces of the third, eighty-seven pieces of the fourth and three pieces of the seventh. Their total production was thus 275 pieces for these four months or nearly one-twelfth of the output of the whole city.

The variations in scale were matched by variations in the status of different producers. Not all professions are cited but most are: ninety-six of those presenting cloth are described simply as merchants, two as 'marchands-détailleurs', eight as bourgeois, two on occasions as bourgeois and on others as merchants, two as consuls, four as pareurs or tondeurs, one as a cardeur, two as dyers, and one as a 'blancher' or bleacher. It is apparent from this list that although various groups of specialized workers at Carcassonne were incorporated and had monopolies over different processes of cloth-making, there was complete freedom for anyone to act as clothier and to finance and co-ordinate the production process. The merchants who invested in cloth production would most probably have been involved in other commercial activities too. This was certainly the case for the two described as marchands-détailleurs but that it was true for other merchants as well is suggested by a memoir, written in the eighteenth century, which described the Carcassonnais industry during this period:

les drapiers ne se mesloient pas tout seulement de vendre des draps, comme il semble que le mot prins de sa propre signification le veuille montrer, mais vendoient aussy soyes et laines tout ensemble, comme font aujourdhuy la plupart de nos marchands; faisoint aussy des chausses comme faisant les chaussetiers, pour les vendre ... tellement qu'ils étoint marchands drapiers, merciers et chaussetiers tout ensemble.[20]

It was to this lack of specialization and of corporative control over participation in cloth production that many were going to attribute the decline in Languedoc's cloth production in the second half of the century.[21]

Apparent, too, from this list of professions and statuses is that at Carcassonne, as at Clermont, there was participation in the cloth industry by members of the social elite. It was possible, it seems, to be clothier and to remain bourgeois.

The evidence drawn from these three different sources – alum imports to the province, notarial acts relating to Clermont's industry, and the subvention charged at Carcassonne – all points to the same conclusion. Languedoc's cloth industry until the mid-seventeenth century was large, advanced and flourishing, possibly *as* large, *as* advanced and *as* flourishing as it had ever been. It was to this moment that Basville was probably referring at the end of the century, after a long period of industrial decline in the province, when he wrote that the cloth trade with the Levant was 'autrefois le grand commerce de la ville de Carcassonne, qu'il rendoit florissante.'[22]

At some stage between 1640 and 1660 a peak was reached and the industry's fortunes turned. In the 1640s there were already complaints about the mis-sale of cloth in the Levant. The blame for this was attributed, by the marchands-facturiers of the province in a memoir which was sent to the 'Etats', to the 'infidélité' of the 'teinturiers' which was occasioning a loss of reputation.[23] Additional difficulties were caused by the war with Spain (which cut off the major source of high-quality wool as well as one of the province's best markets), disturbances to shipping in the Mediterranean by pirates, and renewed English and Dutch competition which was proving damaging to both French and Venetian

20. Mahul, *Cartulaire et archives*, VI, 96, n.1.
21. Wolff, 'Esquisse d'une histoire de la draperie', p. 460: 'C'est cependant surtout l'insuffisance de la police corporative qu'incriminait l'opinion en général.'
22. Boulainvilliers, *Etat de la France*, II, 561.
23. Requête des marchands-facturiers, 10 Nov. 1643, cited in De Vic and Vaissète, *Histoire du Languedoc*, XIII, 166.

trade in the Levant.[24] To these general difficulties which hampered Mediterranean trade must be added local problems in Languedoc. The three scourges of the pre-industrial world – war, famine and disease – struck at once with the province's involvement in the Frondes, rising food prices and severe outbreaks of plague in the 1650s.[25] Clermont suffered particularly severely. An outbreak of plague in 1652 and 1653 gave rise to the death of a quarter of the town's population. The town was besieged and captured, and suffered an extended and costly occupation by three companies of soldiers in 1653, and rising grain prices in the same year brought the situation to a climax of misery.[26] Notarial registers attest eloquently to these afflictions. Those for 1652 and 1653, during the height of the plague, contain few acts other than wills, often unsigned because of problems of contagion. In addition there are details of large payments demanded by the occupying soldiers (200 *livres* a day) and also made to those who acted as doctors or disinfectors during the plague. The town's finances were to be burdened for years by the debts incurred. A sign perhaps of the novelty of the sufferings (they followed some thirty years of comparative prosperity) are the pathetic notes added by the notaries themselves at the end of their annual registers when they looked back on the experiences of the previous year. Notary Pons recorded that 'le peuple a souffert beaucoup par Charité du bled ayant valu jusques à treitze livre le Cestier, [et] diminuon des monnoyes, estirillité ...' at the end of 1653 and Roubert, 'notaire royal', lamented the loss of his wife, son, daughter and a long list of relations from plague at the end of 1654.[27]

The deteriorating outlook in the Mediterranean, and the local problems at Clermont, could hardly have favoured the town's cloth industry. Unfortunately documentation is scarce. The regulations drawn up in 1655 are the only substantial piece of information which I have found about the industry in this decade and these, at least on first appearances, give the impression of continued prosperity. A more detailed analysis of them, however, yields some information about the effects of the crisis. The very motive for the registration of the new regulations, it emerges, was to attempt to combat declining sales by restating the required sizes and qualities of the various types of cloth produced at Clermont as originally prescribed in regulations published in 1622. This restatement was necessary because all the different cloths listed were being made with

24. L. Bergasse, *Histoire du commerce de Marseille*, IV, 8–12, 25, 41–63.
25. P. Boissonnade, 'L'Etat, l'organisation et la crise de l'industrie languedocienne pendant les soixante premières années du XVIIᵉ siècle', *A. du M.* 21 (1909), 195–6.
26. A. Durand, *Annales de Clermont*, p. 37.
27. ADH II E 26 48, 2 May 1653: payment to occupying troops; II E 25 59, 28 Jan. 1653: details about plague; II E 26 71, II E 26 48, at ends of these registers gloomy comments of notaries Roubert and Pons.

too few threads to the warp. Above all what were effectively 'dix-huictains' (it was stated in the act) and 'quatorzains' were being passed off as though they were 'vingtains' and 'seizains'. This was not the only abuse. Mention is also made of the use of inferior, illegal wools: 'pignon aut*ret* esponge' (probably the fleece of sheep dying from natural causes, known as 'pelades' in the eighteenth century), and cloth was being excessively stretched: the new regulations stipulated that facturiers should not be allowed to 'tirasse lesd. draps avec aucune fort distrumans'. These varied frauds had had extremely severe consequences for the town's industry, it was stated: there had arisen 'un si grand préjudice et Intérêt à cauze de ceste déception' that there had been a collapse ('descry') in the market for Clermont's cloth. Penalties were stipulated for abuse of the new regulations: a fine of 30 *livres* for a first offence, and 50 *livres* and the incineration of the loom on which the cloth was made in the case of a second.[28]

Additional evidence for placing the turning-point in the prosperity of Clermont's cloth-industry in the 1650s is to be found in the registers of the conseil de ville. In 1692 a reference was made to the poor state of the town's industry and an explanation for the decline given: it was attributed to the desertion to the rival cloth-making centre of Lodève of one of the town's leading clothiers, Guillaume Jullien, forty-two years earlier – 1650. Jullien clearly became a legendary scapegoat for the industry's decline for on what could have been the centennial anniversary of his departure a similar statement is to be found again in the registers of the conseil de ville. It was claimed that Lodève until eighty years ago had been without a substantial cloth-industry and that it was 'julien mart. de Clermont [qui] La [the art of cloth-making] porta à Lodève où les eaux se trouvant plus abondantes et plus propres elle surpassa bientôt Clermont'.[29]

This explanation for the crisis is clearly unacceptable. Lodève, far from having learnt the art of cloth-making from Clermont, had an industrial tradition which was yet more ancient than hers.[30] But it seems likely that there was a coincidence between the beginning of the decline and the departure of Jullien and that this was the ground for linking the two events. So, inadequate explanation though it may be, the myth does provide additional grounds for attributing the turning-point in Clermont's industrial fortunes to the 1650s. Lodève's better performance in the second half of the seventeenth century is attributable above all, as the statement made in the registers of the conseil de ville records, to

28. ADH 11 E 25 61, 1 July 1655.
29. ACC BB1, 5, 11 Nov. 1692, 2 Jan. 1750.
30. E. Martin, *Cartulaire de la ville de Lodève*, p. 73, prints a regulation for Lodève's industry for the year 1288.

the quality of its water-power. In the eighteenth century there were to be forty-seven fulling mills at work in the town.[31] The market for heavy, well-fulled broad-cloth was to survive the depression better than that for the lighter cloths which Clermontais clothiers made for export to southern markets, and later in the reign was to be boosted by military demands for cloth.

The placing of the turning-point in the 1650s gains extra credibility when the behaviour of textiles is compared with that of other sectors of the Languedocian economy. As Le Roy Ladurie has shown, the price of wheat went into decline from 1656, that of wine from 1660, and that of silk in 1680.[32] The 'tragic' seventeenth century had begun and a sign of its effect on Clermont is the fate of the new *compoix* which had been drawn up in 1646 as a consequence, I have suggested, of the multiplicity of property transfers occasioned by the years of expansion. A mere thirty-four years later this new *compoix* had ceased to be a satisfactory basis for apportioning taxes, but this time not because of land transfers but because of a decline in rent and abandonment of formerly cultivated land. In a petition sent to the King in 1680 the consuls explained that their difficulty in settling the town's taxes was occasioned by the fact that 'Les ... biens et héritages dont ilz Jouissent à présant soient grandement diminués de prix et de revenu à cauze de la misère du temps.' Since the drawing up of the last *compoix*, they added, 'il est arrivé de très grandz changemens dans tout le tailiable de lad ville ... beaucoup de maisons de lad ville quy estoient en bon estat estant tombés en ruyne et plusieurs biens de la campagne quy estoient alors bien cultivés estant maintenant abandonnés et en frishe'. Further difficulties, the memoir continued, were occasioned by the obligation to repay the debts incurred 'pendant les guerres et dautres temps facheux': it was to the early 1650s that they were referring. An edict of 1667 had ordered full repayment of 150,00 *livres* which was still outstanding.[33]

Clermont's plight thus corresponded closely to that observed by Le Roy Ladurie in other parts of the province – there had been a decline in grain prices and hence in rents, a desertion of marginal land, some depopulation, the abandonment of town houses and difficulty in repaying debts and paying taxes.[34]

The fate of Clermont's cloth industry during the depression is sparsely documented. That it declined is revealed by three brief reports made by visitors to the town. An agent of the intendant Henri d'Aguesseau

31. Appolis, *Lodève*, pp. 470–1.
32. *Paysans*, pp. 511–12, 517–19, 525.
33. Archive de la Manufacture, petition of 1680.
34. *Paysans*, pp. 535–7, 585–99.

mentioned the 'facture de toutes sortes de draperies' after a visit in 1674 but another source informs us that this cloth was of low quality above all and for local sale only, at the fairs of Pézenas, Montagnac and Béziers. The agent was clearly more impressed by the 'très bons draps' which he said were being made at Lodève.[35] In the 1690s there were two reports made by members of the growing *corps* of inspectors. In one in 1692 it was recorded that eighteen clothiers were employing twenty-nine looms in the production of cloth of $1\frac{1}{4}$ *aunes* in width (traditional broad-cloths), that successful attempts had been made to imitate Lodève's somewhat narrower (1 *aune* in width), heavier, military cloth, and that one 'entrepreneur' had mounted twelve looms for the production of fine cloth.[36] In the other a fuller description of the town's industry was provided: 'Ce travail est très ancien et très Commun, ils fillent fort gros pour rendre le drap plus fort et n'employent que des laines fort grossières. Cette fabrique a extrêmement diminué depuis plusieurs années parceque les ouvriers de Lodève qui font le même travail y réussissent beaucoup mieux et employent de meilleures laines.' The second report mentioned, too, that the 'entrepreneur', who now directed twenty-five looms, had been joined in the production of fine cloth by three other clothiers.[37]

These reports show that, although there were signs of an incipient revival in the 1690s, Clermont's cloth industry had declined from all points of view since the mid-century. Both the quantity and the quality of production had evidently declined. A small industry, however, had survived. What type of industry was it? In what ways was it distinct from that which we have just described for the first half of the century? It is in an attempt to answer these questions that we have analysed all notarial registers (complete bar occasional lost pages) for the years 1674–1712.

First, acts listing attendances at meetings of the confréries of the marchands-facturiers and tisserands give an approximate idea of the number involved in cloth production at any one moment (Table 5). These figures provide additional proof of the industry's decline (although the rise in the number of weavers towards the end of the century illustrates the beginnings of the recovery just referred to).

If our records show a maximum of twenty-six clothiers producing at any one time (and this figure is probably on the high side) the total of all clothiers who are named either in notarial acts or in the registers of the conseil de ville between 1674 and 1700 is sixty-seven. This is a very low

---

35. BM Toulouse, MS 603, folio 360; *Chroniques du Languedoc*, III, 225.
36. Fontvieille, 'Premières enquêtes', p. 1134. This represents an earlier usage of the term entrepreneur than that of 1709 mentioned by Braudel (*Civilisation matérielle*, II, 288).
37. ADH C2200, Cauvière's report, 1694.

Table 5. *The number of clothiers and weavers present at confrérie meetings in the seventeenth century or recorded by inspectors as producing cloth in the 1690s*

Clothiers			
1633	50	1687	14
1655	48	1688	26
1674	16	1692	19 (including one entrepreneur)
1686	11	1694	16
Weavers			
1633	37	1692	25
1675	9	1696	30

Sources: Clothiers: 1633, ADH C2152; 1655, II E 25 61, 1 July 1655; 1674, ACC BB1, 25 Feb. 1674; 1686, C2199, 'procès-verbal' of meeting of 21 Feb. 1686; 1687, ACC BB1, 24 Feb. 1687; 1688, II E 26 125, 29 June 1688; 1692, Fontvieille, 'Les premières enquêtes', p. 1134; 1694, C2200, Cauvière's visit. Weavers: 1633, II E 25 43, 18 Sept. 1633; 1675, II E 26 92, 21 Sept. 1675; 1692, II E 26 129, 5 Jan. 1692; 1696, II E 25 98, 21 Dec. 1696.

figure if compared with the sixty-six mentioned in a few notarial registers between 1650 and 1655. The industry, it is clear, was relatively static. There were few newcomers to it – there are only three apprenticeship contracts to clothiers registered between 1674 and 1694 – and there were few departures. One of the characteristics of Clermont's industry during these years thus emerges: it was composed of a reduced and relatively static group. One consequence of the depression would seem to have been a loss of the commercial flexibility and optimism, apparent during the period of expansion, which gave rise to investment in cloth-making by a wide range of merchants and even by people of bourgeois status. The industry was very largely in the hands of a restricted, and largely artisanal, group (as we shall see) and its poverty caused it to attract little interest from outsiders just as it deprived its members of the necessary resources to switch to other trades. Such industrial endogamy is observable in other textile industries in periods of depression.[38]

The inspectors' reports for the 1690s and various acts registered before notaries provide a reasonably full picture both of the scale of the activities of, and of the types of cloth produced by, this restricted group of clothiers. If we exclude the activities of the one, exceptional entrepreneur, eighteen clothiers shared twenty-nine looms between them in 1692 and fifteen clothiers shared the same number in 1694. Thus the ratio of looms

38. E.g. Deyon, *Amiens*, pp. 218, 227–8.

to clothiers was rather less than two to one. Some form of clothier-dominated putting-out system survived from the first half of the century but it was clearly a putting-out system on the most humble of scales. The endeavours of these clothiers were confined to six different types of cloth for the main part: *vingt-quatrains*, *vingt-deuxains* and *seizains* and, less regularly, *pinchinats*, *droguets* and *cordelats*.[39] We are already acquainted with all but the last two of these qualities. These were both coarse and hard-wearing cloths, narrower than broad-cloth, and with minimal finish. Their production was of only marginal significance as they were made either with the odd pieces of wool left over from the making of broad-cloth or with *pelades*.[40] The bulk of production consisted, then, in *seizains*, *vingt-deuxains* and *vingt-quatrains* and above all in *seizains*, the lowest quality of these three. An act of 1687 naming the types of cloth produced at Clermont lists these three qualities only but adds that cloths with more threads to the warp were produced when the demand arose.[41] The silence of the notarial archives about cloth of higher counts suggests that this demand, if it arose at all, did so only most infrequently. The type of market for which the majority of the town's clothiers would have been producing is demonstrated by the fact that it was a piece of *seizain* that was the conventional reward given to the weaver's apprentice at the end of his years of service.[42]

What had happened to the production of those higher qualities of cloth produced in the first half of the century with sufficient regularity to justify the presence in the town of cloth commissioners from centres such as Genoa and Lyons? It is clear that it had been abandoned virtually completely, most probably as a consequence of a collapse in France's trade with the Levant, and that Clermont's clothiers had been obliged to concentrate on the production of coarse, heavy, low-quality cloth for local markets despite the fact that their neighbour and competitor, Lodève, was better equipped for this sort of production.

The price paid by apprentices to their masters gives, we have already

39. Mention of the production of these cloths is made in the following sources: *24ains* and *22ains*, ADH ɪɪ E 26 97, 13 July 1680; *22ains* and *16ains*, ɪɪ E 26 129, 19 March and 14 May 1692; *cordelats*, ɪɪ E 26 124, 8 Jan. 1687; *droguets*, ɪɪ E 26 97, 1 Aug. 1680; *pinchinats*, BN FF 8037, Desmaretz's survey, undertaken locally by Paignon, report of 11 Sept. 1708.
40. Thus an agreement between the weavers and clothiers in 1687 stated that the 'pezets', or wool scraps remaining after the weaving process, were to be used to make 'draps mais bien sullement à la lizière ou séparément en cordellat' (ADH ɪɪ E 26 124, 8 Jan. 1687). The *lizière* was the margin of the cloth for which lower-quality wools were used.
41. ADH C2199, Act of 21 Feb. 1686.
42. For instance the contract registered before Delpon, 28 Oct. 1689 (ADH ɪɪ E 26 126). The price of *seizain* was approximately 8 *livres* the *canne*.

seen, some idea of the status of a profession. Descriptions of what the master will teach his apprentices are sometimes also included in acts. Although there are only three apprenticeship contracts registered with clothiers during these years they serve to inform us on these matters.[43] The fees paid were between 24 and 27 *livres*, even less than those paid at the bottom end of the clothiers' profession in the 1650s, and far removed from the large amounts which continued to be paid to merchants. Clothiers usually continued to call themselves marchands-facturiers but it would seem that the emphasis in the title was now on the role of facturier rather than that of marchand. This supposition is supported both by the fact that clothiers were occasionally referred to simply as facturiers[44] and also by the nature of the description given of the duties which the would-be clothier was to be taught in one of the three apprenticeship contracts. André Cayse, apprenticed by his brother Guillaume to Jean Delpon 'marchand facturier de draps' in 1684, was not going to be taught book-keeping skills, it is clear, for neither he nor his brother could sign the apprenticeship contract and his master-to-be did so with evident difficulty, but the 'mestier de facturier ... concistant à carder embourer excardasser emprimer et les teintures ordinaires'.[45] Now we were aware already that at the lower end of the profession the clothiers' main function was the selection, purchase, sorting and dressing of wools before the spinning process, but pressing and dyeing, the presence of specialized cloth-dressers, shearers and dyers had suggested, had not generally been carried out by the clothiers themselves during the first half of the century. It would seem that, in part as an economy measure and in part as a result of the shift to producing lower-quality cloth for local markets whose customers were less demanding about finish, those of Clermont's clothiers who had continued producing had extended their role to include virtually the whole production process apart from spinning and weaving. This monopolization of the majority of production processes by the clothiers would explain the scarcity of mentions of specialized dyers, shearers and cloth-dressers in the notarial registers during these years. Again the contrast with the five-year period 1650–5 is striking. Between 1674 and 1700 only one member of each of these three professions is named in connection with Clermont's traditional industry and even these three, it is clear, could not obtain adequate employment in Clermont. The cloth-dresser mentioned left Clermont to work in a royal

---

43. ADH II E 26 123, 130, acts of 10 Sept. 1684, 8 Feb. 1693 and II E 26 135, 23 Oct. 1692.
44. Three examples among many: Gabriel Pelletan and François and Barthélemy Combettes were referred to as facturiers in the following acts: ADH II E 25 89, 23 Sept., 21 Nov. 1671.
45. ADH II E 26 123, 10 Sept. 1684.

manufacture; the shearer left to work in Lyons and the dyer let his dye-house to a clothier in 1679 as his son too had left for Lyons.[46]

The surviving clothiers in addition to cutting their labour costs by carrying out so much of the production process would seem to have bought their wools on credit. In 1671, for example, there are three cases of clothiers having to surrender property in Clermont in default of payment for wools sold on credit by Montpellier merchants.[47] Labour and raw-material costs were the two major components of circulating capital (invariably far larger than the investment in fixed capital in pre-industrial economies) and thus the economies made with respect to both these items minimized the clothiers' investments. What little outlay there was in fixed capital was partly undertaken by other participants in the production process. The looms, one of the most expensive items, were owned by the weavers. Apart from their own workshops, and the occasional involvement with a dye-house or fulling mill, the only item of fixed capital of any size was what was known as a twisting mill, a machine consisting of a large wheel, turned by a donkey, and designed to rectify inconsistencies in the spinners' yarn and then to wind this yarn onto a large number of bobbins to create the *chaîne* (warp) of the cloth. Such machines were apparently peculiar to the south of France. One was described by John Locke visiting Carcassonne in the 1670s: '*I saw a wheel*', he wrote, '*turned by one ass, which* twisted & wound *at the same time* 64 threads *of yarn*'.[48] These machines cost between 75 and 135 *livres* which, one might have thought, would have represented but a small outlay for a clothier. This was clearly not the case, however, and they were invariably administered by a group of clothiers who, by thus combining, minimized the machine's capital cost as well as ensuring its full utilization. Several such associations for purchasing and operating twisting mills are to be found in the notarial registers and the importance attached to what would appear to be but a minor investment is dem-

---

46. However, from the late 1680s and 1690s, several of these categories of workers are mentioned in connection with Villenouvette's production and Clermont's new production for the Levant (see chapters six and seven). The three mentioned in connection with the traditional industry are Jean Maysonnade, marchand-teinturier, who rented his dye-house for 70 *livres* a year in 1679 (ADH 11 E 25 94, 22 Feb. 1697) and the presence of whose son in Lyons we have noted above (p. 60, n. 38); Barthélemy Delphiere, 'maître pareur de draps', who was to work for Villenouvette (11 E 25 91, 15 Jan. 1674) and Antoine Noudard, pareur, who left Clermont to work in Lyons during the 1680s (11 E 26 122, 123, 126, 16 June 1682, 26 Nov. 1684, 24 Jan. 1689). The temporary presence of a Carcassonnais dyer in Clermont, one Jean Bouissède, in the 1680s was not in connection with Clermont's traditional industry. (See below pp. 111–12.)
47. ADH 11 E 25 89, 23 Sept., 21 Nov. 1671.
48. J. Lough (ed.), *Locke's Travels in France, 1675–1679*, p. 133.

onstrated by the care with which the rights of those involved in the purchases were prescribed. One act registered in 1678 concerned a twisting mill which had cost a mere 75 *livres* to build and yet it was with a formality appropriate to a joint-stock company that it was laid down in the act that the four 'share-holders', a joiner and three clothiers, 'ne pourront vendre led Retorssoir Que par pluralisme de voix'.[49]

So the typical Clermontais clothier in the second half of the seventeenth century, our sources suggest, produced low-quality cloth on a small scale, with a minimal investment in both fixed and circulating capital, for local markets. But although the majority of the sixty-seven clothiers whom we have identified shared these characteristics and would, if one compared them with their predecessors operating before 1650, have been ranked among the poorest of the profession, it would be wrong to regard them as a completely homogeneous bloc. There were distinctions among them, even if these distinctions were probably less sharp than those existing between clothiers in the first half of the century, and an analysis of these will contribute to a fuller understanding of Clermont's impoverished industry during this period.

First, as is already apparent, not all of the sixty-seven clothiers produced simultaneously. This was in part for the obvious reason that included in this figure are some clothiers who died during the period and others who began production for the first time. But there are other reasons too which it is important to clarify. Some clothiers clearly produced with greater regularity than others, for their names crop up repeatedly in notarial acts registered in connection with cloth-making. These producers are of particular interest to us and for the purpose of analysis I have put into a category of 'regular' producers all those for whom there is evidence of production, continuous or not, over a span of at least ten years. There are twenty-four who qualify and it is reasonably certain that they formed the core of Clermont's industry. It is the characteristics of this group which I shall first describe.[50]

Among these twenty-four were a few clothiers with larger resources than the average. There were three families which owned or rented dye-houses – Fraisse, Ménard and Desalasc.[51] In addition Fraisse and

49. ADH II E 26 120, 9 March 1678. Other acts concerning twisting mills are recorded in II E 26 119, 124, 6 Sept. 1676, 10 April 1686; II E 26 97, 134, 13 July 1680, 30 June 1691.
50. In fact there are twenty-six but in two cases it is clear that a son was succeeding to a father's business. The names of the twenty-six; Pierre Almes, Antoine Azemar, Estienne Berthomieu, Mathieu Bonnal, Barthélemy Combettes, Jean Delpon, Pierre Dides, François Domergue, Fulcrand Fraisse, Jean Ginouvés, Géraud Gravié, Jacques and Pierre Laurés, Guillaume, Estienne and Raymond Lugagne, Jacques and Antoine Ménard, Pierre Nayrac, Gabriel Pelletan, Jean and Mathieu Pradier, Jean Ranc, Jean and Pierre Desalasc, Jean Turc.
51. ADH II E 26 185, 1 March 1724; II E 26 98, 9 July 1681, II E 26 126, 27 Aug. 1689.

Desalasc had sons apprenticed at Lyons and Montpellier[52] and all three were referred to in notarial acts as marchands as frequently as they were as marchands-facturiers.[53] The sort of additional interest which justified the superior title is illustrated by the activities of Pierre Desalasc who was tax-collector for Clermont in 1670 and combined cloth production with trading in wools.[54] Far from buying wools on credit he himself had sufficient resources to provide loans to his sister's and daughter's husbands, both of whom were among our group of regular producers but who were, it is clear, less well provided financially than he was.[55] But although these three members of the group of twenty-four enjoyed the possession of slightly larger resources than average, the majority of these 'regular' producers clearly operated their cloth-making concerns in the penny-pinching manner which has just been described. The societies formed to administer twisting mills, illustrative, I have argued, of the frugality of clothiers, were formed uniquely by members of this group. They do indeed demonstrate frugality but they show, too, a certain commitment to production.

A *certain* commitment but probably in no case, a *total* one. The norm, it is clear, was to combine cloth-making with other activities. The property surrendered by those clothiers who could not meet their debts to wool merchants in the 1670s included vineyards and arable land. The transactions suggest then not only a lack of resources, but also an imperfect professional specialization. This is not the only evidence of clothier involvement in non-industrial affairs. The Lugagne family, regular producers throughout the entire period, owned two olive groves.[56] In 1684 another clothier rented land which he promised in the contract to ditch and keep regularly tilled.[57] Pierre Dides traded in mules as well as making cloth[58] and Gabriel Pelletan's skills in iron- and woodwork enabled him to gain temporary employment in 1674 repairing a fulling mill.[59] The dependence on cloth-making was decreased by the existence

52. ADH 11 E 26 131, Pierre Fraisse's presence at Lyons is recorded; 11 E 26 126, Desalasc apprenticed his son to Pierre Astruc, future director of Villenouvette, then a Montpellier merchant.
53. E.g. ADH 11 E 26 131, 1 May 1694, Jacques Ménard is referred to as merchant. Both Ménard and Desalasc are also referred to as merchants in the notarial acts cited in note 51 above.
54. ADH 11 E 26 128, Jan. 1691.
55. ADH 11 E 26 131, 8 March 1694, records the settlement of a loan made to Pierre Delpon, married to Marie Desalasc, and 11 E 26 171, 30 March 1709, records a loan made to Jacques Laurés, his brother-in-law.
56. ADH 11 E 26 101, 8 Nov. 1684.
57. ADH 11 E 26 101, 12 March 1684.
58. ADH 11 E 26 101, 26 July 1684, Pierre Dides, described in the act as a 'marchand-facturier-de-draps', received payment for mules which he had sold.
59. ADH 11 E 25 91, 22 Dec. 1674.

of these alternative sources of income. Even those of Clermont's clothiers who formed the core of the profession thus correspond to what Jean Meuvret has described as the typical industrial producer of the late seventeenth century – a 'gagne-deniers' for whom industrial income 'ne constituait qu'un revenu d'appoint'.[60]

The information on the remaining forty-three clothiers is, inevitably, more patchy. Their failure to be included in our first category is occasioned precisely by the infrequency of their appearances in notarial registers. Some of the forty-three do not qualify as 'regular' producers because they died or retired from production before completing the ten-year requirement – such was the case for example of five clothiers mentioned in the 1670s and present some forty years earlier at the registration of new statutes in 1633.[61] Others fail to qualify because they were only setting up their cloth-making establishments in the 1690s. There were two groups, however, whose irregular production has more significant explanations than old age or youth: there were a few merchants of exceptional wealth who invested in cloth-making for a short period only and there were a considerable number of clothiers who existed on the fringe of the profession and who were clearly too poor to produce cloth with any regularity.

In the case of the first group we encounter rare examples of what we have seen was a regular phenomenon in the first half of the century: the involvement in cloth production of merchants or bourgeois with large resources. There are only three examples of this, Pierre Baille, André Dupoivre and Jean Raymond. Pierre Baille, a Protestant merchant and clothier, was involved in 1672 in the purchase of fifty pieces of cloth at Carcassonne, a speculation which would have required considerable resources and which indicates extensive trading links.[62] He was also manufacturing on some scale in Clermont. An incidental piece of evidence suggests that his warehouses were loaded with wool – in March 1674 he was in litigation with a lady of the town because a bale of wool, thrown from his warehouse, had landed on her head.[63] In 1673 and 1674 Baille was buying old fulling mills and property beside the River Dourbie – the significance of these purchases will be seen later. The two others, André Dupoivre and Jean Raymond, or Jean de Raymond as he frequently called himself, were not only of a fortune but also of a social

60. 'Circulation monétaire et utilisation économique de la monnaie dans la France du xvie et du xviie siècle', *Etudes d'Histoire Moderne et Contemporaine* I (1947), 19.
61. Estienne Astruc, Fulcrand Audran, Quintin Fraisse, Louis Tournal and Jean Berthomieu.
62. ADH II E 25 89, 25 June 1672.
63. ADH II E 25 91, 11 March 1674.

standing far removed from that of other cloth-makers. Each was at one stage first consul.[64] Raymond had a brother, a marchand-droguiste, living in Bordeaux,[65] and in the 1690s he described himself as a banquier and was, indeed, involved in the commerce of Clermont's cloth with Marseilles, allowing clothiers with whom he was dealing to draw letters of exchange on him payable at Marseilles.[66] Dupoivre was Clermont's tax-collector in 1680 and he married the daughter of a doctor and advocate at the 'parlement' of Toulouse who brought him a dowry of 3,000 *livres*.[67] Dupoivre and Raymond were associated for the purpose of cloth-making for a maximum of six years, between 1679 and 1685. During these years, but during these years only, they referred to themselves as marchands-drapiers, or marchands, and they set up a manufacture of a scope which provided a contrast to the activities of their poorer and more cautious colleagues. They rented a well-equipped dye-house, purchased a twisting mill and related equipment, and employed a dyer from Carcassonne.[68] Their cloth-making concern they described as a manufacture but in fact it was just a short-term speculation. They made no cloth after 1685[69] and there is no record of their having joined either the clothiers' corporation or the confrérie (Baille was a member of the corporation – he acted as 'prévôt' or provost in 1674).[70] The motives for their association are not clear but it is possible that they were producing cloth for the Turkish market following the example of two recently founded royal manufactures, Villenouvette and Saptes. The dyeing of the cloth for this market was particularly crucial and it is significant that the Carcassonnais dyer whom they employed came from the village of Conques, the site of Saptes.[71]

The activities of these three merchants stand out because they were exceptional. Exceptional and, to judge from the brevity of their periods of involvement in cloth production, unsuccessful. Their examples are the exceptions which prove the rule: the industry was dominated by the

64. ACC BB1, 26 Aug. 1687, André Dupoivre was first consul; Jean Raymond, a former captain in the army, was first consul in both 1686 and 1696. In the latter year he referred to himself as Jean de Raymond, banquier (ADH 11 E 26 124, 24 Jan. 1686, 11 E 25 98, 30 Jan. 1696).
65. ADH 11 E 26 122, 28 May 1683. His brother was Charles Raymond.
66. ADH 11 E 25 98, 30 Jan. 1696. The particular agreement here was with Pierre Antoine Barthe; its significance will be seen later.
67. ADH 11 E 26 98, Jan. 1681.
68. ADH 11 E 25 94, 25 Feb., 7 March 1679; 11 E 26 97, 13 July, 1 Aug. 1680; 11 E 26 120, 16 April 1679.
69. In that year they sold the dyeing vat for blue colours which they had bought to Pierre Maysonnade (ADH 11 E 26 102, 16 Aug. 1685).
70. ACC BB1, 25 Feb. 1674.
71. See chapters five and six.

small-scale, artisanal producer and for reasons which have yet to be clarified the overwhelming majority of rich merchants and bourgeois of Clermont chose not to invest in industrial production during this period.

With our third group, those clothiers whose irregular production is to be explained by a lack of resources, we are dealing, it is evident, with the clothier at his most humble. At this level the profession of clothier merges socially and economically with that of the salaried worker. The daughters of two of these clothiers married weavers and the brother of another was a weaver.[72] The distinction between weavers and clothiers was evidently so small that a young man choosing a profession would have been likely to have difficulty in deciding on one or the other. This indeed was apparently the experience of one Estienne Soulayrol who was first apprenticed to a marchand-facturier in October 1692 and then, having apparently changed his mind, was apprenticed to a weaver the following April.[73] That there should have been a group of 'temporary' clothiers at Clermont is not surprising. It has been seen that the profession of clothier in the second half of the seventeenth century involved, very largely, manual skills and that the capital investment required could be minimal if credit for wool purchases was granted and so what would seem to have happened is that normally or occasionally salaried workers, when the demand situation for cloth was favourable, undertook their own independent production. This hypothesis is supported by inconsistencies apparent in the titles given in notarial documents to members of this group. Raymond Lhebrard and Michel Valette were described as marchands-facturiers in certain years and as cardeurs à laine in others,[74] while Jean Souvier in 1694 was described as a 'marchand cardeur facturier de draps' in 1694, a hybrid title which is expressive of this ambiguity in the distinction between cardeurs and facturiers.[75] That it should have been the cardeurs who fluctuated between being salaried workers and clothiers was predictable in view of the similarity between the two professions. There does not seem to have been any strictly enforced regulation about who was allowed to produce cloth. In the first half of the century, as we have seen, production was occasionally undertaken by people 'from above', of bourgeois status, and it would also have been undertaken occasionally by people 'from below', cardeurs and their

---

72. ADH II E 26 118, 15 April 1675, II E 25 105, 16 Feb. 1699, II E 26 127, 4 Nov. 1690.
73. ADH II E 26 135, 136, 23 Oct. 1692, 13 April 1693.
74. Lhebrard was provost of the clothier's confrérie in 1688 but in 1690, at the signing of his marriage contract, he described himself as a 'cardeur à laine' (ADH II E 26 125, 127, 29 June 1688, 4 Nov. 1690); Valette, again, was a cardeur à laine when he signed his marriage contract in 1686 but in 1687 and 1688 he is referred to in notarial acts as a marchand-facturier (II E 26 124, 125, 20 Jan. 1686, 8 Jan. 1687, 29 June 1688).
75. ADH II E 26 131, 29 July 1694.

like (and definitely was at Carcassonne as we have seen). Effectively cloth production was open to all, and although evidently there was a core of regular producers who made the bulk of cloth, the occasional involvement by 'temporary' clothiers, when the market situation was favourable, was clearly a regular occurrence. The major difference between the first and second half of the century would have been that the market situation in the second half was generally unfavourable to such temporary involvements and thus deterred bourgeois or merchant investment in industry. Salaried workers, however, whilst being deterred by the unfavourable market situation, might have been encouraged by the similarity of their resources to those of regular clothiers and by the relative ease with which the low-quality cloth being produced in the town could be made. On the whole, though, the practice was evidently rare. As we have noted, there were few movements in and out of the industry which was formed by a relatively stable group of clothiers. Clermont's cloth industry, during these years of depression at least, was no generator of social mobility. The reverse was going to be the case in cloth-making centres when an economic recovery began in the 1720s. Complaints about non-clothiers making cloth became frequent. In 1728, for example, we find the 'gardes-jurés' of Mirepoix complaining that 'plusieurs particuliers s'ingèrent sans aucun titre et sans avoir fait apprentissage de fabriquer de Draps ... et principallement toute sorte d'artizans comme cardeurs, Retorseurs, tisserands, pareurs et affineurs'.[76]

If during the period of expansion, as we have seen, there had been a tendency for social and economic distinctions between employers and employed, clothiers and weavers, to widen, the opposite, it will already be clear, had occurred during the depression. There continued to be two different confréries but apart from that the closeness between the two professions is shown not only by intermarriage but also by the weavers' ownership of an important part of the fixed capital used in cloth production, the loom, and of land. Thus Antoine Thérou, weaver and son of a weaver, who married a clothier's daughter, was given not only a loom in his marriage contract but also half his father's vineyard, and his future wife brought with her a dowry respectable enough to set them both up in comfort – use of her parental house, 200 *livres*, ample household equipment, pewter plates, a walnut bedstead, three walnut chairs, two gold rings, two dresses and a large supply of household linen in a 'coffre bois noyer fermé à clef'.[77] An even fuller picture of the resources of a Clermont weaver is provided by the division of the heritage of Pierre

76. ADH C2129, 11 Jan. 1728.
77. ADH 11 E 26 118, 15 April 1675.

Villasecque between his two sons Jean and Jacques and his daughter Françoise between 1687 and 1691. The daughter received money and vineyards to the value of 120 *livres*, Jean a loom, a bed, household equipment, three barrels of red wine, a choice of gold ring or household chairs, and 40 *livres*, and Jacques 100 *livres* in land, a gold ring, linen and the rest of his father's possessions on condition that he lived with his father, making 'un pot et feu'. Villasecque was able to provide a dowry for his daughter, set up one of his sons with a loom and provide generously for his elder son and heir, and hence for his own old age. The contract with his son endured only for a year: in 1691 'ne pouvant continuer à demurer plus ensemblement' they divided their possessions, and as a result an even more exact inventory of their belongings was made. Jacques was to receive a loom, considerable quantities of furniture, and, most significantly, agricultural implements: a wine-press, two seed-sowers, an axe and a bill-hook as well as the fruits of the weaver's land – three barrels of wine, a large jar of olive oil and flour 'par heus Recully en moisonnant'.[78]

It is probable that the Thérou and Villasecque families were among the richest in the weaving profession and there are certainly no grounds for selecting their cases as typical. But the evidence about their resources does serve to reinforce two points which we have stressed already. First, that the distinction between independent clothier and salaried worker was not sharp – the two professions literally merged from the point of view of the economic and social status of their members – and secondly that virtually no participants in the industry depended on it totally for their livelihood. The weaver's costs, like the clothier's, could be subsidized by income from an agricultural source. Cloth as a consequence was very cheap.

Charles de Loyseau in his renowned survey of French society in the seventeenth century grouped all those involved in any way in manufacturing, all 'gens de métier', in one 'vile' category while merchants, he held, could be qualified as 'honorables hommes', 'honnestes personnes' or 'bourgeois des villes' in view of their 'utilité', the 'necessité publique du commerce' and their 'opulence ordinaire'.[79] In view of what has just been shown about those involved in industrial production at Clermont during the second half of the seventeenth century a stratification of this kind becomes easily comprehensible. And Clermont's example also provides justification for grouping all artisanal trades in one broad category for there is evidence that those involved in cloth production charged and

---

78. ADH II E 26 127, 128, 2 April 1690, 12, 13 Aug. 1691.
79. Cited by R. Mousnier, *Les hiérarchies sociales*, pp. 62–4.

received similar apprenticeship fees as, and were linked socially to, other gens de métier. Two clothiers for example had sisters married to hatters, another had daughters married to a tanner and a carder, another had a tailor, a blacksmith and a tanner among close relations and another was married to a cobbler's daughter.[80]

So Clermont's industry had declined and changed, with respect to both its product and its organization of production. To recapitulate: richer merchants were no longer involved in industrial production; the characteristic producer was artisanal and little separated from the salaried worker; cloth produced was of low quality; skilled, specialized workers had left; clothiers were 'all-rounders' both in that they carried out most of the processes of production themselves and in that they supplemented industrial with agricultural earnings; and the industry was static from all points of view – technologically, in that it was not generating social mobility and in that there were few movements either into or out of it.

Now most of the causes of the depression we have already mentioned: demand, political, monetary, agricultural and demographic circumstances were clearly all unfavourable. Clermont's industrial decline was in no way unique. It was in parallel with that which occurred in the majority of important urban textile centres in France. The structural changes which had occurred in Clermont's industry had, likewise, their counterparts elsewhere. Deyon observes at Amiens in this period, for example, a movement towards 'une organisation plus parcellaire du métier, le repliement vers l'entreprise familiale'.[81] And that developments at Carcassonne were of a similar nature is suggested by retrospective notes in letters from the local sub-delegate written in the 1740s – 'les fabriquands de ce temps là', he wrote, 'ne faisoient qu'un commerce Borné [;] ils possédoint touttes les qualités des maîtres des différends arts et ne Croyoint pas dérogés dêtre continuellement autour de leurs ouvriers'; 'les fabriquands étoint eux même tisserands cardeurs pareurs'.[82]

What is perhaps less clear, and this is a question which we have left pendant, is the way in which these two often-observed phenomena, depression and organizational change, were linked and why, to all appearances, the depression affected those clothiers with large concerns most, giving rise to a process of industrial contraction and to the pre-

80. ADH II E 26 130, 131, 12 Aug. 1693, 27 Dec. 1694, II E 26 141, 8 Sept. 1698, II E 26 171, 30 March 1709, II E 26 136, 102, 14 Oct. 1693, 24 Nov. 1685.
81. *Amiens*, pp. 224–7.
82. ADH C2429, De Murat to Le Nain, 14 March 1742 and 2 July 1746.

dominance of the artisanal and familial industrial concern. Is the explanation economic: larger concerns were less viable? Is it social: a consequence of the retirement of (a 'betrayal' by) the bourgeoisie? Of some interest too (though less easily answerable in view of the Languedocian bias of our evidence) is the question of why French textile centres fared less well than Dutch and English in this period. The check to commercial expansion in the mid-seventeenth century may have been universal but in some areas of Europe the reaction to the depression was more positive than in others and nowhere was this more the case than in Holland and England. The cloth industries of these northern powers not only replaced the Venetians and French as the main suppliers of the Levant market but also successfully competed (to the ignominy of the French cloth industry) in the French domestic market, supplying, above all, the majority of those finer broad-cloths which had previously figured among Clermont's and Carcassonne's production.[83]

To begin with I shall examine the first possibility, that there are economic explanations for the industrial contraction, and for the gains of small concerns at the expense of large.

To explain the behaviour of Languedoc's large-scale wholesale merchants and cloth producers it is necessary to understand their position in what was, as some historians have emphasized recently, effectively a single European if not world economy.[84] If there had been a dynamism in Languedoc's industrial and commercial life in the first half of the seventeenth century it is to be accounted for, above all, by the fact that the province and France in that period were well placed with respect to this European economy. As I have emphasized in chapter two, Languedoc was ideally situated to participate in the Mediterranean economy and the early seventeenth century witnessed not only a general prosperity in Mediterranean trade but also a relative weakening in the situation of the formerly dominating commercial power, Venice, which allowed Marseilles to develop a flourishing trade with the Levant. This trade occasioned a large demand for Languedocian cloth and also made

83. On these Dutch and English successes see D. Sella, 'The rise and fall of the Venetian woollen industry' in B. Pullan (ed.), *Crisis and Change in the Venetian Economy*, p. 120; R. Davis, 'England and the Mediterranean, 1570–1670' in F. J. Fisher (ed.), *Essays in the Economic and Social History of Tudor and Stuart England*, p. 123; R. T. Rapp, 'The unmaking of the Mediterranean trade hegemony', pp. 499–525; M. Priestley, 'Anglo-French trade and the unfavourable balance controversy, 1660–1685', *Ec.H.R.* 4 (1951–2), 46.
84. Especially I. Wallerstein, *The Modern World-System: Capitalist Agriculture and the Origins of the European World-Economy in the Sixteenth Century.*

Marseilles into one of the largest European distributive centres for exotic oriental products which still played a significant role in European trade.[85]

If it was Languedoc's centrality in the commercial circuits of Europe which was the background for that commercial dynamism which we have observed in the first half of this chapter then it was the province's, and much of France's, *exclusion* from these commercial circuits as a consequence of foreign and civil warfare, the rise of commercial and industrial competitors and unwise political decisions which was the background to that disinvolvement and lack of merchant investment which we have just noted in the second half of the century. The Levant trade was taken over by the Dutch and English, the Mediterranean distributive trade in oriental products moved to Leghorn and the Atlantic distributive trade was dominated by Amsterdam and London. As Braudel has shown, for the first time latitudinal (west to east) rather than longitudinal commercial movements began to predominate in the European economy.[86] 'Une Grande Révolution', had occurred, Lefevre, former 'échevin' of Marseilles, wrote in 1682; the English and Dutch had taken over the distributive trade in oriental goods from Venice which had previously been 'comme le Magasin, et Lentrepôt de toutes les Marchandises, et de toutes les Epiceries, qu'on y alloit prendre pour les distribuer dans le reste de l'oeurope'. Oriental products were reaching France in greatest quantities not in French ships via Marseilles but in Dutch ships via Rouen.[87]

Is the behaviour of Clermont's merchants fully explained by this reference to the European commercial circuits in which they were involved? Not entirely, it would seem, for although circumstances were clearly unfavourable for the production of cloth for international markets there continued to exist opportunities in the domestic market for the sale of all grades of cloth. And yet, as we have seen, the market for lower-quality, hard-wearing cloth was supplied by Clermont's artisanal clothiers and by Lodève's cloth industry (which retained an artisanal structure into the eighteenth century), and that for higher-quality cloth was satisfied, increasingly, by Dutch and English cloth-making centres, imports of fine cloth becoming the single most expensive item in the French import bill.[88] Thus if a decline in production for export markets might be

85. R. Collier and J. Billioud, *Histoire du commerce de Marseille*, III, 198–200, and F. Braudel, P. Jeannin, J. Meuvret and R. Romano, 'Le déclin de Venise au xviiᵉ siècle' in *Civiltà Veneziana* 9 (1963), 30–1, 35, 62–3.
86. Braudel (*et al.*), 'Le déclin de Venise', pp. 76–8.
87. BN FF 62431.
88. P. Boissonnade, *Colbert et le triomphe de l'étatisme*, p. 182.

explicable by referring to the general situation of the European economy there would seem to have been a dual failure in the domestic market by richer merchants which requires elucidation.

With respect to the internal market for lower-quality cloth two factors emerge from an analysis of Clermont's experiences. There is a local factor of significance. The town was not particularly well endowed from the point of view of water-power, necessary to full the heavier, coarser cloths which were in demand for popular or military uses in the second half of the seventeenth century. Lodève, as we have noted, was better equipped, indeed had the best facilities in the province. This should not have represented an insuperable problem, however; there were fulling mills close to Clermont and, if necessary, the services of Lodève's fullers could be hired. Secondly, and in this case the factor is of general rather than of purely local significance, there are signs that in the production of lower-quality in contrast to that of higher-quality cloth, the richer clothier held few if any advantages over his poorer colleague. In fact he may have been at a disadvantage. This was above all because the poorer clothier could cut his costs, as we have seen, by carrying out most of the production process himself and effectively granting himself and those of his family who participated in the production process a less than subsistence wage which would be subsidized by combining industrial production with other occupations. The large-scale producer, in contrast, would have been quite unable to carry out even a small part of the manual side of cloth-making himself because of his high status, his lack of manual skills and the large scale of his production, and would have been obliged to employ labour and to pay for it at the market rate which, necessarily, was above the subsistence level. In other words the richer clothier who employed labour would have had great difficulty in competing. Large-scale production units were in addition more vulnerable to a decline in demand for two reasons: they lost the economies of scale which had given them advantages over the concerns of small-scale clothiers, and the commitment of both clothier and his labour force to cloth production was more complete as there was a lack of back-up agricultural sources of income. Clothiers were objected to in Tudor England not only because of their ambition and social mobility but also because of the damaging consequences for social order of their creation of putting-out industries, with large labour forces, dependent totally on undependable markets.[89] The greater resistance of smaller production units at Clermont is apparent not only from the capacity of Clermont's artisanal clothiers to

89. F. J. Fisher, 'Commercial trends in sixteenth century England', *Ec.H.R.* 10 (1939–40), 110–14.

weather the crisis but also in the performance of Clermont's hat-making industry. The nature of its product and technology was such that hat-making was invariably carried out in small artisanal production units and the greater flexibility of such units is implied by evidence of this industry's continuous expansion in the seventeenth century. Present at confrérie meetings were seven masters in 1615, eighteen in 1659 and thirty-nine in 1689 and the high apprenticeship figures for this trade between 1686 and 1700 have already been noted.[90]

The greater success of the small-scale clothier in the production of lower-quality cloth is thus easily explicable in terms of the divergent characteristics of family and market economies. As has been demonstrated, particularly in relation to peasant agricultural concerns, the two did not function according to the same laws and the contrasts were particularly marked with respect to the effective rates of payment for labour. Various studies have shown how the depression in agricultural prices in this period had similarly diverging consequences for different types of agricultural concern – larger farms employing labour at market rates could not compete with peasant households whose members could ignore the market price for labour and in addition supplement their earnings by obtaining either industrial or agricultural by-employment.[91]

In fact the logic of this argument would suggest that, if artisanal urban-dwellers held an advantage over rich clothiers because of their effective 'self-exploitation' and their obtaining supplementary income from other sources, then country-dwellers, with larger supplies of land at their disposal and hence even less dependence on industrial earnings and with similar advantages with respect to labour at their disposition, would have held an even larger potential economic advantage. The exploitation of this potential competitive advantage was, of course, forbidden in many parts of France with exclusive guilds. In addition, country-dwellers would have been hard put to produce higher-quality cloth because of the technical difficulties involved. But, as we have noted, there were no barriers to production in seventeenth-century Languedoc and the low-quality cloth being produced late in the century was easily imitated. And so this would seem to be the explanation for another aspect of Clermont's industrial decline. In contrast to the period of expansion which, as we have seen in an earlier chapter, had led to a decline in rural cloth production and a concentration in favour of the towns, the period of

90. ADH II E 25 70, 19 May 1659. (This register contains a loose copy of the early act, registered before Pelissier, 15 July 1615); II E 26 129, 8 May 1689.
91. The more favourable performance of smaller, peasant properties during periods of labour shortage is revealed in Le Roy Ladurie, *Paysans*, pp. 168–74, and discussed by J. de Vries, *The Economy of Europe in an Age of Crisis, 1600–1750*, pp. 73–5.

depression had led to a certain revival in independent industrial production in the villages of the Lodévois. It was to this 'abuse' that the author of a memoir composed in the 1680s referred. Mentioning the complaints of clothiers from Clermont and Lodève about the development he commented that 'Les Messrs de Lodève et de Clermont . . . n'ont pas tout le tort qu'on pourrait leur donner' in that the inhabitants of neighbouring villages were making cheap, low-quality versions of their principal cloths with which they were having difficulty in competing. Singled out for mention in the memoir are 'ceux de fondements de Seille, de Cornus . . . où il se fait une grande quantité de ses méchans draps', and by chance, Ceilhes is a village for whose industry there has survived a reasonably full description made in the context of the national survey of 'Arts et Métiers' undertaken in 1692. This provides a good idea of the type of concern which would have had costs as low, or lower, than the urban, artisanal producer. There were six marchands-drapiers operating there, selling their cloth on the spot to Lyonnais merchants or at the fairs of Pézenas and Montagnac. Their cloth was selling at between 4 and 5 *livres* the *aune*. The richest of the six was producing between fourteen and fifteen cloths a year and the poorest four to five. There were in addition twenty-six or twenty-seven carders in the village working both for these rustic clothiers and for their urban rivals in Lodève as well as cultivating their land. These carders, the description added, 'vivent avec beaucoup de peine du jour à la journée'. Ceilhes and Cornus were not the only centres in which independent rural cloth-making was taking place. The author of the 1680s memoir added that production was taking place in 'tous les autres endroits, qui sont aux environs de cette ville' and additional replies to the survey of Arts et Métiers for 1692 showed that cloth-making was taking place at St-Guilhem-le-Désert and Gignac.[92]

The balance between urban and rural production fluctuated, this evidence suggests, with the 'conjuncture'. Whereas in periods of commercial expansion the advantages were all in favour of the larger producer who achieved economies of scale, and had the resources to employ skilled worker and the organization to produce a product of the necessary uniformity and presentation, in periods of depression the tables were turned: in the production of low-quality cloth there were few economies of scale to be gained, little skill involved, no premium on standardization and no need to have recourse to expensive, specialized workers and hence the advantages were all in favour of the producer with lowest labour costs – artisan or rustic-clothier.

92. ADH C2200, Memoir of Jacques Journet, marchand, undated but probably composed in late 1670s or early 1680s; ADH C2773, Survey of Arts et Métiers for diocese of Lodève, 1691–2.

The failure in fine-cloth production for the domestic market appears the more complex of the two questions. It is one which has, too, less relevance to Languedoc than to northern France, for the bulk of the Languedocian product consisted in low to middling qualities, and the main markets produced for were to the province's south. There should have existed, though, the possibility of switching to the production of fine cloth for the domestic market. But, as we have seen, this market came to be monopolized by Dutch and English clothiers. Why was this the case? Similarly when attempts were to be made to send fine cloth to the Levant in the 1660s it was found that the regional cloth was inferior to Dutch and English products though more expensive.[93] What had happened to the skills which had existed at Clermont and Carcassonne some twenty years earlier?

There is one consideration which is of relevance to both aspects of the failure, in domestic and export markets, and that is that over-valuation of the *livre* artificially boosted the price of French cloth exports while making cloth imports unnaturally cheap.[94] The same phenomenon though would have had cost-reducing effects – imports of, for example, Spanish wools and cochineal would have been cheapened too. That the problem is more complex than a question of exchange rates is suggested by the lack of immediate response by French cloth-producers to the protective tariffs imposed in 1664 and 1667.

Another possibility, and it is one which has received some emphasis from historians, is that technological and organizational innovations had given northern European products a competitive edge. The progress lay, it is argued, not so much in the basic production processes but more in the development of new types of cloth and in improvements in the organization and commercialization of production. One historian has coined the term 'increasing roundaboutness' to describe what was effectively the development of a greater division of labour in both the production and commercialization of cloth.[95] Such an increased 'roundaboutness' would have led to economies of scale both in the production process and in the transactions sector. That these developments were innovations, though, is arguable for we have observed exactly the same phenomena in Languedoc in the first half of the century – the manufacture of new cloths, greater division of labour, the employment of rural out-workers, the presence of cloth commissioners at Clermont all the year round etc. But if all these developments which favoured the northern producers

---

93. On these difficulties see below, pp. 141–2.
94. Deyon, *Amiens*, pp. 125–32.
95. H. A. Miskimin, *The Economy of Later Renaissance Europe, 1460–1600*, pp. 91–2, and J. de Vries, *Europe in an Age of Crisis*, pp. 95–110.

were familiar to Languedocians why, then, were they abandoned in the second half of the century? The answer, it would seem, lies above all in the fact that all of them required a healthy demand situation in order to be economically viable and that this was denied for a significant period for the combination of reasons already mentioned. The advantage enjoyed by the Dutch and English, then, according to this argument lay not so much in their superior technology and commercial techniques but in their possession of larger markets, both internal and external, which permitted economies of scale both in the transactions sector and, through division of labour, in industrial production.

As has been emphasized by some, in the pre-industrial period, in contrast to the industrial world in which economies of scale are obtained above all in the production of low-quality goods, the nature of both demand and the production process was such as to limit the possibilities of economies of scale to the production and commercialization of high-quality goods.[96] The best prospect of all for obtaining economies of scale lay in the production of high-quality goods for export markets. We are used to a trading system in which participants generally gain the necessary economies of scale for successful intervention with their products by sales on the domestic market. In the pre-industrial period, and this is another sharp contrast with the industrial world, economies of scale were generally obtainable *only* by participation in export trades and thus it was only when an industry had achieved a low-cost situation by participation in foreign trade that successful intervention in the domestic market for luxury goods became possible. In view of this the interruptions to French foreign trade acquire an added significance. The resultant loss of economies of scale would have made participation in the domestic market difficult. The continued monopolization of the lower levels of the cloth market would not have eased the situation for, as we have just shown, a different type of production unit supplied this market. The importance given by contemporaries to foreign trade is understandable in view of its crucial role.

So, as a consequence of the unfavourable demand situation, those 'modern' elements in Languedoc's cloth industry which we have described for the first half of the century disappeared. Skilled specialized workers could not find adequate employment – their existence had presumed a steady production of medium- to high-quality cloth. Skills in the production of special types of cloth were lost. Division of labour decreased. Advanced commercial techniques, no longer required, went

96. On this see especially D. R. Ringrose, 'Comments on papers by Reed, de Vries and Bean', *J.E.H.* 31 (1973), 226.

out of use. By the 1660s it was not only that the demand situation was unfavourable; the lack of success in selling Languedocian fine cloth on the Levant and domestic market showed that the industry had become technologically backward because of the irregularity with which such cloth had come to be produced. So the lack of demand eventually gave rise to technological backwardness too though, and this it is important to re-emphasize, it was not technological backwardness which originally had caused the failure in demand. The loss of technological and commercial skills occasioned by the failure in demand would, however, make recovery, once the demand situation improved, more difficult.

The evidence which we have presented in support of an economic explanation for the changes which occurred in Clermont's industry in the second half of the seventeenth century would appear to vindicate the decision apparently made by a number of merchant and bourgeois families to withdraw from participation in cloth production. Their disinvestment, it would seem, was the wisest course they could have taken.

The nature of their choice of alternative investments was, too, economically justifiable, it would seem. Some, like Jullien and some of the skilled workers, left for other commercial and industrial centres which, unlike Clermont, continued or came to occupy profitable positions in the commercial circuits of the European economy. The Lyonnais was one such area. Lyons, as Jean Meuvret has shown, was one of the few areas in France which was prosperous in the second half of the century: it was the centre for both the import and the distribution of luxury goods and for the commercialization of both French and north European cloth in France, central Europe and northern Italy.[97] Migration to centres such as Lyons was, as we have seen, a regular feature in Clermont's social and economic life but the extent of migration to the Lyonnais region in the second half of the century seems to have been exceptional. We have identified no fewer than twenty-two Clermontais at Lyons, and two near by at Chalon and Grenoble. Significantly seven of this number had family names which were represented at either the 1633 or the 1655 meetings of clothiers in Clermont.[98] Effectively by moving to Lyons the Clermontais merchants abandoned any direct participation in cloth production and became full-time wholesale merchants. To judge from the Galtié/Moulins correspondence the main trades in which Clermontais who established themselves in Lyons involved themselves consisted in

---

97. 'Circulation monétaire', pp. 24–6; the benefits accruing to Lyons from shifting trading patterns are also mentioned by Braudel and collaborators in 'Le déclin de Venise', pp. 77–8. Lyons enjoyed a growing monopoly in the supply of Swiss and German markets.
98. Marcelin, Pélissier (mentioned 1633); Messier, Fraisse (mentioned 1633 and 1655); Chinion, Figuière, Grasset (mentioned 1655).

the purchase of Mediterranean products and of Languedocian cloth and of the distribution of luxury goods in the Midi – including high-quality northern cloth. The economic justification for such a professional switch was this – if the merchant could no longer compete as industrial producer given his higher costs he could use his larger capital resources to monopolize the commercial element in cloth-making which was the only one, we have seen, which required a large capital investment.

So the move to Lyons and the abandonment of cloth-making for a full-time commitment to trading were economically justifiable – Lyons was an island of prosperity in a depressed France, and profits from trading had become greater than those obtainable from manufacturing. Not all of our lost drapiers departed for Lyons, of course. There existed the possibility, too, of abandoning cloth production and opting for a full-time merchant's existence in Clermont itself. The typical Clermontais merchant in the last quarter of the seventeenth century, and the Galtiés are representative of this, took no direct part in cloth, or any other sort of industrial, production, and confined himself to trading activities. In one case we can identify an individual who switched from a combined marchand/drapier role to a full-time commitment to trading. Marc Germain received an apprentice in 1653 when he was a marchand-drapier, but between 1655 and 1689 he was involved in general trading in association with his brother. In the latter year their partnership was divided – the extensive areas in which they had traded we have mentioned in chapter three and they also mentioned in the act dividing their business that until 1685 'il cestoit faict entre eux et à leur profit un guain continuel en leur négosse'; it is doubtful if Marc Germain would have been in a position to make such a statement if he had been continuously involved in cloth production during this period.[99]

As we have seen, the richer participant in cloth production was possibly at a disadvantage in this period because of the lack of economies of scale in the production of low-quality cloth. In contrast in the merchant profession the possession of large resources continued to be an indubitable advantage. Those clothiers who had the resources to set up as full-time merchants did so as there was no advantage in remaining in the cloth industry. It comes as no surprise to discover that two of the three clothiers at Clermont who, we have noted earlier in this chapter, were better off than the average for the profession, apprenticed their sons to merchants in Lyons and Montpellier.[100]

---

99. ADH II E 26 126, 1 May 1689.
100. ADH II E 26 131, 7 Nov. 1694, Pierre Fraisse's presence at Lyons is recorded; II E 26 126, 23 Feb. 1689, Jacques Desalasc, son of Pierre, was apprenticed to Pierre Astruc at Montpellier for a fee of 200 *livres*.

We are still far from having accounted for all the desertions from the cloth industry or, for that matter, from providing a full description of the characteristics of Clermont's elite in this period. Indeed the documentation which would permit us to do so does not exist. There are certain clues which suggest, though, that at Clermont, as in other commercial centres such as Amiens,[101] there was a tendency for elite families, including former rich participants in the cloth industry, to rely increasingly on non-commercial investments – in land, office or 'rentes constituées' – and to define more strictly the necessary qualification for bourgeois status. The most significant clue which suggests that this tendency developed in Clermont consists in the fact that access to the prestigious office of first consul, which entitled its holder to attendance at the Etats, officially open to all imposed for more than six *livres* in the *compoix*, came to be restricted to bourgeois as strictly defined. This, at least, is the impression given by various protests made in the 1720s when renewed upward social mobility occasioned by the economic revival was making it difficult to enforce such a rule. In 1723 a complaint was lodged that Guillaume Mutuel, an apothecary, who had managed to get himself elected to the first consulship, and 'qui prétend à ceste députation [as the town's representative to the Etats] possède un mettier mécanique dapp*re* ayant servy et administré ses remèdes pendant Lannée de son consulat comme il fait actuellement et quil nest pas d'ixample que les app*res* sont de la qualitté pour estre deputtés pour les estats'. The consul for the following year, Pierre Alfonse, *viguier* of Lestagnol, clearly corresponded to the bourgeois requirement but in November 1725 there was another dispute as a consequence, this time, of the election of a marchand-fabricant to the consulship. Alfonse, backed by eight others who described themselves as 'principaux hans' of Clermont (they were all large property-owners), refused to confer the consulship on the marchand-fabricant on two grounds: first that to do so would be to make a mockery of the general cloth regulations of 1669 which gave jurisdiction over the cloth industry to the consuls – if clothiers were elected consul the consequence would be that they might be 'juges de leur propre cauze' – and secondly that the office of first consul 'ne doit estre exercée que par les gentilhommes gradués, et bourgeois vivant noblement comme sest luzage dans touttes les villes de la province'.[102] This evidence would suggest, then, not only that the first consulship had been confined for a number of years to bourgeois but also that the criteria to qualify for the status of bourgeois were being more strictly defined. Involvement in any sort of industrial activity had clearly become excluded and the nature of

101. Deyon, *Amiens*, pp. 273–83.
102. ACC BB3, 19 Nov. 1724, 16 Nov. 1725. The second case was settled in favour of the marchand-fabricant by an order of de Bernage, 21 Nov. 1725.

what were acceptable investments emerges from a marriage contract in which a scrupulous father-in-law-to-be prescribed how his daughter's dowry should be used by her prospective husband – the money would be handed over when the 'fiancé ... trouvera à faire Lacquizition dune terre pour y employer lad somme, ou autrement sil trouve à La placer sur un fond seûr ou solvable comme province diocèze communauté ou autre*mt*'.[103] The Jullien family was one which invested heavily in the latter type of funds, rentes constituées. By an act registered in 1661 Jean Joulhien, described as bourgeois, transferred to his brother Guillaume, likewise described as bourgeois and quite probably the same 'Jullien' who had deserted to Lodève, no less than 7,298 *livres* invested in rentes constituées on the communautés of Clermont and Brignac and on the diocese of Lodève.[104] The only sort of commercial activity which, it seems, would have been in any way socially acceptable was the distant wholesale trading of the type practised by Galtié et fils, and the relative rarity of merchants with such resources and widespread trading links in Clermont in the second half of the seventeenth century is suggested by the lack of qualified merchants whom the Galtiés could find locally to act as arbitrators in a dispute which they had with Moulins in 1704: their account books had to be sent to Lyons where a relation of Galtié's wife, an Archimbaud, served in this role.[105]

The economic wisdom for such a switch to 'rentier' type investments is again undeniable. In a period of falling prices fixed incomes from such sources increased in real terms. Does this, then, finally justify us in discounting as fictitious those accusations which have been levelled at French bourgeois, merchants and industrialists in this period? If we are judging the situation of the individual merchant facing a certain set of economic circumstances the answer is probably yes, but if we are judging the French elite in this period as a collective unit then the answer would be less definite, for it was, after all, the collective behaviour of this elite which contributed to creating the set of economic circumstances which encouraged the type of responses we have just analysed. This is what Le Roy Ladurie is implying when he writes of the sad state of the economy in this period being in part the work and desire of the French. Economic priorities had not yet been given the primacy which they were to receive in the pragmatic century of the 'philosophes' and the civil disturbances, the involvement in international warfare and the persecution of

103. ADH II E 26 144, 19 Dec. 1704.
104. ADH II E 25 84, 15 Feb. 1661.
105. A Clermontais, Gabriel Vallibouze, initially acted for the Galtiés but later Galtié's widow made her cousin, Jean Baptiste Archimbaud of Lyons, her arbitrator (ADR, Fonds Moulins, IV, Letter of 21 July 1704, and XV, Letters of 24 Nov. 1712, 22 Oct. 1714).

Protestants, all damaging economically, were at least indirectly a consequence of the values and actions of the French elite. As Le Roy Ladurie writes: 'L'unité de religion représentait pour beaucoup d'entre eux un bien plus valable du soi que le sauvetage à tout prix du profit ou de bien-être.'[106] Signs of the priority given to glory and to religious unity at Clermont are the singing of Te Deums in the town after any victory of Louis XIV, the care taken in the choice of the preacher selected by the consuls for Lent, the establishment of several religious foundations in the town in the 1660s, and the steady and increasing persecution of the Protestant minority.[107] This persecution was both a sign of priorities and directly damaging to the town's industry and trade. Some of the leading families in the cloth industry were Protestants. An act registered in 1661 lists the 'anciens du consistoire' of the 'religion prétendue réformée' in Clermont and at least four of the nine names were, or had been, involved in cloth-making in one way or another – Jean Baille (father of Pierre Baille mentioned earlier in this chapter), David Michel, who owned one of the fulling mills on the Dourbie, Jean Donnet and Jean Vernet, both present at the registration of the 1655 statutes.[108] Protestants were excluded from political representation – they were allowed neither to stand nor to vote in consular elections[109] – and subjected to increasing harassment. Pierre Villar, a Protestant notary, for example, had soldiers from a regiment of 'Zurlobes' billeted in his house. Some chose to accept at least nominal conversion – Villar's was one of approximately sixty families which did so and, in return, he was given 86 *livres* compensation for the damage which the soldiers had done to his house.[110] Others went into refuge, in most cases before the final Revocation. Among the refugees we find, again, important members of Clermont's commercial and industrial community: the brothers Pierre and Jean Baille, who left for Amsterdam; one Jean Forestier who left under sentence of death for Switzerland leaving substantial possessions in Clermont which were confiscated (possibly the same Jean Forestier described as a 'marchand-drapier et marchand-facturier' in the 1650s); and Jean Vernet left too – a notarial act for 1689 describes him as a 'fugitif et Huguenot'.[111]

---

106. *Paysans*, p. 642.
107. Crémieux, *La vie politique*, pp. 52–3; A. Durand, *Annales de Clermont-l'Hérault*, pp.37–9.
108. ADH 11 E 25 84, 4 June 1661.
109. Crémieux, *La vie politique*, p. 53.
110. ADH 11 E 26 103, 23 Jan. 1686; the conversion of sixty families to Catholicism is noted in ACC BB1, 26 Aug. 1687.
111. P. Gachon, *Quelques préliminaires de la révocation de l'édit de Nantes en Languedoc, 1661–1685*, 'pièces justificatives', pp. cxliv–cxlv; ADH 11 E 26 70, 19 May 1651; 11 E 26 126, 16 Oct. 1689 (Vernet).

So, to conclude our assessment of the value of social explanations of France's economic stagnation in this period, we would emphasize again that, although when we analyse the economic behaviour of *individual* members of this elite as we have done at Clermont we find their behaviour to be rational, when we examine this elite as a whole, as a collective entity, different conclusions are reached. We find that the military disruptions to economic activity which made investments of a rentier kind more reliable than commercial ones, the very existence of so many alternative and guaranteed forms of income – venal offices, rentes constituées, seigneurial dues, positions in the tax-farms, etc. – as well as the expulsion of Protestants, reflected or came to reflect collective interests and priorities of the Catholic bourgeoisie. If the French bourgeoisie had had to struggle to survive, as French artisans certainly did, and had not found such easy, protected and honourable alternatives to commercial and industrial involvement, it is highly unlikely that France's economic decline in this period would have been either so severe or so prolonged.

What, then, were the general characteristics of Clermont's social structure in the second half of the century? In the previous chapter I have argued that Clermont's social structure was of an exceptional kind in that the extent of commercial opportunity, and the lack of administrative and ecclesiastical posts, gave rise to an unusual degree of social mobility, and to status being judged in terms of wealth as much as position. But I also posited (and this in line with the writings of Mousnier) that the town's social structure would be in part conditioned by the state of the economic conjuncture and thus that the extent to which these two characteristics applied would fluctuate. If during the first half of the century, a period of expansion, there had been both high levels of social mobility and a widening gulf, which took on a class nature, among those involved in the production process, in the second half of the century there had been an evident drawing together, and a lack of social mobility among artisanal sections of Clermont's population. And it would seem, too, that Clermont's elite in this period shared these characteristics in so far that the limited nature of economic opportunities and the lack of artisanal upward mobility protected it from penetration from below, while the security which falling prices gave to those living on fixed incomes protected its members from loss of position. The situation, if it has been correctly described, was representative: as Mandrou writes, 'la conjoncture du xviie siècle a certainement servi le renforcement des rapports sociaux traditionnels dans une société qui est loin encore de sa conversion aux valeurs capitalistes'.[112]

112. R. Mandrou, *Louis XIV en son temps*, p. 29.

Once an adjustment had been made to the changed circumstances brought about by the depression Clermont's economy and society would seem to have settled into a fixed pattern which was to last until the 1690s. Both were dominated, it would seem, by a relatively small and stable group of wealthy bourgeois and merchant families. The persecution and eventual expulsion of Protestants, damaging to the interests of the French economy as a whole, inevitably were beneficial to the non-Protestant or 'nouveaux-convertis' members of this elite. They found that, to add to the advantages of the lack of pressure from below because of the low levels of social mobility, they were suddenly freed from the energetic economic competition of their religious rivals. Aspects of the Moulins/Galtié correspondence illustrate this stability. Not only was Clermont involved in the same type of trading relationships with Lyons from the 1650s until the 1690s but the trade was also handled, it would seem, by a relatively small group of families throughout these years. The merchants to whom Moulins was apprenticed, Mathieu Archimbaud and Louis Durand, were already trading with Clermont in the 1650s – there is evidence of several Clermontais merchants drawing up letters of exchange on them in this decade.[113] Moulins when he founded his own trading concern in the 1690s carried on the same trade which he had learnt with Durand and had been practising on Durand's behalf for so many years. Galtié's links with this established social and economic network are shown by his marriage to an Archimbaud and the long period during which he occupied a dominant economic situation in Clermontais society is shown by the references to be found to him in the 1670s – described as a marchand-droguiste, he was farming the town's taxes in 1671.[114]

One is struck by Galtié's confidence and certainty in announcing his son's prospective marriage to Catherine Estienne, niece of Raymond Estienne, ex-Clermontais who was well established in Lyons. As will be remembered, in his letter to Moulins he wrote that it was unnecessary to go into details about the Estienne family in Clermont because '[elle] vous es cogneu que cest la plus honneste la plus reglée et la plus comode de nostre ville':[115] he was confident in his own social position, in that of the family into which his son was marrying, and he was also confident that Moulins, too, would be fully informed about the Clermontais branch of the Estienne family and aware of the social significance of the match. The exact statuses and fortunes of the families dominating both Cler-

---

113. ADH 11 E 25 60, 9 May, 23 June 1654.
114. ADH 11 E 25 90, 20 June 1673, 11 E 26 95, 5 Feb. 1678.
115. ADR, Fonds Moulins, IV, Letter of 3 Aug. 1694.

mont's economy and its society and the links with Lyons in this stable period would have been common knowledge to Galtié and Moulins.

In fact, as we shall see, Galtié's confidence in the security and permanence of his family's position at or near the peak of Clermontais society was misplaced for in the 1690s a period of economic change and commercial revival was beginning which was both to endanger those too firmly committed to the stable trading patterns which had predominated for the last forty years and to generate powerful new merchant dynasties which would challenge the hegemony of his and other bourgeois families in Clermont.

5

Colbert, Languedoc, Saptes, Villenouvette

the first View that Nation had, in erecting those Manufacturies was, to supply their own Occasions, and thereby save a large Sum of Money within the Kingdom, which they had been used to pay to foreign Labour. To effectuate which, besides these positive Encouragements to Undertakers, and their Charters exclusive (which, by the way, are, what would not have been endured in a free Country, as *England* is), they laid high Duties upon *all foreign Woolen Manufactures*, and particularly on the *English*, as their most formidable Rivals. (J. Smith, *Chronicon Rusticum-Commerciale; or Memoirs of Wool* (1757), II, 427, n.)

While there have been many general studies on Colbertian policies there has been little detailed research on the application of Colbertian reforms in different localities. In this chapter we feel justified, thus, in describing but briefly the general characteristics of Colbertian policy but will explore in greater depth the implementation of that policy in Languedoc.

As has been rightly emphasized, the prime-mover in the Colbertian experiment was fiscalism: a realization that the tax-paying ability of the French population was limited by the amount of money circulating in the kingdom. As Colbert explained in a 'Mémoire au Roi', composed in 1670, his main purpose was to 'proportionner ce que [les peuples] payent pour le trésor public avec le nombre d'argent qui roule dans le commerce'. In order that this required proportion be achieved Colbert believed that it was necessary for French merchants and industrial producers both to provide the domestic market with the industrial goods it needed, and thus prevent an outflow of bullion to pay for imports, and also to export French manufactured products and thus achieve a favourable balance of trade.

These goals, Colbert was well aware, were far from being achieved in the mid-seventeenth century. He was conscious that France had suffered a relative economic decline. 'Avant l'année 1600', he wrote, 'les manufactures faisaient gagner une infinité de peuples, l'argent ne sortait point du royaume.'[1] His summing up of the economic situation at the accession of Louis XIV would, it seems likely, have diverged only slightly from the desperate description which Voltaire provides in his *Siècle de Louis XIV*:

Les Juifs, les Génois, les Vénitiens, les Portugais, les Flamands, les Hollandais, les Anglais, firent tour à tour le commerce de la France, qui en ignorait les principes. Louis XIII, à son avènement à la couronne, n'avait pas un vaisseau; Paris ne contenait pas quatre beaux édifices; les autres villes du royaume ressemblaient à ces bourgs qu'on voit au delà de la Loire. Toute la noblesse, cantonnée à la campagne dans des donjons entourés de fossés, opprimait ceux qui cultivent la terre. Les grands chemins étaient presque impracticables; les villes étaient sans police, l'Etat sans argent, et le gouvernement presque toujours sans crédit parmi les nations étrangères.[2]

Holland appeared to be the nation which had gained economically at France's expense and it was the Dutch example which Colbert followed closely in his reform projects for the French economy. Arguably, of course (and this was to be the basis of the Physiocratic criticism of Colbertian policy), the Dutch case was exceptional and its example inapt for a highly agricultural country such as France. But this is another question. Good or bad model though it may have been there is no doubt that it was the Dutch success which was Colbert's inspiration. It is only necessary to read his correspondence with France's ambassador at Amsterdam, in which he shows curiosity about all aspects of the Dutch commercial and industrial success, to be assured of this.[3]

If Holland (and England, too, to an increasing extent) had clearly fared better economically than France during the seventeenth century then the major reasons for this, in Colbert's eyes, lay in the superior organization of all aspects of their trading and manufacturing. Their large fleets and trading companies, efficient diplomatic services, advanced credit systems, technologically advanced and well-regulated industries, large and efficient merchant classes and well-thought-out tariff and trading policies were the keys, it seemed to him, to their successes for in all other matters France was their equal if not their better: with respect to geographical situation, labour supply and natural resources France was clearly well placed.

In view of the nature of this diagnosis the main emphases in Colbert's reforms are understandable. He founded a large number of trading and manufacturing companies (no less than thirty between 1665 and 1670);[4]

1. These quotations, and the general description of Colbertian policies which follow, are largely drawn from R. Mandrou, *Louis XIV en son temps*, pp. 123–45.
2. Vol. I, p. 4.
3. See for example G. B. Depping, *Correspondance administrative sous le règne de Louis XIV*, III, 349–51, 446–7, 449, for letters written by Colbert to the French ambassador in Holland between 1664 and 1670.
4. Mandrou, *Louis XIV*, p. 138.

he encouraged ship-building and reinforced the French navy; he improved the commercial element in the French consular services; he instigated national surveys of, and composed regulations for, French industry; for the enforcement of industrial regulations he set up an inspectorate and encouraged the foundation of guilds; merchants' rights to export bullion were restricted and their participation in the re-export trade was encouraged by the establishment of free ports; use of the letter of exchange and other credit mechanisms was encouraged by a new Commercial Code published in 1673; the import of foreign manufactured goods was restricted by prohibitive tariffs; and finally he (and his successors) attempted, by a variety of measures, to improve the social status of commercial and industrial activity.

It was a revival in *industrial* production, it should be emphasized, that was the central element in the Colbertian reforms, and it was this bias which distinguished French 'mercantilism' from its English variant in which the greatest emphasis was on commerce. And above all by industrial production is meant textiles. As Mandrou notes, the majority of the thirty odd companies founded by Colbert between 1665 and 1670 were for the purposes of textile production. Similarly Markovitch has observed not only that the first industrial surveys, carried out on Colbert's orders, were effectively surveys of cloth production but also that until 1727 inspectors of manufactures were only appointed for the purposes of supervising production of woollen cloth.[5] The priority is easily explicable. It was cloth which was the major industry, in both domestic and external markets. The large share of woollen cloth in English exports until the mid-seventeenth century has been frequently emphasized. And in addition there had been considerable technological developments in cloth production in England and Holland since the mid-sixteenth century (Ill. 9). These consisted not so much in changes in the basic processes but in the development of new cloth types and in improvements and variations in the finishing processes. The most important new products were known as 'new draperies' and 'Spanish' or Dutch-style cloth, the former a type of worsted, the latter a lighter but finer version of the old broad-cloth.[6] Both types had been first developed in the Low Countries (the name 'Spanish' cloth being a consequence of the sovereignty of Spain over Flanders).[7] As we have seen, there are signs that the Dutch-style cloth was being made in Languedoc during the first

5. 'Le triple tricentenaire de Colbert: l'enquête, les règlements, les inspecteurs', *R.H.E.S.* 49 (1971), 308–9.
6. On the 'new draperies' see D. C. Coleman, 'An innovation and its diffusion: the new draperies', *Ec.H.R.* 21 (1968), 416–29. On Spanish cloth see pp. 94–5.
7. This is the theory of the Abbé Prégnon, *Histoire du pays et de la ville de Sedan*, II, 470 n.1, but J. de L. Mann implies that the name is to be explained by the use of fine Spanish wools in this cloth's production (*The Cloth Industry in the West*, pp. xvi–xviii).

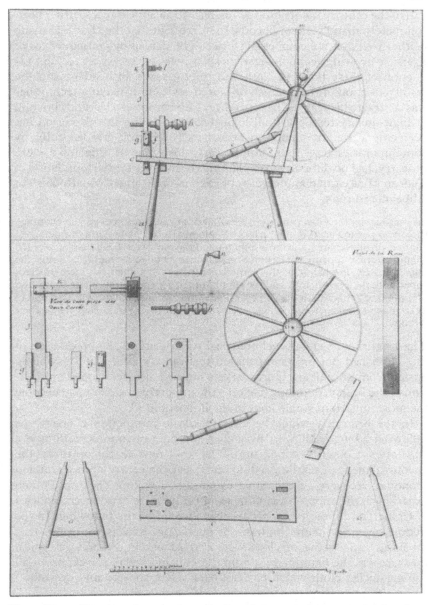

Ill. 9. Large Dutch-style spinning wheel and its constituent parts: drawing designed to facilitate imitation

half of the century but its production had, to all appearances, either been completely abandoned, or become so infrequent that the cloth was made neither well nor at a competitive price. The damaging consequences of France's growing technological backwardness with respect to the production of these types of cloth was fully grasped by Colbert and the re-introduction of the Spanish or Dutch-style cloth-making techniques was central to his plans. The centrality of luxury industries, and above all of high-quality textiles, in all long-distance trading in this period has been emphasized frequently by historians,[8] and it was grasped, fully, by contemporaries too. John Smith, early historian of England's cloth industry, had no difficulty in explaining the motives for the foundation of Cadeau's fine cloth manufacture at Sedan in 1646, and of Van Robais's at Abbeville in 1665:

> the reason why the Government in *France* was at such an Expence, to encourage these two particular Manufacturies, was plainly this: The making of fine broad Cloth is, in all Regards, the most difficult and the most beneficial Part of Woolen Manufacture; requiring the largest Stocks to carry it on to Advantage. In this, the *Dutch* and *English* being, at the Time when these Manufacturies were erected, superior to the *French*, they had the supplying, in a great Measure, the Court and Kingdom of *France* with their finest Cloths; the Expence of which was so much, as to make a considerable Article against them in the general Balance of their Trade . . .[9]

The English and Dutch technological superiority in the production of fine cloth had not only contributed to France's (and Venice's) being ousted from profitable export markets but had also occasioned an invasion of the French domestic market – the import of fine cloth had become the most important single item in the import bill.[10]

In the centrality which he gave to textile production Colbert was following a long tradition. Invariably, not only in France, both before and after Colbert's time, until the mid-nineteenth century, the encouragement of textile production was at the centre of any planned economic recovery or economic expansion. Looking back on French experiences the only contrasts one would emphasize between the policies of Colbert and those of his predecessors would be the following. In the middle ages the main emphasis in such policies was to ensure that finishing and dyeing of cloth were carried out in France. A typical measure was the banning by Philip the Fair in 1318 of the export of all Languedocian cloth which had not been dyed, sheared and dressed.[11]

---

8. Heckscher, *Mercantilism*, II, 190: 'It was the luxury industry which stood in the forefront of official encouragement and basked in state aid.'
9. *Chronicon Rusticum-Commerciale; or Memoirs of Wool*, II, 427 n.
10. Boissonnade, *Colbert*, p. 182.
11. Levasseur, *Histoire des classes ouvrières*, I, 436–7.

The actual types of cloth, however, were evidently relatively uniform (in contrast to Colbert's day). All that was necessary was to ensure that standard cloths were finished in France and thus could be commercialized by French merchants. If we compare the sixteenth century with the seventeenth the major distinction that emerges is that it was on the encouragement of silk rather than on cloth production that the main emphasis was placed and that it was from Italian industrial centres, rather than Dutch, that the relevant techniques were copied.[12]

Both Colbert's assessment of the situation of the French economy and his remedies for its problems have been criticized by historians. It has been pointed out that the weaknesses were more profound and that the roots of the problems lay in the fragility of the agricultural economy and a resultant lack of industrial demand. In addition it has been shown that Colbert's puritanical approach to monetary policy, his persistence with an over-valued *livre*, was deflationary, encouraged imports and made French exports less competitive.[13] That these criticisms have some basis has been suggested in our last chapter in which we showed that the basic cause for the industrial failure was the demand situation, and that the technological backwardness, organizational weaknesses and lack of merchant investment in industry were consequences rather than causes of France's difficulties. But in defence of Colbertian policy it should be added that although by developing a more flexible monetary policy he might have contributed to a revival in the level of demand it is difficult to see how any policy which he might have developed would have influenced greatly the majority, agricultural economy. Some of the criticisms of Colbert smack of an unwarranted hindsight occasioned by our modern experience of, and awareness of the requirements for, industrialization. There was no question of achieving a structural transformation in the French economy in the seventeenth century. What was necessary was to improve France's position in the minority, international, commercialized part of Europe's economic life. And to succeed in doing this some of the technical and organizational changes proposed by Colbert were clearly necessary. These changes would not be prime-movers in a recovery (the demand situation, as it had been in the crisis, was the crucial variable), but they had become necessary and they would facilitate recovery.

Well conceived or not the reforms were put into action, and put into action with extraordinary vigour and persistence. 'Ce programme', Mandrou writes, 'Colbert l'a poursuivi pendant vingt ans, avec une

12. Chaunu and Gascon, *Histoire économique*, I, 352–3.
13. E.g. Le Roy Ladurie, *Paysans*, pp. 597–8; Deyon, *Amiens*, pp. 81–2, 125–8; Braudel and Labrousse, *Histoire économique*, II, 189–90, 351–8.

ténacité extraordinaire.'[14] It was precisely this persistence and thoroughness which distinguished Colbert's work for, as has often been pointed
out, individually his policies were in no case novel.

Languedoc was to play a central role in Colbert's plans for industrial
recovery. This was because its cloth industry was the best situated and
equipped to produce for what remained in the seventeenth century both
France's and Europe's best industrial markets, the Mediterranean zone
as a whole and above all the Levant. The Levant trade's importance to
France was frequently stressed by Colbert. In 1671 he wrote of it as 'Le
seul commerce considérable qui se fasse en France' and, again, in 1682 as
'assurément le plus important du royaume'.[15] And cloth was the only
substantial import item, apart from bullion, which was in demand in the
Levant.[16] The revival of Languedoc's cloth industry and that of the
Levant trade were thus closely linked.

Essentially the situation of France's trade with the Levant in this
period was parallel to that which we have observed in Languedoc's cloth
industry. There had been a dramatic decline in the activities of the large-
scale Marseillais merchants who previously had dominated the trade.
The collapse in their affairs has frequently been emphasized. 'De 30
millions de livres le commerce tombé à 4 millions environ, de 1,000
bâtiments de mer le nombre réduit à 30, tel était le résultat de cinquante
ans de malheurs'; this is Masson's description of the situation in the
1660s.[17] But in counterpart smaller-scale merchants and shippers had
resisted the depression better, if they had not actually benefited from the
crisis in the affairs of the large-scale merchants. Thus Morineau has
shown that despite the decline in the 'grand commerce' with the Levant
the sum at which the *gabelle* of the port was farmed out had continued to
expand into the 1660s as a consequence largely of the activities of small-
scale Languedocian and Provençal shippers and a relative prosperity in
local trades.[18] A study by Dermigny illustrates the same phenomenon:
the minor meridional ports were active, small ships and small-scale
merchants existed in abundance, and there was regular, intense trade
between coastal ports, with the Barbary and, significantly, with Leghorn.
As Dermigny shows, the 'Levant' for these small-scale traders was,
effectively, Leghorn where were to be found all the Levantine products

14. *Louis XIV*, p. 138.
15. Depping, *Correspondance*, III, 534–5, 620–1, Louis XIV to de Nointel, ambassador to
    Constantinople, 20 Aug. 1671, Colbert to Morant, intendant of Provence, 2 Jan. 1682.
16. R. Paris, *Histoire du commerce de Marseille*, V, 543.
17. P. Masson, *Histoire du commerce français dans le Levant au XVIIe siècle*, pp. 130–5.
18. M. Morineau, 'Flottes de commerce et trafics français en Méditerranée au xviie siècle',
    XVIIe Siècle 86–7 (1970), 136–71.

which were required for distribution in Languedoc and Provence.[19] Those merchants and shippers who continued to trade with Leghorn, or the Levant, from Marseilles were little distinct from the small-scale operators based in other Languedocian and Provençal ports. Indeed a description which Marseilles's Chamber of Commerce made in 1665 of the qualities of its merchants would surely fit the majority of small-scale traders and shippers in the Mediterranean zone in this depressed period – 'notre ville est composée d'un grand nombre d'habitants qui n'ont que 500 à 1,000 livres vaillant, qui par leur industrie le négocient et font rouler deux ou trois fois l'année et le retirent quand bon leur semble'.[20] It was indeed the lack of capital resources which was a major reason for the preference shown for trading in specie. A return could be achieved far more rapidly than from selling cloth. Similarly, another problem of the period, the damage caused to trade by piracy, was greatly exacerbated by the smallness of ships and the lack of co-operation among merchants.

The depression had thus caused a decentralization of commercial activity, and had favoured small-scale traders, the reasons for their greater resistance being similar to those accounting for the survival of the artisanal clothier.[21] As René Baehrel has shown, there were, as it were, two competing economies in pre-industrial France: a local one which was small scale, traditional, familial and most sparing in its use of money and a more modern one, concentrated, using advanced credit mechanisms and international. In the second half of the seventeenth century it was the former which was in the ascendancy.[22]

This situation, though it might have been favourable to certain smaller Provençal and Languedocian ports normally controlled by rich Marseillais merchants, was highly unsatisfactory in Colbert's eyes. The Marseillais preference for exporting specie he attributed to lack of national spirit rather than to lack of resources, the small scale of their concerns to an anarchic individualism and refusal to co-operate, and it was their port, he was convinced, that was 'L'endroit du royaume par où s'écoule dans les pays estrangers une bonne partie de l'argent que l'industrie des artisans et des marchands de toutes les autres provinces y attire'.[23] The use of a

---

19. L. Dermigny, 'Une concurrence au port franc de Marseille: armement languedocien et trafic du Levant et de Barbarie', *Provence Historique* 5–6 (1955–6), 248–62, 53–81.
20. Cited by Masson, *Levant au XVIIᵉ siècle*, p. 180.
21. See pp. 119–21.
22. R. Baehrel, *Une croissance: la Basse-Provence rurale*, I, 66–97. Though the turning-point, in favour of the international economy, occurred in the 1680s according to Baehrel. Clermont's example would provide support for this hypothesis.
23. Colbert to Rouillé, intendant at Aix, 3 March, 21 Sept. 1679. (P. Clément, *Lettres, instructions et mémoires de Colbert*, II, pt. 2, *Industrie et commerce*, pp. 695, 706.) On Colbert's opinion of Marseillais see Paris, *Histoire du commerce*, V, 49–51.

certain amount of specie was, in fact, essential for the trade and Colbert's intolerance in this respect was restrictive but from other points of view his judgement of the situation seems perfectly justifiable. The small-scale merchants involved in the Levant trade were similar to the artisanal cloth producer in that they operated on too small a basis to achieve economies of scale and in that as a consequence of competing with each other they neither sold French products well nor succeeded in obtaining imports at a good price. The large profits in the trade would thus have been accumulated by rich merchants at Leghorn – Armenians and Dutch and English shippers were particularly dominant there – in the same way that industrial profits in artisanal cloth industries were monopolized by rich merchant cloth buyers.[24] In other words there was certainly some justification for intervention even though intervention could not have been expected to achieve rapid results in view both of the extent of the commitment to this new pattern of commercial relationships and of the fact that this type of commercial organization, like the 'artisanal' form of cloth production was, at least in part, conditioned by the general level of economic activity – depressed, according to all accounts, between 1660 and 1680.

The Colbertian reforms for France's Mediterranean trade included the following measures. The consular service in the Levant was reformed; a new ambassador was appointed to Constantinople; various experts were sent to the Levant to survey the market situation; Frenchmen were trained as interpreters; new 'Capitulations' with the Sultan were negotiated and eventually granted in 1673; attempts were made to improve French shipping in the Mediterranean; a new franchise was granted to the port of Marseilles; a succession of Levant companies were founded to trade with the Levant; and Languedoc's cloth production was encouraged in a variety of ways.[25]

The importance and complexity of the last three items justifies the devotion of a paragraph to each. The franchise was largely aimed at Leghorn. It made Marseilles into a free port but it effectively, also, gave Marseilles a monopoly in the Levant trade as it imposed a tariff of 20% on all Levantine imports which did not enter France on French ships via either Marseilles or Rouen. The clauses in the franchise making Marseilles into a free port were executed immediately, and likewise the

24. On limitations of artisanal industrial production see above, pp. 31–3. On the trade at Leghorn see R. Davis, 'England and the Mediterranean, 1570–1670' in F. J. Fisher (ed.), *Essays in the Economic and Social History of Tudor and Stuart England*, pp. 135–6.
25. Masson, *Levant au XVIIe siècle*, pp. 137–84; C. Carrière, *Les négociants marseillais au XVIIIe siècle*, I, 309–24; Paris, *Histoire du commerce*, v, 11–15, 49–55, 87–91.

privileges given to French shipping, but the effective monopoly of Marseilles in the Levant trade (Rouen's distance excluded it from participation) was not strictly enforced until the mid-1680s, as Dermigny's study on Sète reveals. Until then Marseilles had neither the shipping nor the mercantile capacity to cope with the entire trade.[26]

There were five different Levant companies founded between 1669 and 1690. Few Marseillais invested in the first three, those of 1669, 1670 and 1678. A capital contribution was made by the Crown but the main investors were financiers from Paris, Lyons and Languedoc. The relative exclusion of Marseillais interests is demonstrated most markedly by the third company's placing its three offices at Sète, Lyons and Paris. The lack of Marseillais participation was attributed again by Colbert to the town's inhabitants' refusal to accept any form of disciplined trading system but a more convincing explanation is that it was a reflection of the lack of commercial capital in the town. A sign that this scarcity was becoming less marked was the gradually increasing Marseillais involvement in successive companies. This suggests that a slow recovery in Marseilles's commercial fortunes was occurring during these years. The fourth company, that of 1685, was effectively dominated by Marseillais and when the fifth company was disbanded in the 1690s Marseilles's commerce had revived to the extent of being able to support a trade much larger than that of the 1660s without the aid of any commercial company. The Levant companies were not given a monopoly of trade but they were less 'liberal' than their Dutch and English equivalents in so far that they were similar in nature to joint-stock organizations, trading as single entities, rather than being (as in the Dutch and English cases) structured associations of independent traders. The primary obligation of these companies was to export French industrial products and above all cloth. Special bounties were granted to encourage this – 16 *livres* a piece to the 1669 company, 10 *livres* to the others. This obligation, it is clear, was not to the companies' advantage and was on occasions relaxed. In the 1670s various special permissions were granted for the export of coin (to the delight of Marseillais merchants so often chastised by the Government for this practice). As Paris writes, the companies were forced to become 'soit des organismes de vente pour les draps, soit même des entreprises industrielles'; and this was a contributory factor in their failure: 'Les ministres dans la préoccupation fort louable de développer les manufactures en France, lui avaient sacrifié la navigation et le négoce.'[27]

The cloth which the Levant companies were obliged to export was

26. L. Dermigny, 'Armement languedocien', p. 254.
27. Paris, *Histoire du commerce*, v, 64.

largely Languedocian. It was two pieces of the province's finest cloth with which the new ambassador, De La Haye, was entrusted by Colbert on his journey out to his new post. But the inadequacy of Languedoc's fine cloth was apparent even to the untrained eyes of the new ambassador. He wrote to Colbert from Marseilles before embarking, informing him that the Languedocian product did not match for either price or quality some English fine cloth which he had bought in Paris before leaving for Marseilles and also that a memoir which he had been given detailing the cloth's production costs suggested that 'il n'y a pas d'apparence qu'elles puissent être vendues à beaucoup près de ce qu'elles coutent'. Marseillais merchants with whom he had conferred considered that a loss of between 12 and 15% would be incurred.[28]

On repeated occasions during the next ten years or so Colbert was to receive similar pessimistic verdicts about Languedoc's cloth. The most frequent criticisms were that cloth was poorly dyed (lack of uniformity in the colour being the major fault) or uneven in quality and finish. This fundamental problem of the inability of Languedoc's industry to produce cloth which matched that of its competitors either in price or quality was stressed by the Chevalier d'Arvieux who had been sent on several investigatory missions to the Levant by Colbert in the 1660s: 'Les manufactures de draps, établies en Languedoc pour contrefaire les draps d'Angleterre de Hollande et de Vénise, étaient bien éloignées de la perfection, et de la bonté de ceux de ces pays là', he wrote, and this defective quality was all the more damaging because 'Les Turcs se connaissent en marchandise pour le moins aussi bien que les Espagnols qui sont de si habiles connoisseurs, que nos plus habiles commerçants ne sauraient les tromper.'[29]

The first evidence that we have of an attempt to remedy these quality defects is to be found in a letter from Nicolas Arnoul, 'intendant des galères' at Marseilles, and a close collaborator of the controller general. He had visited the fair of Beaucaire in July 1666 to assess the economic situation and informed Colbert that although 'il y avoit force draps de Carcassonne et de Beaux', Marseilles's merchants had only bought some four hundred pieces of various qualities, and had not placed further orders. They were continuing to show a preference for trading in silver pieces of 5 *sous*. But Arnoul had one more-promising piece of news. 'Je me suis icy abouché avec un habile homme qui n'est pas Provençal', he told Colbert, 'qui a desjà une grande manufacture de draps; mais on le

---

28. Depping, *Correspondance*, III, 396–7, letter of 24 Oct. 1665.
29. Cited by Masson, *Levant au XVIIᵉ siècle*, p. 205.

maltraite comme estranger. Je croy qu'on se pourroit accomoder avec luy, celuy que j'ay pris pour la manufacture des habits et tentes n'estant si entendu ni si riche.'[30]

The 'habile homme qui n'est pas Provençal' could only have been Pierre de Varennes, a rich Parisian merchant, who, with his brother Jérosme, had taken over that exceptional manufacture of Saptes which we have mentioned in a previous chapter. Since its foundation this concern had had, as large manufactures tended to in the pre-industrial period, a chequered history. It had lost its high reputation after the death of one Maurice de Sapte, descendant of the Sapte brothers who were its founders. A big court case had followed his death and the manufacture had fallen into the hands of one Soubrié who ran it for seven or eight years before it was taken over by Maistre, a Carcassonnais merchant, who had married the Sapte heiress 'en troisiesmes nosses'. It changed hands again in about 1620 when it was bought by a Sieur de Fay and it was this de Fay, or his son, who had leased the concern to the de Varennes brothers. Exactly when they took over the manufacture and who exactly they were is not known (though this secret remains to be discovered, no doubt, in the registers of a Conques notary). Fraisse, a later director of Saptes, believed that both brothers were from Lyons. But he seems to have been misinformed.[31] Pierre de Varennes was referred to on several occasions as 'marchand' or 'bourgeois de Paris'[32] and local evidence suggests that Jérosme (and perhaps the original de Varennes family) was Carcassonnais and possibly linked in some way with the manufacture of Saptes before the 1660s. In the 'registres paroissaux' for Conques for the year 1650 there is recorded the birth of a daughter to Jérosme de Varennes and his wife Jeanne Figole. Some years later it was this same daughter who married 'Noble Pierre de Fay'. Jérosme, who is described as 'marchant et banquier' in the second act, had evidently cemented his and his brother's business relationships with the de Fay family by marrying his daughter to the heir.[33] That Jérosme's links with Conques were of long standing is

---

30. Depping, *Correspondance*, III, 401–3, letter of 21 Aug. 1666.
31. On Saptes see also p. 36. A short summary of the manufacture's history is provided in Mahul, *Cartulaire et archives*, II, 20–1, and another, dating from approximately 1712, by a later director of the concern, Fraisse (ADH C2203, 'Mémoire instructif pour le Sr Fraisse propriétaire et faisant travailler la manufacture royale de Saptes'). Basville's information is largely inaccurate (Boulainvilliers, *Etat*, II, 561), and Boissonnade ('Colbert, son système et les entreprises d'Etat en Languedoc: 1661–1683', *A. du M.* 14 (1902), 11, 44) would seem to be wrong in attributing the foundation to Guillaume de Varennes, uncle of Pierre and Jérosme.
32. For instance Boissonnade, 'Colbert, son système', p. 11.
33. Registres paroissaux of Conques, acts of 11 Aug. 1650, 9 Feb. 1667.

also suggested by his choice as the first 'baile de manufactures' for the village of Conques (which had its own cloth industry) in December 1666.[34]

Saptes was still functioning as a manufacture in the mid-seventeenth century but on a humble scale, with a labour force of about one hundred. As a consequence of the de Varennes' involvement both the scale of its activities and the quality of its product were transformed. The labour force was expanded to about six hundred.[35]

Arnoul wrote to Colbert under the impression (it is clear) that the news of his meeting with so well qualified an industrialist as de Varennes, and of the existence of a large manufacture in Languedoc, would come as a surprise. It is highly unlikely, however, that this was the case. First, Guillaume de Varennes, uncle of Pierre, was one of the nine major shareholders in the 'Compagnie des Indes' and for this reason the de Varennes family must have been known to Colbert.[36] Secondly during 1666 a number of Dutch workers arrived to work at Saptes and it would seem virtually certain that Colbert co-operated in their recruitment. Reich de Pennautier, treasurer of the Etats of Languedoc, immensely wealthy financier, and main industrial collaborator of Colbert in the Midi,[37] recorded in April 1667 that these workers had been present at Saptes for the last six months[38] and the accuracy of his statement is borne out by the parish registers of Saptes. In September 1666 it is recorded that Mathieu Samade, maître-tisserand of Leyden, married Catherine Jean from Conghuxson in the 'pays de Munster'. The act was witnessed by Thomas Nachtels, marchand-drapier of Amsterdam, and Habraam Pitre and Duhacs Galopsin of the town of Razan (Rozendaal?). Additional acts registered between 1667 and 1669 reveal the presence of other Dutch or Flemish workers: Pierre Gabron from the diocese of Rocroi in Picardy, 'Un olandois nommé Carladan pareur de draps', 'Gille hollandois tisseran des draps', 'Léonard Motaribi de la ville de Limbourg', 'Philippe Goffar Holandois'.[39] Basville actually stated in his memoir that 'le Sieur de Varenne . . . proposa à Monsieur Colbert, il y a 30 ans, de lui permettre

34. A new post established in connection with Colbert's first general industrial regulation of 8 April 1666. Depping, *Correspondance*, III, pp. 799–801, letter of Pennautier to Colbert.
35. Boissonnade, 'Colbert, son système', p. 47.
36. *Ibid.*, p. 44.
37. On Pennautier see Boissonnade, 'Colbert, son système', pp. 37–40, and G. Chaussinand-Nogaret, *Les financiers de Languedoc*, pp. 29–30. In addition to being treasurer of the Estates of Languedoc, Pennautier held the post of 'trésorier général du clergé de France'.
38. Depping, *Correspondance*, III, 801–3, letter of 27 April 1667.
39. Registres paroissaux of Conques, acts of 2, 13 Aug. 1667, 28 Oct. 1668, 10 March, 9 Nov. 1669.

d'aller en Hollande, pour y débaucher des Ouvriers: Il y fit plusieurs voyages, & en ramena un nombre considérable',[40] but that Colbert in addition to being consulted actually co-operated on the recruitment of these workers is highly likely for it was precisely during the years 1665 and 1666 that he was employing two agents in Holland, Janot and Dumas, for the purpose of recruiting Dutch workers. Van Robais, accompanied by some fifty employees and all necessary equipment, was their richest catch but the Dutch workers who arrived at Saptes in August or September 1666 were, it seems likely, in part proceeds of their work too.[41] A third factor which makes it appear that Colbert was involved in the transformation of Saptes was the promptitude with which the concern was raised to the status of royal manufacture. This occurred in October 1666 and it seems probable that the de Varennes brothers had obtained assurance that this privilege would be granted before they risked large sums in the manufacture's improvement.[42]

The extent of Colbert's interest in Saptes emerges from his correspondence with Pennautier. The Languedocian financier's letter of April 1667 not only confirmed the arrival of Dutch workers but contained information about their technological contribution to the manufacture which serves to inform us why such importance was attached to their presence.

Nous avons trouvé... que, jusques à ce que nos ouvriers ayent attrapé leur secret nous ne pourrons jamais faire les draps au prix qu'ils les vendent: ils ont l'art de faire un drap égal à ceux de Carcassonne avec un tiers moins de laine, et cette laine encore ils la filent et l'apprestent avec une diligence si grande, qu'un de leurs ouvriers faict plus de besogne en un jour qu'un François dans une sepmaine.

Pennautier was evidently most optimistic about the manufacture's prospects. A representative from Marseilles had just visited it, he wrote, 'et il est convenu avec moy qu'il y a de quoy establir un commerce qui seroit d'une utilité infinie au Languedoc et à tout le royaume'. He concluded his letter by predicting that the de Varennes 'manufacture d'Hollandois' would be 'capable d'instruire toute celle de Carcassonne'. Colbertian expectations from such concerns could hardly have been better expressed.[43]

So it seems justifiable to attribute to Colbert a contributory role in the expansion and improvement of the manufacture of Saptes undertaken in 1666. And further royal support was forthcoming in the following years.

40. Boulainvilliers, *Etat*, ii, 561.
41. See Depping, *Correspondance*, iii, pp. 751–4, letters of Colbert to Janot, Oct. 1665.
42. Statutes of 26 October 1666, Boissonnade, 'Colbert, son système', p. 11.
43. Depping, *Correspondance*, iii, 801–3.

The manufacture received the bounty on its cloth exports to the Levant, and in 1669 20,000 *livres*, half a promised capital loan of 40,000 *livres*, were paid to 'de Varennes, Grandié, André & Cassan [Cusson], marchands, entrepreneurs de la manuf. de draps destinez pour le Levant'.[44] Grandié, André and Cusson belonged to Carcassonnais merchant and clothier families.[45] De Varennes (and by de Varennes is now meant Pierre de Varennes as there are no mentions made of Jérosme after December 1666) had evidently obtained local support for his schemes. Possibly he had been obliged to because of a 'petit désordre … arrivé dans … [ses] affaires' which Pennautier commented on.[46] Later in the same year the royal accounts detail a payment of 1,800 *livres* to de Varennes, the bounty for the export of 180 pieces of cloth to the Levant. Colbert, aware of the public-relations value of such payments, ordered Arnoul 'de faire cette libéralité publiquement afin d'exciter toujours de plus en plus les marchands à faire ce commerce'.[47]

Colbert clearly expected the royal manufacture of Saptes to play a crucial technological role in the improvement of Languedoc's manufactures but it is evident that he did not rely purely on this concern to fulfil his ambitions. On the same day that Saptes was raised to the status of royal manufacture, Carcassonne was made 'draperie royale' and subjected to the new regulations which had been devised in consultation with the various 'corps des métiers' of the town. The regulations were opposed by the weavers, pareurs and other categories of cloth-workers for they were evidently designed to favour the drapiers or marchands-fabricants who were obliged to form themselves into a single corporation which included Conques and Saptes within its jurisdiction. As we have seen in the previous chapter, there had been a great degree of informality about who was allowed to produce cloth in Carcassonne in the 1640s and in that the decay of French manufactures was interpreted by most as being the result of such disorganization and a lack of a strict corporative system – 'C'est … surtout l'insuffisance de la police corporative qu'incriminait l'opinion en général', Wolff writes – this measure can be seen as representative of an attempt to restructure French industry on a stable and lasting basis.[48] Four jurés-gardes or bailes were to be appointed to administer the affairs of the corporation. Jérosme de Varennes, as we have just seen, was appointed for Conques, Guillaume Cusson, who was to

44. J. Guiffrey, *Comptes des bâtiments du roi sous le règne de Louis XIV*, I, column 371.
45. Boissonnade, 'Colbert, son système', p. 44.
46. Depping, *Correspondance*, III, 801–3.
47. Guiffrey, *Comptes*, I, Column 371, Clément, *Lettres*, II, pt. 2, 732–3, Colbert to Arnoul, 7 Dec. 1669.
48. P. Wolff, 'La draperie en Languedoc', p. 460.

Table 6. *October 1666, cloths prescribed and regulated for production by draperie royale of Carcassonne and royal manufacture of Saptes*

Cloth type	Threads to warp	Wool type	Width
Draps façon d'Espagne	3,600	*refleurette d'Espagne*	1½ *aunes*
Draps façon d'Hollande	3,200	Segovian	1 *aune*
Draps façon d'Angleterre	3,200	Segovian	1⅓ *aunes*
Draps de Carcassonne communs	2,600	Finest from Béziers, Narbonne	1⅙ *aunes*
Draps de seau	2,000	Béziers, Narbonne	1 *aune*
Draps seizains de Carcassonne	1,600	Carcassonne, Narbonne, Béziers	1 *aune*

Source: F. Jaupart, 'L'industrie drapière de Carcassonne', p. 190.

become an associate of the de Varennes, was one of the three appointed for Carcassonne. The industry was to be submitted to the surveillance of a 'commis à l'inspection'. The first holder of this position would seem to have been one Marc Cocagne, described in a document dated 8 January 1672 as 'commis général des manufactures de Languedoc et Dauphiné'.[49] Finally the 'règlements' specified and regulated the types of cloth which were to be made in the town. The range and names of these cloths provide added confirmation both of the emphasis placed on fine cloth production in Colbertian plans for industrial revival and also of the extent to which it was the Dutch and English examples which were being followed (Table 6). In addition to providing this general regulative and corporative framework for the collective draperie royale of Carcassonne, Colbert provided financial help to those clothiers who attempted the production of fine cloth (see Table 6, first three qualities): cloth exported received the bounty and a significant quantity was purchased directly by the Crown for sale on the Parisian market. At this stage, however, Carcassonne's clothiers' production was evidently far inferior to that of Saptes which itself was inferior to that of Dutch and English competitors.[50]

As de Vries writes of mercantilist reforms: 'In a world that did not expect long-term growth of foreign markets men pinned their hopes for gain from trade on their ability to control their markets.'[51] The state-

49. ADH C2199.
50. Jaupart, 'L'industrie drapière de Carcassonne', pp. 188–90; Boissonnade, 'Colbert, son système', p. 14; Guiffrey, *Comptes*, I, columns 287, 552, 640.
51. *Europe in an Age of Crisis*, p. 124.

ment is particularly apt for describing the assumptions of Colbert's policies. Specified clothiers, in specified towns, were to produce specified cloths, to be bought by specified companies, operating in specified ports, and selling in specified markets. Colbert believed, like all his contemporaries, that the existing economic opportunities were fixed and limited. If he had lived in a machine age he would have designed machines to produce the exact (unchanging) items required to establish once and for all the French position in the existing fixed and limited markets. As he did not he was obliged to use human agents. He allocated to the corporations of clothiers, in each cloth-making centre he had the administrative capacity to control, the duty of supplying specified cloths for particular markets. The consequence, and it was a desired consequence, was, as Heckscher stresses, 'a more sharply defined exclusiveness between different places'. The belief in a static economic world is also, of course, illustrated by the very idea of narrowly regulating the manner in which industrial goods were to be produced. 'In principle, the regulations were deliberately devised to prevent technical and economic innovations', Heckscher adds.[52]

Carcassonne, in the forefront of Colbert's plans, benefited from a specially designed règlement. The famed general cloth regulation of 13 August 1669, devised after an extensive industrial survey carried out throughout the country by the 'maîtres-des-requêtes', was enforced in leading cloth-making centres throughout France, and it brought a similar system, and a similar executive combination of jurés-gardes and 'commis à l'inspection', to other substantial Languedocian cloth-making centres.[53] Clermont was one such centre and an act recorded in the registers of the conseil de ville in February 1674 demonstrates that the clothiers confrérie had already adapted to functioning along the lines envisaged in the reform, even though there were hardly enough clothiers remaining in the town to provide candidates for the required annual election of two prévôts, two jurés-gardes and two 'juges de police'. A further act recorded the first contact with the new inspectoral system. On 19 December 1686 the commission of Emeric Bosson, 'commis à l'inspection des manufactures', was registered in the town.[54]

The prominence given to Carcassonne in Colbert's plans for the resurrection of Languedoc's industry and the Levant trade needs no extra explanation in view of what has been written in chapter two. The town

---

52. *Mercantilism*, I, 147, 170.
53. Markovitch, 'Triple tricentenaire', pp. 305, 307, 312.
54. ACC BB1, Acts of these days. In ADH C2199 there are details about the appointment of Bosson, formerly a merchant.

was indubitably the most important cloth-making centre of Languedoc, and of France, too, according to some. This certainly was the opinion of Louis Cauvière, newly appointed inspector of manufactures at Marseilles, who, after a visit of Languedoc's manufacturing centres in 1694, wrote of it as 'la fabrique du Royaume la plus Considérable par le grand nombre de draps quil s'y fait, et par la quantité de marchands qui font ce commerce'.[55] But that Clermont-de-Lodève should have been the site of the province's second large manufacture, Villenouvette, was hardly predictable in view of the sad state to which the town's industry had declined in this period.

The background to the foundation of this manufacture is both complex and obscure. An intervention by Colbert can be definitely discounted: at a later date he specifically stated that 'cette fabrique de Clermont n'a pas esté establie par l'autorité du roy'.[56] Clermont would seem to have been chosen as a site for a second manufacture primarily for geographical reasons. It was the nearest significant cloth-making centre to Montpellier and it was financiers from Montpellier who were the main force behind its foundation.

The role of financiers, amongst them Languedocians, in the various Levant companies has already been mentioned. The province's involvement was particularly marked, we have seen, in the 1678 company which had offices at Lyons, Paris and Sète. Sète to all appearances was an anomalous partner to Paris and Lyons, respectively political and economic capital of France. It was still but a village. Its growth as a port had only just begun. The explanation for its involvement in the third Levant Company is as follows. Languedoc lacked, and always had lacked, an adequate port and one had become all the more necessary, and all the more potentially profitable, as a consequence of the completion of the Canal du Midi in the 1660s. (An adequate Mediterranean outlet was required for this canal.) Sète, as a consequence, was developed in the 1660s by financiers from Montpellier and it was they, too, who founded export companies in the port. Two 'Compagnies de Sète' were formed in 1669 and 1676. About one, the 'Ancienne Compagnie de Sète', very little is known apart from the fact that it was set up by six Montpellier financiers. But it seems very likely that these six founders of the first company were among the twelve members of the succeeding 1676 company whose names are known to us. All were drawn from the ranks of rich Languedocian financiers for whom the centre of activities was Montpellier. Several were also members of the 'Cour des Comptes, Aides et

55. ADH C2200, Cauvière's report, 1694.
56. Colbert to d'Aguesseau, 26 March 1682 (Clément, *Lettres*, II, pt. 2, 732–3).

Finances' of Montpellier. All possessed in abundance the item lacking at Marseilles – capital: in mid-seventeenth century France, it is clear, finance was a far more favourable field for entrepreneurial activity than commerce.[57]

Involvement in the Compagnie de Sète, and participation in other interventionist schemes, represented a change of path for these financiers. It was representative of a fairly generalized trend among such groups throughout France which was occasioned, it would seem, by a combination of factors: a shortage of investment opportunities for such groups (possibly brought about by the Colbertian reforms in the taxation system and the stabilization in tax demands); indirect pressure from Paris (it was ultimately on royal concessions that the financiers' fortunes depended); and finally an optimistic innovating spirit which bears comparison with that observed among French financiers in the 1840s and 1850s (peace in the 1660s, the new reign and the new ministry would have all contributed to such a mood). We have already come across the main Languedocian participator in Colbertian schemes, Reich de Pennautier, but among the group of financiers who founded the Sète company were two brothers, André and Honoré Pouget, who rivalled Pennautier in the scope of their affairs, in particular the former: André Pouget combined one of the most important offices in the Cour des Aides of Montpellier, 'greffier-en-chef-civil', with a central position in the tax farms of the province, 'fermier des gabelles', and he was involved in the provisioning of the Navy and had been a major backer of Riquet in the building of the Canal du Midi, investing 600,000 *livres* in this affair. In Boissonnade's words he was a 'brasseur d'affaires entreprenant, un spéculateur aventureux'.[58]

The initial purpose of the Sète companies was the export of wine and eau-de-vie throughout the Mediterranean. This trade was facilitated not only by the opening of the Canal du Midi but also by the introduction to the province in 1663 of a new method of preparing eau-de-vie. But a combination of Pouget's (and his colleagues') ambition, the evident inadequacy of Marseilles's resources for handling the Levant trade, and a temporary buoyancy in cloth sales to the Levant in the early 1670s, clearly encouraged the Sète company to diversify its activities to include participation in the Levant trade.[59] To do this it needed a regular supply of high-quality cloth but Saptes's production was largely being absorbed by the Levant company and so it would seem that the idea occurred to

57. Dermigny, 'Armement languedocien', pp. 252–4, and *Naissance et croissance d'un port: Sète de 1666 à 1880*, pp. 9–12.
58. Boissonnade, 'Colbert, son système', p. 40.
59. Paris, *Histoire du commerce*, v, 55–6.

Pouget and his associates to find an alternative source. This source was to be Clermont-de-Lodève. The link between the founding of the second Compagnie de Sète, which was also known as the Levant Company, and the establishment of Villenouvette is revealed by the fact that no less than five of its members invested money in the manufacture.[60]

In other words a strand of interventionist activity slightly diverging from the one which we have been investigating in the case of Marseilles and Saptes gave rise to the Canal du Midi, the improvements in the port of Sète, the foundation of the Sète companies and the establishment of Villenouvette. It was as if 'Colbertism' approached the Mediterranean in a pincer movement, from two directions – via Toulouse, the Canal du Midi and Sète, and via Lyons and Marseilles. With the foundation of the third Levant company in 1678, in which the Sète Company's Levantine office became a succursal branch, these two separate strands virtually merged. Reich de Pennautier was perhaps the co-ordinator. He had been involved on both flanks of the pincer movement.

Neither the Sète companies, nor Villenouvette, were established in opposition to the Levant Company and Saptes. As we shall see, Villenouvette was effectively a transplant from the first royal manufacture. But there may have been a gentle rivalry among financiers which expressed itself indirectly in the way in which Villenouvette was created. The original memoir from which Basville drew his description of the two manufactures states that Villenouvette was founded by 'des particuliers qui vouloient L'imiter [Saptes]'.[61] But rather than to imitate, Villenouvette, which was built in a most extravagent manner, would seem to have been designed to outdo Saptes. As Boissonnade writes, the manufacture was

---

60. There would seem to be a distinction between the membership of the second Sète company of 1676, which included André and Honoré Pouget ('conseillers et secrétaires du roi', Montpellier), Laurent Bosc, André Boussonnel, Antoine and Jacques Roux ('greffiers au bureau des finances' of Montpellier), Jacques Marcha ('avocat'), Gabriel Creyssels ('trésorier des troupes' of Provence), Guillaume Pujol ('trésorier de France' at Toulouse), Jacques Icher ('receveur général des gabelles'), Pierre Jean Pujol ('trésorier des mortes payes'), Jean Vivens, Gédéon Brutel, Samuel Verchand, Jean Roux, Samuel Fournier, Daniel Pujol and Jacques Cambacérès ('receveurs des tailles' for Nîmes, Mirepoix, Viviers, Le Puy, Albi, Limoux and Toulouse), and those who associated themselves with the third Levant company, who included seven members of the Sète company (André Pouget, Marcha, Icher, Brutel, Verchand, Creyssels, Bosc) and five newcomers – Jean Salgues (bourgeois), Pierre Sartre ('receveur de la Bourse du Languedoc'), Jean Pégurier ('contrôleur au grenier à sel' of Frontignan), Jean Bonnel ('receveur des tailles', Albi), and François Bosc (banquier at Lyons). André Pouget, Jacques Icher, Gédéon Brutel, Samuel Fournier and Jean Bonnel are among the associates who take over Villenouvette. (Dermigny, 'Armement languedocien', p. 253, n.4 and *Sète*, p. 12.) For more details on Villenouvette associates, see pp. 157–8.
61. ADH C2203, 'Mémoire sur les Manufactures de Saptes et de Clermont', *c.* 1690.

established on a 'pied magnifique'.[62] Colbert was later to be highly critical of this extravagance to which he attributed the manufacture's later liquidity problems. 'Je plains le Sieur Pouget', he wrote, 'les bastimens qui ont esté fait par les entrepreneurs ne sont l'effet ni d'aucun ordre qui leur ayt esté donné, ny mesme d'une conduite sage et prudente.'[63]

But we are anticipating slightly for initially the new manufacture was not established on quite so magnificent a footing, and nor were Pouget and his associates directly involved in its original foundation. Initially they acted through one Pierre Baille, marchand/marchand-facturier of Clermont, to whom they loaned large sums of money. For approximately two and a half years Baille had, it seems, virtual freedom to set the manufacture up in the way in which he wanted. The choice of Baille as agent is easily explicable. The associates themselves had no industrial experience and so they needed the co-operation of a local clothier. Baille was an obvious choice both because he was significantly richer, and evidently better qualified to run a large concern, than his artisanal colleagues in the industry and also because he was linked both by his Protestantism and by marriage to the world of Montpellier officials and financiers. In 1667 he had married Izabeau Coulomb daughter of Pierre, 'procureur de Sénéchaussée' in the 'présidial' of Montpellier, and it was his Protestantism which eventually obliged him to flee from Clermont to Amsterdam where (ironic reversal) he was to found a cloth manufacture.[64]

As early as 1673 we find evidence of Baille borrowing large sums from two Montpellier financiers. These were Fulcrand Duffours, involved in the *gabelles* and in the farming of the 'droit de lods et ventes du domaine du roi' and later an associate in the manufacture, and François Jougla.[65] This is the only direct evidence of a loan to Baille which I have found but in a memoir about Villenouvette, composed between 1697 and 1698, it is specifically stated that the manufacture was founded in *1670* by Baille

62. 'Colbert, son système', p. 40.
63. Colbert to d'Aguesseau, letters of 8 May 1681 and 6 Feb. 1682 (Clément, *Lettres*, II, pt. 2, 718, 729–30).
64. On Baille see p. 111. His marriage to Izabeau Coulomb is recorded in ADH II E 25 87, 88, 9 March 1667, 14 Jan. 1668. Before leaving for Amsterdam (Gachon, *Quelques préliminaires*, pp. cxliv-cxlv; De Vic and Vaissète, *Histoire générale*, XIII, 566) he would seem to have offered his services as clothier to the Republic of Venice. Braudel and his collaborators ('Le déclin de Venise', p. 43) record a proposal made in 1676 – the year in which Baille's links with Villenouvette were cut – by one 'Bailie' to introduce to Venice 'La fabrica di Rensi', et tele ad uso di Olanda'.
65. An act of 10 Nov. 1676 records these loans (ADH II E 26 119, 10 Nov. 1676). On Duffours see also II E 25 94, 23 June 1679 and II E 62 86, numerous acts of 1673.

with the help of large sums of money advanced, principally, by Pouget.[66] It was on the basis of this document that Appolis argued that Villenouvette was founded in 1670, rather than 1674 (as others had maintained).[67] But although it is quite possible, even likely, that Pierre Baille's relationship with Pouget dates from this year, and that he produced cloth before 1674 (maybe for the mysterious Ancienne Compagnie de Sète) for export to the Levant, it can definitely be affirmed that the actual foundation of the new manufacture (rather than the date of Pouget's association with Baille's original concern) occurred between 1673 and 1674 because all the acts relating to the original purchase of land and buildings, and to their transformation to form the new manufacture, were registered by the Protestant notary whose service the Baille family used – Pierre Villar.[68] That the new manufacture represented, as it were, an expansion of Baille's original activities in Clermont is suggested by a report made by a visitor to the manufacture in 1674. He was acting on behalf of d'Aguesseau and reported that 'depuis peu à un quart de lieue de la ville on y fait travailler une facture de draps fins de toutes sortes de Colleurs quj sont sy beaux et fins que ceux dholande, on a fait venir de facturiers de ce pays là ... on fait quantité de draps quon transporte du costé de Smirne et autres parties du Levant'.[69] It seems highly improbable that such a level of activity would have been achieved so rapidly if the manufacture had not inherited the momentum of Baille's original concern in Clermont. That it was the financial support of Pouget and other financiers which was the decisive element in the decision to establish a larger concern at about $1\frac{1}{2}$ kilometres from Clermont, on the River Dourbie, is demonstrated convincingly by a contract drawn up between Pouget, his associates, and the Count of Clermont for the payment of the *lods* due on all land purchased by them or on their behalf. The contract begins as follows: 'Guilhem de Clermont de Castelnau ... sçaschant que Monsieur Me André Pouget ... Gédeon Brutel et avec assosiés pour l'establissement dune facture de draps au terroir ... de Clermont ... avoir fait diverses acquisitions tant soubs le nom de pierre Baille que de jean Baille son pare marchans de lad ville de Clermont des deniers desd. assosiés', and this introduction is followed by a list of all the purchases made by Baille (the first being that of a mill in June 1673) and an agreement to pay 4,300 *livres* for all the *lods* due since 1670.[70]

66. ADH C2202.
67. *Lodève*, p. 514. In opposition to Boissonnade ('Colbert, son système', p. 12) who gives the date 1674 and G. Martin (*La grande industrie en France sous le règne de Louis XIV*, p. 97) who gives that of 1678.
68. The relevant registers: ADH 11 E 25 90–2.
69. BM Toulouse, MS 603, folios 360, 366.
70. ADH 11 E 60 90, 26 Feb. 1677.

An examination of Pierre Villar's registers confirms the veracity of the act registered in Montpellier between the Count of Clermont and the associates. On 27 June 1673 a fulling mill on the River Dourbie and adjoining land was bought by Jean Baille for 500 *livres* from Daniel Michel, doctor of theology, and minister in the reformed church at Graissesac, who had been given the property by his uncle David Michel, apothecary.[71] This was the first step taken in the establishment of Villenouvette. The bulk of purchases were made, however, between 1674 and 1675 and it would seem justifiable, therefore, to regard 1674 as the foundation date.

From the outset the manufacture was conceived on what by the standards of Clermont's poor industry was a vast scale. Baille purchased land, houses and fulling mills for a total of 2,063 *livres* between 1673 and 1675, rented property of a value of 16,120 *livres*,[72] and paid out 21,210 *livres* in wages and materials for repairs and construction work and 2,200 *livres* for seed, vine-stocks and agricultural labour for cultivating the land around the manufacture.[73] The buying and repairing were evidently carried out with speed for already in 1675 there was a sizeable labour force lodged at the establishment which was known at this stage as the 'métérie de Dourbie' or as the 'métérie et moulin sur la rivière Dourbie'.[74] This large labour force is revealed by a dispute which Baille had with the farmers of the *subvention* at Clermont over the food which he sold to his workers. The dispute was settled by his promising to pay the sum of 400 *livres* each year to cover 'les chères quil fait tuer et débiter ... pour lui et ses ouvriers'.[75]

Although Baille continued to own property in Clermont, and purchased more such property between 1673 and 1675, his new manufacture was designed to be self-contained and fully equipped with all that was necessary both for making cloth and for housing and feeding its labour force. The repairs and construction work undertaken, and the new equipment made, included the rebuilding and modernization of the

---

71. ADH II E 25 90.
72. The annual rental of the properties (the farms of Mas Rouju and Malavialle in the Dourbie valley and a house in Clermont) was 806 *livres*. I have estimated this to be 5% of their value.
73. Evidence all extracted from ADH II E 25 90–2.
74. These two titles are first used in acts of 5 March, 1 July 1675 (ADH II E 25 92). The enterprise was first termed a manufacture in 1676 – it was referred to as the 'méthérie et manufacture de dourbye' on 28 June 1676, 'la manufacture de cette ville' on 26 July 1676, and as 'la manufacture de Vileneufve de Clermont' on 26 Aug. 1676 (ADH II E 26 119).
75. ADH II E 25 92, 1 July 1675.

fulling mills, the provision of copper and lead cauldrons and furnaces for a dye-house, the construction of large tables for shearing, dressing and burling the cloth, and of cloth-tenters, cloth-presses, twisting mills and looms, as well as the basic repairs to the houses which were designed to make them suitable for the labour force – a labour force which required at least nineteen beds, twenty-one cupboards, seven wardrobes, six kitchen tables and a mill for grinding flour.[76] The manufacture was intended to be not only self-contained but also self-supporting. Baille had bought land and planted it with grain, vines, fruit trees and vegetables[77] and he also bought no less than 381 sheep and goats during 1675,[78] the slaughter of which was no doubt the occasion of his dispute with the farmers of the *subvention*.

Expenditure on such a scale, capital equipment of such quality and so great a concentration of production were evidently not designed to imitate Clermont's traditional cloth industry. It was the new Dutch method of cloth-making which was being introduced. The intendant's agent had noted the presence of Dutch workers at the manufacture and this report is confirmed by the 'registre de catholicité' of the manufacture. Amongst local names appear a Vandyck, a Van Dor, a Trintrop and a Shoemaker, the first two from Holland, the last two from Germany, as well as two other Dutch workers, whose names have been translated into French: a Charron from Leyden and a Capitaine from the Duchy of Limbourg.[79] Two later acts before notaries provide crucial details about the role and the date of arrival of one of these northerners. Jacob Trintrop, from Münster in Germany, married in 1693 and in his marriage contract he recorded that he had been at the manufacture for eighteen years – since 1674 or 1675. In 1681 his name appeared at the head of a list of weavers who were forming a confrérie at the manufacture – a short note explained this precedence: it was he, 'Jacob Trintrop aleman quy a commencé le travalh des draps quy se font en lad Manufacture à la mode dolande'.[80] These workers, according to the 1674 visitor, had been brought from Holland (and Germany). This they evidently had but it would seem that they had come in most cases via Saptes. Jacob Trintrop, for example, originally from the town of Münster, was married to one Anne de Simony from Conques which could only mean that he had spent time at Saptes before coming to

76. ADH II E 25 91–2, 26 Feb., 20, 21, 22 Dec. 1674 and 29 April 1675.
77. ADH II E 25 91, three acts of 22 Dec. 1674.
78. ADH II E 25 92, 19 March and 3 Sept. 1675.
79. Alberge, 'Villeneuvette', p. 32. This register is now held at Montpellier, ADH III E 181[1 bis].
80. ADH II E 26 136, 98, 29 Jan. 1693, 17 Nov. 1681.

Clermont, and the Dutchman Van Dor and his wife de Teysse had definitely worked previously at Saptes for their daughter had been baptized there in 1673 or 1674, the parish register reveals.[81] Saptes by the 1670s, of course, could provide trained Languedocian workers as well as Dutchmen and some of Villenouvette's first workers were evidently such – five ex-Conques families registered births, deaths or marriages between 1675 and 1680.[82]

It was in 1676 that the manufacture was 'taken over' by Pouget and his associates. The expression 'taken over' would seem to be apt. Until then Baille, to all appearances at least, had had complete freedom to use the money which he had been loaned by Pouget and his associates in the manner in which he wanted. But during 1676 friction developed between him and his backers. Colbert, in a letter to Intendant d'Aguesseau, written in July 1676, mentioned 'petits différens entre le sr. Bail et sr. Pouget et les marchands de Montpellier qui veulent fournir leurs deniers pour la soustenir et l'augmenter'.[83] The desire for an expansion would have been occasioned by the formation of the second, and larger, Compagnie de Sète in 1676. It is probable that Baille thought that it was unwise to expand his already large concern further. Anyway Pouget used the dispute as an opportunity to take complete control of the concern. Gédéon Brutel,[84] one of his closest collaborators, acted on his behalf. He paid off Baille's creditors making them cede their claims on Baille to himself in front of a notary. Such transactions are to be found in the registers of both Montpellier and Clermontais notaries. The formula, in each case, was the same. Antoine Paulinier, a Pézenas merchant, for example, was owed 2,800 *livres* by Baille. Brutel paid Paulinier in cash, transferring the obligation on Baille to himself 'à ses risques perils et . . . sans espoir . . . d'avoir . . . garanty ni restitution de deniers contre led Sr. Parlini . . . quand bien . . . led Sr. Baille seroit insolvable et ledit Sr. Brutel ne pourroit estre paýe'.[85] The result of these transactions was that instead of having a large number of creditors Pierre Baille had one, Gédéon Brutel, Pouget's associate. What was being carried out was a take-over bid: Baille's debts were being treated like shares in a joint-stock company, and, as in the case of modern take-overs an element of secrecy was involved: Baille was not present at the signing of any of these acts by

81. ADH iii E 181[1 bis].
82. From the Bassay, Galsen, Sayssigne, Sabatier and Relion families.
83. Colbert to d'Aguesseau, 30 July 1676, cited by Alberge, 'Villeneuvette', p. 21.
84. In addition to his involvement in the collection of *tailles* (see note 60 above) Brutel, like Pouget and Duffours, was involved in the *gabelles*, as receveur général, and was also a conseiller du roi and former 'fermier des glacières' of Languedoc (ADH ii E 60 91).
85. ADH ii E 26 119, a register which contains several other similar acts. Other such acts were registered by the notary Gardel of Montpellier (ii E 60 91).

which Brutel assumed the responsibility for paying off his debts. Baille must have had some idea about what was happening, however, for in September and October of 1676 he was buying and exchanging property which he had bought near the Dourbie for a house in Clermont and land near the Lergue.[86] He was finally forced to relinquish any claims which he had over the manufacture by a cash payment from Pouget. Accounts drawn up later for the running of the manufacture under the new management record the payment of 4,200 *livres* in 1676 'sçavoir 3,000 à Baille pour l'obliger à remettre la Manufacture, et 1,200 à Nourrit son beaufrère comme sa caution'.[87] In the memoir of 1697–8 it is stated that Pouget took over the manufacture 'faute par le sieur baile davoir donné bon compte à ses créanciers'.[88] The appearances are, though, that the take-over rather than being precipitated by Baille's possible insolvency was occasioned by the increased involvement of the Compagnie de Sète in the Levant trade.

The associates who were to run Villenouvette during the next few years included Pouget himself, Brutel, Duffours, Samuel Fournier, doctor, advocate and 'receveur des tailles' for Albi, François Coste, 'receveur au grenier à sel de Montpellier', Jacques Icher, 'receveur général des gabelles' and 'receveur des tailles' for Albi, Jean Vernet, doctor and advocate, Jean Bonnel, banquier, and Jean-André Fredian, négociant of Marseilles. Of these nine Pouget, Brutel, Fournier, Icher and Bonnel were members of the Compagnie de Sète at some stage. The links between the two organizations could hardly have been closer. All, again, apart from Fredian were from the same world of Montpellier finance: four were involved in the *gabelles* and four in the *tailles*.[89] Involvement in these new enterprises did not mean that these financiers had abandoned their normal tax-collecting activities. In 1677 the four involved in the *tailles* formed yet another society together with Honoré Pouget entitled 'La société d'anciens officiers des tailhes et tailhons' and jointly borrowed 100,000 *livres*.[90]

The amount invested by the associates was (for a manufacturing con-

---

86. And as noted above (note 64) he probably attempted to obtain employment in Venice during these months.
87. ADH 1 B 10310, Examination of Villenouvette's accounts undertaken by Jacques Cambacères and Laurent Bosc, both associates of the second Sète company (see note 60).
88. ADH C2202.
89. Sources for additional information on these financiers (additional to that provided in note 60); on Fournier, Coste and Icher, ADH 11 E 60 91, 5 April 1677, 11 E 26 100, 10 July 1683; on Vernet, 11 E 25 94, 28 Aug. 1679; on Fredian, ADH C7214, Etats, 20 Nov. 1682; on Jean Bonnel, ADH 1 B 10310 in which his early participation in the manufacture is mentioned. Involved in the *gabelles* were Pouget, Duffours, Brutel and Icher and in the *tailles* Brutel, Fournier, Bonnel and Icher.
90. ADH 11 E 60 91, 5 April 1677.

cern) very large. Some 40,000 *livres* (it would seem) was the minimun contribution.[91] But some of the associates contributed more. This was certainly the case of Pouget, but Jean-André Fredian, too, provided over 40,000 *livres*, a notarial contract reveals. On 2 August 1678 he withdrew from the concern and part of his original investment was immediately repaid, but the act registered a debt of 50,000 *livres* owed by Pouget, Brutel and the other associates 'pour reste du quart que le Sr Fredian avoit en la propriété et fonds delad. Manufacture'.[92]

The new name which the associates gave to the concern, 'La Manufacture de Villeneuve de Clermont', symbolized their pretensions for it. These were soon turned into physical form for the bulk of the large capital collected was devoted, it is clear, to enlarging and embellishing what was to become the 'Manufacture Royale de Villeneuve de Clermont' on 20 July 1677.[93] The farm of Mas Rouju, the nucleus of Baille's activities, was from now to take second place to a magnificent 'model' manufacture built next to the Dourbie. The basic structure designed by Pouget and his associates has been retained by the manufacture, which only closed down in 1954, to this day (Map 4). A description of both the nature and the cost of the improvements was sent to Pouget in Paris in 1681.[94] The manufacture had been surrounded by walls on three sides (the fourth side being protected by the River Dourbie) and the walls, which formed a large square, were pierced by three impressive gates (Ills. 10 and 11). Inside there were small streets and squares which separated the six major buildings. These provided ample space for all the processes of production as well as for the accommodation of the labour force. There were rooms for shearing, dressing, pressing, dyeing and washing the cloth; there were also spaces to dry and stretch the finished cloth and rooms and spaces for drying, cleaning, sorting, beating, carding and spinning the wool. There was one building entirely devoted to weaving, containing thirty-one looms. There were two fulling mills, a wool-washing basin and a large artificial reservoir supplied by water tapped from the Dourbie and delivered to the manufacture by an aqueduct and long channel. Sixty-six houses had been built for the labour force and an elegant apartment for the associates (described as 'le logement des messieurs'). There was a tavern, with cellars large enough to contain 400

---

91. If we are to judge by the size of Bonnel's investment in the concern which is mentioned in ADH I B 10310.
92. ADH II E 68 73, 16 Jan. 1693; reference is made to the original separation of Fredian from the concern by act registered before the Montpellier notary Gardel, 2 Aug. 1678.
93. Letters Patent of 20 July 1677 (Archive de la Manufacture).
94. Archive de la Manufacture, 'Description de la manufacture envoyée à Mr. Pouget à Paris le 20 ianvier 1681'.

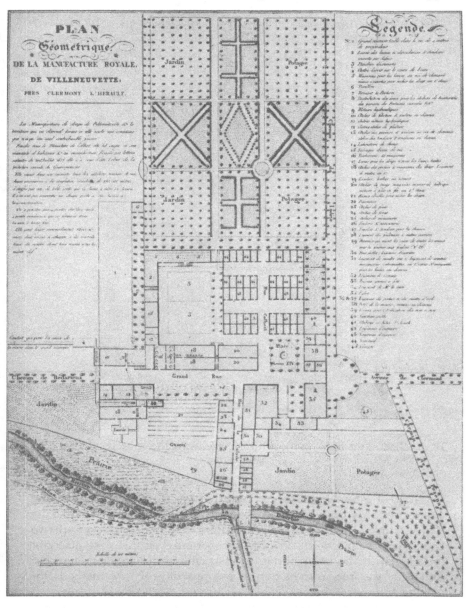

Map 4   Plan of Villenouvette (ADH 1 E, Fonds Villeneuvette)

Ill. 10. View of the inside of the main gateway and of the central building of the manufacture

hogshead of wine, a barn for 2,000 *setiers* of wheat, a room for cultivating silkworms, a hay barn, two rooms equipped with small looms for making coarse cloth, a slaughter-house, a bread and wine shop, a bakery with two bread ovens, a flour mill, a dovecot, a chapel and even an ice-pit, no doubt installed with the co-operation of associate Brutel another of whose 'interests' was the introduction to the province of new methods for making and conserving ice.[95]

95. See above, note 84. On the introduction of ice-making to the province shortly before 1660 see Boissonnade, 'La crise de l'industrie languedocienne', p. 185.

Ill. 11. View of the manufacture from a hill situated on the other side of the Dourbie

No expense had been spared. To make the reservoir and aqueduct alone 30,000 *livres* had been spent and the total cost of all the new buildings was 170,709 *livres*. In addition to this an agricultural estate of 900 *séterées* had been bought around the manufacture, the associates had paid off all Baille's debts and the labour force had been expanded. The memoir sent to Paris in 1681 stated that 'les ouvriers en nombre pour le moins 700 personnes travaillent activement'. Pouget and his associates had created what was always to be regarded as 'la plus belle de toutes les manufactures de Languedoc',[96] a most remarkable creation, matching the other great project in which Pouget was involved, the Canal du Midi, described by Voltaire as 'Le monument le plus représentatif du règne de Louis XIV'.[97]

If the initial contributions of the associates were sunk largely into land purchases and buildings, the working capital for the concern seems to have been provided by Pouget. It was he, in Paris, who discounted letters of exchange drawn up either by the associates at Villenouvette or by Antoine Brutel, brother of Gédéon, banquier and the associates' cor-

96. AN F12 645, 'Mémoire sur le commerce du Levant', *c.* 1756.
97. Cited by J.-Y. Tirat, 'Circulation et commerce intérieur de la France au xviie siècle', *XVIIe Siècle* 70–1 (1966), 78.

respondent at Lyons. Another relation of Brutel, his nephew André Chabert, acted as 'commis' for the concern in Marseilles while Fulcrand Duffours was 'directeur général' of the manufacture itself.[98] There is no evidence of the other associates' having any direct, executive role in the concern though there is record of their occasional presence in Clermont.[99] Pouget, Fredian and Brutel were undoubtedly not only the three largest financial contributors to the concern but those who played the largest role in all financial and commercial aspects of its activity. Pouget throughout was situated in Paris. There he must have had regular contact with Colbert and Colbert's close economic advisers. It is likely that it was he who obtained the edict raising Villenouvette to the status of royal manufacture and Colbert mentions in a letter to d'Aguesseau in 1679 that he had offered to 'servir utilement' both King and minister.[100] That he also had contact with Jacques Savary is suggested by a payment of 1,000 *livres*, recorded in his accounts with the manufacture in February 1681, to 'sieur Savary pour faciliter Lobtention dun arrest en faveur des marchands'.[101] The amount of circulating capital he advanced to the manufacture was large – up to 126,000 *livres* in a single month. A large return on all such loans was demanded. Throughout, 10% interest was charged on all advances made by any of the associates to the company. Brutel was, as it were, the company's sales director. He divided his time between Marseilles and Villenouvette (and probably Sète as well). Some of his time he must have spent at Bagnoles-sur-Cèze where his brother Estienne lived for there were found some of his papers after he had mysteriously disappeared in 1683 when the company was in difficulties.[102] As well as being associate of the manufacture Brutel formed a separate society with Fredian for the export of the manufacture's cloth to the Levant. This, anyway, is what the record of the loading of 255 pieces of the manufacture's cloth for Smyrna on behalf of 'Messrs Brutel, Fredian & Cie' would suggest.[103]

With the financial support of the associates, and an increasingly large credit granted by members of the Levant Company, production was

98. The financial arrangements are revealed by the manufacture's current account with Pouget during these years (ADH I B 10310). Duffours is described as 'intéressé et directeur de la manufacture' in ADH C2202.
99. For instance six of the associates, Brutel, Icher, Fournier, Duffours, Coste and Vernet were present to sign a contract in Clermont on 28 Aug. 1679 (ADH II E 25 94).
100. Cited by Boissonnade, 'Colbert, son système', p. 39.
101. ADH I B 10310.
102. All these details from ADH I B 10310.
103. Archive de la Manufacture, 'Extrait de polices tirés des originaux exibés et retirés par Sʳ Jean André Fredian pour estre collationés par nous Pierre Maillet et Jean Baptiste Amoreux notaires Royaux . . . Marseille, 14 Oct. 1676 – 29 Oct. 1680' (details of export of Villenouvette's cloth).

expanded in 1676 and 1677. A record of exports from Marseilles shows that 256 pieces of cloth were dispatched in the first year, 454 in the second. But then exports declined to 182 pieces in 1678, 224 in 1679, 190 in 1680, and a further 112 until July 1681.[104] It is probable that cloth was being produced for different markets, or exported via Sète, but that there were difficulties in the Levant market during these years, and that these difficulties caused problems to the concern there is no doubt. In 1678 Fredian, the company's main agent in Marseilles, was experiencing some sort of bankruptcy,[105] and in the years that followed trade with the Levant was disturbed by Algerian corsairs, and Marseilles's merchants returned to their old practice of exporting specie instead of manufactured goods.[106] In addition one of the purchasers of the manufacture's cloth, Artaud, who was residing at Smyrna where over half the Company's cloth was sent, failed to pay his debts, and the manufacture was involved for 28,200 *livres* in the bankruptcy of one Billot in March 1681.[107] With sales to the Levant failing the manufacture tried to sell its surplus stock in Paris: in February 1681 Pouget received 31,000 *livres* from the 'marchands-merciers' of Paris for the sale of cloth and a further 7,000 *livres* for another eight bales of cloth which had reached him via Gédéon Brutel at Lyons.[108] These sales were not sufficient to keep the manufacture going, however, and early in 1681 it was in very severe difficulties and appealing for help to Colbert. At this early stage Colbert was prepared to promise his support: 'Vous pourrez mesme faire espérer qu'en cas de besoin Sa Majesté pourra les assister de ses fonds, ou les faire assister par la province d'un prest d'argent sans intérest . . .', he wrote to the intendant, d'Aguesseau.[109] He was not yet aware of how serious the crisis was.

The situation in which Villenouvette found itself was not unprecedented. Saptes, too, had experienced similar crises on two or three occasions before 1682.[110] What was different at Clermont was the severity of the crisis. It was occasioned, as those at Saptes had been, by the mis-sale of cloth, but it was enormously intensified by the fact that the associates had

104. Archive de la Manufacture, 'Extrait . . .', has production up to Oct. 1680; ADH 1 B 10310 records payment of 1,200 *livres* bounty for the export of a further 112 pieces of cloth in July 1681.
105. ADH C7214, Etats, 20 Nov. 1682.
106. Dermigny, 'Armement languedocien', p. 254, and see Depping, *Correspondance*, III, 617–24, and Clément, *Lettres*, II, pt. 2, 692–5 and III, 519.
107. ADH 1 B 10310.
108. ADH 1 B 10310.
109. Clément, *Lettres*, II, pt. 2, 718, n.2, letter of 11 April 1681.
110. ADH C7214, Etats, 20 Nov. 1682, the deputies estimated that Saptes had 'manqué' three times in the previous twenty or thirty years.

invested money in the concern with such extravagance and by the fact that there was a parallel crisis in the affairs of Pouget, the company's main backer. The crisis in Pouget's affairs was to cause his bankruptcy – his losses at Villenouvette were estimated at half a million *livres*.[111] Boissonnade characterizes him as having been a 'financier habile' but a 'mediocre entrepreneur d'industrie'.[112] The crisis in the affairs of the royal manufacture was also nearly to cause its ruin and abandonment. Colbert, when he was aware of the extent of the problems, rapidly withdrew his initial promise of support. In reply to a proposition from d'Aguesseau in May 1681 that the manufacture of Saptes should be joined to that of Villenouvette, he complained of Pouget's extravagance – 'je plains le sieur Pouget' – and gave his opinion that to join the two manufactures would be to ruin them both and that 'celle de Clermont estant foible et ayant trop entrepris, il vaut mieux le soutenir foible que de la joindre à une autre et les faire périr toutes deux'.[113]

Saptes was also in difficulties during 1681, but not so desperate as those of Villenouvette.[114] Colbert continued to show indecision about what course of action to take. He was torn between his desire to save the Treasury from very large expenses and his anxiety to save and support two manufactures which were playing such an important role in fulfilling his mercantilist ambitions. By the end of the year he had thought of a solution which would safeguard both of his scruples: the rich Etats of Languedoc should be encouraged to play the role which the Crown had played until then and support the ailing manufactures. Illustrated by this proposed change in paymaster for the province's industrial effort was the increasing financial strain in Paris. As Mandrou writes of Colbert, 'les difficultés de trésorerie l'ont incité au delà de 1670 à faire appel de plus en plus largement au financement partiel par des autorités locales'.[115] The consequent loss of direct central control was not going to be without its major disadvantages, as will be seen. The powers in the provincial Etats were in some cases the very individuals who were most heavily involved financially in the two concerns. But this factor does not seem to have been considered by Colbert. On the contrary he quite rightly anticipated that

111. ADH 1 B 10310, 'Mémoire sur les loyers de la manufacture de Clermont', 16 March 1683, states that it is certain that 'cette affaire a accablé le Sr. Pouget, et quil y perd environ cinq cens mil livres'. Lavisse's estimate (*Histoire générale du IVᵉ siècle à nos jours*, VII, pt. 1, 222) that Pouget spent 1,000,000 *livres* at Villeneuvette is perhaps accurate, but a part of this sum must have been recovered.
112. 'Colbert, son système', pp. 18, 40–1.
113. Clément, *Lettres*, II, pt. 2, 718.
114. The details of the crisis in the affairs of these two royal manufactures are provided by C. W. Cole, *Colbert and a Century of French Mercantilism*, II, 159–70, and Boissonnade, 'Colbert, son système', pp. 18–26.
115. *Louis XIV*, p. 141.

the Etats would be initially reluctant to commit themselves to providing regular financial support for the province's manufactures. There were no precedents for such provisions and previously the Etats' economic interventions had been minimal. Thus d'Aguesseau, acting in close consultation with Colbert, at the opening session of the Etats in December 1681, was obliged to give this body's members what amounted to a short introductory talk on the importance of 'mercantile' policies for the province's prosperity in order to win them over to supporting Villenouvette. This manufacture was failing, he explained, 'par la fatalité qui est attachée aux commancements de toutes les grandes entreprises'. The loss of the concern would be tragic for the province because of the promise of future wealth which the manufacture could bring, income from industrial sources being more reliable than that from the land. 'Manufactures . . .', he explained, 'ne sont sujettes ny aux révolutions des saisons ny à l'inconstance des élémens, qu'elles dépendent de lart, de l'industrie, et de l'aplication des hommes.' In support of this assertion he pointed out that the richest countries were those whose prosperity was based on manufactures. He was evidently referring to Holland, above all, and to illustrate further the importance of the manufacture at Clermont he insisted that the commerce which enriched the Dutch most was not that of the Indies, as some people believed, but that of the Mediterranean. The royal manufacture at Clermont would enable the province to enjoy the same advantages. D'Aguesseau finished by urging generosity: 'nous ne devons pas traiter cette affaire comme des particuliers régleront leur despence domestique, Mais que nous devons avoir de plus grandes veües . . .'.[116]

No immediate grant was made by the Etats. Instead a commission was appointed to investigate the matter. This reported back to the assembly in January 1682 having analysed a project submitted by the associates of the manufacture. The project showed that the concern had debts of 750,000 *livres*, and to set against these 350,000 *livres* in effects (i.e. circulating capital), 298,583 *livres* of fixed capital (buildings, land, tools), and a sum of 224,739 *livres* owed by Gédéon Brutel with whom the other associates were in litigation. To help them out of their difficulties the associates were requesting an interest-free loan of 400,000 *livres* from the province, and the privilege of not paying any interest on their debts. They anticipated being able to make 500 pieces of cloth a year at a profit of 40,000 *livres* (Table 7).[117]

116. ADH C7214, Etats, 3 Dec. 1681.
117. As can be seen from Table 7 the figures presented to the deputies of the Etats in fact total 39,800 *livres*. This is perhaps an additional illustration of the unreliability of the associates' recovery plan.

Table 7. *Villenouvette's associates' estimate of future annual profits*

Food sold to the workers at the manufacture	14,400 *livres*
Bounty on 500 pieces of cloth	5,000 *livres*
Revenue from their land holdings	4,200 *livres*
Profits from cloth manufacture	16,200 *livres*
TOTAL	39,800 *livres*

Source: ADH C7214, procès-verbaux of Etats, 10 Jan. 1682.

The project of the associates revealed the deplorable state of the manufacture's finances and the deputies were not unnaturally sceptical about the associates' recovery plan in view of the fact that a large part of future profit was expected to come from selling food to the labour force. The commissioners stressed in their report their lack of confidence in the associates and advised against any involvement with them 'à cause du mauvais estat de leurs affaires'. It would be better, they suggested, to form a new company, but they doubted that any merchants in the province would want to involve themselves in such an affair, and they doubted too whether the advantages of such a new company would outweigh the cost to the King and the province, particularly as there was no shortage of cloth manufactures in the province 'establies depuis longtemps et qui sont beaucoup meilleures que celle de Clermont'. The report concluded emphatically: 'la province ... ne doit point entrer dans cette affaire de quelle manière que ce soit'.[118]

The negative reaction of the Etats was certainly predictable but d'Aguesseau was under orders to ensure that the manufacture was provided for and the Etats, having been informed by him that the King desired that 'cette manufacture ne tombât pas', reluctantly granted 70,000 *livres* – 40,000 as an immediate cash injection and 30,000 with which to buy wools for the following year in May. But to avoid the establishment of a precedent they recorded that this grant was only made 'par un pur devoir de plaire au Roy', and in a last attempt to avoid any involvement the King was sent a memoir which was particularly critical of the management of the concern – 'ceux qui l'entreprenoient n'estoient point marchandz et n'avoient pas la Connoissance qui leur estoit necess^{re} pour un establissement de cette qualité' – and warned, again, emphatically against either province or Crown becoming involved in 'une affaire dont l'événement est si incertain'.[119]

118. ADH C7214, Report of the deputies appointed by the Etats to investigate the affairs of Villenouvette, 10 Jan. 1682.
119. ADH C7214, 'Mémoire sur la manufacture de Clermont', 10 Jan. 1682.

This barrage of advice against supporting Villenouvette impressed Colbert and as a consequence at no stage was the manufacture to be nearer to closing than in 1682. Replying to a pessimistic letter from d'Aguesseau, Colbert agreed that it would be too great a burden for the province to buy all the buildings and entrust them to a new company. The money could be used more fruitfully elsewhere and instead he proposed that Villenouvette's looms should be transferred to Carcassonne. In this way, he said, 'tout ce qui est utile de cette manufacture peut estre facilement maintenu'. Venting his spleen against the extravagance of the associates he concluded a second letter with the statement that 'ni l'autorité du roy ni les secours des Estats ne doivent pas estre employés pour les sauver de cette ruine, laquelle ils se sont attirés par leur conduite peu prudente'.[120]

The royal manufacture of Villenouvette appeared to be condemned. Until August 1682 Colbert was relentless and d'Aguesseau was ordered to investigate the possibility of transferring its looms to Carcassonne.[121] During August, however, he changed his mind, almost certainly on the advice of Pennautier and a number of leading members of the Levant Company who stood to lose large sums from the collapse of the manufacture.[122] On their advice, it seems, he wrote to d'Aguesseau with another proposition in August 1682. The Etats should provide a loan of 100,000 *livres*, buy all the tools of the manufacture, pay an annual rent for the buildings to Pouget and pay a bounty of 10 *livres* for each piece of cloth produced, in addition to the bounty paid by the King. Saptes and Clermont would be run by one 'holding company' to which local merchants, prepared to invest 6,000–8,000 *livres*, would be encouraged to join.[123]

This proposition was extraordinarily generous. In fact it was quite unmatched by previous royal support for manufactures in Languedoc or, indeed, in France as a whole. D'Aguesseau was surprised both at Colbert's change of tune and at the generosity of the terms. He guessed what had happened and wrote on receipt of Colbert's instructions:

Je ne sais pas par quels canaux la proposition qu'il vous a plu de me mander par votre lettre ... a été portée mais je suis persuadé qu'elle vient originairement de M. de Pennautier, qu'il l'a concertée avec M. le Cardinal de Bonzy et quelques

---

120. Colbert to d'Aguesseau, 6 Feb., 26 March 1682 (Clément, *Lettres*, II, pt. 2, 729–30, 732–3).
121. Boissonnade, 'Colbert, son système', p. 23, and Cole, *Colbert*, II, 164. Cole cites a letter of early August which shows that Colbert was still planning to abandon Villenouvette.
122. Boissonnade, 'Colbert, son système', pp. 37–9.
123. Cole, *Colbert*, I, 165.

uns des principaux des états qui sont à Paris et par des vues particulières. Comme elle est très avantageuse pour ceux qui y prendront intérêt tout le monde y trouvera son compte. M. de Pennautier qui a sa part dans la manufacture de Saptes et qui est le premier mobile la soutiendra par cette union et se rendra maître de ces deux manufactures (ce que je ne puis m'empêcher de regarder comme un très grand inconvénient).[124]

Pennautier, as well as a major backer of the Levant Company and of the manufacture of de Varennes, was, with the Cardinal de Bonzi,[125] a leading member of the Etats. A weakening Colbert (he was to die within the year) was being pressurized into favouring a type of solution which it is highly unlikely that he would have adopted in his prime. The invitation to local merchants to join the venture was probably insincere. Those who were going to benefit from the immensely favourable terms were some of Pouget's and de Varennes's creditors, who would be assured of payment by formation of the new company, the Levant Company, which would be assured of a regular supply of cloth and, above all, the proposed associates in the new company – de Varennes, Jean-André Fredian and two Parisians, Pierre Thomé and Gaspard Hindret. The last two were unknown quantities in Languedoc but well known in the capital, coming from a restricted, elitest coterie of participators in Colbertian reforms and rich financiers. The former was among the richest men in France and held (at various stages in his career) a string of titles, offices and director-ships in important companies – 'écuyer', 'trésorier général des écuyers', 'conseiller du roi', 'fermier général des aides et domaines', 'trésorier des galères' and director of the Santo Domingo and second Guinea Companies. Notably ambitious, and the term had as yet no virtuous connotations, it was he whom public opinion considered La Bruyère was describing in his *Caractères* when he wrote of 'un homme d'un petit génie ... qui ne rêve qu'à une seule chose qui est de s'avancer ... est ce donc un prodige qu'un sot riche et accrédité'.[126] The latter was écuyer, seigneur de Beaulieu, and son of Jean Hindret, founder and director of the 'manu-facture royale des bas de soie du Château de Madrid', and had worked with his father in this concern.[127] Both had recently joined the third

---

124. D'Aguesseau to Colbert, 5 Sept. 1682, cited by Alberge, 'Villeneuvette', p. 23.
125. Pierre de Bonzi, bishop of Béziers, later ambassador to Florence, Venice and Warsaw, archbishop of Toulouse and ambassador to Madrid, and finally 'aumônier' to the Queen, and archbishop of Narbonne.
126. ADH 11 E 26 100, 15 July 1683; Chaussinand-Nogaret, *Financiers*, p. 110, n.1; Boissonnade, 'Colbert, son système', p. 43; C.-F. Lévy, *Capitalistes et pouvoir au siècle des lumières*, 11, 75.
127. ADH 11 E 26 100, 15 July 1683; G. Martin, *La grande industrie*, p. 55, n.1. Boissonnade, 'Colbert, son système', p. 44, confuses father and son.

Levant Company (together with Fredian) and this (and the exceptional terms proposed) would explain their interest in controlling Villenouvette.[128]

All that remained to be done was to get the Etats to accept the new terms but this they were far from enthusiastic about doing as Villenouvette's situation was deteriorating and the new terms would involve them in a very large expense. They had other grounds too for a lack of enthusiasm about the new proposals. None of the proposed associates was Languedocian. Three of them had never previously produced cloth. Two of them were completely unknown quantities and both of the other two, Fredian and de Varennes, had previously gone bankrupt. No security was to be provided for the province's advances. The proposed investment of 200,000 *livres* by Thomé and Hindret seemed inadequate, and the 10% rate of interest, which they were planning to grant themselves on capital used in the new company, excessive. Neither Thomé nor Hindret had yet arrived in Languedoc. Fredian had arrived but because of his previous involvement with the first Villenouvette company there were doubts about his status. No aspect of the affair seemed satisfactory.[129]

If they had been permitted to do so there is no doubt that the Etats would have turned the project down but before they had time to do so a dispatch was received from the Court demanding that a decision should be immediately reached which should not be other than 'Conforme aux Intentions de Sa Majesté'. They were advised that as the King knew 'parfaitement ce qui est avantageux à ses peuples ilz ne sçauroient prendre un meilleur party pour leur propre intérêt que de suivre aveuglement ses volontez'.[130]

The agreement was confirmed by a royal edict of 8 May 1683. The exact terms granted to the new company which had been formed at the end of the year 1682 were as follows. In return for a commitment to keep at least thirty looms in activity in each of the two manufactures, the four involved were to receive an interest-free loan of 130,000 *livres* repayable in six years: 70,000 of this sum was to go to Villenouvette and 60,000 to Saptes. Some 4,000–5,000 *livres* a year was to be paid in rent to the owner of Villenouvette (who continued to be André Pouget). Two *pistoles*

128. Chaussinand-Nogaret, *Financiers*, p. 105.
129. ADH C7214, Etats, 20 Nov. 1682. Hindret and Thomé were supposed to be coming south to Languedoc. Hindret was ill on the way but had arrived by Jan. 1683. Thomé had still not arrived by then but was present in Clermont in July 1683 (Cole, *Colbert*, II, 165–8 and ADH II E 26 100, 15 July 1683).
130. ADH C7214, Etats, 14 Dec. 1682.

of bounty on production were to be paid, one by the province and one by the King, and finally an annual grant of 6,000 *livres* was to be made for ten years out of the proceeds of customs paid at Lyons.[131] A week after the publication of this edict de Varennes, Thomé and Hindret pacted with the Levant Company for the sale of the two manufactures' production.[132] At vast cost Colbert's aims had been achieved and he seems, thus, to have died with the certainty that Villenouvette had been solidly established: 'je crois cette affaire entièrement terminée', he wrote to d'Aguesseau shortly before his death, 'et que cette manufacture sera en état d'augmenter le bien général de la province'.[133]

Effectively by means of this agreement Villenouvette and Saptes had become semi-public concerns. Saptes was to receive a large share of its working capital from the province and a sign of the new dependence was the establishment of what was termed a 'magasin de nantissement' at the manufacture as a security for the loan. Goods (consisting in wool and cloth above all) to the value of the amount loaned were kept permanently in this magasin which was supervised by a 'contrôleur' who also saw to the payment of the annual bounty on production. The contents of the magasin were declared in the proceedings of the Etats every year.[134] No such magasin was established at Villenouvette until after 1689, when a new company took the concern over, but a contrôleur was appointed as at Saptes[135] and the extent of the Etats' involvement in the concern was yet greater than in the case of Saptes for not only was a large share of circulating capital being provided but, by renting the buildings and tools at 4,500 *livres* a year from André Pouget, the Etats were also effectively providing the fixed capital to the new associates whose responsibility was thus limited to the provision of but a part of the necessary circulating capital. Cauvière, having visited Villenouvette in 1694, stressed the extensive advantages enjoyed by the director of 'un fonds de soixante à quatre vingts mil livres; une maison qui ne luj coûte rien ... [et] une pistolle par pièce'.[136] In return the Etats wanted at least recognition of their property rights. Consenting to an increase in the number of looms at Villenouvette in 1697 they ordered that 'il sera estably des magasins sur la porte desquels il sera mis un escriteau qui marquera que ce sont les magasins de la Province'.[137]

131. Boissonnade, 'Colbert, son système', p. 26.
132. G. Rambert, *Histoire du commerce de Marseille*, VI, 21, n.4.
133. Colbert to d'Aguesseau, 22 July 1683, cited by Alberge, 'Villeneuvette', p. 23.
134. ADH C7222, Etats, 21 Oct. 1683.
135. A post held by André Dupoivre (ADH C7248, 7277, Etats, Nov. 1689, 7 Dec. 1694). On Dupoivre see p. 112.
136. ADH C2200.
137. ADH C7285, Etats, 19 Jan. 1697.

On 15 July 1683 the new company took possession of Villenouvette. The major formality to be fulfilled was the purchase of the remaining stock of the old company – wools, dyes and cloth in various stages of production above all. Representing the old company on the occasion were André Pouget's brother, Honoré, Duffours, Fournier, Coste and Icher. Representing the new were Thomé and Fredian, and representing the major creditors of the old company (listed as Pennautier, Samuel Daliés, Jean du Noyer and Jean de la Porte)[138] was Joseph Prévost, bourgeois of Paris. The value of the stock had been estimated at 63,047 *livres*. Of this sum 57,000 *livres* was paid by a letter drawn on Thomé, payable at his 'domicile' in the 'rue neufve St Agustin', Paris, and a further 3,056 *livres* 8 *sous* by means of a letter of exchange drawn on Bertellet, 'caissier' of the Levant Company at Marseilles.[139] The industrial failure of Languedocian finance could hardly have been symbolized better than by this act of liquidation. The Company of Sète had been unable to help Villenouvette and was to be gradually dissolved during the years, 1683–7. Languedoc's role from now on was to be largely that of cloth-producer. The commercialization of its cloth was to be concentrated in Marseilles which, significantly, began in these years to enforce the monopoly element in its franchise. The revival and reconcentration of 'le grand commerce' of Marseilles was beginning.[140]

138. The notarial act registered on 15 July 1683 (ADH 11 E 26 100) records the titles of these distinguished financiers. Daliés was seigneur of La Tour and Embrun, a conseiller du roi and 'receveur général des deniers' of the Dauphiné; de la Porte was écuyer and 'conseiller sécrétaire du roi maison couronne de France et de ses finances'; du Noyer was conseiller du roi and 'trésorier général de France' of the 'généralité' of Paris. Daliés was also, like Pennautier, a director of the Levant Company (Masson, *Levant au XVIIe*, p. 183).
139. ADH 11 E 26 100, 15 July 1683; act of liquidation.
140. Dermigny, 'Armement languedocien', p. 254.

6

Villenouvette succeeds

At the famous Manufactory near *Nismes* in *Languedoc*, Cloths are made so
admirably well, that some have even thought they outdid the *English*; and
certain it is, they are very good, but want the Substance and Firmness and
Weight of the *English*. (*Atlas Maritimus Commercialis, etc.*, 1727, in
J. Smith (ed.), *Chronicon Rusticum-Commerciale; or Memoirs of Wool*, 2nd
edn, 1757, II, 206)

The initial reactions of local communities to royal manufactures were
generally unfavourable. 'Que de récriminations contre ces manufactures
nouvelles, mieux outillées, qui ... viennent s'ajouter aux anciens! Que
d'intérêts ligués contre elles!' Philippe Sagnac writes.[1]

This hostility was occasioned by a number of relatively predictable
factors. There was first an inevitable feeling of jealousy towards any
member of the local community favoured by the grant of a special
privilege and the donation of financial support. Quite suddenly such an
individual might find himself presented with exceptional and unprecedented economic opportunities denied to all others. In addition, a local
cloth industry would be likely to suffer from the competition of a new
manufacture's cloth and it would certainly suffer, as would all other
industrial and agricultural employers of labour, from the sudden extra
demands placed on the local labour market. Local food prices might rise,
at least temporarily. And what was probably most irksome of all was that
although the new concerns were, as it were, absorbing local factors of
production their fiscal privileges exempted them from paying certain
taxes. Effectively, thus, the local community's *real* level of taxation was
increased by a manufacture's foundation: its tax imposition remained the
same but it lost some of its tax-payers to the tax-exempt manufacture.
Clearly some social groups stood to gain from a manufacture's foundation – wage-earners, small-scale farmers who did not employ labour,
local shop-keepers, builders etc. It was likely to be members of the local

1. *La formation de la société française moderne*, I, 118.

elite who were most adversely affected: as employers of labour, and possible participators in the local cloth trade, they stood to lose economically from the foundations and to this economic loss was added a social threat: the wealth, resources, life-style, values and status of those involved in the privileged concern were likely to contribute to disturbing their hegemony in local communities. Ultimately it may have been the social threat which weighed most heavily. There were to be bitter arguments over claims to precedence over normal clothiers made by the directors of royal manufactures,[2] and the reaction to a director of the manufacture of La Terrasse, founded in 1698 in the diocese of Rieux,[3] was yet more direct. He was attacked by bourgeois from the local town of Carbonne when he was attempting to buy a leg of mutton in a butcher's shop. Complaining to the intendant about the incident he explained that 'La haine que les Bourgeois de Carbonne ont conçüe contre notre manuf*re* estant infinie Ils ne cessent pas de rechercher les occasions pour nous chagriner.' His attackers, depriving him of his mutton, had shouted that 'il ne falloit pas que cette canaille de la manuf*re* en Eussent et quil falloit les chasser hors de leur terroir'.[4] There were similar reactions to royal manufactures in northern France. A strike was fomented in Van Robais's concern at Abbeville, for example, by 'Les bourgeois et les ecclésiastiques, curés et chanoines, qui jalousent le privilège de la manufacture'.[5]

Local hostility to Villenouvette came to a head in 1680 when the consuls attempted to obstruct the enforcement of the right which the associates of the manufacture had been granted in 1679 to separate their land and buildings from the terroir of Clermont and create Villenouvette into a separate 'communauté', or village, with its own *compoix* and paying its taxes separately (Map 5).[6] Before this was done Clermont's consuls demanded that the lands on which the manufacture had been built should be re-assessed – the *compoix* had not been changed since 1646 when these lands had been assessed at a low rate – and made to support a larger share of the town's tax burden. The associates, in reply to this demand, argued that they had invested in Villenouvette on the assumption that it would continue to be taxed at the same rate as previously.

The issue was an important one and in the various petitions and counter-

---

2. ADH C5479, Letter from de Murat, 23 Dec 1730, pointing out that directors of royal manufactures have not been attending the 'assemblées générales du commerce' because of disputes over precedence.
3. ADH C7295, Etats, 5 Jan. 1699.
4. ADH C2123, Massiac to de Bernage, 11 Aug. 1720.
5. M. Courtecuisse, *La manufacture de draps fins Van Robais aux XVIIe et XVIIIe siècles*, p. 116.
6. Right granted by letters patent of 14 Aug. 1679, Appolis, *Lodève*, p. 132.

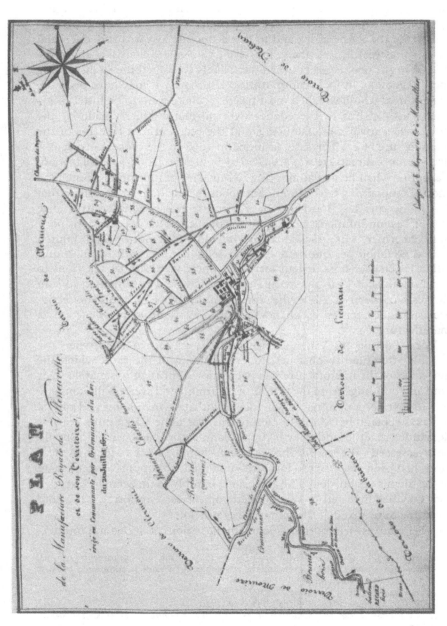

Map 5 Plan of estate, Villenouvette (ADH 1 E, Fonds Villeneuvette)

petitions which were presented by the interested parties to the Cour des Comptes, Aides et Finances (where the question was eventually settled in Villenouvette's favour) the hard feelings of both sides were expressed. The associates complained that the consuls 'par un esprict malicieux de Chicanerie ont mis en oeuvre toutes les Invantions quon puisse simaginer pour traverssez lesds. sieurs Inthéressez dans leur paizible jouissance'; that the request to make a new *compoix* had been made 'à dessaing de surcharger et augmenter sy fort les terres et Bastimants delad Manufacture pour leur donner subject dabandonner ... et les Ruyner entièrement, ce quy est une impertinance sçans exemple'; and that the request in question 'ne procède que de la malice desds sieurs consuls et particullièrement de celle du sieur Guintard [a rich landowner][7] premier diceux'.[8] Included in the consuls' petitions were most of the complaints which royal manufactures generally aroused. It was pointed out that the valley of the Dourbie, where Villenouvette had been built, had been transformed by the associates' investments:

il y a de toutes de mestiers et dartisans, plusieurs hôteleries et cabarets avec quantités de marshandz et de marshandizes lesd Intéresés ont faict déffricher mestre en jardins prairies ollivettes Vignes et en champs à semer du bled toutes les terres qui estoient demurés incultes ... Ilz entretienent plusieurs troupeaux de bestes à laine et autres. Enfin d'un dézert quy estoit inhabité et en friche il ny a pas quinze années ilz ont faict un gros bourg où ilz ce sont procurés des revenues très considérables.

By contrast, the consuls argued, the community of Clermont had lost considerably from the foundation:

il est mesme certain que la ville et communauté de Clermont a souffert souffre et souffrira à ladvenir un grand préjudice de ce nouvel establissement tant parce que plusieurs artisans hosteliers et Cabaretiers de lad ville ce sont allés establir aud lieu de Villeneuve que parce que tous les ouvriers quy avoient acostume de travailler dans la mesme ville de Clermont où il ce fabriquoit au paravant une très grande quantité de draps et autres marshandizes de laines sont allés travailler et demurer à lad manufacture.[9]

The nature of the consuls' case is clear: while the tax-paying ability of that part of their terroir in which the manufacture had been built had been greatly increased, that of the town had been commensurately

---

7. In 1710 Jean Guintard's tax-assessment was 271 *livres* 4 *sols* 6 *deniers*. There were only nine individuals assessed more highly than this. ACC CC14, *Milliaire* for the year 1710 (a *milliaire* was a list prepared each year on which, after analysis of the *compoix*, the tax due by each property-owner was entered). See Appolis, *Lodève*, p. 290.
8. Archive de la Manufacture, 'Minute d'acte pour ... les Inthéressés ... contre les consuls', 1680.
9. Archive de la Manufacture, 'Requête des consuls ... au Roy', 1680.

reduced. On these grounds they pleaded for an equitable redistribution of the town's tax-burden.

In both cases the statements are extreme – it was not pure malice which motivated the consuls, it is clear, and the consuls' attribution of all their town's difficulties to the manufacture, including the decline of their cloth industry, was far-fetched. But that there was friction, and good cause for friction, on both sides at this stage is evident. But with the settlement of this dispute and the creation of Villenouvette into a new and separate communauté, the relationship between town and manufacture would appear to have calmed. Villenouvette became an added curiosity in the varied Clermontais countryside, a popular destination for a Sunday walk,[10] but for a few years (it would seem) very much a separate, self-contained and isolated institution which impinged but little on Clermontais life. Indeed the enclosed design of the manufacture with its high walls and gates, the creation of Villenouvette into a separate village, the consecration of a chapel in the manufacture in 1678,[11] the establishment of a school[12] and the self-dependence in the production of food and clothing had the effect (and it was an intended effect) of isolating the manufacturing village and its occupants.

This enclosing of manufacturing was a new phenomenon and very much a reversal of previous traditions. We have seen, earlier, an example of the mediaeval treatment of industrial activity: artisans were intended to carry out their work under the public eye, in workshops which were so situated that they could be informally supervised from the street.[13] The only precedent for such an enclosing of manufacturing activities is provided by corrective poor-houses in which the poor were put to work; but they were put to work not so much for the sake of what they could produce as for the supposedly morally improving effects of industrial work in itself.[14] The justification for the type of enclosure of production at Villenouvette and elsewhere was primarily technological but there was conceivably a moral element in the experiment, too. It was, as we have seen, to 'infidélité' that France's industrial decline was attributed by some and it seems possible that it was believed that France's industrial

10. As it remains despite the decadence of its once fine gardens. The walk to Villenouvette was often combined with attendance at Mass at the chapel of Notre Dame de Peyrou, which is situated on the road to Villenouvette. A case before Clermont's seigneurial court illustrates this: ADH, Ordinaires Clermont, Case 113, 29 March 1769.
11. Archive de la Manufacture, order of Bishop of Lodève, 7 July 1678.
12. The presence of a school-master, Antoine Roussel, from the diocese of Vabres, is recorded in a notarial contract of 15 April 1700 (ADH 11 E 25 100).
13. See p. 32.
14. See, for example, C. D. H. Jones, 'Prostitution and the ruling class in eighteenth century Montpellier', *History Workshop. A Journal of Socialist Historians* 6 (1978), 14.

reputation could be recovered only by institutions such as Villenouvette in which there was moral, economic and physical control over the labour force.[15]

Whatever the ultimate purpose for the enclosure of their labour forces it was certainly within these isolated concerns of Saptes and Villenouvette that the effort to create a French cloth to rival that of the Dutch and English for both price and quality was made. Not until the 1690s was there very much initiative shown outside these two royal manufactures. Indeed the extent of the aid granted to these two manufactures had become an extra disincentive to the production of fine cloth (to add to the larger cost of such production and the technical difficulties). In 1694 Carcassonnais clothiers complained 'qu'ils ne pouvoient jamais entreprendre à faire de ces draps tandis que les entrepreneurs de Saptes et de Clermont auroint une pistole par pièce'.[16] So it is on this effort made in the royal manufactures that this chapter will focus. We have concentrated above all on the progress of Villenouvette and have grouped the problems which were confronted, and in the main solved, under the following broad headings: entrepreneurial, managerial, labour, technical and financial.

Entrepreneurial

Such colossal undertakings as the royal manufactures were bound to suffer from severe organizational problems, particularly shortly after their foundation. The manufactures were not developed and built up gradually, like the commerce of the normal merchant or clothier, but were large-scale concerns from their inception. Herman Freudenberger, in a study on privileged cloth manufactures in the Habsburg Empire, has demonstrated how Austrian manufactures faced difficulties for the same reason – royal pressure to expand production prevented a natural progression from small to large enterprise.[17] Colbert anticipated, and sympathized with, the sort of difficulties to which such rapid expansions of production gave rise. 'Tous les grands desseins ne peuvent pas réussir sans de grandes pertes dans les commancemens',[18] he wrote in 1670, and, as we have seen, d'Aguesseau likewise rationalized the difficulties experienced by Villenouvette to the Etats of Languedoc in 1681 in terms of 'la fatalité qui est attachée aux commancemens de toutes les grandes entre-

---

15. See p. 100.
16. ADH C2200. The bounty awarded on all fine cloth exported between 1667 and 1670 was no longer being paid. See p. 147.
17. 'The Brno Fine-Cloth Factory', p. 201.
18. Depping, *Correspondance*, III, 428, letter to ambassador in London, 4 July 1670.

Ill. 12. 'It is a taste for pomp and grandeur which almost always ruins the
manufactures of France': decorative fountain at Villenouvette

prises'.[19] But we have also seen that Colbert was less tolerant about
certain of Villenouvette's problems which were, as it were, self-created.
Pouget's and his associates' rebuilding of the manufacture after 1676 if
it left a marvellous monument for posterity did nothing to ease the
concern's liquidity situation. French entrepreneurs were often criticized
for a like extravagance. St-Fond, for example, travelling in England
in the second half of the eighteenth century, was struck by the simplicity
of English manufactures and commented that 'It is a taste for pomp
and grandeur which almost always ruins the manufactures of France'

19. ADH C7214, Etats, 3 Dec. 1681.

(Ill. 12).[20] This contrast in industrial architecture between the two countries was caused, above all, it is clear, by France's relative industrial backwardness with respect to England. Whereas in the latter country most industrial establishments developed naturally, being the product of market forces, and were thus created gradually and, inevitably, economically, French royal manufactures (and many concerns which were not royal manufactures) were not only built from scratch in many cases but were also conceived and planned by people who had often no previous experience of manufacturing activity. This, as we have seen, was the case at Villenouvette and, as a consequence, the manufacture bore the marks of its non-industrial creators. They created a 'model' manufacture but one with some unusual features. There were some resemblances to those massive poor-houses which, as we have noted, shared with Villenouvette the characteristic of enclosing industrial workers, but the manufacture also, with its farm-buildings, gardens, its 'beau pigeonnier couvert de tuilles acrochés en pavillon', its six 'grands degrés à repos' (which had cost 2,000 *livres* alone), its 'belle glazière de pierre' (another 1,000 *livres* this had cost), its herd of sheep (800 head), its two corn mills, its plantations of vines, mulberries, almonds, olives, figs, cherries, apples and chestnuts and its estate of some 900 *sétérées*, must have appeared to contemporaries as a most magnificent example of that central social institution, the *mas* or country estate.[21] And indeed, as we have seen, the manufacture functioned initially as both an agricultural and an industrial concern.[22] In 1682 the project which the associates presented to the Etats showed that they were anticipating making nearly as much profit from their estate as from their cloth-making.[23] This agricultural/industrial combination was intended primarily, we have seen, to contribute to the manufacture's self-dependence, but that it was also designed to make Villenouvette serve as a country house for the associates is suggested by the inclusion of a fine apartment for them overlooking the central square (the 'Place Louis XIV' from which branched the 'Rue Colbert'), and the attentions lavished on a private garden adjoining this apartment which was tended by a gardener brought from Montpellier.[24] Certainly Pouget treated the manufacture both as industrial concern and as country estate: like all city-dwellers with country properties he arranged for regular packages of produce to be sent to him in Paris. One of them included a consignment

20. Cited by S. Pollard, *The Genesis of Modern Management*, p. 64.
21. Archive de la Manufacture, listed in the description sent to Pouget in 1681.
22. Alberge, 'Villeneuvette', p. 34.
23. See p. 166.
24. ADH III E 181[1 bis], Act of 3 June 1677.

Ill. 13. Combination of rural and industrial: dovecot situated at the head of the
Rue de la Calade, leading to the Dourbie

of chick-peas.[25] The same attitude is apparent too in the formula which
the associates used to oppose an attempt by the consuls to impose more
taxation on them: 'il faut considérer lad. Manufacture comme une
maison par^{re} et les ouvriers comme de Domestiques'.[26]

But this attempt to make manufactures combine the roles of industrial
concern and country estate (Ill. 13) inevitably complicated managerial
problems and greatly increased the initial investment. The problem was
intensified yet further by the fact that the non-industrial backers of these
concerns were used to getting a very large return on their investments in
royal finances and expected a similar return on the money which they
advanced to the manufacture. When in 1684 the ex-associates tried to
disentangle their affairs they informed their two colleagues from Montpellier, Cambacères and Bosc, who had been appointed as 'arbitres',
that the financial affairs of the concern had been operated according to
what were, it is to be presumed, the norms operating in the service of
royal finances: Bosc and Cambacères were instructed 'de considérer que

25. ADH 1 B 10310, Pouget's accounts with manufacture.
26. Archive de la Manufacture, 'Inventaire des actes . . . devant . . . Cour des Aydes', 1680.

c'estoit icy une affaire de négoce; Dans laquelle les intérêtz ou changes des sommes empruntées ne devoient pas estre réglez suivant les ordonnances, Ny les parties justifiées avec la mesme exactitude que pour les affaires ordinaires entre particulliers, parceque cella se pratique autrement dans luzage de commerce'.[27]

Such heavy investment in stone, bricks, mortar and land, and such high interest charges on advances, were two reasons for the rapidity with which serious financial problems arose at Villenouvette and at other such manufactures and the difficulty of sorting these problems out was greatly increased by the fact that there was so little knowledge about the exact legal liabilities of the partners in such unprecedented concerns. As a consequence, financial problems were followed generally by long litigations between partners. Pollard has observed the often-repeated pattern – over-investment, large losses and then lengthy litigation.[28] And Villenouvette and Languedoc's manufactures were no exceptions to this rule. Indeed we owe to the phenomenon most of our knowledge about the province's manufactures because the novelty and cost of the judicial cases gave rise to their being transferred to the jurisdiction of the intendant, and as a consequence the intendancy archives have most exceptionally rich dossiers on these concerns.[29]

The memoir sent to Pouget in 1681 in which both the cost and the form of the manufacture were described also details the administrative structure which had been established. A director had been appointed 'pour donner des ordres' and eight sub-directors 'pour veiller en particulier sur chaque nature d'ouvriers'.[30] The position of director was clearly the key one. It was he who played the co-ordinating role. Such was his significance that his death or resignation was likely to cause an immediate loss of confidence in creditors and to precipitate bankruptcy or abandonment. The manufacture of Saptes, after the death of Noël de Varennes in 1691, came to a virtual halt,[31] and the deaths of the entrepreneurs of Grange-des-Prés[32] in 1706, and of Aubenas[33] in 1714 occasioned temporary abandonments: 'cette manufacture est abandonnée depuis la mort de Pelletan père', reported the Etats on the former occasion; 'la mort du

---

27. ADH 1 B 10310, A rate of interest of 10% had been charged on all sums advanced by any parties.
28. *Genesis*, pp. 28–9.
29. ADH C1123, 1124, 2202, on Saptes, Grange-des-Prés and Villenouvette respectively, C1277–84 on manufactures of La Terrasse and Auterive.
30. Archive de la Manufacture and Boissonnade, 'Colbert, son système', pp. 46–8.
31. ADH C1123, the nephew of Pierre de Varennes (a son of Jérosme most probably) who had succeeded to the direction in 1685 (ADA 9 C 23).
32. Founded in 1698 (ADH C7292, Etats, 23 Jan. 1698).
33. Founded in 1707 (ADH C7339, Etats, 20 Jan. 1707).

Sieur Pussant arrivée pendant le cours de cette année a fait cesser la manufacture', they reported on the latter.[34] From experience the Etats learned the importance of the director's role and in 1719, when it was proposed to change the direction of Villenouvette, they advised against it, observing that 'L'Assemblée a déjà éprouvé plusieurs fois dans cette manufacture, et dans les autres de la province combien le changement d'entrepreneur est dangereux.'[35]

The problem was a dual one – not only was the job itself a complex and delicate one but also there was a marked shortage of qualified candidates for directorships. The crisis occasioned by a director's demise was thus often prolonged by the difficulties met in finding a replacement. Roux de Montbel, 'syndic-général' of the Etats, entrusted in 1692 with the task of employing a replacement for Noël de Varennes could find no-one in the Carcassonnais. 'Jay cherché quelqun en ce pays icy et je nay pas trouvé . . .', he wrote to Basville, and he detailed the two men in Languedoc with the rare qualities which were needed and whom he was considering inviting to assume the position jointly: 'le Sr Plauchut[36] . . . qui connoist la bonté et la qualité des draps parcequil a esté longtemps commis à la marque, et dy mettre le Sr Vaudecourt[37] pour tenir les escritures homme entendu et qui prend soin de celles de la compagnie du Levant'.[38] There was evidently a scarcity of men with the capacity or disposition to undertake the direction of the new manufactures. The lack of capacity is explicable by the primitive state of local industries – they were not likely to produce men competent to direct such large and unprecedented establishments. Important too was the lack of inclination. Local clothiers were reluctant to relinquish their own businesses to assume direction of concerns which were prestigious perhaps, but which were notorious for their financial instability. Roux de Montbel, writing again to Basville in May 1692 when a new director had yet to be found, explained the difficulty: 'nous navons point de ressource à Carcassonne car il ny a point de marchand qui y veuille quitter son négoce'.[39] It was not just that Carcassonne's clothiers were reluctant to involve themselves with Saptes, they were actively hostile to the manufacture, because of its privileges. In his earlier letter de Montbel had commented on this

---

34. ADH C7292, 7318, Etats, 20 January 1707, 12 Dec. 1714.
35. ADH C7380, Etats, 30 Jan. 1719.
36. Brother-in-law of Pierre Sartre, an important financier, and with Pennautier a major creditor of Saptes. (ADH C1123; Chaussinand-Nogaret, *Financiers*, p. 45).
37. Or Baudecourt, Jean, a merchant from Castres, another major creditor of Saptes, and a Protestant (M.-L. Puech-Millau, 'Un marchand castrais au xviie siècle d'après ses archives, Pierre Albert 1633–1708', *Revue du Tarn* 5 (1936), 41).
38. ADH C1123, Roux de Montbel to Basville, 13 April 1692.
39. ADH C1123, Roux de Montbel to Basville, 4 May 1692.

antipathy which made the Carcassonnais unsuitable candidates for the directorship: 'les marchands de cette ville ny sont pas propres parceque leur intérest est que cette manufacture tombast'.[40]

As we have seen, one of the associates, Fulcrand Duffours, became director of Villenouvette in place of Pierre Baille in 1676. We have little information on his directorship but Duffours must have adapted reasonably well to his role for he was to carry on in his post under the new company formed in 1683.[41] In 1687 he was succeeded by Pierre Rostain de Berthellet who, like Jean Baudecourt, proposed as successor in 1692 to de Varennes at Saptes, had obtained his experience with the Levant Company where he was caissier in 1683.[42] He was followed by Pierre Barthe of Limoux in 1689, who was to be both director and owner of the third company to operate the manufacture.[43] Barthe died in 1694 and was replaced by his son Thomas for the period remaining of his contract with the Etats.[44] Thomas Barthe was replaced by three associates, Pierre Astruc, Gabriel Pelletan and Pierre Berthellet,[45] and in 1703 it was Pierre Astruc who took entire control of the manufacture until he was replaced by his son in 1720.[46]

This list of directors informs us of two important points. First, the shortage of directoral material was to a great extent solved by the end of the seventeenth century because the royal manufactures, and other 'Colbertian' concerns such as the Levant Company, were themselves turning out increasing numbers of suitable candidates. There were Baudecourt (who did not in fact accept the invitation to direct Saptes)[47] and Berthellet from the Levant Company, Plauchut (he refused the invitation as well) who was employed by the Administration as a cloth-

---

40. ADH C1123, 13 April 1692.
41. The last reference to him as director is in a notarial act of 12 May 1687 (ADH 11 E 26 124). He is described in this act as director and 'intéressé' and thus would seem to have had some stake in the second company.
42. He is described as caissier of the Levant company in a notarial act of 16 July 1683 (ADH 11 E 26 100); the first and last mentions of him as director at Villenouvette are made in acts registered on 1 Aug. 1688 and 8 May 1689 (11 E 26 125, 126).
43. The terms of his agreement with the Etats were approved in Nov. 1689 (ADH C7248) and his presence at the manufacture is first recorded by a notarial act registered on 5 June 1689 (11 E 26 126).
44. The concession was arranged in Pierre Barthe's will which was made on 8 Nov. 1694 and opened six days later (ADH 11 E 26 137).
45. The terms of their contract are recorded by a Montpellier notary (ADH 11 E 60 103, 22 Jan. 1697). It was the same Pierre Berthellet who had acted as director in 1688. Since 1688 he had been 'directeur de la monnoye' at Montpellier.
46. Astruc père died in that year though since 1714 his son had directed the concern (ADH C2200, Astruc fils to Etats, 24 Nov. 1720).
47. Though he was to become involved in the manufacture of *londres* at St-Chinian (ADH C2200, Report of Cauvière and see p. 222).

marker, Pelletan who had worked at Villenouvette since its origin,[48] and Thomas Barthe and Pierre Astruc, both sons of directors and presumably tutored by their fathers. Secondly it is apparent from this list of names that, with the exception of Pelletan, risen (as we shall see) from the ranks of the manufacture's salariat, directors continued to be men of some social distinction. Barthe and Astruc were both rich and well-connected merchants. The former had been first consul of Limoux and in this capacity he was actually present at the meeting of the Etats which authorized the terms of his new company.[49] One of his sons was a trésorier of Toulouse, another a captain of grenadiers in the regiment of Berry and he had a daughter married into the nobility.[50] He himself when he arrived in Clermont was referred to as bourgeois and as 'Maistre de la Manufacture de Villeneuve'.[51] Astruc was possibly of Clermontais origin;[52] a Montpellier merchant, he was previously involved in large-scale cloth purchases on behalf of the troops which were maintained by the province.[53] High rank, it would seem, was another essential qualification for the position of director in a community such as Villenouvette where both social and economic control was exercised over the labour force. That to this social and economic control was added a moral authority is suggested not only by the inclusion of a chapel within the enclosure of the manufacture (Ill. 14) and accounts of the manner in which Villenouvette functioned in the nineteenth century,[54] but also by evidence of a high priority given to religious matters by the directors. Pierre Barthe, for example, although only present in the Clermontais region for a few years before his death in 1694, evidently acquired a considerable reputation for good works. He is described as a 'bienfaiteur' in an act recording a contribution which he made to the Convent of the 'Pères Racolés' in Clermont and in August 1690 he ordered a new altar to be erected in the chapel of 'Notre Dame de Peyrou'. His own children had been given, it is evident, the strictest of religious upbringings. An act of 28 January 1690 records the surrender by one of his sons, Pierre-Antoine, 'clerc tonsuré' of Limoux, of his position as 'prébandier au chapitre et cathédrale' of 'Notre Dame' of Alet to his cousin Thomas who was already 'clerc tonsuré' in the parish of St Martin of Limoux. All the different roles of

48. First described as a 'résidant' of the manufacture on 2 Sept. 1677 (ADH 11 E 26 94).
49. ADH C7248, Etats, Nov. 1689.
50. ADH 11 E 26 137, 14 Nov. 1694.
51. ADH 11 E 26 126, 5 June 1689.
52. Astruc was a common Clermontais name and a Pierre Astruc, quite possibly *the* Pierre Astruc, was a 'marchand-garde-juré' in the town in 1674 (ACC BB1, 25 Feb. 1674).
53. ADH 11 E 60 103, 21 Jan. 1696, agreement between Astruc and André de Joubert, syndic of the Etats.
54. See especially Alberge, 'Villeneuvette' pp. 34–6, Baudrillart, *Populations agricoles*, pp. 267–9, and Reybaud, *La laine*, pp. 125–30.

Ill. 14. Spiritual life of the manufacture: main entrance to the chapel consecrated in 1678

these directors are revealed by their wills. Those of Barthe, Berthellet and Pelletan provide for religious foundations, house servants (two 'servantes' in the case of Barthe, a 'valet' in the case of Berthellet), miscellaneous members of the manufacture's labour force (a 'garçon tisserand' in the case of Barthe, the 'hôte' of the manufacture in the case of Berthellet), as well as, of course, for their own families. Pelletan's will contained a special instruction to the effect that he was to be buried in a chapel of Notre Dame de Peyrou 'laquelle chapelle mapartient'.[55]

55. ADH 11 E 26 127, 28, 31 Jan., 18 Aug. 1690, 11 E 26 137, 8 Nov. 1694, 11 E 25 100, 23 Jan., 21 March 1700.

Ill. 15. 'Logement des commis', Place Louis XIV

Managerial

The directors of royal manufactures were of sufficient importance to leave record of their existence in the correspondence of the controller general, in the intendancy archives and in the records of the meeting of the Etats. Details about the 'sous-directeurs', those appointed according to the memoir of 1681 'pour veiller en particulier sur chaque nature d'ouvriers', are not so easily found. Their role, however, was of undoubted importance and contemporaries, such as Adam Smith and Josiah Tucker, attributed the failure of large trading companies to the weaknesses of middle management. Tucker, for instance, in *A Brief Essay on Trade*, argued that large, privileged companies '*cannot* trade, *if they were so inclined*, upon so *easy* terms, as *private* Adventurers would do, were the Trade *laid open*. So many *Directors*, *Supercargoes*, *Storehouse-keepers*, *Factors*, *Agents*, *Clerks*: – and all the *Pickings* of their *several Dependants* ...'[56] The managers of Villenouvette were, therefore, a crucial, though largely undocumented, group. In default of other evidence the few sparse details revealed in the notarial archives must be used to give some idea of their origin, their role and their efficiency.

56. Cited by Pollard, *Genesis*, p. 24.

From Clermont's notaries the existence of at least thirty-five individuals of managerial status can be traced between 1674 and 1712 and there is, in addition, evidence of nine apprenticeship contracts for the position of marchand-facturier during the same years. Included in this sample are not only two sub-directors[57] but also others of similar status: eleven described as marchands,[58] three caissiés,[59] one financier,[60] one marchand-drapier, seven facturiers or marchand-facturiers[61] and three commis.[62] The profession of seven of the thirty-five is not revealed – they are simply described as 'résidants' (Ill. 15);[63] the types of contract in which they are involved, however, show them to be managerial rather than manual workers. Evidently represented are a variety of different managerial functions which do not seem to fit exactly into the tidy structure of command described to Pouget in 1681.

First, the origins: if the technical skills required for the manufacture of the new style of cloth were imported from Holland, whence the managerial skills required to discipline men, the commercial skills necessary to keep accounts and maintain correspondence, and the entrepreneurial skills necessary to co-ordinate the process of cloth production? Of the thirty-five the origins of twenty-five are revealed: seven were from Montpellier (though one of these seven was in fact a native of

57. Antoine Pagès, Louis Lavremejan, ADH 11 E 25 94, 11 E 26 98, 27 Aug. 1679, 17 Nov. 1681.
58. Fulcrand Bedos (ADH 11 E 26 95, 96, 26 March 1678, 16 Dec, 1679); Barthélemy Besancelle (11 E 25 100, 23 Jan. 1700); Paul Clavel (11 E 26 130, 26 April 1693, 11 E 26 148, 2 May 1710); Adrian Devic (11 E 25 95, 21 July 1681); Jean Irlandier (11 E 25 93, 27 April 1677, 11 E 25 98, 6 March 1695); Laurens Levieux (11 E 25 93, 27 April 1677, 11 E 25 98, 6 March 1695); Antoine Manié (11 E 25 93, 26 March and 24 June 1678); Jean Roux (11 E 25 100, 23 Jan. 1700); Jacques Desalasc (11 E 26 180, 3 Aug. 1719); Estienne Trial (11 E 25 98, 2 June 1697, 11 E 25 106, 16 Sept. 1702); Jean Roustan Villet (11 E 26 147, 3 Jan. 1709, ACCM H 182, 23 July 1698). These individuals are mentioned on many occasions, the references given identify profession, presence in manufacture, and, in most cases, dioceses of origin.
59. Pierre Fournier (ADH 11 E 26 96, 98, 16 Dec. 1679, 29 March 1681); Raymond Martin (11 E 25 95, 22 April 1682); Jean Pailhes (11 E 25 106, 18 June 1703).
60. Jean Cledon (ADH 11 E 25 93, 14 Oct. 1678, 11 E 26 99, 20 Dec. 1682).
61. Jean Cassagnan (marchand-drapier, ADH 11 E 26 137, 8 Nov. 1694); Jean Bonnal (11 E 25 106, 18 June 1703); Barthélemy Combettes (11 E 25 91, 15 Jan. 1674, 11 E 26 136, 29 Jan. 1693); Joseph Goudard (11 E 25 106, 18 June 1703); Géraud Gravié (11 E 25 98, 16 July 1696); Gabriel Pelletan (11 E 26 119, 2 Sept. 1677); Mathieu Pradier (11 E 25 100, 21 March 1700); Antoine Pouget (11 E 25 96, 6 Dec. 1692).
62. Jean Rigaud (ADH 11 E 26 138, 12 Dec. 1695, ADH C1124); Henri Sabatié (ADH C2135, report of Guilhaume Jean, huissier of Aspiran, 7 Oct. 1697). Tranercin (11 E 25 93, 10 Oct. 1678).
63. Jean Cusson, M. Lavigne, Raymond Moffre, P. Monlaur, Ignace Poussanel, A. Rey, B. Vinié (ADH 11 E 26 147, 1 Feb. 1708; 11 E 25 100, 15 July 1683; 11 E 26 125, 1 Aug. 1688; 11 E 25 100, 23 Jan. 1700; 11 E 26 134, 7 May 1691; 11 E 26 147, 1 Feb. 1708; 11 E 26 100, 14 April 1683).

Clermont),[64] eight were from Clermont, two from Lodève, two from Carcassonne, two from Limoux, one from Marseilles, one from Pézenas, one from Champagne, and one from a village in the diocese of Lodève.[65] It was certainly a wide recruitment area but not one which at first glance would seem to reveal any pattern of particular significance. When the details of professions are added to those about origins, however, a coherent recruitment scheme emerges which reflects the particular problems faced by the manufacture in securing the type of management it required.

The perfect manager would have been the genuine marchand-facturier or marchand-fabricant, a man acquainted with both the technical and the commercial aspects of cloth-making and accustomed to controlling a large labour force – the equivalent of the gentleman-clothier of England's West Country.[66] Such men, however, as has been seen, did not exist in or around Clermont at the end of the seventeenth century and were probably rarities within the province. The so-called marchand-facturier was closer to the situation of facturier or cardeur than to that of 'marchand'. Equally there were few commercially literate merchants in Clermont, the most distinguished members of the merchant profession having left for Lyons. So the manufacture could recruit facturiers in Clermont – and six of the eight Clermontais amongst the company's management were facturiers[67] – but they had to look elsewhere for the majority of their commercial skills and significantly the seven individuals who came from or via Montpellier were all merchants, with one exception, the financier. The Lodévois, apart from its facturiers, provided two of the caissiés of the manufacture, both from Lodève, and two merchants, both from Clermont. The seventh facturier was from Pézenas; another merchant came from Marseilles; Limoux, during Barthe's directorship, provided a commis and a marchand-drapier; Champagne's contribution was a military captain (described in 1681 as a directeur)[68] and the professions of the Carcassonnais and the inhabitant of a village of the Lodévois are not revealed. The major fact of significance to emerge from these details is

64. Jacques Desalasc, apprenticed 1689 to Pierre Astruc, future director of Villenouvette and then a merchant of Montpellier, worked at Villenouvette for ten years, after 1695. (ADH 11 E 26 126, 180, 23 Feb. 1689, 3 Aug. 1719).
65. Montpellier: Besancelle, Clavel, Cledon, Irlandier, Roux, Desalasc, Trial; Clermont: Bedos, Bonnal, Combettes, Gravié, Manié, Pelletan, Pouget, Pradier; Lodève: Fournier, Martin; Carcassonne: Cusson, Monlaur; Limoux: Cassagnan, Rigaud; Marseilles: Villet; Pézenas: Goudard; Champagne: Lavremejan; Octon: Vinié.
66. E. A. L. Moir, 'Gentlemen clothiers: a study of the organization of the Gloucestershire cloth industry, 1730–1835' in H. P. R. Finberg (ed.), *Gloucestershire Studies*, pp. 226, 239.
67. Jacques Desalasc, included amongst the 'merchants', was the son of the Clermont clothier Pierre Desalasc.
68. ADH 11 E 26 98, 17 November 1681.

that Villenouvette, in the absence of the perfect candidate for management, was forced to improvise, and whereas it was able to find men with cloth-making abilities amongst Clermont's clothiers, for its commercial skills it was forced to look elsewhere and above all to 'Montpellier ville marchande'.[69] It is probable that this makeshift combination of mercantile, cloth-making and military skills was difficult to co-ordinate during the early years of the manufacture's existence and contributed to the crisis through which the manufacture was to pass.

The variety of managerial functions exercised at the manufacture make it difficult to decipher the exact hierarchy of professions and the structure of command. Van Robais's manufacture in 1714 had a comparatively simple organization – Josse Van Robais (the original Van Robais's younger son) and three of his nephews directed the personnel and the workers, four commis looked after the correspondence and accounts of the manufacture, and ten 'contre-maîtres', the lowest category of management, supervised particular workshops.[70] This manufacture had been in operation for nearly sixty years, under continuous family management, and it had presumably refined and simplified its system of management. The situation at Villenouvette, however, was probably not very different. In the early years there were a director and at least two senior sub-directors,[71] who presided over the manufacture. When Pierre Barthe took over the direction he was assisted by his sons Pierre-Antoine and Thomas, and possibly Louis, another military captain.[72] The Barthes were followed by three associates, all of whom had a hand in the direction of the manufacture, and the last director during the first fifty years of the manufacture's existence, Pierre Astruc, was assisted by his son who eventually succeeded him. So throughout these formative years there were normally two or three individuals exercising the direction of the manufacture. Directly beneath them, at least in the early years when there was a clear distinction between those with commercial and technical skills, came those involved in the financial, mercantile, clerical and actuarial aspects of the manufacture. These activities, which involved skills of an exceptional nature at the end of the seventeenth century, would have enjoyed considerable prestige. It was significant that at least three members of this management group claimed to be bourgeois or

69. The title of L. J. Thomas's history of the city.
70. Courtecuisse, *Van Robais*, p. 103.
71. Pagès and Lavremejan.
72. Thomas took over the direction after his father's death; Pierre-Antoine's skills in cloth-making are demonstrated by his establishment of an independent concern in Clermont and his activities at Grange-des-Prés (see pp. 260–1); Louis was present at Villenouvette in 1694 and 1695 (ADH II E 26 137, 165, 27 Feb. 1694, 17 Feb. 1695).

sons of bourgeois.[73] Lastly there were the facturiers, the equivalent of Van Robais's contre-maîtres, involved in the actual direction of workshops. At the lower level of this category of management it is possible that we are dealing with purely manual workers, such as carders, who might have had a few spinners under their direction: the blurring of distinctions at Clermont has already been noted and a similar confusion is apparent at Villenouvette.[74] At the upper level there was the possibility of considerable responsibility: three facturiers or marchands-facturiers were directing all the weaving in the manufacture in 1681 and were entitled 'Régens et directeurs de la Bouthique et travalh des tisserans'.[75]

How efficient was this managerial team? Clearly the crisis which came to a head in 1681 was largely the result of the extravagance of the associates. The manufacture had certainly achieved its most essential role, the making of cloth, and had exported 454 pieces to the Levant in 1677, its first complete year under the direction of the new company.[76] There is, however, one significant piece of evidence which demonstrates that managerial incompetence contributed to the difficulties. The particular section of management incriminated is the higher-status group involved in the commercial and actuarial activities of the manufacture: keeping a check both on everyday running expenses and on the extensive improvements carried out to enlarge and beautify the manufacture was evidently too much for the caissiers and financiers, and the Etats turn out to have been entirely correct in their opinion, expressed in January 1682, that 'on ne pouvoit prendre nulle seûreté avec les Intéressez . . . et que le compte qu'ils faisoient estoit . . . incertain',[77] for the accounts of the manufacture were in such chaos that the associates, after the dissolution of the first company, had to call on the services of two of their colleagues from Montpellier to help sort out the manufacture's affairs and thus restore their peace of mind – 'leur procurer et à leurs familles le repos dont elles ont besoin', as their two colleagues expressed it.[78] In order to unravel the complicated accounts the two friends of the associates were

73. Clavel, Cledon and Fournier.
74. Thus Jacob Trintrop and Louis, his son, were referred to on occasions as facturiers or even marchands-facturiers (ADH II E 26 98, 29 March 1681, II E 25 98, 16 July 1696). Similarly François Briguibal, a cardeur, is referred to as a marchand-facturier in 1695 (II 25 104, 27 March 1695).
75. ADH II 26 98, 17 Nov. 1681.
76. Archive de la Manufacture, record of exports to the Levant, 1676–80.
77. ADH C7214, Etats, 10 Jan. 1682.
78. ADH I B 10310, Examination of the accounts of the manufacture. On the two colleagues, Cambacères and Bosc, see p. 151, n. 60.

assisted by one Estienne Courcelles, 'employé à tenir les escritures de la cie du Levant ... très entendu en ces matières'.[79] At the head of the account which they prepared with Courcelles's help they were forced to reveal that:

les livres delad. Manuffacture nont pas esté tenus avec toutte la regularité et lexactitude, qu'il eut esté à souhaiter, que les parties dont led. Estat sera composé ny estoient point couchées; que la plus grande partie des lettres de Change tirées par lad. compagnie sur le sieur Antoine Brutel banquier à Lyon en divers payemens, Balinier, et Consté de Paris, endossées par les Intéressez en lad. compagnie ont esté Egarées, que le Sieur gédéon Brutel Lun des principaux intéressez et quy avoit esté chargé de touttes lesd. lettres est absent, et qu'insy il n'estoit pas possible de dresser un compte aussy exact qu'on eut deubte fere ...

The apology which was made by the two friends of the associates was clearly a strong indictment of those involved in book-keeping at the manufacture. There is no similar piece of evidence to show inefficiency on the part of the managers involved in the direction of workshops, but one would imagine that their task must have been difficult, particularly in the early years, as they were dealing with men totally unused to such an organization of production and also unacquainted with the new cloth-making techniques. The title 'régans et directeurs' implies that these men had to play an instructive as well as a directive role,[80] both of which would have been arduous. The concentration of thirty-one looms in a single building was certainly an impressive achievement, and may have aided the supervision of the labour force, but it probably did not lead to comfortable working conditions and the confrérie founded in 1681 mentioned the problem of workers fighting, insulting each other and blaspheming.[81] The elaborate codes formulated by the Van Robais for disciplining the weavers' workshops in their manufacture give some idea of the managerial problems involved in dealing with a large labour force unaccustomed to working regular hours.[82]

Thus the shortage of suitably qualified personnel for management, and the unprecedented managerial problems encountered, were two major difficulties for Villenouvette. Both were gradually alleviated. The solution to the first was similar to the solution found to the shortage of qualified directors – just as Colbertian concerns trained suitable candidates for direction so they produced the genuine marchand-facturier

79. Courcelles and another clerk, Combes, were also ordered by d'Aguesseau to go through the books of the manufacture (ADH C2202).
80. 'Régent' usually meaning school-teacher.
81. ADH II E 26 98, 17 Nov. 1681.
82. Courtecuisse, *Van Robais*, 'pièces justificatives', pp. 135–42.

whose absence had originally contributed to their difficulties. These marchands-facturiers, with both commercial and cloth-making skills, came from three sources: apprenticeship, promotion within the factory and paternal training. There is evidence of nine apprenticeships for the position of marchand-facturier at Villenouvette during these years.[83] The contracts stated that the apprentices were to be taught 'Louvraige et faction des draps' or the 'faction et fabrique des draps quy se font journelement en la Manufacture', and were to obey 'ausd. mestres facturiers delad. manufacture'.[84] Yet it was not purely the profession of facturier, as exercised at Clermont, that these apprentices were to be taught. Firstly they paid far higher apprenticeship fees than their Clermontais counterparts – merchants' apprenticeship fees of between 100 and 400 *livres*[85] – and secondly they themselves were not from artisanal backgrounds. Among the parents of the nine were a bourgeois, an advocate, a conseiller du roi and 'receveur du scel' at Carcassonne, a merchant from Carcassonne and a priest who apprenticed his brother-in-law.[86] These distinguished apprentices were likely to have been taught by both the merchants from Montpellier and the facturiers from Clermont and this awkward combination of merchant and clothier was clearly capable of producing healthy offspring, for the true marchand-facturier was trained within the manufacture. The best example of this was Gabriel Pelletan, who was eventually to become one of the directors and associates. He was of the most humble origin: his sister was married to a weaver and his poverty is attested by the fact that he had property seized in Clermont in 1671 in default of payment of 441 *livres* for wools.[87] Gradually he worked his way up through the hierarchy of Villenouvette's management: described simply as facturier before he joined the manufacture and when he was serving there in 1677 and 1679, he was one of the three 'régans et directeurs' of the manufacture's weavers in 1681 and in the same year he was referred to as marchand for the first time.[88] In 1688

83. Guillaume Almeras, Joseph and Hillaire Tudesq (ADH II E 25 92, 3 Nov. 1676); Jean Anterrieu (II E 26 98, 7 Aug. 1681); Jacques Baffiés (II E 26 103, 15 Sept. 1686); François Bourg (II E 26 105, 15 Sept. 1688); Jean-Gaspard Léotard (II E 26 140, 10 Oct. 1697, II E 25 107, 2 April 1704); Antoine Raissac (II E 26 139, 142, 9 July 1696, 29 April 1700); Jean Verny (II E 26 100, 15 July 1683).
84. ADH II E 25 92, 3 Nov. 1676, II E 26 98, 7 Aug. 1681.
85. 100 livres paid by Almeras and the Tudesq brothers, 400 by Léotard.
86. The fathers of the Tudesqs, Léotard, Baffiés and Raissac. The brother-in-law of Anterrieu.
87. ADH II E 26 108, 10 June 1667; II E 25 89, 21 Nov. 1671.
88. ADH II E 26 119, 2 Sept. 1677; II E 25 94, 23 June 1679; II E 26 98, 17 Nov. 1681; II E 25 95, 11 July 1681.

and 1689 he was referred to as inspecteur of the manufacture and as a 'marchand & intéressé',[89] in 1693 as a 'marchand-bourgeois' and finally in 1697 as directeur général.[90] Pelletan had worked his way up from the lowest managerial position to the directorship and even so august a body as the Etats of Languedoc recognized his merits as a 'fort bon facturier'.[91] His rise was yet more remarkable than that of Jean Hogenbergh at Van Robais's manufacture, described by Josse Van Robais as 'leur principal contremaître, qui ... ne doit qu'à son mérite remarquable l'avantage d'être à la tête de 43 métiers'.[92] Pelletan's case is the most impressive but other Clermontais were to gain an equally valuable experience at the manufacture. Thus both by apprenticeship and promotion within the manufacture highly qualified managers and directors were obtained. The third source of such managerial talent has already been mentioned: two sons of directors were to succeed their fathers in the direction of Villenouvette and a third was to be the first director of the royal manufacture of Grange-des-Prés.[93]

Thus the manufacture had succeeded in training within its own walls the type of management it required, and the task of this newly trained management was gradually eased, too, as the manufacture's population became more settled and accustomed to the new way of life. The managers of the first associate had had not only to keep a check on the labour force but to administer a large estate, provide all the food for the manufacture's labour force and also, it is to be presumed, supervise the massive construction projects of Pouget and his partners. After 1683 there was no more building done and no more estate to be administered by the manufacture's management (the estate was still owned by Pouget);[94] thus the problems of management were immediately simplified. Also, to an increasing extent, managerial responsibilities were sub-contracted – no longer were the managers to have the complete responsibility for each individual and each individual process at the manufacture. From June 1679 the task of providing the manufacture with cards was sub-contracted to two independent card-makers from

89. ADH II E 26 125, 126, 14 July 1688, 27 Feb., 1 May 1689. The titles 'inspecteur' and 'intéressé' pose some problems. The former may signify that he acted as the first contrôleur for the manufacture on behalf of the Etats, before André Dupoivre took over (see p. 170, n. 135). The latter may signify that a cloth manufacture Pelletan was founding in Clermont during these years was in partnership with the associates (see pp. 272–4).
90. ADH II E 26 130, 4 Oct. 1693, II E 25 98, 2 June 1697.
91. ADH C7292, Etats, 23 Jan. 1698.
92. Courtecuisse, *Van Robais*, p. 116.
93. Thomas Barthe, Pierre Astruc and Pierre-Antoine Barthe.
94. See p. 170.

Clermont and their employees. These card-makers were to be given a
rent-free room at the manufacture and free food and were to supply cards
for three years at fixed prices and with complete regularity 'affin que les
ouvriers ni puissent donner en Chaume, ni le travail reculle'.[95] Card-
making was the only process which the notaries record as having been
sub-contracted by the first associates. The directors of the succeeding
companies followed this precedent for card-making[96] and sub-
contracted other duties as well. Thus in August 1684 Jean-André
Fredian, present in Clermont, sub-contracted to Hillaire Tudesq (an
apprentice to the manufacture in 1676), for a payment of 500 *livres* a year,
the monopoly of selling food in the manufacture as well as the duty of
looking after the director's horse. Tudesq was to have the right to use the
manufacture's ice-pit but was to supply fourteen pounds of ice daily from
the pit to the company between 15 May and 15 October. He was also
obliged to carry all merchandise to and from the manufacture for a fixed
daily fee.[97] Other minor duties sub-contracted were the operation of the
manufacture's grain mill and bakery and the duty of providing the
manufacture with tallow for the purpose of dressing wool.[98] Both these
tasks had previously been attended to by the company's management.[99]
But important though these examples are perhaps the most crucial development in easing the problems of management was the incorporation of
the family economy within the manufacture. As the labour force settled
down at Villenouvette and married or brought their families from their
towns of origin the manufacture became a community of families, forming so many productive cells, rather than being composed of seven
hundred individuals. Villenouvette became a manufacturing village
rather than a factory and the management was automatically helped in its
tasks by heads of families, school-teachers and priests. The unit of
production was not necessarily within the family as a worker's wife or
child might be working in a different section of the manufacture but an
informal system of masterships in all the different professions was established, and each master took the responsibility of hiring and training his
own apprentice or 'compagnon',[100] who formed part of his household

95. ADH ii E 25 94, 23 June 1679.
96. ADH ii E 26 137, 21 Dec. 1694.
97. ADH ii E 26 101, 14 Aug. 1684. Hillaire Tudesq was one of the apprentice marchands-
    facturiers. His involvement in providing food for the manufacture demonstrates the
    increasing flexibility of management. By an act of the same day he had rented Pouget's
    estate around the manufacture for five years.
98. ADH ii E 25 99, 98, 9 July 1698 and 28 Nov. 1697.
99. Thus by a contract of 12 Aug. 1682, Jean Ombras, 'mangonier' at the manufacture,
    purchased fat and grease from butchers at Sairas on behalf of the associates (ADH ii E
    26 99).
100. The equivalent of the English journeyman.

and was clothed, fed and sometimes paid at his expense.[101] In addition, in 1681, the weavers formed a confrérie which not only created collective responsibility for good behaviour in the large weaving workshops but also established a regular system of mastership.[102] These developments applied equally to the cloth-finishers and dyers, who were referred to as masters after a certain number of years and who, like the weavers, received apprentices or employed compagnons. In addition there would seem to have been promotion of the most skilful and competent from within the ranks of workers, and those promoted assumed positions of responsibility. Estienne Maysonnade, for instance, was referred to as 'maître-teinturier-en-chef' and presumably exercised some control over the crucial dyeing processes.[103]

The spontaneous development of the family unit within the manufacture, and of the organization of production on the basis of masters, apprentices and compagnons or journeymen, had the result of greatly diminishing the responsibilities of management. A similar structure had developed at Van Robais's manufacture where, as Coornaert writes, 'chaque atelier y forme une unité distincte, comme un atelier artisanal ... les ouvriers y gardent des usages de caractère nettement archaique: droits d'apprentissage ... confrérie corporative, etc.'.[104] The result of these developments was that Villenouvette was eventually to differ very little from normal manufactures which operated a putting-out system on a fairly large scale, the 'usines dispersées' described by Charles Gide.[105] Effectively what was being created was a usine dispersée, but one dispersed within a very small area, within the walls of a single village. A memoir of 1748 showed how simple a managerial and organizational structure eventually developed. The memoir contained a list of all the inhabitants of the manufacture: there was a director and only two commis or assistants who composed the management, and otherwise there was a long list of masters' families in which were included journeymen and apprentices.[106]

101. Thus on 27 April 1692 a master-weaver agreed to employ and feed a 'garçon-tisserand' for two years and to pay him 15 *livres* 'à mezure que led. garçon en aura besoin' (ADH 11 E 26 135).
102. ADH 11 E 26 98, 17 Nov. 1681. It should be emphasized that the weavers worked in the large workshop housing thirty-one looms, which was described in 1681, and not in their homes during this period. This is clear from the report of Cauvière in 1694 (ADH C2200).
103. ADH 11 E 26 134, 12 August 1691.
104. E. Coornaert, 'Les "manufactures" de Colbert', *Information Historique* 11 (1949), 4.
105. C. Gide, *Cours d'économie politique*, pp. 183–7.
106. Archive de la Manufacture, 'Etat des familles que nous avons dans l'Enclos de la Mre Royale ...' 22 April 1748. It should be mentioned that the manufacture was only operating twenty-one looms at this date.

As the organizational structure of the manufacture was simplified the actuarial problems faced by the management decreased. In contrast to the financial confusion under which the first company had laboured Pierre Barthe, on his death-bed, could confidently predict his likely profits for the three years remaining of his contract with the Etats, and adjust his will in accordance.[107] With the manufacture functioning efficiently the directors could afford to extend their activities outside its walls and Barthe and his successors were to operate looms in Clermont and Aspiran.[108] Pierre Barthe even had the confidence and enterprise to cheat the Etats and the Crown who were so generously paying him a bounty on his production; he purchased cloth at St-Chinian, St-Pons and Limoux, only having it finished and dyed at Villenouvette, but claiming his reward as if it had been made there.[109]

Labour

These problems of direction and management were originally secondary to the most basic of all the difficulties faced by the royal manufacture – the creation of a trained labour force. Dutch workers, as has been seen, played an important role in the introduction of the new cloth-making techniques, both at Saptes and Villenouvette, and these pioneers were followed in later years by more of their compatriots; Pennautier reported the arrival of seventeen Dutch workers at Saptes in 1691.[110] Their recruitment was clearly an essential part in the equipment of the royal manufactures; equally essential, however, was the recruitment of French workers, to whom the new methods could be taught. Villenouvette had seven hundred workers by 1681.[111] Saptes was employing approximately six hundred by the early 1690s,[112] and although both manufactures probably possessed nuclei of a labour force before the great expansion (Villenouvette in the form of Baille's employees at Clermont, and Saptes in the form of the employees of the company which preceded de Varennes),[113] these nuclei were evidently not sufficient, for it was not by

---

107. ADH 11 E 26 137, 138 14 Nov. 1694, 17 Dec. 1695: a maximum profit of 27,000 *livres* was anticipated.
108. ADH C2200, Memoir of Cauvière, 1694 and ADH C2135.
109. ADH C2200, Memoir of Cauvière, 1694 and ACCM H181, *contraventions* at the 'bureau de marque' of Marseilles, 16 March 1695.
110. Pennautier to de Pontchartrain, 30 October 1691 (A. M. de Boislisle, *Correspondance des controleurs généraux avec les intendants*, 1, 977n.).
111. Archive de la Manufacture, memoir of 1681.
112. Fontvieille, 'Les premières enquêtes', p. 1125: enquête of 1692, 500–600 workers at Saptes.
113. Boissonnade, 'Colbert, son système', p. 47.

apprenticeships, the normal form of industrial recruitment, that the new labour force was built up, but by the attraction of trained cloth-workers from other parts of the province and other areas of France. The small role played by apprenticeships in the early years of the existence of Villenouvette is demonstrated by the fact that between 1674 and 1681, the years during which the labour force expanded most rapidly, there were only nine apprenticeships to the royal manufacture recorded in the registers of the Clermont notaries.[114]

The founder of a manufacture at Auterive in the diocese of Toulouse in the 1720s, who faced similar problems to those experienced by the directors of Villenouvette, described how he set about recruiting his labour force in a memoir sent to the intendant.[115] Unskilled workers, for spinning and sorting wool, he secured locally. These were all women or children, and were probably previously under-employed. He described them as follows: 'les unes d'une honnête naissance, les autres infirmes par leur âge, les autres d'un âge fort tendre quy sont les enfans de 7: jusqu'à 10 et 12 ans le reste des Fileuzes propres à autre choze sont d'une très petite conséquence'. The second category of semi-skilled workers, cardeurs and cardeuses, he secured in part from the town of Auterive, where there already existed a primitive cloth industry, and in part from other parts of the province. The third category of skilled workers, weavers, shearers, cloth-dressers, cloth-pressers and dyers, whom the director described as 'artizans distingués', had had to be secured from further away – 'de toutes les Provinces à gros Fraix'.[116]

Did Villenouvette have a pattern of recruitment similar to that outlined by the director of the manufacture at Auterive? Unfortunately none of the company's directors left an explanation of how he overcame his recruitment problems and there is no easy source from which to trace the origins of the labour force.[117] Again the notarial archives have to be used. A variety of different contracts reveal the presence at the manufacture of

114. From the notarial registers of Villar, Pons and Delpon for these years, ADH 11 E 25 91–5, 11 E 26 91–98, 118–21.
115. The founder was Marcassus, and the manufacture was to be made into a royal manufacture in 1729 (AN F12 645, 'Mémoire sur le commerce du Levant'). Marcassus was probably the most renowned of Languedoc's clothiers and earlier, in 1711, he had taken over the direction of the manufacture of La Terrasse, previously known as the manufacture of Rieux (ADH C7389).
116. ADH C2127, Memoir of 5 May 1726, sent to de Bernage.
117. In this survey of the labour force I have not made use of the parish register of Villenouvette and Mourèze (ADH 111 E 181[1 bis]) which was not available when I was carrying out my research. Details of Dutch and German workers I have taken from Alberge, 'Villeneuvette', p. 32, and also from notarial contracts. Alberge either had access to the Villenouvette parish register before it was deposited in the departmental archives or used a copy of it kept in the manufacture.

workers who had not previously registered contracts of apprenticeship and who, therefore, it must be presumed, arrived at the manufacture already trained in their particular skills. These contracts sometimes reveal only the name of the worker, sometimes his name and his profession, and sometimes his name, profession and town of origin and even the number of years he had served at the manufacture. By a close examination of all the notarial registers between 1674 and 1712 a large number of people who served for shorter or longer periods at the manufacture are revealed and from these an impression can be obtained of the areas from which different categories of workers were recruited. It is an impression only, however, it must be stressed, as the names have been selected over a period of thirty-nine years and there is no way of calculating how representative the sample is of the total labour force employed at the manufacture during these years.

Apart from the directors and the thirty-five people whom we have characterized as management there is evidence in the notarial registers of at least 224 individuals who were at work at the royal manufacture between 1674 and 1712. Of these 224, the origins of 172 and the professions of 206 are recorded and both the origins and the professions of 156. Twenty-four of the 224 were women.[118] The 206 professions are divided as follows: eight Dutch and Germans, who were instructors in the new techniques, six dyers, thirty-five shearers and cloth-dressers, ninety-six weavers, twelve carders, two operators of twisting machines, two card-makers, twenty-four women who were spinners and domestic servants and twenty-one miscellaneous professions ranging from gardeners, shepherds and apothecaries to 'pâtissiers', shoemakers and chaplains.

Before exploring the origins of the workers in each of these categories and seeing whether a recruitment pattern existed similar to that observed at Auterive an initial sample can be provided by analysing the origins of the forty workers present at the foundation-meeting of the manufacture's confrérie in 1681. The sample has the advantage that all those mentioned were present at the same time in the manufacture. The meeting was presided over by a director and three sub-directors, and forty workers attended, thirty-nine of them weavers and one a cloth-dresser.[119] The dioceses of origin of twenty-seven of the forty workers can be traced. There were eleven from Clermont itself, eight from the diocese of Carcassonne, two from the dioceses of Alet and St-Papoul to the west of

---

118. In fact there are many more female occupants of the manufacture named in notarial acts but their professions and origins are rarely specified.
119. ADH II E 26 98, 17 Nov. 1681: Lavremejan, Hillaire and Joseph Tudesq and Gabriel Pelletan. The Tudesq brothers were apprenticed to Villenouvette on 3 Nov. 1676 (II E 25 92). Mézas, the cloth-dresser, was from Trèbes, close to Carcassonne.

Carcassonne, three from Narbonne, one from St-Pons and two from much further away – from Arras and Münster in Germany. From these details it can be seen that Clermont's depressed cloth industry was fertile recruiting ground for the manufacture and that, apart from Clermont, it was the diocese of Carcassonne and its hinterland which was making the largest contribution.

This initial sample already shows that Villenouvette was securing its 'artizans distingués' from some distance, although it was drawing a significant number of workers from Clermont's cloth industry. The analysis by individual professions reinforces this initial impression. Of all the manufacture's labour force the dyers were undoubtedly those with the most sought-after skills. The importance of the dyer's art in the selling of cloth in the Levant was crucial, as shall be seen, and the chief dyers would certainly be more aptly grouped within the management of the manufacture.[120] There are six dyers mentioned during these years. Two were the sons of the solitary dyer of Clermont, Jean Maysonnade,[121] one, Vital Bernard, was the son of a notary at Lyons,[122] one was from Carcassonne,[123] one from Montesquieu in the diocese of Rieux, to the west of Carcassonne,[124] and the last arrived with Pierre Barthe in 1689 from Limoux in the diocese of Alet.[125] The professions closest to the dyers' in distinction were those connected with the finishing of the cloth: shearing, dressing, pressing and fulling. The thirty-five individuals who performed these tasks have been treated as a single group (twenty-five of them are referred to as tondeurs, two as fullers, five as pareurs, two as 'planquets'[126] and one occasionally as tondeur and occasionally as 'marchand-affineur'). Of the thirty-five the origin of twenty-seven is revealed and Carcassonne and its hinterland accounted for exactly two-thirds of this number (Carcassonne, twelve; Mirepoix, two; Pamiers, two; Alet, one; St-Papoul, one). The dominance of Carcassonne is even more marked than with the initial sample of weavers and those coming from Carcassonne's west had probably in most cases worked at Carcassonne before reaching Clermont. This was certainly the case with Antoine Bartes, a shearer from the diocese of St-Papoul, who declared when he married in 1677 that he had lived nearly thirteen years in Car-

---

120. The dyers were eventually referred to as marchands-teinturiers. The activities of Estienne Maysonnade give some idea of their resources and status, see p. 266.
121. Pierre and Estienne Maysonnade, ADH 11 E 26 137, 134, 27 Feb. 1694 and 12 Aug. 1691.
122. Vital or Victor Bernard, ADH 11 E 26 126, 24 Jan. 1689.
123. Jean Bouissede, ADH 11 E 26 124, 13 June 1686.
124. Philibert Peiron, ADH 11 E 25 165, 17 Feb. 1695.
125. André Massiac, ADH 11 E 26 126, 24 Jan. 1689.
126. A meridional term for cloth-dresser.

cassonne before coming to Clermont.[127] Of the remaining nine, five were from Clermont, two from the diocese of St-Pons, one from Mazamet in the diocese of Castres and one from Narbonne. Thus the dyers and cloth-finishers, with one exception, came from within the province of Languedoc, but from distant dioceses, and certainly from areas which were far removed from Clermont's normal migratory sources. What brought the solitary Lyonnais, Vital Bernard, to Clermont? By chance the link is revealed in this stranger's marriage contract in 1689. Present at the signing of the contract was Antoine Noudard, a Clermontais shearer who had left Clermont to work in Lyons before returning to take up employment at the royal manufacture. He attested to Bernard's Lyonnais origin and added that he had 'mangé et Beu avec luy souventes foix dans laditte ville de Lion maizon et bothique du Sr Bernard mar^t teinturier dud Lion son fraire travailhant ensemble'.[128] Bernard was obviously the younger son of the family and having been told by the Clermontais Noudard of the royal manufacture founded at Villenouvette had decided to try his fortune there.

Finally the weavers, the least skilled of the 'artizans distingués' (Map 6): the diocese of origin of sixty-two of the total of ninety-six is revealed in notarial registers.[129] A large share of this number came, once again, from Carcassonne and its hinterland – twenty-two from the diocese of Carcassonne itself, two from Alet and one each from Mirepoix and St-Papoul but a larger share than in the case of the previous categories came from Clermont itself and neighbouring cloth-making towns: Clermont provided twelve of the group and a further fourteen were provided by cloth centres to Clermont's west: Bédarieux and Roquebrun (Béziers), seven; St-Pons and St-Chinian (St-Pons), five; Lacaune (Castres), two. Of the remaining ten, one was from an agricultural village, bordering Clermont, in the diocese of Béziers, six were from the diocese of Narbonne, and one each from the dioceses of Alès, Vabres and Arras. Carcassonne and Saptes again played a considerable role in manning Villenouvette. The role of Saptes is revealed not only by the fact that seven of the twenty-two Carcassonnais were born in Conques but also by an incidental piece of information which is again provided by a marriage contract. A weaver from Carcassonne who had been working at Villenouvette for three years married in 1687 and two of his fellow-workers and compatriots attested to his Carcassonnais origin, one of them adding that he had actually taught the man in question to weave at

---

127. ADH II E 26 94, 8 Aug. 1677.
128. ADH II E 26 126, 24 Jan. 1689.
129. Included in this number are the thirty-nine weavers present at the establishment of the confrérie in 1681.

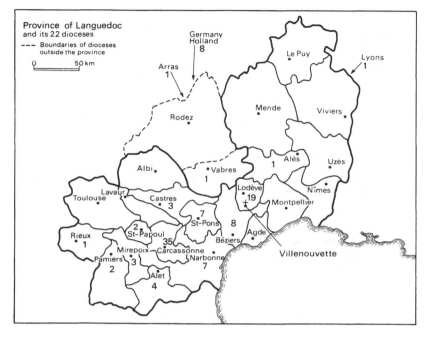

Map 6   Origins of 103 'artisans distingués' at Villenouvette

Saptes.[130] The greater ability of Clermont and neighbouring small-scale cloth producers to supply weavers rather than other categories of specialized workers is fully understandable in view of the structural change which had occurred in the local industry as a consequence of the depression. As we have shown, the groups of workers most affected, and thus most reduced in quantity, were those involved in the costly and specialized finishing processes.

The other categories of male workers which remain to be analysed include carders, operators of twisting mills, card-makers and a variety of secondary professions. There were two operators of twisting mills, both of them from Carcassonne. The two card-makers who worked at the manufacture both came from the ranks of Clermont's artisans. The origin of ten of the twelve carders is revealed. This last is a category of worker of some significance as the carder was not an 'artizan distingué'

130. ADH 11 E 26 124, 19 March 1687. The movement was not in one direction only. There were several examples of workers from Villenouvette leaving for, or returning to, Carcassonne, e.g. Antoine Ramel who returned to Conques after nine years at Villenouvette (11 E 26 127, 24 Jan. 1690).

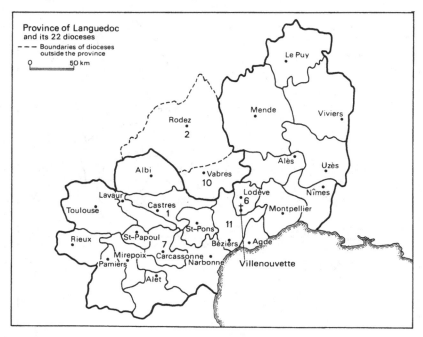

**Province of Languedoc
and its 22 dioceses**
– – – Boundaries of dioceses
outside the province
0 _____ 50 km

Le Puy

Mende

Viviers

Rodez
2

Alès

Uzès

Albi

• Vabres
10

Lodève
6

Nîmes

Lavaur

Castres
1

Montpellier

Toulouse

St-Pons

11

Rieux

St-Papoul
7

Béziers

• Agde

Mirepoix
Pamiers

Carcassonne

Narbonne

Villenouvette

Alèt

Map 7   Origins of 14 less-skilled, and 23 female, workers at Villenouvette

but a worker likely to be available locally, and just as the majority of the manufacture's facturiers came from Clermont's industry so the majority of its carders came from another local industry, that of Bédarieux: five of the ten were from there, one was from Clermont, one from the diocese of Vabres and three from Carcassonne. As was the case with the weavers, a higher proportion of the less-skilled professions could be recruited locally (Map 7). As for the miscellaneous professions, no coherent migratory pattern is likely to emerge, though certain employees with specialized skills did, as was to be expected, come from areas in which those skills were common. There were, for instance, two shepherds and a school-teacher from the Vabres, an area of large sheep herds and also one from which a large proportion of Languedoc's teachers was invariably drawn.[131] There were in addition a gardener from Nîmes, a centre of market-gardening, two bakers from Lodève, an innkeeper, an apothecary, a marchand-droguiste and a pâtissier from Clermont, a shoe-maker from Béziers and a governess from Bédarieux. The information gives

131. E. Le Roy Ladurie, *Paysans*, p. 129, notes this phenomenon.

some idea of the variety of professions at Villenouvette – it was a complete manufacturing village – but the only detail which adds to our knowledge of the technological links between the manufacture and elsewhere is the fact that one of the two carpenters employed at the manufacture came from Conques. Present at the manufacture in 1683 it is possible that he had learned the art of making the new equipment necessary for Dutch-style cloth at Saptes.

The last group consists of the twenty-four women, the origin of twenty-three of whom is known. They are described as servants or spinners, both unskilled occupations. The majority of these women came from the normal migratory source of Clermont, the Massif Central – nine were from the diocese of Vabres, two from Rodez, and one from a village in the north of the diocese of Lodève. Of the remainder, two were from Clermont, six from the diocese of Béziers, one from Castres, and only two from Carcassonne (Map 7). Thus the pattern is completed, and it can be seen that recruitment to Villenouvette did indeed follow the pattern later described at Auterive: the manufacture's 'artizans distingués' came mainly from around Carcassonne and in part from Clermont itself and from local cloth-making towns, and its unskilled labour came almost entirely from the normal migratory sources of the town and from neighbouring villages.

It was a varied and valuable labour force which had been created at Villenouvette, and one which posed numerous problems to the manufacture's directors, some of which have already been mentioned. The labour force had to be fed, and, as has been seen, Pierre Baille and the first group of associates took on themselves the responsibility of providing food for the workers. It had to be clothed, and the existence of 'petits métiers' at the manufacture, recorded in the description of 1681, was for the purpose of clothing the labour force.[132] Later at Grange-des-Prés both these duties were to fall on the shoulders of the director, Pierre-Antoine Barthe – amongst his effects were a hundred shirts 'destinées pour les ouvriers' and amongst his creditors was a baker owed 'pour le pain qu'il a fourni aux ouvriers de la Manufacture et dont ils ont tenu compte au Sieur Barthe sur leur salaire'.[133] The novel conditions in which the workers found themselves could give rise to violence: the statutes of the confrérie founded at the manufacture in 1681 imposed fines 'sil arrive que quelquesuns des ouvriers à sentrebatre dans la Boutique';[134] they could give rise to disease: later the director of Grange-des-Prés was to complain that 'les maladies continuelles avoient fait

132. Archive de la Manufacture, memoir of 1681.
133. ADH C1124, Proceedings connected with Barthe's bankruptcy, 1699.
134. ADH II E 26 98, 17 Nov. 1681.

déserter ses ouvriers';[135] and they could give rise to an exceptional comradeship: frequent were the weddings at Villenouvette at which a worker, far away from his family, was accompanied by 'ses bons amis' from the manufacture.[136]

Probably the best-documented problem is that concerning the conservation of this unique and valuable labour force. There was a constant danger that workers would be enticed away by local or foreign entrepreneurs. Thus the walls and monumental gates had more than just a decorative function at Villenouvette, in the same way that the Swiss Guards posted at the doors of Van Robais's manufacture had a duty to perform in preventing the desertion of the labour force within.[137] When the manufactures experienced one of their periodic crises the problem of the retention of the labour force was that most emphasized by the intendant and controller-general. Thus d'Aguesseau stressed his concern in 1681 that 'les tisserands qui sont de différents pays et quelques uns même étrangers' might abandon the manufacture during its difficulties. He was asked by Colbert to keep a check on Pierre Baille's wife who was still in Clermont and might be attempting to arrange for some of the manufacture's workers to join her husband in Amsterdam.[138] Similarly in 1692, when Saptes was on the verge of bankruptcy, Roux de Montbel, the syndic-général of the Etats, assured the intendant that to prevent the desertion of workers 'la manufacture na pas cessé dun moment et tous les ouvriers ont esté bien payés'. The syndic-général had also warned local clothiers not to attempt to hire workers from the manufacture: 'je leur dis fort rudement', he informed the intendant, 'et je leur annonce quà vostre passage vous le leur dirés encore dune manière à les faire trembler s'ils estoient assés hardys pour en débaucher aucun, ce quils avoient commencé de faire, et je leur ay fait remettre'. Van Robais's manufacture had the considerable advantage of a privilege giving it the monopoly of the passage vous le leur dirés encore dune manière à les faire trembler s'ils made the retention of the labour force less of a problem. Similarly at Carcassonne an order had been made by the local court prohibiting Saptes's workers from leaving the manufacture and local merchants from employing its labour force.

The formation and conservation of a large, specialized, skilled labour force at Villenouvette was a complex and costly process. It was another cause of the great expense which the manufacture occasioned to its backers in the early years. Some precise details of costs involved are

135. ADH C7343, Etats, 26 Jan. 1707.
136. E.g. ADH II E 26 98, 17 Nov. 1681 and II E 26 126, 20 Jan. 1689.
137. Courtecuisse, *Van Robais*, pp. 74–5.
138. Alberge, 'Villeneuvette', p. 32.

revealed in notarial contracts. There are records, for example, of large payments made to Dutch and German workers – no less than 500 *livres* to Jacob Trintrop in 1683 for instance[139] and on another occasion a payment of 40 *livres* by the associates to a 'mettre olandois' is recorded, for the training of a French apprentice.[140] Equally, workers brought from Carcassonne and other cloth-making areas must have been offered high wages to induce them to move. Once the new skills were learned, however, the royal manufacture became less dependent on support from outside and became itself capable of training the labour force it required. The growing independence and maturity of the manufacture is accurately reflected in the growing number of apprentices it trained. There were a total of 125 apprenticeships to the manufacture registered by Clermont's notaries between 1674 and 1712.[141] Of these, 116 were for the position of weaver, eight for those of shearer and cloth-dresser and one for that of dyer. Six of these apprenticeships were in the 1670s, twenty-nine in the 1680s, fifty-eight in the 1690s and thirty-two between 1700 and 1712. Apprentices were recruited by the masters of the manufacture themselves; they were also clothed, fed and rewarded by the masters.[142] A cheap method of labour recruitment and training was thus possible once the manufacture was fully established; the turning-point for Villenouvette came in the mid-1680s, ten years after its foundation.[143]

Already three different migratory patterns have been revealed for the different types of workers at Villenouvette. The skilled came from furthest away, the semi-skilled were largely recruited from local cloth industries close to Clermont, and the unskilled came from Clermont's normal migratory sources, above all from the Massif Central. Yet another migratory pattern is revealed by the apprenticeship records. With very few exceptions the apprentices came from local villages, the majority from within the diocese of Lodève and most of the remainder from the neighbouring diocese of Béziers (Map 8). Of the 125 apprentices, seventy-two were from Lodève, twenty-seven from Béziers, eleven from the dioceses of Vabres and Rodez, three from Narbonne, one from Montpellier, six from various Languedocian cloth-making towns, two from Uzès, one from Alès, one from Nîmes and for one the origin is not stated. Most of the villages which provided apprentices for the manufacture were within

139. By the associates of the first company, ADH II E 26 122, 5 May 1683.
140. ADH II E 26 120, 4 Dec. 1679.
141. Excluding those for the position of marchand-facturier.
142. The reward consisting generally in articles of clothing to be handed over at the end of the apprenticeship. There was rarely an apprenticeship fee for the position of weaver.
143. Of the 29 apprenticeships recorded in the 1680s eleven were in the first half of the decade, eighteen in the second and between 1690 and 1694 there were thirty-seven apprenticeships.

Map 8   Origins of 124 apprentices at Villenouvette

a day's travel of Clermont, and indeed used Clermont as their normal market centre. Thus if the number of apprenticeships to the manufacture revealed its growing efficiency and ability to train its own workers, the details of the origins of these apprentices reveal the integration of the manufacture into the local economy. It was no longer forced to seek its labour force from far away and those apprentices who were not from neighbouring villages were generally drawn to the manufacture by exceptional circumstances, in most cases by the presence of a close relation at the manufacture.[144]

Initially the manufactures had problems in retaining their labour forces. This problem evidently became less crucial when the skills the manufactures were trying to retain became less of a rarity. There is also, however, evidence that the labour force became increasingly stable, a tendency which evidently would have been likely to take place as the

144. The one apprentice from Nîmes was the gardener's son (ADH 11 E 25 94, 9 May 1680); one from Limoux was sponsored by Pierre Barthe (11 E 26 134, 12 Aug. 1691); one from Rodez had first served as a domestic servant to Barthe (11 E 26 136, 24 Feb. 1693) etc.

manufacture successfully integrated the family unit. Thus in 1731, sixty-five years after the arrival of the first Dutch workers at Saptes, the local subdelegate reported that the descendants of these workers still lived at the manufacture, having adopted French nationality.[145] Evidence of a relative stability amongst a considerable proportion of Villenouvette's labour force is provided in the notarial registers of Clermont. The cloth-workers often mentioned the number of years during which they had served at the manufacture when they registered a contract. Thus François Galsen, originally from Conques in the diocese of Carcassonne, when he made his will in 1685, declared that he had been 'résidant et travailhant avec sa familhe à lad Manufacture depuis lannée mil six cens septante quatre'[146] and Jacob Trintrop could boast twenty years of service when he made his will in 1694.[147] Others had lost trace of the passing of time and could only record that they had been present at the manufacture 'despuis longues années'. For others it is possible to make the calculations for them when their names have appeared repeatedly over the years in the notaries' registers. By making these calculations and also using the calculations of the workers themselves it has been possible to identify at least thirteen workers who spent over twenty years at Villenouvette between 1674 and 1712, eleven who spent over fifteen years, and twenty-four who spent over ten.[148] The figures represent a minimum and it is certain that in fact a great many more than forty-eight workers spent more than ten years at the manufacture during this period.

Why this stability? The creation of a community at Villenouvette and the incorporation of the family unit were clearly the main causes. Important also was the commitment to continual production, whatever the state of the market, which ensured regular wages, and also the responsibility which the directors took for the welfare of their labour force (Ill. 16). Regular employment and high wages evidently provided an opportunity for the thrifty worker to build up his or her savings. Jean Millet, for instance, a weaver's son from the diocese of Alet who had worked at Saptes before arriving at Villenouvette in 1678,[149] making his will in 1709 after thirty-one years of service, was able to leave 120 *livres* to each of his two daughters, 173 *livres* to his younger son and 1,010 to his elder, including 650 *livres* 'délivrés en dépost entre les mains de Mrs Pierre Astruc ... entrepreneurs de lad. Manufacture reelle^{mt} en argent

---

145. ADH C4677, Report of de Murat, 1731.
146. ADH II E 26 123, 2 Oct. 1685.
147. ADH II E 26 137, 5 Oct. 1694.
148. These figures do not include those who gave imprecise details ('depuis longtemps' etc) nor those who spent less than ten years at the manufacture and then worked at Clermont.
149. ADH II 26 100, 15 July 1683, II E 26 124, 19 March 1687.

Ill. 16. Rue Colbert, adjoining which weavers' houses were situated

comptant'.[150] Girls who worked at the manufacture were able in many cases to amass a dowry, which was mentioned in their marriage contracts. In 1704 and 1705 three sisters, who had worked for between ten and twelve years at the manufacture, married; two had saved 100 *livres* and one 200.[151] Another girl who married in 1709 brought 90 *livres* as her marriage portion 'quelle a gagniés en travailliant de ses mains à lad. manufacture'.[152] Evidence of the directors' concern for the welfare of their labour force is provided most directly by the special arrangements

150. ADH ii E 26 147, 3 Jan. 1709.
151. ADH ii E 25 107, 2 April 1704, 12, 17 May 1705.
152. ADH ii E 25 108, 21 May 1709.

which were made with the inhabitants of Aspiran when Thomas Barthe set up looms in this village. A 'tronc', or alms-box, was established to which Barthe committed himself and his successors to an annual contribution of 300 *livres* a year 'à faire pourvoir à secourir dans les maladies les ouvriers qui travailleront actuellemt. aud. lieu d'aspiran, et qui n'auront pas de quoy se faire servir'.[153] The royal manufacture thus provided a humane community in which there were possibilities to make savings and the confidence which existed between worker and employer is demonstrated by the fact that it was into the directors' hands that Jean Millet entrusted most of his life's savings.

Technical

It has already been seen that it was Dutch and German workers who brought the new 'Dutch-style' techniques of cloth manufacture to Saptes and Villenouvette. But the production of consistently high-quality cloth, capable of out-selling its Dutch and English equivalents, was not an easy task and was certainly not guaranteed by the arrival of a few foreign workers. The Dutch and English had a firm hold on the Levant market and the French had to establish their reputation by consistent good production before they could hope to compete. Colbert was aware of this and, as early as 1671, Augustin Magy, one of the principal directors of the Levant Company, was sent to Constantinople to study the English and Dutch trade and identify the factors which contributed to their dominance of the market. Magy's report reached Colbert in 1671.[154] The principal reasons for the Dutch and English success were, Magy explained, 'la fidélité qu'ils ont tousiours maintenu tant dans la bonté des draps que dans leurs couleurs. Ils sont si exacts à soutenir cette réputation qu'ils ne voudroient pas mettre en vente une seule pièce qui ne fust de la qualité ordinaire et d'une couleur fidelle.' Unless the French were

153. ADH C2135, Agreement of Thomas Barthe and Jean Dejean, 'vicaire perpetuel' of Aspiran, 29 Nov. 1694. The system was continued until at least 1704, but by then it was being in part financed by deductions from the workers' salaries – an early example of a compulsory insurance system.

154. AN F12 645, 'Mémoire de M. Magy sur le commerce de Levant'. This memoir is undated but references within it as well as the fact that Colbert, in a letter of 28 December 1671 (Depping, *Correspondance*, III, 877), refers to it make it certain that it was composed in 1671. Significantly the memoir presented on the Levant trade in the later editions of J. Savary, *Le parfait négociant* (e.g. 1749 edn, 1, 396–446) is almost identical to this memoir of Magy. Savary claimed (p. xii) that the memoir which was composed in 1679 was the fruit of discussion with friends of his who had traded in the Levant. One of the friends must have been Augustin Magy who might have lent his memoir of 1671 to Savary because Savary's account follows Magy's almost verbatim in places.

equally scrupulous about the quality of their cloth and the consistency of their dyeing there would be no possibility of establishing a similar predominance in the Levant. A consistently high standard of production was particularly important in the early years when it was necessary to 'mettre en réputation nos draps contre la jalousie que les Anglois et les Hollandois en met qui ne manquent pas de les descrier'.

Having emphasized the need to maintain a consistently high standard of production Magy described the characteristics of this standard which had to be adhered to so carefully. The cloth should be fine and supple but this fineness should not cause the warp of the cloth to be revealed, he explained, and in order to secure this effect the weaving should be very firm, the batten of the loom being pressed down hard on the weave,[155] and the cloth well fulled. The shearing had to be so thorough that no nap should be visible and the breadth and length of the cloth always constant. In addition Magy advised that the cloth when pressed should have thick pieces of paper[156] placed between its folds to prevent staining and that at the end of the production process the cloth should be packed completely dry to prevent deterioration of the dye during transit.

Magy's advice was intended for Saptes, the only manufacture producing fine cloth for the Levant, and this first part of his memoir consisted in no more than a description of some aspects of the new 'Dutch methods' of cloth-making. In addition to this advice, however, he warned the manufacture of two major flaws in its manufacturing and also provided some hints about the best methods of presenting and marketing the cloth. The two major defects were of such importance that Magy warned that unless they were rectified it would be impossible 'de pouvoir soustenir la fabrique'. The defects revealed themselves, he explained, because the Levantine tailors did one of two things before they worked on the cloth – either they soaked the cloth completely in water or they sprinkled water on the cloth and then ironed it. The former treatment caused de Varennes's cloth to shrink and its nap to rise, the latter caused the dye to deteriorate, stains and variations appearing. The shrinking was the result of insufficient fulling, the staining the result of a lack of 'fidélité' in the dyeing. The lighter dyes deteriorated most of all and Magy described poetically the effect of the tailor's treatment of the cloth: 'La Couleur se varie et faict comme des nuages dans la presse.' The result of these two major flaws was a continual stream of complaints to the French com-

155. H. Freudenberger in his study on a Bohemian privileged manufacture which introduced the Dutch-style techniques maintains that the Dutch type of weaving required 'the batten to be hit six times against the weave' each time a cross thread was passed with the shuttle through the shed (*The Waldstein Woollen Mill*, p. 29).

156. 'Cartons', the French expression, probably the equivalent of today's cardboard. W. Partridge in *A Practical Treatise on Dying* refers to the need for thick paper for pressing (p. 85).

missioners at Constantinople, complaints which the commissioners were obliged to shrug off with 'des mauvaizes raizons' which caused a loss of reputation to the French and great delight to the English and Dutch merchants who 'ne demandent pas mieux que des occasions pour décrier cette fabrique'. The market was evidently very competitive and the English and the Dutch, apprehensive about the arrival of a newcomer in Constantinople, were not beneath spreading false rumours about the low quality of de Varennes's cloth.

So de Varennes's manufacture was not performing two vital processes of production – the fulling and dyeing – sufficiently effectively to enable the cloth to withstand the journey to the Levant and the attention of the Turkish tailors. Equally the manufacture was suffering from a lack of experience in marketing techniques, a lack which Magy hoped to rectify. He sent samples of the margins of Dutch cloth[157] which he advised Saptes to copy though with a finer-quality wool, and he advised that the cloth once it had been pressed and packed should, if possible, be left entirely alone, to prevent any deterioration in the finish. If it was to be inspected this should be done not at Marseilles but in the manufacture before the packing. De Varennes should also prepare samples[158] of all the pieces of cloth in each bale 'car cella est d'une grande facillité pour la vente et faict éviter la peine qu'on a de les montrer pièce à pièce ce qui porte préiudice à la beauté des draps'. Cloth which did not come quite up to standard, being either coarser or heavier than the rest, should be kept separately, Magy advised, and sent to Smyrna, Aleppo or Cairo, where the lower qualities were in greater demand. De Varennes had not been consistent in the measurement of his cloth, Magy informed Colbert, as he had found considerable variations in the sizes of some of the manufacture's cloth. He advised sending de Varennes a measure of the Paris *aune* as well as one of the *pic* (the measurement used in the Levant) which he enclosed with his memoir. The invoices accompanying the cloth should have the measurements cited both in *pics* and *aunes* – 'cela donnera une grande facilité à la vante', Magy considered.

Magy completed his memoir with advice on the assortment of colours suitable for each bale of cloth,[159] and with descriptions and samples of all the different sorts of cloth being sold in the Levant and the return

157. The *lizière* or margin of the cloth was made of coarser wools than the cloth which would actually be used by the tailor and contained a stripe of a particular colour which identified its quality. Here Magy is advising Saptes to copy the Dutch identification mark for their cloth.
158. *Echantillons* or samples of each piece of cloth in a bale were pasted on a card or piece of paper to aid the merchant charged with the sale.
159. The nature of the assortment of colours was crucial for two reasons: for the sale of cloth as demand for different colours fluctuated, and for profit as darker colours were more expensive to dye than lighter shades.

products which were available for import into France. De Varennes was making *Londrines* or *Londrins*,[160] a type of cloth which had a sale of 2,000 to 2,500 pieces a year at Constantinople, most of which was supplied by the Dutch. Magy was confident that if de Varennes and others succeeded in maintaining a high quality of production 'nous en pourrons débiter la moitié et dans la suitte tout et chasser les hollandois de cette porte qui leur pourfournit d'argent p^r tout le commerce ce qu'ils font en levant'. A second quality, *nims-londrins*, was being attempted with little success by Carcassonne's normal clothiers. Their cloth was displaying the same defects as that of de Varennes and the last bale to have been sold had been of such bad quality that the French merchants had been obliged to accept its return. Magy warned that 'Cette balle a si fort décrié cette sorte de draps qu'il sera bien dificille de leur pouvoir faire prendre réputation et de trouver à les vendre' but he was confident that the 'Messrs de Carcassonne' were capable of making as good cloth as their competitors 'lorqu'ils le voudront faire'.

The memoir from Magy caused Colbert to write alarmedly to Pennautier about the faults in de Varennes's cloth.[161] Clearly Saptes had not yet succeeded in producing cloth to equal that of its competitors and this failure was one of the causes of its difficulties. The memoir demonstrated very clearly the extensive technical and commercial problems connected with the production of new types of cloth for a new and competitive market, and these difficulties were only slowly to be overcome. The hostility and competitiveness of the Dutch, mentioned by Magy, were to be a constant feature of these early and difficult years. The Dutch, according to Basville, sold their cloth at a loss for seven or eight years hoping to 'rebuter nos Français'.[162] A memoir composed on the Levant trade in the mid-eighteenth century emphasized, as well, the long struggle with the English and Dutch who for a long time used 'toutes les menées dont on peut faire usage dans le Commerce pour ruiner un concurrent; insinuation défavorable, avantages secrets, ménages à l'acheteur sur des marchandises d'une autre espèce; baisse excessive de prix, rien n'est épargné'.[163] Villenouvette, too, was to suffer from the same sorts of technical difficulties as Saptes, as well as from the competitiveness of the Levant market, and a contributory factor in the crisis of 1680–3 was the fact that the French were still not able to equal the standard of English and Dutch cloth.[164]

160. 'Londrines' was the conventional spelling during the seventeenth century but I shall adhere to the eighteenth-century usage: *londrins*.
161. Colbert to Pennautier, 28 Dec. 1671 (Depping, *Correspondance*, III, 877).
162. Boissonnade, 'Colbert', p. 18.
163. AN F12 645, 'Mémoire sur le commerce du Levant', c. 1756, p. 13.
164. Boulainvilliers, *État*, II, 562.

With the benefit of advice from Magy and others, however, and with the growing efficiency of its managerial system and labour force, there is evidence that Villenouvette and Saptes gradually, 'par tâtonnements successifs de son modèle',[165] succeeded in improving the quality of their production. By the late 1670s there were already occasional reports stating that Languedoc's production, at its best, was superior to that of the Dutch,[166] and by the late 1680s this superiority was aiding French merchants to make inroads into markets previously monopolized by competitors. De Seignelay, ambassador at Constantinople, wrote contentedly with news of 'La décadence du débit des draperies de Hollande et la préférence de celles de France',[167] and in a memoir of 1694 it was confidently asserted that the French cloth had 'entièrement détruit le commerce que les Anglois et Holandois faisoient'.[168] Cauvière visiting Saptes in the same year commented that the name of de Varennes was 'fort Conneu en Levant'.[169]

Financial

The financial instability of Saptes and Villenouvette is explained in part by the extravagance of directors, the incompetence of managers, the indiscipline of workers and the technical superiority of competitors, but the most fundamental of all reasons was that the royal manufactures' heavy investment in fixed capital and commitment to continuous production went completely against the practice of all other contemporary industrial concerns. Clermont's clothiers' minimal fixed capital investment and their reliance on alternative sources of income to support them in years of difficult trading has been emphasized and the Clermontais were not exceptional. S. D. Chapman, describing the investment policy of English clothiers during the early eighteenth century, concludes that it 'reflected ... the prime concerns of the entrepreneurs of the age: the need to limit their commitment to, and insulate themselves against, the erratic course of industrial change that had been characteristic of the economy as far back as anyone remembered'.[170] Thus the royal manufactures went completely against the logic of all 'pre-industrial' industries and were doomed to suffer crises whenever there was a downswing in the

---

165. The phrase is Pierre Deyon's, 'La production manufacturière', p. 52.
166. Paris, *Histoire du commerce*, v, 544.
167. Marquis de Seignelay to Girardin, ambassador at Constantinople, 4 Jan. 1687 (Depping, *Correspondance*, III, 650).
168. ADH C2202, in a request made by Pouget for the rents of his buildings at Villenouvette to be increased, 15 Jan. 1694.
169. ADH C2200, Memoir of Cauvière, 1694.
170. S. D. Chapman, 'Industrial capital before the Industrial Revolution: an analysis of the assets of a thousand textile entrepreneurs, c. 1730–50' in N. B. Harte and K. G. Ponting (eds), *Textile History and Economic History*, p. 137.

trade cycle because their high overheads and their valuable labour forces forced them to continue production when other cloth-making concerns had closed down.

This was a basic problem which affected all of France's royal manufactures. In addition, however, Saptes and Villenouvette were producing for the Levant, a distant market, and were thus burdened not only by their heavy fixed capital investment but also by the slow turnover of their circulating capital because of the long delay before the price of the cloth sold in the Levant could be realized. This was soon seen to be the fundamental explanation for the instability of these concerns. The Etats, for instance, in 1682, commented that 'Ceux qui fabriquent de draps pour le Levant, ne doivent pas estre chargez du soin de les y envoyer pour leur compte, et que tous ceux qui l'ont entreprise ont ruiné leurs affaires, et ont abandonné le commerce.'[171] Basville explained the dilemma even more fully. De Varennes's first exports were unprofitable, he explained, in part because the competition of the Dutch but also because 'il ne put avoir son débit assez prompt, & pour attendre les retours en Marchandises, il lui faloit nécessairement un an ou 18 mois, n'ayant point de Magasins établis; de sorte qu'il auroit falu qu'il eut des fonds suffisans pour travailler deux & trois ans, sans compter sur le retour qu'en la 3ᵉ ou 4ᵉ année ... cela surpassoit ses forces'.[172]

The nature of the solution to this most fundamental of Languedoc's royal manufactures' problems we have already seen. Saptes and Villenouvette received increasing financial support firstly from the Crown, then from financiers, and finally from the provincial Estates while the succeeding Levant Companies to a greater and greater extent assumed the responsibility for commercializing the cloth. Finally, in the 1690s, the revival in Marseilles trade reached the point where the Levant Companies' interventions were no longer necessary and normal merchants, and associations of merchants, took over their role. This is not to say, of course, that the directors of royal manufactures were deprived of further responsibility for investment. On the contrary the amount which they had to invest was still very large. The provincial loans only provided a part of the circulating capital required, the total amount used being far larger. In the 1690s, for example, between 3,900 and 4,875 *livres* were being spent on firewood alone,[173] and goods deposited in the province's

171. ADH C7214, Etats, 20 Nov. 1682.
172. Boulainvilliers, *Etat*, ii, 562.
173. ADH ii E 26 129, 30 Oct. 1692, Agreement between Pierre Barthe and Henry de Lauriol Vissec, seigneur of Jonquières, for the annual delivery of 'tout le bois chaine servant à la teinture de lad. manufacture' – 12–15,000 *quintaux* at 6 *sols* 6 *deniers* the *quintal*.

Ill. 17. Villenouvette survived until 1954: evidence of the nineteenth and twentieth centuries at the manufacture

'magasin de nantissement' in the manufacture were on occasions of a value of over 200,000 *livres*.[174] Similarly extra building, the purchase of new looms and equipment, and expansion of production such as that which occurred in the 1690s,[175] had to be financed by the entrepreneur himself. But the assurance of a regular and rapid sale for their cloth, and of a significant financial contribution from the Estates, certainly eased the situation.

174. Etats' reports of 1705, 1707, 1708, 1711, 1712, 1718, 1720; capital being used: 90,600, 122,220, 123,000, 125,000, 135,800, 129,000, 205,500 *livres* (ADH C7326, 7339, 7341, 7354, 7359, 7377 and 7385).
175. On this expansion see pp. 223–4.

The success

So the experiences of Villenouvette to some extent vindicates the claims of Colbert and d'Aguesseau that its initial difficulties were teething problems rather than permanent attributes. By the 1690s it had become an efficient manufacture. The crucial dyeing processes had been mastered: 'Les couleurs sy sont belles à cause des Eaus et de la capacité du maîttre teinturier quy Réussit bien à Rencontrer les Couleurs quy sont demandées pour le Levant', reported Bosson in 1692.[176] To Cauvière on his visit in 1694 Villenouvette seemed an ideal manufacture and he reported:

elle a dans son enclos toutes les commodités qu'on peut souhaiter pour une manufacture de draps: des grands lieux pour les fileuses, un grand magasin vouté pour les laines et au dessus des greniers pour les faire sécher à lombre, une grande teinture où toutes les Eaux passent à travers et vont faire tourner trois moulins a draps, au sortir de là . . . 4 presses façon dhollande, et deux à la manière de france, une grande boutique où il y a 31 mestiers à drap; douze à une autre petite.[177]

The manufacture's success was certainly in part attributable to the financial support given by the Crown and Etats, but to attribute all credit for the manufacture's survival to this support[178] would be to ignore the gradual process of adaptation, simplification and improvement which we have just described. And that Villenouvette's long survival (until 1954) owed more to this process than to the extent of its privileges is apparent from the fact that it survived despite a gradual decrease in the amount of official support that it received (Ill. 17).[179]

176. ADH C2513, *c.* 1692.
177. ADH C2200, Cauvière's report.
178. A widely accepted view of royal manufactures is that they survived only as a consequence of receiving such support. E.g. P. Goubert, *Beauvais et le Beauvaisis*, p. 587: 'On sait d'ailleurs que la plupart des créations de ce type ont rapidement périclité, et que celles qui ont survécu l'ont dû aux subventions que leur attribuait le ministre.'
179. After 1728 the only form of assistance received by royal manufactures was a standard annual 'rent' of 3,000 *livres* a year.

7

Villenouvette and Clermont

'Il établit toutes sortes de manufactures qui coûtoient plus qu'elles ne valoient.' (Abbé de Choisy of Colbert, cited by P. Clément, *Histoire de la vie et de l'administration de Colbert*, p. 229)

'L'on peut la regarder comme le modèle & pour ainsi dire, comme la mère de toutes les autres qui sont dans la province du Languedoc.' (Savary des Bruslons, of Saptes, *Dictionnaire universel du commerce*, III, 479)

'And thus have the *French* Policies invited over the most Exquisite Manufacturers into *France* from all parts of the World; these with their Schollars were first imployed at the Charge of the Government; but the Manufactures soon afterwards diffused into the gross Body of the people.' (*Britannia Languens, or a Discourse of Trade*, 1680, reprinted in J. R. McCulloch (ed.), *Early English Tracts on Commerce*, p. 303)

As we have seen in chapter three, the profound cause of the crisis in Languedoc's industrial production was the unfavourable demand situation occasioned by a combination of factors: the general European depression, geographical shifts in Europe's commercial circuits and aggravations of the effects of the European depression occasioned by both France's involvement in foreign warfare and her domestic social and political problems. Commercial and technical backwardness had developed as a consequence of the unfavourable demand situation. They were not its cause. They became, though, a probable barrier to a rapid recovery.

Colbert's reforms, we have argued, were directed largely at the symptoms and the consequences rather than at this profound cause of the crisis which was, clearly, beyond his power to remedy. He attempted to improve the quality of manufacturing and the organization of trade and to enlarge French shipping resources; he strove to change attitudes to trade and to modernize commercial methods; he encouraged investment in trade and industry, and, finally, to ensure that when success was achieved it should endure he devised regulations and entrusted their enforcement to a corps of inspectors and a revived guild system.

In the 1690s this recovery in demand which was beyond Colbert's powers to arrange occurred in France and throughout Europe. It has been noted by historians from points of observation located in all the centres of the European economy. Posthumus's price series for the Amsterdam market record a sharp revival;[1] J. D. Chambers has commented on the quite exceptional prosperity in England during these years;[2] Pierre Léon, from the vantage point of Lyons, notes a moderate price rise between 1692 and 1715 after some thirty years of stagnation;[3] Pierre Deyon, situated in Normandy, registers these price rises too and writes that suddenly, 'quelques années après la mort du grand ministre ... l'esprit d'entreprise gagne une partie de la bourgeoisie française. Ses initiatives parties de Rouen, de Saint-Malo, de Paris, de Marseille, animent le commerce maritime.' This movement he categorizes as a 'cycle interdécennal' within the longer depression (phase B) which had been affecting the French economy since the mid-century and he adds that 'l'ampleur du phénomène, sa généralisation, la participation des prix non agricoles au mouvement de hausse incitent à reconnaître à la période de 20 à 25 ans qui commence en 1688 une certaine originalité'.[4] Finally the revival, and its universality, is noted by Jean Meuvret: 'ces années préparent ou annoncent un renouveau', he writes. 'C'est l'exploration des mers du Sud, et, comme l'a montré Pierre Goubert, l'élargissement de l'horizon commercial de vieilles maisons françaises. C'est le début, décrit par Vilar, de l'essor catalan. C'est la croissance de Marseille et de notre commerce du Levant.'[5]

We have already observed some of the effects of the general recovery in demand on Clermont's industry in the 1690s, a rise in the number of weavers and the production of new types of cloth. It is revealed, too, in the Galtié/Moulins correspondence. Galtié père et fils would seem to have been slightly taken by surprise by the sudden boom in the cloth trade. On 27 November 1691 they informed Moulins that they were unable to acquire cloth from Lodève as all the clothiers there were fully employed working for Parisian merchants who were supplying the army with cloth.[6] Lodève's industry was evidently exceptionally prosperous. The survey of Arts et Métiers, carried out in 1691, revealed that there

---

1. N. W. Posthumus, *Inquiry into the History of Prices in Holland*, I, 39–40, 75, 111–14.
2. *Population, Economy and Society in Pre-Industrial England*, pp. 114, 143–7.
3. 'La crise de l'économie française à la fin du règne de Louis XIV (1685–1715)', *Information Historique* 18 (1956), 131.
4. *Amiens*, pp. 82, 54.
5. 'Circulation monétaire', pp. 2–3. On this general economic revival see also P. Vilar, *Or et monnaie*, pp. 243–8, *La Catalogne*, I, 647–9; P. Chaunu, *La civilisation de l'Europe classique*, p. 394; Braudel and Labrousse, *Histoire économique*, II, 257.
6. ADR, Fonds Moulins, IV, e.g. Galtié to Moulins, 27 Nov. 1691.

were seventy-five marchands-facturiers and seventy-nine master-weavers in the town with eleven apprentices to the former profession and thirty to the latter.[7] The switch to the production of *draps-forts* in the Lodève style by three of Clermont's clothiers in 1692 is, it is clear, linked to this exceptional demand for military cloth.[8] The general expansion in demand continued into 1693. The fair of Beaucaire in 1692 was an exceptionally successful one and in January 1693 the intendant at Montauban was reporting that prices of manufactured goods were rising daily.[9] The demographic and agricultural crisis of the years 1693–4 caused a sharp check to the growth: Cauvière when he visited Lodève in 1694 found one third of the town's looms idle and only between thirty-eight and forty clothiers at work.[10] But the check was only temporary and in 1695 and 1696 the expansion was renewed. Galtié père et fils again found difficulty in obtaining adequate quantities of 'draps en blanc' for dispatch to Moulins in Lyons. These types of cloth were unbelievably 'rescherchés' even though Lodève's production had increased to 24,000 pieces in the previous year, they informed their correspondent in January 1696.[11]

The Carcassonnais region's industry was, likewise, in full expansion. Reich de Pennautier, who still acted as an informal industrial agent in the province, wrote to the controller-general, the comte de Pontchartrain, on 30 October 1691, informing him that 'Le commerce des draperies, dans tout le Haut Languedoc et dans tous les lieux où il s'en fait, ne sauroit estre plus florissant. On travaille partout à force, et les ouvriers manquent plutost que le débit.'[12] There are signs that this revival in Carcassonne's industry had its roots in the 1680s. An inspection carried out in 1688 revealed that the town and its suburbs contained 387 looms of which ninety-six were mounted with medleys and the rest with both common and fine broad-cloths.[13] The survey of Arts et Métiers of 1691 not only provides information on the number of masters in the different industrial corporations in Carcassonne but also gives details of all marchands-fabricants who had been received master during the previous ten years.[14] There were forty-four marchands-fabricants, seventy pareurs, 115 master-weavers, thirty-six cardeurs, thirteen cardiers, sixteen retorseurs

7. ADH C2773, Report of 15 May 1691.
8. See p. 104.
9. Boislisle, *Correspondance*, I, 115, letters from de Pontchartrain, 14 Sept. 1692, 9 Jan. 1693.
10. ADH C2200.
11. ADR, Fonds Moulins, IV, Letter of 22 Jan. 1696.
12. Boislisle, *Correspondance*, I, 977 n.
13. ADH C2199, Inspection by Arnaud de la Marque, 1688.
14. ADH C2773.

Table 8. *New marchands-fabricants*
received at Carcassonne, 1681–90

1681	2	1686	2
1682	2	1687	0
1683	1	1688	3
1684	2	1689	4
1685	3	1690	1

Source: ADH C2773, Survey of Arts et
Métiers, 1691–2.

and fifteen master dyers. The industry was clearly not only large but also well supplied with skilled workers and the existence of a considerable optimism about its future is revealed by the large number of apprentices: eleven to marchands-fabricants, twenty to pareurs, two to cardiers, three to retorseurs, three to cardeurs à laine and three to dyers. The total number apprenticed to weavers is not recorded but it is noted in the survey that five had been taken on in 1691. The details of the reception of new masters suggests that the body of Carcassonne's clothiers had been substantially enlarged or renewed during the 1680s (Table 8). The expansion continued in the 1690s. Pennautier's letter shows the extent of the prosperity in 1691 and the report which Cauvière made after his visit in 1694 suggests that the industry, although its expansion had been temporarily checked in that year, had grown considerably since the inspection carried out in 1688. He commented on 'Le grand débit que les marchands ont eu depuis quelques années' and recorded that 800 looms were being employed by forty-eight clothiers in Carcassonne itself and in neighbouring villages. Cauvière's explanation of the crisis was that it had been caused by 'Laviditté du profit [qui] les a plongés dans un abus quj a fait un tort considérable à leur fabrique'. The marchands-fabricants blamed it on the war, informing Cauvière at a special meeting which had been summoned in the hôtel de ville that 'leur commerce avoit beaucoup diminué du Costé d'allemagne, piedmont et millan par la guerre'. A petition made to the Etats by two merchants shortly after this visit provides further confirmation of the extent of the temporary crisis: 'La manufacture de Carcassonne a entièrement diminué despuis une année par le peu de consommation', they wrote.[15]

Cauvière's report, and various industrial surveys carried out between 1690 and 1710, inform us of what cloths were being made for what

15. ADH C2200, Cauvière's report and ADA 9 C 19, 'Mémoire des sieurs Castanier, Poussonnel et Cie, marchands, Carcassonne', *c*.1695.

markets during these years. It is evident that there had been a significant recovery in the town's industry and that, as at Amiens,[16] the recovery had taken the form, above all, of a rise in the production of the range of high-quality, specialized cloths for distant markets, the provisionment of local markets with coarser cloths (which was the role the industry had sunk to during the depression) being left increasingly to less important cloth-making centres (Table 9). Not all these cloths were being made at the same time. Indeed the production of some types (the *londrins*) clearly replaced the production of others (*draps façon d'Angleterre*, largely, it would seem). Average production was in the region of 10,000 pieces (not including cloth which was only finished at Carcassonne). Carcassonne's cloth-making centres (Table 9). Not all these cloths were being made at the same time. Indeed the production of some types (the *londrins*) clearly town's cloth were sold in Paris, making Carcassonne the fifth largest supplier in the kingdom, and in a survey of the Languedocian cloth industry carried out in approximately 1695 it is reported that the town was selling cloth in some of the major industrial centres of northern France – Brittany, Picardy, Champagne and even Normandy.[17]

The expansion in the Levant trade, and in the demand for Languedoc's cloth in the Levant, can, likewise, be traced to the late 1680s. As we have noted in the previous chapters it was in 1687 that it was reported by the ambassador at Constantinople that Languedocian cloth was at last selling better than Dutch and within a few years the English trade too was suffering from the inroads of French competition: 'It is scarce imaginable how great a trade the French drive all over this empire', wrote Ambassador Sutton from Constantinople in 1702, '[they] . . . make such considerable advances daily in their traffick and incroach so much upon our cloth trade, that unless some effectual means be used to prevent it they will be able to get it out of our hands past all recovery.'[18] A sign of the more favourable demand situation in the Levant was that Marseilles's merchants in the 1690s finally began to participate fully in the Levant trade. Their involvement was on such a scale that it was found to be unnecessary to found a new 'Compagnie de la Mer Méditerranée', as the Levant Company was now called, when its 1685 charter expired in 1690. As Basville explained, 'la facilité que l'on trouve maintenant à les [Languedocian cloth] vendre aux Marchands de Marseille en a empêché le renouvellement'.[19]

16. Deyon, *Amiens*, pp. 174–8.
17. Deyon, *Amiens*, p. 146, n.4; ADH C2513, 'Commerce des draperies du Languedoc', c.1695.
18. Cited by A.C. Wood, *A History of the Levant Company*, p. 119.
19. Boulainvilliers, *Etat*, II, 562.

Table 9. *Cloth produced and finished in Carcassonne in the 1690s*

Types Threads to warp	Number of pieces Markets	Price per *aune* Wools used
Draps façon d'Hollande and *façon d'Angleterre* (3,000–4,200)	2,000–3,000? Italy (until 1698) Interior	Up to 17 *livres* Segovian
Draps façon d'Elbeuf (2,800–3,000)	Few Interior	Second ségovie Alborazin
Vingtsixains *Vingtquatrains* (2,400–600)	About 6,000 Interior Switzerland Italy Flanders Germany Spain	$8\frac{1}{2}$–11 *livres* Béziers, Narbonne, and, for higher qualities, Soria or Second ségovie
Droguets façon d'Angleterre	600–700 Germany Switzerland	
Cloth for overcoats	400–500 Interior Spain	$16\frac{1}{2}$–17 *livres*
Finished at Carcassonne *Draps de Montagne* (i.e. from villages of Lagrasse, Montréal, Labastide etc.) (1,600–2,400)	About 3,000–6,000 Interior Flanders Germany Switzerland Italy	
Produced after 1695 *Londrins-premiers* (3,200) *Londrins-seconds* (2,600)	2,000–3,000 Levant	11–$11\frac{1}{2}$ *livres* Segovian $8\frac{3}{4}$–9 *livres* Soria or Second ségovie

Sources: ADH C2200, Cauvière's report, 1694; C2513, memoir on 'Commerce des Draperies du Languedoc', *c.* 1690; ADA 9 C 17, 'Coppie fidelle du procès verbal per la reddition des comptes des droits de bouïlhe devent les marchans de Car^ne^ et ceux de la Montaigne', 1692–1711; BN FF 8037, fo. 71, survey of 1708; Fontvieille, 'Les premières enquêtes', p. 1125.

The first reaction in Languedoc to the improved situation in the Levant market consisted in the establishment of the manufacture of *londres*, a coarser version of the *londrins* and *nims-londrins* which were being made by Villenouvette and Saptes. A privilege allowing Noël de

Varennes to undertake the production of this new type of cloth in and around the town of St-Chinian was granted in 1688. The Estates were obliged once again to act as paymasters: in 1689 they made a ten-year, interest-free loan of 30,000 *livres* to de Varennes. By 1694 there were sixty-five looms producing this new cloth.[20] The manufactures of Saptes and Villenouvette expanded their production too to meet the rising demand. Pennautier in his letter of October 1691 informed de Pontchartrain that both manufactures were in full expansion:

J'ai vu la manufacture de Saptes qui n'avoit d'ordinaire ... que trente métiers battans. Elle en avoit, le 2ᵉ de ce mois, cinquante trois, et on alloit établir d'autres. Si elle ne fait pas la quantité de pièces de drap pour le Levant qu'elle devoit faire, c'est parce que les ouvriers lui manqueront, quoyque, depuis peu, il luy soit venu dix-sept familles hollandoises, toutes catholiques, Je n'ay pas eu le temps d'aller à celle de Clermont; mais j'apprends qu'elle travaille aussy considérablement.[21]

That his information on Villenouvette was correct is demonstrated by the sharp rise observable in the number of weavers' apprenticeships to the manufacture: 1687, two; 1688, six; 1689, seven; 1690, two; 1691, seven; 1692, twenty-one; 1693, four; 1694, six. New workshops were opened in Clermont and in the neighbouring village of Aspiran to house extra looms. The total number of looms used was increased from forty-three to sixty-three in 1691 and to seventy in 1696.[22]

Until 1695, however, there was little participation in the growing trade by unprivileged clothiers. This reluctance to switch to producing for the new market has various explanations. First, there was no great economic pressure to do so for, as we have just noted, demand for cloth from established markets was strong during these years. Secondly the switch to *any* new market was a costly, risky and difficult process. New tools were required, there were technical problems involved in making new types of cloth, new types of raw material had to be secured, new cloth buyers contacted etc. (We have seen in previous chapters the difficulties which well-funded royal manufactures experienced in such matters.) And finally there was a reluctance because it was felt that it would be impossible to compete with the royal manufactures, which enjoyed the advantages of subsides and interest-free loans. Not unnaturally the consequence of the trade being handled for so long by these vast and spectacular concerns had been that most normal clothiers had come to feel that

20. ACCM H 159, copy of edict of 19 Oct. 1688; ADH C7248, Etats, 1689; ADH C2200, Cauvière's report.
21. Boislisle, *Correspondance*, I, 977 n.
22. Apprenticeships as recorded by Clermont's notaries. Expansions of looms recorded in memoir of *c.*1697–8 on manufacture held in ADH C2202.

participation in the trade was something quite beyond their resources. This, indeed, was the main reason for their hostility towards the concerns which we have noted previously. As Cauvière reported after visiting Villenouvette in 1694, the grant of a bounty to the royal manufactures for the production of cloth for both the domestic and the Levant markets 'fait murmurer tous les fabriquants de cette province, les uns n'osent pas travailler pour le Levant, ne Croyant pas y pouvoir trouver leur compte, et les autres de ce quil [Barthe] touche et devarenes aussy, une pistolle de chaque drap quils font pour France ou ailleurs qui ne leur est pas deüe et qui ne laisse pas de leur faire un grand tort'.[23]

Despite these economic and psychological barriers to production some unsubsidized clothiers tried the new market in the early 1690s. One was the entrepreneur whose sudden appearance with twelve looms in Clermont we have noted in chapter four. He was Gabriel Pelletan, who had served at Villenouvette since 1677 or earlier, and his enterprise in Clermont would appear to have dated from approximately 1686.[24] It was largely his labour demands which led to an expansion in weavers' apprenticeships in Clermont in parallel to that at Villenouvette: 1687, none; 1688, two; 1689, seven; 1690, four; 1691, eleven; 1692, ten; 1693, ten; 1694, two. The contrast with the preceding period was striking; between 1674 and 1686 there had been only four weavers' apprenticeships. As we have seen Pelletan was joined in the production of fine cloth for the Levant by three other Clermontais in January 1694.

At Carcassonne there does not seem to have been such a spontaneous growth in the production for the new market. In contrast to Clermont, the town's large industry had a wide range of expanding markets for which to produce and this must have been the main reason for the lack of movement. Only one Carcassonnais produced for the market before Cauvière's tour of the province (by this time Clermont had forty looms producing), Joseph Gaja, who founded a manufacture in Narbonne in 1692 (transferred to the neighbouring village of Bize in 1698), and he only did so, it seems, on the understanding that his production would be subsidized by the Etats. In January 1693 he was awarded a 6 *livres* bounty.[25] But between 1694 and 1695 the situation changed radically. Whereas there was a sharp depression in the Italian and German markets which, we have just seen, absorbed a significant part of Carcassonne's production, the demand for cloth in the Levant, which had been expanding already, was boosted yet further because various French naval suc-

23. ADH C2200.
24. By a contract of 13 Jan. 1686 he rented a workshop in Clermont, close to the Rhonel (ADH II E 26 103).
25. ADH C7267, Etats, 15 Jan. 1693; ADA 9 C 19, memoir of Gaja, c.1732.

cesses obstructed the delivery of English and Dutch cloth. The position in the Levant market had been helped throughout these years of expansion by the unusual successes of the French fleet. The Etats' awareness of the advantages accruing from the victory at Beachy Head in 1689 is apparent from their statement, made when they approved the establishment of de Varennes's manufacture of *londres* in 1689, that the project would be 'd'autant plus heureux présentement par la mer Méditerranée qu'elle n'est pas libre aux Anglais qui le faisoient cy-devant'.[26] But the situation between 1693 and 1695 became even more favourable. The English Levant Company's 1690 convoy had reached its destination safely but no other voyage had been risked until after the English naval victory of La Hogue in 1692. In view of the depletion of stocks of cloth in the Levant the convoy then sent in May 1693 was 'the richest that ever went to Turkey'. It was composed of over four hundred Dutch and English ships which were carrying 50,000 pieces of cloth. This vast convoy was caught by the French fleet in Lagos Bay and virtually totally destroyed; eighty merchant-men were captured and many others burned or sunk and as a consequence of the losses Constantinople was to receive no English cloth for four years.[27] English exports of cloth to the Levant were to recover but the effective monopoly which French suppliers enjoyed in the market for some four years not only contributed to the rapid expansion just observed but also established, once and for all, the reputation of Languedoc's cloth in the market. The contemporary opinion that the Turks were conservative buyers, reluctant to try new cloths but persistent in their tastes once they had accepted a product, was probably not without foundation. The fillip provided to France's Levant trade by these four years of monopoly conditions was clearly of great significance. Significantly in the sixteenth century too the Venetian loss of supremacy and the Dutch acquirement of a dominant position in the Levant trade had occurred during a period of warfare which had greatly hampered Venetian trade.[28]

The coincidence of the collapse of their own trades in Italy and Germany because of the war with this opening of the Levant market clearly impressed Carcassonne's clothiers. At the meeting summoned by Cauvière they declared that:

puisque leur commerce avoit beaucoup diminué du Costé d'allemagne piedmont et millan par la guerre, la même guerre leur offroit une occasion favorable pour travailler en draps fins pour le levant qui empêchoit les anglois et les hollandois dy

26. ADH C7248, Etats, 1689.
27. Wood, *Levant Company*, pp. 108–13.
28. R. Collier and J. Billioud, *Histoire du commerce de Marseille*, III, 198–9.

envoyer leurs convoyes qui y portoient beaucoup de draps de toutte qualité questant éclairés dans la fabrique Ils ne manqueroint pas de les Imiter, en sorte que la paix venant elle ne leur empêcheroit pas de continuer ce négosse quils peuvent faire avec autant de facillité et moins de fraix qu'eux.

Referring to Carcassonne's former involvement in production for the Levant they wrote that 'leurs pères avoint travaillé autresfois pour ce pais avec succès', but they still hesitated to commit themselves to the new market 'tant que les entrepreneurs de Saptes et de Clermont auront une pistolle par pièce'.[29]

This last barrier to participation in the expanding trade was effectively removed by the Etats in January 1695. They had been informed that the King 'désiroit que la province facillitât le commerce des draps fins pour le Levant' and, on the advice of Cauvière, had decided 'qu'on ne pouvoit mieux faire que de se servir des marchands de Carcassonne et du Sr Pelatan de Clermont pour faire ces sortes de draps'. The marchands from Carcassonne were Castanier and Poussonnel (described as 'fort riches') who had established a manufacture in the suburbs of the 'cité' of Carcassonne (the faubourg known as La Trivalle, which was also to become the name of their manufacture) and two others (described as 'fort expérimentés'), Pignol and Cusson. These merchants and Pelletan had come to Narbonne where the Etats were being held but had declared that they would not produce for the Levant unless they received the same subsidy as Villenouvette and Saptes. This the Etats granted for a total of four hundred whole pieces to be produced by Pelletan and Poussonnel and Castanier and a hundred pieces each by Cusson and Pignol.[30]

This decision by the Etats represented a turning-point for two reasons. It was from this moment that the province's exports to the Levant 'took-off'; production for the eleven months of 1695 for which there are records was 11,262 half-pieces, nearly six times that recorded for 1688.[31] And it was by this decision the Etats confirmed and consolidated a policy of subsidizing manufactures which, to judge from the success of Pelletan and three of Clermont's ordinary clothiers before 1695, and of many other unsubsidized clothiers between 1695 and 1707 (when the subsidy system was extended yet further to include *all* clothiers producing for the Levant), was not strictly necessary. As the cost of supporting a growing number of manufactures grew, the Etats made several attempts to escape from their obligations. In 1708 they petitioned the Crown unsuccessfully to abolish the subsidy system, enclosing with their petition evidence of the rising unsubsidized production (Table 10).[32]

29. ADH C2200, Meeting of 3 July 1694.
30. ADH C7277, Etats, 15 Jan. 1695.
31. See pp. 228–9.
32. ADH C7341, Etats, 14 Jan. 1708.

Table 10. *Statistics, showing growing importance of unsubsidized production, sent to King by Etats of Languedoc*

	Subsidized cloth sent to Levant	Unsubsidized cloth sent to Levant
1700	3,582	2,749
1701	5,108	3,580
1702	5,179	5,909
1703	5,410	7,313
1704	4,452	6,601
1705	4,024	7,924

Source: AN F12 645.

The Etats' evident preparedness to subsidize manufactures producing for new markets gave rise to a number of propositions for the founding of new manufactures, and to a variety of requests for financial support from established concerns in the following years. Manufactures producing for the Levant market which were granted support between 1696 and 1720 included two royal manufactures established in 1698 in the châteaux of Grange-des-Prés, near Pézenas, and of La Terrasse, in the diocese of Rieux; a manufacture at Pennautier, near Carcassonne (founded by Reich de Pennautier) in 1699; one at Aubenas and one in the Hôpital de la Grave of Toulouse in 1707; one at Cuxac in 1711 and one at Bédarieux in 1713.[33] By the late 1690s it was clear that there were fortunes to be made from producing for the Levant, and there is a sharp contrast in the nature of the foundations made before and after 1695. Whereas there had been an element of the heroic in the struggle to establish Saptes and Villenouvette it was clear, from the identity of those granted the right to found manufactures in 1698 and 1699, that privileges were now being conceded to those with influence in high places: it was the Prince de Conti who founded the manufacture of Grange-des-Prés, this château being his Languedocian residence. A proposal for the privilege granted to him to found this concern reads: 'Le Prince de Conti prince de notre sang nous a fait représenter qu'il auroit dessein d'établir dans une de ses terres . . . une manufacture de draperie.' La Terrasse was founded by the syndic-général of the Etats, Pierre Roux de Montbel, seigneur of La Terrasse,[34]

33. The registers of the Etats for these years contain information on these new foundations as well as recording their production.
34. AN F12 1380, has details on both Conti's and Roux de Montbel's requests. The latter's cultivation of favour with influential ministers in Paris is emphasized by Boissonnade ('Colbert, son système', p. 43). The privilege to found this royal manufacture may have been the reward for this assiduity.

Table 11. *Exports to the Levant, 1688–1725 (in ½-pieces of 15–16 aunes)*

1688	2,000–2,400	1710	16,167
1695	11,262 (11 months)	1711	22,199
1696	9,560	1712	28,729
1697	7,514	1713	32,240
1698	3,834 (6 months)	1714	31,271
1699	7,130	1715	15,060
1700	6,331	1716	11,340
1701	8,688	1717	21,820
1702	11,088	1718	24,620
1703	12,723	1719	28,780
1704	11,053	1720	20,000
1705	11,948	1721	24,300
1706	unknown	1722	19,500
1707	unknown	1723	27,780
1708	10,731	1724	25,700
1709	13,924	1725	31,200

Sources: 1688: J. Savary des Bruslons, *Dictionnaire universel du commerce*, III, 371–4; 1695–8: ACCM H 174, 'Etat des draps ... fabriqués dans les manufactures de Languedoc et de Marseille, 1695–1698', Cauvière, 11 July 1698; 1700–5: bureau de marque, Marseilles, 1708–14: record of exports from Marseilles; 1715–25: bureau de marque, Montpellier, from M. Morineau and C. Carrière, 'Draps de Languedoc et commerce du Levant au XVIIIᵉ siècle', *R.H.E.S.* 56 (1968), 109. On p. 111 of the same article there is information on cloth sizes: the size of a piece of Languedocian cloth was 30–2 *aunes*, and it was on the basis of pieces of this size that the bounty was awarded. After weaving, pieces of cloth were divided into two and were sold as half-pieces. During the eighteenth century production was generally recorded in numbers of half-pieces. It was also occasionally recorded in whole pieces, in *balles* of ten whole or twenty half-pieces and in *ballots* of five whole or ten half-pieces. On English cloth sizes see R. Davis, *Aleppo and Devonshire Square*, p. 99.

and Pennautier's influence both in Paris and in the Etats has been emphasized in a previous chapter.

The figures above show the total of subsidized and unsubsidized cloth exported to the Levant until 1725 (Table 11). In the Clermontais region there were four different sources of production of the new cloth: Villenouvette, Pelletan's privileged manufacture, unsubsidized clothiers and Grange-des-Prés. The inclusion of Grange-des-Prés (which in fact only produced between 1700 and 1709) in the Clermontais region is justified not only by its proximity to Clermont but also by the fact that it was built, manned and directed largely by Clermontais. Its directors, were, in succession, Thomas Barthe, Pierre-Antoine Barthe, Raymond Budin, Gabriel Pelletan, Jean and Antoine Pelletan and Pierre Astruc[35].

35. On this manufacture see ADH C1124 and registers of Etats.

Table 12. *Production of Villenouvette, Grange-des-Prés (1700–9 only),*
Gabriel Pelletan and Clermont's clothiers, 1700–25 (in ½-pieces)

1700	2,372	(1713	1,809)
1701	2,316	(1714	1,412)
1702	3,044	1715	6,423
1703	2,430	1716	4,302
1704	3,852	1717	5,039
1705	4,061	1718	6,130
(1706	3,024)	1719	—
(1707	2,380)	1720	5,380
(1708	1,590)	1721	6,504
1709	3,450	1722	4,360
1710	3,365	1723	5,435
1711	3,569	1724	4,380
(1712	1,864)	1725	5,540

N.B. Figures in parentheses do not include Clermont's production (for which figures are incomplete). Grange-des-Prés's production is not included in the figure for 1703. Gabriel Pelletan's concern abandoned production between 1717 and 1719. Clermont's production for 1715 and 1717 has been calculated by quadrupling and doubling figures recorded for a quarter and half of these years' productions respectively.

Sources: Procès-verbaux Etats, 1700–20; ADH C2208, 2231, 'cochineal passports' 1712–25; AN F12 645, Cauvière's figures recorded at Marseilles, 1700–5; C2212, figures for Feb.–May 1715; AN F12 556, 1380, visite générale de Montpellier, 1716, 1717, 1718.

All, bar Budin (a bourgeois, of St-Chinian originally, who had moved to Pézenas),[36] were from Villenouvette. The comparison of the production of the Clermontais region with that of the province as a whole shows that it contributed between one-quarter and one-half of the total exports to the Levant during most of these years (Table 12).

The rapidity of the growth is striking. No sector of the French economy grew more rapidly than Languedoc's cloth industry in the first half of the eighteenth century, no trade as rapidly as the Levant. The extent of the success seems to surprise historians as it did contemporaries. 'Par un ravivement des plus inattendus, qui étonna les français eux-mêmes, leur triomphe fut aussi rapide que complet', Masson wrote of the success in the Levant market. It is in the Levant trade that 'paradoxalement, on rencontre du neuf: la remarquable montée des exportations de draps de Languedoc', write Léon and Carrière in the new *Histoire économique et sociale de la France*.[37]

36. On Budin's origins ADH C1124, ADH 11 E 79 103, 14 June, 26 July 1688; 11 E 68 73, 17 Jan. 1693.
37. P. Masson, *Levant au XVIIᵉ siècle*, p. 367; Braudel and Labrousse, *Histoire économique*, II, 198.

Before analysing in greater depth what, as the nature of the quotations at the beginning of this chapter will have suggested, is the major theme of this chapter – the role of Colbertian policy in the revival of Languedoc's cloth industry for the Levant – it is necessary to emphasize two characteristics of this growth. First, as we have seen, the commercial expansion was fairly general in the 1690s. But we have also noted that demand for particular types of cloth, produced in particular towns, was especially intense. Cloth production was highly specialized, different markets requiring different types of cloth, and it was only certain varieties of production which were in demand. The rise in demand for *londrins* for the Levant was the most spectacular example of this and, as a consequence, a large premium was placed on the possession of those still relatively rare skills necessary for the production of this type of fine cloth. The same was true of Lodève's military cloth. If Clermont's traditional production had been in as great demand as Lodève's cloth it would not have been necessary for three Clermontais clothiers to change to producing cloth of the same kind as that produced in Lodève. Clermont had the advantage of proximity to Lodève and to Villenouvette, which enabled it to participate in the production of the two best-selling cloths of these years. Other cloth-producing towns lacked these advantages. In the same year of 1691 in which Lodève's industry could sell all the cloth it could produce it was reported that the twenty-two facturiers who formed St-Pons's humble cloth industry, who made *seizains* for the main part, 'vont aux foires de pézenas et montaignac pour la débite des draps de leur facture, nestant pas mesme ordinaire quils sy trouvent tous à la foire à cause du peu de draps quils fons, soit parce quils nont pas des fondes que pour le peu de débitte'. Eighty-nine cardeurs existed at St-Pons, the same report continued, but they had no maîtrise 'à cause de la diminution et de la Rétribution du travail de ce misérable mestier comme estant le plus peauvre de tous les mettiers'.[38] It was the towns producing specialized cloths for international markets who stood to gain most from the expansion: those towns whose industries had been the object of Colbertian reforms.

The second 'characteristic' of this expansion will, it is likely, already have suggested itself as a result of a perusal of the production figures. It is apparent that the expansion in production and in the number of apprenticeships was at a hectic rate in some years but it is evident, too, that the expansion was unsteady and that downturns in production could be as sharp. There is non-quantitative evidence for these fluctuations too. Until 1697 the trade was buoyant, the progress satisfactory. So much so that the Etats at their meeting of 23 January 1697 decided not to grant any

38. ADH C2774, report of 16 July 1691.

more aid to new manufactures.[39] But in 1699 and 1700 there was a sharp crisis. As a consequence of this first major setback a mood of pessimism and gloom spread among clothiers. A memoir was sent to the Etats stating that 'il leur paroissoit quils ne pouvoient continuer le commerce pour que les anglois et les hollandois le font avec beaucoup plus d'avantage qu'eux et peuvent par conséquent bailler à meilleur marché les draps de même qualité quils fabriquent dans leur pais'. Included too in the memoir were complaints about the high dues on wools and dyes, about Marseilles's trading monopoly, and about the damage which inspectors caused to cloth when they unpacked it for examination.[40] From 1701 to 1706 there was a steady recovery. In the latter year the Etats again expressed their belief that the subsidy system could be abandoned as the trade was so well established: 'puisque cette gratiffication n'avoit pas été accordée que dans un tems où la fabrique de draps fins pour le Levant n'étoit pas connüe … mais que le nombre d'ouvriers qu'il y avoit présentement dans la province … qui fabriquoient de draps fins pour le Levant sans aucune gratiffication ne laissoit pas lieu de craindre que ce commerce peut tomber'.[41] Apprenticeships at Villenouvette and Clermont had reached an unprecedented level in 1706. In the following year they slumped. Already in January, Astruc, director of Villenouvette, was warning d'Aguesseau, president of the conseil de commerce, of a loss of reputation in the Levant and of large unsold stocks of cloth in Marseilles.[42] But the crisis was at its worst in 1708 and 1709. 'Les manufactures sont sur le point de tomber. Celles des draps du Levant, qui, depuis quarante ans s'est perfectionée et est devenue très belle court beaucoup de risques', wrote Intendant Basville on 12 April 1708.[43] The Etats were forced to think again about abolishing subsidies. On 26 January 1709 they recorded that 'La conjoncture du temps et L'interruption du commerce du Levant, ne permettent pas de suprimer présentement les gratifications.'[44] Production picked up again, however, during 1709 and expanded continuously until the end of 1714, the quantity produced more than doubling and large numbers of new apprentices being taken on in these years. In 1715 there was another collapse. In January 1716 the Etats recorded that 'L'estat de tous ces fabriquans est très facheux parcequ'ils ne peuvent se défaire de leurs draps';[45] Inspector Carbon recorded the same phenomenon in September 1716: 'la cessation des fabriques qui tombent tous les jours non

39. ADH C7292.
40. ADH C7301.
41. ADH C7339.
42. AN F12 1380, Letter of 23 Jan. 1707.
43. Boislisle, *Correspondance*, III, 40 n.
44. ADH C7343.
45. ADH C7370.

seulement par la disette dargent, mais encore par le défaut de Consommation'.[46] The Etats in January 1717 commented gloomily on the protracted decline: 'ils n'ont pas fabriqué à beaucoup près un aussi grand nombre de pièces qu'en l'année 1715 à cause de la cessation du commerce, et en . . . 1715 on avoit fait . . . [moins] qu'en . . . 1714'.[47] In the same month Cauvière reported from Marseilles that 'il ne s'est vendu aucune balle dans cette place, qui ait donné du profit'. Cloth was sold in the Levant at a profit of 20–25% but 'la perte qu'on fait sur les marchandises de retour qui en proviennent . . . absorboit ce gain'.[48] During 1717, however, another recovery began. Apprenticeships and production figures rose steadily and in 1719 were nearly as high as they had been in 1713 and 1714. The last major crisis occurred in 1720 and 1721. This time it was occasioned by the plague at Marseilles, which blocked the export port, and the failure of Law's scheme and resultant monetary problems. De Bernage writing on 10 March 1721 to de Machault of the 'triste situation' of the province's cloth industry informed him that there remained a backlog of cloth produced in 1719 which had yet to be sold.[49] This, though, was to be the last major crisis. As the production figures reveal, in 1723 an expansion began which was to be virtually continuous until 1763. What checks there were to expansion were minor in comparison with the dramatic fluctuations of these early years which had caused production to be halved or doubled within a year.

In the space of some thirty years the expanding Languedocian cloth industry was thus shaken by four major crises – 1699–1700, 1707–9, 1715–17 and 1720–1. It was also, we have seen, a crisis in other cloth markets which was partly responsible for the rapidity of the expansion in 1694 and 1695. That the trade was dominated by the prosperity of the domestic economy is demonstrated not only by the coincidence of these crises with the major financial, demographic and agrarian crises of the end of the reign of Louis XIV and of the Regency, but also by the remark of Cauvière just quoted; the losses in the trade did not come from the sale of cloth in the Levant but from *the low price at which return products sold in France* in these years of general crisis. The period was one of exceptional economic opportunity – at no later stage was demand to experience such rapid rises, cloth selling at speculative prices in some years – and at the same time one of exceptional perils as each crisis brought its trail of abandonments of production and bankruptcies. Deyon's study on Amiens shows the same violence in fluctuations – years of record produc-

46. AN F12 1382, Report to Controller-General de Noailles, 20 Sept. 1716.
47. ADH C7373.
48. AN F12 645, Cauvière to de Noailles, 14 Jan. 1717.
49. ADH C2123, De Bernage to de Machault, 10 March 1721.

tion, followed by slumps, the number of looms in use varying by up to 300 in a year. His conclusion could be applied to Languedoc's experiences: 'Tout se passe, dans cette deuxième partie du règne de Louis XIV, comme si une contradiction était apparue entre les possibilités techniques et commerciales nouvelles d'une partie de nos manufactures, et les entraves apportées à leur activité par la fragilité de l'économie agricole du royaume, et par la mégalomanie de la politique extérieure.'[50]

But to return to the major question which interests us: the link between 'Colbertism' and the recovery. As we have already acknowledged, the Colbertian reforms were not, and could not, have been responsible for the revival in the general demand situation. The causes of this are slightly obscure – a variety of monetary, fiscal, climatic, agricultural and demographic factors seem to have been involved – but a wide range of historians have quite rightly insisted on the autonomy of these factors of governmental decisions: 'les mouvements profonds des négoces d'Ancien Régime ne s'expliquent pas par des décisions de pouvoir', writes Charles Carrière.[51] There is a second possibility, though, and that is that the Colbertian reforms so raised the level of technical ability in the French economy that this autonomous expansion in demand could be responded to more readily than would otherwise have been the case. In other words if Colbertian reforms were not prime-movers did they not at least contribute to accelerating the expansion when it occurred as well as ensuring its permanence? (Languedoc, for example, was to dominate the Levant market for most of the eighteenth century.) And there is a third possibility too. Was the expansion, accelerated or not by Colbertian intervention, in any way marked by Colbertian organizational reforms (guilds, inspectors, privileged manufactures etc.)?

There are two points of view on these questions. Holders of a traditional view would not only credit Colbert and Colbertian reforms with the expansion but would also, in some extreme cases, argue that he was the prime-mover in the recovery. Thus Arnould in his study of France's balance of trade published in 1791 concluded that in Languedoc 'ces encouragements [to royal manufactures] prolongés, et étendus jusqu'au commencement du 18ᵉ siècle, à de nouvelles manufactures de même espèce, amènèrent les plus heureux succès, lorsque les Turcs eurent pris goût à nos draps londrins'.[52] Boissonnade wrote in a similar vein:

50. *Amiens*, pp. 171–2, and 'Variations de la production textile aux XVIᵉ et XVIIᵉ siècles', *Annales* 18 (1963), 954.
51. In E. Baratier (ed.), *Histoire de Marseille*, p. 210.
52. A. M. Arnould, *De la balance du commerce et des relations extérieures de la France dans toutes les parties du globe*, I, 248.

'L'effort prodigieux de l'Etat pour restaurer et développer l'industrie nationale, avait, sous la direction de Colbert, donné sur presque tous les points des résultats étonnants, qui provoquaient l'envie, l'émoi, l'admiration des envoyés étrangers.'[53] And T. J. Markovitch, somewhat surprisingly, feels that his discovery of a 1.6% growth rate in the French cloth industry between 1670 and 1710 is 'une confirmation chiffrée de la supériorité de la politique de Colbert sur celle de ses successeurs'.[54]

This traditional view is held but rarely now. Quite rightly, in view of the discoveries made in recent years about the strength of agricultural and demographic determinants of the demand situation in the French economy, the role of governmental decisions in causing profound movements is discounted. But there is a tendency, too, to discount the secondary and tertiary possibilities which we have just posited and to argue that Colbertian reforms did not act as prime-movers in the recovery, nor contribute to its speed, nor significantly mark the form it took.[55] It is Charles Carrière who has adopted this position with respect to Languedoc's cloth production. In a short revisionist article he attempts to disprove the view held by contemporaries, and accepted by historians such as Boissonnade, Masson and Sagnac, that the Colbertian reforms and royal manufactures were responsible for the expansion in Languedoc's cloth production, and claims that they influenced only a minute proportion of the province's cloth production and that even this minor role was 'sans grand succès, il faut en convenir'. Instead, he argues, the bulk of cloth exported consisted of the type of cloth Languedoc had always produced, and had continued exporting to the Levant throughout the century – low-quality broad-cloth. In comparison with this enormous 'production "commune"' the few hundred pieces of cloth marked with the ministerial seal 'n'ont qu'une place insignifiante'.[56]

Evidence which has already been presented in this book would suggest that such a view is over-simplified. It would seem to ignore the fact that fine rather than coarse cloth was, and always had been, the most important and profitable branch of the Levant trade and was to form in the

53. *Colbert*, p. 203.
54. 'Le triple tricentenaire', p. 312. See also Masson, *Levant au XVIIe siècle*, pp. 207, 485; E. Martin-St-Léon, *Histoire des corporations de métiers*, p. 398; Heckscher, *Mercantilism*, I, 190–2; J. Koulischer, 'La grande industrie aux xviie et xviiie siècles', *Annales d'Histoire Economique et Sociale* 3 (1931), 13–14.
55. See especially H. Sée, *Histoire économique de la France*, I, 240; E. C. Lodge, *Sully, Colbert and Turgot*, pp. 167–8; Crouzet, 'Angleterre et France', p. 257; Braudel and Labrousse, *Histoire économique*, II, 188–90, 354–6.
56. 'Draperie languedocienne', pp. 161–4; and with Morineau, 'Draps de Languedoc', p. 114: 'ne soulevons pas le problème des origines où s'imprime la marque de Colbert, en qui nous croyons peu, pourtant'.

eighteenth century the great majority of Languedoc's exports to the Levant.[57] It ignores the need, which we have emphasized, of acquiring a good reputation with Turkish cloth buyers. It implies that cloth bought and sold in pre-industrial Languedoc was undiversified and uniform when this, as we have seen, was far from the case. It ignores, too, the evident technical and commercial backwardness of France at the time of Colbert's ministry. It judges the royal manufactures purely in terms of their *own* production (which is also under-estimated) and not in terms of their possible contribution to the cloth industries in their vicinity. In fact the position adopted seems to be one of 'conjunctural-determinism' – 'mouvements profonds' dictated all.

That significant technical changes were involved in the switch to producing for the Levant is apparent from Cauvière's reports after his visit in 1694. As mentioned, he recorded the production of three of Clermont's clothiers for the Levant, and their efforts, by which he was clearly impressed, he described in detail. Their production would have been of a low quality compared with that of the royal manufactures but, as is apparent from the description, it was quite distinct from that of Clermont's traditional industry:

> trois des marchands et ouvriers ... ont cessé leurs fabriques ordinaires depuis le mois de Janvier dernier pour faire des draps de londres ordinaires pour le Levant, et ont demonté quinze mestiers de leur ancienne fabrique pour les faire travailler à celle cy, ces nouveaux draps me paroissent fort bien faites, avec des laines du pais qui est fort belle, ils font filler au grand tour ou grand roüet à la manière dhollande, le fil en est plus fin que dans tous les autres endroits ou on fait de pareils draps et où on ne fille qu'à la manière de France, au petit tour ou petit roüet les draps en sont plus beaux, montrent moins la corde et Il y entre moins de laines mais ils coûtent aussy plus à filler et à tisser, l'un remplace l'autre. Ce commencement m'a sy fort plu que je les ay engagés à augmenter leur travail leur promettant de contribuer à les mettre en réputtacion à Marseille. Ils n'ont encore fait que des Londres de 2,000 fils d'une aulne un sixième de large au nombre de soixante quatorze pièces, Ils feront des larges à l'advenir de 2,400 fils à une aulne un quart.[58]

Cauvière's detailed description proves that it was not Clermont's traditional product which was being sent to the Levant but cloth made according to the new Dutch-style techniques imported to the province by de Varennes, Pierre Baille, André Pouget and others.

---

57. Carrière and Morineau refer to *londrins-seconds*, which formed, they note, the bulk of Languedoc's exports, as middling quality ('Draps du Languedoc', p. 119). *Londrins-seconds* was a fine, light-weight cloth made with Spanish wools, of 'middling' quality if compared with *mahous* or *londrins-premiers* but of high quality if compared with the bulk of the province's production between 1660 and 1690.
58. ADH C2200.

How had Clermont's clothiers learnt these skills? What was the origin of the improvement in the quality of Carcassonne's production which we have observed? It is to the answering of these questions that the rest of this chapter will be devoted. *Prima facie* the role of Colbertian manufactures and reforms would appear to have been fundamental. Until the mid-eighteenth century, production for the new market was virtually confined to Carcassonne, Clermont and St-Chinian, the three towns adjacent to the three privileged manufactures founded before 1690. We shall attempt to show more precisely, though, how the techniques developed in these manufactures were proliferated.

As has been emphasized at an earlier stage in this work, industrial techniques in the pre-industrial period were manual, and depended on the transference of skilled workers for their proliferation. Dutch skilled workers had brought the new cloth-making techniques to Saptes; it was by a transference of trained Dutch and Languedocian workers from Saptes that Villenouvette developed the new techniques. Saptes's ability to expand production in the 1690s was partly a result of the recruitment of a further seventeen Dutch families, we have just seen. How else but by the movements of both management and skilled workers from Villenouvette could the new cloth-making techniques have been developed at Clermont? We shall analyse the contribution of the manufacture to the different cloth-making professions.

Firstly the clothiers themselves. Two documents relating to the industry in 1708 reveal that the body of Clermont's clothiers had been substantially changed by this date and the scale of industrial concerns increased. Few of the clothiers from the town's traditional industry would seem to have continued producing cloth and their place had been taken, in great part, by ex-members of Villenouvette. The two documents in question are a survey of French industry carried out in 1708, and new corporative statutes which Clermont's clothiers registered in the same year.[59] The industrial survey reveals that sixteen clothiers were operating 104 looms. In other words the size of the industry (judged by looms) had doubled since the 1690s while the number of clothiers had remained virtually stationary. The average number of looms to the clothier had increased to slightly over six. If those recorded as producing in the industrial survey are added to those present at the registration of the new corporative statutes we obtain a total of twenty clothiers, at least nine of whom had served at Villenouvette: two of Gabriel Pelletan's sons, Antoine and Jean,

59. ADH ii E 25 108, 1 Aug. 1708; BN FF 8037, Desmaretz's survey, folio 56. (A summary of this survey is provided by P. M. Bondois, 'Etat de l'industrie textile en France d'après l'enquête du contrôleur général Desmaretz (début du xviiie siècle)', *Bibliothèque de l'Ecole des Chartes* 114 (1943), 165–6.)

five ex-apprentices to the manufacture, Joseph Tudesq, Antoine Raissac, Jean Verny, François Bourg and Jean-Gaspard Léotard, and two Clermontais who had worked for a number of years at the manufacture, Mathieu Pradier and Jacques Desalasc.[60] In addition a tenth member of the new corporation, Estienne Mathieu, had served his apprenticeship with Pierre-Antoine Barthe,[61] and thus owed his skills indirectly to the royal manufacture, and an eleventh, Pierre Desalasc, was associated with his son Jacques who had served ten years at Villenouvette.[62] Of the remaining nine, five were from Clermont's traditional industry (François Pouget, Raymond and Estienne Lugagne, Estienne Berthomieu and Jacques Ménard),[63] two others (Guillaume Santoul and Pierre Aumières) had connection neither with Villenouvette nor with the town's traditional industry, both being sons of prosperous farmers,[64] and finally there were two wholesale merchants who had diversified to cloth-producing – Jacques Galtié of Galtié père et fils and Pierre Estève, one of Raymond Moulins's correspondents.[65]

These marchands-facturiers in most cases not only themselves had ability in, and knowledge of, the new techniques but could also make use of the skills of some of the members of the large labour force trained at Villenouvette who, like them, left the manufacture during these years to set up independent workshops in Clermont. Some of these cloth-workers adopted new titles to distinguish themselves from those of Clermont's traditional weavers who continued to make the old style cloths – they are referred to in notarial documents as 'maîtres-tisserands à la manière d'Hollande'.[66]

The move from the manufacture to the town, in the same way as the move from the town to the manufacture, can be traced from the notarial registers. Cloth-workers originally mentioned as employees of Villenouvette are later found to be working in Clermont. The notarial registers are not so sensitive a source as to register each such movement but again they provide an accurate impression of the change which was taking place. Three acts involving the weavers' corporation at Clermont reveal a

60. See pp. 186–92.
61. ADH ɪɪ E 26 133, 1 Dec. 1690.
62. ADH ɪɪ E 26 167, 20 Aug. 1705; ɪɪ E 26 180, 3 Aug. 1719.
63. See p. 109.
64. Santoul was received master in 1706, Aumières in 1707 (ACC BB2, 10 Oct. 1706, 29 Aug. 1707). Aumières was the son of a ménager of St-Amans, diocese of Castres (ADH ɪɪ E 25 107, 27 Sept. 1704). Santoul not only was the son of a ménager but is himself described as such in 1704 (ɪɪ E 26 144, 8 March 1704). On the status of ménagers in the diocese of Lodève (in some cases a high one), see Appolis, *Lodève*, pp. 373–4.
65. ADR, Fonds Moulins, ɪv, Pierre Estève mentions his manufacture in several letters, e.g. those of 13 Aug., 27 Sept. 1714.
66. E.g. ADH ɪɪ E 26 139, 15 Aug. 1696.

gradual infiltration of the town's industry by former employees of
Villenouvette. In 1687 three out of fourteen, in 1692 seven out of twenty-
five, and in 1696 nine out of thirty weavers who attended these meetings
had served at the royal manufacture.[67] (These figures are minimal as
some of the other weavers may have served at Villenouvette without
leaving record of their presence there.) In total the notarial registers
reveal the names of fifty ex-employees of Villenouvette who established
themselves in Clermont during this period (until 1712). This number
was formed of thirty-three weavers, ten shearers and cloth-dressers,[68] six
dyers[69] and one carder. A large supply of the 'artizans distingués', so
essential for production for the new market, was coming from Villenouvette and the boast of a later director of the concern, that it was only as a
result of the royal manufacture's presence 'que la plus grande partie des
ouvriers de Clermont s'est formée, et qu'on a peu travailler pour le
Levant', can be seen to have been in part justified.[70] Only in part,
however, for the royal manufacture was not a sufficient source of labour
for an expansion as rapid as that which was occurring at Clermont.
Besides the fifty ex-members of Villenouvette, the presence of seventy-
five other non-Clermontais workers is revealed in the notarial registers
during these years. Amongst this number there were thirty-five weavers,
fifteen cloth-dressers and shearers, nine carders, ten operators of wool-
twisting machines, four dyers, a joiner and a cauldron-maker. These
individuals, as in the case of Villenouvette, came mainly from other
cloth-making areas of Languedoc. They served no apprenticeships and
so it is to be presumed that they arrived at Clermont equipped with the
skills required for their particular professions. A sizeable proportion
came from Carcassonne and its hinterland: eleven from the diocese of
Carcassonne itself, two from the diocese of Alet and one from Mirepoix.
Carcassonne did not make such a preponderant contribution to
Clermont's new industry as it did to Villenouvette's, however, for the
majority of these workers came from cloth-making towns to Clermont's
west (Map 9): thirteen were from the diocese of Castres (eleven of these
being from the cloth-making town of Lacaune), six were from Bédarieux
(Béziers), eight from the diocese of St-Pons (from the towns of St-Pons,
St-Chinian and Riols, all cloth-making centres), one from Lavaur, and
six from Lodève. The remaining twenty-seven were divided as follows:

---

67. ADH II E 26 104, 5 Jan. 1687, 5 Jan. 1692; II E 25 98, 26 Dec. 1696.
68. Jacques Bonneville, Paul Cathala, Pierre Delpon, Jean Estève, François Laborde,
    Antoine Maurel, François and Mathieu Mézas, Antoine Noudard and Joseph
    Tarbouriech.
69. Vital Bernard, Jean Bouissede, André Massiac, Estienne and Pierre Maysonnade and
    Philibert Peiron.
70. ADH C2131, Bourlat to de Bernage, 7 July 1730.

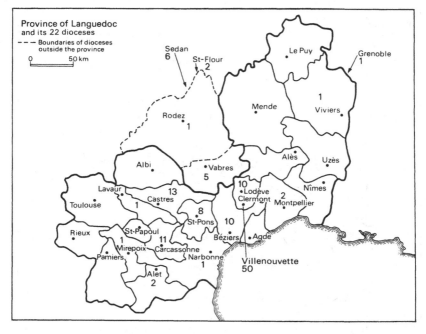

Map 9   Origins of 125 cloth-workers at Clermont

nine were from different parts of the Massif Central, eight were from villages in the diocese of Béziers and Lodève, two were from Montpellier, one was from Bize in the diocese of Narbonne, one was from the diocese of Grenoble, and no fewer than six were from Sedan, the site of the first Dutch-style manufacture in France. There was not such a sharp distinction between the origins of the skilled and semi-skilled workers as there was in the case of Villenouvette. Six of the fifteen shearers and cloth-dressers, however, came from the Carcassonnais region, a higher proportion than for the other less-skilled professions, and Clermont had to look far for its dyers: two were Carcassonnais, one was from Rodez and the other from Montpellier.

Thus Clermont, like Villenouvette, recruited the majority of its new labour force from other cloth-making areas of Languedoc, though a significant proportion came from the royal manufacture itself. Villenouvette played the role for Clermont which Saptes, Carcassonne and the Dutch and German workers had played for it, providing the essential nucleus of workers equipped with the new skills. As in the case of Villenouvette the new industry once established was able to train an

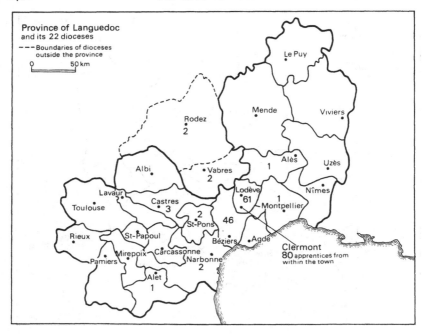

Map 10   Origins of 201 apprentices at Clermont

increasing number of apprentices and thus to ensure its future self-sufficiency as regards labour-supply. The rise in apprenticeships has already been examined and the new apprentices came largely from within the diocese of Lodève, or from the neighbouring diocese of Béziers (Map 10). Of the total of 202, 141 were from within Lodève, eighty being from Clermont itself, and forty-six were from neighbouring villages in the diocese of Béziers. Only fifteen remain to be accounted for: three were from Lacaune in the diocese of Castres; Rodez, Vabres, Narbonne and St-Pons provided two each; Alet, Alès and Montpellier one, and the origin of one is not recorded.

The movement of so many workers to Villenouvette and then to Clermont from other parts of France and of the province of Languedoc illustrates that there was a quite exceptional mobility of labour between the cloth-making towns of France during this period. The mobility was occasioned by professional factors and it ignored normal migratory patterns. A large number of 'cloth-making mercenaries' were prepared to work wherever a high wage was offered and thus helped to cause a rapid diffusion of the new cloth-making techniques. The workers who came to

Clermont very often did not expect to stay. Particularly in the 1690s, when new manufactures were being opened throughout Languedoc, they were prepared to move again if the opportunity offered itself. The most abundant and suggestive evidence of this mobility is provided by the apprenticeship contracts themselves. The industry was developing so rapidly, and the Clermontais entrepreneurs (particularly Pelletan, the Barthes and Astruc) were so ambitious, that even the most home-loving of master-weavers could not be sure that he would be working in the same place at the end of his contract with his apprentice as at the beginning. Thus to avoid disputes with apprentices the procedure to be followed in the event of the masters' movement away from Villenouvette or Clermont was defined in a number of contracts. There were a variety of different formulas for these 'mobility clauses'. Sometimes the apprentice promised to follow his master wherever he should work; one promised to serve Mevic Requy, a Carcassonnais working at Clermont, 'soit icy ou alheurs à lendroit que led Requuy travalhera'.[71] In other contracts it was only to certain areas, or named manufactures, that the apprentice was obliged to follow, normally around Clermont. A contract of 1698, for instance, stated that 'lapranti sera teneu de suivre son maistre pour travalher en lad manufacture Royalle de Vileneuve, aud Clermont et en la Grange-de-Préds de Pézenas et non alheurs'.[72] A contract of 1692 prescribed a wider range – the apprentice was to follow his Villenouvette master 'en cas led maître voudroit aller travalher à béziers St-Chinian ou Clermont'.[73] Several contracts for 1697 stipulated that should the master move more than four leagues from Clermont the apprentice was not obliged to follow him.[74] In some contracts the apprentice was specifically relieved from the obligation of following his master,[75] and in others the master claimed the right, should he leave for another town, 'de bailher ledit. apprantis à tel maître tisserant quil voudra'.[76] The variety of different ways in which the possibility of the master-weaver's departure was catered for is of interest, but the essential conclusion to be drawn from all these contracts is the same: particularly during the 1690s, the moment when Languedoc's production for the Levant started to expand, the weaver's mobility was such that he could not predict his future working place for even the short period of an apprenticeship. It was perhaps inevitable that there should have been such mobility within the

71. ADH 11 E 26 135, 8 April 1692.
72. ADH 11 E 26 141, 19 Jan. 1698.
73. ADH 11 E 26 135, 15 June 1692.
74. ADH 11 E 26 165, 18 May and 24 June 1697. Grange-des-Prés and Villenouvette were both safely within a radius of 4 leagues.
75. ADH 11 E 26 135, 12 May 1692.
76. ADH 11 E 26 126, 5 June 1689.

immediate region of Clermont but, as has been seen, workers had originally come to Clermont from all over Languedoc, and there is evidence, too, of workers from Clermont moving large distances to work in new manufactures. Seven of the employees of Barthe at Grange-des-Prés in 1699 had left to work at the new manufacture of La Terrasse[77] and there is abundant evidence of movements to Carcassonne, the centre of the new industry.[78] All types of workers were affected: the Barthes and Pelletans, for instance, recruited all categories of workers as well as management for Grange-des-Prés in Clermont and at Villenouvette.[79] One example of managerial mobility is the case of Cazals, a marchand-facturier of St-Chinian. He was recruited by Barthe to work at Grange-des-Prés but disgraced himself there by impregnating one of the manufacture's spinners, so in 1699 he left to work for Gabriel Pelletan at Aspiran.[80] Another example is that of Joseph Goudard: son of a marchand-bourgeois of Pézenas, he was apprenticed at the manufacture of La Trivalle in Carcassonne.[81] In 1703 he was employed as a facturier at Villenouvette;[82] later in that year he was employed as a facteur by Pelletan at Grange-des-Prés;[83] in 1708 he was received master at Clermont;[84] in 1715 he was producing cloth in partnership with Pierre Estève at Clermont,[85] and he finished his career as a director of Laporte's royal manufacture at St-Chinian.[86]

So Clermont's example shows that royal manufactures were capable of playing the role for which they had originally been intended by Colbert: the forming of 'travailleurs qualifiés capables d'exercer leur métier pour leur propre compte'.[87] It shows, also, that in this formative period of Languedoc's Levant trade there was virtually a province-wide labour market for cloth-workers equipped with the new skills and it provides an added illustration of what has been observed in our previous chapter; once a nucleus of skilled workers had been formed its reproductive powers, via the apprenticeship system, were strong. It is clear, however, that the example is an extreme one in that given the poverty of Clermont's industry there was little possibility of an autonomous indus-

77. ADH C1124, list of 'créanciers privilégiés', 1699.
78. See p. 201, n. 130.
79. ADH C1124.
80. ADH C1124.
81. ADH C2153, has details of his career including evidence of his reception as master on 25 Sept. 1708.
82. ADH 11 E 25 106, 18 June 1703.
83. ADH 11 E 26 145, 7 Dec. 1705.
84. ADH C2153.
85. ADH C2212, Production details for 1 Feb.–1 May 1715.
86. ADH C2153.
87. Coornaert, 'Les manufactures', p. 2.

trial expansion and the role of the royal manufacture inevitably was preponderant. The assessment of the role of Colbertian reforms, and of the royal manufacture of Saptes, in the evident improvement in, and expansion of, Carcassonne's industry is more complex for in this case we are dealing with a large industry with an evident autonomous growth capacity, which did not expand its production purely for the Levant in this period but also achieved successes in several different markets. I shall first analyse the ways in which the town's industry changed during these years, secondly show how the demand situation contributed to these changes, and thirdly suggest how Colbertian reforms and manufactures interacted with the improved demand situation.

The changes that occurred in Carcassonne's industry from the mid-1680s were parallel to those which occurred at Amiens and elsewhere in this period.[88] Whereas between approximately 1660 and 1680 the industry had been stagnant, producing low- or medium-quality cloth for sale, largely, in local markets or for purchase 'in the white' for finishing at Lyons, and the predominating production unit had become small scale and familial, by the mid 1690s the town's industry was emerging in quite a different guise: some fifty clothiers, operating for the most part on a large scale (they shared 800 looms between them), were producing a large amount of cloth of which a growing, and already large, share consisted in select, fashionable, high-quality cloth intended for distant markets. The most significant figure in the industry had become the marchand-fabricant. It was his ambition, ability and resources which were crucial to thse changes. Deyon, who observes a similar growing prominence of the large-scale manufacturer at Amiens during this same period, emphasizes this cruciality: 'Les seuls progrès que nous ayons constatés intervinrent là où les fabricants mêmes disposaient de quelques réserves monétaires', he writes.[89] The marchand-fabricant's combination of merchanting and manufacturing roles had the consequence that profits, instead of being creamed off by merchant-buyers as was the case when industrial production was in the hands of a large number of small-scale producers, went in great part to the industrialist who, by reinvesting, could expand and improve the quality of his production.

So these were the changes, and the nature of the economic background to them is evident. As we have emphasized in a previous chapter in which we noted the gradual disappearance of all these characteristics of an advanced industry, such techniques and high-quality production were

---

88. Deyon, *Amiens*, pp. 149, 171–2, 174, 178–9.
89. *Amiens*, p. 191.

economically viable only if the demand situation was favourable, as they were liable to considerable economies of scale. And so the background to this improvement was, indisputably, the improving demand situation and rising prices for cloth. The situation was all the more favourable to large concerns in that wages were rising more slowly than cloth prices.

Equally indisputably, however, such production methods and industrial skills did not develop automatically from an improved demand situation. We have seen that only certain towns in Languedoc were equipped to respond to the call from re-opened or expanding markets. There clearly had been, then, a necessary process of learning forgotten or new skills for the expansion to take place and the assistance which 'Colbertism' had given in this process could only have been positive. It seems justifiable to infer from the way in which Villenouvette influenced Clermont's industry that the manufacture of Saptes, which had functioned eight years longer than Villenouvette, had had a considerable technological influence on Carcassonne's industry. Our previous chapter on Villenouvette's success shows how the necessary skills for production in the new market could, within the family economy and via the apprenticeship process, multiply quite rapidly. We have seen also how Villenouvette itself was, as it were, an off-shoot of the older manufacture. That Carcassonnais clothiers looked to Saptes as a source for the skills necessary to produce fine cloth is apparent from the attempts by Roux de Montbel in 1691 to prevent clothiers from poaching members of its labour force during the temporary difficulties occasioned by Noël de Varennes's death.[90] But this was only the most obvious example of the Colbertian influence. Who were these enterprising clothiers with the resources to emulate Saptes's production and to take on its highly paid, skilled workers? A group created by the 'conjuncture' which was favourable to large-scale producers? Yes, but the formation of such a group had clearly been much favoured by the controversial policy of reviving, or introducing, the guild system. As we have observed, in the 1640s there were no restrictions on participation in cloth production. The creation of a corporation at Carcassonne ensured control over entry into the trade of clothier and hence greater professionalism. The trade could thus be exercised only by full-time, specialized clothiers, and the emergence of rich marchands-fabricants, and the increase in the scale and quality of production, in part a consequence of the improved 'conjuncture', was also contributed to by a corporative system which, in the (theoretical) interests of the quality of production, ensured that only a limited selection of qualified, specialized clothiers should be allowed to

90. See p. 204.

respond to the rising demand. And these marchands-fabricants benefited not only from the existence of skilled workers at Saptes. It was Colbertian trading companies and manufactures which had established the reputation of Languedocian cloth in the Levant and contributed to the re-establishment of regular trading links. It was the protective tariffs imposed by Colbert which had provided a new incentive to the production of fine cloth for the domestic market. It was agents employed by the trading companies, such as Augustin Magy, who had carried out the necessary market research to ensure that the right types of cloth were made. Magy, whose mission to the Levant in 1670 we mentioned earlier, corresponded with the controller-general regularly in the 1670s and 1680s, advising on further improvements which could be made in Languedoc's production.[91] It was he, too, who was responsible for introducing the Dutch-style cloth-making techniques and tools to St-Chinian, and he was described after his death by Cauvière as 'fort entendu en la fabrique des draps, et fort Capable d'augmenter le commerce du Levant par les lumières qu'il avoit tiré des soings quil sestoit donné'.[92]

Clearly it is impossible to measure the exact contribution of either 'conjuncture' or 'Colbertism' to the rapidity of the advance. The only acceptable course is to recognize the interaction of both in the success, and to emphasize, as Pierre Deyon does, that Colbertian reforms should not be judged in terms of their immediate consequences only: 'Un progrès technique considérable avait ... été acquis', Deyon writes, 'et, dans ce domaine tout autant que dans celui de la production manufacturière, on aurait tort de négliger les réalisations économiques de l'époque de Colbert parce qu'elles ne s'inscrivent pas immédiatement dans les statistiques des prix ou de la production.'[93] The revival in the 'conjuncture' activated a machine built, and well oiled, by Colbert.

In 1694 Carcassonne's clothiers, *invited* on the King's behalf by Cauvière to produce for the Levant, showed in their response to the invitation that it was not only the favourable demand situation which had given rise to this invitation but also their skills. They assured Cauvière 'que la manufacture de lad ville est dans la meilleure disposition qu'elle aje jamais esté, les marchants estant fort appliqués sérieusement de travailler en draps fins depuis que l'entrée des draps estrangers en a été deffendu ... on ne trouve presque pas de différence avec ceux d'Hollande et dangleterre'.[94]

91. AN G7 1684, letters of Guilleragues to Colbert, 22 Dec. 1679, 16 Jan. 1680, mention Magy's continued co-operation during these years.
92. ADH C2200, Cauvière's report.
93. *Amiens*, p. 103.
94. ADH C2200, Cauvière's report on Carcassonne's clothiers' meeting of 3 July 1694.

So we would argue that there is strong evidence for the second of our two 'possibilities'. The success of French manufactures in this period was unquestionable. As Heckscher writes, the results of Colbertian policy were 'in many cases ... brilliant and French luxury industries during these years became the envy of and admiration of Europe'.[95] The rapidity of the transformation of France's status as industrial competitor surprised and alarmed competitors in England. And it seems certain that it was Colbertian reforms which facilitated this rapid recovery of a powerful position in so many markets which occurred once the demand situation became more favourable.

It is also possible, and in raising this point we progress to our third possibility, that Colbertian intervention affected the form the industrial revival took, that the reforms had, to a great extent, pre-determined the trades and industries which would benefit from the improved demand situation. In other words it is possible that although the economic revival was general the reforms, subsidies and preparations had made it more advantageous to produce for certain trades than others. This would seem to have been the case in Languedoc. The growing advantages in producing for the Levant were to occasion, for example, a gradual abandonment of production for those other markets which, as we have seen, were profitable in the 1680s and 1690s. This tendency, as we have observed at an earlier stage, would not necessarily have been regarded unfavourably by Colbert who desired such an industrial specialization, different towns being entrusted with the provision of different markets. There was clearly a long-term danger in it, however, if the Colbertian belief in a world of fixed and unchanging markets should turn out (as it was to) to be untrue. Structural problems might develop and might develop all the sooner in so far that the model on which the Colbertian reforms were based was the Dutch economy, and the Dutch economy in the *mid-seventeenth century*. But by the end of the seventeenth century it was already apparent from the beginnings of the Dutch economic decline, which was not entirely attributable to French and English competition, that this Dutch model, satisfactory though it may have been for dominating the European economy in the mid-seventeenth century, provided no recipe for permanent industrial success.[96] It has been argued that the French industrial and commercial expansion of the sixteenth century was too much based on the example of a Venetian economy on the point

95. *Mercantilism*, I, 190–2.
96. J. de Vries, *Economy of Europe in an Age of Crisis*, pp. 251–2; C. H. Wilson, 'The economic decline of the Netherlands', *Ec.H.R.* 9 (1939), 111–27.

of decline.[97] The expansion which began on the basis of the Dutch model in the 1690s could be criticized on the same grounds. As we have seen, pride of place in Colbert's plans was given to the revival of a dominant situation in the Mediterranean. Indeed it was to this purpose that was owed the extent of the support given to Languedoc's royal manufactures. But the exceptional importance of the Levant trade to the Dutch and English in the mid-seventeenth century was a consequence of impermanent factors – the disruption of the Baltic, Russian and German trades above all[98] – and by the end of the century a decisive shift towards Atlantic trading was beginning to take place in these northern economies.

It is only hindsight that enables one to speculate in this manner. To contemporaries the success was complete and satisfactory: 'on travaille mieux en Languedoc qu'on ne travaille en Angleterre', boasted the Etats of Languedoc in 1712,[99] and it was fear of French competition which governed economic debates in England in the first half of the eighteenth century and, quite probably, the fact of French competition which checked the growth in cloth production. The success seemed to justify Colbertian-type policies, indeed seemed to give grounds for their intensification in order to prevent the acquired position in markets being lost. As the right sort of cloths had been developed then they should be regulated. In 1697 and in 1708 new regulations were published for Languedoc's cloth industry.[100] Since there was a danger that overproduction might develop, other cloth-making centres should be allowed to register new guild statutes and production should be confined to those areas already producing. As we have just seen, new corporative statutes were approved for Clermont in 1708 and in 1715 production of fine cloth for the Levant was confined to members of the clothiers' corporations of Carcassonne, Clermont and St-Chinian.[101] Because the production of low-quality textiles in the areas where fine cloth was made could

97. Chaunu and Gascon, *Histoire économique*, 1, 302, refers to the Italian banks at Lyons orientating sixteenth-century France 'dans les grands courants du commerce international mais ce fut davantage dans l'Europe du passé – celle de la Méditerranée et des Italiens – que dans l'Europe de l'avenir, tournée aussi vers l'immensité neuve de la mer océane'.
98. Deyon, *Amiens*, p. 158; G. D. Ramsay, *English Overseas Trade during the Centuries of Emergence*, p. 60; F. J. Fisher, 'London's export trade in the seventeenth century', *Ec.H.R.* 3 (1950), 151–61.
99. ADH C7339, Etats, 13 Jan. 1712.
100. The regulation of 1697 is published in *Les règlemens des manufactures et teintures des étoffes qui se fabriquent dans le royaume* (Paris, 1701).
101. AN F12 55, Registers of Bureau de Commerce, folios 320–1, 25 Jan. 1715.

adversely affect the quality of both, then certain areas should specialize in fine cloth and certain in coarse. By the same 1715 measure Carcassonne, Clermont and St-Chinian were barred from producing any but fine cloth. As clothiers showed a lamentable tendency to cheat, then more inspectors should be appointed. The number of Languedocian inspectors was increased from two to four in 1697 and a fifth was appointed for Montpellier in 1714.[102]

There had been a degree of flexibility in industrial policy until the turn of the century while the right formula for economic success was sought but now that success had been achieved the mould was set.

102. Boislisle, *Correspondance*, I, 1673, letter of de Pontchartrain to Basville, 9 Dec. 1697.

8

The first thirty years, 1695–1724

I believe that, for each period into which our economic history may be divided, there is a distinct and separate class of capitalists. In other words, the group of capitalists of a given epoch does not spring from the capitalist group of the preceding epoch. At every change in economic organization we find a breach of continuity. It is as if the capitalists who have up to that time been active, recognize that they are incapable of adapting themselves ... In their place arise new men, courageous and enterprising who boldly permit themselves to be driven by the wind actually blowing and who know how to turn their sails to take advantage of it. (H. Pirenne, 'The stages in the social history of capitalism', *American Historical Review* 19(1914), 494–5)

Few of the men who entered the trade rich were successful. They trusted too much to others, too little to themselves. (P. Gaskell, cited by Pirenne, p. 514, n. 31)

That the French trade with the Levant should have expanded rapidly from the 1690s is no cause for surprise. The circumstances which had led both to the extent of its decline, and to the strength of the English and Dutch involvement in the Mediterranean, were of a temporary rather than a permanent nature. As we have seen, the French trade had been particularly severely affected by a variety of factors: shifts in European commercial circuits, internal disorders, involvement in foreign warfare, piracy in the Mediterranean, the decline in domestic demand and hence in that for return products from the Levant and the over-valuation of the *livre*. And we have suggested too that, although the importance of the Levant trade to the European economy justified the interest shown in it by Dutch and English merchants, the extent of their involvement in the trade in these years was exceptional and occasioned, likewise, by disruptive factors which were to turn out to be of an impermanent nature: the collapse of the Baltic, German and Russian trades in the first half of the century as well as interruptions in the maritime routes to the East Indies which, temporarily, caused a revival in the importance of the overland spice routes to Turkey.[1] During the last fifteen years of the century

1. See pp. 117–18, 247.

circumstances became far more favourable to France's trade. It was again a period of warfare but the theatre of war was largely in northern Europe and, as we have seen, naval successes on this occasion actually favoured French attempts to re-establish her situation in the Levant market. In addition it was a period in which a Europe-wide recovery in prices occurred and, on this occasion, devaluation of the *livre* and a carefully devised trading policy ensured that it should be French traders who would benefit from the expansion in the domestic economy. New and favourable trading terms had been negotiated with the Sultan. France's industrial and commercial skills had been improved. A degree of domestic social stability had been achieved and was to last until the second half of the eighteenth century. The French East and West Indian trades were not yet sufficiently developed to occasion much competition to the Levant as a source for exotic products and raw materials. The Turkish empire itself was at peace, and prospering during these years.[2] All, therefore, was set for a great expansion in the French trade and the situation which had given rise to the extent of Dutch and English involvement in the Mediterranean no longer applied. As Ralph Davis has shown, the recovery of the East Indian and West Indian trades and the availability of 'colonial' raw materials and exotic products caused a gradual decline in the demand for return products from the Levant and hence a gradual decline in the trade during the first half of the eighteenth century. Indeed the contrast between the states of the French and English trades could hardly have been sharper. By 1707, when the French trade was just establishing itself, the English trade was said to be past its heyday; in 1760, when the French trade was entering its most productive decade, an English factor leaving Aleppo was to report that the trade 'was far down the hill in decline, and its reputation as a source of great merchant fortunes dying . . . due to influences beyond the control of the merchants engaged in the trade or the Levant company'. The major 'uncontrollable' cause, as Davis writes, was 'the falling demand for Levant silk in England'.[3] In France, though, demand for Levantine products was rising rapidly and giving rise to speculatively high prices in some years. Silk and cotton bulked large among products imported, the latter product in particular: by the mid-century thirty million pounds of cotton were being imported a year, representing one-third of the total value of imports.[4] The continued importance of the industrial produc-

2. Paris, *Histoire du commerce de Marseille*, v, 91, 547, refers to both the good relationships between France and the Ottoman Empire (temporarily interrupted in 1697) and the growing prosperity of Ottoman markets during the first half of the eighteenth century.
3. *Aleppo and Devonshire Square*, pp. 26, 30.
4. Paris, *Histoire du commerce de Marseille*, v, 505.

tion of the southern half of France must have contributed to the suitability of the Levant as a source for industrial raw materials. Lyons and Nîmes were the largest French silk-producing centres and Montpellier was developing a large cotton industry in the first half of the eighteenth century. It was the Levant which was the French 'Eldorado' in the first half of the eighteenth century, a fact which partly explains the intensity of the cultural curiosity shown in the area.[5]

To the fact that general background factors were favourable to the French trade needs to be added one further consideration. This is that France had most obvious economic and geographic advantages in producing for the Levant, advantages of a kind which would have meant that even under equal conditions (and conditions were not equal) the French would have been likely to have enjoyed a competitive edge over rival producers. Labour costs by all accounts were about a third lower in France than in Holland or England, and Languedoc was ideally sited for industrial production for the Levant being close both to the source of the major necessary raw material – Spanish wool – as well as to the market itself. Even before the trade was well established commentators predicted that the French, on the basis of these advantages, would oust the Dutch and English from the market. Jacques Savary, in his *Le parfait négociant*, wrote in 1679 that the Languedocians 'ruineront [the trade] d'Hollande parcequ'on le [cloth] peut donner à meilleur marché & que l'on a la facilité d'assortir les couleurs dans trois ou quatre mois, au lieu qu'il en faut une année entière aux Hollandois'. The careful assortment of the range of colours included in each bale of cloth, and a rapid response to change in taste for different colours, were crucial in securing a rapid sale. As Savary emphasized, 'il faut remarquer que les Turcs, les Arméniens & les Persans sont très difficiles pour les couleurs ... La vivacité des couleurs en cause le débit'.[6] 'Surtout il faut observer les assortimens des balles pour les couleurs qui changent Icy presque deux fois Lannée, on aura soing de les Envoyer tous les six mois',[7] it was stated in a memoir sent from the Levant in 1680. Basville, in his memoirs on Languedoc, summarized the advantages enjoyed by his province in production for the new market:

On ... pourroit porter le Commerce aussi loin que l'on voudroit, & même faire entièrement périr celui des Hollandois dans le Levant; parce qu'on le fait en

---

5. Paris, *Histoire du commerce de Marseille*, v, pp. 100–5. But as Paris points out this interest, together with the importance of the Levant trade, had lapsed by the second half of the century: 'les "chinoiseries" avaient remplacé les "turqueries" et la littérature allait chercher ses décors exotiques dans les pays tropicaux'.
6. *Le parfait négociant*, pp. 402–3.
7. AN G7 1684, 'Mémoire pour le commerce des draps de Levant', *c.* 1680.

France avec beaucoup d'avantages sur eux. 1° La facilité d'avoir les Laines d'Espagne & du Pays. 2° La situation favorable, qui fait que toutes les Saisons sont propres à en faire le trafic; au lieu de la longue navigation où les Anglois & Hollandois sont obligez. 3° La bonté des eaux qui servent aux teintures & à la preparation des laines; ce sont aussi ces mêmes moyens qui ont fait parvenir ce Commerce si promptement au point qu'il est.[8]

The second advantage which Basville listed, the possibility of maintaining a more regular contact with the market, had been greatly reduced in the seventeenth century, of course, because the small, French trading ships were often the victims of privateers who were particularly abundant in the Mediterranean in this period. The eighteenth century, though, saw a great decline in Mediterranean piracy and the possibility of making frequent, small-scale voyages to the Levant gave the French a distinct advantage over the Dutch and English with their cumbersome convoys which took six to seven months to arrive, and up to fifteen or sixteen months to complete a round trip. There was certainly no question of a rapid response by the Dutch and English to a change in fashion in the Levant. The importance of dyeing, and of the rapid response to changes in the demand for different colours in the Levant, to the French success is illustrated by the fact that the English when they attempted to copy Languedocian cloth gave their imitations the name 'French colours'.[9]

Languedoc's only major disadvantage was its clothiers' poverty which was a consequence of the industrial decline and disinvestment which had occurred since the mid-century. A memoir sent from the Levant in the early 1680s emphasized this one handicap: 'le travail est Incomparablement plus facile et à meilleur marché en Languedoc que en Hollande, Il n'y a que la différence des maistres des fabriques qui fasse la différence du prix, ceux d'hollande estant assez riches pour faire rouler leur fabrique sans prendre de l'argent à Inthérest'. De Varennes, it was stated, was having to borrow money at interest rates of up to 16%.[10] The main justification of the policy of granting interest-free loans lay in the need to compensate for this handicap.

So the rapidity of the revival of the Levant trade is easily explicable. The French trade was favoured both by temporary conjunctural factors and by permanent geographical advantages. And this rapidly expanding trade, without any doubt, offered most exceptional economic opportunities both to those at Marseilles, involved in the commercial side of the trade, and to those in Languedoc, involved in the industrial, just as the

8. Boulainvilliers, *Etat*, ii, 562.
9. Davis, *Aleppo*, p. 103.
10. AN G7 1684, 'Mémoire', c. 1680.

English trade in its prime in the seventeenth century had generated exceptional fortunes among the 'Turkey merchants' in London and the 'gentlemen clothiers' of the West Country.[11]

The Levant trade was an example, probably the most impressive example, of the new *élan* observable in the French economy from the 1690s, and which we have commented on in the previous chapter. New industrial and commercial dynasties were formed during this period throughout France. As Léon wrote, despite the economic disruption 'nouvelles aristocraties marchandes' arose in this period. Sagnac observed, likewise, the formation of 'un grand patronat, une aristocratie manufacturière' which with its large capital resources, privileges and market links succeeded in dominating 'Le vieux métier du moyen âge', and Levasseur registered the contrast between the artisanal clothiers of the seventeenth century and the new species of entrepreneurs developing in these years: 'celles des directeurs et des propriétaires d'usine et de grande fabrique, riches négociants qui correspondaient avec les ministres, traitaient avec les intendants et occupaient dans l'industrie la même position que les armateurs de commerce'.[12]

In no sector of the economy was this newly generated wealth more remarkable than in textiles and, above all, in woollen-cloth production. The phenomena which we have already observed at Carcassonne and Clermont and which Deyon has observed at Amiens – industrial growth and a concentration in favour of a rising class of rich clothiers – have been observed too at Le Mans, Beauvais, in the Norman cloth centres and indeed in cloth-making centres throughout France during this period.[13] It was the misnamed 'industries du passé' which were at the forefront of France's exceptional growth in the first half of the eighteenth century (trade grew at a rate of 4.1% per annum until 1745 in contrast to the 0.5% growth rate observed in England). As Dornic writes, 'on va ... au commerce de draperie comme au meilleur moyen de faire fortune'. And he shows in support of this assertion that the eight purchasers of masterships in the textile industry at Le Mans in 1722 were all already qualified practitioners of other professions: a 'chapelier', a baker, a 'vinaigrier-chandelier', a 'practicien', a 'barbier-perruquier', a 'tailleur-couturier', a

11. Davis, 'England and the Mediterranean', p. 126: 'the title of "Turkey merchant" was later a general synonym for vast riches'.
12. Léon, 'La Crise', p. 133; P. Sagnac, *La formation de la société française moderne*, p. 119; Levasseur, *Histoire des classes ouvrières*, 11, 402.
13. Deyon, *Amiens*, pp. 171–8, 226–8; 'La concurrence internationale des manufactures lainières aux xvɪᵉ et xvɪɪᵉ siècles', *Annales* 27 (1972), 31; 'La production manufacturière', pp. 55–6; Crouzet, 'Angleterre et France', p. 269; Markovitch, *Les industries lainières*, pp. 21–3, 125, 148, 153, 225.

'vendeur de blé' and a 'tisserand en fil de chanvre et en lin'.[14] To change professions in mid-career, a risky and costly procedure, could only mean that opportunities in cloth-making were quite exceptional.

Why was it that textile production was so important a means for social mobility in this period? In addition to a fact that we have already emphasized – the exceptional weight of this sector in pre-industrial economies and its crucial role in foreign trade – textile production had another characteristic which distinguished it from purely trading activities. Whereas the essential and only major requirement for successful participation in commerce was the possession of large financial resources, in industrial production the possession of capital was an important but not nearly so preponderant element. Labour input into textile production could amount to 50% or more of the final costs.[15] There was no machinery which could obviate this fact and while the rich producer was at no disadvantage with respect to labour which both he and his artisanal rivals hired on the open market, the artisan, as we have seen, enjoyed the additional resources of his own and his family's labour. In other words the artisan's chances of competing with the merchant were more favourable in industrial production than in pure commercial activities.

In few places was this speculative surge into cloth-making more marked than in those three Languedocian towns equipped for producing for the Levant – Carcassonne, Clermont and St-Chinian. At Carcassonne in 1722 it was reported that the number of clothiers had increased from 100 to 180 in the previous six years, and it will be remembered that there had only been forty-eight clothiers in 1694. Old clothiers were reported to be 'au désespoir de voir que toute sorte de novice se mêlent du métier'.[16] This growth was confirmed by another report made two years later: the number of clothiers had doubled since 1708 and it was lamented that (as at Le Mans) masterships had recently been purchased by three individuals 'engagés depuis long temps dans d'autres professions'.[17] At Clermont it was not to be expected that the expansion should have been quite as hectic as at Carcassonne. There was a far smaller base from which to build and, besides, Lodève's industry, as

14. Braudel and Labrousse, *Histoire économique*, II, 503–5; Crouzet, 'Angleterre et France', pp. 263–4; F. Dornic, *L'industrie textile dans la Maine et ses débouchés internationaux (1650–1815)*, pp. 49–55.
15. Some idea of the weight of textiles in the 'pre-industrial' industrial sector is given by the estimate made in Braudel and Labrousse, *Histoire économique*, II, 528, that they formed 47.9% of total industrial production in France in 1786. On the varying proportions of production costs which consisted in labour charges see Deyon, 'Concurrence internationale', pp. 20–3.
16. ADH C2125, Montferrier, syndic of Etats, to de Bernage, 14 May 1722.
17. ADH C2126, Gardes-jurés to de Bernage, 29 Oct. 1724.

we have seen, was in full expansion during the period of warfare, absorbing local labour resources. But despite these limitations the expansion was at an impressive rate. The evidence of the growth in production we have given and the number of looms used by Clermont's clothiers, which had doubled between 1694 and 1708, more than doubled again between 1708 and 1723; in that year an inspector recorded that 228 looms were in use.[18] There is evidence, too, of a considerable movement into the trade. Production figures are unfortunately very patchy for this period but there is evidence that forty individuals definitely produced for the Levant during this period and that a further eight probably did so in view of the fact that they joined the new restrictive clothiers' corporation founded in 1708.[19] The forty-eight came from thirty-one different families. The figure does not include those members of Clermont's traditional industry who continued to produce for their old markets and for whom there is no evidence of a switch to production for the Levant, nor does it include a number of others, described as marchands-facturiers in the notarial registers, but for whom we have found proof neither of membership of the corporation nor of production for the Levant. It is thus a net rather than a gross figure.

This chapter is largely devoted to identifying which of these thirty-one clothing families, from what backgrounds, succeeded and which failed and to establishing, on the basis of clothiers' varied experiences, the nature of the qualities necessary for success in the new market. Of particular interest will be the comparison that it will be possible to make of the efforts of clothiers from rich merchant backgrounds with those from humbler social strata. Which type was best suited for the expanding trade? To appreciate the significance of this question, it is necessary to remind ourselves of the state of Clermont's trade, industry and society at the end of the seventeenth century. We have shown that industrial production was monopolized by artisans, merchant involvement being minimal and that profits in industrial production were very small, and so the industry did not generate social mobility. We have shown that Clermont's trade was presided over by a relatively static group of rich merchants, among them the Moulins and Galtiés, whose dominance had apparently been uninterrupted for a long period, and who so controlled

---

18. ADH C2128, Production figures for 1728.
19. In compiling this figure the registers of the conseil de ville, in which the reception of the majority of new masters is recorded, have been used (ACC BB2,3). In addition the industrial survey of 1708 (BN FF 8037), attendance lists at corporative meeting (ADH II E 25 108, 1 Aug. 1708, C2153, 25 Sept. 1708) and a list of masters made in 1728 (C2131, 19 Sept. 1728) have been consulted.

the wholesale trade that they could share out those few economic open-
ings which existed among their dependents. We have shown that these
rich merchant families, and their landed and bourgeois relations, dominated the social life of the town and that something akin to a static society
of orders had come into existence because of the lack of social pressure
from below and the relative lack of competition among members of the
elite. And in view of this situation the development of the local cloth
industry for the Levant was a factor of some novelty and represented,
indeed, a challenge to the local elite, in the same way as the original
foundation of Villenouvette had done. Some members of the elite (the
Galtié family above all) responded to the challenge by themselves producing for the new market. Their major advantages over artisans who
attempted the same was the possession of capital. Who was going to
succeed those with large capital reserves, like the Galtiés, or the artisanal
producers with the advantages of low living and production costs? This is
the basic question that we shall be answering.

The struggle for success was all the harsher in that, as we have shown in
the previous chapter, conditions in the new market were so unsteady
during these years. The failure rate was high. In the survey carried out in
1708 on the orders of Desmaretz mention is made of the fact that several
clothiers had abandoned production for the new market 'despuis quelque
tems' and the gardes-jurés of Carcassonne's cloth industry in 1716 listed
no less than twenty-seven clothiers 'qui ne travaillent plus'.[20] It was the
apparently only temporary involvement of so many clothiers in production for the new market which was the grounds for Pierre Astruc, director
of Villenouvette, criticizing 'les petits fabriquants [qui] à la faveur de
quelque conjuncture favorable font des mauvais draps de France dans le
Levant'[21] and it was the grounds, too, for both controller-general and
Etats of Languedoc favouring the continuation of the policy of subsidizing royal manufactures which were obliged by their contracts either to
maintain a certain prescribed number of looms in action or to complete a
certain number of pieces of cloth each year.[22] As was concluded in Paris,
after the far steadier figures for privileged manufactures' production for
1709 had been noted, it was only on the royal manufacture 'que l'on doit
compter p^r soutenir ce commerce', and it was in the province of
Languedoc's interests to continue to support them in order to preserve
the links with, and reputation in, the Levant and also to serve as
'Modelles et dazilles aux ouvriers quy se Disperseroient par toute

20. BN FF 8037; ADA 9 C 17, List accompanying letter to intendant, dispatched on 6 Dec.
    1716.
21. AN F12 645, Pierre Astruc to d'Aguesseau, 27 Jan. 1705.
22. See for example ADH C7343, Etats, 26 Jan. 1709.

L'Europe dans une cessation de travail'.[23] The crucial decisions on subsidy policy were thus made in years of crisis; there was a tendency for crucial economic questions in the pre-industrial period to be decided in such circumstances, as several historians have shown.[24] The formulation of industrial policy on the basis of the exceptional experiences of crisis years was to have interesting consequences.

But if the struggle was to be fierce, and the difficulties were to be exceptional, the prizes were large. By the 1720s a new type of industry, and a new type of clothier, had emerged. The fifteen or so of the thirty-one clothing families which had attempted production for the Levant and had succeeded possessed an average of between fourteen and fifteen looms each, which would have meant that they would have employed an average of three hundred workers. Clermont's marchands-fabricants had become 'gentlemen clothiers', and the nature of the profession had changed from being largely manual (as it had been in the late seventeenth century) to being largely entrepreneurial, managerial and commercial. The main tasks of the marchand-fabricant of the 1720s were the purchase of raw materials, the supervision of his large, widely spread labour force (done on horseback), account-keeping and letter-writing in his 'bureau', and the sale of his cloth. That there was potentially both an economic and a social distinction between the old industry and the new is apparent from the high status of some of the apprentices to the trade and the high apprenticeship fees charged ('merchant' fees of up to 400 *livres*)[25] by those clothiers qualified to teach the new skills who, like the weavers, to distinguish themselves from Clermont's traditional producers, adopted the high-sounding title of 'marchands-facturiers pour les échelles du Levant'.[26]

In order to identify the qualities which had enabled this comparatively small group of clothiers to achieve this situation, and the failings which had deprived others of success, I shall provide case studies of some of the most significant participators in the new industry. I shall present these in the order which would have been observed in the period. I shall respect contemporary rules of precedence by starting with the most dis-

---

23. AN F12 645, 'Mémoire sur le Dépouilhement de L'Estat Général envoyé par M. Cauvière', *c.* 1708–9.

24. For example, B. E. Supple, *Commercial Crisis and Change in England, 1600–1642*, pp. 228–35; G. Martin, *La grande industrie en France sous le règne de Louis XV*, p. 1.

25. Up to 400 *livres* in place of the 24–7 *livres* paid in the traditional industry (e.g. ADH II E 26 167, 7 March and 16 June 1706, II E 26 144, 8 June 1704). A similar contrast is noted by H. Heaton between the fees paid by apprentices to Yorkshire's traditional clothiers, abut 30 shillings, and those paid to worsted manufacturers, about 16 guineas (*The Yorkshire Woollen and Worsted Industry*, pp. 302–3).

26. E.g. ADH II E 26 172, 26 Nov. 1711.

Table 13. *Varying fortunes of clothiers in and around Clermont 1695–1724*
(arranged in approximate order of social status at the beginning of the period)

	Social Background	Source of Skills	Fate
Pierre-Antoine Barthe	Bourgeois	V	B
Jacques Galtié } Bernard Galtié } Jean Galtié	Wholesale merchant	Ass. Raissac, Fraisse	B
Raymond Budin	Wholesale merchant	Hires assistants	B
Louis Tartary	Apothecary	Buy cloth in white	W
Estienne Maysonnade	Merchant/dyer (Villenouvette) }	?	W
Marc Nougaret	Ex-Lyonnais merchant	?	W
Jean-Gaspard Léotard	Bourgeois (son of advocate)	A Barthe	W
Estienne Maysonnade	Merchant	A Barthe	W
Pierre Estéve	Merchant	Ass. Goudard	W
Joseph Goudard	Son of 'marchand bourgeois'	A La Trivalle (royal manuf.)	W
Claude Bonnal	Merchant	Ass. Raissac	W
Guillaume Santoul	Substantial farmer	?	PNP
Pierre Aumières	Substantial farmer	?	
Pierre Desalasc	Clothier/merchant	C	S
Jacques Desalasc	Clothier's son/merchant	V }	S
Georges Desalasc	Clothier's son/merchant	C	S
Jacques Ménard	Clothier/merchant	C	W
Pierre Flottes	Tanner/merchant	Ass. Jean Roustan Villet (V)	S
Pierre Flottes	Merchant's son	A Pradier	S
Jean Flottes	Hatter's son/merchant	A Tudesq	$\frac{1}{2}$ S
Jean Verny	Professional background }	V	S
Thomas Verny	Clothier's son	V	
Gabriel Verny	Clothier's son	V	
Joseph Tudesq	Professional or merchant?	V	B
Hillaire Tudesq	Professional or merchant?	V	W
François Bourg	Merchant	V	PNP
François Audran	Substantial farmer?	A Pradier	S

Name	Occupation	Service / association	Status
Guillaume Liquier	?	A Desalasc	S
Gabriel Pelletan	Clothier	CV ⎫	S
Jean Pelletan	Clothier's son	V ⎬	
Antoine Pelletan	Clothier's son	V ⎭	
Mathieu Pradier	Clothier	CV ⎫	S
Mathieu Pradier	Clothier's son	V ⎭	
Antoine Raissac	Merchant?	V	S
Raymond Fraisse	Clothier	Worked for Raissac, Pradier	W
Mathieu Bonnal	Clothier	CV	PNP
Estienne Berthomieu	Clothier	C ⎫	S
Antoine Berthomieu	Clothier's son	C ⎭	
Estienne Berthomieu	Clothier's son	C	S
Jean Bernard	Dyer's son	A Pelletan	S
Jacques Bonneville	Innkeeper's son/shearer	V	S
François Pouget	Clothier	C	PNP
Raymond Lugagne	Clothier	C ⎫	S
Arnaud Lugagne	Clothier's son	C ⎭	
Estienne Lugagne	Clothier's son	C	W
Estienne Lugagne	Clothier	C ⎫	W
Guillaume Lugagne	Clothier's son	C ⎭	
Jean Lugagne	Clothier's son	C	W
Pierre Delpon	Clothier	C	W

Key: V – served at Villenouvette, A – apprenticed, C – served in Clermont's industry, Ass. – associated with, S – successful, B – bankrupt, W – withdraws, PNP – possible non-producer (i.e. no direct evidence of having produced cloth on own account). Brackets indicate partnership.

Notes:

(1) Fifty-one names included on this list: the forty-eight referred to on p. 255 and also Raymond Budin, entrepreneur of Grange-des-Prés, and Maysonnade and Tartary, neither of whom were clothiers.

(2) By 'fate' is meant situation in 1725. Some clothiers apparently successful in 1725 were later to go bankrupt (e.g. Georges Desalasc, Estienne Berthomieu, François Audran); others, apparently unsuccessful in 1725, were later to return to cloth-making (e.g. Joseph Tudesq's son, Antoine, at least one Lugagne).

(3) It should be emphasized that the calculations of status are approximate and would no doubt have been hotly disputed by these clothiers themselves. The only members of the profession about whose status there is some certainty are those in the top quarter of the list (Goudard and above).

tinguished members of the new industry and ending with the most humble (Table 13).

Pierre-Antoine Barthe came to Villenouvette to work with his father in the late 1680s. The high status of his family we have mentioned in a previous chapter and we have also seen that the move to Villenouvette represented a distinct change of course for him. The fact that he had been made a tonsured clerk at Limoux suggests that it had originally been intended that he should have a clerical career. His father died in 1694, leaving him 13,000 *livres*, and it was this sum, and his own accumulated resources, which he used to create with great speed a large cloth-making concern in Clermont. Six thousand *livres* of his inheritance was paid directly in wools in January 1695; in February 1695 he rented a house for his manufacture; in April 1695 he accepted Jean-Gaspard Léotard, younger son of an advocate of the parlement of Toulouse, as an apprentice; in July he accepted a second apprentice, Estienne Verdier, son of a bourgeois of Aspiran; in September he purchased the house of Jean de Léotard, the father of his first apprentice, 'pour y construire une manufacture de draps', for 2,460 *livres*; in December he took on a third apprentice, Estienne Mathieu, who came from a merchant background; in January 1699 he made Jean de Raymond, 'banquier' and first consul of Clermont, his commissioner to receive all the cloth which he had previously sent to Pierre Remusat, merchant of Marseilles, empowering him to 'vendre, engager, et négossier Icelles, et faire desd draps tout ce que [il] … trouvera à propos'; in August 1696 he extended his 'facture' to the house of Pierre Baille which had been seized by the community for non-payment of *tailles*; in October he rented a dye-house for 100 *livres* a year and the act reveals, from the list of witnesses, that he had taken on two facteurs, Antoine Raissac and Jean Degua: the former, the son of Vincens Raissac of Carcassonne, had been apprenticed to Villenouvette in 1690 and had been working there as facteur since the end of his apprenticeship, and the latter, it seems likely, was the son of Bernard Degua, a marchand-facturier of Barthe's home-town, Limoux; in March 1697 he arranged for Claude Fraisse, master-carpenter of Clermont, to make two cloth presses 'lun à mode dolande et lautre pour le catisage' for a price of 316 *livres*. In October 1697 he contracted with Jean Estève, tondeur, for the finishing of the four different types of cloth which he was making: *mahous, londrins, londrins-seconds* and *meuniers*. Estève and his employees were to work for him alone for six years and were to follow him should he leave Clermont. This, indeed, is what Barthe did during 1698: in January his brother Thomas, relieved of the directorship of Villenouvette by the society formed by Gabriel Pelletan, Pierre Astruc and Pierre Berthellet, had become the founding director of Grange-des-Prés, and in September Pierre-Antoine Barthe took over this role from his older brother. There is no doubt that the direction of a royal manufacture was the most prestigious situation in the new industry but Barthe's timing had been disastrous for it was during 1699 that the reviving French Levant trade experienced its first serious setback and the combination of the large expense of establishing Grange-des-Prés and of the problems occasioned by mis-sale of his cloth ruined Barthe. In March 1699, only six months after taking over from his brother, he was obliged to hand over all his possessions, including the manufacture, to two of his major creditors, Raymond Budin and Jean de Raymond. The disastrous state of his affairs obliged Barthe, at least temporarily, to disappear. In April he was not present at the fair of Montagnac to pay letters of exchange which he had drawn up. One of his major creditors, Jacques Lapierre, a merchant from Aspiran, was responsible for the official 'protestation' of the letters of exchange. Lapierre had called as his witness one 'lorange', 'hoste de pézenas quj fait cabaret aud Mon^{ac} pendant ces foires'. Asked if Barthe had lodged with him, as was his wont, during the fair this witness replied 'quil y logeoit autrefois pendant les foires mais quil ne la pas veu de celluy'. Several searches for Barthe had been made among those attending the fair but none had met with success. Barthe was still absent six months later; in October 1699 his creditors were obliged to dispose of his possessions without his being present. He was to re-appear; in 1701 he was living in Pézenas and he made a brief visit to Clermont to settle some debts. The last mention we find of him in the registers of Clermont notaries is for the year 1711. The house which he had bought from Jean de Léotard was sold on his behalf by a group of his creditors. It was noted in the act that 'led S^r barthe auroit heu un mauvais succez dans ces affaires et commerce de draps pour le Levant'.[27]

The status of the Galtié family, too, we have assessed at some length in a previous chapter. Their involvement in production for the Levant began after 1700 but in order to understand the background for this

27. Pierre-Antoine Barthe: father's will, ADH 11 E 26 137, 8 Nov. 1694; payment of inheritance by his brother in wools and cash, 11 E 26 138, 3 Jan. 1695; contracts 1695–7 linked to the establishment of his manufacture in Clermont (references in chronological order): 11 E 26 165, 22 Feb. 1695; 11 E 26 140, 10 Oct. 1697 (act refers to original apprenticeship of April 1695); 11 E 25 98, 6 July 1695; 11 E 25 98, 6 Jan 1696 (act refers to sale made in Sept. 1695); 11 E 26 143, 1 Feb. 1701 (act refers to original contract of 1 Dec. 1695); 11 E 25 98, 30 Jan. 1696; 11 E 26 139, 23 Aug. 1696; 11 E 26 139, 29 Oct. 1696; 11 E 26 140, 18 March 1697; 11 E 26 140, 10 Oct. 1697. All information relating to Grange-des-Prés is drawn from ADH C1124. Barthe's re-appearance in 1701 is recorded in a notarial act registered on 1 Feb. 1701 (11 E 26 143) and the last transaction in which his former manufacture in Clermont was sold is recorded in 11 E 26 172, 30 July 1711. Earlier references to, see pp. 184, 189.

diversification in their activities we shall first provide further information on the response of the family to the favourable trading circumstances of the 1690s. The decade was clearly a prosperous one for the family. Jacques Galtié fils married well, we have noted, in 1694 and he was given what was (for Clermont) a spectacular donation by his father on the occasion of his wedding – 8,000 *livres*. In the following years he lavished considerable sums of money both on his wife and on the property of his father-in-law with whom he and his wife co-habited. Presents which he gave to his wife included her 'habits nuptiaux', a diamond cross and various other diamond jewels, and among the improvements which he made to his new home was the conducting of water from a spring to the house. Galtié fils evidently felt that the prosperous state of the family business justified his making these expenses. It is clear that he had increased considerably the scale of his affairs during these years. The relationship with Moulins was proving most fruitful and in recognition of this he sent two, large Roquefort cheeses to his correspondent in November 1698, instructing him to 'boire à nous en les mange'. Perhaps, though, the family firm had expanded the scale of its affairs too rapidly, or perhaps during the difficult years 1699 and 1700 it ran up some large losses, for there are signs at the turn of the century that the son was experiencing misgivings about having expanded so rapidly. In 1700, referring to the shipwreck off Nice of a boat which had been carrying some of their goods, he wrote to his cousin Jean Moulins that 'cest peut estre un frain que la providence peust donner à N^{re} ambition et cest de là que nous avons à réflechir quelle doit estre reglée [,] moderée'. It may well have been the cousin Moulins, situated in Provence, who was the driving force behind the expansion. On the 2 May 1701 Galtié fils wrote to him from Lodève advising him to be more cautious: 'au nom de Dieu changer de manière & retrosissons les affaires plustost que de les augmenter'. Two weeks later he wrote again in similar terms: 'nous navons pas assez de bien pour soutenir vostre ambition'. By 1702 affairs were going badly: 'Jai par ces affaires ruinés La santé de mon père', wrote Galtié fils to his cousin from Montpellier. In 1704 the Galtiés became involved in litigation with Jean Moulins. As a consequence the relations with Raymond Moulins of Lyons, which for years had been so cordial, became distinctly strained. In October 1703 Moulins wrote to Pouget, notary, and procureur, who was transacting business in Clermont on his behalf, informing him that the 'escritures', which Galtié pere et fils had composed summarizing their claims against his nephew, were 'assurément Inpertinantes et dignes de leurs Autheurs', and he added threateningly, 'Je naurois jamais Creu ces M^{rs} quy affectent un air de probité dans le Monde, capables de dire ... des Choses quy ne sont pas Vraÿes ... ils se sont forgés des Chaînes par leur Mauvaise foy quils ne rompront pas quand Ils voudront.' In 1704 Moulins and his nephew travelled to Clermont to settle the dispute. A special passport was granted on 20 March 1704 by the intendant at Lyons for 'Remond Moulin marchand drapier de la Religion Catollique natif de Clermont de Lodève et Jean Moulin son neveu qui vont aud lieu Pour les afaires de son Comerce'.

It seems probable that it was their break with the Moulins family that finally decided Galtié père et fils to begin cloth production (without abandoning their other affairs), a course which they must already have been considering in view of the local evidence at Clermont of the very high profits obtainable. There are only indirect references to the matter in the Moulins correspondence which, naturally, slackened considerably because of the dispute. But a note added at the bottom of one of the letters of Galtié fils, written in October 1703, suggests that production had begun in that year. The note added transmits good wishes to Moulins from 'Raissac'. This was the Antoine Raissac, who had served at Villenouvette and in Barthe's concern. Since Barthe's bankruptcy he had been making cloth for the Levant in association with his father-in-law, Claude Bonnal. In July 1703 he had withdrawn from this association to form another, it would seem, with Galtié père et fils. Jacques Galtié fils was to die in 1704 but the father, with the assistance of his youngest son Bernard, carried on and their association with Raissac is mentioned in the registers of the conseil de ville for 1706. In the citation it is also stated that they were employing Raymond Fraisse, an ex-clothier of St-Chinian, as 'commis'. At some stage Raissac withdrew from his society with the Galtiés to found his own concern. This, no doubt, was the reason for Galtié's forming a second society on 25 July 1708 with his former commis, Raymond Fraisse.

Like Barthe, Galtié created a large-scale concern most rapidly. The 1708 survey reveals that he was using fifteen looms in his production of two hundred whole pieces of cloth and by his death in 1710 he had become the largest cloth producer at Clermont apart from Gabriel Pelletan and the second largest unprivileged clothier in the province. He had invested heavily in fixed capital. During the few years of his involvement in the trade he had created a fully equipped manufacture with looms, spinning wheels, a cloth-finishing shop with three Dutch-style cloth presses, a fully equipped dye-house, a cloth-dressing shop, storage rooms and four tenters for stretching the cloth into shape. The business had clearly not salvaged the family fortunes, however. Profits were made in some years. Raymond Fraisse, by his agreement with Galtié, was to receive one-quarter of the profits and to be liable to none of the losses. One-quarter of the profits between July 1708 and October 1709 had amounted to 1,455 *livres* and total profits would thus have been 5,820 *livres*. But during 1710 the concern found itself in difficuly. In February of that year Galtié père informed Moulins in a letter that he and his youngest son, Bernard, who had never left home, were working in the business and that he was 'un peu Incomode' and he added, 'assurément les affaires où je me trouve y a bien à travalher et à les souttenir pourront faire des advances à Limitaon de nos voizins qui ont commansé avec moings de fonds que nous et peutestre moings damis'. Clearly he was becoming increasingly dependent on advances from both cloth buyers and wool merchants to carry on his concern and thus found himself in the same situation as poorer clothiers ('nos voizins') who had begun their businesses without the advantages which he had enjoyed of having a large capital of his own and extensive commercial contacts ('amis'). Galtié père died in 1710 and left his affairs in a lamentable state. Raymond Moulins wrote to his widow on hearing the news of the death expressing his 'vive doulleur' adding that 'lamityé dont il ma honnoré depuis mon Enfence me rendra sa mémoire chère toute ma vye', but, in keeping with one of Moulins's own favourite maxims, 'les hommes ne se connoissent que par leurs actions', his reaction to the death is probably better judged by his immediate attempt to claim repayment of some debts from Galtié's estate. An uncharitable remark he made in another letter sent to the widow in June suggests that Galtié's affairs had been going badly for some time: 'les négociants de Languedoc de provence et de Clermont ... ont Reconneu depuis fort longtems que Messrs Galtié père et fils faissoient un Négoce forcé, avec peu de Crédit, et un bezoing pressant dargent tous les jours pour leur Manufacture'. Galtié père had justified his laxity towards the entrepreneurial decisions of his oldest son shortly before his death in a letter to Raymond Moulins:

je fais mon possible pour pouvoir avoir le continuaon de vivre le Reste de mes jours sans reproche comme jay faict jusques à prézant et sy le sort a voullu qu'à la fin de ma vie feu mon fils maje endossé daffaires quj me faut soustenir audellà de ce que je savés faire cest toujours avec un Exprict de rendre à un chasseur ce quj luy appartient de sy bon coeur que je solicite quon le fasse à moy mesme.

In fact Galtié's widow and surviving children were to find it difficult to be indulgent towards the father's memory once they had involved themselves in sorting out his affairs. An arrangement had to be made with Galtié's creditors, who were only paid one-third of their debts. The economic situation of the 'maison Galtié' had clearly been greatly damaged by the failure of father and oldest son. The losses incurred by her former husband, the widow wrote to Moulins in May 1710, 'me mettent dans un estat souffrant le reste de mes jours après avoir travalhé autant que femme de mon estat laje fait et sans avoir ansj cauzé une dépance'. The youngest son, Bernard, wrote to Moulins in similar terms; his father's affairs had caused him 'des terribles embarras que jespère de me sortir mojenant lajde de celluy quj connoit Lintérieur des hommes et quj en punit tost ou tard la Mallice Sj cella nest pas en ce Monde Infalliblement cella sera en Lautre'. Christian resignation did, indeed, seem to be the only course open, for Galtié's descendants found themselves involved in a series of legal disputes occasioned by the failure of the family enterprise. In October 1714 Galtié 'veuve' wro.e again to Moulins informing him of 'le pitoyable Etat de mon Malheur ... me voyant opressée par raport aux Malheureux affaires de feu mon Mary, que lhonneur et la persuasion de Mes parens mont fait obliger. Je me voÿs auiourdhuy Acablée, et Meprisée de Ceux quj devoit me loüer, puis que je nay pas Epargné mes Soins pour soutenir la maison malgré lorage Impétueux.' She was referring to her daughter-in-law, Catherine Estienne, the widow of Jacques Galtié fils, who had sent bailiffs round to seize some of her possessions in order to ensure payment of the rest of her former husband's wedding donation.

The widow and youngest son continued to produce cloth until 1712 but after this date there is no further record of production by their concern. In a letter written in 1717 to Moulins, Jean Altayrac mentioned the sale of their cloth presses to a shearer. Evidently the manufacture had been liquidated. Bernard Galtié became a marchand-épicier, a profession which would probably have involved retailing and, hence, a distinct decline in status from the original parental profession of wholesale marchand-droguiste. Jean Galtié, although at some stage he was received marchand-fabricant, never, it would seem, produced cloth. In 1710 and 1711 he was without employment but at some stage, having 'rien eu de sa maison ny en état den jamais rien avoir', he was employed 'par charité' by his brother-in-law, Paul Reboul, who had established himself in Provence.[28]

28. The Galtiés: marriage of Galtié fils, ADH 11 E 26 131, 24 Aug. 1694; expenditure on wife and father-in-law's property mentioned in letter of Galtié veuve to Moulins, 22 Oct. 1714, ADR, Fonds Moulins, xv; on the business relationship between the Galtiés and Moulins between 1698 and 1702, Fonds Moulins, iv, letters of 4 Nov. 1698, 25 Dec. 1700, 2 May 1701, 15 May 1701, 2 Jan. 1702; on the dispute between the Moulins and Galtiés, Fonds Moulins, xv, xvi; Moulins's letter to Pouget is in the Fonds Moulins, xvii, Livre de copies de lettres, 25 Oct. 1703; Passport: Fonds Moulins, xxiii; note about Raissac, Fonds Moulins, iv, letter of October 1703; on Raissac's association with Bonnal: 11 E 26 142, 29 April 1700, 11 E 25 103, 9 Nov. 1709; and with Galtié: ACC BB2, 8 April 1706; society with Fraisse: 11 E 25 108, 4 June 1710; on the size of Galtié's production: BN FF 8037, ADH C 7350, 7354, Etats, Jan. 1710, 1711; on the fixed capital investment: 11 E 26 172, 13 Oct. 1711; profits made with Fraisse, 11 E 25 108, 4 June 1710 (this act suggests that profits were significantly less

Pierre-Antoine Barthe and the Galtié family are the two major examples of involvement in industrial production by families belonging to Clermont's elite. In addition there are a few cases of very short-term participation and others of production by individuals whom one could only describe as being of middling status. Sometime in 1694 a society was formed between a rich 'maître-chirurgien', Louis Tartary, and Estienne Maysonnade, one of the sons of Jean Maysonnade, who was, we have noted, dyeing at Clermont in the 1650s, and who, having spent some years living at Pézenas in the 1680s, had become 'maître-teinturier-en-chef' at Villenouvette in the 1690s. The purpose of the society was to purchase cloth 'in the white' and to resell at Marseilles once dyeing, pressing and dressing had been carried out. The initial investment consisted in 3,000 *livres* but decidedly more had been invested by March 1695 when Maysonnade took over the entire direction of the society. Among those from whom the society bought cloth were Pierre Delpon and Estienne Berthomieu, two of Clermont's artisanal clothiers who must have been among those who had switched to producing *londres-ordinaires* for the Levant in 1694. The scale of the society's affairs was clearly of a completely different order from those of these humble clothiers. During 1695, though, Maysonnade left to work in Carcassonne, leaving his business in the hands of his brother Jean Louis who had returned from Lyons. After April 1695 there is no further mention of the society to be found in the notarial registers.[29] Another example of a short-term involvement in the trade is that of Jean de Raymond, who had shown momentary interest in cloth production in the 1680s, we have seen in chapter four, and who in 1696 was acting as cloth commissioner for Pierre-Antoine Barthe in Marseilles. He would seem to have provided some financial backing to Barthe for in January 1699 it was he, and one Raymond Budin, who were among Barthe's largest creditors and who took over the manufacture of Grange-des-Prés. Raymond's links with Grange-des-Prés lasted about five months only for in May 1699 it was decided that Budin should have entire control of the manufacture. Raymond Budin, too, came from a rich background. He originated in

than 5,820 *livres*. Accounts had been falsified by Fraisse, Galtié's widow claimed, and profits had in fact been only 480 *livres*); on the crisis and collapse of the concern: Fonds Moulins, IV, Galtié père to Moulins, 8 Feb. 1710; XVII, Moulins to Galtié veuve, 14 May, 12 June 1710. Arrangement with Galtié's creditors: II E 26 171, 172, 24 April 1710, 13 Oct. 1711; reaction of surviving Galtiés to ruin, Fonds Moulins, IV, letters of 23 May, 24 June 1710, 22 Oct. 1714; disappearance of concern: ADH C7359, Etats, 13 Jan 1712, no record of Galtié production. Altayrac's letter is of 3 May 1717 (Fonds Moulins, IV); Bernard Galtié's fate: ACC BB 3, 1725; and Jean Galtié's: Fonds Moulins, IV, Jacques Galtié (cousin) to Moulins, 12 March 1727.
29. Maysonnade-Tartary Association: ADH II E 26 139, 30 March, 14 April 1695.

Carcassonne but moved to St-Chinian and later to Pézenas. His wife Catherine de Martin of Pézenas brought him a dowry of 8,000 *livres* at their marriage in 1686. His move to St-Chinian may have been linked to the decision to make *londres* for the Levant. In 1686 together with his father-in-law he purchased a fulling mill in this town for 1,400 *livres*. But in 1688 he took up residence in Pézenas and, while retaining some cloth-making interests at St-Chinian, he would appear to have devoted himself largely to trading there. In notarial registers of Pézenas he is referred to as bourgeois and some idea of his resources is given by the fact that he invested 60,000 *livres* in Grange-des-Prés when he took it over. But the concern was to be as ruinous to him as it had been to Barthe. In 1704 the manufacture was handed over to Gabriel Pelletan, Budin having sustained large losses. Since 1701 he had become involved, too, in a costly and complex legal wrangle with some wool merchants at Toulouse who had accused him of forging commercial documents. Disputes concerning his affairs at Grange-des-Prés were to continue until 1730. At one stage in 1706 he was sentenced to be hanged in the main square of Pézenas. Like his predecessor Barthe he was obliged to disappear until his name was cleared.[30]

Those of middling status who produced for the Levant during these years include Marc Nougaret, who, like Jean Louis Maysonnade, had worked at Lyons for a while and been attracted back to Clermont by the good prospects of producing for the Levant;[31] Jean-Gaspard Léotard, second son of an advocate at the parlement of Toulouse, who after serving for Barthe and at Villenouvette was producing at Clermont in 1708;[32] Estienne Mathieu, an ex-merchant, who associated himself with Nougaret, and likewise was producing in 1708;[33] Pierre Estève, a merchant, who associated himself with Joseph Goudard, son of a prosperous marchand-bourgeois of Pézenas, who had served in several privileged manufactures;[34] Claude Bonnal, another merchant, who associated himself with his son-in-law, Antoine Raissac, between 1699 and 1703;[35] Guillaume Santoul and Pierre Aumières, both sons of substantial farm-

30. Raymond Budin: for details about Budin's earlier career in St-Chinian and Pézenas see ADH 11 E 79 102, 14 Dec. 1686 and 11 E 68 73, 17 Jan. 1693. The transfer of Grange-des-Prés to Pelletan is recorded by the Etats ADH C7322, 22 Jan. 1704. All the rest of this information is drawn from ADH C1124. See also pp. 112, 228–9.
31. Producing in 1706 in association with Estienne Mathieu (ADH 11 E 26 146, 10 Oct 1706: they receive an apprentice). See also p. 60, n. 38.
32. Production recorded in 1705 survey (BN FF 8037).Presence at Villenouvette recorded 2 April 1704 (ADH 11 E 25 107).
33. ADH 11 E 26 146, 10 Oct. 1706; BN FF 8037, survey of 1708.
34. Producing 1708 (BN FF 8037). On Goudard see p. 242.
35. ADH 11 E 26 142, 29 April 1700, 11 E 25 103, 9 Nov. 1709.

ers,[36] and Pierre Desalasc and Jacques Ménard, whom, as we have seen, were both from the top levels of Clermont's traditional industry.[37] Apart from Desalasc none of these men of middle rank succeeded. There is no evidence of dramatic bankruptcies as in the cases of Barthe and Galtié but production for the Levant had clearly not benefited any of them very much. Pierre Estève, we know from his correspondence with Moulins, having failed as clothier[38] took up soap production while his partner, Goudard, was obliged to leave Clermont to work at a new royal manufacture in St-Chinian in a managerial capacity because of the 'dérangement dans ses affaires'.[39]

Pierre Desalasc's success is of some interest to us. For a participant in Clermont's traditional industry, we have seen, he possessed considerable resources. But by the late 1680s, we have also seen, he was apparently disenchanted with industrial production. Not only did he apprentice his elder son Jacques to Pierre Astruc, a Montpellier merchant, but he also in 1689 sold his dye-house to Jean Bouissede, a dyer who was working for Gabriel Pelletan. In the 1690s, however, the improving prospects in the cloth trade must have encouraged him to resume production (if he had indeed stopped making cloth) and there is evidence that in 1695 his cloth-making concern was functioning. In addition his son, Jacques, returned to Clermont to work at Villenouvette, arriving possibly with the Montpellier merchant to whom he had been apprenticed in 1689, Pierre Astruc, who became one of the partners in the concern in 1697. Jacques worked at Villenouvette until 1705. Since his apprenticeship in 1689 he had been independent of his father but in that year he was married again (his first wife whom he had married in 1695 had died) to Izabeau Fayet, who brought him a dowry of 3,000 *livres*. In return for his father's donation of half his possessions, this half being valued likewise at 3,000 *livres*, he agreed to work in the family business and live in the family household, 'ne faisant qu'un pot et feu, La bourse régie par led. Desalasc père'. The Desalasc concern, in which the younger brother, Georges, was already working, expanded rapidly from this moment. Desmaretz's industrial survey of 1708 shows that it was employing the same number of looms as Galtié – fifteen – and that it had made two hundred whole pieces of cloth in the previous years. The Desalascs already lived in the industrial heart of Clermont, in the Rue de la Fregère, in one of the

36. Both present at registration of new guild statutes on 1 Aug. 1708 (ADH 11 E 25 108). See p. 237.
37. See pp. 109–10.
38. ADR, Fonds Moulins, IV, letter to Moulins, 30 July 1721.
39. Or so claimed Clermont's gardes-jurés when Goudard's son attempted to obtain permission to manufacture on the basis of his father's mastership in 1747 (ADH C2153).

Ill. 18. Industrial expansion in the Rue de la Fregère in the early eighteenth century: doorway of 1707

houses which backed onto the Rhonel (Ill. 18), but in 1711 they clearly required extra space in this quarter for their enterprise: an act of 1711 records that Pierre Desalasc, 'marchand fabriquand de draps mode dolande', had purchased for 3,170 *livres* from the creditors of Pierre-Antoine Barthe the house which Barthe had purchased for his manufacture in 1695. Later in the same year Pierre Desalasc emancipated his younger son Georges who wanted to handle his own affairs, and donated 3,000 *livres* to him which became his portion in a formal association entered into between the two sons and their father on 30 November 1711 (father and elder son had invested 11,651 *livres* 12 *sols* 1 *denier* between them). In 1713 Georges Desalasc married Marguerite Quintard who brought him a dowry of 4,000 *livres* and, conveniently, a house in the Rue de la Fregère. By this time his original stake in the family association had grown to 10,000 *livres*, as a consequence of 'les profits . . . de lad sossiété'. The act recorded both this increase in wealth and also the fact that Georges de Salasc left his 10,000 *livres* in the family business to match the 10,000 *livres* each which his brother and father held now in the family concern. Conditions were less favourable for the Desalascs in the years 1715 and 1716 and this decided the younger brother to separate his affairs from those of the family. In an act in which the 'mauvais subceds de profit ou accroissement de pertes' in the Levant trade is mentioned, this separation is recorded as well as the dispute which arose between the brothers as a consequence of the complex process of separating their affairs. The act settling this dispute reveals that the Desalasc concern owned not only looms and spinning wheels but also, like Galtié's manufacture, fully equipped shearing and cloth-dressing shops, a fully equipped dye-house, a spinning and carding shop and tenters for stretching the cloth. Another consolidated manufacture had been established at Clermont. Both Jacques and Georges Desalasc were among those clothiers producing in 1725 on a large scale (though Georges Desalasc was to go bankrupt a few years later).[40]

Two branches of the Flottes family worked for the Levant during these years. Their statuses were not dissimilar to that of Desalasc. In both cases they were from superior, artisanal backgrounds comparable to those of the leading families in Clermont's traditional cloth industry. The first Flottes to involve himself in cloth production was Jean, son of Thomas, a hatter. He had originally been apprenticed to a merchant and had worked some years as a 'garçon marchand' in Clermont and Montpellier. Like others, however, he was clearly impressed by the large profits which were being made from cloth production and on 24 January 1707 he not only was apprenticed to an ex-Villenouvette facturier, Joseph Tudesq, in order to be trained in the métier of 'marchand facturier des draps pour le Levant et autres draps qui se fabriquent dans le présant royaume', but also drew up a marriage contract with Tudesq's daughter. Tudesq had a medium-sized concern with four looms, which produced eighty pieces of cloth in 1708. In March 1708 Flottes requested his inheritance of 2,385 *livres* from his uncles (Thomas Flottes had died in 1690) and he invested this in what had become his family business. It was not a good investment. Tudesq, whose affairs were going badly, was obliged to go bankrupt in 1709. The act by which he settled with his creditors records 'la doulleur où il avoit esté par le dérangement de ses affaires'. Flottes himself was one of the principal sufferers from his father-in-law's failure: he had not received any of his wife's 1,500 *livres* dowry and it seems doubtful whether he was able to recover any of his investment in the

40. Desalascs: apprenticeship of son to Pierre Astruc and selling of dye-house, ADH II E 26 126, 23 Feb., 27 Aug. 1689; working in 1690s: there is evidence that in August 1695 a St-Pons carder was employed by him (II E 26 131); Jacques Desalasc's presence at Villenouvette: II E 26 180, 3 Aug. 1719; marriage and association with father, II E 26 166, 20 Aug. 1705; purchase of additional house in Rue de la Fregère: II E 26 172, 30 July 1711; emancipation of, association with, Georges Desalasc, II E 26 172, 26 Nov., 9 Dec. 1711, Bobo, 'Une communauté languedocienne', p. 24; favourable situation of 1713, difficulties 1715–16, fixed capital of concern, and the dispute with Georges are all recorded in an agreement of 12 Aug. 1724, (II E 26 185). Georges Desalasc's bankruptcy: a meeting of his creditors is recorded in II E 25 117, 8 March 1731.

concern. After this failure he gave up cloth production and probably resumed his career as merchant. In the 1720s, however, and again in the 1730s, he took up cloth production again and his descendants were to be among Clermont's important cloth-making families.[41] Pierre Flottes, an uncle of Jean Flottes, was a leather-bleacher in the 1690s but became a wool merchant in the first decade of the eighteenth century. This change in itself represented a progression (a move from an artisanal to a merchant profession) and Flottes was clearly profiting from the general expansion and rise in the demand for wools. The biggest profits were to be made in cloth production, though, and this was doubtless his reason not only for placing his oldest son Pierre in this profession (apprenticed to Mathieu Pradier in 1714, received master in 1718) but also for himself purchasing for 1,650 *livres* one of the four special masterships created by the King in 1722 which exempted their purchasers from serving an apprenticeship and completing a *chef-d'oeuvre*. Both father and son produced cloth in the 1720s. The extent of their resources is shown by the father's donation of 4,500 *livres* in Spanish wools and 1,500 *livres* in tools to his son when he made an advantageous marriage in 1722 to Catherine Tartary, daughter of a rich apothecary, and niece of Louis Tartary whose temporary involvement in the trade in the 1690s we have noted. Both branches of the Flottes family were thus survivors and their role in the industry was to be substantial not only because of their large resources but also because of their prolificity. Pierre Flottes père purchased a mastership not only to produce himself but also to give his three other sons the right to become clothiers without paying mastership fees. And his sons were to be equally prolific. 'La Providence mayant donné neuf enfans cinq garçons et quatre filles, jay élevé quatre de mes garçons dans la fabrique', wrote Jean Flottes 'aîné' modestly in 1747. The 'providential' abundance of Flottes was to cause a Montpellier engraver difficulty in the second half of the century in devising distinct coats of arms for all the different branches of the family: 'comme je sçay que vous êtes une famille nombreuse et quil faut pour le bon ordre que vous soyés distins les uns des autres', he wrote to one of his Flottes customers, 'jay crue prendre sur moy de rendre votre armorial en règle . . . et que pour rendre plus vray le nom de flottes au lieu dun vaisseau jen ay mis deux qui représente mieux une flotte'.[42]

41. Jean Flottes (later referred to as Jean Flottes vieux): original apprenticeship in Montpellier, work as garçon-marchand, apprenticeship to Tudesq, marriage to master's daughter: ADH 11 E 25 103, two acts of 24 Jan. 1707; receives inheritance: 11 E 25 103, 5 May 1708; Tudesq's bankruptcy: 11 E 26 171, 1 June 1710; movements in and out of industry recorded in production statistics.
42. Pierre Flottes: progression from leather-bleacher to merchant: ADH 11 E 26 126, 129, 22 May 1689, 26 May 1692, ACC CC14, Jalaguié's account book; mastership for himself and son: ACC BB2, BB3, 8 Aug. 1718, 29 Dec. 1724; son's marriage: Bobo,

The most impressive, and the earliest, example of success in production for the new market is that of Gabriel Pelletan. His early poverty and humble social background have already been recorded. It was he who had property seized by Montpellier merchants for failing to meet engagements for wool purchases in 1671, and whose sister was married to a weaver. Likewise we have described his gradual advancement through the ranks of Villenouvette's management. His ambitions, however, evidently extended beyond playing a senior role within the manufacture for in 1686 he once again started to manufacture cloth in Clermont, renting a house and 'boutique' on the Rhonel for 35 *livres* a year. From its inception the concern was evidently planned on a scale different from those of Pelletan's colleagues in Clermont, and was producing different cloths. From an early stage Pelletan was employing labour from outside Clermont – an act of 1687 reveals a carder from Grenoble working for him – and in 1688 and 1689 he expanded his activities, either from his profits or with help from the directors of Villenouvette, buying a house for 1,000 *livres* in the 'rue qui va au Rhonel', buying a half share in a twisting mill, and entering a six-year agreement with Jean Bouissede, a dyer, who had formerly worked at the royal manufacture, for the dyeing of all the cloth 'soit à colleur descarlatte que en autres colleurs', which came from his 'manufacture'. Between 1690 and 1694 Pelletan extended his activities yet further. In 1690 he rented a fulling mill for 165 *livres* a year on the River Lergue, and in 1691 he sold to Paul Cathala, an ex-Villenouvette shearer and cloth-dresser, a 'grande presse à Mode dolande' as well as another, 'Mode de France', for 1,000 *livres*, which was to be paid over a period of six years during which, it is to be presumed, Cathala was obliged to work for him. Also in 1691 he rented a dye-house, probably because his dyer had left for Carcassonne, and in 1693 he purchased for 568 *livres* the dye-house left empty by his former employee and hired another dyer from Rodez. By this stage the house which he had bought in 1688 was evidently no longer large enough for his manufacture. In 1692 he had extensive repairs and improvements carried out to it and in 1695 bought two neighbouring properties in the Rue de la Fregère, with yards and gardens, which gave him a large, consolidated unit on the Rhonel. The last purchase, which completed the complex, consisted of a small stretch of land for his cloth tenters. It seems highly probably that in the case of several of these purchases Pelletan was buying properties which had served cloth-making functions earlier in the century. The house which he bought in 1688 had belonged to Raymond Grasset, a

'Une communauté languedocienne', p. 36; Flottes's prolificity: ADH C2049, petition of Flottes père et fils, 9 Nov. 1747, C5545, Jean Jean (Montpellier engraver) to frères Flottes, 15 May 1782.

Table 14. *The growth of Pelletan's manufacture, 1686–95*
(prices in 'livres')

Year	Rented		Bought		Repaired/Sold	
1686	House	35–42 p.a.				
1688			House	1,000		
1689			½ Twisting mill	67		
1690	Fulling mill	165 p.a.				
1691	Dye-house	40 p.a.			Sale of presses	1,000
1692					Repairs	1,324
1693			Dye-house	568		
1695			Two houses	1,300		
			Strip of land	50		

Final investment (purchases and repairs) – 4,309 *livres*

Clermontais now living in Lyons, and the one he purchased in 1695 had belonged to the former Jacques Chinion, described as 'Capitaine' in the act, and most probably the same Jacques Chinion, bourgeois, who had been making cloth in the 1650s (Table 14).

It was clear that in a decade Pelletan had created a manufacture that bore no resemblance either to his own former concern before he joined the royal manufacture or to the artisanal activities of his fellow clothiers at Clermont. In 1692 and 1694 visiting inspectors met Pelletan. Bosson, on the former occasion, described Pelletan as an entrepreneur, rather than a facturier, reporting that he was making a hundred pieces of fine cloth a year with twelve looms, and that his manufacture was 'en bon Estat' and possessed its own dye-house for scarlet colours. Cauvière in 1694 found that Pelletan had more than doubled the number of his looms since Bosson's visit and that his aim was to expand his production yet further ('augmenter tous les ans'), an ambition which Cauvière did not doubt him capable of achieving because 'son travail m'a paru très beau et luy fort habille'. Cauvière also mentioned the skills of Pelletan's dyer and reported that Pelletan had ceased, at least temporarily, working at Villenouvette, and was making three varieties of cloth for the Levant and for the domestic market, *meuniers, londrins-larges* and *londrins-seconds*. Cauvière's report was sent to the Etats of Languedoc and it was on the basis of his recommendation that Pelletan was granted the *pistole* bounty. This was not to be the height of his achievement, however, for he not only expanded his production yet further so that by 1698 he was making 1,200 half-pieces of cloth a year, but also in 1697 became a partner in, and director-general of, Villenouvette and for six years ran both his own concern in Clermont and the royal manufacture. When Astruc took over the sole direction of Villenouvette in 1703, Pelletan took over that of Grange-des-Prés, and he ran this royal manufacture as well as his own privileged manufacture in Clermont until his death in 1706. It was not for nothing that the Etats referred to Pelletan as a 'fort bon facturier'.

It must have been Gabriel Pelletan's exceptional success which encouraged many others to produce for the Levant. He became, rather like Magy, a technical expert in the new trade. It was he who assessed the value of the cloth left by Barthe when he abandoned Grange-des-Prés, for example. He had accumulated a large fortune remarkably rapidly and it was a sign of the relative flexibility of Clermont's elite that they accepted this 'nouveau-riche' into their number. In 1691 he was elected first consul and from this year he was referred to as marchand-bourgeois. His children achieved honourable marriages amongst Clermont's elite. His son Antoine married Jeanne Jaurions in 1697 and thus became related by marriage to both the Estienne and Galtié families as Jeanne Jaurions was the daughter of Jeanne Estienne, sister of Raymond Estienne of Lyons. Pelletan gave his son 5,000 *livres*, his son gave his wife-to-be a diamond valued at 100 *livres*, and Jeanne Jaurions was given all her father's possessions, bar 1,200 *livres*, and 3,700 *livres* in silver as her dowry. The marriage was of sufficient note to be mentioned in one of the Galtiés' letters to Moulins: 'le mariage du Sr Peletan avec Mad^{le} Jaurions fust consomé Il y a quelque temps', they wrote on 10 December 1697. Pelletan's other son, Jean, likewise was married well in 1704 to Marthe Vallibouze, daughter of Gabriel Vallibouze, a wholesale merchant, and of 'Demoiselle Dorothée de Julien'. This was another family closely linked to the Galtiés. It was Gabriel Vallibouze who was chosen as their referee in the dispute with the Moulins in the same year. Pelletan's oldest daughter Marie had been married two years previously to noble Philippe François de Lozières, and given a dowry of 6,000 *livres* as well as a gold cross mounted with diamonds worth 300 *livres*, and his other four daughters were left with good prospects for prestigious matches after his death in 1706: they were left 4,000 *livres* each in his will. One of them, Anne, married Paul Clavel, son of Jacques Clavel bourgeois of Montpellier, in 1710; another, Jeanne, married Pierre Rouquet, a rich merchant later in the same year. The total value of the marriage contract was 22,500 *livres* of which 12,000 *livres* were paid in *louis d'or*.[43]

43. Gabriel Pelletan: assembly of manufacture, employment of skilled workers: ADH 11 E 26, 124–31, 13 Jan. 1686, 19 Aug. 1687, 15 March, 12 Aug. 1688, 8 Sept. 1689, 17 May 1690, 1 July 1691, 5 Jan. 1692, 24 Jan., 29 July 1693, 10 Feb, 7 Sept. 1695, 11 E 26 134, 28 Oct. 1691; references to Grasset and Chinion see pp. 96, 124, n. 98; inspectors' visits 1692, 1694: Fontvieille, 'Premières enquêtes', p. 1134, ADH C2200, Cauvière's visit;

Mathieu Pradier, Gabriel Pelletan's brother-in-law, was likewise one of the earliest successful producers for the Levant. Like Pelletan he came from a humble background. One of his sisters was married to Pelletan, the other to a master-tailor. His father in 1680 is described simply as a 'facturier de draps' and his mother was illiterate. He himself was a member of Clermont's traditional industry but may possibly have been involved in some way in Pelletan's early manufacturing activities in the late 1680s. Certainly the link with his brother-in-law was very close: Pelletan presented his wife-to-be with a diamond valued at 10 *écus* when his marriage contract was drawn up on 10 October 1689. During the 1690s, though, he clearly expanded his own cloth-making activities, renting a house in the Rue de la Fregère for 50 *livres* a year in 1694 and buying two other houses in the same street for 740 *livres* and 850 *livres* in 1697. It was also in 1697, it seems probable, that he joined the manufacture of Villenouvette in which his brother-in-law Pelletan was now a partner. He is described as a resident of the manufacture in 1700. Whether he ceased producing cloth in Clermont or not whilst working at Villenouvette we do not know, but certainly in 1708 he was producing on a large scale. Like the Desalascs and Galtiés he was working fifteen looms and producing two hundred whole pieces of cloth a year. Mathieu Pradier *fils* was another of the survivors into the 1720s and like Pelletan he had achieved a remarkably rapid social ascension. In 1707 he was elected second consul and purchased the position of 'lieutenant de maire héréditaire' which gave him the right to the title of conseiller du roi. Between 1719 and 1728 he and his son, likewise called Mathieu Pradier, assembled a large estate around an elegant country house which they had purchased at Camplong, devoted considerable attention to improving this estate, and spuriously adopted the title 'seigneur de Camplong et de Creyssels', the names of the two farms which had been purchased.[44]

We have already followed the early stages of Antoine Raissac's career,

granting of bounty, production in 1690s, involvement royal manufactures: ADH C7292, 7295, 7322, Etats, 23 Jan. 1698, 5 Jan. 1699, 22 Jan. 1704; assessment Barthe's cloth: ADH C1124; first consul, marchand-bourgeois: 11 E 26 128, 130, 9 Dec. 1691, 4 Oct. 1693; children's marriages: Antoine, 11 E 25 98, 19 Nov. 1697 (Galtiés' comment ADR, Fonds Moulins, IV, letter to Moulins of this date); Jean: 11 E 26 144, 22 Nov. 1704; Marie: 11 E 25 101, 22 May 1702; Anne: 11 E 26 148, 2 May 1710; Jeanne: 11 E 26 171, 26 Sept. 1710; Pelletan's will: 11 E 26 146, 17 Jan. 1707. Earlier references to, see pp. 192–3, 224.

44. Mathieu Pradier: family background: ADH 11 E 25 89, 94, 4 April 1672, 12 Oct. 1680, 11 E 26 125, 14 July 1688; participation in Clermont's traditional industry, close links Pelletan, marriage: 11 E 26 124–6, 19 Aug. 1687, 29 June 1688, 10 Oct. 1689; establishment of manufacture: 11 E 26 131, 5 March 1694, 16 May 1697, 11 E 25 98, 7 April 1697; resident Villenouvette: 11 E 25 100, 21 March 1700; production 1708, BN FF 8037; municipal offices: ACC BB2, 12 Sept., 16 Oct. 1707; land purchases etc.: Appolis, *Lodève*, pp. 374, 429, 441, 512.

his apprenticeship to Villenouvette in 1690, his employment by Barthe in 1697, his marriage into, and association with, the family of Claude Bonnal, and his second association with Galtié in 1703. When he married Marguerite Bonnal in April 1700 his total assets were valued at 1,660 *livres* but his associations with his father-in-law and Galtié evidently enabled him to increase his resources for when he separated himself from the latter he was able to establish a manufacturing concern of some size. He had established his own shearing-shop in 1702 or 1703; in 1707 he purchased his father-in-law's dye-house (built in 1704 and situated just outside the Porte de la Fregère, at the end of the street of that name) and between 1707 and 1708 he created a large enclosure next to this dye-house and the River Rhonel (Ill. 19). An act of 22 September 1710 records a large payment in wages for work carried out between August 1707 and January 1708:

pour la construction et bâtisse dune muraille ... despuis la Maison à faire tinture ... jusques au lit du Rhonel quy forme Lenclos dud. Raissac ... et pour aider à faire un grand puids ... atenant aud Ruisseau de Ronel ... et faire un couvert à icelluy et bastir aussy despuis dud. puids et le long dud Ruisseau de Ronel ... y ayant fait un grand portal à pierre de taille couvert Icelluy à tuilhes à canal et continuer led. bastimant pour entièrement fermer et former Lenclos le long dud. Ruisseau de Ronel.

In 1708 Desmaretz's survey records that Raissac, like Desalasc, Pradier, Pelletan and Galtié had a substantial cloth-making concern, boasting fifteen looms, and with two hundred whole pieces of cloth to its credit in the previous year. Raissac was another survivor into the 1720s. By then he, too, had adopted habits of a bourgeois kind: notarial acts of 1721 record large payments to workmen for improvements carried out since 1719 to 'lenclos maison et pigeonnier de campagne que led Sr Raissac a acquis de demoiselle Suzanne Rigaud ... Dit de fon rouge'.[45]

Estienne Berthomieu was the son of a facturier in Clermont's traditional industry and, as we have seen in an earlier chapter, himself one of the regular producers in that industry. His resources were rather smaller than those of Pierre Desalasc, however, and he himself was of slightly lower status and barely literate: it was with evident difficulty that he signed his name at the bottom of notarial acts. During the 1690s, as we have seen, he undertook the production of *londres-ordinaires*. But as neither he himself nor his two sons (who worked with him in the family concern) had either had training at Villenouvette or been apprenticed to

45. Antoine Raissac: establishment of his manufacture: ADH II E 25 108, cancelled act of 1706, II E 26 146, 28 July 1707, II E 26 171, 22 Sept., various acts October, 1710; purchase and improvement of Fon Rouge, II E 26 183, 16 March 1721. Earlier references to, see pp. 260, 263.

Ill. 19. Gateway, and 'enclos' backing on to the Rhonel, of 'maison de fabrique' in the Rue 'de la Fregère

an ex-Villenouvette clothier he confined his production initially to the lower-quality cloths for the new market and continued to produce cloth for Clermont's traditional markets. Two acts recorded in 1701 and 1703 in connection with the building of a 'rétorsoir' or twisting mill show not only that the Berthomieus were continuing to adopt a co-operative approach to cloth-making by sharing the necessary investment in this piece of equipment but also that as well as *vingt-deuxains* 'façon dolande' they were still making traditional-style *vingt-quatrains, vingt-deuxains* and *seizains*. Several bales of this traditional product were bought from Berthomieu by Galtié père et fils in 1700 for dispatch to Lyons. Theirs was the best such cloth available on the local market, the Galtiés stated.

In 1705 Berthomieu père purchased a lead dyeing vat 'pour servir aux teintures des écarlattes'. Again he made this investment in co-operation with another clothier, on this occasion with Pierre Desalasc to whom he was related. Desmaretz's survey shows that the Berthomieus were working four looms and had eighty pieces of cloth to their credit for the previous year. Between 1709 and 1712 they expanded their production. Recorded in the registers of the Estates of Languedoc for these years is a production of sixty-nine pieces of cloth in 1709, ninety-nine pieces in 1710 and 170 pieces in 1711. The father died in 1712 but widow and sons continued to expand production: 230 pieces of cloth in 1713, 280 in 1714. The expansion was then checked by the crisis of the years 1715–17 , to be resumed again between 1718 and 1725. The younger son, Estienne Berthomieu, undertook independent production from 1720 with substantial financial backing from his uncle, Jean Altayrac of Lyons, who had returned to Clermont. Some idea of the resources of the family is provided by Berthomieu's will of 26 May 1706 by which he left 1,200 *livres* to his daughter, Françoise and 1,000 *livres* each to his other three children and made his wife his 'héritière universelle'. The total value of his fortune was estimated to be 8,400 *livres* (probably an underestimate). By the time of Berthomieu's death the family's resources had grown; the effects of the manufacture alone were valued at 12,000 *livres*. The Berthomieu brothers were two other survivors. Their rising social position is apparent from Estienne's marriage to Jeanne Banes, daughter of a bourgeois (she brought him a 5,000 *livres* dowry), and from Antoine's election to the first consulship in 1725.[46]

In two cases important Clermontais clothier families were founded by individuals who originally were employed as skilled workers at Villenouvette. One of these individuals was Vital Bernard. He was the second son of a Lyons notary and he came to Villenouvette at the age of twenty-seven to work as a dyer, a trade which he had learnt from his brother who was a marchand-teinturier at Lyons. His ambition to found his own independent dye-house is apparent from the fact that after four years service at Villenouvette he set himself up as a dyer in Lodève where the industry was in expansion during these years. In 1696, though, he returned to Clermont and purchased for 600 *livres* a house and garden outside the Porte de la Fregère, adjoining the Rhonel. There he practised

---

46. Estienne Berthomieu: signs with difficulty, ADH II E 26 143, 2 Feb. 1701; involvement new and old industry: II E 26 143–4, 9 Oct. 1701, 18 Feb 1703; Galtié's purchase of their cloth: ADR, Fonds Moulins, XVII; purchase of vat: II E 25 102, 30 March 1705; production: BN FF 8037, ADH C7350, 7354, 7359, C2208, C2231; Estienne Berthomieu fils produces: ADH C2231; backing from Altayrac: II E 25 237, 30 Oct. 1731; estimates of family's fortunes: II E 25 103, 26 May 1706; II E 26 156, 19 May 1721; Estienne's marriage: II E 26 156, 8 May 1721. Earlier references to, see p. 266.

his trade for several years, taking on new apprentices, who paid 100 *livres* apprenticeship fees in 1701 and 1707. In 1708 he apprenticed his son Jean, who had reached the age of fourteen, to Jean Pelletan. The son worked for Pelletan for a total of eight years and was finally received marchand-fabricant in 1722. The first record of his production is for 1724 and his concern was to expand steadily in the following years. A sign of his social arrival was his marriage in 1729 to Marianne Tartary, sister of Catherine who had married Pierre Flottes fils a few years earlier.[47] The other clothier family whose founding member worked his way through the ranks of Villenouvette's labour force was that of Bonneville. This was an old catering family. François Bonneville was the landlord of the Logis du Cheval Blanc at Clermont and it was a son of his, Bernard, by profession a pâtissier, who set up a tavern at Villenouvette. One of Bernard's sons, Pierre, succeeded his father as inn-keeper at the manufacture while another, Jacques, became a cloth-shearer, served at the manufacture until the turn of the century, and worked at Grange-des-Prés before buying in 1706 a small property in the Rue de la Fregère, backing onto the Rhonel and directly adjoining the enclosed manufacture which Raissac was building for himself in these years. The cost of this building, which was in a poor state, was 550 *livres* and during 1707 Bonneville converted it into a 'boutique de tondeur'. In 1724 he became a master in the clothier's corporation by purchasing for 1,650 *livres* another of the special masterships which had been created by the King in 1722.[48] The role of both the Bernard and the Bonneville families in the trade was going to be significant.

At the bottom of our social scale of those who produced for the Levant during these years are some members of the town's traditional industry who had fewer resources than either the Desalascs or the Berthomieus. Among these were various members of the Lugagne family, which was among our group of 'regular' producers for the period 1674–94, and Pierre Delpon, a poor relation of Pierre Desalasc. We shall follow the history of the Lugagnes. In order to support the extra cost of producing for the new market, Estienne and Raymond Lugagne, who had worked

47. Vital Bernard: at Lodève: ADH 11 E 26 130, 29 July 1693; dye-house and apprentices in Clermont: 11 E 25 104, 106, 108, 12 March 1696, 4 May 1701, 28 July 1707; apprenticeship, mastership of son: 11 E 26 147, 17 Aug. 1708, ACC BB3, 24, 25 April 1722; production: ADH C2231; Jean Bernard's marriage: Bobo, 'Une communauté languedocienne', pp. 198–9.
48. Jacques Bonneville: grandfather's, father's and brother's careers: ADH 11 E 26 124–5, 27 June 1687, 9 May 1688, 11 E 25 99, 26 Dec. 1699; his career: at Villenouvette, 11 E 25 99, 8 Dec. 1699, and Grange-des-Prés, 11 E 25 107, 15 Sept. 1704; establishes workshop in Clermont, 11 E 26 167, 18 Aug. 1706, 11 E 25 108, 16 Oct. 1707, 11 E 26 146, 30 Dec. 1707; mastership: ACC BB3, 29 Dec. 1724.

individually for Clermont's traditional markets, associated themselves. In 1697 Raymond Lugagne had bought a property in the Rue de la Fregère which must have provided the centre for their concern. It was they who, with Berthomieu and Jacques Ménard, administered jointly a twisting mill between 1700 and 1703, and in 1708 they were working six looms and had produced one hundred pieces of cloth. They do not seem to have had the means, however, to produce cloth for the new market regularly. Quite probably they varied their production and in years of difficulty concentrated entirely on traditional cloth for local markets. But this recourse was taken from them (as it was from other surviving members of Clermont's traditional industry) by a royal edict in 1715 which forbade the manufacture of any other than fine cloth at Clermont. The sons of Raymond and Estienne Lugagne, all of whom were received marchands-fabricants, attempted at various stages to produce cloth for the Levant but, with one exception, that of Arnaud Lugagne, oldest son of Raymond, these attempts were unsuccessful. Estienne Lugagne, for example, second son of Raymond, produced for a few years in the 1720s but was obliged because of his losses to abandon production and to take up a post as manager in Seimandy's privileged concern at Bédarieux. As he informed the intendant in February 1746, he had made cloth 'dans un tems où bien loin de gagner on perdoit dans la fabriquation'.[49]

The unsettled trading conditions, and the edict banning the production of the traditional coarse broad-cloths in Clermont, were the decisive elements in excluding the poorer participants in the trade. The edict of 1715 was an unprecedented measure which set the seal on the fate of the poorer members of Clermont's traditional industry. The registers of the conseil de ville in 1717 record the protest of some of their number: it was reported that 'pluzieurs mart⁵ qui faisoint travallier en londres larges saizains et vingtdeuxzains qui ce sont fabriqués de tout temps dans led. Clermont demandent quil leur soit permis de continuer led. traval attandu quils ne sont point en estat de pouvoir faire travallier en londres seconds'. These poorer clothiers had urged that 'les marts puissent chacun travaillier suivant ses forces et sa portée'.[50] This liberty had never previously been denied at Clermont; now it was, and the clothier with insufficient resources to produce fine cloth for the Levant was obliged either to change profession or to accept a salaried position in the new industry. The latter was the course which several of the town's traditional

---

49. Lugagnes: association: recorded in survey of 1708, BN FF 8037; property Rue de la Fregère; II E 25 104, 15 Dec. 1697; twisting mill, II E 26 143–4, 9 Oct. 1701, 18 Feb. 1703; edict of 1715: AN F12 58; Estienne Lugagne's lament: ADH C2052, Letter to Le Nain. Earlier references to, see p. 110.
50. ACC BB2, 20 June 1717.

clothiers had in fact already resorted to. Raymond Delpon was received marchand-facturier at the same time as his brother Pierre in 1693 but was working as a cardeur for Barthe at Grange-des-Prés in 1699.[51] Pierre Laval, described in 1694 as a marchand-facturier, became, too, a commis of Barthe's.[52] In other cases it was the son who chose a more humble profession: Hillaire Souvier, whose father had had the ambiguous status of 'marchand-cardeur-facturier', was apprenticed to a weaver in 1689.[53] The descent from the status of poor facturier to salaried worker was not a particularly abrupt one. We have seen in an earlier chapter how the profession of clothier in Clermont's traditional industry blended, as it were, economically and socially with those of the various categories of salaried workers.[54]

Our survey has shown that the fortunes of those who produced for the Levant during these years were most mixed. Those at the top and at the bottom of the social scale seem to have had least success, those at or just below the middle, most. The failure of the poorest clothier is easily understandable. Not only were market conditions most unstable during this period but also the production of fine cloth required skills and resources which poorer clothiers, unless they had served at Villenouvette, did not possess. And while production for the new market was so hazardous, the expansion in the affairs of successful clothiers offered abundant opportunities of salaried employment. The failure of the rich is more complex. Why was it, to use Gaskell's words, that 'few of the men who entered the trade rich were successful'? Galtié père was conscious, we have seen, that he had set out with distinct advantages over his artisanal neighbours in the size of his capital and the number of his 'amis'. It is difficult to give a conclusive answer to this question on the basis of so few examples but we shall risk making some general observations about the more obvious entrepreneurial failings of the wealthy participants in the trade.

Some of the disadvantages of the rich participants are fairly obvious. Gaskell states that they 'trusted too much to others, too little to themselves' and that this was the case at Clermont can be seen from the need of Barthe, Galtié and others to hire commis or to make use of associates trained in the royal manufacture. They were thus deprived of a share of their profits, and a substantial share: the terms which Galtié granted to his associates (a quarter of profits and no share in losses) were most

51. ACC BB1, 2 Feb. 1693; ADH C1124, List of Barthe's creditors.
52. ADH 11 E 26 131, 5 June 1694; ADH C1124.
53. ADH 11 E 26 126, 7 Aug. 1689.
54. See pp. 113–16.

generous, far more so than those granted to non-investing associates later in the century. (A rich merchant in 1726, for example, contracted to give his cloth-making partner one-tenth of profits while the later was to be liable for one-twentieth of losses.)[55] Extra-familial associations were, besides, invariably risky in the pre-industrial period. The ambition of the junior associate was usually to build up his resources as rapidly as possible in order to establish his own concern and very often he had few scruples about how this was done. Galtié's association with Fraisse ended in a court case: Fraisse, claiming a larger share of profits than he had been granted, had absconded with ten pieces of *londrins-seconds*.[56] Raissac's association with his father-in-law, likewise, ended abruptly and bitterly in legal wranglings.[57]

In addition to the fact that the practice of employing commis had possibly damaging consequences there are signs that, in Barthe's case at least, the actual choice of commis or apprentices was not optimal. One is struck by the fact that Barthe's apprentices were mainly of rather high social standing. They included Estienne Verdier, son of a bourgeois, Jean-Gaspard Léotard, son of an advocate, and Estienne Mathieu, from an honest merchant background. It may be unfair to cast aspersions on these apprentices' capacity for work but one wonders whether Barthe would not have been wiser to have resisted his evident preference for apprentices from backgrounds similar to his own and chosen instead sons of artisanal families. This, certainly, was the course taken by the far more successful Antoine Raissac. In 1708 he took on the son of a shearer from the royal manufacture, Jean Jacques Tarbouriech. His satisfaction with him was such that in 1710, when the apprenticeship was completed, he waived payment of the 300 *livres* apprenticeship fee.[58] He chose another apprentice in that year from a similar, artisanal background. This was Jean Delpon, son of Pierre Delpon, a clothier from Clermont's traditional industry. Again the apprenticeship fee was waived in view of the 'bonne amitié' existing between Raissac and the Delpon family and the promise of Delpon père to feed and clothe his son during the two-and-three-quarter-years' apprenticeship.[59]

Comparing the activities of our few rich participants in the trade with those of their competitors of more humble origins one is struck by the exceptional speed with which their concerns were built up and the scale of production increased. All the clothiers whose careers we have surveyed

55. Terms recorded in ACC BB3, 3 Feb. 1727.
56. ADH 11 E 25 108, 4 June 1710.
57. ADH 11 E 25 103, 5 Nov. 1709.
58. ADH 11 E 26 172, 31 Oct. 1710.
59. ADH 11 E 26 172, 13 Dec. 1711.

substantially increased their investments in fixed and circulating capital during these years but none as rapidly as Barthe and Galtié. It would seem that their attitude towards the new trade was in some ways conditioned by their merchant background. A merchant's reaction to rising demand was to benefit from the expansion as fully as his resources permitted and they would appear to have treated their cloth production in a like manner. But cloth production, unlike pure commercial affairs, required both a large labour force and a significant fixed capital investment and the maintenance of both clearly occasioned large losses to Barthe and Galtié when the demand for cloth collapsed, as it did on several occasions during these years. It would seem that they committed themselves too fully, at too early a stage, to a market which, as we have seen, was subject to most severe disruptions in this period. We have argued in an earlier chapter that periods of depression favour small-scale concerns, periods of expansion, large. The 'conjunctural' background between 1690 and the 1720s was confused, being exceptionally favourable in some years and exceptionally unfavourable in others, and it would seem that the concerns which could survive in these circumstances were those which were sufficiently flexible to respond to both types of situation. The concerns of Galtié and Barthe were geared for the years of expansion only.

Two of our merchant participants in the trade continued their traditional trades in addition to cloth-making. This was the case of the Galtiés and also of Raymond Budin. Budin's correspondence with various Toulousain merchants shows that in addition to making a wide range of cloth for the Levant at Grange-des-Prés, he was involved in trading in wool and in large purchases of Lodève's and of other varieties of cloth which he had dyed and finished at his manufacture.[60] One doubts the wisdom of this combination of manufacturing and trading activities. The examples of those clothiers who succeeded shows that the new breed of successful entrepreneurs were pure industrialists, who gave their undivided attention to cloth-making. General trading thus distracted an entrepreneur from his industrial role and the use of a manufacture's dyeing and finishing facilities for processing a wide range of cloths quite probably caused the labour force to be less expert in preparing that narrow range produced for the Levant. Significantly a part of Budin's large losses was occasioned by the fact that a number of bales of his cloth had to be down-graded – *londrins-premiers* sold as *londrins-seconds*,

60. ADH C1124, Letters of Mirande and Bermond (Toulouse merchants) to Budin, especially those of 23 Sept., 19 Dec., 26 Dec. 1699, 30 July 1700 and memoir entitled 'Raisons contre divers articles des comptes reçus par Monsieur Mirande', 24 Dec. 1701.

londrins-seconds as *londres-larges* etc. – in view of their poor quality.[61] As we have seen in an earlier chapter, the characteristic commercial arrangement which had predominated during the period of depression had been one in which a host of small-scale producers sold 'in the white' to a handful of rich merchants who carried out the dyeing and finishing processes. It was this pattern which Budin continued to adhere to in part and which Maysonnade and Tartary followed in their 1695 association. But it seems that this system was no longer applicable and certainly unsuitable for competitive and specialized markets such as the Levant. Cloth needed to be of consistent quality and of standard sizes, dyes had to be uniform, and it does seem that the clothier who supervised the whole production process, from the purchase of wool to the sale of the cloth at Marseilles, had become essential in order to ensure that this sort of quality control was achieved. Merchants perhaps under-estimated the technical difficulties of producing for the new market. Colbert evidently had been aware of the importance of the specialized clothier, on the other hand. As we have seen, his corporative reforms had been specifically designed to favour the emergence of the full-time, specialist entrepreneur who was to take the place of the less fully committed merchant participators in cloth production.[62]

We have seen that a number of the clothier families who succeeded in these years made use of the labour of all the members of the family. In the contract by which Georges Desalasc associated himself with his father and his brother it was laid down that 'tous les trois soccuperoit et donneroit leurs entiers soins et aplications aud. négosse sans pouvoir soccuper à autre choze',[63] (re-affirming what we have just stated about the importance of the concentration on a single trade.) In fact, though, such contracts were made only when one of the members of the family, as in the case of Georges Desalasc, had been emancipated and wanted to participate on his own account in the family business. Before such emancipations the participation of sons and other children in the economic affairs of their maison was mandatory and required no special contract to be enforced. The participation of members of rich merchant families in their family affairs was, however, likely to be more limited. This for two reasons. First, considerations of status would, it seems certain, have prevented any extensive involvement in physical work by any members of the family. Galtié's widow told Moulins in 1710 that she had supported her husband's maison 'autant que femme de mon estat

---

61. ADH C1124.
62. See p. 244.
63. ADH 11 E 26 185, 12 Aug. 1724.

laye fait';[64] this 'estat' would have ensured, it seems certain, that her support would not have included physical work and she may indeed be implying that her support could have been only of a moral kind. The second reason is this. The co-operation which we have observed, among members of Clermont's traditional cloth-making families in a previous chapter, and among artisanal producers for the new market in this, was occasioned by an economic need. In the case of the traditional industry there was the need to work to survive and in the new one to this consider-ation was added the real possibility that the co-operation would provide the means to advance considerably the wealth and standing of the family. The possession of large resources had, as we have seen from the example of the Galtié family, very different consequences. The priority in all such families was placed on the need to conserve the family patrimony and status of the maison and the greatest risk to this conservation was, precisely, the existence of too many sons. In rich households, therefore, from an early stage, while the heir-apparent (the oldest son) was in-corporated into family affairs attempts were made to place younger sons in such a way that they should no longer be dependent on the family patrimony. We have seen this policy carried out with respect to Jean Galtié who was clearly conscious of the importance of his not being a charge to his maison. So if poverty drew members of a family together for survival purposes wealth, ironically, obliged their economic separation. Such rules were likely to be particularly harshly applied in periods of economic depression in which the likelihood of families' significantly increasing their wealth was small. Families like the Galtiés, which had flourished in a period of depression, would have had difficulty in relaxing such a system in order to profit from the improved conjuncture all the more so in that the privileging of the oldest son at the expense of the others (as was the case in the Galtié family) inevitably gave rise to intense, if repressed, fraternal rivalries. The contrast between the co-operative approach of the families of artisanal clothiers and the evident tension in the Galtié household could not have been sharper. Jacques Galtié before his death was obliged very often to correspond with his cousin and Provençal business contact, Jean Moulins, when he was *away* from Clermont because of the tensions in his home. From Lodève in May 1701 he wrote 'jai ma teste Rompue de reproches et cest à toi à me consoler par la vigilance & à bien prendre le sens de tout aujourdhuy que je suis escarté de la maizon et en estat de Dire ma pensé sans croire rien risquer de la part de la familhe'; 'je tembrasse', he added at the end of his letter, 'et te recommande sur tout pour mon repos dans la familhe destre exact car tu

64. ADR, Fonds Moulins, IV, Letter of 23 May 1710.

cognois Nos Génies et je suis tourmenté comme un Chien'.[65] As for Jean Galtié, far from being in a position to help his declining maison after his father's death in 1710, he was *persona non grata* in his family home: 'on ne le veut plus voir', wrote one of Moulins's correspondents. A letter which Jean Galtié sent to his cousin shows his absolute exclusion from family affairs: 'Vous sçavez très bien que je naj jamais eu la moindre connoissance des affaires qui ce sont faitz et encore moins de ce quils pouvent estre puis quabsolument Il me lestoit Defendu.' This exclusion at least had the advantage of enabling him to wash his hands of any blame for his family's misfortunes: 'Je naj rien à me reprocher Il seroit à souhaitter que bien de gens fussent aussj tranquilles que je le suis sur semblables affaires.'[66]

The Galtiés and Moulins are the only rich merchant families for which we have detailed information in this period and it would not, therefore, be wise to be over-emphatic about what may conceivably be atypical cases. Reading the correspondence it does seem that the relationship of Jacques Galtié fils with his cousin was extraordinarily intense. Likewise Jean Galtié's ejection from the family household in 1710, though not his exclusion from all family affairs, was in part linked to his impregnating a 'fille de la ville' in that year.[67] It does seem, though, that rich families were run differently from poor ones, and that in so far as their rules had been devised to conserve an acquired position they had difficulty in responding to new opportunities.

It seems likely that the relationships between the merchant participants in the trade and their labour forces were more distant than those between the poorer clothiers and their employees. The attitude of a Galtié to humbler members of Clermont's population is as well illustrated by the casual reference by Jacques Galtié père to his son's impregnating a 'fille de la ville' as it is by a remark in a letter of Jacques Galtié, the cousin, to Raymond Moulins. This Jacques Galtié, as will be remembered, had left Lyons to work in Paris in some banking capacity in 1708. During the Regency he had made large sums most rapidly by speculating in some of John Law's schemes and then lost this fortune, equally rapidly, with the collapse of the 'systeme'. He had returned to Clermont 'en debte comme un Bouché' and convinced that there was no 'sort plus triste que le mien par la confiance aveugle que jay eu aux billets de banque'. In 1722 he was considering establishing a cloth manufacture, having recuperated, it would seem, a part of his lost capital. It may have

65. ADR, Fonds Moulins, IV, Letter of 2 May 1701.
66. ADR, Fonds Moulins, IV, VII, Rigal to Moulins, 25 Nov. 1710, Jean Galtié to Jean Moulins neveu, 20 Feb. 1711.
67. ADR, Fonds Moulins, IV, Letter of 8 Feb. 1710.

been for that purpose that he apprenticed his nephew Denis Guion to a marchand-fabricant in 1722. (In the contract he is described as a banquier of Paris.) The distance which separated this banquier from a working member of Clermont's community emerges from a remark made in connection with one Antoine Martin, to whom he owed money. Martin was the son of a laboureur and would therefore have been socially on a par, if not superior, to salaried cloth-workers. Galtié had been unable to settle his debt because of his temporary lack of liquidity and he wrote to Moulins saying 'je vo lay renvoyé [Martin] affin que vous eussiez votre part Du plaizir quil y a de devoir *à ces sortes de gens là* lors quon ne peut pas les payer. Je croy que sil vous a écrit il doit vous lavoir marqué de même cas [;] avec moy il ny a point de porte de der*ʳᵉ*.' Jacques Galtié returned to Paris in the late 1720s and clearly did not undertake production for the Levant. This, at least, was a wise decision for it is difficult to believe that he would have been successful. His priorities were for good living, not hard work. As he wrote to Moulins soon after his arrival in Clermont, 'ce pajs cy est un assez bon pays et nous nous divertirions assez sy nous avions de largent'. Martin's response to his temporary failure to repay his debt was not, in fact, as violent as he clearly expected it would be. Martin simply asked Moulins to clarify who was supposed to pay the debt (which Galtié had incurred transacting business on Moulins's account) and added 'ne prenés pas de mauvaize part M*ʳ* quand je vous escris car M*ʳ* Galtier ce moque entièrem*ᵗ* de moy'.[68] There is no direct evidence that the merchants involved in the new trade experienced labour problems but it is evident that it was impossible for them to live in 'bonne amitié' with their employees in the manner of their artisanal rivals, who not only participated in the physical process of cloth-making, but came themselves from the lower strata of Clermont's population.

The nature of the necessary ingredients for success in the new market has been emerging slowly as we have specified some of the entrepreneurial qualities which richer participants in the trade apparently lacked. We shall now elaborate on these qualities at greater length by analysing the successes of the group of clothiers who survived the violent fluctuations in the trade in its first thirty years to emerge as a rich and powerful entrepreneurial group in the 1720s.

A first and evident shared characteristic of those who had succeeded

68. Jacques Galtié (cousin): ADR, Fonds Moulins IV, Letters to Raymond Moulins of 26 Dec. 1720, 9 Jan., 10 Feb. 1721, 21 May 1722, Letter of Antoine Martin to Moulins of 7 May 1722; mention of the possibility of his founding a manufacture is made by Moulins in a letter of 19 May 1722 (Fonds Moulins, XXII); apprenticeship of nephew: ADH II E 26 183, 22 Dec. 1722. My emphasis in letter concerning Martin. Earlier references to, see pp. 60–3.

was the link with Villenouvette. Of the thirteen principal families which formed the industry in the mid 1720s – the Desalascs, the two branches of the Flottes family, the Pelletans, the Pradiers, the Berthomieus, the Bernards, the Bonnevilles, the Raissacs and four families whose histories I have not followed, the Audrans, Vernys, Bouissons and Liquiers – members of seven had served at the manufacture, and of the six others only the Berthomieu and Bouissons do not appear to have had members apprenticed to an ex-member of the manufacture.[69] The technological contribution of the manufacture was thus vital to their formation. The importance of the acquirement of a high level of technical skills in the production for the new market cannot be over-emphasized. What is more, Villenouvette would seem to have provided a particularly full and effective training. Ex-members of the manufacture not only showed themselves capable of making the full range of cloth for the new market but they also received a training in all processes of manufacture. Antoine Raissac, for example, was not merely a qualified marchand-facturier, he was also, an act records, 'maître tondeur de draps et maître teinturier' and, if we are to believe Raissac's own words, his shearing shop, one of six existing in Clermont in 1706, was 'des plus parfaites'.[70] Jacques Bonneville and Jean Bernard when they became marchands-fabricants likewise continued to do their own shearing and dyeing and Gabriel Pelletan, in dispute with the weavers' corporation in 1705 because several of his weavers were working without having been received master, claimed that he himself had been received master in their profession and that these weavers could thus be regarded as his assistants. The validity of this claim was disputed, but that Pelletan, after his years directing the main weaving workshops at Villenouvette, would himself have been capable of weaving there is no doubt.[71] Clermont's traditional industry had provided its members with a similar wide range of skills (it has been noted that its members carried out most of the processes of production themselves) as well as the advantages of the great economy of the artisan's way of life. The skills in the case of Clermont's traditional clothiers were clearly not as refined as those possessed by ex-members of the manufacture and so the tendency, we have seen, was for Clermontais who had not

69. The Desalasc, Pelletan, Pradier, Bernard, Bonneville, Raissac and Verny families had had members employed at Villenouvette. The two branches of the Flottes family, the Audran and the Liquier families had all had members apprenticed to ex-Villenouvette clothiers. François Audran and Pierre Flottes were both apprenticed to Mathieu Pradier (ADH 11 E 26 167, 7 March 1706), Jean Flottes to Joseph Tudesq (11 E 25 103, 24 Jan. 1707) and Guillaume Liquier to the Desalasc concern (11 E 26 167, 16 June 1706). For details of other families' links with Villenouvette see pp. 236–7.
70. ADH 11 E 25 103, 16 Feb. 1709; 11 E 25 108, cancelled act of 1706.
71. ADH 11 E 25 107, 12 July 1705.

received training at Villenouvette to apply the Dutch methods initially to the highest qualities of their traditional cloths – *vingt-deuxains* or *vingt-quatrains* – and then to improve the quality of their workmanship in order to be able to make *vingt-sixains* or *londrins-seconds*.

There were additional advantages to the excellent technical formation which accrued to these clothiers from their long years of service at the royal manufacture, or in the concerns of Villenouvette-trained clothiers. By serving these long 'apprenticeships' they were effectively following the advice which Jacques Savary gave to all would-be merchants and achieving a 'connaissance parfaite ... du Commerce dont ils se meslent [et une] ... grande expérience ... en servant longtemps les autres Marchands, auparavant que de faire leur établissement'.[72] The importance of a thorough knowledge of the trade as well as of another factor which we have emphasized as being necessary for success in production for the new market – a complete control by the entrepreneur of all parts of the production process – was emphasized by Mathieu Pradier fils in a memoir composed in 1732: 'Né dans ce commerce, l'ayant pratiqué moy même pend.' 20 années faisant moy même l'achat de mes laines teignant moy même mes draps, ils n'ont point de léger défaut que je n'y découvre d'un coup d'oeuil.'[73] The importance of the principle that many years should be served in a subordinate position before independent production be undertaken can be gauged as well from the failure of the Galtiés, Budin and Barthes as it can from the success of, for example, Pelletan and Raissac. Pelletan established an enormous cloth-making concern at Clermont but he did so only after years of production at Clermont as a normal clothier, ten years experience at Villenouvette, and ten years gradual expansion of his activities in the town. Likewise we have seen that Raissac undertook independent production only after some seventeen or eighteen years during which he had served successively as apprentice, facteur and associate to wealthy producers.

We have emphasized that the 'conjunctural' conditions during this period were exceptionally unstable. This factor added to the difficulty of producing for the new market and was probably fatal, we have shown, to those rich participants in the industry who had over-committed themselves to a trade which was not yet dependable by the rapidity with which they had built up the size of their labour forces and fixed capital investment. The concerns best equipped to survive, we have argued, were those which were sufficiently flexible to adapt to both sorts of circumstances. The rising generations of clothiers were by no means totally immune to

72. *Le parfait négociant*, p. 37.
73. ADH C4676, Memoir on Levant trade, 1732.

the sorts of the problems which beset Galtié and Barthe. The losses of
the Desalasc family between 1715 and 1717 we have just mentioned and
even Gabriel Pelletan's son, Jean, suffered some momentary financial
embarrassment during these years: 'la loi du commerce et sa loyauté lui
a toujours permis de remplir ses engagements', he recorded in a notarial
act registered in 1717, 'mais le mauvais état et le continuel dérangement
du commerce continuant d'être, cela lui fait craindre d'être en défaut de
la convention'.[74] But in general these rising clothiers had a better chance
of survival because they had not yet entirely shed those artisanal qualities
which had enabled them, or their like, to carry on producing cloth during
the depressed years of the seventeenth century. Their living costs were
low; a significant part of the labour input into their concerns was provided by themselves and members of their families; they could (until
1715) switch to the production of other types of cloth; and they would
not yet have lost the ability themselves to cultivate any land which they
might own.

As was to be expected given the closeness of social and familial links
between members of Clermont's artisanal population, members of the
rising generation of clothiers were in many cases closely related. In
addition the shared experience of residence at Villenouvette, or of producing for the Levant in Clermont, gave rise to numerous additional
familial alliances between these clothier families. By the 1720s not one of
the surviving families was without some relationship to another. Pradier
was Pelletan's brother-in-law, we have seen, and was closely related to
the Desalascs. The Desalascs and Berthomieus were linked by the marriages of members of their families to the Altayracs. Pradier's sister had
married Joseph Tudesq (a failed fabricant) and a Tudesq daughter had
married Jean Flottes whose cousin Pierre Flottes together with Jean
Bernard had married daughters of Maximilien Tartary. Jean Verny and
Joseph Tudesq married Gély sisters (in the case of Tudesq this was a
second marriage) and one of Verny's daughters married François Audran.
Antoine Raissac's daughter married a son of Pierre Flottes. Guillaume
Liquier's daughter married a third member of the Tartary family, Maximilien, brother of Catherine and Marianne. Jacques Bonneville by his
marriage to Lucy, daughter of Mathieu Palot and Jeanne Bonnal, had
become a relation of Pradier, Tudesq and Pelletan, who were all cousins
of his bride, as well as of Paul Cathala, a shearer in the new industry.
The Bouissin family was closely related to the Bernards. Similar family
links united the clothiers with the skilled members of their labour forces.
Paul Cathala, who was a native of St-Chinian, had married an aunt of

74. Cited by Bobo, 'Une communauté languedocienne', p. 31.

Mathieu Pradier, and thus was a close or distant relation to the majority of the clothiers. Similarly the brothers Pierre and Jean Ramy, a cloth-dresser and a shearer, both married into clothiers' families, the former to Marie Altayrac, niece of Pierre Desalasc, and the latter to Marie Lugagne, daughter of Raymond, marchand-facturier. Thus the clothiers and the skilled workers in the new industry were enmeshed in a network of relationships the complexity of which has only been hinted at here. The relationships and links were sufficiently strong for a group of strangers to the profession to declare in 1725 that 'la plus grande partie desd. fabriquands sont parans ou alliés'.[75]

Some of the advantages which Clermont's new generation of clothiers acquired from their close family links with each other have been seen. They provided the basis for partnerships and for mutual co-operation. Tudesq and Flottes, Verny and Audran, Pradier and Pelletan, the Lugagne brothers, the Flottes, Berthomieu and Desalasc families were all associated at various stages in their efforts to achieve success in the new market.[76] In addition, clothiers had inherited that tradition of mutual aid which had existed in the town's traditional industry. We have seen several manifestations of this: the continuation of the practice of joint utilization of twisting mills, for example, until the scale of individual clothiers' affairs was sufficiently large to make full use of these machines possible, and the fact that in the 1690s Pierre Desalasc lent money to his son-in-law, Pierre Delpon, and his brother-in-law, Jacques Laurés, for the purchase of wools. Additional manifestations are provided by the fact that Pierre Desalasc and Estienne Berthomieu jointly purchased a dyeing vat for 1,075 *livres* in 1705 and that Mathieu Pradier lived with his brother-in-law Gabriel Pelletan during the years in which the latter was founding and expanding his manufacture in Clermont.[77] The marriages of members of this closely related group invariably drew a large

75. Pierre Desalasc's sister was married to Jean Altayrac, a hatter (ADH 11 E 26 130, 27 Dec. 1693) and their son Jean was married to Françoise Berthomieu, daughter of Estienne (11 E 25 124, 29 March 1738, will of Jean Altayrac); marriage of Tudesq to Pradier's sister: 11 E 26 127, 7 Sept. 1690; marriages of Verny and Tudesq to Gély daughters: 11 E 26 124, 12 May 1687, 11 E 25 102, 10 Feb. 1703; Audran/Verny link: 11 E 25 153, 27 Oct. 1749; Raissac/Flottes: 11 E 26 188, 21 June 1728; Liquier/Tartary: Bobo, 'Une communauté languedocienne', p. 189; Bonneville/Palot: 11 E 26 131, 11 March 1694; Bouisson/Bernard: 11 E 25 153, 20 Jan. 1750; Cathala/Pradier (aunt's name being Bonnal): 11 E 26 123, 22 Oct. 1685; Ramy/Altayrac, Ramy/Lugagne: 11 E 25 102, 2 Oct. 1702, 11 E 25 108, 13 April 1706; comment on closeness of clothiers' links: ACC BB3, 16 Nov. 1725.
76. All their associations previously mentioned apart from that between Audran and Verny which is recorded in production statistics for years 1714–21 (ADH C2208, 2231).
77. These links have been already recorded apart from Pradier's residing in Pelletan's house. This is documented in acts of notary Pouget for the year 1700, e.g. ADH 11 E 25 101, 8 Sept. 1700.

selection of participants in the new industry. The closeness of the links which a combination of intermarriage, co-residence at Villenouvette (in several cases), and joint participation in the new industry had contributed to, as well as the optimism and prosperity of this rising generation, is shown by the generous donations which were frequently given on these occasions. Jacques Bonneville and Lucy Palot, marrying in 1694, in addition to their parental portions received 100 *livres* from Paul Cathala, 50 *livres* from Mathieu Pradier and from Gabriel Pelletan, and 30 *livres* from Joseph Tudesq.[78]

One factor which all these successful participants in the trade lacked at some stage was capital. This collective lack, we have emphasized, was the major handicap of Languedoc's industry during this period. And as we have seen too it was a lack of 'moyens' which excluded the poorer clothiers of Clermont's traditional industry from participating in the new trade. What made it possible for clothiers to produce in years of expansion was the availability of credit. The industry was part financed in its early years by a number of wool merchants who granted long credits on the expensive wools which they sold. The centres for the importation of Spanish wools were Toulouse and Bayonne and a group of rich merchants from these towns clearly played an important role in the financing of Languedoc's industry. The names of Bermond, Colomez and Mirande, merchants of Toulouse, and of Laborde, a merchant of Bayonne, figured prominently amongst the creditors of Saptes in 1692 and Grange-des-Prés in 1699, and equally Bermond was a creditor of the Desalascs in 1724 for a total of 5,677 *livres* 10 *sols*, the price of nine bales of wool, Colomez and Mirande were the largest creditors of the Galtiés in 1710, and Colomez a creditor of Tudesq in the same year. The actual capital cost of production was also reduced by the readiness with which Marseilles's merchants purchased the cloth in the early years of expansion.[79]

Such aid, however, was not generally available in years of depression and this was an additional cause of the sharpness of the cyclical crises in the industry in the early years. Gradually, though, this capital shortage was overcome by the clothiers' strict policy of ploughing back profits into their businesses. Such a policy was axiomatic for the artisanal producer who rarely had the skills necessary to calculate his profitability accurately. The Desalascs' family association demonstrates such a process at work. The lack of regular account-keeping is shown by the fact that they needed to make a complete inventory of all their equipment and raw

78. ADH II E 26 131, 11 March 1694.
79. ADH C1123, 1124, record their links with Saptes and Grange-des-Prés; links with Desalascs, Galtiés, Tudesq, recorded in ADH II E 26 185, 172, 12 Aug. 1724, 24 April, 1 June 1710.

materials on each occasion on which they wanted to ascertain their liquidity position. That the ploughing-back of profits became, as it were, part of an accepted code of business techniques is apparent from the terms of a society drawn up by two clothiers in 1746: the society was to last five years, stock-taking was to take place every September, a maximum of 500 *livres* a year could be 'borrowed' by the associates from the society though 5% interest was to be paid on such sums, none of the profits were to be used until the society had been dissolved, and no salaries were to be drawn by either associate.[80] By the 1720s the majority of the surviving clothiers had adequate means and this, as well as the more stable trading conditions, contributed to the greater steadiness apparent in the industry's output. The clothiers' enrichment meant too that they had overcome their only major disadvantage *vis-à-vis* their Dutch and English competitors and merchant-entrants to the trade.

Essentially the secret of the success of the rising generation of clothiers lay in their combining basically artisanal attributes (capacity for hard work, low living costs, co-operative approach to production etc.) with the technical, commercial and entrepreneurial skills propagated by the royal manufactures and made serviceable by the changing economic climate. As artisans, clothiers and their families had frugal life-styles and were accustomed to the most minute economy in the processes of production, processes to which they themselves, as well as the members of their families, contributed.[81] The ploughing-back of profits was virtually automatic and fixed capital costs were kept to a minimum as the clothier's home was his workshop. The whole lives of these clothiers and of their families revolved around the profession which was practised in their midst: it governed marriages, generally arranged for professional reasons, and it governed both social and religious life, which revolved around the activities of the confrérie or the corporation. Labour problems were virtually inconceivable, for the clothiers lived and worked in the midst of their workers who, at least in these early years, were sep-

---

80. ADH C2047, Terms of association between Jean Martin and Gabriel Verny, 2 Feb. 1746.
81. That all members of the families of the new clothiers participated in production has been revealed by some of the son–father and fraternal associations. It is also shown by the details of Joseph Tudesq's bankruptcy proceedings. Tudesq's mother and his partner's wife (the partner was Jean Flottes) were owed money for menial work connected with the production process ('pour avoir trié trois cent neuf livres laine . . . et litage de vint quatre pièces draps', ADH ii E 26 172, 1 June 1710). Another clothier married a girl who operated her own laundry business. She brought with her as part of her dowry a 'boutique de blanchissage quelle a fait elle même et gagnoit par son travail industrie et négoce' (ii E 26 152, 28 Oct. 1717). A laundry girl would probably have been an able assistant to a clothier; she would certainly have had no inhibitions about involving herself in manual labour.

arated little either financially or socially from their masters. Lastly, as artisans, they were contented with their lot and totally committed to their trade. The ambition to seek a higher position in society was unlikely to occur to them as they had been brought up to manual work.[82] The new generation of successful Clermontais clothiers operated with all the advantages of the artisan's way of life and method of production, without the disadvantages of his limited markets and primitive techniques. It is not surprising that richer merchants found it difficult to compete. The rising generation did indeed correspond closely to that type described in Pirenne's brilliant, intuitive article quoted at the head of this chapter. The group which had emerged to a situation of prominence in Clermont's cloth industry by the mid 1720s consisted of 'nothing else than parvenus brought into action by the transformations of society, embarrassed neither by custom nor by routine, having nothing to lose and therefore the bolder in their race toward profit'. There are signs too, we have seen, that members of Clermont's previous commercial elite were 'incapable of adapting themselves'[83] to the new economic circumstances.

The rapid, and early, economic success and social promotion of Gabriel Pelletan does not seem to have caused alarm among members of Clermont's elite. Indeed, in permitting him to become first consul in 1694, considerable flexibility was shown and the Galtiés commented uncritically on the marriage of his son to Demoiselle Jaurions. In the 1720s, however, there were distinct signs of tension between newly enriched clothiers and members of the traditional elite. We have mentioned these in a previous chapter without going into detail. In November 1724 there was a dispute over the rights of Guillaume Mutuel, an apothecary, to attend the Etats. In November 1725 there was a sharp reaction from a group claiming to be the 'principaux hans.' of the town against the election of a marchand-fabricant, Antoine Berthomieu, to the first consulship. This office should only be occupied by 'gentilhomes gradués et bourgeois vivant noblement', it was claimed. Antoine Berthomieu, even though he was now describing himself as an 'ancien capp^{ne} de milice et mar^t bourgeois', was clearly not acceptable to this group. For the rest of the decade there were bitter disputes over the consular elections, the

---

82. The close relationship between clothiers and employees is illustrated at marriage ceremonies. Clothiers frequently attended the marriages of their employees (particularly in the early years of the new industry) and gave presents. On 9 Dec. 1691 a carder and servant of Gabriel Pelletan married and were presented with a ring and a bed by Pelletan's wife; on 2 Jan. 1689 a weaver employed by Pelletan married and was presented with a gold ring valued at 6 *livres* (ADH II E 26 128, 126).
83. 'Stages', pp. 494, 515.

intendant having to step in and name a consul in 1725, 1727 and 1728 in order to 'empêcher les Brigues et Cabales qui ce fait chacque année'. Sometimes clothiers were elected and in other years traditional bourgeois. Jean Roustan Villet, a clothier, followed Berthomieu as first consul in 1727; Antoine Maistre, bourgeois, succeeded to Villet in 1728; in 1729 Estienne Berthomieu was made first consul and Jacques Bonneville second; in 1730 the pendulum swung in the opposite direction again with the election of Pierre Landier, one of the 'principal inhabitants' who had opposed Antoine Berthomieu in 1725. But in the 1730s the struggle was decisively won by the rising generation. By an edict of November 1733 Louis XV made the post of first consul venal and created new offices of 'maire' and 'lieutenant-de-maire', and it was members of the rising generation, without exception, who purchased these offices. Jean-François Bouisson purchased the position of lieutenant-de-maire, Jean-Pierre Desalasc, oldest son of Jacques, that of first consul, and Antoine Berthomieu and Jean Altayrac became 'maires alternatifs et mitrienals' by their payment of 18,450 *livres* each for half shares in the post of mayor. Both Berthomieu and Altayrac were aged fifty-one. After some thirty or forty years of hard labour they had attained the pinnacle of Clermontais society.

That the social arrival of the rising generation of clothiers in the 1720s should have given rise to such hostility and resistance, whereas that of Pelletan in the 1690s apparently passed by without comment, is fairly easily explicable. The circumstances were quite different. In the 1690s an intact, still confident and dominating elite could quite easily admit one parvenu. Pelletan's social rise was exceptionally precocious. In the 1720s, however, as we have seen, it was a whole group of clothiers, all closely-related, who were rising to ascendancy in Clermont. The traditional elite's consciousness of this is apparent from the fact it was they who described the clothiers as being for 'la plus grande partie ... parans ou alliés'. In their petition they complained that 'lesd. fabriquands veullent ce perpétuer dans la maison de ville', which was indeed the case, and to oppose this, in addition to their claim that the post was intended for bourgeois only, they used the subtle argument that if clothiers were allowed to hold the post they would be both judge and party in any disputes concerning cloth production, for the general règlement of 1669 (which had been devised in a period in which it would have been highly unlikely that a clothier would achieve a senior position in the magistracy) gave jurisdiction over the cloth industry to the consuls. The alarm of the traditional elite was added to by other consequences of the emergence of this powerful group of clothiers with their large labour forces. The new industry represented an economic as well as a social threat to them for it had occasioned a general rise in wages in the region and this affected large land-owners, who employed labour, particularly severely. Significantly complaints about this phenomenon were frequent too in the 1720s. In 1728, for example, it was recorded in the register of the conseil de ville that 'lad Commt^é ressoit des notables préjudices par lad. fabrique qui cauze les vallets quj estoint pour lors à gages à dix escus sont présentement à trante escus, que les gages de servantes en sont de mesmes et à paine on en peut trouver et que les hommes et fammes pour travailler les terres et travaux nécess^res ont augmanté de deux tiers'. It was decided to request the intendant to instruct cloth manufacturers to 'cesser pandant les Culiettes du bled vandanges et ollivier pour que les hans peussent trouver plus aizément des hommes et des fammes'.[84]

The rise of these new clothing families (Ill. 20) would have been more acceptable to and containable by the old elite if their own fortunes had grown in the same proportions as those of the clothiers, but the lack of members of this elite among purchasers of municipal offices in Clermont in the 1730s is not the only evidence that this was far from having been the case. It would seem that it was not only in the cloth industry that members of the traditional elite failed to distinguish themselves, and that the Galtié, Budin and Barthe families were not the only ones to 'go under' during these years. Raymond Budin's correspondence reveals that 1699, a year of general crisis, saw a number of commercial failures and, amongst them, that of the Vallibouze family of Clermont: 'bien dafferes ce tournent de travers dieu en soit Loué les faillites des quelles vous nous parlés nous surpennent tout à fait et particulièrement celle de Vallibouze dautant que avons peu comprandre [qu'il] ne fesoit daffere que par comission', wrote the Toulousain wool merchant Mirande to Budin on 23 September 1699.[85] And Moulins's letters to his various correspondents reveal that several participants in that stable network of Clermontais families which had dominated the Lyons/Clermontais trade during the second half of the century met similar fates. Raymond Grasset, ex-Clermontais and Lyonnais merchant, disappeared during these years leaving his affairs in great disorder (it was rumoured that he had gone to the Levant). The Mathieu family, which had been closely related to that group of drapiers which had presided over Clermont's industry in the 1650s and then dispersed to more prosperous commercial centres in the second half of the century, was in desperate straits in these years. Moulins corresponded with a member of this family who had remained in Clermont. This Mathieu, who described himself as bour-

---

84. ACC BB3, BB4, 19 Nov. 1724, 16 Nov., 21 Nov. 1725, 15 Nov., 15 Dec. 1726, 15 Jan., 1 Nov. 1728, Nov. 1729, Nov. 1730, Dec. 1734, 27 Feb., 8 May, 11 Oct. 1735.
85. ADH C1124.

Ill. 20. By the mid-1720s a group of enriched clothiers challenged the supremacy of Clermont's traditional elite: elegant living in the manufacturing suburb of the Rue de la Fregère

geois, explained that the family patrimony had been entrusted to his older brother who had been associated with one Villard in Lyons and had died recently. Villard had gone bankrupt and there seemed no way to recover their family funds. No help was expected from his cousins, another branch of the Mathieu family which had moved to Chalôn-sur-Saône, because of 'L'estat dérangé de leurs affaires'. The situation of the Mathieus was desperate, their decline sudden: 'convenés Monsieur que mon sort est à plaindre mais bien davantage cellui dune vieille mère de 86 ans ou plus qui tout à Coup se trouve depourveüe de tout secours humain', wrote Mathieu to Moulins on 20 September 1717; 'en un mot nous voilà absolument à Lhôpital si dieu na pitié de nous'.[86] The period was one of change: commercial circuits were shifting (it was Marseilles not Lyons which was from now on to be Clermont's immediate commercial superior); new merchant families were rising; the use of credit was becoming more extensive; the rules of the game had changed, and there are signs that numerous families which had grown accustomed to the stable economic environment that had prevailed in the second half of the seventeenth century failed to adjust. As Turle, a traditional Carcassonnais merchant wrote to Moulins in November 1712:

je vous avoue que la fidélité et bonne foy dans le commerce est bien différente de celle de nt^{re} temps car pour sy peu quon ne travaile on ne trouve point cette franchise dautre fois elle me paroît sy différante que je crains que sy elle dure il faudra cesser de rien faire on ne songe à présent que à tromper son compagnon il mest arrivé assez souvent de cas et avec des maisons de Lyons.[87]

Among the Moulins papers is a small cloth-bound volume which contains, amongst a variety of other material, a number of curious herbal cures, recipes, quotations, comments and maxims which, Moulins noted, he had found among his former employer Louis Durand's papers after his death in January 1696. The maxims are of no great profundity but they are clearly formulated by a man who believed that both economic success and moral salvation would come from the observance of relatively elementary semi-religious rules.

Dans les affaires faut simprimer pour Maxime quil n'y a rien de bon que ce quy est honnête, ny rien de mauvais que ce quy est dezhonnête, tout ce que dieu a préveu nécessairement arrive par nécessité, et tout ce quil a préveu Indifférément arrive par Indifférence, or est il que tout ce quy dépend de notre liberté.

Quand on sengage témérairement dans une meshante affaire on Commence par où lon devrois finir, Car on ne conte la raison qu'après que le Malheur est arrivé au lieu que sy on leust escoutée auparavant on le pouvoit Eviter.

Nul ne doit avoir part aux affaires que Celuy quy Les peut servir et quy luy peut donner sy faut dire de gages de son industrie et fidélité.

Il faut estre dans toutes ces actions, au dessus des pations cette grâce ne peut venir que de dieu sans laquelle on ne peut rien la nature de lhomme ne pouvant rien de luy même.[88]

---

86. ADR, Fonds Moulins, IV, Letters of Mathieu to Moulins, 22 June 1716, 20 Sept., 22 Dec. 1717.
87. ADR, Fonds Moulins, III, 15 Nov. 1712; Turle's belonging to Carcassonne's traditional merchant elite is revealed not only by his reaction to the changing nature of business habits but also by the fact that it was a Turle (he himself, his father, or a close relation it seems certain) who was made one of the *bailes* of Carcassonne's new clothiers' corporation in December 1666 (Depping, *Correspondance*, III, 799–801).
88. ADR, Fonds Moulins, XXIII.

One feels that such maxims were no longer of much service in the changing circumstances of these years. The connection of morality and religion with economic behaviour occurred extensively only among those small groups of the population whose business affairs had long passed the stage of being dictated by pure, economic need: the circumstances which applied to the majority of the French population. The advice and example offered by the notary Pouget, another of Moulins's Clermontais correspondents, were without doubt more instructive about the qualities required to prosper in the new period. 'Vous savez Monsieur', he wrote, 'que nous sommes dans un siècle, où Il faut travaillier pour pouvoir survenir à payer les taxes, et Impôt, ce quy moblige estant procureur, notaire, et beaucoup dautres charges quon me fait prandre, de prandre le party du négosse, ce quy fait ayant tenu quelques foires ...'[89] But it is clear that Mathieu, bourgeois, was incapable of following this advice. He wrote repeatedly to Moulins in an attempt to recover his dead brother's capital explaining that, it was 'le pain unique dune vieille mère de 86 ans, et dun fils unique qui *sans nul talent* n'a dautres resources'.[90] Nor, apparently, was Jean Galtié in a position to react; he must have been in his thirties by the time of his father's death but he still had no permanent employment (though, as mentioned, he was later employed out of charity by his brother-in-law, Reboul). Galtié's desperation in these years emerges in a letter written in 1711 to his cousin Moulins in Genoa: 'Du moins avoit ils [some others to whom he is referring] la consolation Davoir D'employ et Moj Men Estes je Allé justement à la boucherie où lon conduit ses pauvres agniaux sur la promesse que vous maviez Donné De menvoyer ce quil me faudroit pour j pouvoir Exercher quelque Emploj.'[91] Nor were Moulins's own decadent nephews and nieces residing in Clermont and its neighbourhood in a position to follow such advice. One refused Moulins's offer to transfer to him all the remaining family land in the region: 'je vous remercie de loffre que vous me fettes de me laisser les biens sils estoint à ma portée', he wrote to his uncle, 'mais comme il ne les sont pas vous fairés bien de les vendre et il en sera mieux d'en passer par la vente que de les affermir pour ne rien porter de profit et ils dépérissent tous les jours et il faut en presser les ventes avant que les terres achèvent de dépérir'. He was obviously incapable not only of working the land himself, but also of finding an adequate tenant to farm it for him, and land in the Mediterranean region, as we have emphasized in an earlier chapter, declined rapidly in quality if left uncultivated. The nephew was relying on the services of Antoine Martin for liquidating the

89. ADR, Fonds Moulins, IV, 1 April 1705.
90. ADR, Fonds Moulins, IV, 17 June 1717, my emphasis.
91. ADR, Fonds Moulins, VII, 20 Feb. 1711.

family patrimony, a man whom he considered was 'honnête homme et fort dans nos inthérêts'. It seems more likely though that Martin, who was buying up some of the Moulins's property, was acting against the family's interests. Another of Moulins's correspondents warned him that Martin was deliberately neglecting land which he was renting, by leaving it uncultivated, in order to buy it at a lower price. Accused of doing this by Moulins, Martin replied: 'je ne suis pas assés Riche pour payer la taille dune terre pour n'en tirer une Rente'. That the same applied to the Moulins family, that they were not sufficiently rich to neglect their family patrimony in Clermont, is evident too. The bankruptcy of Raymond Moulins, head of the 'maison Moulins', occurred in 1725.[92]

92. ADR, Fonds Moulins, IV, Moulins neveu to Raymond Moulins, 11 July 1725; Lacroix to Moulins, 3 July 1724; Martin to Moulins, 4 Sept. 1724. On the decline, and 'disappearance', of the concern of Raymond Moulins to which we owe the survival of the Moulins papers, see P. Léon (ed.), *Papiers d'industriels et de commerçants Lyonnais*, p. 284.

9

The second thirty years, 1725–54

> ... every class of capitalists is at the beginning animated by a clearly progressive and innovating spirit but becomes conservative as its activities become regulated ... soon the primitive energy relaxes. The descendants of the new rich wish to preserve the situation which they have acquired, provided public authority will guarantee it to them, even at the price of a troublesome surveillance. (Pirenne, 'Stages', p. 515)

> The French sustain some Disadvantages by their *Monopolies and exclusive Charters* ... And there is good Reason to conclude, there is something of the same nature for the *Turkey* Cloth at Carcassonne. (Josiah Tucker, *A Brief Essay*, pp. 28–9)

Between 1725 and 1753 at least sixty-six new masters were received into the clothing profession at Clermont.[1] This fact is in itself a sign of the growing prosperity of the town's industry and is all the more impressive in view of the fact that between 1737 and 1753 access to mastership was restricted to sons, or sons-in-law, of masters.[2]

Fifteen of the new marchands-fabricants, all received before the 1737 measure, were new to cloth-making. In five cases individuals previously involved in other activities took up manufacturing: Pierre Martin, who became a master in 1729, had worked as a 'marchand-d'étoffes' before he was apprenticed to Jean-François Bouisson in 1726,[3] and Jacques Martin, his brother, who produced cloth briefly in the 1750s, was a négociant, previously involved, amongst other things, in tax-collecting;[4] Pierre Jalmes, who became master in 1728, was a 'marchand-trafiquant'

---

1. Most receptions were inscribed in the registers of the conseil de ville. Some were not and so I have supplemented this source with details on masters provided by Delagenière in 1739 (ADH C2036). I have not included the year 1754 in this survey as the rules concerning admission to mastership were changed in this year. See below p. 367.
2. See pp. 321–2.
3. Pierre Martin: apprenticeship: ADH 11 E 25 112, 26 Dec. 1726; reception as master: ADH C2036, 9 Aug. 1729.
4. Jacques Martin: he produced cloth only from 1752 to 1754. There is no record of his having served an apprenticeship or of his having been received master. Described as négociant, and involved in tax-collecting in 1746: ACC BB5, 15 April 1746.

before he was apprenticed into the cloth industry;[5] Jean Roustan Villet and Jean Astruc, who became masters in 1729 and 1731, had originally been merchants, the former in Marseilles and the latter in Montpellier, and joined Clermont's industry after service at Villenouvette.[6] In seven cases it was the father who had apprenticed his son to a marchand-fabricant in order to give him the necessary qualifications for producing for the Levant. Pierre Bruguière, received in 1729, was the son of a merchant who had been apprenticed in 1712 to Goudard and Estève.[7] Laurens Bouisson, received in 1728, was the son of a prosperous ménager who had been apprenticed (with his brother Jean-François) to Guillaume Santoul in 1708.[8] Estienne Desalasc, received in 1736, was the son of a marchand-cardier who had been apprenticed to Antoine Raissac in 1721.[9] Jean Gairaud, received in 1731, was the son of a merchant who had been apprenticed to Antoine Berthomieu in 1725.[10] Pierre Gayrand, received in 1749, was the son of a merchant who had been apprenticed to Jean Roustan Villet in 1735.[11] Antoine Toucas, received in 1729, was the son of a 'marchand-savonnier', who took advantage of the opportunity offered by a royal edict of June 1725 to buy a mastership for 350 *livres* in 1729;[12] Joseph Vieules, received in 1734, was the son of a wool merchant.[13] One of the new masters, Pierre Vernazobres, was the son of an ex-member of Villenouvette who had never made cloth at Clermont. He was received in 1731 having been apprenticed to Estienne Berthomieu.[14] In the case of two new masters, Jean-Louis Perette and Antoine Viala, I have found no information on background.[15]

5. Pierre Jalmes: professional background: ADH 11 E 26 148, 26 Aug. 1710, 11 E 25 109, 124, 13 May 1713, 5 Sept. 1738; reception: ADH C2036.
6. Jean Roustan Villet: professional background, presence at Villenouvette: ADH C2158, petition of Pierre Jean Villet to be allowed to manufacture, 1745, and ADH 11 E 26 147, 1 Feb. 1708, 3 Jan. 1709; purchased mastership on 14 July 1729, ACC BB3. Jean Astruc: professional background, presence at Villenouvette: 11 E 25 112, 22 Feb. 1726; apprenticeship: 11 E 25 118, 30 March 1732; reception: 15 May 1732, ADH C2036.
7. Pierre Bruguière: professional background and apprenticeship: ADH 11 E 26 168, 6 Jan. 1712; reception: ADH C2036.
8. Laurens Bouisson: professional background and apprenticeship: ADH 11 E 26 168, 147, 8 March 1704, 21 Oct. 1708; reception: 24 Jan. 1728, ADH C2036.
9. Estienne Desalasc: background: ADH 11 E 25 132, 12 Sept. 1740; apprenticeship: 11 E 26 183, 25 Oct. 1721; reception: 8 Dec. 1736, ADH C2036.
10. Jean Gairaud: background and apprenticeship: ADH 11 E 25 117, 30 Jan. 1731; no record of reception, but must have been in 1731, year in which he began to produce.
11. Pierre Gayraud: background: ADH 11 E 25 127, 6 May 1741, ACC BB4, 9 June 1740; apprenticeship and reception: ACC BB5, 28 June 1749.
12. Antoine Toucas: background: ADH 11 E 25 113, 9 Jan. 1728; purchase of mastership: ACC BB3, 14 July 1729.
13. Joseph Vieules: background and apprenticeship: 11 E 26 188, 167, 27 Oct. 1727, 16 May 1709; reception: 7 April 1734, ADH C2036.
14. Pierre Vernazobres: background: ADH 3 E 181[1 bis], act of 9 April 1708; apprenticeship: ADH 11 E 25 113, 29 June 1727; reception: 29 Nov. 1731, ADH C2034.
15. Jean-Louis Perette: reception: 26 Sept. 1731, ADH C2050; Antoine Viala: reception:

In no case were these new, for-the-most-part-merchant entrants to the industry of a status, or resources, to match those of a Barthe, a Budin or a Galtié. Not one of them was a wholesale merchant and if one were to fit them into that hierarchical list of clothiers assembled in the previous chapter their place would be in the middle, alongside those families of middling or upper-artisanal status such as the Flottes or Desalascs. Quite possibly these families, like the clothiers', had benefited from the commercial expansion which had been in progress since the 1690s. In three cases at least, those of the sons of the marchand-cardier, marchand-savonnier and wool merchant, the new masters came from trades which would have directly benefited from the expansion in cloth production. It would seem likely, given their similarity in origins, that these new masters would have shared some of the qualities of the successful generation of clothiers which we have described in the previous chapter. If this was indeed the case then they would have represented potentially useful additions to the growing industry.

We have sufficient evidence to plot the experiences of one of these new cloth-making families, the Martins. They were Protestants and became the only Protestant family in the industry. Antoine, father of Pierre, we have encountered at a previous stage in this book. It was he who employed the two commercial travellers, mentioned in chapter three, who sold goods in the diocese of Lodève.[16] His trade was largely in cloth but, unlike the Galtiés, he did not work on a wholesale basis, but distributed goods, which he would have purchased for the main part at local fairs, in Clermont's immediate commercial hinterland. Some idea of the family's moderate resources is provided by Pierre Martin's marriage contract; his bride had a dowry worth just over 2,000 *livres* and Antoine Martin's total possessions were valued at 7,600 *livres*.[17] Between 1713 and 1726 it is evident that the family grew considerably in wealth for when in 1726 the father, Antoine, at the age of seventy-eight, associated himself with a master-clothier, Jean-François Bouisson, to make cloth, it was he who provided all the funds and within two years production had reached a total of 240 half-pieces.[18] A considerable investment would have been required for so rapid an expansion in output to have been achieved. The cloth-making concern was run in the name of this associate initially as no member of the Martin family had yet been received master but in 1730, after the reception of Pierre Martin, it was transferred to his name. Like the concerns of the clothiers described in the previous chapter it was a

25 June 1733, ADH C2036.
16. See p. 66.
17. Bobo, 'Communauté languedocienne', p. 134.
18. ADH II E 25 112, 113, 5 Aug. 1726 and 12 Jan. 1727; ACC BB3, 3 Feb. 1727; production ADH C2231.

co-operative family business; 'j'ay cinq enfans que j'ay élevés dans la fabrique . . . avec leur secours j'ay en fait jusques à cent soixante Ballots londrins seconds dans une seule année', wrote Pierre Martin ('homme entreprenant', it was reported) to Intendant de Bernage in 1743.[19] The Martins, likewise, built up the size of their plant rapidly. A report of 1739 shows that their concern was housed in a 'grande maison de fabrique' and equipped with its own dye-house, shearing shop and a large open space for stretching cloth.[20]

This reinforcement of the industry by these fifteen new masters was dwarfed in significance by the massive recruitment of sons of masters who, by the corporative statutes of 1708, were relieved from the obligation of serving apprenticeships, paying mastership fees and completing a *chef-d'oeuvre*, being entitled to become masters at the age of sixteen 'en faisant seulement une expériance' in front of the gardes-jurés.[21] There were no stipulations to ensure that the examining gardes-jurés should be unrelated to the applicant for mastership and it is thus not surprising that virtually all clothiers' sons became masters. We have records of a total of fifty-one masters' sons who were received between 1725 and 1753.[22] The fact that these fifty-one shared only seventeen different family names illustrates the extent to which the industry was confined in this period to that limited range of families which had produced successfully during the first thirty years. Eleven came from the two branches of the Flottes family, five from the Bonneville and Martin families; there were four Bouissons and Vernys, three Lugagnes, Delpons and Pelletans, two Desalascs, Léotards, Ménards and Liquiers and one Bernard, Berthomieu, Raissac, Tudesq and Villet.

It will be the experiences during the years 1725–53 of these new clothiers, and of the old clothiers who were still producing, that we shall be analysing in this chapter. Our survey will be divided as follows. We shall first describe the general characteristics of the growing industry and the nature of the entrepreneurial qualities which continued to be necessary for success within it. We shall then describe the various measures by which the corporative, inspectoral and regulative systems were made more restrictive during this period. This description will be followed by an analysis of why these systems were made more restrictive when their original purposes had been fulfilled. Our principal answer to this ques-

---

19. ADH C5545, letter of 12 Jan. 1743; description of Martin is that of Tricou, 9 Sept. 1743 (same source).
20. ADH C2036.
21. ADH II E 25 108, 1 Aug. 1708, statutes of clothiers' corporation.
22. From register of conseil de ville, ADH C2036 (1739) and ADH C2050 (1748).

Table 15. *Languedoc's cloth production for the Levant 1725–54*
(in ½-pieces)

1725	31,200	1735	59,830	1745	53,010
1726	26,980	1736	59,980	1746	57,750
1727	31,800	1737	61,120	1747	62,600
1728	49,400	1738	62,790	1748	60,220
1729	52,120	1739	54,250	1749	62,790
1730	41,560	1740	51,890	1750	56,710
1731	43,000	1741	52,810	1751	62,600
1732	48,530	1742	45,790	1752	63,950
1733	57,760	1743	55,290	1753	64,330
1734	60,280	1744	44,500	1754	69,110

Source: M. Morineau and C. Carrière, 'Draps de Languedoc et commerce du Levant au XVIIIᵉ siècle', *R.H.E.S.* 56 (1968), 109–10: figures for bureau de marque of Montpellier.

tion is that it was to achieve stability in the industry and in our next section we shall describe how this ideal was attained by the mid-century and how the industry, to all appearances, had reached a magnificent peak by 1750. Appearances, we shall argue, were deceptive and in our last section we shall demonstrate how the intensification of these systems, combined with the action of the 'Buddenbrooks effect' (that aspect of entrepreneurial decline emphasized by Pirenne in the quotation placed at the head of the chapter), had contributed to eroding that 'primitive energy' which we have observed in the previous chapter. This loss of primitive energy, we shall argue in the concluding section of the chapter, was all the more damaging in that Clermont had become totally dependent on the industry and had developed a serious 'law and order' problem by the mid-century.

The industry continued to expand in size as is apparent from the production figures (Tables 15 and 16). The number of clothiers producing at any one time remained relatively small but a gradual increase is observable: there were fourteen clothiers working in 1725 and thirty-five in 1753.[23] These clothiers, for the most part, corresponded with the type of rich 'gentleman clothier' described in the previous chapter. That it was the production of high-quality cloth, for distant markets, which had favoured the predominance of this type of producer (for reasons that will have emerged in previous chapters) is apparent from the fact that the neighbouring industries of Bédarieux (producing low-quality cloth for local markets) and Lodève (producing coarse *draps forts* for local markets

23. ADH C2231.

Table 16. *Clermont's industry 1725–54: production (in ½-pieces)(a) and number of clothiers (b)*

	(a)	(b)		(a)	(b)
1725	4,100	14	1740	7,636	20
1726	4,100	13	1741	7,634	21
1727	5,480	14	1742	5,066	20
1728	4,600	17	1743	5,408	20
1729	3,852	18	1744	5,110	26
1730	5,480	19	1745	6,378	24
1731	5,020	22	1746	7,470	28
1732	5,480	22	1747	7,610	29
1733	6,420	23	1748	7,570	30
1734	6,220	22	1749	7,130	31
1735	6,314	22	1750	7,410	32
1736	7,080	25	1751	8,020	34
1737	7,938	25	1752	7,690	34
1738	7,012	24	1753	8,000	35
1739	4,234	16	1754	8,440	36

Source: ADH C2231, 'cochineal passports', 1720–54.

and military uses) retained 'artisanal' structures. Whereas Clermont's 214 looms in 1724 were divided between eighteen clothiers, Lodève's 180 looms in 1724 were divided between no less than 140, and Bédarieux's thirty-two clothiers, in the same year, had only thirty looms at their disposition.[24] The bankruptcy laws which had to be refined and extended to cope with the complicated affairs of the new clothiers did not apply to the traditional, artisanal clothier, who was unlikely to keep accounts. As late as 1760 a bankrupted Lodève clothier excused himself from presenting accounts to the consular jurisdiction at Montpellier on the grounds that 'en qualitté de fabriquant, je nay point tenu des livres parceque étant dans la classe des artisants je ne puis pas être dans la disposition de lordonnance'.[25]

The extent of the concentration of capital ownership was gradually increased (Ills. 21 and 22). We have witnessed the growth in individual clothiers' investment in plant and by the end of the 1730s virtually all the tools and buildings involved in cloth production were in their hands. As inspector Delagenière reported in 1739, 'tous les maîtres fabricans ... fournissent aux cardeurs et tisserans, les métiers et autres ustenciles nécessaires à la fabrique'. In addition all the 'maisons de fabrique', all seven dye-houses, and some of the shearing and finishing shops were

24. AN F12 1380, Production figures for département of Montpellier, 2nd half of 1724.
25. ADH 8 B 403, Bilan Joseph Teisserenq.

Ill. 21. 'A concentration of capital ownership': 'maison de fabrique' viewed from
the Rue de la Fregère

owned by the clothiers.[26] The only parts of production which escaped
their control (in some cases) were the finishing processes: the cloth-
finishers had succeeded in founding an exclusive corporation, like that of
the clothiers, which restricted the performance of shearing and cloth-
dressing to their members.[27] Some of the clothiers were already, or
became, qualified as 'maîtres-affineurs', however, which entitled them to
have their own finishing shops.[28]

In the seventeenth century we have observed a process of de-
specialization and de-centralization of industrial production as a large
industry declined; its remaining members survived by combining cloth
production with other activities, and independent rural producers, with
exceptionally low costs, competed successfully in supplying the coarse
cloths which were the only ones which continued to be in demand. The
reverse process had been occurring since the beginning of the revival in
the 1690s, and continued to do so during the period which we are now
analysing. That Clermont's industry had become a full-time one has

26. ADH C2036.
27. ADH ii E 25 107, 5 Dec. 1705 (registered by parlement of Toulouse, 13 Jan. 1706).
28. Antoine Raissac, Jacques Bonneville and Jean-Pierre Desalasc were among those in
    this category (ADH C2036).

Ill. 22. 'Maisons de fabrique' viewed from the bed of the Rhonel

already been revealed by the complaints of farmers about the shortage of labour for harvesting local crops. Visiting Inspector Le Mazurier commented in 1741 that 'les ouvriers de toutes espèces travailloient comme dans une fabrique qui ne se trouvoit point dans de circonstances à souffrir aucune interruption'.[29] Cloth production had also become, far more than it had been, the overwhelmingly predominant activity both in Clermont and in the surrounding countryside. As a clothier noted to the intendant in 1746 (with slight exaggeration), 'il n y a point à Clermont dautre Industrie ny dautre Commerce'.[30] And Delagenière observed too in a description of Clermont made in 1740 that 'la plus grande partie des

---

29. ADH C2142, Letter to de Bernage, 13 Nov. 1741.
30. ADH C2048, Jacques Martin to Le Nain, *c.* 1746.

Table 17. *Clermont's labour force, 6 July 1732*

	Number	Wages in *livres* and *sols*
Laveurs	50	18s a day
Batteurs	30	16s a day
Assortisseurs	30	18s a day
Trieuses	400	6s a day
Embriseuses	400	12s a day
Cardeurs de chaîne	200	15s a day
Cardeurs de trame	150	15s a day
Fileuses	3,000	7s a day
Retorseurs	15	15s the *naucade*
Their garçons	15	9s a day
Tisserands	600	11s the *livre* (of wool woven)
Canoneuses	300	6s a day
Epotoyeuses	150	25s the *naucade*
Foulonniers	10	30s the *naucade*
Their garçons	10	15s a day
Pareurs	15	7 *livres* the *naucade*
Their garçons	40	15s a day
Affineurs des apprêts	10	27 *livres* the *balle*
Their garçons	30	15s a day
Rentrayeurs	12	4 *livres* the *balle*
Liteuses	50	12s a day
Teinturiers	7	6 *livres* 10s $\frac{1}{2}$-piece
Their garçons	15	15s a day
Cardeurs de lisières	12	20s a day
Cardeurs	15	20s a day
Their garçons	15	12s a day
Faiseurs de lisses	5	20s a day
Lainiers	4	30s a day
Fabricants	29	—
Garçons-fabricants	30	—
TOTAL	5,649	

Source: ADH C5595

habitans sont employés à la fabrique et ne subsistent que par le travail que les fabricants leur fournissent'.[31] By 1732, Delagenière's calculations show, the industry was employing 5,649 people (Table 17).

To provide this vast labour force other trades had either declined or been completely absorbed. The two other major industrial activities practised at Clermont, hat-making and tanning, had shrunk considerably in importance.[32] And the industry's rapid growth had had significant

31. ADH C2498.
32. AN F12 565, Roland de la Platière, memoir 1766, reports on decline of hat industry in

effects on rural areas too. Rural areas provided the majority of female labour, which accounted for over three-quarters of the total labour force, and the employment of such a large proportion of local disposable female labour created severe problems for those involved in agricultural production. Land was abandoned. In 1750 there were 3392 *sétérées* of land uncultivated in the terroir of Clermont, much of it abandoned (it was noted in the registers of the conseil de ville) because of the 'rareté des journaliers causés par les fabriques'.[33] Similarly the expansion affected that independent cloth-making which had been in expansion during the depression. These rural producers were absorbed into the growing industry's labour force. As an inspector noted in 1727, 'les ouvriers qui sont dans le voisinage de Clermont et de Lodève ne s'occupent plus . . . à la fabrique des cadis'.[34] The whole region was becoming a vast cloth manufacture. A survey carried out by Inspector Tricou in 1754 revealed that the inhabitants of fifty-six different villages or towns, in six different dioceses, were weaving, spinning or carding for Clermont. A similar colonization of the countryside had been carried out by Carcassonne's clothiers for whom no less than eighty-one different villages were working.[35] As the sub-delegate at Carcassonne recorded in 1731:

On ne fait autre chose dans la même ville et dans touttes les paroisses du diocèse que de donner les façons nécessaires aux draps, ce qui occuppe même le peuple dans quatre ou cinq diocèzes voisins et par là à proprement parler Carcassonne nest dans un sens quune manufacture de draps remplie de cardeurs tisserands fileuses et tondeurs de draps, toutte la campagne fourmille et des fabriquands et douvriers.[36]

The nature of the clothier's role, changing already between 1695 and 1724, was fully transformed by the end of this period. Those local administrators who had lived through these years of growth and structural transformation in the industry showed their awareness of the extent of the changes. De Murat, sub-delegate at Carcassonne, in a letter written in 1746 to Le Nain, intendant, in which he had described the artisanal roots of the town's industry, wrote:

Il en est bien autrement aujourdhuy, les fabriquands sont de gens comerçans ils font leurs affaires dans leur bureau et peu vont chés leurs ouvriers, ce sont des commis ou des facteurs quon y envoye, je veux croire cependant que nos fabriquands tous gros seigneurs quils sont et bien différends de ces gens mécha-

Clermont; ACC BB4, 18 Feb. 1737, at a meeting of shoemakers and leather-bleachers it is revealed that the number of masters has halved since 1712.
33. ACC BB5, 6 Jan. 1750.
34. AN F12 74, folio 314, 24 April 1727.
35. ADH C2090.
36. ADH C4677, De Murat, 1731.

niques du siècle passé ont acquis des lumières et des connoissances dans la fabrique qui peuvent les mettre en état de conduire leurs ouvriers comme le faisoint ceux des temps des anciens Règlemens.[37]

Not all clothiers at Clermont corresponded to this description – as we have seen there was some movement into the industry by people who had yet to make fortunes and needed to build up the scale of their concerns gradually – but the restrictions on the reception of new masters had the consequence that increasingly the type of clothier described by de Murat became the norm. Raissac, whose participation in all processes of production we have emphasized in the previous chapter, was employing a commis by the 1740s. He complained in 1742 of the loss of profits occasioned by 'les appointements d'un commis quil est obligé de tenir ne pouvant pas agir par luy même à cause de son âge avancé'.[38] Jean-Pierre Desalasc, son of Jacques and grandson of Pierre Desalasc, did not have old age to excuse his use of three commis in 1741: he was only 28. They were necessary to him in part because of the scale of his affairs but also, it would seem, because of his involvement in local politics. In 1735, we have seen, he had purchased the office of first consul at the age of 21, and in 1740 Antoine Berthomieu, who had become his father-in-law in 1736, graciously allowed him to attend the annual meeting of the provincial Etats in his place.[39] It had become, it appears, a sign of social distinction for rich clothiers to employ commis rather than performing the more menial cloth-making tasks themselves. This, at least, is the impression given by a remark in a letter of Desalasc to the intendant in 1742 in which he compared 'les fraix qu'il est obligé de faire pour trois commis quy luy coûtent environ 1,200 *livres* par an avec la médiocrité de ceux de la plupart de *ces nouveaux fabriquants qui font tout par eux mêmes*'.[40] In addition to hiring commis, Desalasc no longer carried out his own dyeing – he had let his dye-house out to a master-dyer in 1740[41] – but he was not alone in doing this: of Clermont's seven dye-houses, all owned by clothiers, two in 1740 were out of use and the other five had all been let out to master-dyers.[42] Some of the original clothier purchasers of these dye-houses had, as we have seen, carried out their own dyeing. But it would be wrong purely on the basis of this information to conclude that the quality of Clermont's entrepreneurs had declined. As we shall see, the nature of their role had changed and, quite possibly, the renting-out of dye-houses

37. ADH C2429, 14 March 1747.
38. ADH C2040.
39. ACC BB4, 11 Dec. 1740.
40. ADH C2039, Request of *c.* 1739. My emphasis.
41. ADH II E 25 128, 26 June 1742.
42. ADH C5569, *c.* 1740, survey of dye-houses.

was a sensible course allowing them to concentrate their energies on more crucial aspects of their job.

These possibly more crucial aspects of his job confined the clothier, above all, to his 'bureau'. His regular presence there was necessitated by the fact that many of his duties were now of a commercial and actuarial kind. Clothiers' inventories listing the contents of these 'bureaux' provide some insight into what exactly these duties were. Among the items to be found in the clothiers' offices were generally a few technical manuals. Jean Baptiste Laussel, for example, possessed *Le manuel des négociants*, published in three volumes at Lyons,[43] and the Bourlat brothers, who had taken over the direction of Villenouvette in 1729, had a large, well-furnished technical library in the royal manufacture which included the *Dictionnaire oeconomique*, the *Dictionnaire universel de commerce*, *La méthode de dresser toutes sortes de comptes*, *Le traité général du commerce*, *Le négoce d'Amsterdam*, *La pratique des échanges*, Jacques Savary's *Le parfait négociant*, *Le dictionnaire de Michelet*, *Le dictionnaire universel des drogues simples*, *Le traité du commerce de terre et de mer*, *Le banquier français*, *L'instruction sur la manière d'élever les bêtes à laine*, *Le traité de poids et mesures des principales places de commerce de l'Europe*, *Le tarif des poids des piastres* and *L'art de la teinture de la laine et des étoffes de la laine*.[44] There had clearly been something of a revolution in the quantity of technical publications at merchants' and clothiers' disposal. But above all the 'bureaux' contained account- and letter-books. Jean Baptiste Laussel was far from being among the town's leading clothiers – he only produced for a few years in the 1760s – but among his possessions were some forty different account- and letter-books: separate account books for each different category of worker, 'grands livres', a 'journal de fabrique', a book for copies of letters, a 'brouillard pour des marchandises en société', a book recording all 'outils chez les ouvriers', 'livres d'expédition', a 'livre d'échéance', a 'livre pour la dépense de la maison' etc.[45] So it was in the 'bureau' that the complex functioning of these large but scattered industrial concerns was co-ordinated. If the skills necessary for success in the first years of the industry had consisted in great technical ability combined with a capacity for hard work and an artisanal thrift, those necessary for success during these years consisted, above all, in commercial, financial and actuarial skills and managerial ability. The clothiers' large fixed and circulating capital was not, for the most part, enclosed in their maisons de fabrique but was in the hands of a large number of widely dispersed rural out-workers. The clothier's actuarial and managerial

43. ADH, Ordinaires Clermont, Case 781, 11 June 1766.
44. ADH, Ordinaires Clermont, Case 787, 1 Dec. 1787.
45. ADH, Ordinaires Clermont, Case 781, 11 June 1766.

roles involved him in keeping a check on all his materials, and co-ordinating the activities of his dispersed labour force, to ensure the necessary steady output of cloth.

The role was without doubt an extremely difficult one. To gain an idea of what exactly it involved one would need to consider the nature of the role of the managing director of a modern enterprise, with a labour force of two or three hundred and a large fixed and working capital, and then to consider in what ways this role would be complicated should this labour force and fixed and circulating capital, instead of being concentrated in a factory, be dispersed over up to fifty square miles in up to three hundred different houses. Assiduity in the attendance to his paper-work was surely a cardinal obligation for the rich clothier and it is highly probable that the sub-contracting of the dyeing processes to master-dyers or the use of commis for routine visits to the labour force were wise policies.

This is to describe the clothier's duties in a static manner. All clothiers, it is evident, fulfilled these necessary duties and would have possessed the basic commercial and actuarial skills necessary to control their manufactures. But there were still sharp distinctions, of which the clothiers themselves and the inspectors were quite conscious, in the effectiveness of different clothiers. Delagenière reporting on Clermont's industry on 17 May 1731 wrote as follows:

il y a dans l'ordre des fabricants en draps pour le Levant trois classes différentes: des riches, des aisés, et des mal aisés, dans chacun de ces trois classes, il y en a de très habiles et d'un goût parfait jusques dans les moindres opérations qui concernent cette fabrique, d'autres qui travaillent avec capacité et fidélité, mais qui n'ont pas encore atteint le goût de la propreté et de la perfection et enfin il y en a plusieurs qui ne travaillent qu'à la faveur d'un crédit qui leur est onéreux, sans capacité et très éloigné de l'exécution des Règlemens, parcequ'ils ne les ont jamais étudiés, ces derniers mettent ordinairement le désordre dans la fabrique.

Explaining why this last type of clothier gave rise to 'désordre' Delagenière continued: 'chaque fabriquant est bien aisé de profiter des avantages que le commerce et le débit leur présentent alors le fabriquant de la dernière classe pour remplir ses engagem⁵ tâche de s'attirer tous les ouvriers qu'il peut gagner en augmentant inconsidérément leur salaire'. The consequence of this was a rise in wages and the spread of bad workmanship among all employees in the industry 'comme une maladie contagieuse, sans pouvoir l'éviter'.[46] Delagenière's short description identifies for us both the major qualities necessary for successful participation in the trade, and also some of the major difficulties and hazards encountered by clothiers. The possession of large resources was clearly a

46. ADH C2132, Report of 17 May 1731.

major advantage to a clothier but it was not essential for there existed excellent credit facilities for the purchase of wools, and finished cloth might be paid for in advance in years of good trading by cloth commissioners at Marseilles. In addition, the fixed capital investment necessary for participation in the industry remained small in comparison with that in circulating capital. Thus poorer clothiers could produce, and might indeed be able to compensate for the interest which they paid for their credit by the economies which they made in labour costs by avoiding the services of commis. Technical skills remained of great importance, it is clear. Even if clothiers got by with low-quality production in some years, it was such cloth which was first rejected in a year of crisis in the trade. But possibly the most important skill of all in a trade which continued to be afflicted by sharp fluctuations in the level of demand was the judgement of the right level of production, the ability, to use Delagenière's words, 'de profiter des avantages que le commerce et le débit leur présentent'. More was involved in doing this than might appear. Good market sense was necessary, it is clear, but the clothier also had to make financial preparations to expand or contract production. (Few clothiers, if any, operated purely with their own capital and thus, for a rapid expansion in production, credit had to be both obtained, and then returned, which meant that it had to have been used, and turned into cloth. Likewise a contraction in production, if the expansion had been undertaken on the basis of credit, was only possible when the raw materials bought on credit had been processed and made into cloth, and the cloth sold to give the clothier the means of repayment. This is what Delagenière meant by meeting 'engagements'.) In addition, and this was perhaps the most problematic matter of all, the clothier needed, when expanding production, to have the necessary workers at his disposal, and this, as it was unlikely that only one clothier would have sensed an improvement in market conditions, gave rise generally to competition for workers, and the 'disorder' described by Delagenière. Contraction in production, from the point of view of the clothier, was an easier process but if it was undertaken too sharply then he could find himself without an adequate labour force to participate in the next revival in demand.

The trade required a wide range of skills from the clothier, therefore: it was an evident advantage for him to have large resources, and he required technical ability, actuarial skills, commercial flair and managerial ability to mobilize his production to respond to this flair. Given the still unsteady nature of the trade, it was perhaps these last two elements which were the most important. Inspectors, concerned with the quality of production, tended to emphasize the damaging consequences of that 'avidity' which caused clothiers to undertake too large a production; 'le fabriquant plus attentif à son intérêt mal-entendu, qu'à perfectionner son ouvrage', Delagenière complained, 'prend des engagements au dessus de sa portée, en s'obligeant de remettre un certain nombre de balles de draps dans un tems limité';[47] 'On peut dire en général que les fabriques et commerce de france seroient très florissant et souhaité par préférence si le génie de la nation n'étoit naturellement plus porté à ses intérests qu'à travailler avec attention à perfectionner les arts, il faut que des connoisseurs mettent un frain à l'avidité des fabriquans', wrote Pradier in 1732.[48] These two commentators were right to stress the damaging consequences, both for the clothier himself and for the industry as a whole, of the speculative activities of clothiers who over-estimated the production of which they were capable, but they would have conceded too that the essence of entrepreneurial skill lay in the right judgement of the market situation and the ability to ensure that that judgement was effectively, and rapidly, translated into cloth produced.

If the skills necessary for success were varied there is no doubt that the clothier's major role, whether it was exercised from his 'bureau' via commis or directly by visiting his workshops, was the management of his manufacturing activities. His function had taken on some 'merchant' characteristics but his essential role remained that of cloth-maker. Workers had to be formed and trained, controlled and conserved; the output of workers involved in different processes had to be co-ordinated so that a steady through-put was achieved; production had to be accelerated when the demand situation was favourable; workers had, if possible, to be conserved when demand declined; workers had to be supervised to ensure that they did not steal raw materials etc. And all these tasks were made more difficult by the competition for the service of workers from other clothiers at Clermont and from other textile centres.

The 'forming' of workers had been the principal task of the first generation of clothiers but it was a continuing necessity as the industry expanded. In the survey on the areas working for Clermont made in 1754, mention is made of the recent formation by Clermont's clothiers of several 'très bons filoirs pour chaisne' in distant villages of the diocese of Castres, and it is added that 'il leur en a coûté beaucoup pour les mettre au point de perfection où ils sont'.[49] Pierre Martin, when he began production in the late 1720s, must have found that the majority of local labour was already employed by other clothiers and so he established new workshops at St-Gervais, again in the diocese of Castres, where as the sole employer he could effectively control the local labour force. One of his sons resided at St-Gervais to supervise the spinning carried out there,

47. AN F12 1382, Letter of Delagenière, 19 Jan. 1731.
48. ADH C4676, Memoir on Levant trade, 1732.
49. ADH C2090.

and the survey of 1754 recorded that 'on y file beaucoup et très bien'.[50] One explanation for the rapidity with which the Martin family was able to expand its production lies in its foresight in developing these new workshops. St-Gervais was some 30 kilometres from Clermont and other workshops set up were yet further from the town, up to 50 kilometres away. The establishment, at considerable cost and risk, of these workshops was another positive facet of the entrepreneurship of Clermont's clothiers in this period.

The clothier's managerial role had only begun, however, once he had established his workshop. He was still faced with all those other difficulties which we have just listed. What he desired, it is evident, was a dependable labour force which would work for him only, and at a regular pace. To achieve this aim he used various means. A first step was the purchase of the loom which, as we have noted in an earlier chapter, had tended to belong to the weaver in Clermont's traditional industry. The loom once purchased remained generally in the weaver's house but its ownership provided the clothier with a relatively direct means of controlling his employees. The contracts of sale generally stated that the purchasing clothier reserved the right to remove the loom 'quand bon luy semblera' and that the weaver was to work for none other than him.[51] The ownership of all tools was clearly not a sufficient discipline, however – the increasing number of clothiers producing at Clermont, the rising production of Villenouvette and Lodève and, from the 1740s, the rapid expansion in cotton production at Montpellier, led to the services of workers being competed for amongst clothiers and between different producing centres. From the point of view of clothiers this competition for labour had several damaging consequences – it led to a rise in wages; it led to a decline in workers' productivity (the phenomenon of the backward-sloping supply curve for labour applied to Languedoc as it did to other textile-producing areas in the pre-industrial period), and it led to a decline in quality – as Pradier *fils* emphasized, in a memoir written in 1732 to improve his chances of being made inspector, 'il faut que la main de l'ouvrier soit habituée à la même nature d'ouvrage et qu'elle ne soit pas déréglée par des qualitez de laine inférieure'.[52] The use of cloth-making equipment for processing cotton was especially damaging because small pieces of cotton inevitably became mixed with the wool when the equipment was returned to cloth-making and, as cotton took a different dye from wool, showed up like an infection on the finished cloth. The survey of 1754 revealed that several of Clermont's traditional working areas had had to be abandoned. The inspector explained in a note added at the end

50. ADH C5545, 2090.
51. E.g. ADH 11 E 26 129, 131, 4 May 1692, 8 Feb. 1694.
52. ADH C4676.

of the survey that 'les fabricants de cette jurande se voyant tous les jours resserrés par la filature du coton, ils ont été forcés de chercher dans la Montagne des endroits propres à fournir des filoirs . . . pour ne pas estre tous les jours exposés à avoir des draps barrés de fils de coton'.[53]

The response of the individual clothier to these sorts of problems varied. Antoine Raissac's name appears in a number of notarial acts signed with workers, and it is clear that he used a variety of means to ensure a regular output and faithful service from his employees. One method was to lend money to a worker. An act recorded in 1715 shows that Raissac was owed 518 *livres* 9 *sols* by one Nicolas Berthellet, a weaver who had in his house a variety of pieces of industrial equipment belonging to Raissac, all marked with the initials A. R.[54] Berthellet's house was the security for the loan. Another method was to offer a reward in return for a certain amount of work completed within a specified time. In 1727 Raissac 'gave' a loom valued at 49 *livres* to Jacques Bascou in return for Bascou's promise to work for no other than him until he had made fifty pieces of *londrins-seconds*. The contract had a penalty clause: the loom was to be returned and a penalty of 60 *livres* was to be paid 'sil arrive que avant que led bascou aie . . . remis et fait titre lesd. cinquante pièces draps . . . aud. Raissac quand bien mesme led Bascou auroit faittes quarante neuf que led Bascou travailhe pour autre que pour led Sr. Raissac'.[55] Bascou would have had to work for approximately two years for Raissac in order to keep his loom. But the most frequent method adopted by clothiers to obtain a commitment to regular work from their employees was by making a simple cash payment. On 3 February 1733 Raissac paid 99 *livres* 15 *sols* to Jacques Aubouy, master-weaver, who committed himself to 'faire aller deux métiers' on Raissac's behalf until he had made forty pieces of cloth;[56] similarly Antoine Berthomieu paid a cardeur of St-Félix-de-Lodez in September 1732 the same sum in return for his commitment not to work 'pour autry ny vacquer à autre choze Jusques à ce quil aye cardé et fait filler . . . quatre vingtz chaisnes pour draps londrin second'.[57] These labour contracts varied slightly in the wording of their conditions – a weaver living in the village of Ceyras who was working for Villenouvette promised in 1733 to 'travalher continuellem^t et sans interruption . . . et de fair valoir un mestier sans pouvoir vacquer à autre choze directement ny indirectement pour quelque cauze Raizon ny prétexte que ce soit ou puisse estre'[58] and a 'rétorseuse' promised (unwisely) in

53. ADH C2090.
54. ADH II E 26 176, 19 May 1715.
55. ADH II E 25 117, 28 Feb. 1731.
56. ADH II E 25 119, 3 Feb. 1733.
57. ADH II E 25 118, 24 Sept. 1732.
58. ADH II E 25 119, 12 June 1733.

1731, in return for the favour shown by Guillaume Liquier in selling her a twisting mill 'à bon Marché [,] de rétordre aud Sr Liquier[59] deux chaînes pour drap par semmaine pendant la vie dud. Sr Liquier' – but their basic purpose was invariably the same, to ensure a regular output from workers who were under no legal obligation to work continuously nor, very often, with any pressing economic need to do so.

Although the practice of giving bonus payments to workers was disapproved of by the authorities it was clearly resorted to by most clothiers and represented, effectively, a very normal entrepreneurial response to the problems presented by the character of the labour market and by the working conditions in an extended putting-out system. The variety of carefully phrased notarial acts which tied workers to their employers is yet one more example of the creativity of Clermont's clothiers in this period. The poaching of each others' workers, also frequently resorted to, was likewise, although perhaps unethical, by no means illegal, and not only was favourable to the worker in question but contributed to a competitive environment which was advantageous to the industry as a whole. The competition for workers, like the original efforts put into the formation of a large trained labour force, join, therefore, our growing list of *dynamic* characteristics of Clermont's industry during this period. There were few signs before the end of the 1730s of that loss of 'primitive energy' to which all industrial elites were subject according to the Pirenne thesis.

If competition among clothiers was, as I have argued, a necessary discipline to ensure that the province's industry remained competitive, to clothiers themselves, and particularly to the less efficient, it seemed a threat, and on many occasions they showed a preference for a less-competitive environment. A first step in the creation of such an environment was made when the new clothiers' corporation was founded in Clermont in 1708. The most novel feature in the statutes of this new corporation was the replacement of the six *livres* mastership fee, which was that charged according to the rules of the general règlement of 1669, by a fee of 450 *livres*. It is quite evident that by increasing the traditional mastership fee by a multiple of seventy-five, and giving exceptional privileges to their sons and sons-in-law, Clermont's rising generation of clothiers had aims which were only in small part altruistic. They were largely concerned to reserve, if possible, the developing industry for themselves and their progeny.

The clothiers made use of a Clermontais notary, Azemar,[60] to compose

59. ADH II E 25 117, 28 Feb. 1731.
60. ADH II E 25 108, 1 Aug. 1708.

and register their act. Azemar had clearly become a local specialist in corporative matters, for his services were used by other groups of workers who registered statutes during these years. Where he, or the clothiers, had obtained the necessary expertise for drawing up such a document it is not clear but the original source, direct or indirect, of the principle, if not the method, of founding a restrictive guild was Lyons. As a visitor to the province's industry was to observe in the 1750s: 'en examinant les Statuts et Règlemens des Jurandes de Carcassonne, Clermont-de-Lodève, St-Chinian &c on trouve que l'esprit de ces jurandes a été comme celui des marchands fabriquans de Lyon depuis 1702, d'éloigner les ouvriers de la maîtrise, de réduire le nombre des maîtres'.[61] That both notary and clothiers were aware of the novelty of their action is apparent from the care with which they composed the prologue of the new statutes: an unprecedented measure had to be made to appear precedented in order to obtain the statutes' registration by the parlement of Toulouse. The prologue consisted in a short (and distorted) resumé of the town's industrial experiences during the previous hundred years, intended primarily to show that the decline experienced in the industry had been a consequence of too easy access to the profession of clothier. It was explained that a long period of virtually uninterrupted prosperity for Clermont's cloth industry was interrupted in the early seventeenth century by civil war and plague. The disturbances not only damaged the town's industry but caused the loss of the confrérie statutes. In order to give rise to a rapid recovery it was decided that only a very moderate sum would be demanded from new aspirants to mastership. Unfortunately this generosity was misguided for it resulted in an influx of new masters who 'tant de leur incapacité que de leur peu de moyen auroint Employé dans leurs factures de laines non permises' which occasioned 'un préjudice nottable à lad. fabrique quy dans les suites auroit eu presque un Entier desfait'. The new clothiers were thus blaming the crisis of the seventeenth century on the excessively 'liberal' statutes of 1633,[62] and claimed to be re-establishing continuity and guaranteeing the future stability of the industry by 'restoring' a high mastership fee. In fact, of course, the reverse was the case. The new statutes represented a decisive break in Clermont's long cloth-making tradition for until 1708 there had always been easy access to mastership: this has been seen to have been the case at Clermont, and the south of France generally, as Coornaert observed, was an area of open corporations.[63] As for the statutes of 1633, to which the

---

61. Vincent de Gournay (ADH C5552).
62. It is presumably to these statutes (see p. 91) that reference is being made. Clermont had suffered from plague in 1629 and 1630, and was occupied in 1632 (Durand, *Annales de Clermont-l'Hérault*, p. 35).
63. See pp. 99–100 and Coornaert, *Les corporations en France*, pp. 26, 252.

clothiers referred, these, far from having been excessively 'liberal', had represented a first step away from equality and easy access to mastership.

In addition to this historical justification for the imposition of a high mastership fee the clothiers stressed that the corporation required extra funds for the fulfilment of those religious obligations which it had inherited from the confrérie, to pay interest on the sums which they had been obliged to borrow to pay various taxes imposed on their profession during the war, and to finance future tax demands. Stricter control over entry to the profession would have beneficial consequences for the quality of production too, it was argued: the statutes would serve to 'maintenir lad. fabrique et ny recevoir que de personnes dignes et capables dune entière connaissance conformem* aud Règlement gnal. de 1669'. Again one doubts the veracity of either of these two motives. The general règlement of 1669 prescribed exactly the same measures for controlling the competence of new clothiers as those included in the new statutes, and had the financial needs of the corporation been so pressing they would not, surely, have disposed of the 400 *livres* which they received from the first new master to be received in accordance with the new statutes in the way in which they did: 100 *livres* was kept for celebrating religious services but the remaining 300 *livres* was shared out between sixteen clothiers 'pour remboursement de partie de sommes par eux fournie'.[64]

The high mastership fee acted as an additional financial barrier to producing for the Levant to that which the high costs of such production already occasioned. The strict enforcement of apprenticeship requirements, and the high standard which could be demanded of an applicant for mastership in the completion of his *chef-d'oeuvre*, would have served, too, as a means of limiting entry to the profession. The high value which came to be placed on the possession of a mastership will have emerged already from the fact that Pierre Flottes and Jacques Bonneville paid 1,650 *livres* each to purchase the position in 1724.[65] Production for the Levant was so profitable, however, that despite these controls there was a rapid increase in the number of masters. In view of this, attempts were made to ban the reception of all but sons and sons-in-law of masters. The clothiers' corporation at Carcassonne was the first to achieve this end in Languedoc. Again the idea for the introduction of such a measure came from other textile centres. Such limitations had already been applied at Rouen, Arnétal, Elbeuf, Louviers and Orival and the Carcassonnais requested the same concession 'avec d'autant plus de fondement que

---

64. A copy of this act of 25 Sept. 1708 is contained in ADH C2153. The mastership fee had been moderated to 400 *livres* on the instructions of the parlement of Toulouse.
65. See p. 271.

notre communauté jadis composée tout au plus d'Environ soixante marchands fabriquants cest a présant de plus de cent soixante'.[66] This
request was granted. In January 1725 an edict stating that no masters or
apprentices were to be received for three years was duly registered,[67] and
this ban was renewed repeatedly until the 1750s.[68] Evidently Clermont's
clothiers soon heard about the success of the Carcassonnais in obtaining
this limitation for in 1727 they registered an act before a notary by which
they added five new clauses to their statutes which would have had the
same effect. Claiming that they were acting purely to remedy 'aux abus
qui se coulent dans leur fabrique', and to bring their cloth 'au poin de
perfection', the clothiers arranged that no apprenticeships should be
entered into, or new masters received, for three years, that no Protestant
should ever be accepted as master, and that the mastership fee, moderated to 400 *livres* by the parlement of Toulouse in 1708, should be raised
to 450 *livres*. Two of these clauses had a specific target, the Protestant
Martin family which had started producing under the name of another
master in 1726. All the existing masters were Catholics and they evidently desired to maintain the 'purity' of their profession.[69] Apparent
again from this act is that Clermont's clothiers were using a supposed
concern about the quality of production as their principal justification for
measures which were designed primarily to give them and their descendants a monopoly in the trade. Only two of these additional clauses were
finally submitted for approval to the parlement of Toulouse: those banning the reception of new masters and raising the mastership fee. These
were registered by the parlement and Clermont's clothiers then sought
royal assent. This was a fault in protocol – 'ils finissent où Ils devoient
commencer', it was noted – and so the extra clauses were not accepted.
This rejection was sustained despite petitions from Clermont. These
petitions again illustrate that clothiers were prepared to use arguments of
more than doubtful veracity to attain their ends. A list of forty-five
clothiers was sent to the intendancy in 1728 and it was stated that this
'nombre des martˢ est fort considérable pour la ville de Clermont atten-
deu quon manque d'ouvriers et par conséquent le trop grand empressement des martˢ cause qu'on ne peut pas perfectionner l'ouvrage'. Of the
forty-five only twenty-two were actually producing cloth, the others
having retired from the industry. The limitation of entry into the profession was to be delayed ten years because of the clothiers' fault in proto-

66. ADH C2126, Gardes-jurés of Carcassonne to de Bernage, 29 Oct. 1724.
67. AN F12 71, folios 340–2, edict of 16 Jan. 1725.
68. ADH C2210, Memoir on 'Fixation', *c.* 1755 – renewed for three years on 16 March
    1728, 19 Dec. 1730, 27 May 1734 and for six years on 12 March 1737.
69. ADH II E 26 188, 31 July 1727.

col.[70] It was an edict published in 1737 which banned the reception of masters who were not sons or sons-in-law of clothiers both at Clermont and St-Chinian for six years. This ban was repeatedly renewed until 1754.[71]

The increase in the number of corporations, the introduction of high mastership fees and finally the ban on the reception of new masters were not the only ways in which the competitive elements in the industry were limited and the clothiers' activities restricted artificially. We have seen in a previous chapter that the regulative system, once the right formula for success in the Levant had been found, had been tightened by the two special règlements for the Levant industry published in 1697 and 1708, and we have seen too that the inspectoral corps, appointed to enforce these regulations, was gradually enlarged. This process was what I have described in a previous chapter as the 'setting of the mould'. But stringent though these varied restrictions already were, they were added to considerably during these years.

The inspectoral corps, it was found, was not large enough to exercise an adequate control over clothiers. It was intended, of course, that the elected officers of the clothiers' corporations should play a subsidiary role in enforcing regulations. But it was found that their probity for this task was questionable. As an intendant was to remark: 'Les gardes-jurés marquent tout ... Ils font d'ailleurs que ce qu'ils désirent que leurs successeurs fassent pour eux.'[72] An inspector had been appointed at Montpellier in 1714 but he rarely had time to visit Clermont himself, normally sending there an assistant, to check that regulations were being observed. This assistant, it emerges from the registers of the conseil de ville, was bribed by clothiers to approve their cloth.[73] In order for a proper control over the enforcement of regulations to be maintained it was necessary for each leading production centre to have its own inspector. This ideal was achieved gradually. In 1727 Clermont was given its own inspector with authority over the industry in Clermont and in neighbouring towns.[74] And in 1740, as this inspectorate was still too large for one man to control, it was divided into two and a new inspector was appointed to reside at Lodève. It was thus during the administration of Controller-General Orry that the inspectoral system reached its height: a total of thirteen inspectors were concerned with Languedoc's woollen manufactures.[75]

With an inspector resident in Clermont the possibilities of control over

70. ADH C2131 has details of this affair.
71. ADH C2139, Letters of Orry to de Bernage, 21 Oct. 1737, and de Bernage to Orry, 24 Jan. 1738.
72. ADH C2223, St-Priest memoir, 1779.
73. ACC BB2, 24 Sept. 1718.
74. ADH C2477, Le Peletier to de Bernage, 23 June 1727.
75. Dutil, *Etat économique*, pp. 300–1.

the industry increased enormously. The clothiers were without doubt aware of this for in 1729 they launched a campaign to have the first appointee, Delagenière, removed.[76] They were backed by the clothier-dominated conseil de ville which described the inspector as 'extremem' intéressé et Capricieux ce faizant un plaisir de faire de la peine au général'.[77] The clothiers failed in their attempt, however, and Delagenière remained at his post. His reports soon betrayed the reasons for the hostility to his presence. In most cases the clothiers were using wools which were not permitted by the regulations and they were also making the coarser *londres-larges* in villages outside Clermont despite the legislation of 1715 which forbade the production of such cloth. One of Delagenière's first acts, therefore, had to be to undertake a complete reform of the industry: a period of grace was allowed during which clothiers could use up their low-quality wools and then the regulations were enforced to the letter.[78]

With the presence of Delagenière the severity of regulation reached its height at Clermont. The same developments occurred in other areas of France. Controller-General Orry was rigorously orthodox in his policy. As Pierre Deyon noted, Orry revived Colbert's policy, 'renforce la rè-glementation industrielle, orchestre le progrès du commerce'.[79]

Parallel to the increasing severity of the regulative system was a gradual tightening of control over who was allowed to produce cloth, and eventually over how much cloth was produced. Because of the way in which the industry had been fostered it was likely that the new cloths would be produced only in and around Carcassonne, Clermont and St-Chinian, but in 1715 the privileged position of these three towns was made definite, when they, and the royal manufactures, were granted the monopoly of the production of the fine cloth sold in the Levant. At the same time the right to manufacture the coarser *londres-larges* was granted in the dioceses of St-Pons, Limoux and Castres, and denied to Carcassonne, Clermont and St-Chinian.[80] The policy, again, was intended to encourage the maintenance of a high standard of production for it had been found that the quality of workmanship declined when spinners and weavers worked with both coarse and fine wools. The result of the policy was a narrow specialization in different towns on the production of particular types of cloth, which Heckscher described as a 'more sharply defined exclusiveness between different places'.[81] This specialization

---

76. ADH C2498, 2131.
77. ACC BB3, 15 June 1729.
78. ADH C2129–30 have details of this reform.
79. *Mercantilisme*, p. 78.
80. AN F12 58, folios 320–1, Bureau de Commerce, 25 Jan. 1715.
81. *Mercantilism*, I, 147.

was intended. The policy also had the result, however, of further enhancing the monopolistic position of the clothiers in these different towns.

During the late 1730s the industry again, despite all the controls which had been imposed upon it, went through a considerable crisis which is revealed by the production details for Clermont and Languedoc.[82] It was in reaction to this crisis that the regulation of industry was extended to its maximum. A first edict of 13 January 1736 forbade clothiers who had gone bankrupt from manufacturing until they had paid all their debts, and from that year an annual list was prepared of those clothiers who were allowed to produce. From this list were excluded not only bankrupts but also all those who practised a second profession, were still under parental protection, had never worked previously for the Levant, or who were considered by the local inspector to have insufficient resources to work well.[83] In 1741 these restrictions were extended yet further when a series of measures known as the 'fixation' were enacted.[84] Fixation was quite simply a quota system which was designed to control not only those who were allowed to manufacture, but also how much cloth each clothier might produce. It was designed to ensure stability for the industry and to balance the so-called 'arrangements', or cartel of merchants, which had been organized at Constantinople in 1736 by the ambassador Villeneuve for the purpose of limiting cloth purchases and sales in the different Levantine markets.[85] Fixation represented the apotheosis of administrative interference with the industry. Control was virtually complete and stability this time *was* assured, as the production figures reveal. Not even sons or sons-in-law of masters were now allowed to produce without obtaining special permission from the intendant, a permission which was not easily obtained,[86] and clothiers who were producing could not be certain of having their quotas renewed. Each year a new 'tableau', which announced the quotas for the following year, was prepared after extensive consultations between the inspector, intendant and controller-general. Some clothiers might have bales knocked off their quotas for having produced bad-quality cloth. Some might have some added for having produced efficiently and 'faithfully'. Such small changes were intended to encourage emulation amongst clothiers (there

82. See pp. 305–6.
83. ADH C2210, Memoir of *c.* 1755, C2036, tableau for 1739.
84. ADH C2040. On administration of this system see Appolis, *Lodève*, pp. 501–5.
85. ADH C2201, Memoir of Le Mazurier, 1739; C. Roure, 'La réglementation du commerce français au Levant sous l'ambassade du marquis de Villeneuve (1728–1741)' in J.-P. Filippini *et al.* (eds), *Dossiers sur le commerce français en Méditerranée*, pp. 33–101.
86. See the opposition to reception of the son of Joseph Goudard, ADH C2153, and to Pierre Gayraud, son-in-law of Jean Flottes aîné, C2152.

was now no other stimulus for such emulation). Dominique Tricou,[87] Clermont's new inspector, reported that some minor changes made for 1747 (three clothiers had been penalized for slackness and had had part of their quotas removed) had given rise to 'beaucoup d'Emulation à nos fabriquants et il en a résulté un grand bien'.[88] Equally, if market conditions permitted, the total production quota for the town or the province was increased, again giving scope to the intendant and inspector to penalize or to reward, or to grant quotas to new clothiers. The clothiers themselves abetted (and sometimes prejudiced) their chances of large quotas by sending petitions to the intendant, or arranging for distinguished relations or friends to write to the intendancy, in order to obtain favourable treatment. Liberal presents of fruit and game sometimes accompanied letters.[89] In theory it was the clothier's skills as manufacturer that were respected in the allocation of quotas. The control over these was such that by 1749 the inspector at Montpellier had a list of all clothiers producing for the Levant on which each one was graded according to his skills from one to four.[90]

As we have emphasized in the first section of this chapter, the major entrepreneurial task of the clothiers, despite the importance of their commercial roles, remained that of cloth-making and, as cloth-making remained an extremely labour-intensive activity – improvement in quality had been achieved but no changes in the nature of the basic processes – a great part of their time was devoted to controlling their labour forces, and, as workers were neither confined in manufactures nor under any legal obligation to work either continuously or for one master, controlling their labour forces was no easy task. We have shown some of the spontaneous individual entrepreneurial responses to this situation. These individual responses were to be supplemented first by various collective actions of the clothiers' corporation, and secondly by official intervention. The 1715 edict restricting Clermont's production to that of fine cloth served, effectively, as a means of preventing the town's labour force from accepting work not only from participants in Clermont's traditional industry but also (and this was more important) from clothiers producing *draps forts* at Lodève. In practice it proved difficult to enforce this measure when Clermont's industry was without work and Lodève's in

---

87. Son of Gaspard Tricou, a merchant of Montpellier, appointed to Clermont in 1745, ADH C2499.
88. ADH C2050, Tricou to Le Nain, 2 Nov. 1747.
89. See for example correspondence between Pierre Gayraud and Dr Haguenot, 1752–3, in the new Fonds Villenouvette (ADH).
90. ADH C2049, this bundle contains a list, compiled by Vassal and Gaja, of clothiers about whose qualifications they disagree.

expansion. This was the case in 1716 and 1717, soon after the edict's first
publication, but despite this the attempt was made. On 20 June 1717, at
6.00 in the morning, leading members of the corporation made a surprise
visit to all the carding and spinning workshops in the town, seized all the
wools belonging to Lodève clothiers, and arrested one of the cardeurs,
imprisoning him in the hôtel de ville, 'ce qui auroit cauzé une tumeur
dans notre ville et une cessaon du traval de tous les autres ouvriers qui
travaillent en laine'.[91] Differences with Villenouvette over labour questions were settled in a more amicable manner. On 13 February 1720
Astruc, director of Villenouvette, was given the right to use the labour of
the villages of Nébian, Péret, St-André, Montpeyroux, Adissan,
Lézignan-la-Cèbe, Gignac, Vissec, Ceyras and Pouzols. The occasion of
this agreement was also used by Clermont's clothiers' corporation to
settle some disputes over labour among their own members. Guillaume
Liquier and Estienne Berthomieu were given the right to share labour
with Astruc in the villages of Caux and La Vacquerie, Pradier was given
the exclusive right to the labour of St-Jean-de-Fos, Raissac to that of
Aniane, Pelletan was to share Ceyras and Pouzols with Astruc, and the
remaining clothiers were granted Pouget, Vendémian, Cazes, Poulhian,
Gabian, Neffiès, Cabrières, Puechabon and some other villages to share
between them.[92] If anything it would seem that this agreement sharp-
ened the disputes with Lodève's clothiers, some of whose preferred
working areas had been shared out between Clermont and Villenouvette.
Confrontations between rival employers occasionally gave rise to violence and disputes reached such an intensity that the intendant was
obliged to step in. After the carrying out of a survey in order to 'remédier
aux suites facheuses que toutes ces contestations peuvent causer au commerce par le mélange des fabriques' an 'ordonnance' was published in
1722 which gave to Lodève all the villages and hamlets of the mountainous areas north of the Rivers Lergue and Salagou, apart from
Montpeyroux, St-André, Octon, Ceyras, St-Félix-de-Lodez and Jonquières which, in addition to the rest of the dioceses of Lodève and
Béziers, were granted to Clermont. Villenouvette was not included in
this agreement and this was the grounds for further disputes and a further
intervention by the intendant in 1729.[93]

    These collective actions on the part of clothiers, and interventions by
the intendant, must have eased the labour problems faced by clothiers.
That it did not totally solve them is apparent from the information which
we have already presented showing that clothiers continued to offer

91. ACC BB2, 20 June 1717.
92. ADH II E 26 181, 13 Feb. 1720; ADH C2202, confirmed by de Bernage.
93. Appolis, *Lodève*, pp. 538–40.

bribes to their workers. The disputes between rival producing centres may have been solved; those between competing clothiers still remained. We have argued that such competition was normal and indeed necessary. It gave the worker a certain bargaining position and independence and thus served to retain his interest in the industry, and it was a discipline for the clothier necessitating efficiency. However it is quite clear that these sorts of considerations, if they occurred to clothiers, did not impress them. For them this independence of the labour force, and this competition with colleagues, were the major factors which complicated their entrepreneurial tasks and thus they showed, from an early stage, that they favoured the passing of some measure which would have removed, or inhibited, workers' ability to change employers. What they desired was a universal system, backed by the administration. Pradier in his memoir of 1732 proposed that there should be legislation binding each worker to his employer, and denying the right to change master without specific permission: 'C'est le point de la fabrique qui mérite le plus d'attention', he insisted. The same prominence was given to the problem by the clothiers at Carcassonne who published a special pamphlet on the question. Referring to the decline in the quality of production, they wrote:

Ce mal vient du grand nombre des fabriquants agissant sans concert & courant les uns sur les autres pour s'enlever les ouvriers: & on a trouvé que pour guérir ce mal radicalement, il falloit changer cette multitude d'actions divisées & contraires les unes aux autres, en une seule qui en laissant à un chacun toute sa liberté pour les opérations particulières de son commerce, produisit pourtant le même effet, que s'il n'y avoit qu'un seul Fabriquant dans Carcassonne.[94]

The desire to escape from a competitive system could hardly have been better expressed.

Once again the clothiers' desires were catered for. At the same time as fixation the 'billet de congé' system was introduced by two edicts of 1740 and 1749. The system deprived workers of the right to leave their employment without written permission and, despite the shearers' guild's privileges, gave clothiers the right to operate their own independent finishing shops.[95] To regulate fully the labour market it was necessary to share out the weavers in accordance with the quota of each clothier. Permission to do this was granted too in August 1746 by the intendant and in October the distribution was carried out by the inspector. This measure avoided two evils, Tricou emphasized: over-payment and a consequent 'diminution de travail parceque l'ouvrier gratiffié va Employer au Cabaret pour manger cet argent le temps quil Employoit à

94. ADH C2134, 21 Jan. 1730.
95. ADH C2090, 2497, Edicts of 18 Oct. 1740, 2 Jan. 1749.

son travail'; and rivalry between clothiers 'qui tous les jours sont à la veille d'avoir des querelles particulières pour un ouvrier qu'on leur aura pris'. The right to set wages unilaterally was granted to the clothiers at the same time. This last measure was all that was needed to end all competition for labour. The clothiers, anxious to demonstrate the generous spirit with which they would exercise their new powers, immediately conceded small wage increases, which they justified by the high food prices. It was with an equal condescension that Carcassonne's clothiers assured their labour force of 'le juste tempérament qu'on prendroit dans la fixation de leur salaire'.[96]

The grounds for the original authorization of corporations, subsidizing of manufactures, publication of regulations, and appointment of inspectors have been explained in previous chapters. These measures had had first an educative and reformatory function, being designed to improve the technical level of France's industrial production, and they had come to have a controlling purpose, to ensure that a certain technical level having been achieved it should not be allowed to deteriorate. The intensification in regulative policy, the increases made in the size of the inspectorate, the continuation of the subsidy system and the privileging of new manufactures, the official sanction given to measures which limited competition and the final adoption of a quota system are matters which are more difficult to explain, however, in view of the fact that these initial goals had already been fulfilled. In the new *Histoire économique et sociale de la France* the apparent illogicality of the revival of 'mediaeval' policies in a period of growth is recorded, and it is also stressed that Colbert himself had regarded 'le dirigisme industriel' as an 'expédient temporaire'.[97] The causes of this apparently paradoxical intensification of what were intended originally to be temporary expedients lay primarily in the interaction between concrete problems encountered by all French cloth-making centres in this period with what can be described as 'mercantilist' conceptions of the nature of the economic system within which these industries were functioning.

The nature of the concrete problems we have described already: production was liable to violent cyclical swings, quality of production tended to deteriorate sharply during years of expansion because the processes of manufacture were rushed, labour was undisciplined and particularly so when well paid, different cloth-making centres competed for the same workers to whom they entrusted different types of material which occasioned a loss of specialized skills, clothiers without adequate re-

96. ADH C2394 has full details of this distribution.
97. Braudel and Labrousse, *Histoire économique*, II, 224, 251.

sources or cloth-making qualifications attempted to produce cloth with the aid of credit during years of expansion etc. The one factor which all these problems had in common was that they affected the quality of production. This was the unifying factor and it was one of profound significance because, as we have observed already, it was believed that to lower quality was to risk losing a trade. Indeed it was believed by many (and again we have seen signs of such a belief in the previous century) that the main cause of fluctuations in trades was the greed of clothiers and the decline in quality to which this greed (which took the form of over-production) gave rise. Examples of this way of thinking are manifold: 'cette fabrique et ce Comerce diminuent chaque jour par la trop grande quantité de ces draps quon a faits passer en Levant depuis quelques années', wrote de la Chapelle from Carcassonne in 1729, for example. The consequences would be disastrous, he added: 'on estime que ce Comerce se perdra totalement ... si on ne limite bientôt l'ambition démesurée du fabriquant'.[98] Insecurity was increased, of course, by two factors: first the fact that France had experienced so sharp an industrial decline in the seventeenth century, a decline which, as we have seen, was believed by contemporaries to have been caused by precisely these kinds of abuse – the memory of the industrial and commercial collapse of the seventeenth century would seem to have exercised as great a dominance over industrial policy in France until the 1750s as the memory of un-employment in the 1930s did on economic policy in industrial countries in Europe after 1945 – and secondly by the fact that trading conditions were so exceptionally disturbed during the first thirty years of this expansion which we have been studying. We have already seen that this latter consideration was probably the decisive factor in persuading the Etats to continue with the costly bounty and privilege system. Finally faith in regulation, guilds and inspectors was increased by the fact that contemporaries, unlike recent historians, attributed to them the revival which had occurred in French trade. They lacked completely the statis-tical data which have caused historians to emphasize the importance of 'mouvements profonds' in the economy and, understandably, accredited the recovery to those factors about which they were informed, the acts of government intervention. Consequently the new 1708 regulation for the Levant trade was treated as a cloth-maker's Ten Commandments in Languedoc in more than the figurative sense:[99] clothiers on occasions

98. AN F12 557, 'Reflections sur l'état des Manufactures et du Commerce de Carcassonne', 1729.
99. ADH C2201, 'déliberation' clothiers' guild 22 April 1763: 'les confesseurs Refusent absolution aux fabricants des draps attendu qu'ils ne suivent pas les Règlements et qu'ils ont fait serment de les suivre lorsqu'ils ont esté reçus à la maîtrise'.

were refused absolution for disregarding its clauses. As it was stated in a memoir composed in 1768: 'L'arrêt de 1708 est regardé comme un chef-d'oeuvre, tout le monde convient qu'on lui doit la perfection des draps et l'état florissant où ce commerce est parvenu.'[100]

By 'mercantilist' conceptions of the economic system we mean that contemporaries, unlike historians, were unaware that the Industrial Revolution was going to take place. The only world they knew was the only world which existed, one in which there was a limited range of markets, without significant capacity for expansion, one in which as Defoe, equally 'mercantilist' in his outlook, wrote, 'if one place sinks, another advances; and if one kind of manufacture declines, another advances'.[101] Contemporaries, then, had no awareness that there might be advantages in possessing industries which were flexible, highly competitive and with a significant capacity for expansion. Their ideal, on the contrary, was that production should be stabilized in order to consolidate positions in markets which, they believed, were of an invariable, stable nature. And in that they judged abuses of quality to be the major danger for this situation of stability they were prepared to intervene in industrial production to stamp out such abuses.

If it was the constant pre-occupation, that the valuable new trade might be lost as a consequence of a decline in quality and a return to the depressed circumstances of the seventeenth century thus occasioned, which was the major cause for interventionism and the sanctioning of restrictive practices, there were two subsidiary factors which contribute to explaining why clothiers' requests to administrators were so frequently responded to. The clothiers' corporations were most convenient bodies to tax (we have observed the Clermontais clothiers' emphasis on their need for funds to meet tax demands) and administrators were probably sensitive to this as well as to the fact that by allowing masterships to become difficult to attain they were creating the opportunity, which was to be exploited in the 1720s and 1730s, of selling special masterships which exempted their holders from completing an apprenticeship or *chef-d'oeuvre*. The other factor which gave both directors of royal manufactures and normal clothiers an added influence over administrative decisions was the fact that their manufactures had become so essential both for the prevention of poverty and for the regular payment of taxes. As Delagenière wrote on 28 August 1728 to the intendant, 'on peut assurer que la plus grande partie des habitants de ce Diocèze tomberoit dans une affreuse misère par la seule cessation du commerce et

100. ADH C2223, Memoir on Levant trade, 1768.
101. Cited by C. H. Wilson, 'Cloth production', p. 221.

de la fabrique qui en est la principale ressource'.[102] The rise of these large cloth-making concerns had, without doubt, contributed to alleviating local poverty and to increasing the regularity with which taxes were paid but it had, for the very same reasons, given rise to a certain dependency of the local administration on these concerns' owners. Clothiers again showed that they were sensitive to the importance given by administrators to their indirect role in the relief of poverty and used it to justify requests for privileges. For example the director of one manufacture justified his request for the status of royal manufacture on the grounds that his concern acted as 'la mère nourrice d'une vaste contrée' and two other requests for this status were supported by the Bishop of St-Pons on the grounds that the two 'fabriquants ... font un Bien infini dans mon diocèse'.[103] The political system in France in the eighteenth century was a curious combination of extreme centralization and local anarchy and clothiers, with their large resources, their vast labour forces, their dominance of local politics and their social connections, had become powers on the local level which had to be reckoned with.

To outward appearances administrative intervention in the industry had been successful for with the establishment of 'fixation' in the 1740s not only did production first stabilize and then expand steadily but also the quality of production improved. The trade cycle had apparently been legislated out of existence and Inspector Tricou was able to write to Intendant Le Nain on 25 August 1749 in the following terms:

j'auray l'honneur de vous observer avec plus de vérité que la fabrique de Clermont est montée de façon qu'il ne soit fabriqué que de beaux et bons draps, bien teints, et bien aprêtés, qu'il y a encore plus d'uniformité dans cette fabrique que dans toute autre, que les draps en sont recherchés et vendu par préférance pour les Echelles du Levant dans les quelles ils sont en très grande réputation.[104]

An apparent sign of the health of the industry was the interest which was shown in technical progress. In 1748, for example, not only were clothiers introduced by Inspector Le Mazurier to a new method of garnishing two pieces of cloth at a time, but the services of a furnace-maker, one Klimbert of Besançon, were utilized to reconstruct the furnaces used for heating dyeing vats in order to achieve significant economies in fuel. Twelve furnaces were rebuilt, at a cost of 48 *livres* a furnace, after a successful experiment had been carried out at Pierre

102. ADH C2129.
103. ADH C5544, Laporterie (of Roquecourbe) to St-Priest, 2 Feb. 1757; ADH C2122, Letter of 16 Aug. 1720.
104. ADH C2159, 28 Aug. 1749.

Martin's dye-house.[105] A Clermontais ironsmith, one Pauze, presumably as a consequence of his encounter with Klimbert, became a regional expert in furnace design, it would seem, for two years later he reconstructed three furnaces at St-Pons, 'chacun, à grille, souppage & ventouse à l'imitation de ceux que le S' Kleiberg [Klimbert?] fait dans touttes les Raffineries des Salpetre'.[106] In the same year (1748) Clermont became the first Languedocian textile centre to be introduced to the flying shuttle. A demonstration was given by weavers from the manufacture of Moüy. The Martins and Desalascs were the first to utilize the new shuttle and expressed their satisfaction to the intendant. The experiment had been carried out in front of the inspector, clothiers and weavers and Martin père informed Vassal at Montpellier that all parties 'ont trouvé cet ouvrage parfait. ils ont tous convenu qu'avec cette Navette l'ouvrage étoit beaucoup mieux et se faisoit avec plus de diligence.' Albert, a doctor from Montpellier, who had been charged with the introduction of the shuttle at Carcassonne and who acted during these years as the chief technical adviser to the intendant on all aspects of cloth-making, informed Le Nain on 4 December 1748 that the Martins were 'si satisfaits qu'ils ont desjà donné l'ordre à leur menuisier de travailler à tout ce qui est nécessaire pour quatourze métiers qu'ils vont faire monter à Bédarieux pour les sayes'.[107] The flying shuttle was equally well received at Carcassonne: 'Nous ne sçaurions dire à votre grandeur, combien cette Nouvelle navete a été curieusement examinée, et moins encore luy exprimer comment elle a été reçüe des personnes intelligentes, soit fabriquants ou Ouvriers', the local gardes-jurés informed the intendant.[108] Albert meanwhile was carrying out further experiments in dyeing techniques and in the use of different types of soap for fulling cloth. He informed the intendant on 9 July, 1749 that he had examined 'les operaisons du foulage et dégraissage avec des yeux de phisicien'.[109] The skills, confidence and enthusiasm of the Enlightenment were being mobilized to improve yet further Languedoc's brilliant industry.

The leading families amongst the clothiers had become fabulously rich by the mid-century. Even in a period of expansion, such as that which was occurring throughout France during these years, the fortunes which

105. ADH C2502, Le Mazurier to Le Nain, 24 Oct. 1748; C2381, Report of clothiers on dyeing experiment.
106. ADA 9 C 11, Report Fontanes, 5 Sept. 1750.
107. ADH C2158, 4 Dec. 1748. On introduction of flying shuttle to France see C. Ballot, *L'introduction du machinisme dans l'industrie française*, pp. 247–9.
108. ADH C2159, 30 June 1749.
109. ADH C2159, Albert to Le Nain, 9 July 1749.

they had accumulated gave rise to a certain notoriety. Sub-delegate Bonnafous, commenting on the imposition of the *vingtième* in the diocese of Lodève in 1750, noted that at Clermont 'Le commerce ... en draps pour les échelles du Levant est très avantageux et brillant, les marchands senrichissent tous les jours. Il y en a dont la fortune les met au rang du plus opulant du Diocèse, et dans la seconde clase bien dautres qui tendent à la première.'[110] It was to the clothiers that the visiting military captain referred in 1749 when he wrote that the 'négossients ... fait icy noblesse'.[111] The best evidence of their status and resources is provided by marriage contracts. The policy of making strictly professional marriage alliances was now less closely adhered to. In the 1730s, for example, Marie Altayrac, daughter of Jean Altayrac, married Dominique de Serres, conseiller at the Cour des Aides of Montpellier, and Jean Bernard, whose career we have followed since the arrival of his father from Lyons to work as a dyer at Villenouvette in the 1680s, married both his daughters into the nobility in the 1750s, one to Jacques Etienne de Causse and the other to Etienne Désclaux, 'trésorier de France' at Toulouse.[112] Generally, however, despite the occasional marriage clearly motivated by a social ambition which had outgrown the limited possibilities of Clermont, the majority of matches continued to be made amongst the clothiers themselves. That co-operation which we have observed among these families in their cloth-making activities was now being extended to consolidating their social position in the town. Appolis writes of the tendency, as at Lodève, for clothiers to marry 'entre eux'. Some of the most important of these marriages were those of Jean-Pierre Desalasc with Marie Berthomieu, only daughter of Antoine (bride's dowry 18,000 *livres*), of Gabriel Pelletan with Françoise Altayrac (bride's dowry 45,000 *livres*), of Jean Pelletan with Mathieu Pradier's daughter (dowry of 30,000 *livres*) and of Jacques Martin with Scholastique Berthomieu (bride's dowry 18,000 *livres*; Martin given 50,000 *livres* by his father).[113] A sign of the recognition given to at least one of these enriched families by those whose status was based on more traditional criteria was the presence of the bishop of Lodève, Souillac, at the marriage of Jean-Pierre Desalasc and Marie Berthomieu in 1736 to confer his blessing on the couple. Souillac became an ardent patron of the Desalasc family with whom he invariably stayed when he visited Clermont.[114]

The profession of clothier had become both rich and elegant: 'se n'étoit

110. ADH C1744, Etats for *dixième*, 29 Nov. 1750.
111. ADH C6763, 29 May 1749.
112. Bobo, 'Communauté languedocienne', pp. 45, 56; ADH 11 E 25 154, 19 Jan. 1750.
113. Appolis, *Lodève*, pp. 509, 511, 513; Bobo, 'Communauté languedocienne', p. 49.
114. Appolis, *Lodève*, p. 16.

alors que peruqués; gens de Bon sens', a Clermontais recorded later in the century.[115] The large profits accumulated from cloth production were invested in land purchases (the clothiers' entries in the *compoix* grew longer and longer), or in beautifying their houses. A notarial act records for us that Estienne Berthomieu in 1727 refaced his house with freestone and installed 'fenêtres à l'italienne'[116] and in another act it is recorded that Pierre Vernazobres had been granted special permission to make an 'arceau et des fenêtres', extending from his house to a neighbouring building and overlooking the Planol.[117] The majority of rich clothier families owned houses either in the Rue de la Fregère, backing onto their manufactures (the Pradiers, Pelletans, Raissacs, Bonnevilles and Bernards were housed in this part of the town), or overlooking the Planol (in addition to Vernazobres, the Martins and Desalascs had substantial houses in this quarter). The purchase of municipal offices in the 1730s we have described in a previous chapter, and in the 1740s and 1750s the most successful clothier families were thinking in terms of buying 'seigneuries'. Marie Berthomieu, daughter of Antoine, purchased the seigneurie of Lauzières and in the 1760s and 1770s was to refer to herself (pretentiously) as 'Baronne de Lauzières, Seigneuresse d'Octon, d'Arièges et autres places'.[118]

The accounts of Clermont's clothiers' corporation for the years 1743–50 survive and these provide additional insights into the circum- stances of the industry in this decade of stable trading conditions and growing prosperity. The corporation had a comparatively large budget (expenditure of up to 7,000 *livres* a year) and this was financed in part by a due of 5 *sols* which was raised on each piece of cloth produced and, in years of exceptional expenditure, by borrowing. Richer clothiers were the main source of loans. In 1746, for example, a year in which the purchase of an office of 'contrôlleur et Inspecteur' was made for 4,415 *livres*, Antoine Berthomieu and la veuve Bernard each loaned 3,000 *livres* at a rate of interest of 6%. Not only did richer clothiers have capital to spare but, as their purchase of land and offices has already suggested, they were not averse to supplementing their profits from their manufacturing concerns with income of a rentier kind. Many of the corporation's expenses were of a routine nature: payment for repairs to the town's bureau de marque; tips given to the town's valets de ville; the purchase of stationery; charitable donations (bread given to the poor, cloth donated to the hospital etc.); expenses incurred in the fulfilment of the social and religious duties which the corporation had inherited from the confrérie

115. ADH C5592, Pezet to St-Priest, 25 Aug. 1782.
116. ADH 11 E 26 188, 17 Jan.–6 Feb. 1727.
117. ACC BB5, 6 June 1753.
118. Appolis, *Lodève*, p. 571, ADH, Ordinaires Clermont, Case 457, 1771.

(payments to bell-ringers, for wax, to the priest for saying masses, for the purchase of 'pains bénis', etc.); the payment of a salary of 400 *livres* to a commis employed by the corporation and of part of the salary of the inspector; the financing of a postal service between Pézenas and Clermont. Other expenses were incurred on behalf of the collective economic interests of the corporation. Almost every year deputations were made to the intendant at Montpellier to influence decisions relating to the industry; for example a deputation was sent in 1743 to gain the intendant's support for an attempt to oppose the reception of a new master in the corporation and in 1746 it was another deputation which negotiated the right to share out all the weavers among clothiers. Large expenses were also incurred in what might be described as public-relations exercises, designed to enhance the corporation's favour with the administration. No less than 839 *livres* 7 *sols* was spent in connection with expenses made during 'la convalescence du Roy' in 1745 and a further 472 *livres* 19 *sols* in 1749 in connection with 'la dépense faite à l'occasion de la rejouissance de la convalescence de M. Le Nain'. Other expenses were more directly related to cloth-making. Various measures designed to contribute to the control of the labour force were financed. In 1746, 65 *livres* was spent on 'Pluzieurs Journées de cheval pour la tournée des ouvriers faite par M[r] L'Inspecteur assisté des jurés-gardes'. Money was spent in attempts to discourage the embezzlement of raw materials: 27 *livres* 19 *sols* in 1745 on one 'farie surpris en vol et nourry en prison', and no less than 1,931 *livres* 16 *sols* 8 *deniers* in 1748 on the trial of two men accused of purchasing stolen wools. There was some financing of technological experiments. Those of Klimbert in 1748 were paid for in part by the corporation. There are signs that the corporation was building up some sort of technical library for its members: 18 *livres* 19 *sols* was spent on the purchase of books in 1750. Finally there were expenses incurred for social reasons. Visiting inspectors were, it is clear, lavishly entertained. A payment of 93 *livres* to Tournal, inn-keeper, is recorded in 1743 on the occasion of a visit made by Paul Pailhoux, a total of 57 *livres* was spent in 1748 in connection with some sort of celebration made at the métairie of one of the clothiers, Mathieu Pradier, to 'baptize' a spring which he had tapped, and finally 3 *livres* 2 *vols* were paid in 1749 to the valet de ville of Lodève 'envoyé ici par les jurés-gardes dud Lodève à L'occasion d'un fripon'.

Most of the characteristics of Clermont's clothiers in this period are illustrated by the varied nature of these expenses: their wealth (the budget of their corporation was large and certain expenses were clearly unnecessary); their cultured interest in technological matters; their charitable but undemocratic attitude to poorer members of society; their use of their corporation as a pressure group on behalf of their collective interests in the industry; and their evident desire to enjoy the occasional festive occasion on which their shared interests were celebrated socially.[119]

Despite appearances, and despite the evident confidence of clothiers and inspector, all was not well with Clermont's industry for the Levant. The various aspects of 'interventionism' which we have described may have contributed to short-term stabilization of production but they had had damaging consequences for the industry's long-term prospects. We shall now examine, in turn, the effects of the increasing severity of regulations, the restrictions on the right to produce cloth and the increase in the legal power which clothiers possessed over their labour force.

The very existence of regulations limited the job of the entrepreneur. Regulations served not merely to discipline; so complete were they that they served as a virtual technical guide to cloth-making. This was clearly an advantage in a period when the new techniques were unknown, but ultimately it gave rise to a lack of initiative, and to the dominance of routine. Above all the growing strictness in the enforcement of the regulations concerning wool qualities – this was the very kernel of the regulative system – must have had a deleterious effect for as every cloth manufacturer knows it is in the mixture of wools that half the art of cloth-making lies. The use of wools other than those prescribed by regulations was regarded as cheating when in many cases it should have been appreciated as a necessary part of the process of cloth-making. This suppression of initiative applied also to the process of manufacture and to the tools used in manufacturing. Everything had to be done according to the rule-book, and any innovation which involved a change in the nature of the production process was looked upon as fraud or as an abuse to be stamped out. Significant in this context were the official reactions to two machines invented by Languedocian artisans. In 1728 a device called a *tone* or *tonne* was being used by cloth-dressers in the dioceses of Carcassonne, Lavaur and Castres to finish their cloth. It was clearly similar in concept to a gig-mill, consisting of a large roller, driven by water-power, with brushes attached. There was probably truth in the report that these machines were capable of damaging the cloth but this was not sufficient grounds for ordering their destruction: damaged cloth would surely not have been sold and the machines' destruction, if necessary, could have been left to market forces.[120] There was a similarly hostile reaction to a machine called a *sabot*, which was being used by weavers in 1732. The device must have been remarkably similar to the

119. ADH C2523, Accounts of bureau de marque, Clermont, 1743–50.
120. ADH C2129, 2130, Report of Carbon, Carcassonne, 1728, Letter of de la Chapelle to de Bernage, 14 May 1728.

flying shuttle, 'invented' one year later in England, judging from the description of the local inspector: he explained that the *sabot*, attached to one corner of the loom, 'Renvoye le coup de navette à Louvrier, qui est de lautre Côté du métier'. There was a virtually instinctive hostile reaction: the inspector described it as a 'machine très préjudiciable et dont louvrier ne sçauroit faire que de très mauvais draps' and reported that the 'abuse' of its utilization was spreading 'avec fureur'.[121] The documentation about these machines is not sufficient for a judgement to be made about their technological importance but it can be seen that, in general, official policy was hostile to any innovations made by the worker himself, as opposed to those which were sanctioned officially,[122] and as such it was frustrating precisely the sort of empirical technological progress which has been noted as having been of such importance on the other side of the Channel.

An equal reluctance to accept local initiatives is apparent in the royal policy towards the adoption of new types of cloth. The cloths which Languedoc's clothiers were allowed to produce for the Levant did not change during the first half of the century with two exceptions. First a new type of cloth was devised in 1741: it was a coarser version of the *londrin-second* called *nims-londrins* which never enjoyed very much success.[123] Secondly, and more significantly, some of Clermont's and Lodève's clothiers started to produce a cloth called *sayes* during the late 1730s and the 1740s. *Sayes* were distinct from *londrins-seconds*: they were an imitation of a Venetian product and were stronger and heavier than all other cloths for the Levant although made with similar, high-quality, Spanish wools and having the same finish. The cloth was in demand, and the two towns achieved considerable success in its manufacture, but despite this when news of its production was received in Paris clothiers were banned from making it (it was feared that a deterioration in the quality of *londrins-seconds* would result from its manufacture) and a monopoly was granted to a Parisian merchant, Vallat, to produce it instead. Orry's reaction to the new cloth provides a perfect example of administrative inflexibility: 'La qualité de ces draps n'étant pas désignés dans le Règlement de 1708', he wrote to de Bernage, 'et la fabrique des draps pour le Levant n'étant déjà que trop étendüe en Languedoc, l'introduction de cette nouveauté seroit également dangereuse pour notre commerce dans le Levant et pour les fabriques des draps de Lodève par le dérangement qu'elles pourroient en souffrir.'[124] Vallat's privileged

---

121. ADH C2134, Procès-verbal of Paul Pailhoux, inspector, 1 Dec. 1734.
122. The contrast with the enthusiasm shown when the flying shuttle was officially adopted is striking.
123. ADH C2047, Regulation of 17 June 1741 for the production of *nims-londrins*.
124. ADH C5522–4, 5545, 5585.

manufacture was never to function efficiently and the opportunity provided by the new cloth was lost. A small note in the margin of a memoir about Languedoc's cloth industry registered the failure and pronounced the moral to be learnt from the experience: it was necessary to 'rendre la liberté et ne plus accorder de privilège exclusif'.[125] This demand was to be made more and more frequently.

The new cloth and the technological innovations mentioned were rejected in each case because of concern over the effect which their introduction would have on the quality of production and on France's position in export markets which she already dominated. The dominant characteristic of the policy of these years, as we have stressed earlier in this chapter, was an attempt to stabilize and consolidate successes which had already been attained rather than preparing the ground for new developments. But there was worse than this for not only were new cloths not developed; old trades which had long traditions of prosperity were abandoned in favour of production for the new market, and of the five cloths prescribed by the regulations only one was made in any quantity: Carcassonne, Clermont and St-Chinian by the mid-century had abandoned their traditional trades and were concentrating almost entirely on one cloth, *londrins-seconds*. The banning of the production of *londres-larges* and the varieties of coarse cloth which were made on small looms has already been mentioned. In addition the manufacture of *cadis* and of other coarse cloths in the diocese of Lodève, for sale at local fairs, was neglected,[126] and there was a decline in the production of medleys at Carcassonne. Trades neglected at the expense of the growing industry were conveniently ignored by most contemporaries who commented on the economic progress of the province, as they have been by most historians when describing the 'astonishing' expansion of Languedoc's cloth exports to the Levant, but the loss of the medley industry at Carcassonne was a matter of some significance. The loss was an indirect consequence of state intervention. The monopolistic position of the clothiers for the Levant brought excess profits and these affected the traditional medley industry in two ways: first, clothiers from this industry were tempted to start production for the Levant, and secondly those clothiers who continued to produce medleys experienced problems of labour shortage as those producing for the Levant could afford to pay higher wages. These problems affected wide areas, for the influence of the new industry spread far. In 1729, for example, a year of expansion in the Levant trade, the clothiers of Lavaur and Limoux found that they were

125. AN F12 557, Memoir of 1744.
126. See p. 310.

losing most of their workers to Carcassonne's Levant industry.[127] Originally the existence of this traditional industry had provided alternative employment for Carcassonne's clothiers in years of difficulty in the Levant market.[128] Gradually, though, the skills necessary for these and other cloths, and the contacts with other markets, were lost. A memoir composed in 1744 described the medley industry as 'absolument tombé'.[129] The dangers of this total dependence on the Levant market did not go totally unremarked by contemporaries. Gilly, deputy of commerce for Languedoc, writing on the province's cloth industry in 1725, stated that it would have been better if fewer royal manufactures had been founded and there had thus been less concentration on the Levant market, 'car on n'est parvenu à faire ce si grand nombre de Draps qu'on fait aujourd'huy qu'au détriment des plus Anciennes fabriques'.[130] The almost total concentration on the production of *londrins-seconds* was also noted by contemporaries: Pradier was to comment in 1744, for instance, that Clermont, in contrast to most manufacturing towns which had 'différentes qualités détoffes à faire', made only *londrins-seconds*.[131]

This last factor, the overwhelming concentration on a single type of cloth, cannot of course be entirely attributed to administrative intervention. It was also a consequence of the nature of demand in the Levant. The Ottoman Empire experienced a period of peace and prosperity during the first half of the eighteenth century and there was an actual increase in the demand for middling-quality cloth in this normally stable market.[132] It is this phenomenon which provides the explanation for the concentration on *londrins-seconds* as well as providing part of the general background for the success of Languedoc's clothiers. The results of this concentration were clearly dangerous, however: the towns of Languedoc were not merely dependent on one market, they were dependent on the sale of one cloth in one market, and the skills necessary for the production of other cloths, skills possessed by the first generation of clothiers, had gradually been lost.

If the regulations caused an excessive concentration on a single cloth and a single market the limitations on production, as will have already

---

127. ADH C2131, Report of de la Chapelle, 27 April 1729, AN F12 557, 'Reflections', Carcassonne, 1729.
128. E.g. in 1725 and 1731 there were revivals in the production of medleys at Carcassonne, AN F12 1380, ADH C2134, Reports of de la Chapelle, 3 Feb. 1725, 19 Nov. 1731.
129. AN F12 557, 'Mémoire concernant l'Etat actuel du Commerce ... en Languedoc en 1744'.
130. ADH C5517.
131. ADH C5533, Pradier to Le Nain, 5 Oct. 1744.
132. Paris, *Commerce de Marseille*, v, 54; Masson, *Histoire du commerce dans le Levant au XVIIIᵉ siècle*, p. 479.

become apparent, caused this limited trade to be concentrated in the hands of just a few clothiers. Appolis in his study on the Lodévois noted this tendency: 'les drapiers', he wrote, 'déjà peu nombreux, tendent à constituer une caste fermée, afin de se réserver jalousement les bénéfices'.[133] The extent to which the industry had become restricted to a 'caste fermée' is demonstrated by the fact that of the twenty-two masters entitled to produce by the 'fixation' of 1741 two were surviving 'founders' of the industry, fourteen were sons of masters, one was a founder's widow and only five could be described as new blood, having attained their masterships by the completion of an apprenticeship and *chef-d'oeuvre*.[134]

The normal and healthy situation in any cloth-making industry in the pre-industrial period was for there to be a slow but continuous turn-over in the body of clothiers. An industry would be reinforced at its bottom end by sons of masters and by ex-apprentices, and it would lose members as a consequence of either the bankruptcy or the retirement of its older members. Retirement by an industry's richest participants, provided that there were rising clothiers to take their place, far from being a vice was an important contributory agent to this continuous process of renovation. The restrictions imposed in the corporative statutes of 1708 were a first measure impeding this natural turn-over but there continued to be some movement into and out of the industry. In the last chapter we have given several examples of social mobility within the industry (for example the rise of the Bernards and Bonnevilles from positions as dyer and shearer respectively). And we have shown that between 1725 and 1737 there were some fifteen new entrants to the industry. Movements out of the industry there were too but these were occasioned in all cases by business failure rather than by the withdrawal of richer clothiers. Mathieu Pradier was one clothier who abandoned production after sustaining large losses. In 1731 it was reported that it was 'notoire que les affaires du Sr Pradier sont ... en désordre au point qu'il a esté obligé de s'absenter pour éviter les poursuites de ses créanciers'. With the help of his father-in-law, Joseph Trail, bourgeois of St-Pons, Pradier was able to reach a settlement with his creditors and he then sought alternative employment in the service of the Crown.[135] In April 1731 he was in Paris in pursuit of this aim[136] and during 1732 he attempted to obtain the inspectorate at Montpellier which had fallen vacant. It was to favour his

---

133. Appolis, *Lodève*, p. 510.
134. ADH C2039, 'Etat des Fabricans', 1741.
135. ADH C2132 has full documentation on this affair. Pradier, before abandoning production, attempted to gain the status of royal manufacture for his concern. See also C5495, Correspondence between Orry and de Bernage.
136. ADH 11 E 25 117, 9 April 1731.

chances of obtaining this appointment that he sent an excellent memoir on the Levant trade to de Bernage during 1732,[137] but the post was finally given not to Pradier but to one Fondière who had been working as an industrial spy in England.[138] He was more fortunate in his search for employment at Paris, however. A notarial act registered in his absence from Clermont in 1733 describes him as 'intéressé dans les affaires du Roy' and a further act registered in 1737 informs us of his position: he had become 'fermier général des biens des religionnaires réfractaires'.[139] But Pradier's ambition remained, it is clear, to obtain employment in the inspectorate and in this he was finally to be satisfied; he was first appointed as inspector to Beauvais and later promoted to the position of 'inspecteur-général'.[140] Other examples of clothiers moving out of the industry (on a temporary or permanent basis) include Gabriel Verny and Pierre Vernazobres who attempted, like Pradier, to obtain positions as inspectors.[141] The course of seeking employment in the administration of industry was one which several clothiers were to take (as some failed British industrialists in the nineteenth century were to do). Another clothier, François Audran, who went bankrupt in 1738, obtained employment at the royal manufacture of La Trivalle;[142] Villet, bankrupt also in 1738, became a retail merchant (a 'marchand-mercier et -clinqualier');[143] Estienne Berthomieu, bankrupt in 1737, was charged with supplying Clermont's butchers with meat in 1740;[144] and Jean Astruc obtained what he himself described as a mediocre job in the 'fermes du Roy'.[145]

If the enforcement of the 1708 corporative statutes had caused a significant slowing-down in that natural and necessary turn-over in Clermont's body of clothiers, the combination of the 1737 measure, which restricted mastership to sons or sons-in-law of clothiers, and the 'fixation' of 1741, brought this turn-over to a complete halt. There was now *no* possibility of new blood entering the industry, nor was there any likelihood, given the high level of profits, that there would be any movement out of the industry. It had even become difficult for sons and sons-in-law of masters to get permission to produce. The industry had thus

137. ADH C4676.
138. ADH C2200, Rouillé to de Bernage, 2 Feb. 1733.
139. ADH 11 E 25 119, 21 Sept. 1733; Appolis, *Lodève*, p. 513.
140. ADH C5533, Orry to Le Nain, 27 Jan. 1744, C2499, Pradier to Le Nain, 24 Aug. 1748.
141. Appolis, *Lodève*, p. 529; ADH C5585, letters of Vernazobres, 11 Feb., 15 May 1759, and of Trudaine, 19 Sept. 1758.
142. ADH C2036, Tableau for 1739, 11 E 25 153, 27 Oct. 1749.
143. ADH 8 B 396, Bilan, 24 Nov. 1738, 11 E 25 129, 4 July 1743.
144. Bilan: ADH 11 E 25 118, 10 April 1732, ACC BB4, 9 June 1740.
145. ADH C2048, Request of Jean Astruc, *c.* 1746.

become totally static. And this was not the only damaging consequence of 'fixation'. The restrictions on entry to the profession, the quota system and the legislation tying workers to their employers destroyed almost entirely the risk-element in cloth-making: that competitive environment which I have described earlier in the chapter and which was necessary to ensure that the industry continued to be efficient. Profits had become so automatic to those with the right to manufacture that this right to manufacture came itself to have a marketable value and to be treated as a private possession. An illustration of this is provided by an act registered by a clothier who had been allowed to make use of someone else's quota. He declared that although he was using the quota 'néanmoins il reconnoît & déclare que la propriété de la permission de travailler en draps' belonged to the other clothier 'pour en jouir lui & les siens'.[146]

The fact that profits had become virtually automatic in the industry had the consequence that the intendant was plagued continually by requests to be included in the annual 'fixation'. Some of these requests were made with some justification by people who had served apprenticeships and now wanted to be received master and allowed to pursue the career which they had chosen. But there were also numerous demands made by people who under normal circumstances would not have been interested in producing cloth. One type of applicant was the ex-clothier who had produced for the Levant but retired from the industry generally because of lack of resources or financial failure. Mathieu Pradier was one such who requested, and obtained, a large quota for his former manufacture in the 1740s. He provides thus an example, and it is not a surprising example given the artificial condition of the industry, of a movement away from office into industrial activity. Many other applicants were complete outsiders to Languedoc's industry. As production for the Levant had become a sinecure, which was in the patronage of administrators, predictably those social groups in French society who habitually sought sinecures attempted to obtain permission to produce for the Levant. Among those who demanded the right to produce for the Levant were the King's private doctor and the Duchess of Béringhen and the list of distinguished people who supported clothiers' requests to manufacture included the Duchess of Lorges, the Count of Maillebois, the Duchess of Mazarin, the Duke of Noailles, the Count of Rohan, the archbishop of Embrun and the bishops of St-Pons, Lodève, Alès and Carcassonne.[147] As a priest at Paris observed, when he himself requested the right to manufacture for one of his nephews: 'Les uns et les autres

---

146. ADH II E 25 136, 20 June 1746.
147. Appolis, *Lodève*, pp. 503–4; ADH C2048, 2051, 2053, 2055, 2057, 2065.

emploient ici les seigneurs de la Cour et les princes même auprès de M. le contrôleur général pour la même chose.'[148]

It was to this period that Roland de la Platière (who was to be inspector at Clermont between 1764 and 1766) referred under the entry 'Draps du Languedoc' in the *Encylopédie méthodique*:[149]

La permission de faire des draps fut une faveur signalée, que pourtant les personnes en place abandonnèrent à leurs gens: on agiota cette permission; elle fut portée, de la part du fabricant, jusqu'à cent pistoles par ballot; & les maîtresses de Messieurs les commis de Bureau, des valets & femmes-de-chambres, des comédiennes, se faisoient, celui-ci mille écus, celle-là deux mille écus, cet autre dix & jusqu'à douze mille livres de rente de cette gentillesse. ... Par ce seul trait, qui est l'historique le plus exact, qu'on imagine ce que le droit de travailler exigeoit, des manoeuvres, des intrigues, des séductions, des corruptions, des bassesses, des infamies; & qu'on juge & de la probité de ceux entre les mains de qui étoit restée cette branche de commerce & l'économie dont ils étoient obligés d'user dans la fabrication de leurs draps, & du prix au quel il falloit qu'ils les vendissent pour se tirer d'affaires.

Roland de la Platière's account of 'fixation' is not 'exact', as he maintained, but that it is at least based on truth is apparent from the manner in which the system was administered at Clermont.[150] Though requests to manufacture from total outsiders to the industry were invariably rejected there were a number of demands made by clothiers already producing who wanted a larger quota, and by masters who had not previously been included on the 'tableau' either because they had not previously worked independently or because they had abandoned production, and decisions as to which of these requests should be granted were clearly affected by the influence which applicants, or applicants' backers, could marshal on their behalf. There are several examples of clothiers wielding influence to good effect. The prime example is Mathieu Pradier and his case we shall describe in detail for it illustrates facets of Clermont's industrial experience in this period which are of interest to us.

Pradier was particularly well placed to gain administrative favour. His years in the royal service would have acquainted him with the leading figures in the Bureau de Commerce as well as giving him an understanding of how decisions were made and how they could be influenced. He was also able to rely on local support in Clermont for any request which he might make. He was related to the majority of Clermontais clothiers and had particularly close relationships with the Pelletan family which because of its seniority in the industry wielded a significant influence not

148. Cited by Appolis, *Lodève*, p. 503.
149. *L'encyclopédie méthodique*, I, 407.
150. And that intrigues of the nature described by Roland de la Platière did take place is suggested by a mysterious case of bribery and corruption involving, above all, one Mourrèze. This affair is fully documented in ADH C5596.

only over other clothiers but also over the inspector of manufactures, Delagenière. Jean Pelletan père was Pradier's first cousin, and Pradier had provided temporary employment for Pelletan's second son, Jean Pelletan fils, when he had been working in the ferme des biens des religionnaires réfractaires.[151] The extent of the Pelletans' power in Clermont is illustrated by the fact that when Pierre Delagenière was suddenly incapacitated in 1739 as a consequence of a stroke which paralysed him completely it was Jean Pelletan père who was chosen to assist the oldest Delagenière son, Jean-Pierre, to fulfil his father's duties until a decision was made about a successor. Jean-Pierre was appointed as inspector for Bayonne and Oleron in 1740 and the inspectorate was granted officially to the second son, Pierre-Marie. The extent to which the second Delagenière son was under Pelletan's influence is revealed by an extract from the journal which he kept to record his activities as inspector. Soon after his appointment he had summoned a meeting of clothiers and it was Pelletan père, rather than he, who 'à cette occazion [a] fait un discours très Etandu sur le devoir des fabricands et sur l'obligation où ils sont dexécuter les Règlements et il les a menacés de toute la Rigeur des arrêts et ordonnances prononcées'.[152] It was an awareness on the intendant's part of Pierre-Marie Delagenière's lack of independence that led to his transfer to another inspectorate in 1744 and to the appointment of Dominique Tricou in his place. Le Nain explained the circumstances of this transfer to Controller-General Orry in a letter of 9 March 1744:

Sr de Lagenière qui est un jeune homme d'environ 22 ans seulement, et qui n'a ni encore l'expérience ni la fermeté nécessaire pour le maintien d'une fabrique aussy essentielle que celle de Clermont, inquiète souvent malapropos les fabriquants par l'inspiration du Sr Peletan qui a été chargé de le diriger dans ses fonctions; celuy cy auquel il est absolument devoüé ainsy que toute sa famille.[153]

Pradier's intention was to use both his Parisian and his Clermontais sources of influence to obtain permission to produce several types of cloth which had not previously been made in Clermont in his abandoned manufacture. This manufacture he was planning to entrust to Jean Pelletan fils, who since finishing his employment in the fermes des biens des religionnaires réfractaires had been working at Marseilles where his father had established a commercial house. Pelletan had had no experience of cloth manufacture but had had himself received master in 1743, no doubt in anticipation of directing Pradier's concern.[154] Pradier's original request for permission to make these various cloths was made in January 1744 but the demand was opposed by the majority of

151. ADH C5533, Memoir of Louis Martin, 16 Feb. 1744.
152. ADH C2498.
153. ADH C2148, 9 March 1744.
154. ACC BB4, 29 Aug. 1743.

Clermont's clothiers and, in addition, a Lodévois producer of one of the types of cloth which he was planning to make informed the intendant that his manufacture was not of the size which he had claimed that it was: 'les propriétés ne consistent que dans son imagination', the Lodévois wrote, and Pradier's manufacture 'ne seroit sulement pas suffisante pour y exploiter une des six fabriques quil préthend y Réünir'. In view of this dual opposition, Pradier changed his tactics and in March 1744 'moderated' his original demand by suggesting that the new varieties of cloth which he had been proposing, instead of being produced purely in his concern, should be shared out among all Clermont's clothiers. But there was a price for this concession for he added that if the new types of cloth were distributed in this way 'il seroit raisonnable dun autre Côtté en me privant de cette partie quon affectât à ma maison de Clermont un travail par année de 30 balles londrins seconds, et de 20 balles de nims afin que mon Etablissement soit occupé'. Pradier had opened this request by claiming that he was acting for 'Le bien de L'état' but it is clear that at least one person in authority who read this request was aware of the hypocrisy of this claim. In the margin of Pradier's memoir the following statement is to be found: 'c'est la première fois qu'on a veu un Inspecteur demander la permission de fabriquer pour son compte, ce n'est pas là son métier, et il doit se contenir dans les bornes de ses fonctions, qui consistent à surveiller le fabriquant, et non pas à être fabriquant'. But Pradier pursued his aim to share in the new profits available in production for the Levant as persistently as he had pursued his ambition to become an inspector ten years previously. He came down to Clermont in October 1744 to campaign for support for his scheme and soon succeeded in winning over some of the clothiers who were tempted by the prospect of being granted a share in the production of the new cloths. Soon two hostile camps formed among the clothiers, those favouring Pradier and those opposing him. The latter informed the intendant about Pradier's, and his relative, Pelletan's, scurrilous tactics: 'ils vont de porte en porte', they wrote, 'capter les suffrages d'un chaqu'un et ils n'ont peu encore parvenir qu'à faire signer leur mémoire, qu'à leurs parens ou leurs alliés'. Pradier's allies likewise were abusive about his opponents. Whereas they themselves formed 'la partie la plus saine, la plus ancienne' of the corporation, they claimed, their opponents consisted of no more than 'six à sept fabriquants qui ne font que de Naître dans notre manufacture où partie même ne sont entrés que par lachapt des maîtrises'. Pradier finally mobilized much of Clermont to support his project. A 'conseil-général' of the communauté met on 3 December 1744 to endorse his plans.[155]

Predictably Dominique Tricou found the presence of this corrupt

155. All details contained in ADH C5533.

Clermontais fellow-inspector in the town most irksome. He wrote frankly to Massol, a secretary at the intendancy, on 22 January 1745, describing the situation:

je ne dois pas vous laisser ignorer que notre Marchand de Cervelle [Pradier] a fait répandre icy par ses adhérans que les Etats avoint été si satisfait des Mémoires qu'il leur avoit donné que tout d'une voix on luy avoit accordé tout ce qu'il avoit demandé et que sa maison travailleroit, et fairoit tout ce quelle voudroit, et qu'il avoit pris des arrangements pour me faire changer ce que sûrement je ne resterois pas longtems à Clermont, et pour apuyer ce raisonnement la vielle Me Lagenière au lieu d'aller joindre son fils à Castres pour le convenir et pour ne pas brusler la chandelle par les deux bouts vient d'arrenter une maison et a passé police pour deux ans, vous ne sauriez croire ... combien cette manouvre fait d'impression sur les esprits la plus part des fabricants s'immaginent qu'au premier courrier je vais recevoir lordre de passer à quelqu'autre inspection et que Pelletan et luy seront icy les maîtres et les tiendront dans les fers comme par le passé, ce qui les met dans une consternation des plus grandes ... je ne vous cacheray point que tout cela m'inquiette et que je crains que la patience ne m'échape à la fin et ne me porte à quelque facheuse extrémité contre ce faquin et que je ne luy coupe le visage.[156]

Despite Tricou's fears neither was he removed from his inspectorate nor was Pradier's first request granted, but, and it is here that would seem to lie the subtlety of Pradier's tactics, the controller-general while he refused the first request accepted the second (which was far more useful to Pradier personally), and Jean Pelletan fils was included on the 'tableau' for 1745 for a total of 60 *ballots* which made him the largest individual producer at Clermont.[157] The concession granted to Pradier and Pelletan fils was all the more remarkable in view of the latter's lack of training as a clothier. Ironically Pradier had obtained a larger quota for his concern than Jean Pelletan was actually able to produce. In October 1746, when all other clothiers were clamouring to be allowed to produce more cloth, Pelletan had to write to Le Nain requesting to be allowed to produce the rest of his quota during the following year.[158] Pradier, though, was still not satiated. During 1746 a proposal had been accepted to enlarge the total quota of Languedoc's production for the Levant by 500 *ballots*. Pradier demanded his share, claiming that, 'les 60 Ballots qui ont étté accordés à la maison du Sr Pradier, sous le nom de Jean Pelletan fils ... se trouveroint diminués sil navoit part aujourdhuy à Laugmentation'.[159]

In 1748 Pradier set the seal on his long association with Jean Pelletan

---

156. ADH C2499, 22 Jan. 1745.
157. ADH C2043, Pradier announces controller-general's decision in letter to de Bernage, 27 March 1745.
158. ADH C2047, J. Pelletan to Le Nain, 8 Oct. 1746.
159. ADH C2047, Anonymous memoir in Pradier's hand.

fils by marrying his daughter Monique to him.[160] Possibly it was at the celebration held at his métairie in this year (and financed, we have noted, out of the corporation funds) that the prospective marriage was announced to clothier colleagues. Pradier was able to give a dowry of 30,000 *livres* to his daughter, as much as the wealthiest clothiers who had never ceased to produce gave in wedding donations. Pradier had been 'en faillite' seventeen years previously. Clearly he had rebuilt his fortune in the royal service and by the favours which he had obtained for his manufacture. Despite his fortune Pradier was to complain in 1755 that the 30 *livres* capitation with which he had been imposed was excessive. The reply of the conseil de ville to his complaint informs us fully about the advantages of his situation:

il n'a pas Eté trop cotisé puisqu'à travers tout ce quil dit Il paroît quindépendament de sa pention de 3,000 [livres] sur laquelle on na point porté la vue lorsquon a fait le Rolle de la capitation Il jouit encore de son propre aveu trente Balles de draps sous le nom dud Sr Pelletan fils, son Gendre dont personne nignore quil Retire un bon Revenu, quil jouit aussy une Belle maison, et des Biens fonds assés Considérables à la porte de la ville quil vient dy Etablir un Lavoir de laines qui lui porte sept livres dix sols par jour lorsquil travaille. Et quil y a fait Bâttir une Belle maison de plaisance, qu'outre tout cela il jouit Encore dune Rente de quatre cens livres quitte de vingtième sur le Sr Jean Flottes aîné mart. fabriquant . . . à cause dune vente que led. Sr Pradier lui fit . . . dans ces circonstances il est surprenant que led Sr Pradier qui a de grandes facultés, ce qui figure plus que personne de cette ville, se plaigne.[161]

The Pradier saga is of interest to us because it exposes the darker side of the experiences of Clermont's cloth industry during the 'fixation' period. The industry appeared to be prosperous and stable, but corruption had set in. The inspectoral system was being manipulated by clothiers, and tensions and divisions were emerging between different families as success ceased to be the reward of entrepreneurial qualities and became a consequence of privilege, influence and bullying. Pradier and Pelletan fils were typical representatives of a new type of entrepreneur whose skills lay as much in influencing administrators and extracting concessions as they did in cloth-making. In a thoughtful chapter in the seventh volume of the *Cambridge Economic History of Europe* Jürgen Kocka contrasts the entrepreneurial qualities apparent in those areas of Germany which had experienced industrial and commercial develop-

160. Bobo, 'Communauté languedocienne', p. 52.
161. ACC BB5, 6 Dec 1755. Pradier's 'patron' in Paris would seem to have been intendant de commerce de Montaran. It was he who supported Pradier's request for a quota in 1745. He commented in a letter to Intendant Le Nain of Pradier's 'zèle et . . . capacité qui me sont souvent d'un grand secours' (ADH C2047, 10 Dec. 1745).

ment spontaneously, under the discipline of the market, with those which existed in areas subjected to strong mercantilist intervention. Whereas there was some continuity between the enterprises of the former areas and the concerns which developed during the industrialization of Germany, this was seldom the case in the latter areas where entrepreneurs, Kocka writes:

side-stepped problems of large-scale management which were ... appearing for the first time, and which were to become typical of the later factory system too ... adopted known technical advances, but seldom ... initiated them themselves ... absent is not concern for profits, market-orientation, or an aptitude for political dealings, but abilities and motivations for rational, systematic, steady entrepreneurship and for innovatory control over the technological processes.[162]

Clermont's entrepreneurs were coming to correspond to this type but this, as we have seen, had not been their primitive state. The increasing restrictions on their production, legal control over their labour force and regulation as to how they should produce cloth had created en environment in which traditional entrepreneurial qualities had become less and less necessary and exercise of political influence more and more important. There was a certain irony that a son and a grandson of two of the creators of the industry, whose entrepreneurial qualities had been of the purest, should have been two of the most expert practitioners of the new arts necessary for economic success.

We have till now confined our analysis to the effects of the restrictions of production on the clothiers. Our justification for this is that it was on the clothiers' abilities and resources that the industry largely depended. It was they who owned virtually all the capital and it was they who had the necessary market contacts and commercial, actuarial and managerial skills to make the industry function. Clothiers themselves certainly considered that they were the only participants in the production process worthy of administrative consideration. But clothiers were not justified in neglecting the state of the industry's labour force, any more than we are. It was ultimately on the labour force's willingness to produce cloth that the industry's future depended and this willingness was certainly diminished, even if the clothiers' powers of compulsion were enlarged, by the introduction of the billet de congé system. We shall follow briefly the reactions of skilled workers (those involved in finishing processes) and the less-skilled (weavers) to their loss of independence.

The reaction of cloth-finishers to the growing power of the clothiers

---

162. 'Entrepreneurs and managers in German industrialization' in P. Mathias and M. M. Postan (eds), *Cambridge Economic History of Europe*, VII, pt. I, 507.

was to be more violent. A first conflict occurred in 1730. An attempt was made in this year by clothiers both to reduce the price of the finishing processes and to increase their control over them by stipulating that all cloth had to be presented at the bureau de marque after shearing and after receiving the last dressing before the dyeing process. The reaction of the cloth-finishers to this dual threat to their profession was to strike. As members of the clothiers' corporation reported, cloth-finishers refused to work at the new prices and 'par un complot entr'eux [ont] portés toutes les forces à tondre les draps chez la veuve Cathala enfermées sous la clef afin d'empêcher, par cet expédient facheux et contraire à l'ordre de la police que doit être observée dans la fabrique, les ouvriers qui auroient été dans le dessein de travailler au prix que leur avoit été proposé'. The tondeurs, defending themselves, claimed that 'ils estoint les maîtres de les [their shears] enfermer là où ils vouloint', but the intendant clearly disagreed; he fined their corporation 200 *livres* for their action.[163] Resistance to the 1740 measure which permitted clothiers, despite the cloth-finishers' corporative statutes, to establish their own finishing shops which could be operated by cloth-finishers who had not been received masters, was to be sharper. The dispute came to a head in 1746. The cloth-finishers' corporation first sent a pitiful memoir to the intendant in which it was claimed that its members now lamented their choice of a trade which had declined in status. The profession was composed now of 'des misérables qui ont vieilli dans un métier où ils ont mangé tout ce qu'ils ont Reçeu de leurs Pères'. Their plea was backed by the Bishop of Lodève who both confirmed that the situation of the members of the corporation had become desperate ('aucune d'eux n'avoient comme autre fois les facultés de fournir à l'entretien de sa famille') and gave the cause of this sad state (the clothiers were avoiding using their services and 'n'employent que des garçons de tous les païs'). Inspector Tricou, however, was less sympathetic and in reply to Intendant Le Nain's queries he explained that only five or six of the clothiers had established their own finishing shops, that the rest were using the services of the independent shearers and cloth-dressers, and that it was only the worst workers in the corporation who were unemployed; these few had been complaining since 1740, he pointed out, because 'ils sentirent combien cet arrest les gênoit et ils prévirent que dès lors qu'il n'y auroit que les bons ouvriers quy auroient du travail'. Far from regretting the edict of 1740, Tricou described it as an absolutely essential measure 'par raport à la subordination quil doit y avoir entre le fabriquant et l'ouvrier'. Tricou was supported by the clothiers themselves who maintained that only since the edict of 1740 had

163. ADH C2132 has all details.

they been certain of being able to make cloth of a consistent quality, 'parce que nous sommes maîtres des ouvriers ... ce n'est que la crainte où l'ouvrier est que nous le renvoyons sil fait mal son ouvrage ... qui le rend plus soigneux et plus atentif à ce qu'il fait; en conséquence nos Draps en sont plus beaux'. Tricou and the clothiers thought only in terms of the quality of their cloth; the local priest, La Romiguière, took a moral viewpoint. He wrote to the intendant asking him to lend a sympathetic ear to the case of the cloth-dressers: 'Les voilà réduits à L'aumône ...', he emphasized, and putting words into their mouths he wrote, 'Comment payer les droits et les taxes qu'on nous demande? Que deviendront nos femmes et nos enfants? et quel parti tireront nous des grandes dépences que nous avons fait pour nous établir? Si les marchands absorbent tout par leur avidité insatiable'.

Realizing that petitions were not going to achieve anything a few of the cloth-dressers decided to intimidate those members of their corporation who were working in the clothiers' workshops. On the evening of 23 March they waited outside the workshop of the veuve Bernard and when her workers left they advised them to stop working or to face the consequences. On the 24th they waited outside another workshop and having asked Pierre Mézas to come outside they warned him to stop working there because 'sil continuoit, on luy donnerat tant de coups de Bâton, qu'il resteroient une année au lit'.

This was the extent of the rebellion and there was little likelihood of its being successful. In fact the rebel cloth-dressers seemed more concerned about concealing what actions they had taken than in carrying out their threats, for on 25 March one of them warned one of those who had been threatened not to reveal what had happened or 'il luy feroit couper Bras et jambes'. Their actions did not remain secret for long, however, for after evidence had been gathered on the 26th, orders were given on the 29th by the viguier of Clermont for the arrest of the two cloth-dressers involved. The affair would probably have ended there but Tricou sent such an exaggerated account of what had happened to Le Nain (he translated threats of violence into violence perpetrated, writing that the threatened cloth-dresser 'fut assommi par ces coquins qui l'attandoit dans la rue et ils l'auroient infailliblement tué s'il ne fut venu du secours') that the intendant sent an order to the maréchaussée of Lodève to arrest two other cloth-dressers, who had in fact nothing to do with the original threats. The injustice was flagrant and La Romiguière and a number of leading inhabitants of Clermont (but no clothiers) signed petitions requesting the release of the innocent cloth-dressers. As a result of these the two men were soon returned to Clermont but they still had to suffer the indignity of paying for their own arrest, despite the fact that their innocence had been proved. Tricou was little concerned with the justice or injustice of the case but he was delighted with the effect that the incident had had on labour-relations. He wrote contentedly to the secretary of the intendancy that 'la parition de la mareschaussée à Clermont . . . a fait un grand effet sur l'esprit des ouvriers, et que chacun se tient dans son devoir . . . tout est calme à présent dans la fabrique'; he was of the opinion that this state of affairs would continue 'pourvue toute fois que Mr le prieur de Clermont ne se mesle point des ouvriers ni de la fabrique'.[164]

That the cloth-finishers should have reacted violently to the growing power of the clothiers is easily explicable. As we have seen, in the early years of the industry their profession had been neither economically nor socially distinguished from that of clothier. Intermarriage between their own and clothiers' families had been frequent and members of the profession had had the possibility of becoming clothiers should they so desire.[165] Gradually, though, their trade had declined in status as clothiers became more wealthy and exercised a greater control over all aspects of the production process. The possibility of rising to the status of clothier became more and more remote and was to be removed entirely by the 1737 measure. Finally the labour legislation of 1740 deprived the corporation of its most significant privilege, the right of its masters to have a monopoly over the finishing processes. Growing poverty and dependence as this measure came to be enforced, and an awareness of loss of status, combined to activate the revolt.

It was the weaver who was the prime target of the labour legislation of 1740 and 1749. As an inspector noted in 1732, 'le tisseur . . . fut de tous les temps l'ouvrier le plus Indomptable, et toujours pour ainsi dire, la pierre d'achopement pour le fabriquant'.[166] If the system solved the clothiers' labour problems in the short term its long-term effects, as was the case with other aspects of state intervention, were undoubtedly damaging. The decrease in the competition for the services of the labour force which the measure occasioned may have contributed to an improvement in the quality of production, and an easing of the entrepreneurial task, but it was at the cost of alienating the weavers for whom the measure was all the more repugnant in that there was no technological justification for it – it was introduced for purely disciplinary reasons – and in that it imposed a treatment on them which was distinct from that given to any other category of labour. Inevitably the system was used by clothiers to decrease wages and by 1745 the weavers' situation was becoming desperate.

164. ADH C2424, 2427 have all details; see also Appolis, *Lodève*, pp. 549–54.
165. See pp. 290–1.
166. ADH C2508, Vallon, inspector Carcassonne, to de Bernage, 15 Oct. 1732.

At a meeting of their corporation which was attended by eighty-five masters it was complained that they were being treated 'avec plus de rigeur que les esclaves' and declared that 'les tisserands seront exposés à mourir de faim, tandis que les Marchands accumulent tous les jours de Richesses'. But there is no evidence that the weavers used their collective strength, expressed at this meeting, in order to confront their employers as the cloth-finishers had done. They limited their action to petitioning the intendant for the abolition of the billet de congé system and to requesting that Clermont's clothiers should be allowed to make an additional type of cloth in order to provide more employment.[167] Administrative intervention, it would seem, had contributed to diverting weavers' attention from the direct conflict of interests which existed with their employers. That the administration, and clothiers, feared the collective strength of the labour force, however, is apparent from a new clause added to the second general edict regulating labour questions published in 1749: expressly forbidden was the right of 'Compagnons et Ouvriers de s'assembler en Corps sous prétexte de Confrairie ou autrement'.[168] The confrérie, an institution which had existed 'de temps immémorial' to serve the social and spiritual needs of its members, had become a social danger in the divided industry of Languedoc. This clause in the 1749 edict would hardly seem to have been necessary for the weavers' 'protest' against their working conditions most frequently took an indirect form: if they were able to they deserted their profession. From Carcassonne it was reported that weavers, 'voyant leur métier tombé dans l'esclavage', were seeking alternative employment 'où l'on puisse en la faisant être libre'.[169] If for reasons of age, or lack of alternative employment, it was impossible to desert the profession, weavers at least ensured that their sons should enjoy better destinies. The inspector from St-Chinian reported in 1747 that 'La pluspart des pères et mères qui ont cette profession sopposent formellement que leurs enfans la prenent.'[170] A shortage of labour inevitably resulted. At Clermont in 1753 it was reported that fifty looms were deserted for lack of weavers and that 135 masters between them had not found a single apprentice willing to be taken on in the previous year.[171] The contrast with the situation of the profession during the expansion of the industry was striking: a 120 *livres* mastership fee had been imposed in 1711 to prevent too rapid a rise in the

167. ADH II E 25 134, 3 Jan. 1745. See also C2394, Petition of weavers to intendant, 12 Nov. 1746.
168. ADH C2497, 2 Jan. 1749, clause 3.
169. ADH C2156, Weavers to Le Nain, 13 March 1748.
170. ADH C2153, Memoir of Cazaban, inspector Carcassonne, 20 May, 1747.
171. ADH C5552, Memoir of de Gournay, 1753.

number of weavers[172] and on 19 February 1729 four would-be weavers had paid 142 *livres* 15 *sols* each for special masterships which had been offered for sale.[173] There could hardly have been a more fundamental industrial problem than this abstention of the labour force.

So, behind an impressive façade, all was far from well with Clermont's industry during these years. Stability of production and regularity in quality had been achieved but the health of the industry in the long term had been jeopardized. The industry had become over-committed to a single market, its labour force was oppressed, alienated and declining in numbers, its entrepreneurial class was too restricted and unsuitably rich, the promotion of fresh talent was not accepted, the 'fixation' system had led to corruption – profits had been too easy and 'patronage' had resulted in some of the largest profits being accumulated in the least worthy, and least useful, hands – and lastly the likelihood of colossal over-production had been created for there were literally dozens of would-be clothiers, dazzled by the fortunes made by those already producing, who were waiting to undertake production as soon as the system of 'fixation' was abolished. All these problems were mainly, if not entirely, due to administrative intervention in Clermont's industry.

These weaknesses were all the more potentially dangerous to Clermont in that it had become so dependent on its cloth industry. This we have emphasized before but what we have not emphasized is that the cloth industry had significantly changed the character of the town, and made it far more vulnerable than it had been at the end of the seventeenth century to any major economic disruption. The town at the end of the seventeenth century was impoverished but, as we have seen, the majority of its population owned some property and had adjusted to the depression by drawing income from a variety of different sources: petty trading, artisanal activities or cultivation of the soil. The town does not seem to have contained much serious poverty. The diocese of Lodève as a whole was punctual in the payment of its taxes (we have noted) and the serious agricultural and demographic crises at the end of the seventeenth century clearly affected poor areas of the Massif Central far more than they did Clermont's population. The conseil de ville in January 1698, for example, recorded difficulties in paying the town's taxes but complained, above all, of the repercussions for Clermont of the far more serious subsistence problems of the Rouergue; a number of families had had to

172. ADH II E 25 109, 26 Oct. 1711.
173. ACC BB3, 19 Feb. 1729.

leave the neighbouring province to beg their bread and 'certains establys den la prézent ville coupent les olliviers, southes et autres arbres en particulier, se portent à voler de jour et de nuit les olliviers'. A request was sent to the intendant for an ordonnance to be issued 'de faire sortir de lad ville lesd. familles estrangères honteuzes et de mauvaize vie quy sy sont Réfuggiés'.[174] The growth of the cloth industry, however, had had the consequence that an increasingly large proportion of Clermont's population owned *no* property and was totally dependent on its industrial wage. It was to remedy this, and to contribute to the payment of the town's taxes, that in 1750 it was proposed that those without land should be obliged to cultivate the many *sétérées* of waste or abandoned land. The consequence of the growth of a large, propertyless class was that Clermont developed an internal problem of lawlessness. The major threat to property had previously resulted from Clermont's situation on a main route of communications from the Rouergue; disorder was now regularly occasioned by members of the town's own population. Disruptions to the town's peace became more and more regular. In 1712 the theft of olives, firewood and other agricultural products was again complained of but this time attributed to 'des estrangers quj ce sont retirés dans ceste ville à cause des manufactures ou par dautres hans quj nont aucun bien en fonds dans led. terroir'. In 1717 there were similar complaints. On 6 February 1729 it was recorded again that 'il y a personnes quj ce sont establis dans la p[nt] ville najant aucun Compoix quj ravagent la Campanie en coupant toute sorte darbres et souches et vollent les fruits'. In 1731 a 'sédition du menu puble' occurred in protest against the imposition of a *subvention* to pay the town's debts. In the registers of the conseil de ville it was reported that:

dans le temps que le conseil salloit assembler ... ce seroient attroupés environ deux cents artizants hommes ou femmes lesquels seroint venus dans Lhôtel de ville, criant hautement quils ne voulloint point de subvention ... et la nuit du même jour la porte du Bureau delad subvention (qui est à la place du Planol) feut Brullée la Barrière des dominiquains partie abattue ensemble la Bâtisse qui avoit esté faitte au coin du jardin de la dem[lle] de Salasc qui avoit esté construite la dernière et les autres Bâtisses aiant aussy eu le même sort.

The mob was categorized as 'menu puble La plus part estrangère', but the pretence that all disorderly elements in the town were strangers was becoming difficult to sustain: cloth-workers who had lived a generation in Clermont, despite being propertyless, had become Clermontais and their problems had become the town's, as the increasing regularity of disorder was revealing. In 1734 there were troubles again and a request was made

174. ACC BB2, 20 Jan. 1698. For situation of town in seventeenth century see pp. 103–16.

to the commander of the province to authorize the formation of a bourgeois patrol in the town. Guards had to be placed at the gates of the town in August 1737 to prevent the theft of grapes and in November of the same year another bourgeois guard had to be formed after many complaints about the theft of agricultural products, the burning of a bakery and the destruction of the trees in the garden of the new mayor, Jean Altayrac. In the Summer of 1738 it was again found necessary to appoint a bourgeois guard to patrol the town between 8 p.m. and 5 a.m. each night. During the 1740s, the decade of maximal prosperity and stability in the Levant trade, outbreaks of disorder occurred almost every year, in 1740, 1742, 1743, 1744, 1747, 1749 and 1750. Robberies at harvest time had become such regular events that the appointment of guards at the gates of the town to control ingoings and outgoings was referred to by 1739 as a 'coutume'.[175]

That these repeated disorders as well as being motivated by economic factors contained what might be termed a 'social' element is evident from the symbolic forms which protest on occasions took. It was surely not without significance that the property of purchasers of the offices of mayor and first consul should have been damaged in the 1730s, and the destruction of the gate of the Dominican monastery in 1731 must have had some explanation. The 'bâtisses' destroyed during the same 1731 uprising were small enclosures made in front of those elegant houses which faced onto the Place du Planol. The mob in selecting these as one of its targets was expressing, it seems likely, its consciousness of the wealth of the occupants of these houses as well as its resentment at the fact that to embellish these residences what had previously been communal property had been enclosed. On at least one occasion the cloth industry as a whole was the target of popular discontent. In April 1749, requesting a detachment of troops from the commander of the province on account of 'le cours des assassins, des vols et des désordres qui arrivent fréquament', the consuls stressed that the military presence was above all necessary in order that:

la fabrique des draps ne soit pas expozée aux domages quelle vient d'éprouver ces fêtes de pâques, car les fabriquans étant obligés d'étendre la nuit leurs draps soit dans les enclos de leurs maisons, soit dans des jardins pour leur faire prendre l'air, ils ont eu le malheur d'en avoir quantité de déchirés et de dégradés, en sorte quils ont tout lieu de craindre quils ne leur soient volés.[176]

175. ACC BB2, 29 June 1712, 20 June 1717, BB3, 6 Feb. 1729, 26 July 1731, BB4, 12 Nov. 1734, 25 Aug., 1 Nov. 1737, 31 Aug 1738, 24 Feb. 1740, 29 Aug. 1742, 15 Sept. 1743, 26 Sept. 1744, BB5, 29 June 1747, 14 Jan. 1750; ADH C6763, consuls request to commander of province, 8 April 1749.
176. ADH C6763, 8 April 1749.

So Clermont had changed from being a relatively peaceful community to one which was becoming more and more prone to disorder, from one which had few members without property, and thus without some interest in the preservation of order, to one with a large propertyless population who were especially vulnerable to years of depression in the cloth industry and likely, in desperation, to abuse the property rights of the better-off. And the law and order problem was exacerbated by the fact that the new magistrates in the town, who owed their enrichment and their posts to the very same economic process which was the fundamental cause of this unstable situation, lacked authority. They were new men, much hated by the traditional elite, and had yet to win, it is clear, the love and respect of the generality of Clermont's population who had not, of course, had any say in their appointment. The reaction of the military captain to the town's magistrates we have quoted already, but we will do so again. Clermont, he had written, 'goûteroit tous les dousseurs de la vie dans son genre montagnare si les chefs de la police, savoit mettre les mains à leuvre'. They did not because they were terrified of a public reaction to any measure which they might take. As the bishop of Lodève wrote after the mayor and consuls had failed to take any action against a notorious polygamist: 'les magistrats craignent quils ne leur ravagent leurs biens et leurs récoltes'. The newly appointed 'prieur' of Clermont, La Romiguière, after only four months in the town wrote to the commander of the province with a similar tale: 'il y règne des désordres si affreux que je n'ay pu jusqu'ici y remédier'. He was mainly concerned with disorders of a moral kind but he included in his letter information on disorders of a more general nature: 'ces jours passés on a volé un marchand dans la nuit qui n'a osé rien entreprendre dans la crainte qu'on n'atteint à sa vie. il n'y a pas devant les maisons un banc de pierre qui n'ait été renversé depuis que je me trouve dans cette ville. Chacun commende et fait ce qu'il veut tant le consulat est foible et timide.'[177]

---

177. ADH C6763, Letter of Dampierre, 29 May 1749, C6762, Letters of bishop of Lodève and of La Romiguière of 7 Oct. 1742, 29 Aug. 1744.

10

A change in policy and its consequences, 1754–9

France, though no doubt a richer country than Scotland, seems not to be going forward so fast. It is a common and even a popular opinion in the country that it is going backwards. (A. Smith, *The Wealth of Nations*, I, 108)

Monsieur Jars should above all investigate why English industry is so much in advance of that in France and how far the difference, as may be assumed, rests on the fact that the English are not saddled either with règlements or an inspectorate. (Instructions to Gabriel Jars, French engineer, in connection with his visit to metallurgical concerns in England, 1764, cited by Heckscher, *Mercantilism*, I, 199)

Cette différente façon de penser qui détermine Ladministration politique dun estat, demande des règlements, un frain pour les françois, dans le temps même que la liberté peut convenir aux anglais; incy notre routte doit estre différente pour venir à la même fin. (Mathieu Pradier, ex-Clermontais clothier and retired inspecteur-général to secretary at intendancy, 21 October 1753, ADH C2520)

'Fixation' and the various other measures which limited competition between clothiers had always had their opponents. Négociants at Marseilles were naturally critical of a system which caused cloth prices to be abnormally high;[1] old masters, denied the right to make cloth, grew increasingly bitter about the existence of a monopoly whose fruits they were disqualified from enjoying: 'je nignore point les sourdes pratiques que l'envie excité par la cupidité metoit en usage contre les malheureux qui voulloient prendre part aux avantages dont les Riches sont en possession',wrote Pierre Delpon to Intendant Le Nain in the fifth successive year in which his request to obtain a quota was refused;[2] ex-apprentices were likewise frustrated by the ban on the reception of new masters and expressed in numerous letters both their desire (they used a regular formula) to 'faire fructiffier à [leur] ... proffit les lumières ... acquises sur

---

1. ADH C5552, De Gournay to St-Priest, 13 Aug. 1751. In this letter de Gournay mentions a memoir he has just received from Marseilles in favour of 'le rétablissement de liberté'. See also Dutil, *Etat économique*, pp. 350–1.
2. ADH C2160, 6 April 1749.

la fabriquation en travaillant pour les autres'[3] and their opposition to a system in which they were 'réduit tout le temps de [leurs] . . . vie [s] à servir de comis';[4] and finally, and crucially, 'mercantilist' policies as a whole, of which the 'fixation' system adopted for Languedoc's Levant trade was a prime example, were increasingly criticized by 'liberal' thinkers.

In this chapter we shall discuss the reasons for a loss of confidence in mercantilist policies, detail the measures taken to liberalize Languedoc's industry for the Levant, and describe the apparently disastrous consequences of this lifting of restrictions.

A first reason for criticism of mercantilist policies was that the administrative network, established for their enforcement, showed signs of corruption. But more fundamental – a corrupt administration could have been purged and renewed – was a loss of faith in interventionism in itself as a means for sustaining France's economic growth. This loss of faith was occasioned by several, complex, interwoven factors. First, mercantilist policies had been criticized, and liberal alternatives posited, by a number of largely English and Scottish political economists whose works were rapidly translated and circulated in France. Ideas of a liberal nature had achieved a wide circulation by the mid-century. This is evident if only from the vocabulary with which clothiers, always receptive to arguments of a theoretical kind which might carry influence with politicians, began couching their petitions and requests: 'liberté' was more and more frequently demanded and regulations, formerly revered, came to be regarded and described as an awkward legacy of 'un siècle dignorance'.[5] A second factor contributing to this loss of faith in the interventionist system was a growing awareness that in certain significant aspects the English economy, administered on liberal lines, was progressing more rapidly than the French. Evidence of a growing French pre-occupation with this phenomenon is provided by the dispatch of agents, such as Jars, to England in order to investigate the causes of this success. Certainly by the mid-eighteenth century it was the English, rather than the Dutch (as had been the case at least until the turn of the century), who were regarded as the principal economic rivals and this change in itself posed problems. Mercantilist policies in France had been devised to achieve success on the basis of a 'Dutch models', as it were, and England's growing success meant that this model had become an anachronistic one.

3. E.g. ADH C2087, Requests of Pierre Rouquet, 26 Nov. 1755, and of Louis Bernard Dutheil, c. 1755.
4. ADH C2080, e.g. Request of Joseph Berthomieu (son of Estienne), 1 Jan. 1756.
5. ADH C5533, Petition of Delpon, Rouquet, Bouisson and others to de Montaran, 6 May 1757.

In addition, it was becoming apparent that the very nature of economic success was changing and now required qualities of a different kind, which could not be created by legislation. Whereas Holland's economic success of the seventeenth century had in some major ways been a repetition of those artificial, monopolistic economic dominances exercised by the Italian city-states,[6] and, as such, imitable by the enforcement of protective policies, that of England, though in part a consequence of protective trading policies, seemed too, and seemed pre-eminently, to have profound social causes: the flexibility, competitiveness and inventiveness of its entrepreneurs operating within a *laissez-faire* system. To add to the significance which was inevitably given to this last matter was the growing internal evidence that French business classes, nurtured within a mercantilist system, lacked these qualities, judged more and more as essential for the achievement of economic progress. French businessmen still, it was apparent, treated their commercial activities in the wrong spirit, valuing them not for themselves (as it was sincerely believed that the English and Dutch commercial classes did) but purely as a means for leaving their 'état'; 'nos françois', wrote Mathieu Pradier in 1753, 'sont empressés de pousser leur fortune, sans s'embarasser jusques à un certain point de la réputasion de leurs fabriques, qui forment simplement leurs moyens de gain pour sortir de leur estat, et passer à des charges ... Voilà le goût général.'[7]

This last factor, which Pradier described as 'inconstance', was not, of course, a fresh phenomenon. As we have mentioned in an earlier chapter, a similar scepticism about French entrepreneurial qualities had existed at the end of the seventeenth century.[8] But it had been believed, we have also seen, that a combination of regulations, strengthened corporations, an inspectoral system and the granting of a raised status to manufacturing activities would check these failings. What *was* new in the 1750s was a growing realization that the failings had persisted despite these reforms, and that the reforms themselves had made the French economy too rigid. Entrepreneurs had indeed been encouraged to stay longer in trade, as we have seen at Clermont, but at a cost: trade itself had become corrupted. Entrepreneurs had been encouraged to stay too long in trade and were becoming increasingly slack as a consequence of the security from competition given to them by their monopolistic corporations.

The importance attached by contemporaries to these social and attitudinal factors in explaining economic performance was very large. It was

6. See on this in particular D. Sella, *Crisis and Continuity: The Economy of Spanish Lombardy in the Seventeenth Century*, especially pp. 136–46.
7. ADH C2520, Letter of 21 Oct. 1753.
8. See pp. 41–2.

the primary influence behind the desire to reform the mercantilist system. Little concern was yet expressed about technical backwardness in France. (Probably there should have been more concern about this question but it was not yet apparent how significant a lead England had established in the coal-based technologies.)[9] On the contrary there is plentiful evidence of a widespread belief among the French that, in the textile and luxury-goods sectors at least, a technological edge had been achieved over English rivals: 'les orientaux préfèrent nos draps Londrins Seconds, aux draps des anglois, d'abord par leur bonne qualité, et par nos couleurs qui sont si bien variées que les anglois ne pourront jamais nous imiter', Jean Marcassus, director of two royal manufactures, those of La Terrasse and Auterive, wrote confidently to Intendant Le Nain in February 1749.[10] What is more, there was confidence that even if new techniques were developed elsewhere they could be imitated and then rapidly proliferated within France. We have seen this process occurring, in the last chapter, and it was indeed the case that there had been developed in France a most effective method of introducing new techniques: inspectors were increasingly being deployed as technological as much as regulative agents and the royal manufactures had been given a new role as pilot establishments for experimentation with, and introduction of, new techniques or cloth styles. It was this purpose which served to justify the continuation of their privileges. No, the pressure for reform was occasioned by a belief that new, competitive, flexible qualities were required for success in an economic world which now (in contrast to the Colbertian period) was believed to be capable of significant, if not infinite, expansion[11] combined with a growing realization that the corporative and regulative system, devised to achieve success in the seventeenth century in what was believed to be a stable trading world, tended to repress precisely these necessary qualities.

Criticisms of the system and of French entrepreneurship became more frequent as abuses became more pronounced and the awareness of both the new economic philosophy and England's competitive advantages

9. On this see the following works of J. R. Harris: *Industry and Technology in the Eighteenth Century: Britain and France*, pp. 1–22; 'Skills, coal and British industry in the eighteenth century', *History* 61 (1976), 167–82; 'Saint-Gobain and Ravenshead' in B. M. Ratcliffe (ed.), *Great Britain and her World, 1750–1914: Essays in Honour of W. O. Henderson*, especially pp. 45–56.

10. ADH C2159.

11. On infinite progress see J. Tucker, *Four Tracts*, p. 23: 'No Man pretend to set Bounds to the Progess that may yet be made both in Agriculture and Manufactures . . . is it not much more natural and reasonable to suppose that we are rather at the Beginning only, and just got within the Threshold, than that we are arrived at the *ne plus ultra* of useful Discoveries.' I owe this reference to Alice Shackleton.

became more widespread. Pierre Gout, a Carcassonnais clothier, for example, in two extraordinary memoirs which he composed in 1751 described in exact detail how the majority of his colleagues at Carcassonne were cheated at every stage of the manufacturing process because of their failure to direct personally their cloth-making activities. He believed, it is evident, that entrepreneurs in England and Holland behaved differently; 'cy tous y metoit le main', he wrote, 'comme en hollande et en angleterre. Nos draps seroit dans leur perfection et même il ny auroit pas tant davanies dans les Echellés du Levant'; 'louvrier ou artizant', he added, 'est plus sûr voyant le marchand riche et que Marchand ne met pas la main à loeuvre en laissant touttes chozes à son facteur ou Commis, pour lors lartizan songe à ce refaire sur le marchand . . . cy le marchand est volé il le mérite'; continuing his comparison with foreign competitors Gout stated that 'cy messieurs les hollandois ou anglois vendent plus les draps que nous ils sont actif, les premiers à chaque ouvrage et sapliquet de leur junesse à connoire les deffaux qui peut arriver au drap, et nos marchands, poudrés à blanc et le commis aussy comme le maître, et même il y a Beaucoup des marchands qui ne sont pas connoisseur'.[12] A report made by Natoire, inspector at Limoux and Chalabre, confirms most of Gout's points. The profession of clothier, Natoire maintained, was a complex one: 'Quelque mécanique que soit le métier de fabriquant, et quil paroisse que ceux qui L'entreprenent, nont pas besoin d'une grande supériorité de génie pour y réussir, il est cependant vrai, quil exige une infinité de dispositions, et de connoissances, de la part de celui qui si engage.' A knowledge of the qualities of all different types of wool was an absolute necessity for the clothier, Natoire continued:

Mais où les trouverons nous aujourd'huy ces fabriquans, entièrement pourveus de cette supériorité de lumières, sur une chose aussy importante à la perfection des fabriques; avoüons le de bonne foy, et à notre honte, ils sont très rare dans le siècle où nous vivons disons au contraire que pour trois ou quatre qu'on en voit dans une jurande, de ce caractère, on en distingue cent autres, qui seroint fâchés d'être dans ces favorables dispositions.

Vital for the formation of clothiers was the quality of the instruction given to and the application shown by apprentices but, Natoire continued, neither masters nor apprentices seemed conscious of this: he noted a 'négligence . . . dans tous les maîtres, pour instruire leurs Elèves, et le peu de soin de ceux cy à sempresser d'Etre instruits'. The conse-

---

12. ADH C2514, 'Traité sur la fabrique des londrins seconds de Carcassonne', 23 Nov. 1751.

quence for new clothiers of this lack of attention to their training was judged by Natoire to be disastrous:

je naurois jamais fini, si je détaillois ici, tout ce que je juge d'une conduite si peu sensé, on diroit à les voir agir, qu'ils ont honte de paroître cequils entreprenent de devenir un jour; nulle application à leur devoir, une extrême indifférance pour les premiers élémens de leur métier qu'ils regardent comme tout à fait inutile, et indigne de leurs soins; ils comptent folement que leur père, aient de fonds sufisans pour fournir à leur fabrique, ils en ont de reste avec ce secours, pour travailler aussi bien que les autres, il est cependant constament vrai, que ces vicieuses dispositions entraînent tôt ou tard leur ruine.[13]

Such reports had implications of revolutionary significance for the administration of industry: in contrast to those presented in earlier years in which the major remedy advocated for industrial problems had consisted in the tightening of règlementation and of the corporative system in order to favour the established entrepreneur in his attempts to ensure a high-quality production, these implicated the entrepreneur himself and caused the regulative and corporative system to be judged not so much from the point of view of their possibly positive effects on quality, but from their evidently deleterious effects on the extent of competition and thus on the efficiency of entrepreneurs. To accept these views, and to act on them, involved a complete reversal in policy for French administrators. As Michel de Montaran, intendant du commerce and member of the Bureau de Commerce, wrote to St-Priest in August 1753, when the policy to be adopted towards the restrictions operating in Languedoc's cloth-industry for the Levant was being discussed, 'ne s'agit il pas moins que de refondre toute la manutention de ce commerce'.[14]

It is in the late 1740s that the beginnings of a changed attitude towards economic policy are to be noted among members of the Bureau de Commerce. Orry's controller-generalship had been characterized, we have seen, by an expansion in the regulative and corporative systems which attained their maximal severity. His successor in 1745, however, Machault d'Arnouville, although no 'liberal', was more receptive to the new political economy and he showed this in no more important way than by his acceptance of the appointment of Vincent de Gournay as 'intendant du commerce' in 1751. As Turgot was later to write in his *Eloge de Vincent de Gournay*, 'son entrée au bureau de commerce parut être l'époque d'une révolution'. De Gournay, after a career in trade, had dedicated himself since 1748 to travel in the most advanced areas of the

13. ADH C2380, 'Mémoire sur les diverses qualitez des draps destinez pour les Echeles du Levant', 18 Nov. 1750.
14. ADH C5552, 22 Aug. 1753.

European economy – England and Holland above all – in order to verse himself in the new political economy, both in theory and practice. Once a member of the Bureau, the liberal ideas which he favoured gained rapidly in support. It was he who became the mentor and close friend of the influential Daniel Trudaine, 'intendant des finances' and director of the Bureau de Commerce.[15]

It would seem that de Gournay was already aware of the abuses which existed in Languedoc's cloth industry. Long before his appointment as intendant du commerce, returning from a tour in the Midi, he wrote, 'je reviens de ce pays très convaincu que les règlements ont repandu le découragement dans la fabrique ... et qu'ils ont arrêté les progrès qu'une grande concurrence, beaucoup de génie et d'emulation auraient immanquablement produits'.[16] 'Fixation' must have appeared to him as a prime abuse in France's increasingly corrupted and restrictive industrial system and this would explain why one of his first actions after his appointment was to examine the situation of Languedoc's Levant industry. This examination was most thorough, it is evident. On 13 August 1751 he told St-Priest, Languedoc's new intendant, that 'afin de prendre moy même des Instructions plus amples sur la fixation du commerce du Levant, Jay lu tout ce qui a été allégué en faveur de ce règlement'. The nature of his verdict on 'fixation' was hardly to be doubted: 'tout ce qui en a résulté dans mon esprit', he continued, 'est qu'il est absolument oposé à l'augmentation de notre Commerce & à la concurrence si nécessaire pour le faire fleurir, & pour empêcher les étrangers d'Introduire leurs draps dans le Levant à la faveur de la cherté des Nôtres'. De Gournay, it is evident, expected a rapid decision on this question: he informed St-Priest that 'cette affaire n'a point encore été mise sur le tapis au Bureau de Commerce' but that he believed that it would be 'après les vacances'.[17]

In fact it was not until the summer of 1753, it would seem, that de Gournay's influence had caused that necessary fermentation in the Bureau de Commerce for decisions of a liberal nature to be taken and de Gournay himself was absent from the final discussions for in July 1753 he had set out from Paris on the first of three general tours of French manufacturing centres which he undertook in order to 'y voir par lui-même l'état du commerce et des fabriques, et reconnaître les causes des progrès ou de la décadence de chaque branche de commerce, les abus, les besoins, les ressources en tout genre'.[18] Lower Languedoc formed part of

15. Turgot, *Eloge de Vincent de Gournay*, in P.-J. Vigreux (ed.), *Turgot*, pp. 141–57.
16. Cited by Levasseur, *Histoire des classes ouvrières*, II, 570.
17. ADH C5552.
18. *Turgot*, p. 158.

his itinerary and de Gournay's continued concern with the question of 'fixation' is revealed by the visits which he made to Clermont and Carcassonne. He reached Clermont in October. There he met, among others, Mathieu Pradier who, predictably, differed in his ideas from de Gournay. 'J'ay eu l'honneur de voir icy M. de Gournay', Pradier informed a secretary at the intendancy. 'Je n'ay point eu de la peine à comprendre que le fonds de toutes ses vues est la liberté sans bornes, et que son grand argument roulle sur la pleine liberté des fabriques donnée en angleterre quil prend pour modelle.' The consequences would be dire, Pradier predicted, 'sy les barrières de la fixasion qui ont relevé et soutiennent son canal le plus utille au peuble, qui sont nos manufactures, sont brisées par la liberté'.[19] From Clermont de Gournay proceeded to St-Chinian and Carcassonne and then, before he left the province (it would seem), he composed two remarkable memoirs which summarized most incisively and brilliantly the major abuses to which some sixty years of restrictions had given rise.[20] That on Clermont-de-Lodève's industry I quote at length:

En examinant les Statuts et Règlemens des Jurandes de Carcassonne, Clermont de Lodève, St-Chinian &c. on trouve que l'esprit de ces jurandes a été comme celui des marchands fabriquans de Lyon depuis 1702, d'éloigner les ouvriers de la maîtrise, de réduire le nombre des maîtres et la fabrique, afin de faire en sorte que l'acheteur fût obligé de venir chercher la marchandise et de recevoir la loy, au lieu que notre intérêt celui de l'Etat, est que le fabriquant aille au devant de l'acheteur, et que celui ci ayant toujours un grand choix sur la marchandise préfère celle qui lui plaît, lorsque le fabriquant est forcé par la concurrence à aller au devant de l'acheteur, il en résulte nécessairement deux grands biens, le premier une plus grande économie dans la façon de vivre du fabriquant et de tout commerçant, le second de l'émulation dans la fabrication afin d'obtenir la préférence en offrant meilleur marché à l'acheteur, mais comme ce n'est pas là le Compte du fabriquant, il a représenté l'Etat de concurrence, qui est gênant pour lui, comme un mal pour l'Etat, et a surpris la Religion du Conseil en persuadant que l'Etat de Soufrance où il se peignoit, et où il étoit peutêtre même réellement, étoit un mal pour l'Etat; de là est venu l'arrêt de 1725 qui empêche de recevoir de nouveaux maîtres, ou de recevoir des apprentis, arrêt qui se renouvelle toute les trois ans jusques à aujourdhui, de là la deffense de faire des commendites avec d'autres que des maîtres fabriquans, vice commun aux jurandes de Languedoc avec la fabrique de Lyon, et qui éloigne l'homme opulent de venir au secours de l'homme industrieux et d'allier l'industrie et l'argent; de là enfin le tableau et la fixation, qui en

19. ADH C2520, 21 Oct. 1753.
20. There are copies of these memoirs held in the departmental archives of the Aude and the Hérault (ADA 9 C 21 and ADH C5552). They are dated simply 1753 and are not signed by de Gournay. They are written in his hand, however, and given the ideas expressed, and the evidence of his visits to Clermont-de-Lodève and Carcassonne, could only have been composed by him. The emphasis given to a part of the report on Carcassonne is mine.

favorisant l'un et rejettant l'autre, est une source de division perpétuelle entre les privilégiés et ceux qui ne le sont pas, et fait que les hommes qui n'eut peut être jamais fait de drap pour le Levant, s'il lui eut été permis d'en faire, se dégoûte d'être exclus, et ne fait ni drap pour le Levant ni pour ailleurs.

J'ai cru qu'un fabriquant de Clermont de Lodève étoit un fabriquant de drap, mais jai apris sur les lieux quil n'étoit qu'un fabriquant de Londrins Seconds et que les autres qualités lui étoient interdites ... c'est un malheur pour nos fabriques, et pour nos fabriquans d'avoir si fort subdivisé les différents parties de leur profession, qu'on les a pour ainsi dire renfermé comme dans un étuy, et que leur bien être dépend absolument du sort qu'aura cette partie de leur profession à la quelle on les a fixé, par là on tient leur génie dans des bornes étroites, et on les empêche de tenter diverses branches de fabrication vers lesquelles ils pourroient se jetter, quand quelqu'une ne leur réussit pas.

De Gournay's memoir exposed clearly that incompatibility of interests between the clothier and the State mentioned in the introduction and summarized admirably the ill effects to which the administrative response to the former's demands had given rise at Clermont. A monopolistic guild and a narrow specialization on a particular type of cloth were preventing competition amongst clothiers and were causing a dangerous over-concentration on a single market. He added some details on the effects of the billet de congé system on the labour force. At Clermont weavers were comparing their conditions unfavourably with those of slaves and no new apprentices were presenting themselves, and at Carcassonne (he revealed in a second memoir) cloth-workers were embittered and impoverished: before 'fixation' (local priests had assured him) there were some weavers and other categories of cloth-worker who were comparatively prosperous, with possessions valued at up to 4,000 *livres*, with land which they cultivated themselves and with sufficient resources to eat meat every day, whereas now extreme poverty was universal. At Carcassonne de Gournay was also informed of the fact that the manufacture of *nims*, an intermediate quality between *londrins-seconds* and *londres-larges*, had been disallowed. In reacting to this information he expressed eloquently the essence of the new liberal philosophy:

La supression des draps Nims et la deffense d'en fabriquer paroîtra un jour fort extraordinaire aussi bien que la raison qu'on en donne, que cette qualité prenoit sur celle des Londrins seconds et des londres larges ... *nous ne saurions trop laisser varier les différentes qualités de nos draps, chacune est une arme et un moyen de plus que nous employons contre nos Rivaux; elles laissent d'ailleurs un Champ plus vaste au génie du fabriquant,* qui se jette sur une qualité, quand il ne trouve pas son compte à en fabriquer une autre et par ce moyen la fabrique ne chaume jamais.

The consequences of State intervention were without exception bad, therefore, according to de Gournay. The counterpart to this belief was a great optimism about the prospects of the industry if greater freedom were allowed. Thus in his memoir on Carcassonne's industry he stated that he did not doubt that this town 'ne puisse infiniment pousser son comerce et le varier, les fabriquans sont en Etat aujourdhuy de faire des entreprises et de les soutenir, ils ont acquis des grands Connoissances sur le commerce, que la liberté leur donnera des moyens d'étendre encore davantage'.

In fact the receipt of Gournay's devastating reports about the consequence of administrative intervention on Languedoc's industry for the Levant was not necessary to persuade the members of the Bureau de Commerce that 'fixation' should be abolished. This emerges from a letter of de Montaran, written before de Gournay's visit to Languedoc, notifying St-Priest that the matter was under discussion: 'M^{rs} les Députés et jusqu'à present M^{rs} les commissionaires du Bureau de Commerce', de Montaran informed Languedoc's intendant, 'penchent beaucoup pour la liberté indéfinie tant dans la fabrique que dans le commerce.'[21] The other members of the Bureau de Commerce were, it is clear, already converted to the liberal philosophy. St-Priest was in fact a solitary opponent to the abolition of 'fixation' and, new to his office, he had not sufficient experience or confidence to form a very powerful one.

A peinne initié dans ce qui regarde le comerce, nous recognaisons notre insufisance, et si nous élevons la voix, c'est bien moins dans l'espérance d'étaller une érudition que nous n'avons pas, que dans celle que l'aveu que nous en faisons nous mérittera quelque indulgence et qu'on voudra bien ne pas oublier, que forcé en quelque sortte par la place que nous avons l'honneur d'occupper, nous ne parlons, que par obéissance aux ordres supérieurs par lesquels il nous est prescrit de donner notre avis.[22]

This was hardly an opening to inspire much confidence, or indeed interest, in its readers, and St-Priest's advice was all the less likely to be acted upon in view of the fact that the Etats of Languedoc had sent a strong memoir to the Bureau in opposition to 'fixation'. (The timid St-Priest, alarmed to discover that the Etats were in favour of a policy so opposed to his own, wrote hurriedly to the syndic-général, de Montferrier, informing him that there was no man in the Kingdom less 'partisan de son avis que je le suis du mien'.)[23]

'Fixation,' and the industrial system which had had such significant effects on Clermont's cloth industry, were thus without strong advocates. In addition, in 1754 Machault d'Arnouville was replaced as controller-general by Moreau de Séchelles. This change had the consequence that

21. ADH C5552, 22 Aug. 1753.
22. ADH C5552, 'Minute d'un avis donné par Mr. de Saint-Priest sur la fabrication et le commerce des draps . . . adressé au conseil le 25 août 1752'.
23. ADH C5552, 21 May 1753.

the final decision instead of resting with a man 'médiocrement accessible aux nouveautés en matières industrielles' was now in the hands of someone 'qui les accueillait volontiers'.[24] Thus between 1754 and 1760 a series of reforms was made which prepared the industry for liberty. The first important edict was one of 27 August 1754: this permitted clothiers from Riols, a village near St-Pons, and from all other towns to send any variety of cloth they wanted to the Levant.[25] This measure was followed in October by one suppressing the edict of 1737 which had forbidden the reception of new masters at Clermont and St-Chinian. In February 1755 clothiers were granted the right to dye *londres* (the lowest-quality cloth exported) any colour they chose,[26] and in April 1756 the controller-general announced to St-Priest what was to be the most basic of all the reforms. The war having caused difficulties for shipping in the Mediterranean, the Bureau de Commerce had decided to allow the export of French cloth on foreign as well as national ships. The result of this permission was that the 'arrangements' amongst French merchants in the Levant for the controlled sale of cloth were made inoperable and that the 'fixation', originally devised to ensure a production in line with the controlled sales in the Levant, had to be abolished too. Thus clothiers were once again given the freedom to produce as much cloth as they wanted.[27] This measure stopped short of allowing all masters to produce for the Levant, but this concession was not to be long delayed: on 10 November 1756 a royal order announced the suppression of the tableau, allowing 'tous les Maîtres d'une Jurande, de Fabriquer les Draps et autres Etoffes qui leur sont permis par les Règlemens'.[28] The order was received in Clermont on 24 November and the town's consuls informed St-Priest by return that the new system, that of 'liberty', had been announced by the town crier 'par tous les coins & carrefours accoutumés'.[29]

These measures established liberty in the traditional areas which had produced for the Levant. Between 1756 and 1760 other Languedocian towns, too, were granted the right to participate in the trade which until then had been the guarded preserve of Carcassonne, Clermont and St-Chinian. First, in 1758 Bédarieux was granted the right to make *londres-larges*.[30] This privilege was then extended to Limoux, Saissac and Mas-

---

24. Levasseur, *Histoire des classes ouvrières*, II, 518.
25. ADH C2170, Edict of 27 Aug. 1754.
26. See Dutil, *Etat économique*, pp. 350–4, 380–2, on this measure and on all other aspects of the change of policy.
27. ADH C2089, De Séchelles to St-Priest, 3 April 1756.
28. ADH C2087, Ordonnance of 10 Nov. 1756.
29. ADH C2057, Note from consuls of Clermont, 24 Nov. 1756.
30. ADH C5539, St-Priest to Boullongue (controller-general), 18 Sept. 1758.

Cabardès,[31] and finally in 1759 and 1760 edicts were passed allowing all jurandes of Languedoc to make fine cloth. The Etats participated in this general process of liberalization by ceasing to pay bounties on cloth exported to the Levant in 1758 – this was a practice which (as we have seen) had originated in the 1660s.[32] By 1760 something approximating to the intentions of the Bureau de Commerce – 'liberté indéfinie' – had been established in Languedoc's industry for the Levant.

The members of the Bureau de Commerce expected favourable results from the new freedom. The trade had grown despite the abuses which de Gournay had described, so, clearly, without the restrictions its expansion should know no bounds. The system of 'fixation' was thought to have held back the industry: the controller-general commented that the extent to which 'fixation' had restrained competition was observable from 'le nombre des maîtres fabriquans qui demandoient à être inscrits sur le tableau et par l'empressement avec lequel ils tâchoient d'y parvenir'.[33] The reformers did, however, appreciate that there was *some* need to proceed slowly with the changes. De Gournay as early as 1751 had warned that it would be necessary to carry out the reforms with 'ménagement pour éviter L'Inconvénient de passer subitem' d'une extrémité à une autre',[34] and Trudaine too recorded that the policy of the Bureau de Commerce was to move gradually towards complete liberty, taking care to make reforms 'avec mesure et par degrés sans occasioner des révolutions trop subites'.[35] As has just been seen it took five or six years for the restrictions in Languedoc (apart from regulations) to be abolished. Reform was thus carried out with some 'measure' and 'by stages'. The restrictions in the industry had been so severe, however, that even this comparatively slow pace of reform was like the revolution which Trudaine was anxious to avoid.

If the reformers in Paris thought that the new freedom would cause an expansion in the trade, many clothiers, inspectors and local observers considered that it would cause its destruction. As early as October 1754, when the only concession which had been made was the permission for clothiers to send any varieties of cloth they wanted to the Levant, a merchant from Montpellier was writing pessimistically to St-Priest that if even before this new edict there had been abuses without number

31. ADH C2535, Faucher to St-Priest, Saissac, 23 June 1759.
32. Despite abandoning the bounty system the Etats continued to record production for the purpose of granting exemption on cochineal import duties (ADH C2216–2218, 2232–2234).
33. ADH C5553, De Moras to St-Priest, 12 Oct. 1756.
34. ADH C5552, Letter to St-Priest, 13 Aug. 1751.
35. ADH C5553, Note at the end of a memoir of Jean Pelletan fils, 1760.

'quest ce qu'il en sera aujourdhuy avec cette permission ... nous redevenions [redeviendrons] en Levant marchands de Bonnets'.[36]

Events were going to show the pessimists to be right, not because the principles of de Gournay were intrinsically unsound but because the many years of regulations and restrictions had created an abnormal situation in Languedoc, at Marseilles and in the Levant. In Languedoc the abnormalities consisted first in the enormous number of masters, and would-be masters, who wanted to produce for the Levant, and secondly in the state of mind of the province's clothiers: so long had they been regimented by regulation that they tended to react in most cases to any decrease in the rigour of the system by abuse of cloth standards. At Marseilles and in the Levant the 'abnormality' consisted in the fact that cloth-buyers and cloth-commissioners had grown accustomed to accepting the royal mark on the cloth as a guarantee of its quality (so long had this been the case) and thus had not developed skills in judging cloth qualities. In addition the reformers, partly through caution, had not reformed the entire regulative system: the inspectors remained in place (although reduced in number)[37] and continued to put a royal seal on the cloth although this seal no longer guaranteed quality and the regulations themselves remained officially in force although in practice they were increasingly ignored by clothiers and were no longer consistently enforced by the inspectors. The result of this was that cloth made under the new system, whatever its quality, carried the official seal guaranteeing it to be of the quality prescribed by the regulations.

All of these abnormalities can be observed at Clermont in the response of clothiers to the new situation. The mere visit of de Gournay to the town and rumours of movement towards *laissez-faire* were sufficient to cause disregard for regulation and disorders among the labour force. The gardes-jurés of the clothiers (who, admittedly, had an interest in painting a black picture of the consequences of the abandonment of 'fixation', a system from which they were benefiting so much) reported that on hearing the news of the possible end to 'fixation', 'Dans l'instant la subordination (si nécessaire) de l'ouvrier au fabriquand a été Rompüe et tous les Désordres qui sont une suitte Infaillible de celui là sont arrivé. Louvrier sollicité par le fabriquand, qui veut augmenter sa fabriquation est devenu Indocile, le fillage sest gâtté.' The gardes-jurés warned that if the mere suspicion of 'liberté' had caused such disorder, how much greater the danger if 'fixation' were actually abolished.[38]

The greatest perils lay in the ambitions of the clothiers, rather than in

36. ADH C2170, Vassal to St-Priest, 31 Oct. 1754.
37. Thus the inspections of Clermont and Lodève were reunited in 1755 (ADH C2502).
38. ADH C2499, Report of gardes-jurés, 23 May 1754.

the irregularities of the labour force, however, as events were to show. First, production was expanded at what can only be described as a hectic rate. In the space of a year, between 1755 and 1756, Languedoc's total production rose by slightly less than a third, from 66,630 pieces to 83,270, and Clermont's clothiers provided more than their share of this increase: the town's production rose from 9,400 pieces in 1755 to 12,662 in 1756. In order to make this extra cloth Clermont's clothiers made use of a large part of the labour force of the neighbouring cloth-making centre of Bédarieux: eighty of this town's looms were being employed by Clermontais in 1756.[39] If this increased production had been of good quality then the expansion could only have been regarded as positive but this was far from the case. The freedom to send cloth of any quality to the Levant, granted in 1754, was utilized by a few unscrupulous clothiers to pass off lower-quality cloth, dyed in the same colours as *londrins-seconds*, as *londrins-seconds*. Low-quality rather than Spanish wools were used by clothiers despite the regulations which still, officially, were meant to be followed. As early as 1755 Lodève's clothiers were complaining that their supplies, for making coarse *draps forts*, were being bought up by Clermontais.[40] The general standard of production declined rapidly. The inspector of the Etats of Languedoc, visiting Clermont in 1756, noted with alarm the decline in quality: 'la fabrique en Draps Londrins Seconds est toujours plus deffectueux, soit par la légèreté du Drap qui na pas assés de corps, soit par le trop grand aprêt qu'on luy donne pour Eviter qu'on n'y découvre bien d'autres deffauts', he reported, and he warned that the good clothier would be carried along with the bad for he was not getting a better price for his cloth, despite his use of more expensive raw materials, and was thus effectively 'la victime de l'autre'.[41] A pattern was establishing itself: the greatest profits were going to those who expanded their production and decreased their quality most rapidly because *londrins-seconds* from Clermont (which for so many years had been of an assured and constant quality and which still carried the seals of the inspectors) received a uniform though slowly declining price at Marseilles from undiscerning buyers.

This immediate expansion of production and decline in quality were the work of those clothiers who were already on the 'tableau de fixation'. As has been noted, free entry into the industry was not granted until

---

39. Morineau and Carrière, 'Draps de Languedoc', pp. 109–11; ADH C2231–2234; C2502, Tricou to St-Priest, 15 May 1756.
40. ADH C5512, 'Mémoire sur le dépérissement de la manufacture de Lodève causé par les enlèvements des laines que font les fabricants de londrins seconds à Clermont', 1755.
41. ADH C5596, Mémoire, 1756.

1756. The right to manufacture was, however, granted more readily after 1754 and during these years the number of clothiers at work at Clermont expanded rapidly from the figure of thirty-five in 1754, which was the last normal year of 'fixation', to forty-six in 1756.[42] More alarming was the large number of clothiers, or would-be clothiers, who were evidently preparing to make cloth as soon as the tableau was abolished. St-Priest warned of this. Before the abolition in 1756 he sent a list to the controller-general of all those who had requested to make *londrins-seconds* during the last year of the functioning of the controls: 'Je ne puis m'empêcher de vous Représenter que le nombre en est très considérable',[43] he noted, and effectively the lists included sixty-six names for Carcassonne and forty-two for Clermont (proportionately a larger figure than for Carcassonne).[44] Amongst the Clermontais wanting to manufacture were clothiers who had long ago left the trade, shearers and cloth-dressers anxious to improve their status and fortunes, ex-apprentices long prevented by the controls on mastership from producing cloth, an army captain, a notary, an avocat from the parlement of Toulouse and a 'secrétaire du roi' and member of the Cour des Comptes of Montpellier.[45] The truth of de Gournay's remark, that the fixation system had caused 'tel homme qui n'eut peut être jamais fait de drap pour le Levant, s'il l'eut été permis d'en faire' to be disgusted about his exclusion from production, is apparent. All sorts of explanations were sent to the intendant and controller-general by these clothiers in justification of their attempts to obtain permission to manufacture. The notary, Fulcrand Bruguière, for example, perhaps sensitive to the slight incongruity between the nature of his present profession and that to which he aspired, explained that 'le notariat est un parti que la Circonstance des deffenses de Recevoir de nouveaux maîtres l'obligea de prendre dans le tems, pour ne pas rester oisif'.[46] The restrictions on entry to mastership were relaxed before the abolition of the tableau and the vast influx of new masters to the profession which this change caused is recorded in the registers of the conseil de ville at Clermont. The figures for receptions of masters during these years are given in Table 18.[47]

42. ADH C2231, 2232, 2234.
43. ADH C5523, St-Priest to de Séchelles, 22 April 1756.
44. ADH C2089, 1756.
45. The captain, notary, advocate and secrétaire du roi were Jean Delpon, Fulcrand Bruguière, Vital Bernard Bouisson and Jean Bernard respectively.
46. ADH C2087, Request, 1758.
47. ACC BB4–5. Between August 1757 and December 1764 there is a gap in the registers of the conseil de ville. Figures, thus, are incomplete for these years though an approximate idea of the number of new masters can be obtained from lists of contents of the registers made before those for these years were lost (ACC BB9).

Table 18. *Receptions of masters, 1743–58*

1743	13	1751	2
1744	0	1752	3
1745	4	1753	3
1746	2	1754	13
1747	1	1755	22
1748	6	1756	0
1749	3	1757	0
1750	0	1758	c.8

Those received in 1753 and before were all sons or sons-in-law of cloth-iers (even this limited source of supply could give rise to a large number of new masters, as the figure for 1743 reveals). Those received in 1754 and 1755 were not in most cases sons of masters: their large number demonstrated forcibly the abnormal situation to which the years of 'fixation' had given rise. Amongst these new masters were the same categories of clothier or would-be clothier as described above; in addition, however, the inspector of manufactures, Jean-Baptiste Tricou, no doubt aware that the very fact that there was free entry to the trade was an ominous sign for the future of the inspectorate, had himself made master, and was excused the normal 400 *livres* mastership fee in consider-ation of his position.[48] The number of new masters threatened to swamp the new industry for, it is important to emphasize, the decision to take up cloth production was not made frivolously. Each new master paid the full fee for his mastership unless he had married the daughter of a clothier, and each one was prepared to invest his capital in the industry in the illusion of making a fortune to rival those of the clothiers who had prospered during the period of 'fixation'.

So rapid an increase in the number of clothiers,[49] and so great a temptation to decrease the quality of production, would have caused problems even in the most favourable trading conditions. In fact, of course, the new freedoms coincided with the outbreak of the Seven Years War, and this time, in contrast to the early 1690s, when French command of the sea contributed to the first great expansion of Languedoc's produc-tion for the Levant, it was the English fleet which dominated and which obstructed the export of French cloth. The war also contributed to a

48. ACC BB5, 2 April 1755.
49. ADH C2089, the number of clothiers allowed to produce in 1756 was fifty-eight at Clermont, 105 at Carcassonne and twenty-nine at St-Chinian (letter of de Moras to St-Priest, 18 May 1756).

general depression in the French economy which occasioned a decline in the demand for return products from the Levant,[50] and the result of these two factors was that Languedoc's over-extended industry found that its cloth was unsaleable. Only the credit which was provided by Marseilles's merchants prevented the crisis from being far worse than it was.[51] There were bankruptcies,[52] large-scale unemployment for all types of cloth-worker[53] and the number of clothiers producing had declined to thirty-three by 1759.[54] Report after report from Clermont and from the other clothing towns of Languedoc informed of the extent of the crisis. Tricou writing from Clermont in 1759 informed the intendant that the town's manufactures were 'dans un Etat de misère inexprimable' and that they would perish completely:

ainsi que tous les ouvriers qui n'ayant point du travail d'aucune Espèce sont à la faim et à la mendicité. Tout languit, tout est dans l'inaction; la plupart des fabriquants sont ruinés, et la plus grande partie de ceux qui restent sur pied, a cessé tout travail; ainsi je crois pouvoir assurer que jamais notre commerce des draps pour le Levant, n'a éprouvé une crise plus fâcheuse et plus malheureuse (grâces à M. De Gournay) que celle qu'il Eprouve actuellement ...[55]

50. ADH C2537, Tricou to St-Priest, 8 March 1759: the inspector wrote that English merchants were buying French cloth that had accumulated at Leghorn, and that 'Etant Maîtres de la mer Ils ne payent point d'assurances'. On the general depression throughout France see Crouzet, 'Angleterre et France', p. 264; on other textile regions affected like Languedoc see Labrousse, *Esquisse*, II, 320, 330, 546–50.
51. This is shown to be the case by Morineau and Carrière who, by comparing the figures for cloth production and exports, demonstrate that the Marseillais effectively kept the Languedocian industry in action during these years by anticipating a recovery of demand when peace was made, 'Draps de Languedoc', p. 105.
52. For instance those of the frères Rouquet and Pierre Rouaud, 1758–61 (Bobo, 'Communauté languedocienne', p. 58), of Raymond Ferlus, dyer, in 1758 (ADH 8 B 401), of Jean Rous (11 E 25 160, 10 May 1758), of Gabriel Verny (11 E 25 160, 6 June 1758), of Jean Estimbre, dyer (ADH 8 B 404), etc.
53. A report from Clermont made in 1758 listed by name 224 adults who were out of work with at least 249 children dependent on them (ADH C5600). On this see pp. 433–4.
54. ADH C2232.
55. ADH C2537, 8 March 1759.

II

The last thirty years, 1760–89, 'The Age of Iron': an explanation

Ce n'est plus l'âge d'or dans ce pais là mais l'âge de fer. (The gardes-jurés of Clermont's clothiers' corporation, memoir of 2 Dec. 1784, ADH C2592)

à la vérité le Corps de fabricands a bien changé de ce qu'il étoit . . . se n'étoit alors que peruqués; gens de Bon sens, tous les anciens sont morts, et il leur a succédé une troupe de Bandits; tous fils d'artisans ou douvriers de fabrique, il reste fort peu d'Enfands des anciens. (Pezet, 'juré-auneur' to Clermont's clothiers' corporation, letter of 25 Aug. 1782, ADH C5592)

The industrial crisis of the 1750s was far from the first in the long history of Languedoc's involvement with the Levant. It was, however, probably the most sudden and severe, and it was also distinct from others in that there was to be no proper recovery. There were to be short, speculative expansions in production in some years, and some recovery in cloth prices (as the figures presented in Tables 19–22 demonstrate), but the total value of Clermont's production only rarely attained the levels achieved in the good years of the first half of the century (when fewer clothiers were producing) and the trade was never again to be the source of great fortunes. On the contrary it was to cause the ruin of many of those who continued to produce, and Clermont's clothiers acquired a fame in the years leading up to the Revolution not for their wealth but for their insolvency. They were known as 'les banqueroutiers' and the memory of their humiliations is retained to this day.[1]

The town, the extent of whose dependence on the cloth industry we have emphasized in a previous chapter, suffered greatly from the industrial decline. The annual pleas to the Estates of Languedoc which the consuls made in order to obtain a reduction in the town's tax burden provide a sharp contrast with the descriptions of exceptional wealth made in the first half of the century: 'cette Communauté gémit depuis trop longtemps sur le poids de la plus grande Misère, que bien loin de sadoucir alloit chaque jour en augmentant, que la ville était réduitte à une

---

1. I owe this information to Gaston Combarnous, local Clermontais erudite.

Table 19. *Languedoc's production for the Levant, 1755–89 (in ½-pieces)*

1755	66,630	1767	94,530	1779	75,135
1756	83,270	1768	95,080	1780	86,690
1757	79,410	1769	87,860	1781	91,337
1758	71,610	1770	68,720	1782	98,696
1759	71,150	1771	77,600	1783	72,763
1760	79,790	1772	89,680	1784	52,887
1761	84,000	1773	97,680	1785	54,858
1762	92,000	1774	96,260	1786	55,774
1763	115,200	1775	102,120	1787	57,160
1764	106,000	1776	106,840	1788	62,226
1765	85,690	1777	100,140	1789	63,430
1766	80,530	1778	77,364		

Sources: 1755–88: Bureau de marque of Montpellier, 1789: Etats (Morineau and Carrière, 'Draps du Languedoc', pp. 110–11).

Table 20. *Clermont's industry 1755–89: production in ½-pieces (a) and number of clothiers (b)*

	(a)	(b)		(a)	(b)
1755	9,400	36	1773	11,280	20
1756	12,662	36	1774	9,700	20
1757	11,348	46	1775	10,290	20
1758	7,090	45	1776	13,050	20
1759	6,937	33	1777	11,900	22
1760	7,335	36	1778	5,320	12
1761	8,514	35	1779	4,750	8
1762	9,203	36	1780	11,040	13
1763	19,705	43	1781	15,850	25
1764	13,420	47	1782	8,930	24
1765	21,070	45	1783	8,740	21
1766	6,640	24	1784	5,840	12
1767	10,030	28	1785	7,320	11
1768	13,420	33	1786	8,980	14
1769	11,330	30	1787	11,570	14
1770	10,040	26	1788	12,510	16
1771	10,020	15	1789	10,390	17
1772	10,750	19			

Sources: For years 1755–63 I have used here figures recorded by Roland de la Platière (ADH C2213 'Réflexions' on Clermont, 10 Sept 1764); the other figures are those recorded by the Etats (C2232–4, 2216–18).

Table 21. *Approximate prices of Clermont's 'londrins-seconds',
1683–1784 (per 'aune', in 'livres', 'sous', and 'deniers')*

1683	7/8/0 ·	1758	6/6/0–7/4/0
1694	8/19/6	1759	6/0/0–6/15/0
1716	8/10/0	1760	6/1/0–6/15/0
1718	9/0/0–9/10/0	1761	6/6/0–6/16/6
1720	9/0/0–17/0/0	1762	6/15/0
1722	12/12/6–12/15/0	1764	4/14/0–5/17/0
1723	12/15/0–13/10/0	1765	4/10/0–5/12/0
1724	10/10/0–12/10/0	1766	7/5/0
1725	7/10/0–7/15/0	1767	7/0/0
1726	7/5/0–10/4/0	1768	5/4/0
1727	9/0/0–9/15/0	1769	6/5/0
1728	9/5/0	1770	5/15/0–6/10/0
1729	8/5/0–10/5/0	1771	5/15/0–6/0/0
1731	9/5/0	1772	5/15/0–6/0/0
1732	7/15/0–9/5/0	1773	6/0/0
1733	8/15/0–8/17/6	1774	5/7/0–6/16/0
1734	8/2/0	1777	5/5/0
1744	8/10/0–9/10/0	1778	5/15/0
1746	8/5/0	1779	5/10/0
1749	8/0/0	1780	5/2/6–5/4/0
1750	8/14/0–8/19/0	1781	3/4/0–3/5/0
1752	8/14/0–8/16/6	1784	4/19/0–7/0/0
1757	6/19/0		

Sources: 1683: Masson, *Levant au XVIIe siècle*, p. 191; 1694: ADH C2200, Cauvière's report; 1716–81: inspectors' reports; 1784: ACCM Fonds Roux, LIX, 281–4. N.B.: for years in which a variety of prices are recorded maximum and minimum prices have been calculated. The list is composed of 'cash' prices. It was customary to sell on credit, 6% per annum generally being paid on outstanding amounts. Prices until the mid-century would often be given as follows: 9 *livres* payable in twelve months. In this case the 'cash' price would be in the region of 8 *livres* 10 *sous*. After 1756 pricing becomes more complex. Prices were falling but this was disguised by referring to the lower price as a discount or 'escompte' and the practice of granting credit facilities continued. Thus a price might be given as follows: 9 *livres*, escompte 30%, payable in 12 months. In this case the cash price would be calculated as follows: 70% of 9 *livres*–6%, i.e. about 5 *livres* 18 *sous*. On prices see Morineau and Carrière, 'Draps de Languedoc', pp. 120–1. The correspondence of clothiers with Roux frères of Marseilles provides a far more sensitive register of price variations. I have not used this correspondence as the prices are probably not representative of the town's industry as a whole (whereas inspectors' figures are). Roux frères, described by one correspondent as 'des négociants délicats', would seem to have traded with the better clothiers, and in particular with Flottes Raissac.

Table 22. *Approximate value of Clermont's productions 1716–84*
(in 'livres')

1716	491,895	1759	624,330–702,371
1718	625,590–660,345	1760	665,651–742,669
1720	496,800–887,400	1761	804,573–868,428
1722	613,575–619,650	1762	931,804
1723	813,769–861,638	1764	946,110–1,117,605
1724	554,400–660,000	1765	1,422,225–1,769,880
1725	461,250–476,625	1766	722,100
1726	445,875–627,300	1767	1,053,150
1727	739,800–801,450	1768	1,046,760
1728	638,250	1769	1,062,188
1729	476,685–592,245	1770	865,950–978,000
1731	696,525	1771	864,225–901,800
1732	637,050–760,350	1772	927,188–968,040
1733	842,625–854,663	1773	1,015,200
1734	755,730	1774	923,925–989,400
1744	651,525–728,175	1777	937,125
1746	924,413	1778	458,850
1749	885,600	1779	391,875
1750	967,005–994,793	1780	848,700–861,120
1752	1,003,545–1,017,964	1781	760,800–772,688
1757	1,183,029	1784	433,620–613,200
1758	670,005–765,720		

Method: The calculation is quite simple: maximal/minimal prices per *aune* × 15 (a ½-piece of cloth was 15 *aunes* in length) × production recorded for relevant years.

situation qui neut jamais de Semblable', it was pleaded in 1770; 'il nest point de Communautté qui aÿt autant souffert que la nôtre'; 'Ha! quelle communautté fut jamais aussi tristement célèbre que la nôtre? toute la province retentit du Bruit de ses malheurs depuis dix ans que son enceinte est investie d'un déluge de Maux', the petitions read in 1773 and 1780.[2] So the 1750s represented a definite turning-point in the industry's fortunes. Michel Morineau and Charles Carrière are the first historians to have appreciated this. 'Les choses sont plus profondes: elles ont duré', they write, 'le marasme s'installe d'une manière grave et prolongée dans la draperie languedocienne.'[3]

The cause of the turning-point has been the subject of debate ever since it occurred. As early as 1758 St-Priest was attempting to explain the crisis but admitting his difficulty in penetrating a question which was

2. ACC BB7, 25 Nov. 1770, 4 April 1773, 11 May 1780.
3. 'Draps de Languedoc', pp. 119, 121.

'soumis à la variété d'une infinité de circonstances'.[4] However one factor had evidently impressed St-Priest, as it had done many other contemporaries, and that was that the crisis had immediately followed the lifting of restrictions on production. It was but a short step from noting this coincidence to casting the liberal reforms as the principal cause of the decline and this, indeed, was the conclusion which St-Priest had evidently reached by the 1760s. De Gournay's influence, he affirmed in a letter of 29 August 1765 to de Montaran, was 'la cause première du désordre qui s'est glissé dans la fabrique'.[5] Similarly, in a large memoir which he drew up on the Levant trade in 1779, he recorded his opinion that 'depuis que le désordre a été introduit dans les fabriques par le sistème de liberté, on s'est jetté sur les laines les plus grossières ... et au lieu de draps, on n'a fait que des flanelles'.[6] Inspectors, clothiers, merchants and even members of the labour force, if they were not all as convinced as St-Priest that the crisis had been precipitated by the abolition of restrictions, came to believe, at least, that the type of administrative framework within which the industry functioned was a particularly crucial variable which undoubtedly affected its prosperity. The abuses of the 'fixation' period gradually, it would seem, faded from people's memories and in years of crisis in the industry all that was remembered was that the quota system had brought prosperity and stability to the town. Clermont's clothiers, in a pathetic memoir submitted to the Estates in 1770 for example, requested a return to 'cette heureuse fixation qui fit pendant quinze ans leur fortune'.[7] Equally, though, in years in which the demand for cloth was in expansion clothiers tended to attribute the problems of the industry to those elements of the interventionist system which had survived and which still served to inhibit (they argued) their entrepreneurship: the (out-dated) regulations, inspectors, the corporative system and Marseilles's commercial monopoly for trading with the Levant. Thus a total of twenty-one clothiers addressed a memoir to Trudaine on 5 September 1764 opposing the continuation of the inspectoral system and the practice of marking cloth and declared that 'la vraie liberté consiste à vendre un drap relativement à sa qualité, et à ne pas les confondre toutes par un plomb quy m'est le mauvais à niveau du Bon'.[8] Likewise, Clermont's corporation responded enthusiastically to Turgot's reforms in 1776. 'Permetez nous', the gardes-jurés wrote to him, 'dans ces jours heureux consacrés à la Restauration du

4. ADH C5553, Letter of 17 May 1758.
5. ADH C5554, 29 Aug. 1765.
6. ADH C2223.
7. ADH C2187, 24 Dec. 1770.
8. AN F12 557.

commerce de vous exprimer notre joye sur l'Edit portant suppression de jurandes, maîtrises et règlements que la bonté et la sagesse du Roy vient de donner à son peuple'.[9]

Percipient observers noted that the opinions on regulation of those involved in the trade varied in accordance with the nature of their economic interests and fluctuated, too, according to the market situation. Thus St-Priest was warned in a memoir written in April 1765 that:

Les fabriquants se diviseront dans leurs représentations: ceux qui auront le plus soutenu la qualité de leurs draps s'écrieront contre le mauvais prix de Marseille, contre l'abondance demanderont des gênes & peut être la fixation sans en connoître les suites, ceux dont la fortune et Lambition leur faira voir dans la liberté un employ plus utile de leurs fonds, demanderont d'être libres . . . il arrivera enfin de tous ces différents avis qui ne seront autre chose qu'une discussion d'intérêts.[10]

This warning was not heeded. The belief that the crisis in the trade was largely attributable to the change in industrial policy, and that the solution to the problems would come from the concoction of some new system, was not easily shaken and as a consequence there occurred that continuous variation in industrial policy which was referred to in the introduction to this book. The intendant, inspectors, clothiers and merchants compiled, laboriously, innumerable memoirs in which the industry's crises were diagnosed, and administrative remedies put forward, and each succeeding intendant des finances or controller-general attempted to apply his own formula for industrial regeneration. Trudaine's principles, for example, had consisted in a virtually complete 'liberté' but (he insisted) with 'point d'abus';[11] L'Averdy's policy was a 'juste milieu' between regulation and liberty;[12] Turgot favoured a complete abandonment of all controls and Necker a reversion to a 'système intermédiare', between liberty and regulation.[13] The result of the continual variations in policy was confusion and uncertainty, not recovery. St-Priest's son, who had worked with his father as intendant-adjoint since 1764,[14] complained in 1783 of the repeated changes in policy which confused inspectors, clothiers and cloth-buyers alike. 'Depuis longtemps', he recorded, 'l'administration ne fait que varier sans cesse de principes et de marche, sans rien conclure.'[15] After some thirty years of

9. AN F12 842, 18 May 1776
10. ADH C2178, Composed by one Gallinier.
11. ADH C2212, Le Blanc to St-Priest, 24 Aug. 1764.
12. ADH C5554, L'Averdy to St-Priest, 8 Sept. 1765.
13. Dutil, *Etat économique*, pp. 316–17.
14. V. Gruder, *The Royal Provincial Intendants*, p. 87.
15. Cited by Dutil, *Etat économique*, p. 372.

experimentation it was becoming apparent that more was involved in Languedoc's industrial crisis than a simple question of too much or too little regulation.

It is perhaps the evidence for the failure of these various administrative attempts to revive the industry's fortunes which has caused the majority of historians to discount the view that administrative intervention was responsible for the crisis. If none of the interventionist formulas concocted was capable of solving the crisis, the assumption would seem to be, then the nature of the administrative framework could not have been the crucial, causal factor. In fact Paul Masson, writing in 1911, has been the only historian to follow contemporaries in attributing importance to the consequences of state intervention. The abuse of regulations, and the decline in the quality of production which followed liberalization, demonstrated, he argued, that Languedoc's clothiers had not been ready to take proper advantage of the liberty which they were granted in the 1750s. The long years of regulation had so conditioned their behaviour, and restricted their enterprise, that the freedom gave rise not to new initiatives but purely to the abuse of the regulations which had so long restrained them.[16] Léon Dutil, on the other hand, although his book was published in the same year as Masson's, interpreted the crisis largely in terms of the demand situation in the Levant. In contrast to the stable and prosperous conditions which had prevailed in the Levant during the first half of the century, he argued, the post-1756 period was characterized by crises and warfare. What is more, the supplying of the Levant market was more actively competed for than it had been during the first half of the century. Not only were all French cloth-making centres now entitled to produce for the Levant, with the result that the traditional suppliers had to face competition from a large number of other (largely Languedocian) cloth-making centres, but also foreign competition in the Levant had revived. The English had again become a force to be reckoned with. They had always retained a hold over the very top sections of the market for luxury broad-cloths but now intervened successfully, in competition with Languedoc's *londrins*, with a lower-quality product, shalloons, made in Yorkshire rather than in the West Country. In addition areas of Germany and the Habsburg empire began to produce for the Levant for the first time with some success. The Dutch-style cloth-making techniques had been introduced there by methods very similar to those used for their introduction to Languedoc in the seventeenth century and significant success was achieved with a cloth called *leipziks*. Thus

16. *Levant au XVIIIe siècle*, p. 489.

Languedoc was over-producing for a market which had lost all capacity to expand and which was being more actively competed for by other cloth-producing centres. As Dutil concluded, the two elements in the problem were 'D'un côté un marché limité, de l'autre une fabrique qui produit de plus en plus'. The only one of the contemporary arguments attributing the crisis to interventionism to which Dutil gave credence was that concerning the supposed heavy cost to Languedoc of Marseilles's commercial monopoly of the Levant trade. The cost of sending cloth to the Levant via Marseilles (in terms of commissions, fees and transport) was indeed large, he calculated.[17]

In recent years historians have widened the scope of the debate. Paris and Rambert, in their respective volumes of the history of Marseilles's commerce, have provided further evidence of the declining demand for cloth in the Levant, of the revival of foreign competition and of the decline in quality of Languedocian production. They also, however, relate Languedoc's and Marseilles's trade with the Levant to the general pattern of economic development in Europe, and with the benefit of this wider perspective demonstrate how the growing trade with North America and the West Indies was prejudicing the future of the trade with the Levant. Languedoc's cloth sold well only if the demand for return products from the Levant was high in France and many of these return products (largely raw materials and luxury items) were being obtained more cheaply in the New World by the second half of the eighteenth century. In view of this Languedoc and Marseilles were more fellow-sufferers than antagonists and Rambert strongly disputes the traditional idea of a conflict of interest between merchant town and manufacturing province. Clothier and merchant co-operated, the former being dependent on the latter for advances on his cloth as soon as it was made, Rambert points out, and concluding on the accusations against Marseilles he writes that he does not gain the impression that the clothiers were the victims of merchants but that on the contrary a healthy competition appeared to exist for the purchase of Languedoc's cloth.[18]

Louis Dermigny also addressed himself to the general problem of the decline in Languedoc's trade. In his chapter in the *Histoire du Languedoc* edited by Philippe Wolff he attributed the crisis to the same factors as Dutil: the Russo-Turkish war which disturbed the Levantine market, the

17. *Etat économique*, pp. 376–8, 399–400. On Austrian competition see Freudenberger, 'Brno Fine-Cloth Factory', pp. 123, 158, 244, 278–9. Shalloons were worsteds of a medium quality which competed successfully with *londres-larges*, *londres* and lower-quality *londrins-seconds*. *Leipziks* were of the finest quality and competed with Languedocian *mahous* and *londrins-premiers*.
18. Paris, *Commerce de Marseille*, v, 549–64; Rambert, *Commerce de Marseille*, vii, 308–9.

decline in the quality of production and the increase in foreign competition. But in an earlier article on the relationship between the ports of Sète and Marseilles he had hinted at the possible long-term consequences of the collapse of the efforts of Languedocian financiers in the 1670s and 1680s to develop a direct trade via Sète to the Levant in competition with Marseilles. The result of this failure was that Languedoc's exporters to the Levant found themselves dependent on a comparatively distant commercial centre, and the danger of this was that the relationship was one of choice for Marseillais merchants (it could be abandoned should the export of cloth no longer prove profitable), but of obligation for Languedocians. This failure of the province (and it serves to emphasize the artificiality of regarding the province as in any way a separate entity economically) to ensure the security of its economy was mentioned again by Dermigny in his chapter in Wolff's history: 'l'économie languedocienne', he wrote, 'est pour une part commandée, sinon commanditée, de l'extérieur. Comme si la province était incapable de trouver à suffisance en elle-même les voies et les moyens de son développement.'[19] Michel Morineau makes exactly the same point in a review of the seventh volume of Rambert's *Histoire du commerce de Marseille*. Marseilles's commitment to Languedoc's cloth production lasted as long as the market situation was favourable for the sale of cloth in the Levant, he explains, and 'A n'importe quel moment, le capital marchand conservait la faculté, la liberté de retirer sa mise: il n'était pas concerné par le maintien d'une production industrielle qui l'aurait immobilisé.' Thus when profits in cloth sales declined in the seond half of the century Marseilles's merchants changed the nature of their investments, returning in some years to their former practice of exporting coinage (and particularly a new Austrian coin, the 'thaler') in preference to cloth. Increasingly neglected by Marseilles's merchants Languedoc's clothiers were helpless, Morineau argues. But he adds that there was nothing unusual in their fate. It was in the nature of the capitalism of this period that industrialists were totally dependent on merchants: 'Il s'agit d'une situation qui correspond à un état précis du capitalisme, dans lequel l'industrie reste subordonnée au négoce et ne constitue pas, en elle-même, un facteur puissant, suffisant d'accumulation des bénéfices, du capital.'[20]

The most recent contributions to the debate have come from Charles Carrière. It is he, we have seen, who, in collaboration with Morineau, has

19. 'Armement languedocien', pp. 254–61, 57–8, *Histoire du Languedoc*, pp. 359, 406.
20. 'Marseille et Europe', *R.H.E.S.* 56 (1968), 105–6; on the revival in the trade in bullion in the last years of the Ancien Régime see F. Rébuffat and M. Courdurié, *Marseille et le négoce monétaire international* (*1785–90*).

identified the turning-point in the fortunes of the trade and in his large work on Marseilles's merchants he has offered his interpretation for the crisis. His view is in conformity with his explanation for the original expansion of Languedoc's industry. The importance of administrative decisions he denies – 'ce qui est majeur se trouve à côté et en dehors des mesures administratives', he argues – and like Dutil, Rambert, Paris and Morineau he sees the demand factor as fundamental. The Languedocian clothier is thus cleared of all blame: 'L'explanation n'est pas dans le Languedoc, qui subit, qui est victime: la baisse de la qualité, tant incriminée, est plus une conséquence qu'une cause'; Marseilles, too, is exculpated: 'Pas davantage à Marseille qui a tout à perdre dans un fléchissement de ces exportations, longtemps soutien majeur de sa prospérité'; the crisis is Levantine: 'Elle est dans les Echelles: la crise est levantine.'[21]

There is thus a certain amount of common ground amongst historians who have written about the crisis and if there is an orthodoxy about the nature of its causes it is approximately as follows. The crisis was not a consequence of administrative changes, nor a consequence of a conflict of interests between Marseilles and Languedoc, nor a consequence (as contemporaries would have argued) of 'infidélité' on the part of the clothiers in the wools they used and their general production standards, rather it was reflection of problems in the Ottoman Empire which caused a decline in demand for cloth and caused Marseilles's merchants to change the direction of their speculations.

That there was a crisis in the Levant, and that the pressure of foreign competition intensified problems for Languedoc, there can be no doubt. This, and its relevance to the mis-sale of Languedoc's cloth, will not be disputed. The crisis is moreover fully documented by Svoronos in one of the few local studies made on a Levantine market.[22] What does perhaps need some qualification is the categoric rejection of the idea that the nature of the Marseilles/Languedoc link, the actions of clothiers themselves or the abuses of the regulative and guild systems were in any way to blame. In their anxiety to avoid reliance on the sorts of arguments put forward by contemporaries for the crisis, historians have gone to an opposite extreme, disregarding the supply situation altogether. Even if one were to debate the question purely in the terms chosen by holders of the new orthodoxy, however, it would seem that some importance needs to be attributed to the effects of administrative intervention. One example of this is the question of the controversial Languedoc/Marseilles

---

21. *Les négociants marseillais*, I, 329, 406. For Carrière's interpretation of original success in the Levant see pp. 233–5.
22. *Commerce de Salonique au XVIII* siècle.

link. Clearly Dermigny and others are correct in arguing that there was
nothing unusual in there having been a division of labour between the
province and the port, the former producing and the latter exporting
cloth. It was just such a relationship that existed between England's West
Country industry and the Blackwell-Hall factors in London. (There was
a similar tendency, too, for West Country clothiers to attribute any
difficulties which they might be suffering to the activities of London cloth
factors.)[23] Morineau refers too to the dependency of Hondschoote's
industry in the sixteenth century on Antwerp and of Leyden's in the
seventeenth on Amsterdam. Evidently too (and this is a matter which we
have discussed earlier in this work) the nature of the merchant's role gave
him far greater freedom in his choice of investment than the clothier who
was tied by his larger fixed capital investment, his employment of a very
large labour force, the slowness of the production process which had the
consequence that any decision about the quantity of cloth to be produced
could only be implemented gradually, and the technical difficulty of
switching from one type of production to another. But granted these, as it
were, universal characteristics in the relationship between cloth-making
areas and merchant centres it would still seem that there were particularly
disadvantageous features for Languedoc in the Marseilles link. Firstly it
should be emphasized that, although merchants behaved in a similar way
in all merchant centres, and although there was considerable conformity
in the nature of all merchant/clothier relationships, a cloth industry was
likely to secure considerable advantages from being dependent on a local,
rather than a distant, merchant centre. Yorkshire's industry certainly
gained from the proximity of Leeds and from the presence there of a
group of merchants with no other interest than the sale of cloth, and R. G.
Wilson has argued that it was this, the different way in which the West
Riding trade was handled from that of any other cloth-producing area in
England, which accounted 'in good measure for Yorkshire's growing
supremacy in the 18th century'.[24] Carcassonne's and Clermont's clothiers thus lost their equivalent of Leeds when Montpellier ceased to take
part in the Levant trade. Secondly, if the point is accepted that *any* cloth
industry was exposed to the lack of commitment of merchant investors,
then it is clear that Languedoc's clothiers suffered from this but suffered
more acutely because of the administrative policy which had caused them
to concentrate uniquely on particular markets, and which had also
obliged them to make use of a single port. These types of factors need to
be considered in conjunction with the others which affected demand and

---

23. Davis, *Aleppo*, pp. 58, 115.
24. 'The supremacy of the Yorkshire cloth industry' in Harte and Ponting, *Textile History*,
    pp. 241–5.

we would argue too that the rejection of any consideration of the supply side, of a Languedocian role in the crisis, is unwarranted and is occasioned by a misconception of the characteristics of Languedoc's industry. Morineau's assumption that all 'pre-industrial' industrial centres were, in the nature of things, totally dependent on commercial centres seems extreme. His grounds for making this statement are his belief that industrial producers, at this stage in the development of capitalism, lacked capital resources. This, though, as we have seen, was far from having been the case in an industry such as Languedoc's which was dominated in the mid-century by exceptionally rich merchant-manufacturers. Additional factors, therefore, need to be brought into consideration in order to answer the question which Morineau himself poses (and believes that he has explained): 'cette curieuse impuissance du Languedoc à prendre son destin en mains, à s'émanciper, à assurer de manière autonome l'avenir de sa draperie'.[25] And the question is all the more complex in that this statement needs qualifying. It was not the case that the entire Languedocian cloth industry failed in the second half of the century. The industries of those towns which had prospered in the first half of the century decayed but several other cloth-making centres, such as Castres and Mazamet, far from declining, expanded rapidly on the basis of satisfying the rising demand for cloth in the New World. Indeed even the Levant market could provide a basis for industrial expansion. This is demonstrated by the experiences of Bédarieux: while the old producers for the Levant were bankrupting themselves the clothiers of this town, allowed to export to the Levant for the first time in 1758, were building up fortunes as impressive as those amassed at Clermont during the first half of the century. Formerly a mere tributary to the activities of Clermont's clothiers, by the Revolution Bédarieux's industry dwarfed that of its near neighbour, and when the Wars of the French Revolution interrupted the French trade with the Levant it adapted to producing for the domestic and Italian markets, competing successfully with Elbeuf and Sedan in the production of the finest-quality broad-cloths.[26]

It would seem, therefore, to be inaccurate to absolve the clothiers of towns like Clermont of all blame for the decay of their industries and that the view that all is explained by the demand situation is untenable given the fact that a uniform market situation gave rise to varied responses in different textile centres. We would emphasize again then the centrality of the clothier, the entrepreneur, in textile production in the pre-industrial period. In an epoch in which industries operated without significant fixed

25. 'Marseille et Europe', p. 105.
26. On Bédarieux and Mazamet see Wolff (ed.), *Histoire du Languedoc*, p. 406. See also pp. 426, 433, 449.

Table 23. *Summary of the fate of cloth-making concerns producing in Clermont in 1754, arranged approximately according to wealth (clothiers' successors' names in brackets)*

	Still producing in Clermont, 1789	Retired to become 'rentier'	Moved to superior profession	Ruined or moved to inferior profession	Ceased production but fate unknown
Antoine Berthomieu		1758			
Jean-Pierre Desalasc		1758			
Antoine Martin		1761			
Pierre Martin		1757			
Jacques Martin			1757		
Jean Martin			1757		
Jacques Martin (oncle)		1754?			
Jean and Gabriel Pelletan			1769		
Jean Pelletan (fils)		1765			
Veuve Jean Bernard		1764			
Guillaume Liquier		1758			
Pierre and Denis Flottes (père et fils)		1764	1773		
Pierre Flottes (jeune)		1773			
Denis Flottes (oncle) (Jean Antoine)		1788			
Jean Antoine Flottes		1788			
Jean Flottes (aîné) (François)				1778	
Mathieu Flottes				1778	
Jean Flottes (fils)				1775	
Thomas Verny (Jean)					1766
Gabriel Verny				1758	
François Verny		1789	1757		
Pierre Vernazobres				1758	
Estienne Desalasc	1789				

Pierre Gayraud (Jean-Pierre-Denis)	1789		
Laurens Bouisson (Jean, then Laurens)	1789		
Arnaud Lugagne (Estienne)			1770
Mathieu Bonneville (et fils)		1769	
Bernard Bonneville (Jean and Jacques Bernard)	1789		
Antoine Viala (veuve et fils Antoine)			1769
Antoine Tudesq		1757	
Jean Astruc		1769	
Joseph Vieules		1758	
Pierre Delpon		1758	
Pierre Jalmes		1758	
Estienne Lugagne (Estienne and Jean-Baptiste)			1764
Pierre Jean Villet		1764	

capital, without machinery and with dispersed labour forces, it was the clothiers who acted as linchpins to the whole productive system: it was they who co-ordinated the process of manufacture, it was their capital which financed the industry, it was their experience and skills which ensured production of a good quality and it was on their business contacts and correspondents that the industry depended for its orders. That Vincent de Gournay was aware of this is evident. His grounds for confidence in the fortune of Languedoc's industry lay in his belief that 'les fabriquants sont en Etat aujourdhuy de faire des entreprises et de les soutenir'.[27] *A priori*, given this centrality of the entrepreneur, we would argue that the failure of Clermont's industry in the second half of the century was a consequence of entrepreneurial weaknesses. In order to establish whether this prediction is correct we shall plot the experiences of the majority of those clothiers whom de Gournay met when he visited Clermont in 1753 and whose qualities provided the grounds for his optimism.

As can be seen from the list presented above (Table 23), only four of the thirty-six cloth-making concerns which had been in existence at the time of de Gournay's visit were still producing cloth by the 1780s. A closer scrutiny of the list reveals that richer clothiers (near the top of the list) had largely retired to live off *rentes* or the proceeds of offices, whereas the majority of poorer members of the profession had been either ruined or forced to abandon production, their sons in several cases changing profession. We shall follow in detail the activities of a selection of these clothier or ex-clothier families during these years and our survey will contribute, I hope, to explaining the fate of the industry in the town.

Why this sudden desertion of the industry? The answer, I think, is fairly self-evident. It is provided for us anyway by the first clothier whose actions we shall follow – Mathieu Pradier. Pradier was not actually making cloth in 1754, but in 1756, with the trade in rapid expansion, he had been planning to resume control over his concern, it would seem, for early in 1756 he had requested that he and his daughter should be included on the tableau for 60 *ballots* of cloth.[28] The abolition of 'fixation' in April 1756 caused Pradier to change his mind quite abruptly. He decided to sell his manufacture, informing St-Priest that 'il ne ma jamais convenu dentrer dans la fabrique, et de me trouver confondu avec tant de nouvelles spèces dhommes, et il me convient aujourdhuy moins que

27. ADH C5552.
28. ADH C2087, Request reported on to St-Priest in a letter from de Montaran, 3 March 1756.

jamais'.[29] The identity of those to whom he was referring emerges in another letter: 'il se trouve 51 fabriquands sur le tableau de cette jurande et 40 Maîtres Reçeus depuis Larrest qui la permis, joignés à cella une Légion dapprentis de tout état quon Recevra maîtres avec La même Rapidité au Bout de leurs temps'. Pradier had no scruples about airing his views on these new clothiers: 'tout cest assemblage fait dabord un très mauvais composé', he wrote, 'et bien Loin quon doive en attendre le bien, on peut être assuré du contraire'. Pradier, thus, had both social and economic grounds for not wanting to return to cloth-making. He disdained the new entrants to the profession, and was pessimistic about the future of the industry: 'il faut Monsieur que la fabrique périsse par Ce seul deffaut, de trop de Maîtres, et du manque dommes'. As usual Pradier claimed complete objectivity in his views: 'dieu ma donné des sentiments trop vifs pour le bien publicq pour nestre pas pénétré de tout ce que je prévois . . . Je souhaite destre mauvais prophète, mais je suis persuadé que je souhaite en vain; un commerce illimité qui demande des bornes ne pouvant que périr.'[30]

Few clothiers were to abandon all hope for the trade as rapidly as Pradier but his attitude was symptomatic, and illustrated what must indeed have been the typical reaction of those clothiers who had enjoyed a privileged position for so long. Within a few years a number of other clothiers were to follow his example. One of these was Jean-Pierre Desalasc. The last year in which he produced cloth was 1758 and his desertion of the industry was all the more significant in that in 1754 it was he who had effectively taken over his father-in-law Antoine Berthomieu's concern.[31] Berthomieu had left no male heir though his nephew, Joseph Berthomieu, son of Estienne who had gone bankrupt in 1732, had clearly expected that his uncle's cloth-making concern and, as important, production quota would be bequeathed to him. He complained to the intendant that it was 'Bien plus naturel et plus juste que les draps fussent donnés à un neveu qu'à des Etrangers'.[32] The withdrawal of Jean-Pierre Desalasc thus deprived Clermont's industry of two of its most important cloth-making concerns. The Desalascs. like Mathieu Pradier, did not need to work any more. Their colossal fortune provided them with a more than adequate income and their seigneuries (Jean-Pierre Desalasc had inherited the titles of baron of Lauzières, and seigneur of Octon and Arièges from his mother in 1757) and their ownership of the office

29. ADH C2087, Letter of 17 April 1756.
30. ADH C5553, 26 April 1756.
31. Evidence of this, and other, abandonments has been drawn from the production figures for these years: ADH C2216–18, C2232–4.
32. ADH C2086, Petition of Joseph Berthomieu, 4 Jan. 1756.

of mayor (bequeathed by Antoine Berthomieu) assured them of an unmatchable social position in Clermont.[33] A few letters sent by Desalasc's oldest son to the secretary of the commander of the province in the 1760s demonstrate that the family was living in a leisurely manner, dividing its time between its main country estate at Octon and its town house in Clermont, and involving itself in intrigues in connection with communal politics. These letters to the secretary (in which confidential information was requested) were frequently accompanied by presents of fruit from the country estate.[34] Jean-Pierre Desalasc succeeded in dominating Clermontais politics even after the abolition of his office as mayor in 1766 and his to-all-appearances corrupt manipulation of Clermont's local politics led to protests in 1769 and 1770. It was complained that he disposed of the consulate 'comme sil en étoit propriétaire, quil ny fasse apeller que ses parens, et quil exclue de cette charge et de celle même de conseiller tous ceux des habitants qui ne sont pas de sa cabale'. The two first consuls since the suppression of the mayorship had both been close relations of his: Antoine Berthomieu and Jean-Gabriel Vallibouze, a cousin, and the brother-in-law of a cousin, of his wife. In fact it was his wife who was the major power in his household. St-Priest, reporting on the disputes in Clermont's municipal politics on 3 November 1769, wrote

une seule personne cause par ses intrigues tout le trouble quil y a dans la Comm^té cest la dame de salasc fille et femme d'un fabriquand quon titre de marquise parcequelle possède la terre d'octon quelle a acquis de M. de jougla à qui le titre de marquis étoit personnel, qui jouit dune fortune d'environ quatre cent mille Livres, et dont le père et le mari ont été successivement maires ... ces différents circonstances réunies luy ont acquis une crédit si grand ... que ... elle a fait entrer dans les charges municipales ... tous ceux quelle a voulu.[35]

If Jean-Pierre Desalasc's existence would have appeared extremely leisurely to his austere and hard-working grandfather, Pierre Desalasc, who founded the family's fortunes, that of Jean-Georges-Antoine, his oldest son, would have appeared, it is quite certain, dissolute. The boy's education had been entrusted in the 1750s to the Recollets, a Franciscan order of monks in Clermont. The monks, it would seem, were quite incapable of disciplining him. In July 1756 the 'gardien' of the order complained to the commander of the province of 'les insultes atroces que

33. Appolis, *Lodève*, p. 513.
34. ADH C6764, Desalasc to Coste, letters of 3, 14 Sept. 1764 and C6765, Letters of 14 Jan. 1766, 23 May 1768. E.g. letter of 14 Jan. 1766: 'Me voicy de Retour de la campagne où j'étois depuis Bien longtemps.'
35. On this affair: ADH C949, 'Mémoire pour les habitants de Clermont contre les consuls et conseillers ...', 1769; letter of St-Priest to Terray, 3 Nov. 1769.

vomit journellement contre ma communauté, le fils de Mr Salas maire de Clermont'. The incident which had finally induced him to have recourse to authority he described in detail:

un de mes prêtres professeur de philosophie voyant ce Libertin lui faire mille ingeries Lui Dit: que signifie cela, Monsieur? à quoi il Répondit en expressions Dures, grossières; le medecin [his cousin, Antoine Berthomieu, son of Estienne] lui Représenta le Respect Dû au sacerdoce, et à L'habit de Religieux; s'il ne vouloit en avoir pour la personne même à ce, il Répliqua qu'il se mocquoit et Du Caractère, et de Revêtu ne valoit Rien; il ajouta même que le couvent de cette ville n'étoit occupé que par la canaille.[36]

It would seem likely that as a consequence of this complaint Jean-Pierre Desalasc was obliged to withdraw his son from the monastery: there is evidence that at a later date he was employing a 'précepteur' for him.[37] Jean-Georges-Antoine Desalasc had been received marchand-fabricant in 1752.[38] Possibly, had 'fixation' not been abolished, he might have taken over his father's concern. There was no question of his producing cloth under circumstances of free competition.

The Martin family was distinguished by the speed with which it enriched itself. Pierre Martin, and his five sons who worked with him, had formed an exceptional entrepreneurial team. We have seen evidence for this already and by the 1740s the family had already established itself as one of the richest and most powerful in the industry. To the honest prieur La Romiguière this Protestant family's growing wealth was one other disturbing feature in the disordered community in which he found himself and he wrote to Le Nain:

si votre Grandeur avoit à sévir contre ceux qui abusent de leur fabrique je vous en marquerois qui étant étrangers à notre Religion sont la perte de ma paroisse par la corruption de leurs moeurs et par leurs usures criantes. Les profits immenses qu'ils ont fait les rend téméraires et audacieux ennemis du bien public. ils veulent tout tourner à leur avantage comme s'ils étoient seuls au milieu de la terre.[39]

By the 1750s, after only some twenty-two years of cloth production, the Martins had amassed a fortune sufficiently large to allow father and all five sons to choose between continuing cloth production or living off rentes. We shall provide details of how the different members of the family reacted to the opportunities which their large fortunes gave them.

The first step in what was to be a general movement in the Martin

---

36. ADH C6600, Jean-Antoine Durand to the commander of the province, 22 July 1756.
37. ADH C6765. Desalasc fils refers in a letter to Coste to his former précepteur, 23 May 1765.
38. ACC BB5, 29 Nov. 1752. At the age of fourteen.
39. ADH C2043, 6 Dec. 1744.

Ill. 23. Investment in buildings: hôtel of the Martins

family away from cloth production was taken by the father. In 1751 he purchased the office of conseiller secrétaire du roi in the Cour des Comptes, Aides et Finances of Montpellier. This office, which would have cost in the region of 30,000 *livres*, conferred nobility on him, and the status of écuyer to his five sons during their life-times.[40] In 1771 his sons, by paying 6,000 *livres* each, made this status hereditary.[41] After the death of Martin père in 1755 his office passed to his son Pierre who gave up cloth-making in 1757 and moved to Montpellier in order to dedicate himself to his new post. In Montpellier Pierre Martin fils took up

40. Appolis, *Lodève*, p. 512.
41. ACC BB7, 10 March 1772: Registration of an edict signed in June 1771 by Bertin.

residence in an elegant house in the Rue de l'Argenterie and moved in the highest social circles.[42] His family was well connected. Intendant St-Priest, it is clear from several letters, was on cordial terms with him, referring to him on one occasion as 'un fort honnête homme',[43] and in addition the Martins were, and had been since the 1740s at least, on the closest of terms with some of Montpellier's most distinguished merchant families, among them the Vassals who were most influential and vastly rich.[44] Pierre Martin's two sons, Jean and Pierre, were to follow their father's new destiny, both becoming owners of honourable offices. A distinguished Martin dynasty had been established in Montpellier: two descendants, Martin de Vignolle and Martin de Campredon, were to become generals during the First Empire and a third, Martin de Choisy, an important judge in the Cour d'Appel of Montpellier.[45]

Antoine Martin, who was, it would seem, the oldest brother (he was the first to be received master, in 1731), abandoned cloth production in 1761 but despite this he remained in Clermont, resisting the draw of the rich social life which would have been open to him in Montpellier. His continued residence in Clermont may well be explained by the fact that it was he who was given the superb house which his father had built in the old walled town, overlooking the Place du Planol (Ills. 23 and 24). It would seem that he lived there a life of absolute leisure; there is no evidence of his having been involved in any sort of regular economic activity, apart, occasionally, from lending money (on one occasion, at least, above what was the legal maximum interest rate). His children's education was entrusted to a précepteur and the only regular habit which surviving documents show him to have had was card playing and gambling.[46]

Jacques Martin, like Pierre, was to leave Clermont. He ceased cloth production in 1757, but he was not to cut entirely his links with cloth-making for it was to Marseilles that he went to establish himself, in

---

42. Bobo, 'Communauté languedocienne', p. 127.
43. ADH C2179, St-Priest to L'Averdy, 4 June 1766.
44. Thus in 1746 it is a Vassal who supports Jacques Martin's request to be given a 'fixation' quota (ADH C2047, Vassal to Le Nain, 5 Dec. 1746). On the wealth of the Vassals see Thomas, *Montpellier*, pp. 171–4, and Wolff (ed.), *Histoire du Languedoc*, p. 434.
45. L. Dermigny, *Cargaisons indiennes, Solier et Cie*, I, 60, n. 2; M. Louis de La Roque, *Armorial de la noblesse de Languedoc: généralité de Montpellier*, II, 152, 181–2.
46. Antoine Martin: on his house: Combarnous, 'Clermont-l'Hérault', pp. 268–9; his money-lending: ADH, Ordinaires Clermont, case 185, 10 Oct. 1770 (at 6%, above the legal maximum, his creditor claims) and ACCM, Fonds Roux, LIX, 281–4, Letters of Jean-Antoine Gély and Rousserie fils to Roux frères, 30 March, 3 June 1769; précepteur for children: Ordinaires, Case 514, 26 June 1768; gambling: Ordinaires, Case 514, 26 June 1768 (playing 'lansquenet' on which see Appolis, *Lodève*, p. 356), Case 465, 1771, present at 'académie de jeux' of Louis Portes.

Ill. 24. Detail of the hôtel of the Martins

association with a Marseillais négociant, Lazare Téard, as cloth-commissioner. He and his new associate were particulary well equipped for exercising this role in view of their influential family links in the two major bureaux de marque for Languedoc's cloth production: Estienne Gaja, inspector at Montpellier, was a close friend of the Martins, and Artaud, inspector at Marseilles, was a cousin of Téard. These family links with cloth inspectors were, as we shall see, to be of some significance.[47]

47. Jacques Martin: on the move to Marseilles see Carrière, *Les négociants*, ii, 948 and ACCM, H 176, production statistics for 1756–7 which show Martin receiving cloth on commission in Marseilles from 1756 onwards. On the association with Lazare Téard,

The two remaining brothers, Jean and Barthélemy, retained the closest links with cloth manufacturing. Barthélemy had not in fact ever produced cloth on his own account (although he was received master in 1743). He had worked for his father's concern until 1748, and it was possibly he who had been entrusted with the family's interests in St-Gervais – they had been producing there under what was effectively the 'prête-nom' of Jacques Rouvière. In the second half of the century he continued to live in Clermont, working as a négociant, but also, it is evident, devoting a large part of his time to the study of geology and natural history. The author of a memoir on the diocese composed in 1768, who had been shown samples of copper ore by him, reported that 'Mr. Barthélemy Martin Neg^t . . . est très bon à entendre sur les productions naturelles et sur le commerce de son pays.' His continued link with the town's cloth industry took the form of buying and reselling wools, lending money to clothiers and buying their finished cloth. These activities he was to carry out in a discreet manner. As Taillardat de St-James, inspector at Clermont in the 1770s, explained, it was his 'politique de n'agir jamais qu'indirectement pour ne pas s'exposer à un certain point', and another observer commented likewise on 'l'air calme qui lui est ordinaire'. His influence, though, over the town's industry was at certain stages quite considerable. As Inspector Taillardat reported to St-Priest on 26 October 1777, 'Le S. Barthélemy Martin par l'influence très grande quil a dans la jurande de Clermont où plus de la moitié des fabriquans ne le sont que par lui et pour lui, a contribué plus que personne au relâchement dans lequel cette fabrique est tombée, et à la mauvaise réputation qu'il s'en est suivie.'[48]

It was Jean Martin who was to become the most notorious of the five brothers. He too by the 1750s had sufficient resources to live off rent but it is evident that he obtained immense satisfaction, and profits, from prolonging his links with cloth manufacture. As he explained in a letter addressed to L'Averdy in 1764, 'jay assés du Bien qui pourroit Bien m'empêcher de travailler [mais] jaime le commerce'.[49] He continued producing cloth until 1757 and then abandoned direct involvement in

and Téard's links with Artaud, inspector at Marseillès, see ADH C2177, letter of Jacques Boyer [?] to St-Priest, 6 Oct. 1766. The closeness of the Martins' relationship with Gaja was frequently commented on, e.g. ADH C2177, Suquet (Clermontais clothier and ex-director of the royal manufacture of La Penne) to St-Priest, 29 Sept. 1766: 'Gaja n'est qu'un avec le sieur Jean Martin, puisqu'ils mangent très souvent ensemble, et quils ne ce quittent pas de toute la journée.'

48. Barthélemy Martin: on production at St-Gervais: ADH C5545 and see p. 315; as natural historian: C6554, Memoir on Lodève, 1768–9; as négociant: C5533, Memoir of Pezet, 7 April 1771, C2180, Letter of Taillardat fils.
49. AN F12 1380, 8 July 1764.

cloth production to become a négociant. This new role, like his brother Barthélemy's, involved him primarily in servicing the credit needs of the new generation of clothiers allowed to produce since 1756.[50] Unlike Barthélemy, though, he played this role in a manner which was in no way discreet. He was to be the veritable scourge of inspectors, and of all others involved in the administration of industry, until his dying day, indeed until beyond his dying day: cloth of his was seized at Beaucaire after his death.[51] No-one managed to control him: 'il est d'un caractère si indocile, que ni moi, ni mon fils, ni tous ceux que nous avons fait agir, n'ont pu y parvenir', wrote St-Priest to Trudaine on 2 August 1767 after a long three-year struggle had been waged to make Martin respect regulations.[52] His brother Pierre was occasionally obliged to intercede on his behalf as a consequence of his misdemeanours. As he admitted in a letter to St-Priest written on 30 June 1766, 'mon frère est malheureusement d'un caractère trop vif et trop peu considéré'.[53]

There is an extraordinarily full documentation about the activities of Jean Martin to be found in the intendancy archives, and one which attests to the futility of the continued existence of the inspectoral and regulative systems. The failure to control a man who devoted himself quite openly to abusing these institutions demonstrated that the system, in addition to any other faults it might have had, was both corrupt and ineffective and as such could not possibly be of any value. This exceptional documentation would make possible a virtual day-by-day description of Jean Martin's activities (at certain stages of his career). Here, though, I shall purely provide an outline of the changing basis of his business activities.

Jean Martin began producing cloth on his own account in 1745. He was not a particularly gifted clothier: in 1745 he was described as a 'fabricant médiocre'.[54] But if he never shone as a manufacturer he soon demonstrated definite skills of a financial nature. It was he who was the most regular provider of financial backing to clothiers who lacked the resources necessary to carry out their own production. In 1746 he associated himself with Gabriel Verny who was establishing a new concern. He subscribed all the capital and while Verny was charged with all the tasks connected with the actual manufacturing of cloth in the articles of the society, it was declared that Jean Martin:

50. His name does not disappear from the production registers until 1762, but St-Priest mentions the ceding of his manufacture to Jean Lugagne in a letter of 5 Nov. 1757 (ADH C5585).
51. ADH C5528, Petition of Stanislas Martin, younger son of Jean Martin, 1786.
52. ADH C2179.
53. ADH C2179.
54. ADH C2049.

aura la direction de l'achat de touttes les matières nécessaires à la fabrique, et de la vente des draps qui en proviendront auquel effet il aura seul la correspondence avec ceux de qui l'on achetera, et avec le commissionaire de Marseille que le Sr Martin choizira pour la vente des draps, auquel effet Il tendra les Livres Journeaux, en bonne et Deue forme.

The contract was highly advantageous to Martin who, in addition to obtaining a 5% return on his capital, was to obtain half the profits of the association, profits which, as we have seen, were virtually automatically high during the period of 'fixation'.[55] It was likewise Jean Martin who in 1756 loaned money to Joseph Vieules and Pierre Jalmes, two clothiers who were in some financial straits.[56] Money-lending remained secondary to his cloth-making activities still, however. This priority given to cloth-making is apparent both from the fact that one of the conditions of his granting a loan to Joseph Vieules in 1756 was that 6 *ballots* of cloth from Vieules's quota should be transferred to his and also from the production statistics which demonstrate that Jean Martin, more than any other Clermont clothier, took advantage of the first relaxation in the strictness of regulations in 1754 to expand his production. The way in which he profited from this liberalization is of some significance. The first measure by which the regulative system had been relaxed was, as we have mentioned in the previous chapter, the edict of August 1754 which permitted clothiers to send types of cloth to the Levant which were not included in the 1708 regulation in any quantity they wanted. It was not anticipated that this measure would have very significant consequences; the difficulties involved in introducing new cloths into the Levant market have been seen at earlier stages in this work. The sharper and less scrupulous clothiers (and Jean Martin above all), however, were to profit from the measure in a manner which had not been anticipated by reformers. Rather than sending new types of cloth to the Levant they sent slightly altered versions of the regulated cloths to which they gave different names. This was potentially a most profitable deception: this cloth could be made in unlimited quantities, it could not be inspected as it was not regulated for, and it would fetch the same inflated prices which were being paid for quota production. By February 1755 St-Priest had realized what was happening and warned inspectors that he had noted that:

plusieurs fabriquans ont moins cherché à prendre la véritable interprétation qu'Ils devoient donner à cet arrest, qu'à étendre, et même à abuser de la liberté qu'il leur accorde en cherchant à se raprocher des qualités de draps prescrites par

55. ADH C2047, Agreement signed at Montpellier, 2 Feb. 1746.
56. ADH C2088, Petition of Vieules, *c.*1756; II E 25 158, 16 July 1756: records debt of 4,720 *livres* to Jean Martin.

l'arrest du 20 9bre 1708 . . . et en rendant par là inutiles les arrangemens qui ont été pris . . . dans . . . [les] Echelles.[57]

Impressive was the scale on which Jean Martin took advantage of this loophole in the regulative system. A survey made by Tricou, who described Martin as 'remply d'ambition', showed that in March 1755 he was in the process of making some 550 pieces of *nims* and *26 ains à lisière bleue* and had bought a further 160 pieces of *nims* from two Bédarieux clothiers. The *nims* and *26 ains* were virtually identical to *londres-larges* and *londrins-seconds*, both subject to quotas. In addition to this production Martin was also producing his regular quota which consisted of 23 *ballots* of cloth. To achieve this vast production he had put work out to the hospitals and 'maisons de bon pasteur' of Montpellier, Béziers and other towns in the region.[58]

The nature of Jean Martin's activities until 1756 was effectively dictated by the same factors which governed those of Mathieu Pradier and Jean Pelletan fils. In a period of artificial restraint of production, and artificially high cloth prices, the largest profits were to be obtained not from the quality of production, but from the size of the quota that a clothier could obtain. Martin's loans to Verny and Vieules, and his reaction to the August 1754 edict, were designed primarily, it is evident, to enable him to profit from a situation of exceptionally restricted supply. However, the end of 'fixation' and of the restrictions on the reception of masters in 1756 radically altered the supply situation in the industry. Martin, like Pradier, reacted rapidly but rather than simply withdrawing from the industry he turned the new circumstances to his advantage. Effectively what had been a subsidiary aspect of his affairs, his financial and commercial activities, he now developed into his principal role. He became a full-time négociant, handing over his own manufacture to a close collaborator, Jean Lugagne fils, in 1757, and fulfilling similar functions to those exercised by his brother Barthélemy: buying and reselling wools, lending money to clothiers and other participants in the production process, buying and selling cloth. Several clothiers were to be totally financed by him and although production was registered in their names they were effectively Martin's commis. What is impressive once more is both the scale on which he acted and the rapidity with which he adjusted to the new circumstances. Already in 1757 he had acquired a commercial house in Smyrna, under the name of Delmas, to ensure a rapid sale of the cloth which he bought and by 1765 production in his

57. ADH C2170, St-Priest to inspectors, 19 Feb. 1755.
58. ADH C2170, Tricou to St-Priest, 28 Feb., 15 March 1755; C2086, Jean Martin to de Séchelles, 15 Dec. 1753.

name, or by clothiers whom he financed, was said to amount to between three and four thousand pieces.[59]

There was, of course, nothing necessarily reprehensible about this new role which Martin had developed for himself in Clermont's industry. On the contrary it might be argued that the liberalization measures had been designed to give men like Martin, with great commercial flair, a free rein for their enterprise. Why then the widespread condemnation of Jean Martin? The answer has been provided in part in the last chapter, but a fuller analysis of Martin's activities will throw more light on this matter. The liberal reforms had not been complete, regulations and inspectors remained in place, and inevitably they had not served to undo the effects of sixty or seventy years of interventionism. As we have emphasized, there were two ways in particular in which the industry had been marked by the years of interventionism. First, customers were used to buying cloth simply on the faith of its mark, and standards of cloth had been so uniform that it had become customary for a standard price to be given for a particular town's production, and secondly there were a quite exceptional number of people anxious to produce cloth. Martin's definite entrepreneurial qualities were directed to profiting to the maximum from both of these exceptional circumstances. It was he who was the trend-setter with respect to the gradual deterioration of production which occurred – the production of the manufactures which he financed and that of his own concern (under Jean Lugagne's direction) were reported to be of the worst quality in Clermont – and he lent money, at what was reported to be usurious rates, to those clothiers whose long exclusion from production had made them desperate to found their own cloth-making concerns. It might be thought that both types of action could have ended disastrously for Martin. The low-quality cloth which he was producing could, quite legitimately, have been stopped by inspectors, and the clothiers to whom he loaned money, many of whom were ruined by their involvement in the Levant trade, might have defaulted on their loans. The reasons for these actions not ending in these ways throw light on what were evidently some of Martin's special entrepreneurial qualities. With respect to obtaining governmental approval for what was effectively illegal cloth, local inspectors proved either ineffective or corruptible (with the notable exception of Roland de la Platière with whom

59. AN F12 1380, Letter from Jean Martin to L'Averdy[?], 10 Oct. 1764, in which he states that he has owned a commercial house in Smyrna since 1757 and claims to be employing 3,000 workers to make more than 3,000 half-pieces of cloth a year. The accuracy of this claim is confirmed by a report of Roland de la Platière of 18 Feb. 1765 (ADH C2180) concerning efforts of Jean Martin to manufacture cloth at Bédarieux. In this report it is stated that he is already responsible for the manufacture of 3,000–4,000 pieces of cloth at Clermont.

Martin was to have a long and violent struggle). The inspector at Mont-pellier, Gaja, was under Martin's influence ('sa recommandation [that of Martin] vaut mieux au Bureau de Montp. que votre plomb et votre signature', wrote Roland de la Platière acidly in 1765), and his brother Jacques's associate's relationship with Artaud, inspector at Marseilles, ensured that there would be no trouble in this quarter ('on soupçonne M. Artaud de s'entendre avec J. Martin', wrote Roland and his was not the only report of such connivance).[60] With respect to the second factor, the security of the money he loaned, the following factors go to explaining this. First, his personal acquaintanceship with all those to whom he lent money had the consequence that he must have been fully informed about their financial situation. He was thus better placed to lend money than, for instance, a Marseillais cloth commissioner. Houses were frequently given in security for loans; the houses of both Joseph Vieules and Pierre Jalmes, for example, ended up in Martin's hands.[61] Secondly, the risk was diminished by the fact that the loans were made for a specified purpose, the manufacture of cloth, and in case of default Martin could always seize the cloth once it had been produced. And finally it becomes clear from reading through a number of court cases brought before the seigneurial justice of Clermont, as well as from a variety of other types of documentation, that Martin and his henchmen used the utmost brutality in obtaining repayment from debtors who threatened to default and inspired considerable fear among certain sections of Clermontais society. The statement of one Pezet,[62] 'juré-auneur' at the bureau de marque of Clermont, that 'tout homme qui tombe entre les mains des Martins, est un homme perdu sans ressource, ce sont de gens qui corromproit toute la terre sils le pouvoit pour parvenir à ces fins', would seem to have con-tained more than a grain of truth.[63] The majority of those who borrowed money from Martin were eventually ruined and came much to regret their original association with him. Louis Gayraud who borrowed money

---

60. ADH C2215, Comparison of Gaja's and Artaud's judgements on cloth, 1765.
61. ADH, Ordinaires Clermont, Case 13, 21 Sept. 1790; C6765, Jean Martin to com-mander of the province, 1767 (mentions in letter that he has been forced to take over the house and garden of Jalmes).
62. Henri Pezet: came to Clermont in 1765 to take up the post of juré-auneur and visiteur des étoffes which was financed by the clothiers' corporation. He was invited to take up this position by Mathieu Pradier with whom he was on close terms. He retired from this post in 1782 and sought a pension from the Crown. Throughout his years of service he sent a stream of letters and memoirs to the intendancy. These were mainly critical of the behaviour both of Clermont's clothiers and of inspectors. Not unnaturally Pezet became a most unpopular figure in Clermont. (ADH C2190, Memoir of Pezet on himself, December 1784; on the attempt by the clothiers' corporation to dismiss him from his employment, see correspondence in C5592.)
63. ADH C5533, Memoir of 7 April 1771.

from Martin in 1763 and who was en faillite by 1765 wrote of having linked himself 'Malheureusement' with Martin and of the latter having held his 'pied dans leau pour Largent nécessaire'.[64] Pierre Vernazobres, whose relationship with Martin had ended in physical assault ('coquin fripon je veux te faire pendre', Martin had shouted at Vernazobres before pelting him with stones and finally attacking him with a sword), had complained in 1759 of 'les usures excessives que le Sr Jean Martin ... a exercée à mon égard'.[65] Louis-Joseph Manié likewise, who was brought to court over a 2,000 *livres* loan, stated that Martin's 'aviditté' was 'sy grand quil n'est pas capable de Refflexion'. He maintained that an account which Martin had presented to the court was false and that he had treated all other people who had borrowed money from him in a similar way.[66]

Martin's violence, and his fearlessness of any correction from those in administrative authority, are apparent from his relationship with Roland de la Platière. Roland was subjected to repeated verbal abuse. He was shouted down at meetings which he summoned; 'le Sr J^n Martin ne voulant, ni entendre, ni que les autres entendissent cria ... à pleine tête jusqu'au point que je fus obligé d'abandonner la partie', Roland complained to St-Priest on 6 April 1766 after failing to announce orders which he had received to a meeting of clothiers.[67] And at various stages of his period in Clermont he was threatened with physical assault and on account of this lived in veritable fear for his life. The climax to this conflict was reached in 1766 when Roland refused to mark a large quantity of cloth owned by Martin. As a consequence Roland was threatened with immersion in a vat of boiling water. Martin, Roland reported, had declared 'hautement en place publique' to his dyer, Jean Delpon, 'qu'il n'avoit quà tenir toujours une chaudière d'eau bouillante, et nous y jetter, moi et les gardes jurés, à la première fois que nous retournerions chez lui, et quil le garentissoit des événements'.[68] This was not the only occasion on which Martin made such threats. In February 1766 Roland informed St-Priest that 'cet homme met aujourd'huy tout en combustion, qu'il coure sans cesse d'atelier en atelier pour animer les ouvriers, vomissant partout et sans cesse toutes les horreurs imaginables, jusqu'à leur conseiller publiquement, les garantissant, dit-il, de tout événement, de m'attaquer ouvertement'.[69] The repeated promise to guarantee his 'satel-

64. ADH C2215, 'Mémoire pour le Sieur Gayraud', Sept. 1765.
65. ADH Ordinaires Clermont, Case 149, 24 Feb. 1765; C5585, Vernazobres to St-Priest, 15 May 1759.
66. ADH Ordinaires Clermont, Case 142, 23 July 1759.
67. ADH C2213.
68. ADH C2213, Roland to L'Averdy 13 April 1766.
69. ADH C2177, Roland to St-Priest, 18 Feb. 1766.

lites' (Roland's description of Martin's supporters) from the consequences of their actions is of significance. On what grounds did Martin feel that he could assume responsibility for their breaking the law? The answer is that his wealth, his noble status, and the established social position of his 'parents', did give him a degree of immunity. Also, in addition to his Montpellier connections, he enjoyed 'protection' in Paris, having married the daughter of a courtier, Marie Louise Adélaïde Agogné, who herself became a lady-in-waiting at Court.[70] Despite this protection, Martin's duel with Roland ended in what was to all appearances the latter's triumph. In May 1766 Martin was summoned to Montpellier and obliged to make a public apology for his behaviour, and to promise to amend his ways, in front of the intendant; shortly afterwards, on 31 July 1766, he was banned from all involvement in cloth production. 'Martin a paru fort humilié; je lui ai parlé comme il méritoit', wrote St-Priest contentedly to L'Averdy.[71] In the longer term, though, the triumph was to be Martin's. Roland left Clermont in late 1766. It was comparatively easy for Martin to claim that it was his influence which had led to Roland's removal: 'ce qui est fort singulier', wrote Roland to St-Priest in September 1766, 'ce sont les bruits que les Martins répandent: ce sont eux; c'est leur Crédit; C'est par la voie de M' Vassal, disent ils, que je suis renvoyé d'ici.'[72] Likewise Jean Martin was able to gain indirect revenge on St-Priest. Shortly after the ban on his manufacturing he purchased the newly created office of governor of Clermont and offered impudently to assist in the re-imposition of regulations in the town's industry. An infuriated St-Priest reported on Martin's move to Trudaine; 'ce qu'il a fait depuis peu', he wrote, 'est une nouvelle preuve de la Bizarrerie de sa façon de penser: malgré son interdiction, il a eu l'effronterie d'acheter le gouvernement municipal de Clermont et la folie d'écrire aux consuls qu'il viendroit Bientôt travailler avec eux au Rétablissement de bon ordre'.[73] The nature of the prerogatives which Martin believed that the purchase of this office had given him is revealed by a slight change in the vocabulary which he used to abuse his opponents, and victims, in Clermont: 'drôle, coquin, fripon', he shouted at

---

70. ADH C2179, Morineau [?] to St-Priest, 10 March 1768; C5528, 1786, Plea of Stanislas Martin. Some idea of the extent of influence which Martin was believed to wield is given by the following letter from the gardes-jurés of Bédarieux. Referring to a Bédarieux clothier working for Martin they write: 'Ce qui donne tant d'arrogance à ce fabriquant est la protection dont il croit être honoré par le Sr. Jean Martin; Il croit que celui-cy a autant de pouvoir, ainsy qu'il le publie partout, que M. le Contrôlleur Général et M. l'Intendant et que quelque chose qu'il fasse ou qu'il dise tout doit lui être toléré.' (C2213, Martel and Fabregat to Le Blanc, 14 Oct. 1764.)
71. All details in ADH C2179.
72. ADH C2215, 7 Sept. 1766.
73. ADH C2179, St-Priest to Trudaine, 2 Aug. 1767.

Joseph Pouget in 1770, 'je veux te faire banir de ce pays-ci!'[74] The ban on manufacture was lifted within a year and Martin returned to his former practices but on a larger scale, and with even less respect for the remnants of the regulative system than before. In 1765 he had taken over the royal manufacture of Brioude in the Auvergne and he now used the privileges of this concern to escape all inspectoral control in an unprecedented manner.[75] He was to continue to do so until his death. Taillardat de St-James, inspector at Clermont between 1774 and 1780, was to report to St-Priest in 1777 that:

le S. Jean Martin entrepreneur de la Manufacture de Brioude en Auvergne, fait dans Clermont en Languedoc toutes les opérations de fabrique, sans que personne ose approcher de ses atteliers, il ne seroit même prudent de le faire sans des ordres précis et beaucoup de précautions, il y a des Magazins d'où il s'expédie journellement des Draps dont on ignore la destination, sans passer par aucunes visites, ni par aucuns Bureaux. aucunes Manufactures royales ni privilégiées n'ont jamais joüi de pareilles prérogatives.[76]

In a political system as confused and irrational as that of Ancien Régime France there was always the possibility of clashes between individuals with opposing interests and distinct, but equally valid, sources of status and power. Martin had become too powerful an individual to be handled by inspector or intendant.

The Pelletan family's reaction to the liberalization of the trade in the 1750s was similar to that of the Martins: in 1758 three Pelletans had been manufacturing – Jean Pelletan père and his elder son Gabriel, who were associated, and Jean Pelletan fils, who was still operating Mathieu Pradier's concern – but by 1770 all had withdrawn from direct involvement in cloth production; Jean Pelletan fils had abandoned production in 1765, and his brother Gabriel in 1769. Cloth-making had by then become a subsidiary activity for this family whose main interests lay in the concern which they had been operating at Marseilles since the 1730s for the export of cloth to the Levant. This concern, after the death of Jean Pelletan père, was run by the elder son Gabriel. Jean Pelletan fils, before he abandoned production, extended the range of his activities acting, like the Martin brothers, as négociant for poorer clothiers, and buying finished cloth on behalf of his brother's Marseillais establishment. Like the Martins too the Pelletans had close personal links with inspectors, and particularly

---

74. ADH, Ordinaires Clermont, Case 177, 6 July 1770.
75. It was rumoured that Martin was taking over this concern in April 1765 (ADH C2214, Roland to St-Priest). In 1768 Martin was attempting to obtain permission to send cloth straight from his manufacture to Marseilles without passing by the bureau de marque of Montpellier (C2179, L'Averdy to St-Priest, 11 May 1768).
76. ADH C2180, Letter to St-Priest, 26 Oct. 1777.

with Gaja, at Montpellier.[77] The importance of Pelletan's commercial activities gradually, it is evident, came to supersede that of his cloth-making and, again like Jean Martin, it was on the commercialization of the cheapest cloth that he concentrated, and he thus fell foul of the virtuous Roland. Soon after his arrival in the town Roland commented on the existence of a group of 'gens riches, qui tiennent tous les avantages du mal général, sans qu'on puisse les en soupçonner à lair de candeur et dassurance quils portent dans la société'.[78] That Pelletan was among this number is apparent from another comment of Roland's: against Pelle-tan's name on a list of Clermont's clothiers he wrote, 'avec J. Martin le per. auteur du Bouleversement de cette jurande homme d'autant plus Dangereux, qu'ayant de l'esprit et des Connaissances, il a séduit le peuple fabriquand et les a tous induit à mal faire'.[79] Jean Pelletan fils, as Roland's comment suggests, had adopted an approach to his business affairs similar to that of his father-in-law, Mathieu Pradier – an approach less direct than that of Martin. While he himself was profiting to the maximum from the ambiguous situation in which the liberalization measures of the 1750s had left the industry, he was communicating comparatively regularly with the authorities, giving what he claimed to be his disinterested advice about the solution of the industry's problems.[80]

It is clear that Pelletan was increasingly attracted by the prospect of leading an existence of leisure, and devoting himself fully to activities of a mildly intellectual and cultural kind. (One of the attractions of writing memoirs to administrators clearly consisted in this and Pelletan must have been particularly gratified by Trudaine's reaction to a memoir which he sent to Paris in 1762. 'Jay lu Monsieur', Trudaine informed St-Priest, 'avec une véritable satisfaction le mémoire de M. Pelletan fils.')[81] A letter from Pelletan to the secretary of the intendancy at Montpellier written in 1762 illustrates his intellectual pretensions and the increas-ingly apologetic posture which he was adopting towards both his con-tinued involvement in cloth production and his provincial existence at

77. On the Pelletans' Marseillais company see Carrière, *Négociants*, II, 948. The closeness of the family's links with inspectors is illustrated by the manner in which Gabriel Pelletan concludes a letter to Gaja: 'jauray Lhonneur de vous embrasser en passant' (ADH C2214, 9 Sept. 1765).
78. ADH C2213, Letter to Trudaine, 27 Sept. 1764.
79. ADH C2215, Comparison of Gaja's and Artaud's judgements on Clermontais cloth-iers, 1765.
80. See for example ADH C5566, Jean Pelletan fils to Trudaine, 16, 24 June 1760 and C5553, Memoir of Pelletan fils, March 1760, copies of which were sent both to St-Priest and to Trudaine.
81. ADH C5553, Trudaine to St-Priest, 11 May 1760.

Clermont. The letter concerns an exchange of verses between himself and his correspondent:

Mad^e Pauze ma remis votre épître Mon cher Monsieur elle sappercevra combien je suis rempli de zelle pour tout ce qui peut vous plaire. Mais vous ne deviés pas raillier Impitoyablement un pauvre campagnard, qui sennuye sur la laine et sur la luzerne. Enfin ce n'est pas d'aujourdhuy que les tristes Vilageois sont exposés aux Epigrammes des heureux habitans des grandes cittés. Je viendray le plutost que je le pourrai y montrer ma face maigre et palée.[82]

Jean Pelletan's gradual disinvolvement from all aspects of cloth-making (including the provision of financial backing to poorer clothiers it would seem) did not, this letter and other evidence suggest, involve him in a very brusque change in life-style. Exactly when this retirement occurred it is difficult to establish but it would seem that Pelletan, unlike the Martins, played little if any role in the town's industry after the major industrial crisis which coincided with Roland's inspectorate, between 1764 and 1766. Continued involvement in the town's trade was barely necessary to him financially for, in addition to his own considerable fortune, he and his wife were the only heirs of Mathieu Pradier. Pradier must have died in the early 1770s and his inheritance included not only a significant capital sum but also his superb country house of Camplong as well as his elegant town house/ex-cloth manufacture in the Rue de la Fregère. After Pradier's death Pelletan divided his time between these two residences and also adopted the title 'Jean Pelletan de Fontanilles'. In retirement it seems probable that the only shadow on his happiness was occasioned by the comportment of his only son. Named Mathieu, like his grandfather Pradier, the boy had qualified himself as an avocat but clearly failed to fulfil his father's hopes for him. In 1772 he impregnated a girl of the town and in 1774, for some obscure reason, he was damaging the interior of his grandfather's former house, to which he himself was heir. Pelletan felt it necessary to disinherit his son and as a consequence his nephew Antoine became his heir.[83] Jean Pelletan must have died in the late 1770s for we find his nephew living at Camplong in the 1780s, referring to himself as the 'seigneur de Camplong',[84] and leading, it is evident, a life of great comfort and total leisure. His most energetic pursuit, it would seem, was hunting on his large estate (he

82. ADH C2531, 8 June 1762.
83. ADH, Ordinaires Clermont, Case 788, 2 Jan. 1772, 'plainte de grossesse' against Mathieu Pelletan and Case 780, 26 April 1774, verdict reached that 'Mathieu Pelletan le fils pour cause de dissipation et de démence demeurera interdit de la gestion et administration de ses biens.' These were to be controlled by Jean Pelletan, his father. See also letters of Jean Pelletan to the Commander of the province, January 1774, in ADH C6766.
84. ACC BB8, 4 Sept. 1789.

employed a game-keeper to protect his hunting rights) and his most taxing intellectual employment, it seems likely, was the composition of letters and memoirs to the commander of the province in order to complain about the abuse of his hunting rights by groups of poachers from Clermont.[85] Symbolic of the extent to which Pelletan had separated himself from the industrial activities of his ancestors is a petition which he made to those charged with imposing a *vingtième* on Clermont in the 1780s. He requested to be relieved of paying the tax on the old dye-house contained in what was formerly Mathieu Pradier's cloth manufacture, and what was now his elegant town house. He described the dye-house as a 'vieux cazal sans utilité' and complained about having to pay a tax of 2,000 *livres* for 'des objets qui ne luj rendent pas ... autant que la contribution'.[86] In 1788 Antoine made an extremely advantageous marriage with Dame Louise Sabine Rostan, recent widow of Jean Antoine Flottes Raissac, who had been Clermont's richest surviving clothier.[87] This match too was symbolic. The final step in the transformation of Clermont's new generation of industrialists from a creative, rising class to a static, leisured caste came when their fortunes came to depend not on commercial or industrial sources but on the careful choice of marriage partners and the dispositions of wills. The emphasis had changed from a desire to *improve* social positions, to one to conserve and consolidate them. Antoine Pelletan now occupied a situation which had some similarities to that occupied by the static elite which his ancestors had contributed to displacing at the beginning of the century.

The Bernard family withdrew completely from production in 1764. In fact, though, the family's involvement in the town's industry had been less than total for some time. After Jean Bernard's death in 1746 the family concern had been run in the name of his widow but much of the direction and management had evidently been carried out by the two commis whom she employed.[88] The Bernard children's involvement with their family concern could only have been minimal for in 1752 Jean Bernard (fils) purchased an office of conseiller in the Cour des Comptes, Aides et Finances, and in 1750 and 1759 the two daughters were married prestigiously into noble families.[89] Jean Bernard fils, on the other hand, perhaps in order to recoup the capital lost from the family patrimony by the payment of large dowries to his sisters, was married more humbly,

85. ADH C6768, Pelletan de Camplong to the commander of the province, 27 July 1788.
86. ADH C4932, Petition of Antoine Pelletan de Camplong, *c.* 1780.
87. ADH, Ordinaires Clermont, Case 31, May 1788.
88. ADH C2050, List of clothiers, 1748, the two commis, Malafosse and Jean-Baptiste Flottes, are named.
89. Appolis, *Lodève*, p. 512; ADH 11 E 25 154, 22 Jan. 1750; Bobo, 'Communauté languedocienne', p. 56.

but financially most advantageously, to Françoise, the daughter of Estienne Desalasc, an up-and-coming clothier of humble origins who had been received master in 1736. This marriage brought him a dowry of 20,000 *livres*.[90] If three different examples are sufficient to establish a trend then it would be warrantable to write that there was a general decline in paternal authority among bourgeois families in Clermont in the second half of the eighteenth century for Bernard, like both Jean-Pierre Desalasc and Jean Pelletan fils, suffered considerable embarrassment from the extravagant behaviour of one of his sons. The son in question, Charles, had obtained the position of 'gendarme' in the royal service and was, it is evident, a rake. His behaviour was so scandalous that his father finally petitioned the commander of the province to be allowed to have him locked away. In his petition Bernard père complained that he was 'menacé Depuis longtems dans son honneur dans sa fortune et même dans sa vie par les Déprédations et les vices de toute espèce d'un fils qu'il Reçut du ciel dans sa Colère'.[91] Another son, Jean, was evidently more conformist however. In 1788 he made an extremely advantageous marriage to the daughter of a négociant from the West Indies: she brought him a dowry of 50,000 *livres*.[92] The Bernards, like the Pelletans, had come to depend financially on matrimonial policy rather than on commercial activity by the second half of the eighteenth century.

The discontinuance of the Liquier family concern in 1758 was due in part to the lack of a male heir. Guillaume Liquier died in this year and his widow wound up his concern. But this was not the only reason. Widows during the first half of the century had been known to continue running their former husbands' concerns for a number of years with the aid of assistants[93] and Liquier's son-in-law, Maximilien Tartary, who had been trained as a clothier, received master in 1754 and had produced cloth since 1756, might also have absorbed his father-in-law's concern had he so desired, but he too withdrew from production in the same year. Two factors were clearly influential in this joint abandonment. First, 1758 was a year of maximal crisis and so to continue in the trade would have been risky, and secondly both the Liquier and Tartary families were in the comfortable position of having sufficient resources to enable them to live without working. The extent of their resources is revealed by a will drawn up by Guillaume Liquier's daughter, Françoise, in 1761. She made her uncle, Jean Liquier, a priest, her 'héritier universel', left her husband Maximilien Tartary an income of 800 *livres* a year and a capital

90. ADH II E 25 163, 12 Aug. 1761. On Estienne Desalasc see pp. 421–2.
91. ADH C6768, Bernard to commander of the province, 10 June 1788.
92. Bobo, 'Communauté languedocienne', p. 71.
93. Veuve Bernard ran a large concern from 1746 to 1764 for example.

Table 24. *Family of Jean Flottes vieux, with dates of mastership*

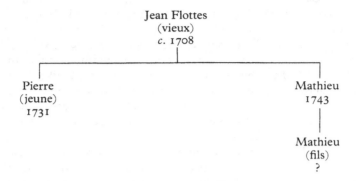

Jean Flottes
(vieux)
c. 1708

Pierre
(jeune)
1731

Mathieu
1743

Mathieu
(fils)
?

sum of 5,000 *livres*, left 12,000 *livres* to the hospital of Clermont, 4,000 *livres* to the fabric of the parish church, 400 *livres* to divide among a number of religious foundations and (rashly?) offered two *cannes* of 'serge grise à chacun des pauvres qui assisteront à mon enterrement'. All her furniture she left to her husband with the exception of the contents of one room. This room, and its contents, she described and her description provides some idea of her comfortable life style:

la chambre de damas bleu complette de douze couverts d'argent; de deux flambeaux d'argent avec leurs épargnes; d'une cévelle d'argent avec son couvercle, de deux cuiliers d'argent à ragout, de quarante huit draps de lit, de deux cens quatre vingts huit serviettes, de vingt quatre napes ...[94]

There were seven Flottes producing cloth in 1754, no less than ten doing so in 1760, and there was no year before 1789 in which less than two members of this large family appear on the registers of Clermont's cloth production. Even in the disastrous year of 1779, when only eight clothiers continued to produce in the town, Jean Baptiste Flottes and Jean-Antoine Flottes-Raissac were among their number. The Flottes were thus the most persistent of Clermont's cloth-making families and provide a partial exception to the general tendency to desert the industry. A partial exception only, however, for a decline from ten cloth-making Flottes in 1760 to a mere two by the end of the 1770s was evidently quite a drastic one.

The experiences of different members of this large family were most diverse – some withdrew from manufacture, some continued to produce and prospered and some continued to produce and were ruined. The

94. ADH II E 25 163, 13 April 1761.

explanation for the wide range of experiences becomes clearer when the varying resources of the different branches of the family are considered. As mentioned in an earlier chapter, there were two branches of the family which initially involved itself in the trade.[95] In this period there were, effectively, five: Jean Flottes vieux who first produced in association with Joseph Tudesq in 1707, left two clothier sons, Pierre Flottes jeune and Mathieu Flottes, and Pierre Flottes (who was received clothier in 1718) left three, Pierre, Denis (oncle) and Jean aîné. I shall first deal with the cases of Pierre Flottes jeune and Mathieu Flottes and then with the more complex experiences of the sons and grandsons of Pierre Flottes. I shall provide details from the family trees of both branches of the Flottes to prevent confusion (Table 24).

Jean Flottes (vieux) died in 1733. His elder son, Pierre (jeune), had begun producing cloth in 1730 and his second son, Mathieu, in 1746. Both were producing in 1754, both were to cease production in the 1770s, Pierre in 1773, Mathieu in 1778. They ceased, though, for different reasons; Pierre had accumulated a large enough fortune to retire and live off rent, Mathieu had virtually ruined himself. Pierre's greater success was in part to be explained by his being the elder son (which would have meant that he would have received a larger inheritance), and in part to his beginning production at an earlier date than Mathieu and thus gaining from the exceptionally profitable state of the trade until the mid-1750s. But his success, too, was due to a talent which, to the trade's great disadvantage, had become a decreasingly essential quality: he was a most proficient clothier and even as harsh a judge as Roland de la Platière conceded this, describing him in 1765 as the 'meilleur de tous de Clermont ... sans tâche'.[96] That he had already accumulated a sizeable fortune by 1762 is revealed by his giving a dowry of 35,000 *livres* to his daughter who married Louis Chauvet, from a well-connected medical family, in that year.[97] By 1773 Pierre Flottes must have been in his late fifties or early sixties and, as he had sufficient resources to live off rent, he retired to Montpellier, taking up residence with his son-in-law, and leaving no heir to continue his business.[98] Mathieu Flottes was possibly less talented than Pierre[99] and in addition, as a second son, the size of his inheritance would have been smaller and he had begun production later. He expanded production in the 1760s and suffered considerably, it would seem, from the crisis in the town's industry which occurred during

95. See pp. 270–1.
96. ADH C2215.
97. Bobo, 'Communauté languedocienne', p. 59.
98. ADH C2189, Pierre Flottes jeune to St-Priest, March 1773.
99. He is described as a 'bon fabricant et honnêt' by Roland (ADH C2215).

Roland's inspectorate and again from another severe crisis which hit the trade in 1774. He suspended his concern temporarily in 1767 and 1768 and from 1771 to 1773, and a sign of his growing difficulties was that it was only with the aid of Barthèlemy Martin that he returned to producing in 1774. Pezet, juré-auneur, reported in 1777 that he was in Barthélemy Martin's employment.[100] His name finally disappears from the production registers in 1779. A case in which his son was involved before the seigneurial court of Clermont vividly illustrates the shame resultant on industrial failure. It suggests, too, that Mathieu Flottes fils may have succeeded in recouping some of his father's losses by means of his skills at 'boules'. The court case concerned insults shouted at the Flottes son by Françoise Desalasc, wife of Jean Bouisson, a rich and successful clothier: 'fripon voudrois tu faire aller mon fils à l'hôpital comme toy vas y toy seul voudrois tu que mon fils mangeât comme toy le Bien de tout le monde', she had shouted. One of the witnesses explained that her insults were occasioned by the fact that Mathieu Flottes, 'quy se trouve un des plus fort joueurs au Balon de ce pays cy', had won 120 *livres* from her son the previous year.[101]

Pierre, the oldest of the three sons of Pierre Flottes, was producing in association with his son Denis in 1754 (Table 25). He was the richest of the three brothers having, like his namesake Pierre Flottes jeune, had the dual advantages of being his father's heir and of having produced cloth continually since 1720. He died in 1756 and the distribution of his estate between his heirs gives a reasonably full idea of the extent of the resources of a rich (but not the richest) Clermont clothier.[102] His heir, Denis, was regarded as a wealthy man locally. In 1768 he was described in the registers of the conseil de ville as 'fort riche soit en maisons soit en Bienfonds quil a dans cette ville', and in addition mention was made of his ownership of a large estate at Pouzols, in the diocese of Béziers, which included noble land.[103] Significantly no mention is made in this description of his cloth-making concern. Denis Flottes had withdrawn from production in 1764 and was, as the statement implies, living largely from landed rent. His younger brother, Jean-Pierre, however, had continued production, on his own account to begin with, and then in association with his

---

100. ADH C2180, Pezet to St-Priest, 30 Oct. 1777, Mathieu Flottes included in a list of 'fabricants qui travaillent sous la direction du Sr B^{my} Martin'.
101. ADH, Ordinaires Clermont, Case 210, 23 Sept. 1780.
102. ADH 11 E 25 160, Sept. 1756: Pierre Flottes's will had been registered with a Canet notary, André, in 1740 and this act consists of the distribution of the major legacies by Flottes's widow, Catherine Tartary, who was to enjoy the usufruct of the inheritance.
103. ACC BB6, 28 Dec. 1768. The estate had been purchased for 22,000 *livres* on 20 March 1756 (ADH 11 E 25 158).

Table 25. *Cloth-making members of second branch of the Flottes family, 1718–89, with dates of mastership*

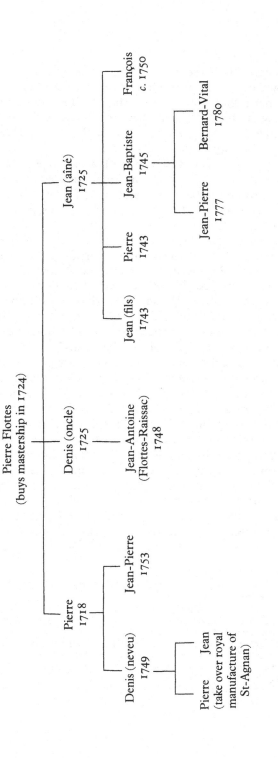

brother-in-law, Estienne Lugagne.[104] The major reason for Denis Flottes's withdrawal from production would have been that which had induced other richer clothiers to withdraw. The trading circumstances were not favourable, and particularly for those of Clermont's clothiers who wanted to produce cloth of quality. Such cloth tended to fetch a price the same as, or only slightly superior to, that of the generality of the town's cloth, so long had the town's cloth been treated as though it were a standardized item. In addition he no longer needed to produce (whereas his younger brother probably did) and may well have regarded producing in the capacity of a normal clothier as beneath his dignity; he referred to himself now as the 'seigneur' of Pouzols.[105] In 1773, however, an opportunity presented itself which effectively obviated all these reasons for not producing: the lease of the royal manufacture of St-Agnan at St-Chinian, which belonged to Roussel de St-Amans, fell vacant.[106] The direction of a royal manufacture had always been regarded as the most distinguished type of employment in the cloth industry and in addition royal manufactures' cloth, unlike that of normal clothiers, tended to be priced individually. Denis Flottes took over the lease of this manufacture, therefore, in June 1774, in association with his brother Jean-Pierre.[107] The renting of this manufacture turned out to be a satisfactory proposition both economically and socially. Economic success resulted from the Flottes brothers' persistent good production which gained a high reputation for their concern. As Tricou, inspector at St-Chinian, reported in 1782, 'Cette manufacture [St-Agnan] est sur le plus grand pied, et jouit de la plus haute réputation. Pour ce l'aquérir cette réputation, ces M^{rs} [the Flottes brothers] firent les plus grands sacriffices en débutant. aujourd'huy ils commencent à jouir du fruit de leurs travaux, et ce réparer des pertes passées.'[108] Denis Flottes must have significantly enlarged his already substantial fortune by the 1780s for it was he who purchased St-Chinian's other royal manufacture, that of 'Ayres', from Bermond, who had gone bankrupt in 1784.[109] His social success is illustrated by his choice of second spouse: he married Sophie de Grandsaignes, who came from a

104. This association is mentioned in ACC BB7, 17 March 1770.
105. For example in a notarial act registered on 4 May 1757 (ADH 11 E 25 159).
106. It was a Roussel who was one of the first St-Chinian clothiers to produce for the Levant. In 1704 Roussel frères were granted the privilege of sending *londres* to the Levant and awarded a bounty of 3 *livres* a piece. Roussel's St-Agnan was one of two manufactures raised to the status of royal manufacture in St-Chinian in 1720 (ADH C7326, 7390, Etats, 17 Feb. 1705, 3 March 1720). On the Roussel family see A. Delouvrier, *Histoire de St Chinian-de-la-Corne et de ses environs*, p. 61.
107. ADH C5545, Tricou to St-Priest, 17 May 1774.
108. ADH C5545, Tricou to St-Priest, 10 June 1782.
109. ADH C2432, Report of Tricou, 22 June 1784.

noble family and, a break in a tradition which had endured in the Flottes family for many centuries, he gave the children of his second marriage classical names – Alphonse, Hector and Helène.[110] Unlike his sons by his first marriage, Pierre and Jean, who took over the direction of St-Agnan from him, it does not seem that any of the progeny of his second marriage was directed towards an industrial career.[111]

Denis (oncle), Pierre Flottes's second son, was wealthy too, though the size of the fortune which he left to his only son, Jean-Antoine, owed as much to his marriage to Antoine Raissac's daughter, Jeanne, who became Raissac's only heir, as it did to his own inheritance and long years of cloth production (he began to produce in 1731). His son's awareness of the importance of his maternal inheritance is revealed by his adoption of the name Flottes-Raissac. Flottes-Raissac provides a rare example of a rich clothier continuing to produce cloth in Clermont despite the possession of a fortune large enough to have allowed him to live comfortably without working. His considerable resources gave him distinct advantages over his impoverished fellow-clothiers. Inspector Vaugelade commented on his circumstances in 1777: he had inherited Antoine Raissac's consolidated manufacture in the Rue de la Fregère which was equipped with 'tout ce qui est nécessaire' and he was, Vaugelade reported, 'à son aise, et même Riche ... [in a position to make] les achats des Laines à propos, et faire les avances Nécessaires pour une Bonne fabrication'.[112] Unlike poorer clothiers he was able to weather the bad years in the trade without withdrawing completely from production. He was not obliged to manufacture on credit, and he had sufficient resources both to dispatch cloth at his own expense for sale in the Levant (he did this during the Seven Years' War) and also to vary the nature of his production in order to experiment with new cloth types and markets.[113] He explained the advantages which he enjoyed over poorer clothiers in a letter to his cloth-commissioners, frères Roux:

Le commerce du Levant me paroît annoncer une Révolution qu'en pensés vous? je vous prie de men Dire votre avis pour que je Diminue mes dispositions en ce gendre. jay éprouvé dans toutes les Révolutions une demande pour mes draps et

110. A. Delouvrier, *Histoire de St Chinian*, pp. 64–5.
111. ADH C5545, Bruté to St-Priest, 31 Aug. 1782: in this letter he explains that the manufacture of St-Agnan is being run in the name of 'frères Flottes', Denis Flottes's sons Jean and Pierre, both minors at this stage.
112. ADH C5535, Vaugelade to St-Priest, 10 April 1773.
113. Production figures reveal that there were no interruptions in his manufacturing. Flottes-Raissac mentions sending cloth at his own expense to the Levant in a letter to Roux frères of 23 Nov. 1762 (ACCM, Fonds Roux, LIX, 281). In 1775 Flottes-Raissac was making *londrins-premiers* as well as *londrins-seconds* (see ADH C5535, Flottes-Raissac to St-Priest, 18 Oct. 1775).

j'ay eu l'avantage de pousser ma fabrication alors tandis que les autres faisoint peu mais à ne vendre qu'avec peine et à des mauvais prix il faut aller Doucement.[114]

Flottes-Raissac's became the only surviving manufacture of any importance in Clermont. It was his concern around which a visitor from Venice was shown in July 1776, for example, and by this stage, indeed, it is doubtful whether there were any other manufactures which would have merited a visit.[115] His example suggests that had more rich clothiers continued in the trade Clermont's experiences in the second half of the century might have been quite different from what they were. Clearly, though, circumstances had dictated against this and it was Flottes-Raissac, not those who withdrew from the trade, who was the exceptional case. His example is interesting precisely in that it provides a contrast, and serves to illustrate the two crucial factors lacking among the new generation of clothiers, capital and experience. Flottes-Raissac himself grew increasingly conscious of the exceptional nature of his concern (it did, of course, become more of an isolated phenomenon as other rich clothiers withdrew from production) and on several occasions between 1770 and 1780 he attempted to obtain a special title for his manufacture to distinguish it from those of other clothiers. In May 1778 he explained to de Montaran his grounds for requesting such a distinction: 'Ma Manufacture est la seule qui a travaillé sans interruption depuis son ettablissement qui Datte de l'origine du commerce du Levant à Clermont de Lodève . . . Réunissant les opérations de Fabrique les plus essentielles, que les autres n'ont pas, ou ne Font pas Valoir', he wrote, and added that the granting of a special title (he wanted to be allowed to mark his cloth 'Manufacture de draps de France en toute qualité autorisée ou protegée par le Roy') 'animeroit mes talents, et me determineroit à continuer ce commerce, et à ne pas fermer cest ettablissement comme L'ont fait tant d'autres'.[116] His request was refused and, as he told de Montaran a year later, the refusal had nearly caused him to 'quiter ce Commerce, et de me Retirer des affaires'.[117] In fact such a move would have accelerated only by a few years the virtually inevitable disappearance of his concern. Flottes-Raissac continued to produce cloth because he knew no other life than that of clothier but there was absolutely no question of his heirs' doing so. He had married into the Marseillais nobility, kept a carriage (for his wife's use largely?) in Marseilles, and his life-style, as much as the size of his cloth-making concern, increasingly separated him from the run of

114. ACCM, Fonds Roux, LIX, 281, 3 May 1787.
115. ADH C5601, Taillardat de St-James to St-Priest, 18 July 1776.
116. AN F12 1382, Letter of 21 May 1778.
117. AN F12 1382, Letter of 7 Oct. 1779.

clothiers in Clermont. He died in 1788 leaving a large fortune (land which was immediately rented out for 1,200 *livres* a year, 30,000 *livres* each for his two daughters' dowries and far more for his son who was to be his héritier universel). His children were minors and he had named his first cousin Denis Flottes (of frères Flottes) and his brother-in-law, Jean-Louis Teisserenc (of Lodève), to be their guardians. A meeting of guardians, and relations of both Flottes-Raissac and of his widow, decided in 1789, without demur, that 'il ne convenoit point de continuer la fabrication des draps'.[118]

Jean Flottes aîné was the youngest of the three brothers. This and two other factors contributed to his, and his sons', being the poor cousins in the Flottes clan: he did not begin cloth production until 1736 (as opposed to 1720 and 1731 in the case of Pierre and Denis) and he had the largest family of the three, a total of nine children of whom four, Pierre, Jean (fils), Jean-Baptiste and François, became clothiers. This is not to say that Jean Flottes aîné was impoverished. In January 1763, for example, he handed over goods to the value of 34,000 *livres* to his son François. But his resources were certainly slighter than those of his brothers while his family responsibilities were considerably greater: François Flottes, in return for this donation of 34,000 *livres* and of goods and land valued at not more than 16,000 *livres*, committed himself to feeding his father, mother and brother Pierre, paying Pierre's inheritance of 3,000 *livres*, paying 2,000 *livres* each to two sisters, Gabrielle and Rose, and feeding his brother Denis, a priest.[119] These were heavy responsibilities. This relative lack of resources meant that the sons of Jean Flottes aîné did not have open to them the alternative of leaving the industry to live off rents. Their commitment to the industry was thus, of necessity, greater. If they wanted to leave the industry they needed to find themselves alternative employment. Roland de la Platière, writing in September 1764, described the choice open to clothiers in the face of falling prices for cloth. Most clothiers would have liked at least to suspend production, he wrote, but such a course had its problems:

ils le feroit en effet sil en étoit dune fabrique comme dun moulin à eau dont en ouvrant et fermant l'écluse, on suspend, on renouvelle à la fois le jeu de toutes les

---

118. ADH, Ordinaires Clermont, Case 584, 31 May 1788 , 28 July 1789. Flottes-Raissac's widow was Dame Louise Sabine Rostan, daughter of Honoré de Rostan, écuyer, former sub-delegate of Marseilles. Included in this dossier is a long inventory of all Flottes-Raissac's effects and property.
119. ADH II E 25 165, 15 Jan. 1763. The standard of care had to be high too: a clause in the act stipulated that the father maintained the right to recover his property '[s'il] n'est point content de la nourriture et de l'entretien que le sieur Flottes le fils donataire fournira'.

machines; mais les ateliers, les outils nen dépérissent que plus; les commis, les ouvriers quittent, se dispersent, changent la manière de travailler . . . la réputation se perd, le nom s'oublie . . . on ne ramène rien de tout cela qu'à très grand frai.

It was better he argued to 'quitter pour toujours, à 40, 50, 60 ans prendre un nouvel état, ou se déterminer à ne rien faire', and he added that *'ceux qui ont gagné précédemment, et qui sont sans famille, n'ont pas hésité; les autres gémissent et s'exténuent'*.[120] The family of Jean Flottes vieux, numerous and with an insufficient fortune, was in the latter position. The oldest of the sons was Jean Flottes fils. He had begun production in 1751 and continued, with some interruptions, until 1768. By then, it is clear, he was anxious to find alternative employment and in this he was eventually to be successful; in 1775 he established himself as cloth-commissioner and merchant in Montpellier.[121] Pierre Flottes's cloth production was brought to an untimely halt by his death: his widow was finishing off his raw materials and completing a few pieces of cloth in 1765.[122] Jean-Baptiste and François were the two members of the family whose involvement in the trade lasted longest. Jean-Baptiste was the more proficient clothier of the two (according to Roland who described him as an 'assez bon fabricant' whilst categorizing François as 'mauvais')[123] and it was he who was to be the more successful of the two. He produced continuously, without interruption, and that he did so with some success is suggested by the voluntary payment of 800 *livres* which he made towards the *contribution patriotique* raised in Clermont in 1789.[124] Like Flottes-Raissac's, his example demonstrates that a clothier with a moderate capital, experience and skills could, even in the difficult conditions of the 1760–89 period, prosper. It is of some significance, though, that despite his success Jean-Baptiste Flottes attempted to ensure that his sons were qualified in a trade other than cloth-making. It would seem that both were apprenticed to merchants for in 1782 one was working in Rome and the other in St-Jacques de Compostella. A year later one was working as an assistant to a négociant at Marseilles and it is probable that the other one associated himself with his father in 1784 for the firm Flottes et fils took the place of that of Jean-Baptiste Flottes in the annual register of Clermont's production in that year.[125]

François Flottes, we have noted, though not the oldest son, became

120. ADH C2213, Roland to Trudaine, 27 Sept. 1764. My emphasis.
121. ADH C5535, Jean Flottes to St-Priest, Feb. 1775.
122. ADH C2215, Comparison of Gaja's and Artaud's judgements, 1765.
123. ADH C2215, Comparison of Gaja's and Artaud's judgements, 1765.
124. Bobo, 'Communauté languedocienne', p. 128.
125. ADH C5545, Pezet to St-Priest, 28 July 1782; AN F12 1378, St-Priest letter of 14 Sept. 1782; ACCM H158, Memoir of 16 April 1784.

effectively his father's héritier universel in 1763, and it was he who took over the parental cloth-making concern (a large proportion of the 34,000 *livres* donation took the form of cloth-making equipment and materials). That François was a man of some ambition is apparent from the speed with which he expanded the production of his father's former concern. Between 1763 and 1764 he raised output from 140 to 620 half-pieces of cloth. In 1766, however, having sustained heavy losses, he withdrew from the trade and until 1768 his concern was idle. During this time he devoted a part of his energies to winding silk, establishing a workshop in his house in the Rue de la Coutellerie.[126] In 1769 he re-established his cloth-making business and expanded the scale of his activities at what was a surprisingly rapid rate. By 1772 he had already achieved an annual production of 1,130 half-pieces which made him Clermont's third-largest producer. Production on such a scale was not prudent, for the market situation for Languedocian cloth at Marseilles remained extremely unstable in the 1770s and François Flottes's efforts rather than enabling him to recover the losses which he had sustained in the 1760s clearly aggravated his financial situation. That all was not going well was suggested by his abandonment of production for a second time in Clermont in 1774 (a particularly bad year). On this occasion he did not withdraw from the trade but transferred his concern to the villages of Roquebrun and Cessenon, to Clermont's west. The advantages of doing this lay partly in the fact that wages in these isolated villages were lower than in the vicinity of Clermont but also, and perhaps more importantly, in that his isolation would enable him to escape the vigilance of the local inspector and also change the mark on his cloth and avoid using the name 'Clermont' which had become a signal for bad quality. A sign of Flottes's growing financial difficulties was the fact that it was Barthélemy Martin who was selling him wools and advancing him some of the capital which he required to effect this production.[127] That François Flottes was a suitable collaborator for the Martins, the disreputable nature of whose business affairs has already been mentioned, is revealed by the commentaries of both the gardes-jurés of St-Chinian and an independent observer in Clermont. The former (in whose inspection Flottes was now operating) complained in 1774 that their workers were frequently being poached 'par quelques fabriquants ambitieux ... entre lesquels le S^r. Flotes tient le premier rang, et que Bien loin de les porter à Bien faire et à perfectionner les ouvrages leur Recommendent au contraire uniquement le célérité de L'imperfection',[128] and the latter, Pezet, juré-auneur at

---

126. ADH, Ordinaires Clermont, Case 289, Oct. 1767.
127. ADH C2189, Pezet to St-Priest, 13 Feb. 1774.
128. ADH C5535, Letter to St-Priest, 1 March 1774.

Clermont's bureau de marque (not, agreed, the most impartial of observers), was yet more critical of Flottes. 'C'est un impoteur, un homme de mauvaise foi qui par sa conduite entrenera un désordre affreux', he wrote. 'Il ne seroit pas prudent de laisser prendre racine à de pareils hommes.'[129] François Flottes soon demonstrated that there was some accuracy in these accusations. His new production he marked under three different names, those of Flottes-Laneige (his mother's maiden-name), and of Jean Hérail and Simon Fraisse of Roquebrun (two of Flottes's assistants). The purpose of marking cloth in different ways was, it seems, quite simply to confuse the buyer. Once production of poor quality had led to the discrediting of one name then a switch could be made to another. In 1776 Flottes introduced a further refinement. He began to mark his cloth 'draperie royale' of Flottes Laneige, Simon Fraisse and Jean Hérail. This time he was to be checked by the administration: the cloth in question was stopped and justifiably, for Flottes was abusing all the remaining elements of the regulative code and doing so not from high principles (as he repeatedly argued) but purely to deceive the consumer.[130] Flottes was to run into further trouble with inspectors in 1778, when a large quantity of his cloth was stopped on a variety of different grounds. He complained vociferously that these stoppages were causing his ruin. They certainly did not facilitate his economic situation but the growing crisis in his affairs can be traced far further back and it was above all the decline in the price of Languedocian cloth in 1777 and 1778 which was aggravating his situation. His fellow-clothiers were well aware of this: as the gardes-jurés of St-Chinian informed St-Priest in September 1778, 'le S. Flottes est un homme dont les affaires sont dérangés et qui fera incessamment faillite, suivante toute apperence. peutêtre ne demandera til pas mieux que d'avoir le prétexte de l'arrestation de ses draps pour excuser sa Banqueroute.' Later in the year he was to go bankrupt; his creditors were to lose 70% of the 200,000 *livres* which he owed.[131]

Thus François was the least successful member of the large Flottes clan and the contrast between his failure and the growing success of his brother Jean-Baptiste and of his various cousins was clearly difficult for him to come to terms with. Of this we have evidence. In 1774 he had moved to St-Chinian on account of the expansion of his activities in the

129. ADH C5535, Pezet to St-Priest, 27 Feb. 1774.
130. ADH C5556, Report of D'Huc, Estorc and Rey, 'adjoints' at the bureau de marque of Montpellier, 1 May 1776 and AN F12 842, François Flottes to Trudaine, 7, 9 May 1776.
131. ADH C5535, Taillardat de St-James to St-Priest, 12 Feb. 1778; C5590, Report of adjoints of bureau de marque, Montpellier, 1778, and letter of gardes-jurés of St-Chinian, 1 Sept. 1778.

vicinity of this town. This made him a virtual neighbour of his first cousins the frères Flottes and he began to collaborate with them in business affairs, having some of his dyeing and cloth-finishing carried out by them. The Flottes brothers must have realized by 1778, though, that their cousin had become an unreliable debtor and in January of that year they were obliged to assign him before the Chamber of Commerce of Montpellier for non-payment of fees charged for services rendered by their manufacture. Denis, who was responsible for this assignation, stopped in Clermont on his way back to St-Chinian from Montpellier. There he had been invited to dine in the house of Gabrielle Flottes, sister of François, who was married to Pierre Gayraud, another clothier. Also present for the meal, together with his wife, was Jean-Baptiste, François's brother. François himself was present in Clermont too and he was both aware that he had just been assigned by his cousin and also conscious, it is evident, that he had been excluded from this Flottes family reunion. Enraged he entered his sister's house, brandishing a cane, and threatened Denis Flottes shouting 'tu veux me perdre . . . est il possible qu'un couzin Germain veuille me Détruire'. Denis Flottes reacted calmly and ruthlessly. Having deprived his cousin of his cane he commented to those present that 'Ce Mʳ· cy a envie Daller voir les galères.'[132]

The founding member of the Verny family, which provided a number of clothiers to Clermont's industry, was Jean Verny. He came from a professional Montpellier family and was most probably a poor relation of that Jean Vernet who was among the associates of the company headed by André Pouget which ran Villenouvette in its early years.[133] Producing in 1754 were two of his sons, Thomas and Gabriel, and a grandson, François, son of Thomas. Their fortunes, like those of the Flottes family, were to be mixed. Gabriel, who had been associated with Martin in the 1740s (a bad omen), went bankrupt in 1758: 'depuis que la fixation qui avoit été faite du nombre des draps londrins seconds qui se fabriquoient chaque année dans cette ville fut suprimée, ce qui fut la cauze de la décadence de cette manufacture, il a fait des pertes si considérables sur les draps qu'il a fabriquez qu'il se trouve devoir Beaucoup plus qu'il n'a', he explained in his act of bankruptcy.[134] Thomas Verny, the elder son, was

132. ADH, Ordinaires Clermont, Case 337, 13 Jan. 1778.
133. Jean Verny was apprenticed to Villenouvette in 1680 (ADH II E 26 100, 15 July 1683). His father was Mathieu Verny of Montpellier, we discover from his marriage contract (II E 26 124, 12 May 1687). That he came from a professional background is suggested by the fact that his brother was a doctor (C2208: it is his brother who acts as his agent for securing a 'passport' to ensure redemption on duty for the import of cochineal in 1713).
134. ADH II E 25 160, 6 June 1758.

the richer of the two brothers but he had a large family of four sons and three daughters. Two of his sons, Thomas and François, had obtained qualifications as avocats and in 1755 Thomas was living in Toulouse, practising this profession, in the company of one of his sisters,[135] but François (despite his legal qualifications) and his other two sons were to become clothiers. François produced cloth at Clermont between 1751 and 1757 and then took over the royal manufacture of Aubenas. Mathieu was to co-operate with François in the direction of Aubenas, and Jean was to take over his father's concern in Clermont in 1758, but abandoned production in 1766. François, by his successful involvement with this royal manufacture, to all appearances succeeded in crossing that all-important, and much-sought-after threshold which permitted a clothier to choose between continuing production or living as rentier. By 1789, it is evident, it was the latter alternative that he had opted for as we find that he had returned to Clermont and been elected as mayor, having left the direction of Aubenas to his brother Mathieu.[136] Some idea both of the extent of his resources and of his public spirit is provided by the donation of 1,900 *livres* which he made to the *contribution patriotique*. This was the largest individual payment.[137]

Pierre Vernazobres had a chequered career as clothier. He went bankrupt in 1733 but between this date and 1741 repaid all his creditors and thus regained his commercial reputation.[138] Production during the period of 'fixation' brought him growing prosperity and by the 1750s he was vying for prestige with the richest of his clothier colleagues, having been appointed as lieutenant-de-maire, an office which entitled him to describe himself as conseiller du roi, and improving his fine house overlooking the Planol.[139] Disaster then struck. He had reacted to the deteriorating market situation in Marseilles after the outbreak of war in 1756 by shipping his cloth at his own expense and risk for sale in America. The ship in which his cloth was loaded was captured by the English. This loss transformed Vernazobres's financial situation and he had to undergo a second bankruptcy.[140] He was to make several attempts to revive his fortunes once again but to no avail. As was recorded in the registers of the

135. ADH 11 E 25 157, 29 Sept. 1755.
136. All these details obtained from production lists. On his election to mayoralty see ACC BB8, 8 Oct. 1789.
137. Bobo, 'Communauté languedocienne', p. 128.
138. ADH 11 E 25 119, 5 Sept. 1733: Concordat between Vernazobres's creditors; C2039 contains (1) a copy of his 'bilan' of 3 July 1734, (2) a report of July 1741 of Bonnafous, sub-delegate of Lodève, stating that Vernazobres had paid off his debts.
139. ADH C6763, Dampierre letter of 29 May 1749; ACC BB5, 6 June 1753, for details of improvements to his property.
140. ADH C5585, Petition of Vernazobres, 11 Feb. 1759, Trudaine to St-Priest, 19 Sept. 1758, St-Priest to Trudaine, 29 Sept. 1758.

conseil de ville, in connection with his tax imposition in 1766, 'La communauté . . . certiferoit volontiers que le sieur Vernazobres na pas du bien.'[141] One course which he tried was (like Pradier in the 1730s) to obtain employment in the administration of industry. In 1758 he petitioned Trudaine for employment, offering his services to 'rétablir la fabrication des draps pour le Levant'. This request was turned down as was a similar one made in 1766. Two bankruptcies were not a good qualification for the inspectorate. As St-Priest informed de Montaran in 1766, 'ce n'est point un sujet convenable pour ces sortes de places'.[142]

Estienne Desalasc's career is of some interest to us for he was the last ex-apprentice, unrelated to established clothiers, to be received master before the ban of 1737. He was the son of a card-maker and had actually worked in this trade himself before being apprenticed to a clothier in 1721.[143] His long training (a sixteen-year gap between being apprenticed and setting up his own concern) and artisanal background should have equipped him with exactly the sort of entrepreneurial qualities which, we have argued, were essential to the original success of Clermont's clothiers at the beginning of the century. Had there been more clothiers of his type, our argument goes, the fate of the town's industry in the second half of the century would have been quite different. And the nature of Desalasc's experiences in the second half of the century provides support for this argument. He produced continuously, and with success, until he died at the ripe age of eighty-five in 1789. All inspectors concurred on his skills as clothier. Roland de la Platière categorized him as 'bon' and noted his reputation for honest dealing[144] (a notable quality in Clermont in the 1760s). Taillardat fils likewise recorded that Desalasc's production in 1777, a year of very low prices, was 'tout ce qu'on peut demander dans les circonstances'.[145] That his persistence and excellence as clothier may well have made him less interesting in other ways is suggested by a remark made by Pezet, juré-auneur, in a letter written to St-Priest in August 1782. 'Le Sr Est^{ne} Desalasc est et a toujours été un très Bon fabricand', he wrote, but added that 'pour lui personnellement, ce n'est pas un homme'.[146] Desalasc would seem to have been a pure industrial-

141. ACC BB6, 28 Oct. 1766.
142. ADH C5585, Trudaine to St-Priest, 19 Sept. 1758; C2177, Vernazobres to de Montaran, 4 Jan. 1766, St-Priest to de Montaran, 12 Feb. 1766.
143. This is revealed by a Desalasc family agreement of 12 Sept. 1740 (ADH 11 E 25 132) in which mention is made of 'travail que led. Sr Estienne Desalasc avoit fait . . . du mestier de cardier, jusqu'à ce quil fut mis en aprentissage de celluy de marchand fabriquand'.
144. ADH C2215.
145. ADH C5534, Report of April 1777.
146. ADH C5592, Letter of 11 Aug. 1782.

ist, absorbed and obsessed by his craft, and with few of the graces which
Pezet observed and admired in clothiers, or ex-clothiers, of older stock.
Such men were in short supply in Clermont in the second half of the
eighteenth century.

Joseph Vieules was received master in 1734 and began production in
1736. His career as clothier was to be punctuated by a succession of
disasters. In 1738 he was banned from production on some obscure
grounds which are not documented, but by 1740 the ban had been lifted
and he was granted a small quota during the years of 'fixation'.[147] In
1747, however, this quota was reduced by three *ballots*. Again the reasons
for this penalty are obscure. Inspector Tricou expressed his bewilder-
ment to the secretary of the intendancy: 'je ne sçay pour quoy ... il
travaille mieux qu'il n'avoit jamais'.[148] It was perhaps these repeated
upsets which were the cause of Vieules's not enriching himself during the
'fixation' period as his colleagues were doing and in the mid 1750s, when
the trade became more hazardous and competitive, he was obliged to
undergo what he himself described as an 'espèce de faillite'.[149] He was
'saved' by Jean Martin, who lent him money with which to liquidate his
debts on the security of property which he owned in Clermont, but then
experienced the habitual fate of those clothiers who became involved
with the Martins. He was obliged to abandon production in 1758 and his
house ended up in Martin's hands.[150] In 1773 he became involved in a
dispute with Inspector Vaugelade and the correspondence to which this
altercation gave rise not only reveals his activities in this year but also
gives an approximate idea of how he had survived since abandoning
regular production for the Levant. The dispute arose as a consequence of
a piece of *vingtain*, belonging to Vieules, being found by the inspector.
The cloth evidently did not conform to regulations and Vaugelade believed that it had been made out of stolen wools for sale in the Levant.
Vieules denied the accusation, maintaining that the cloth was intended
for sale to his son who had established himself as a marchand-détailleur in
Béziers, and questioned the justice of Vaugelade's picking on him – 'un
pauvre misérable qui na quune seule et unique demy pièce de drap qui ne
voit pas le moment quelle soit finie et vandue pour avec ce produit fournir
du pain à sa famille pour quelques jours' – when there were some forty
looms in Clermont mounted with cloth which was of only marginally
higher quality than his. Writing to St-Priest to defend himself, Vieules
provided a synopsis of his experiences since abandoning production in

147. ADH C2040.
148. ADH C2049, 28 Jan. 1747.
149. ADH C2088, Vieules, petition of *c.* 1756.
150. ADH, Ordinaires Clermont, Case 13, 21 Sept. 1790.

1758. He had initially found alternative employment at Lodève. (The same war which had disrupted Clermont's trade with the Levant had expanded demand for Lodève's military cloth.) 'Le besoin m'obligea daller à Lodève', he recorded, 'à servir de comis dans un fabrique de tricots, heureuse encore de trouver cette place.' This concern had then failed like his own and he had been obliged to return to Clermont but had maintained links at Lodève and had been given orders to make 'tricots' in Clermont by a merchant who provided him with the necessary funds and wools. This enterprise had collapsed too, however, and, as Vieules explained, the piece of *vingtain* under discussion had been made 'du débris de ce qui me restoit de la laine que jemployois à ces tricots'. Despite this sad tale gardes-jurés, inspector and Clermont's consuls were adamant. An example had to be made of Vieules to discourage other such marginal producers. He was fined 100 *livres* and the cloth in dispute was confiscated.[151]

We have accounted for the majority, twenty-four out of thirty-six, of the clothiers producing at Clermont in 1754. In addition we have described the experiences of a few clothiers, related to members of this 1754 group, who had not started to produce by that year. What conclusions arise from our survey?

First, it is evident that the information we have assembled throws significant light on the causes of the long crisis which afflicted Languedoc's cloth-making centres during the second half of the eighteenth century. Our *a priori* assumption turns out to have been justified. There is, indeed, the survey has revealed, an entrepreneurial explanation for the industrial decline. De Gournay's confidence that the province's entrepreneurs would respond positively to the abolition of the administrative system which was restraining them was, we have discovered, quite misplaced. This administrative system, which gave them privileged status, turns out on the contrary to have been in many cases the only factor which was inducing them to stay in the trade and Clermont's most fundamental problem in the second half of the century was, it is evident, a consequence of the sudden loss of the bulk of its entrepreneurial elite.

The significance of this discovery is enlarged by the fact that Clermont's example was not an isolated one. Parallel behaviour by the clothier elites of St-Chinian and Carcassonne was predictable, of course, in view of the identical nature of these towns' development cycles, and such behaviour was noted by contemporaries. In 1758, for example, St-

---

151. ADH C5536, Vaugelade to St-Priest, 3, 5, 16 July 1772; Vieules to St-Priest, 5 July 1772; judgement of 17 July 1772.

Chinian's gardes-jurés wrote that they and their colleagues, 'Détrompés par une funeste expérience de deux ans, de L'espoir d'un meilleur sort, Instruits par les pertes passées, accablés par les présentes, et effrayés encore par un avenir plus menaçant', were suspending their trades in order to salvage the 'Débris' of their fortunes. The 'desertion' of the industry would appear to have been yet more rapid and complete than in Clermont. A memoir from the town's clothiers' corporation written on 1 September 1778 recorded that a decline in membership from thirty-four to four or five had been experienced.[152] That there had been a similar 'desertion' at Carcassonne, and that the wealth of those clothiers who had withdrawn from the industry was in some contrast to the desperate state of the trade, is suggested by the comments of an inspector made in 1770. 'Carcassonne m'a paru tantôt animé & tantôt triste', he wrote, 'selon qu'on juge ... en observateur de l'état du Commerce, on y voyoit concours d'équipage issu d'un Négoce resplendissant alors, & offusquant la noblesse presque toute retirée à Narbonne où elle forme une société non moins distinguée par elle même que choisie.'[153] As early as 1758 de Montaran had written to St-Priest expressing his fears that 'les meilleurs fabriquants se dégoûtent' and that the old industry was being ruined to build a new one which would not be its equal.[154] By the end of the 1760s, it would seem, these fears had already materialized.

By the 1770s, then, a new industry had developed and production for the Levant was largely in the hands of a new generation of clothiers. Of this new generation we have said little although it was from its members, rather than from among retiring clothiers, that the majority of victims of the crisis came. The survival rate in the new industry was low. Turgot's 1776 survey of Arts et Métiers revealed that Clermont clothiers' corporation had twenty-two active members but no less than sixty-eight inactive ones.[155] Those who did survive, however, became the 'representative' clothiers of the new industry. The percipient comment by Pezet which we have presented at the beginning of this chapter illustrates this. Clearly regretting the passing of the industry's richer members, he informed St-Priest that 'à la vérité le Corps de fabricands a bien changé de ce quil étoit dans les premiers années que je fus ici, se n'étoit alors que peruqués; gens de Bon sens, les anciens sont morts, et il leur a succédé une troupe de Bandits; tous fils d'artisans, ou douvriers de fabrique il

152. ADH C5545, 5590, Letters to St-Priest of 2 March 1758, 1 Sept. 1778.
153. ADH C5519, Inspector Rodier, 'Mémoire sur le travail de drap', c. 1770.
154. ADH C5539, 23 Aug. 1758.
155. ADH C2792.

reste fort peu d'Enfands des anciens'.[156] The transformation which had occurred in the make-up of Clermont's body of clothiers, and the characteristics of old generation and new, could hardly have been better expressed.

That the continued involvement of rich and experienced clothiers, with wide commercial links, would have eased the situation of Clermont's industry in the second half of the century seems fairly self-evident. Besides it is illustrated by two factors: the success of those few rich, or moderately rich, clothiers, such as Flottes-Raissac, Jean-Baptiste Flottes and Estienne Desalasc who did persist with their concerns, and the nature of the problems encountered by the new generation of clothiers. These new clothiers lacked experience, were in too great a haste to imitate the successes of their predecessors, received little help from a demoralized and impoverished labour force, suffered from Clermont's low industrial reputation among cloth-buyers, but, above all, experienced difficulties because of their shortage of capital. These artisans' sons rather than disregarding regulation from principle did so because they could not afford to maintain the quality of their cloth in the face of falling prices. They continued producing for the declining Levant market not from inertia and lack of enterprise but from a want of resources. They were able to produce for a market only when merchants paid for their cloth in advance, or at least as soon as it left the cloth-dresser's workshop. Finally the poverty of these clothiers caused them to be unable to produce cloth continuously, in bad years as well as good, and this explains the continual fluctuations in the number of clothiers at Clermont (and at Carcassonne) during the second half of the century.[157] An inspector's report for 1771 illustrates these consequences of the clothiers' poverty. Production had decreased in Languedoc because of difficulties in the Levant market, he reported, but it had decreased more abruptly at Clermont than elsewhere because 'les fabriquants moins riches qu'ailleurs ne peuvent faire des draps qu'à mesure qu'ils les vendent, hors d'Etat de les garder longtems dans leurs magasins comme font ceux de Bédarieux'. The same factor, the inspector continued, caused them to 'diminuer chaque jour un peu la qualité de leurs draps forcés de suivre la modicité du prix courant'.[158] The extent of the change in the level of the resources of Clermont's clothiers is striking. Remember the report of the sub-delegate of Lodève twenty-five years previously: 'les marchands

---

156. ADH C5592, 25 Aug. 1782.
157. Apparent from production figures and commented on by Dutil, *Etat économique*, pp. 393–8.
158. ADH C5588, Report of Vaugelade, 20 Feb. 1771.

senrichissent tous les jours, Il y en a dont la fortune les met au rang du plus opulant', he had written. Now they were poorer than the clothiers of other towns in the province, significantly more so than those of Bédarieux, a town whose industry a mere fifteen years earlier had been virtually totally dependent on that of Clermont. The disparity between the state of Clermont's and her neighbours' industries was noted by other inspectors. One recorded in 1784 that he had found 'Clermont dans la misère, Lodève en bon état et Bédarieux riche', and offering his own explanation for the contrasts he continued, 'La prospérité s'y rencontre en proportion avec la conformité aux règles d'une bonne fabrication.'[159] The real explanation was of course more profound. Clermont's industry had undergone a revolution in the mid-century whereas for Bédarieux there had been continuity, and there are signs that the reasons for Bédarieux's success were similar to those for Clermont's at the beginning of the century: its clothiers had received their original training as artisanal producers of coarse cloth for local markets, they had learned the techniques necessary for production for the Levant from the clothiers of Clermont and the privileged manufacture of Aaron Seimandy (in Bédarieux), and were combining their artisanal inheritance of caution, economy and hard work with the new technical skills in order to produce successfully for the Levant.[160] The same inspector described Bédarieux as 'admirable par son industrie'. There were certainly a variety of factors at play but the fact that a neighbouring town was able to prosper by producing cloth for the Levant trade during the second half of the eighteenth century certainly discourages belief that the crisis at Clermont was any more than in part a consequence of developments outside the town.

Now it would be out of place to criticize Clermont's entrepreneurial elite for having moved out of the industry. First, withdrawal was most probably a wise entrepreneurial decision given the difficulties encountered by those who remained in the trade. And secondly, such retirement from industrial production was, we have argued, a regular, acceptable and universal phenomenon in all 'pre-industrial' industrial centres in which the possibility of amassing wealth existed. All such centres experienced development cycles which bore some similarities to that which we have

159. ADH C2190, Brisson to St-Priest, 2 Dec. 1784.
160. Roland de la Platière reported to Trudaine on 4 Sept. 1764 that 'les fabriquants de Bédarieux en honestes gens et en bons citoyens commencent à imiter ce qui ont resté de vrais fabriq^{ts} ici, les meilleurs de toutes les jurandes, et les manuf^{res} royales mêmes' (AN F12 557). Seimandy's manufacture was privileged by the Etats on 11 Jan. 1713 (ADH C7363).

observed at Clermont. But what needs emphasis, and what it has been a major purpose of this book to show, is that it was administrative intervention which had intensified this natural cycle and caused its economic consequences to be particularly disastrous. It was intervention which had caused profits to be concentrated amongst an exceptionally restricted group of clothiers; it was intervention which had encouraged these clothiers to stay longer in the trade than would normally have been the case; it was intervention which had prevented social mobility in the industry (and the value of the existence of a sizeable group of rising entrepreneurs is illustrated, we have argued, by the details of Estienne Desalasc's career); and finally it was intervention, or rather a sudden decision to reduce the level of intervention, which had contributed to this unnaturally rich clothier elite's withdrawing from the trade, and to their doing so *en masse*. As a consequence the industry had been denuded of both capital and leadership and left, in the most difficult of circumstances, in the hands of a large group of poor and inexperienced clothiers whose most obvious quality (and there must be doubts about how positive a quality it was) was a marked precipitancy in the expansion of their production which attested to their anxiety to build themselves the fortunes which they believed only the restrictions on entry to the trade had been denying them.

This destabilizing of the industry because of interference with its natural developmental cycle was, we would argue, the major harmful consequence of administrative intervention. But there were other consequences too which merit consideration. Two, which are particularly vividly illustrated by Clermont's sad experiences, are the over-commitment to the Levant market and the confusion occasioned both by the survival of engrained habits among clothiers and cloth-buyers, and by the prolongation of much of the regulative system, despite the change of policy in the 1750s.

The question of over-commitment to the Levant has been raised at previous stages in this work. Other trades had been surrendered, and Clermont's merchants and clothiers for some sixty years had done little else than produce for the Levant. This concentration had been encouraged by the exceptional profits which the town's semi-monopoly situation had given rise to, and had been in part enforced by a variety of measures designed, we have seen, to stabilize, and to ensure the quality of, the town's production for the Levant. All cloth-making skills, apart from those necessary for the production of *londrins-seconds*, had been lost, and the range of the town's commercial contacts restricted, and oriented above all to Marseilles. And to these commercial and technological restrictions needs to be added some consideration of the psychological consequences of so long a dependence on a single market. It is clear from the large number of entrants to the industry in the 1750s and 1760s, and the long persistence of some in producing under what were almost hopeless circumstances, that clothiers, in addition to lacking resources, commercial contacts and technological skills to produce for other markets, had difficulty in even conceiving of the possibility of producing for elsewhere. Above all they were mesmerized, it would seem, by the impressive fortunes which had been made from production for the Levant in the first half of the century. The Martins and Pelletans, it is evident, were able to speculate on this unnatural keenness to produce for the Levant. There were many takers for the money which they were prepared to loan for the production of cloth and once over-production had occurred (in part in consequence of the credit which they had granted), and prices had collapsed, they could buy up the proceeds of their debtors' investments at knock-down prices. It was the spectacular size of their own, and their colleagues', fortunes that was the chief inducement to new clothiers to undertake production for the Levant and they were able to expand their fortunes yet further by providing these clothiers with the necessary financial backing to pursue their ambitions. We have already seen that a number of clothiers had difficulty in repaying the sums they had borrowed and as either houses or land were the usual pledges for these loans the Martins, Pelletans and other creditors found, as a consequence of their debtors' defaulting, that the size of their investments in land and buildings gradually increased: their transformation to full rentier status was thus an almost automatic consequence of the collapse in the trade.

The confusion occasioned by engrained attitudes, and by the survival of elements of the regulative system, has been mentioned in previous chapters and was also, we have noted, selected by Paul Masson as one of the major explanations for the industry's decline. He categorized the problem as arising largely from the state of mind of clothiers: so conditioned were they by rules and regulations that they could only react to a relaxation in the strictness of enforcement by cheating. But this theory does clothiers an injustice for their production of technically illegal, low-quality cloth, rather than being attributable to their state of mind, is explicable first by their realization that profits on such cloth were likely to be highest, and secondly by the impossibility of continuing to produce cloth according to the regulations profitably. Clermont's cloth during the period of restrictions had tended to sell at a uniform price and, despite the system of liberty, it continued to do so. Could clothiers have been expected to have taken any other course than profiting from this situation? This point was made forcibly by an anonymous observer in Clermont who explained to St-Priest that 'le plus habille fabriquand a été celui qui a sçu mieux éluder le règlement, et mieux engager les Inspecteurs à justiffier aupprès des achetteurs, qu'il les avoit observés'. In other words it was the sharpest (not the dullest as Masson would seem to imply) entrepreneurs who seized these opportunities.[161]

So the sudden change in administrative policy in the mid-1750s not only precipitated mass retirement by Clermont's industrial elite, it also created the possibility of cheating on an unprecedented scale. And this particular 'structural' problem had consequences of a long-term kind. Clermont's reputation as a manufacturing centre was to be almost permanently blackened as a consequence of the extent to which buyers' good faith had been abused. Evidence of this we have seen in the attempts by François Flottes and Flottes-Raissac to escape the town's bad reputation by marking their cloth under different names (and they were far from the only clothiers to do this).[162] In addition to causing the town to lose its good name it gave rise to a (lasting?) aura of disreputability to the profession of clothier in Clermont, created a justified cynicism (given the bias, and susceptibility to bribery, of inspectors) about the impartiality of the administrative system, and clearly contributed to the bitterest of feelings between members of the profession.[163] Because success had become dependent on a combination of skills in eluding regulations and cultivating inspectors and usury, that high consideration in which, it is evident, clothiers themselves and observers had held the cloth-making profession was lost. That confessors shared this view is illustrated by their refusal in years of crisis to grant absolution to clothiers who were guilty of abusing regulations. Roland de la Platière's reaction to the situation at Clermont when he arrived exposes dramatically the atmosphere reigning in the industry. 'Vous m'avés envoyé parmi un peuple de bêttes féroces. Jamais on n'a vu les honnêtes gens autant opinionés par la canaille qu'ils le sont ici', he wrote to his patron Trudaine in September 1764. 'Ou vous ne connaissiés pas cette urgence', he added, '. . . ou vous avés voulu me faire éprouver tous les dégoûts et toutes les amertumes qui peuvent être attachés à une fortune trop médiocre . . . Aucune raison de sentiment, d'honneur ni de justice refleurera jamais la bassesse de leurs âmes: elles sont inaccessibles à tout ce qui cest honête. non, il n'y a rien à

161. ADH C5533, Anonymous memoir of *c.* 1757.
162. AN F12 1387, Rabaud Solier et Cie to Necker, 13 Nov. 1780; 'Le titre de Clermont est à Marseille comme dans toutes les Echelles le passeport de la plus mauvaise qualité des draps du Languedoc.'
163. ADH C5535, in a letter of 23 Dec. 1777 François Flottes and Jean Bouisson d'Ancely note 'Lenvie qui nest que trop répandue parmi les personnes de la même profession, & notamment dans ce pais'.

attendre de pareils gens.'[164] As the author of an anonymous pamphlet
sent to Intendant St-Priest emphasized, to remedy this situation:

il faudroit faire en sorte, que la fortune du fabriquand se trouvât attachée à la
perfection de son drap, et à la bonne foy avec laquelle il faisoit son commerce . . . et
Croyés Monseigneur que si le Meilleur prix du Drap étoit la Récompense du plus
habille fabriquand, le mot d'honneur pourroit se faire entendre, aux fabriquands
de Draps pour le Levant comme aux autres proffessions.[165]

Thus an analysis of Clermont's experiences in the second half of the
eighteenth century provides strong grounds for rejecting the view that
Languedoc's industrial crisis was largely occasioned by factors external
to the province. The view is based on an incorrect assumption that the
cloth-producer was invariably submitted to the merchant, and besides
cannot account for the fact that a uniform demand situation evoked
distinct responses in different Languedocian cloth-making centres. The
analysis of Clermont's experiences has illustrated both the centrality of
the entrepreneur in proto-industrial production, and the manner in
which variations in the nature of administrative intervention, besides
leading to considerable over-specialization and confusion, affected the
quality of entrepreneurship in numerous ways, above all by decreasing
the competitiveness of the industry, encouraging corruption, and syn-
chronizing and accelerating the industry's natural development cycle
and thus encouraging a general abandonment of industrial activity
during the 1750s and 1760s.

164. ADH C2213, 13 Sept. 1764.
165. ADH C5533.

12

Conclusion: the end of the cycle

Il existe entre la draperie du nord et la draperie du midi de la France, un contraste bien marqué. La nature du produit diffère comme les habitudes des populations. (L. Reybaud, *La laine* (Paris, 1867), p. 105)

The distortions occasioned by administrative interference were so great that it was a number of years before a degree of normality returned to Clermont's cloth industry. By the 1780s, however, the level of the town's production, and the number of clothiers producing, had stabilized and although the industry was far from prosperous, and the social climate in the town in no way tranquil, the situation was less desperate than it had been in the previous two decades. An analysis of the nature of the process of adjustment which had occurred in the town's social and economic state will provide a satisfactory epilogue to this long industrial history as well as contributing to assessing the significance of what we have discovered about Clermont's development for both Languedocian and French economic and social history.

There were two sides to this process of stabilization. The cloth industry gradually adapted to a more competitive market situation by cutting costs, and the town as a whole adapted to the increasing unreliability of what had been for so long its main source of income by diversifying its economic activities and returning to a more balanced situation, similar to that which had existed before the expansion of the industry for the Levant. These two developments we shall illustrate in turn.

For Clermont's cloth industry to survive in the more competitive environment which prevailed after the mid-1750s it was necessary that there should be a return to some of those cost-cutting practices which had characterized the endeavours of the clothiers' and weavers' ancestors before the expansion for the Levant began. Then, we have seen, low costs were assured by a combination of factors: first, industrial incomes were supplemented by earnings from other sources and dependence on the industry was thus lessened and costs were effectively subsidized; second-ly, the fixed capital investment in the industry was minimized and shared among clothiers; and thirdly, labour costs were decreased by clothiers' and cloth-workers', and their families', physical involvement in most parts of the production process.[1] There was not going to be a total return to this 'depression model' for industrial production. It was not necessary, for example, for those few remaining richer participants in the trade. But in the case of poorer members of the industry an adaptation of this kind did occur, not so much as a consequence of any conscious decision on anyone's part but, more painfully, by the elimination of those who failed to adapt in these ways.

We shall examine first the case of the cloth-workers. The collapse of the industry had been sudden and it had left the labour force, long accustomed to reasonably steady employment (labour shortage had been the predominating problem in the first half of the century) in a quite desperate situation. In 1758 a list was drawn up in Clermont of the 'ouvriers ... qui se trouvent actuellement sans travail et de leur famille qui sont dans la misère'. It included the names of eighty-two weavers, seventeen carders, nineteen dyers, and thirty-three affineurs. The ma-jority of these workers were married and between them (excluding the carders) they had 249 children dependent on them. The carders em-ployed seventy-three spinners and, in addition to the omission of their dependents the list did not include, the compilers noted, 'un nombre infiny Douvriers qui sont premièrement les journaliers pour laver et battre la laine, trieuses, droseurs, cardeurs, fileuses, épotoyeuses, liteuses, et déliteuses qui sont sans ouvrage depuis long tems'.[2] The industrial crisis of 1765–6 was to cause unemployment on a similar scale. De Montaran, intendant de commerce, when he visited Clermont in October 1765 was moved by what he found: 'la désolation étoit si grande dans cette petite ville, qu'en nous rendant au lieu de l'assemblée des fabriquants', he reported, 'le peuple en foule ne cessoit d'implorer la protection du Roy'. Three to four hundred workers had gathered to meet him and he had ordered them to send forward four of their number. These 'se jettèrent à nos pieds tout en pleurs et nous exposèrent leur misère extrême'; they were, they explained, 'réduits à la mendicité par le manque de travail depuis 18 mois'.[3] The years 1758 and 1765 were ones of exceptional crisis. There were to be years of industrial expansion, too, but overall it is evident first that the trade could no longer be relied upon

---

1. See pp. 103–16.
2. ADH C5600.
3. ADH C2176, De Montaran, memoir on his 'tournée' of 1765–6.

to provide steady employment, as it had done before 1750, and secondly that, in so far as the industry survived at all, it did so as a result of cheapness, and there was thus a downward pressure on wages. Clermont's large labour force was over-dependent on its industrial earnings to survive under these circumstances.

There are two questions which we need to answer then. First, how was this over-large, dependent labour force reduced in numbers? And secondly, how did those cloth-workers who remained at Clermont adapt to surviving in an industry which was no longer capable of providing regular employment? The reduction in numbers occurred in the most tragic of manners. There was no question of the town's adequately solving its unprecedented problem of structural unemployment even though private and communal charity alleviated a part of the suffering.[4] Nor was there any question of a large number of these workers', who had grown old in their profession and been suddenly confronted with poverty, developing those techniques for survival which were so brilliantly exercised by the inhabitants of poor areas of France whose apprenticeship in the art of poverty began at birth. Even to *ask* for assistance was too great an admission of failure to some of these cloth-workers; there were cases of families dying quietly in misery in the privacy of their homes.[5] Some workers left the town to seek employment elsewhere, in several cases abandoning their families to their fates. On the list of the unemployed drawn up in 1758 the words 'a décampé' or 'a quité sa famille' follow several workers' names.[6] Their destinations? Some obtained employment in more successful clothing towns. Mazamet was described in 1786 as 'la ressource d'une foule d'ouvriers de la jurande de Carcassonne',[7] and in addition there existed the possibility of crossing the frontier – there was a considerable emigration of French textile workers to Spain during these years – or even of emigrating to the New World.[8]

4. Thus in December 1764 a *subvention* was proposed to raise extra revenue for the town's hospital (ACC BB6, 18 Dec. 1764).
5. ADH C5471, Clermont's consuls to de Montaran, 12 Jan. 1766: 'La faim la Nudité la Rigueur du froid font périr dans leurs maizons un nombre infini de ces mizérables on les trouve morts aussy sur les chemins parcequ'ils sefforcent de se traîner pour aller mandier dans les villages voizins.'
6. ADH C5600. See also AN F12 557, 'Avis des deputés du commerce', 21 Aug 1784; 'on se plaint à Carcassonne d'une émigration de 5 à 600 ouvriers' and C2227 in which there are details of general survey carried out into the question of the desertion of workers. Le Blanc estimated on 16 Dec. 1774 that more than 12,000 workers had already emigrated (AN F12 676A, Letter to de Cotte, 16 Dec. 1744).
7. AN F12 1380, Memoir for Etats by Louis Valade, avocat, Mazamet, Jan. 1786.
8. Thus ADH C2227, Sub-delegate at Uzès to St-Priest, 15 Sept. 1784; 'on ne peut point ... se dissimuler, qu'il ne passe journellement beaucoup de nos ouvriers chez l'Etranger. Il est à craindre que cette émigration n'enrichisse nos voisins de notre industrie

Table 26. *Mortality in Clermont 1757–74*
(*figures in brackets, number of children of 10 and under included*)

1757	90	(37)	1766	141	(80)
1758	158	(85)	1767	278	(75)
1759	170	(88)	1768	136	(63)
1760	145	(70)	1769	102	(49)
1761	137	(65)	1770	210	(160)
1762	149	(97)	1771	145	(89)
1763	123	(58)	1772	145	(68)
1764	128	(61)	1773	126	(63)
1765	237	(164)	1774	107	(52)

Source: ADH 3 E 81^1–83^1
N.B. In some cases (about 5%) no age at death is cited. In such cases, unless it is specifically stated that the deceased is a child, I have assumed that adults are being referred to.

Such recourses would generally have been open only to younger workers, however. Older workers, in addition to lacking the strength to make the rounds of alternative cloth-making centres for employment, would have been less likely to be granted employment, and would have had stronger ties in Clermont. In addition, and this was remarked on by contemporaries, they were generally unsuited to agricultural employment. They had been debilitated by long years of largely indoor activity of a repetitive and enervating nature.[9] The parish registers suggest that it was death, a direct or indirect consequence of growing poverty, which accounted for a number of these unemployed cloth-workers (Table 26). The swollen mortality rates for 1765 and 1767 were undoubtedly linked to the industrial crisis. The figures for 1765 suggest that children, always more vulnerable than adults, were affected most by the growing poverty in Clermont. The high mortality of 1767, which was occasioned by the outbreak of a severe epidemic, clearly affected adults most severely, however (although it is possible that there was a considerable under-recording of infantile mortality because of the confusion occasioned by the epidemic). That it was Clermont's poor who were the major victims of the epidemic, and that the cause of the outbreak lay in the low quality of

nationale.' See also AN F12 557, 'Avis des députés du commerce', 21 Aug. 1754: 'Cette émigration [from Carcassonne] tient aux espérances que l'indépendance de l'Amérique présente à tous les peuples de l'Europe.'
9. ADH C5471, Dat (sub-delegate Carcassonne) to St-Priest, 17 Feb 1781: 'ces ouvriers accoutumés à ce travail nont peu s'en procurer dautre qui peut leur fournir de quoy vivre attandu qu'adonnés à ce travail depuis leur enfance ils ne peuvent plier leur corps à tout autre ouvrage pénible'.

their food, is apparent from the registers of the conseil de ville. Antoine Berthomieu, consul and qualified doctor, recorded in January 1767 that 'il règne actuelement dans Clermont des maladies murtrières qui attaquent les pauvres gens et que la cauze de ces maladies est évidamment la mauvaise nourriture dont ces infortunés font uzage'. Plotted in the same source is the course of the epidemic: by March its intensity had built up and there had been so many deaths that it had been found necessary 'd'entasser les corps les uns sur les autres dans le petit cimetière'. By July the worst was past and the consuls took stock of the extent of the town's sufferings. They calculated that an eighth of Clermont's population had been afflicted by the epidemic.[10]

Whether it was a case of those cloth-workers who survived adjusting to the nature of the new industry by obtaining alternative sources of income, or of those who survived being those who were less dependent on their textile earnings, is not completely clear but, in either case, it is apparent that the typical cloth-worker after the crises of the 1760s was not as dependent on his industrial earnings as his predecessors had been. The most normal source of extra income was from the land – 'tout tisserand possède au moins une parcelle de terre', Bobo writes[11] – but we also find evidence of weavers, and members of their families, employing themselves in a wide range of activities within Clermont, acting as day-labourers, working as servants, fripiers, couturières and midwives, keeping hens, rabbits and silkworms, running wineshops, selling fish, making and selling pâtisseries etc.[12] This policy of supplementing textile wages with earnings obtained from other sources was followed by those cloth-workers who desired to remain permanently in Clermont. Younger workers, it would seem, found that their best insurance against the unreliability of the industry lay in minimizing their commitment to it by geographical mobility. A sign that a considerable part of the labour force adopted this policy is the fact that the size of Clermont's population came to fluctuate with the prosperity of its cloth-industry. Charles de Ballainvilliers, St-Priest's successor as intendant,[13] in a memoir which he composed on the province in 1788, mentioned this unstable charac-

---

10. ACC BB6, 9 Jan., 1 March, 29 June, 14 July, 26 July, 2 Sept., 20 Sept. 1767.
11. 'Communauté languedocienne', p. 86. The same phenomenon at Carcassonne according to sub-delegate Dat who reported in 1787 that 'Beaucoup d'ouvriers partagent leur temps entre la Lanéfice et la culture des terres; pendant les trois mois consacrés aux moissons et aux vendanges presque tous les ouvriers abandonnent les ateliers' (cited by Dutil, *Etat économique*, p. 290).
12. ADH, Ordinaires Clermont, Cases 150, 247, 240, 775, 788, 74, 213, 788, 73, 96, 775, 11 March 1765, 31 May 1787, 27 April 1787, 23 July 1781, 2 Aug. 1774, 3 Oct. 1763, 24 Oct. 1780, case of 1778, 29 June 1763, 2 Aug 1764, 31 Jan. 1779.
13. Appointed in 1785.

teristic of both Lodève's and Clermont's populations: Lodève's population he estimated at 8,000 but added that 'il est des années où ce nombre varie, en raison de l'activité ou de l'inactivité de la manufacture' and Clermont's population of 4,500, he added, 'éprouve de variations pour les mêmes Raisons'.[14]

Clothiers, like cloth-workers, were in excess supply after the liberalization of the 1750s. As de Gournay originally noted, and as we have stressed, one of the structural problems created by administrative intervention in the industry was that far too many Clermontais were unnaturally anxious to make cloth. A shedding of numbers was a necessary prerequisite for the stabilization of the industry. The movement out of the industry from what might be described as its 'top end' has already been described. But the losses from its 'bottom end' were in fact far larger. Unlike rich clothiers, who left the industry generally to live off rents, these failed members of the new generation of clothiers were forced to find alternate sources of income. Evidence exists about the choice made by a few of them. Some, like the cloth-workers, left the town. Jean Baille, who abandoned production in 1764, declared in 1766 that he was about to 'quitter la ville pour aller résider ailleurs'.[15] Likewise Louis Gayraud, whose fruitless relationship with Jean Martin was mentioned earlier, left Clermont to try his fortune in the West Indies.[16] Fulcrand Delpon, a dyer, who was described (disparagingly) by St-Priest as 'un avanturier', left to establish his trade in Florence.[17] Other failed clothiers obtained salaried employment. Such was the case, we have seen, of Joseph Vieules, and Nicolas Audibert and Pierre-Marc Berthomieu, after several years of independent production, obtained employment with Barthélemy Martin and Roux-Fouscais, a Marseillais négociant, respectively.[18] Some clothiers attempted to survive on the fringe of the profession, producing occasional pieces of cloth with the cheapest of materials. Again Vieules was of their number and his fate was representative: such production, despite the change in the nature of the industry, was not tolerated.[19] In at least one case an ex-clothier obtained agricultural employment. Jean-Jacques Dutheil, who had made cloth in 1763 and 1764, was tenant of a métairie in 1771.[20] In many cases, it is

14. BM Montpellier, MS 48, *Mémoire manuscrite sur la province de Languedoc*, I, 167.
15. ACC BB6, 1 Nov. 1766.
16. ADH, Ordinaires Clermont, Case 56, 16 Jan. 1789; ACC BB8, 1 March 1789.
17. ADH C2189, Letters of Trudaine to St-Priest, Vaugelade to St-Priest and St-Priest to Trudaine, 11 Sept., 3 Oct., 30 Oct., 1769.
18. ADH C2179, Roland to St-Priest, 31 Aug. 1766; Clermont Ordinaires, Case 206, 4 April 1776.
19. ADH C5536: Vaugelade, in his report of 5 July 1772, mentions the names of two other clothiers, Léotard and Vidal, suspected of being guilty of the same practice.
20. ADH, Ordinaires Clermont, Case 469, 27 March 1771.

clear, the exercise of the alternative profession, which failed clothiers were obliged to adopt, involved a definite decline in status. Jean-Antoine Gély, for example, set himself up as a marchand-droguiste after going bankrupt in 1777. A court case in 1783 reveals that he manufactured his own candles on the roof of his house. His involvement in such menial activity would have represented a significant decline in status for him as he came from a distinguished family: his father had served as second consul and he himself was described as bourgeois in 1763 and had married a sister of Flottes-Raissac.[21] Jean-François Rouaud Tartary, who likewise came from an excellent background, was forced too, after going bankrupt in 1770, to accept a distinct decline in status. He had inherited a considerable amount of property and this he was obliged to sell – he parted with no less than five houses in Clermont – and he became a 'marchand-épicier', a retail-merchant. His son, too, by his apprenticeship to a tanner in 1787, was launched on a less distinguished, but no doubt securer, career than that originally chosen by his father.[22] There are, finally, three cases documented of 'académies de jeux' or, less euphemistically, gambling-dens being established by ex-members of the clothier profession.[23] This particular switch in employment is not as surprising as it might sound. As we have seen, the approach of a number of the new entrants to the industry had been that of gamblers as much as of clothiers – a miraculously rapid enrichment had been expected.

As was the case with the weavers, it is not absolutely clear whether those clothiers who survived the crises, and continued to produce, did so because they successfully adapted to the new conditions in the industry, or did so because, for a variety of reasons, they were better suited from the beginning for production under the new circumstances. Evidence suggests, though, that the second of these two grounds for survival was the predominating one. Roles were rigid in the pre-industrial period, and the fate of clothiers like Rouaud Tartary and Gély suggests that richer, or higher-status, entrants to the trade had difficulty in developing the necessary artisanal qualities to cut costs and besides tended to be those *most* likely to expand the scale of their concerns recklessly. The clothiers best equipped to survive, it seems, were those, most scorned by Pradier and Pezet, who came from artisanal backgrounds and who possessed not

21. ADH, Ordinaires Clermont, Case 561, 19 Feb. 1783. On Gély's family background: referred to as bourgeois: 11 E 25 165, 7 Sept. 1763; served as second consul: ACC BB4, Nov. 1741; marriage: Ordinaires, Case 665, 12 April 1782; bankruptcy: 8 B 420.
22. Bankruptcy: ADH 8 B 413, 6 Feb. 1770; sold houses (valued at 5,198 *livres* 17 *sols*) between 1767 and 1774: ADH C5037; marchand-épicier: Clermont Ordinaires, Case 206, 20 July 1780; son's apprenticeship to tanner, Ordinaires, Case 245, 24 May 1787.
23. Set up by Louis Portes (ex-dyer), Philippe Levasseur and Pierre Rousserie (ex-clothiers): ADH, Ordinaires Clermont, Cases 215, 775, 514, 29 Oct. 1780, 5 Dec. 1788, 26 June 1768.

only a capacity for hard manual labour and the advantage of the active support of members of their families, but also in a number of cases specialized skills in one particular production process. Dyers, shearers, cloth-dressers and fullers were among the most successful of the clothiers in the new industry and their combination of their traditional trade with that of clothier enabled them both to cut production costs and to gain extra income by carrying out specialized processes for other clothiers.[24]

It should be stressed again that there was not a complete return to that immobile situation which had characterized Clermont's industry in the 1670s and 1680s. There is, however, abundant evidence of a strong tendency in that direction. We find clothiers once again involving themselves in the physical as much as the commercial side of cloth production, members of clothiers' families participating in the production process,[25] clothiers obtaining income from sources alternative to cloth-making (and above all from the land),[26] and finally clothiers attempting to minimize their fixed capital investment in the industry: the non-utilization of the majority of the fine industrial buildings made in the first half of the century has been referred to already and in addition there is evidence of looms, ownership of which had been concentrated entirely in clothiers' hands in the first half of the century, being sold to weavers.[27] One clothier, offered the possibility of purchasing a loom by a weaver, replied that 'bien loin de vouloir lacheter il n'en avoit qu'un qu'il vouloit ... vendre'.[28]

The result of this gradual process of adaptation by both clothiers and cloth-workers was that by the 1780s Clermont's industry was better equipped than it had been in the mid-century to face the difficult conditions in the Levant market. The parallels with the form industrial decline took in the town in the second half of the seventeenth century extended even to the type of cloth produced. Already the *londrins-seconds*, produced for the Levant at less than two-thirds of the cost of

24. Shearers who became clothiers included members of the Cathala, Fraisse and Bonneville families. Two dyers who took up cloth production (successfully) were Jean and Fulcrand Delpon.
25. E.g. ADH, Ordinaires Clermont, Case 545, 21 Nov. 1753: evidence given reveals that cloth belonging to Mathieu Cathala after coming back from the fulling mill was worked on by his daughters: 'Les Demlles Cathala ont les soins de les liter'. The same operation was carried out by female members of the Flottes/Tudesq household in the early years of the century. See p. 293.
26. E.g. on 27 July 1786, at five in the morning, Gaspard Beaumier, marchand-fabricant 'faisoit fouler des gerbes de bled' in Clermont. Both an agricultural link and participation in manual labour are thus revealed.
27. ADH, Ordinaires Clermont, Case 250, 8 June 1787, sale of loom by Jean Bouisson to weaver.
28. ADH, Ordinaires Clermont, Case 652, 14 April 1788.

those made until the 1750s, were distinct from the cloth produced in the
past century only in their superior finish, and with the wars of the French
Revolution Clermont's clothiers virtually ceased production for the
Levant and produced military cloth instead. The sort of cloth required by
the army was the undistinguished, hard-wearing, coarse product which
had been Clermont's speciality during the previous century. After one
hundred years the manufacture of the fine 'Dutch-style' cloth ceased in
the town and the skills necessary for this type of cloth were lost as workers
became accustomed once again to spinning and weaving coarser wools.[29]
There had been a complete turn in the circle.

As mentioned in an earlier chapter, the extent of the industrial expansion in Clermont in the first half of the century had led to the neglect of
agriculture. It was, therefore, a fairly natural response to the industrial
collapse for the town's population to pay more attention to its landed
resources, and all the more so in so far as agricultural activities were
favoured by the steady rise in agricultural prices noted throughout
France in this period. The agricultural revival was given a further boost
by the physiocrat-inspired edict of 5 July 1770, which granted tax-
exemption for a period of fifteen years on abandoned land brought back
into cultivation.[30] A growing number of exemptions granted for this
reason are recorded in the registers of the conseil de ville of Clermont.
There was an ironic element in this agricultural revival for, it will
be remembered, the original grounds given to the Etats by Intendant
d'Aguesseau for supporting Villenouvette had been that industrial
revenues were more reliable than agricultural, being 'sujettes ny aux
révolutions des saisons ny à l'inconstance des élémens'. In the long run, it
is clear, Clermont's experience had fully demonstrated the fallacy of this
mercantilist belief, at least with respect to the pre-industrial period. The
land, as the physiocrats predicted, was proving a surer resource, and
Clermont's future was to depend increasingly on agricultural sources.[31]
The land recovered was being utilized for many purposes but there was
already an auspicious concentration on the cultivation of the vine. Wine
was described as the town's principal crop by the 1780s, and in the 1760s
and 1770s there was a considerable development in its distillation in the

29. Clermont did not cease producing for the Levant completely but in the year 11 of the
    revolution it was reported that clothiers were having difficulty in finding labour for the
    Levant in view of the fact that workers had become accustomed to making a new type of
    cloth, known as *quatreforts*, and preferred this new type of work to the old (report of 21
    pluviôse, year 11, AC unclassified).
30. A. Soboul, *Les campagnes montpelliéraines*, p. 5; see also ADH C47, Memoir on diocese
    of Lodève, 1787.
31. See p. 165.

diocese of Lodève for use in the manufacture of eau-de-vie, perfumes and verdigris.[32] That expansion in viticulture, which was to make the département of the Hérault, in which the diocese of Lodève was to be included, 'le plus vinicole de France' by the 1860s, had begun.[33]

There is less evidence about the performance of other sectors of Clermont's economy during the second half of the century. It would seem, however, that in contrast to the period up to 1750 a more varied and diversified economy was developing. Some of the neglected trades, particularly tanning, were being revived, and there is evidence of the presence of stocking-makers and of hand-loom weavers, using the small loom, in the town. At the end of the Ancien Régime there was cotton being spun and silk being wound in Clermont, and during the Revolution the manufacture of blankets was developed. There was a revival, also, in the 'petit commerce' which had always been of such importance to the town's economy and, significantly, it was Clermont, rather than Lodève, which was designated as the site for a tribunal de commerce, on the grounds of the great variety of its economic resources. There would hardly have been valid grounds for such a selection in the mid-century when the cloth industry, we have seen, was regarded as the only considerable trade in the town.[34]

By the end of the Ancien Régime Clermont's economic problems were far from being completely resolved (there was an uprising in the town in 1788, for example),[35] but there had been some recovery from the tragic situation of the 1750s and 1760s. This had been achieved partly by a revival in some of the town's traditional activities, which had been dropped or neglected at the expense of cloth production, and in part by the adaptation of the cloth industry to the new circumstances in which it found itself. With the return to dependence on traditional trades and traditional crops, with its cloth industry reduced to more moderate proportions, and with the re-establishment of the balanced economic structure which had existed before the great expansion in the industry for

32. ACC BB8, 1 June 1786 and ADH C6554, Report on the diocese of Lodève, 1774.
33. L. de Lavergne, *Economie rurale de la France depuis 1789*, p. 264.
34. The new intendant, Ballainvilliers, noted the importance of the town's tanning industry (BM Montpellier, MS 48, *Mémoires*, I, 173); stocking makers and weavers using narrow looms noted in ADH, Ordinaires Clermont, Case 55, 2 Nov. 1789; cotton-spinning and silk-winding noted in ADH C47, Memoir of 1786; manufacture of blankets: L1259, Procès verbal of 7 pluviôse, year 4; 'petit commerce': see C6554, Memoir for Prince de Beauveu, 1769 (trading in 'épicerie', wools, wheat, almonds, oil, silk, dyeing-drugs etc. mentioned); on Clermont's selection as site of tribunal de commerce (established 6 Jan. 1791) see L1259.
35. Mentioned in ACC BB8, 11 Dec. 1789. See also ADH, Ordinaires Clermont, Case 36, 23 April 1789: mention made of the establishment of a garde bourgeoise because of an 'émotion populaire quil y eut le quinze de ce mois et dont on craint les suittes'.

the Levant, Clermont found again the relative prosperity and economic stability which it had always enjoyed and these were assured now not by monopoly but by its natural advantages as a market and communications centre.

The information already provided in this, and the last, chapter about those who left the industry and those who stayed in it, and about the gradual change in the nature of industrial production and in the make-up of Clermont's elite, will already have served to throw light on the 'social conjuncture' in Clermont in the years leading up to the French Revolution. In contrast with the situation pertaining in the first half of the century, characterized, we have noted, by high levels of social mobility, by social divisions which increasingly took on a horizontal, 'class' nature and by the dominance of the town by an elite whose income came largely from trade, with the industrial decline there was a return to a situation not markedly dissimilar from that which had characterized Clermont's social structure at the end of the seventeenth century.[36] With lower profits from industrial activity there was less possibility of social mobility, and social divisions within the cloth industry became less marked while the gap between industrial producers and members of Clermont's elite most certainly widened. And this elite, composed largely of ex-clothiers and their close relations, was coming to depend far less on trade for its income and was becoming more exclusive and more rigid in its observation of a traditional bourgeois code of behaviour. Symptomatic, as always, of the changing characteristics of the town's elite was the choice made of municipal officers. No longer were there clothier-mayors. The mayoralty became again, as it had been in the seventeenth century, the preserve of the bourgeoisie. The Desalasc family's monopolization of the post until the municipal reform of 1766 we have traced, and a candidate for election after this reform described his qualification for office in the following terms. He was, he maintained, 'des premiers Bourgeois de cette ville quil vit et a toujours vécu noblement et quil est enfin généralement Reconnû pour estre de la première classe'.[37] The same man's son, also mayor of Clermont, was instructed by his father-in-law when he married in 1784 to invest at least two-thirds of his wife's 60,000 *livres* dowry in land, buildings ('immeubles'), offices or rent on the clergy or Etats of Languedoc. The parallels with the investment policy of bourgeois families in the stable circumstances of the late seventeenth century are striking.[38]

36. See pp. 129–31.
37. ACC BB6, 25 Nov. 1766.
38. Bobo, 'Communauté languedocienne', p. 71 and see p. 127.

What was involved in living 'noblement' and observing a traditional, bourgeois code of behaviour? An analysis of some of the activities of members of Clermont's elite will contribute to clarifying this question. Normal industrial work was barred, it would seem. The lack of privilege now attached to the status of clothier, and the entry into the trade of so many people of humble origin, besides making cloth-making less profitable, had made it less respectable. Pradier's reaction, which we have quoted, was representative.[39] The only remaining institutions which provided industrial employment of an honourable kind were royal manufactures, which continued to be privileged in various ways until the passing of the Allarde law of 1791, and, significantly, we have noted, three families from among Clermont's clothier elite prolonged their involvement in cloth-making by taking over royal manufactures.[40] Significantly, too, one of the rare members of this group who continued to produce in Clermont, Flottes-Raissac, expected that what he clearly regarded as somewhat of a sacrifice on his part, should be officially recognized and rewarded by the granting of special status.[41] That the French Government was aware that it was becoming necessary to grant special encouragements to persuade rich entrepreneurs to stay in trade is apparent both from the new policy initiated in the last years of the Ancien Régime of giving special recognition to concerns which had been functioning from father to son for three generations,[42] and also from a final twist given to the often-changed policy towards royal manufactures. The privileged status of these concerns – initially granted to introduce new techniques and prolonged, we have argued, to conserve the bearers of these techniques, skilled workers, during years of trade depression – was finally being justified (and it is a sign of desperation) on the entirely negative grounds that without such privileges entrepreneurs of royal manufactures would not remain in trade.[43]

39. See p. 389.
40. Jean Martin and the Flottes and Verny brothers.
41. See p. 414.
42. On this policy see des Cilleuls (*La grande industrie*, p. 237) who records the decision of the Bureau de Commerce to write to local intendants to discover which entrepreneurs were worthy of ennoblement because of 'l'ancienneté des familles, dans le commerce ou l'industrie, les capitaux mis en valeur, le nombre d'ouvriers occupés et les succès obtenus'. Records of a survey carried out in Languedoc to identify such individuals are held in ADH C2296. Inevitably few members of Clermont's industry qualified for consideration.
43. Thus two of the grounds for supporting the request of the Carcassonnais, Rolland, for the status of royal manufacture for his concern at Roquecourbe, were that the grant of the privilege cost nothing and that the bad state of trade 'paroissent exiger que l'on protège singulièrement ceux qui cherchent à en étendre ou même à en rétablir la réputation, ce quils feroient peutêtre pas ...' [if not granted a privilege] (ADH C2182, Opinions of Gaja and Le Blanc on the request of Rolland, 4, 10 July 1765).

Various alternatives to industrial production proved attractive to members of this elite, we have noted. Some were drawn to participating in local politics (the Desalasc, Berthomieu and Verny families). Others were clearly attracted by the rich social opportunities, and high prestige, available to holders of offices in the local sovereign court of Montpellier (Pierre Martin and Jean Bernard). Others obtained employment in, or became linked to, the professions: Pierre Flottes jeune, who retired to live with his medical son-in-law in Montpellier, Antoine Berthomieu, nephew of Jean-Pierre Desalasc, who qualified himself as a doctor, the Verny brothers, Thomas and François, both avocats, the former practising his profession in Toulouse, and Georges-Antoine Desalasc, described as an 'avocat en Parlement' in 1789.[44]

Daughters' possibilities were, of course, more limited but one option (apart from marriage) was open to them – participation in charitable work. Two ex-clothiers' daughters, Angelique Verny and Marguerite-Monique Flottes, acquired considerable renown for their good works in attempting to alleviate the poverty to which, our argument has been, the withdrawal of their own families from cloth production had contributed. The latter according to the abbé Durand, a local historian, was a 'parfaite Dominicaine ... Qu'elle était heureuse', he wrote, 'quand elle pouvait soulager quelque infortune.'[45]

Other clothiers, we have seen, were attracted by diversions of a mildly intellectual nature: Mathieu Pradier, who discussed political economy with de Gournay during his visit to Clermont, and who continued to correspond with the intendant on industrial problems, Jean Pelletan, who according to Roland possessed 'esprit et des connaissances',[46] in addition to corresponding with administrators, exchanged verses with Montpellier correspondents, and Barthélemy Martin was famed for his knowledge of the botany and geology of the Lodévois region. Flottes-Raissac, too, to judge from the contents of his library, well stocked with the works of the philosophes, was of a similar bent.[47] It is of some interest that these types of interest were unquestionably stimulated by clothiers' (regular) contact with an administrative system which not only forced them continuously to rationalize their economic behaviour, but also put them into direct contact with individuals who were generally of superior culture to themselves. Writing memoirs provided, in the cases of Pradier and Pelletan, an undoubtable stimulus to their intellectual pretensions.

44. ACC BB8, 8 July 1789.
45. *Biographie clermontaise*, pp. 81–2, 170.
46. ADH C2215.
47. ADH, Ordinaires Clermont, Case 584, 31 May 1788: inventory of Flottes-Raissac's possessions.

That Roland de la Platière's culture was superior to that of the run-of-the-mill clothier has emerged from statements of his quoted in the previous chapter. Clearly he was very much a paradigm of 'Enlightenment Man', and as such an impressive example for Clermont's clothiers, several of whom continued to correspond with him after he had left the town in 1766.[48] Roland's values, intellectual pretensions and scorn for Clermontais society emerge forcefully in a letter which he wrote in a fit of melancholy to St-Priest shortly after his arrival in the town:

Après avoir vécu pendant dix ans dans le sein de la plus douce amitié cultivant par choix la philosophie et les arts; quand l'âge n'est pas celui qui émasse tout le sentiment, que le coeur sait encore parler au coeur, quel spectacle que de me voir lutter pour conserver des goûts, les seuls dont je puisse désormais attendre quelqu'agrément. Quel état que d'être forcé à chaque instant de détester celui où l'affreuse idée me vint d'entrer dans ce maudit métier! . . . Jugés de ma situation, Monsieur, si je ne puis mettre un Racine à ma poche qu'il ne faille mettre un pistolet dans l'autre; si lorsque je veux prendre un Plutarque, un Newton, un Rousseau, je rencontre une arme à feu, et qu'au lieu de me délasser par le charme de l'étude, je suis forcé d'avoir des idées de meurtre . . .[49]

A less intellectual outlet was provided by hunting. Antoine Pelletan and a Desalasc grandson, apparently no less unruly a youth than his father had been, distinguished themselves in this field, it is apparent.[50] It was a pastime which was not unlinked to what was unquestionably a universal characteristic of members of the new elite, a universal characteristic and one which links them with the elite whom they themselves had contributed to displacing in the 1720s and 1730s. This was a strong interest in rural life, expressed in many cases by the purchase of rural properties (which were particularly valued if noble land was attached to them). The ideal was to own both an urban and a rural property. Thus Mathieu Pradier, and later his heir Jean Pelletan, enjoyed the ownership of both what was described as a 'maison de plaisance' on the demesne of Camplong and a fine town house; Denis Flottes, likewise, maintained two residences, his rural estate being in the village of Pouzols; the Desalascs owned, among other rural properties, a large estate at Octon, and Flottes-Raissac inherited his grandfather Antoine Raissac's fine manufacture and his rural property of 'Fon Rouge'. For Jean Bernard and Pierre and Jacques Martin, all of whom left Clermont for the city , it must have been their families' properties in Clermont itself which acted, as it were, as their rural retreats. If expenditure on land and buildings

---

48. These letters are held in the Bibliothèque Nationale, among the Papiers Roland (nouvelles acquisitions 6242–3).
49. ADH C2212, Roland to St-Priest, 23 Oct. 1764.
50. See ADH, Ordinaires Clermont, Cases 238, 239, 27 March 1787. On Pelletan see p. 405.

absorbed the major part of the elite's surplus income a large share went too, it is evident from inventories, on clothes. The inventory made after Flottes-Raissac's death reveals that he possessed a wardrobe of immense variety and luxury. Travel, too, clearly held a growing attraction for members of the elite and although it was generally limited to the bounds of Languedoc and neighbouring Provence – Montpellier, Marseilles (where Flottes-Raissac kept a carriage), local spas (Bagnoles and Lamalou-les-Bains) etc. – there are cases recorded of ex-clothiers travelling further afield. Flottes-Raissac was staying in Paris in 1778 at the Hôtel Montauban, in the Rue Gille of the Faubourg St-Germain, whilst he pursued his attempt to gain a special title for his manufacture; Jean Martin's visits to Paris were regular and it was there that he died in 1784.[51] As the widening net which was cast by its members in their selection of marriage partners has revealed, the elite, whilst loosening its links with other social groups in Clermont itself, had strengthened those with the provincial bourgeoisie, and thus joined that cosmopolitan network of bourgeois families which must have been growing in size and strength during the prosperous eighteenth century.

This ex-clothier elite had clearly progressed far beyond the stage at which economic need in any way dictated the way its members used the hours of the day and like all those placed in this position they needed to develop alternative patterns and habits: a schedule for each day, which needed to be satisfactorily divided between eating, talking, sleeping and minor diversions, and one for the year, with time spent in the country, regular visits (perhaps) to the provincial capitals of Toulouse and Montpellier, and 'cures' in watering places. Certainly there were abundant examples from whom to copy the art of leisure in France, an art, incidentally, which Arthur Young admired in some of those whom he visited during his travels and demonstrably lacked himself.[52] One social

---

51. Visits to Marseilles and Montpellier were clearly made most frequently. Presence at local spas is recorded on two occasions. On 20 July 1780 it was stated in a case before the seigneurial court that Roux-Fouscais, a Clermontais who had established himself as a négociant in Marseilles, had just left the town to take 'les eaux de Bagnols' (ADH, Ordinaires, Case 206) and on 9 Sept. 1765 Gabriel Pelletan informed Inspector Gaja of Montpellier that his cousin (probably Jean Pelletan fils) had just left for Lamalou-les-Bains (ADH C2214). Flottes-Raissac's presence in Paris: see AN F12 1382, Flottes-Raissac to de Montaran, 21 May 1778. Jean Martin's death in Paris: AN F12 1378, Plea of Stanislas Philippe Martin, June 1786.
52. See for example Young's reaction to ten days spent in the company of the Count de la Rochefoucauld and friends (*Travels in France*, pp. 32–5). He disapproved of the amount of time wasted by this group, absented himself from some of their socializing (impolitely?) ('I need not add, that I absented myself often from these parties, which are ever mortally insipid to me in England, and not less so in France') but admired the group's good temper and polished manners: 'the advantages of an unaffected and

innovation in Clermont which was designed to cater for the ample leisure-time of members of the elite was a so-called 'salle de compagnie', opened by one Pierre Louis Arnihac, bourgeois. There Clermont's wealthy could talk, play 'jeux de commerce' and read newspapers in comfort and privacy. Rights of entry were restricted, it is clear. A court case of 1776 serves to reveal not only the names of some of the regular users of this facility – Flottes-Raissac, Antoine Martin, a Maître Perouze, avocat-viguier of Ceyras, Roux Fouscais, ex-inhabitant of Clermont who worked as a négociant in Marseilles – but also the identity of one man for whom, it is clear, it would not have been proper to do so. Antoine Martin in his testimony reported that he had seen François Rouaud (Jean-François Rouaud Tartary, ex-clothier who had gone bankrupt in 1770) entering the house 'ce quil navoit pas coutume de faire'.[53]

Clermont's social structure, like its economy, had experienced a full cycle. The town's elite had stabilized and had ceased to be creative economically. A sign of this, we have pointed out, was the increasing extent to which its members' fortunes depended on dispositions of wills and the choice of marriage partners. In accordance with Max Weber's hypotheses the economic stagnation of the second half of the century had contributed to a return to a social stratification based on 'orders' or 'status' rather than on 'class'. In accordance with Weber's ideas, too, it is evident that the attribution of status among members of Clermont's elite, although there was a qualifying principle that all should possess sufficient resources to enable them to live without working, was governed by a number of non-material elements too, connected with life-style, intellectual attainment, political influence, the possession of titles, links with other families etc., the unifying element being provided more by consumption patterns than by production. These characteristics separated the group from those whose claims to distinction rested purely on wealth, and it was they which gave the elite the characteristics of 'status order' as much as of 'class'.[54] Members of the elite had had to pay dearly for these distinctions. Large dowries had had to be given to daughters in order to develop honourable family links, and large payments made for land and for the purchase of offices and political positions. Now the advantages of their position could be capitalized on for they in turn could charge high sums to, and demand sacrifices from, those anxious to be included in their number. The experiences of the Bernard family are representative.

---

polished society, in which an invariable sweetness of disposition, mildness of character, and what in English we emphatically call *good temper*, eminently prevails'.
53. ADH, Ordinaires Clermont, Case 206, 20 July 1780.
54. M. Weber, *Economy and Society* in H. H. Gerth and C. Wright Mills (eds), *From Max Weber: Essays in Sociology*, pp. 192–4. This reference I owe to William Outhwaite.

We have traced this family's gradual ascension from the original appointment of Vital Bernard as dyer at Villenouvette in 1689 to his grandson's elevation to the position of conseiller in the Cour des Comptes, Aides et Finances of Montpellier and his granddaughters' marriage into noble families in the 1750s. His great-grandson, Jean Bernard, was married in 1788 to Gabrielle, daughter of Jean Marreaud, a retired négociant from the West Indian island of Grenada. She brought him a dowry of 50,000 *livres*. The Bernards had become an established part of the town's elite and as such could charge a high admission price to a family anxious to be included in their number. The source of Gabrielle Marreaud's dowry is of some significance too. There was no longer any question of cloth production in Clermont for the Levant generating such fortunes and enabling a general infiltration of the elite by rising clothiers.[55]

In the introduction some of the ways in which Clermont's example was of more than local significance were suggested. We shall now return to the question of the relevance of what we have discovered about the town's cyclical growth pattern. We shall first assess the significance of our discoveries for the interpretation of Languedocian history. We shall then (briefly) consider the light which is thrown by this detailed analysis of a 'pre-industrial' industrial centre on the general characteristics of economic development in the pre-industrial period. Finally, we shall conclude with an assessment of the implications of the study for the interpretation of eighteenth-century French economic and social history.

Clermont-de-Lodève, as was emphasized in our third chapter, was, and remains, a representative town of Lower Languedoc. It has shared fully in the general process of de-industrialization which has occurred in most parts of the region since the eighteenth century to become largely dependent on its agricultural resources, and above all on the vine. The causes of the region's de-industrialization have been frequently discussed and explanations have varied sharply. At one extreme the phenomenon has been attributed to the region's climate and the personality of its inhabitants,[56] and at the other it has been accounted for by material

---

55. Bobo, 'Communauté languedocienne', p. 175.
56. See for example the views of J. Sion (*La France méditerranéenne*, p. 149) and M. Blanqui (*Des classes ouvrières en France pendant l'année 1848*, p. 166). The former wrote that 'La discipline des manufactures et la vie des cités noires conviennent peu au tempérament méridional', and he commented too on the region's inhabitants' 'individualisme excessif et ... peu d'esprit de suite'; the latter remarked that 'L'industrie même change de caractère lorsqu'elle pénètre dans ces contrées favorisées du ciel, où la seule chaleur du soleil suffirait pour expliquer une foule de phénomènes de l'ordre économique.' See also Stendhal's views, p. 45, n. 67.

factors: by the nature of the industrialization process, occurring gradually in France between the eighteenth and twentieth centuries, which necessitated regional specialization; by the distance of the region from the centres of the Industrial Revolution, and by its unfavourability for the new coal-based technology; and, above all, by the fact that the same process of economic integration which exposed its (by the mid-nineteenth century) frail commercial and industrial entreprises to the full brunt of national and international competition gave a vast boost to its viticulture, causing a sharp rise in wages (and the industry had become dependent on low wages) and, concurrently, giving rise to a strong incentive for large scale industrial disinvestment because of the sudden exceptional profitability of rural investment.[57]

Our study on Clermont contributes to an elaboration of both these types of argument. In the case of the first we have emphasized at the end of the first chapter, and demonstrated by our survey of Clermont's experience, that the long industrial and commercial tradition of the lower province, and the length of the period in which industrial expansions (and contractions) had occurred within a society still fundamentally dominated by pre-industrial values, had had the consequence of creating a deep-seated, instrumental view of trade and industrial activity, regarded invariably as means to an end, and as having little intrinsic value in themselves. This attitude, it seems, endured and was if anything strengthened by the example of the eighteenth-century industrial expansion in the province. It was certainly not eradicated by the administrative effort to create a greater commitment to industrial activity by the revival of the guild system. On the contrary the proliferation of these institutions, which were not natural to the region, purely created new economic opportunities which were exploited by local business classes in a similar instrumental manner. The second type of argument is clearly accurate. It was, indeed, the building of the railway system, and the boost which this gave both to viticulture and to industrial competition, which gave the *coup de grâce* to much of Languedoc's cloth industry, just as it destroyed the languishing fair of Beaucaire. As important as this final blow, though, we would argue, was the process by which several of Languedoc's leading cloth-making centres became marginal in the first place,[58] and it is on the nature of this process, it is to be hoped, that the description of the experiences of Clermont will throw light. The industry for the Levant was the most prosperous in the province in the eighteenth

57. See especially Fohlen, 'Vigne contre draperie', pp. 290–7, and Dugrand, *Villes et campagnes*, pp. 377–402.
58. On the marginality of Languedoc's cloth industry in the nineteenth century see M. Lévy-Leboyer, *Les banques européennes et l'industrialisation internationale*, pp. 103–4.

century, leading to the most significant accumulation of capital, and providing the greatest stimulus to technological and commercial progress. It could have provided a basis for further industrial advance and failed to do so, we would argue, in great part because of a mistaken policy of continued government interference. The argument is supported by the success, despite the ubiquitous presence of the vine, of those industrial centres, such as Castres, Bédarieux and Mazamet, whose industries received less attention from the State.[59] Likewise the illustration in this study of the importance of the entrepreneurial role in industrial production, which finds further proof in the examples just cited, clearly represents a strong argument against the view that demand factors, or the process of industrialization, inevitably condemned the region to pastoralization. The possibility of a Mediterranean region playing an important role in the industrialization process is, besides, fully illustrated by the Catalan example. Catalonia enjoyed an industrial and commercial tradition similar to Languedoc's, and a similar geographical situation, and its population consolidated these advantages during the industrialization process.[60]

According to our cyclical theory of economic development the damage done to the industrial potential of towns like Clermont need not have been permanent. There had been similar industrial declines in past periods, for instance in the mid-seventeenth century, but, as we have seen, recovery was possible and indeed the form which the decline took provided a basis for a future recovery; the return to the familial unit of production, and the cost-cutting techniques enforced by the depression, provided the necessary artisanal qualities which could be exploited when favourable trading circumstances returned. But the possibility of these factors' engendering a new industrial dynamism after the mid-eighteenth century were excluded by two things. First, an Industrial Revolution was

59. A memoir of January 1786 (AN F12 1380) records that by that date Mazamet was producing about 20,000 pieces of cloth of more than twenty different qualities and employing more than 10,000 workers. Clothiers from Bédarieux wrote to Intendant Ballainvilliers on 13 Jan. 1787 (ADH C2190) of 'la réputation dont jouissent les draps de cette jurande non seulement dans le Levant, mais encore dans l'Inde, dans l'Amérique septentrionale et dans l'intérieur du royaume'. On Mazamet's and Bédarieux's growing prosperity in the nineteenth century see Reybaud, *La laine*, pp. 120–5. Equally the industries of the towns of Chalabre and Limoux fared better in the early nineteenth century than the eighteenth-century capitals of the provincial industry. See Baron Trouvé, *Description générale et statistique du département de l'Aude*, pp. 608–12.
60. P. Vilar, *La Catalogne*, especially vols II and III; J. Vicens Vives, *Manual de historia economica de España*, especially pp. 486–90, 504–5, 597–9, 609–13; J. Nadal, 'Spain, 1830–1914' in Cipolla (ed.), *Fontana Economic History of Europe*, IV, pt. 2, pp. 606–16.

occurring in Britain which was giving industrialists a new method, apart from those provided by labour costs, raw material prices and entrepreneurship, of retaining a competitive advantage: investment in machinery. In these new competitive circumstances the advantages gained by the artisanal clothier from his low cost of living and his commitment to his trade were clearly relatively diminished. And secondly such industrial revivals, and such growths of new entrepreneurial elites, had habitually been much facilitated by the declining authority and effectiveness of the previous elite. Several circumstances made such a decline unlikely (and there are signs indeed that it did not occur).[61] The lack of demographic disasters in France after the mid-eighteenth century was one such factor, and another was the fact that the French Revolution effectively gave power to such groups. The bourgeoisie, which had in great part been created by the eighteenth-century industrial and commercial expansion at Clermont, remained in place, it would seem. And if members of it wanted to return to industrial production that option was always open to them, and they could do so under greater advantages than their predecessors in previous centuries, for the events which were occurring in Britain were reducing the relative importance of the labour and entrepreneurial input into industrial production, whilst increasing that of capital, one factor with which the bourgeois participant in industrial production was better supplied.[62]

So although the industrial cycle whose revolution we have witnessed at Clermont was a repetition of previous cycles it was the last such repetition, and at its termination it left the town's industry not, as would have been the case in previous centuries, prepared for another growth period, but, on the contrary, ill-equipped to survive because of its poverty and lack of market links. It could only survive, indeed, as a marginal industry, concentrating on the lowest ends of the market, using old equipment and paying low wages and this is how it did survive, well into the twentieth century. Those qualities which in previous periods would have provided a basis for a steady enrichment and improvement in the industry – the artisanal characteristics of its entrepreneurs – became, instead, permanent characteristics.[63] That lack of total dependence on cloth production, which I have argued contributed to the stabilization of the industry in the second half of the eighteenth century, became, like-

---

61. Continuity is observable in some of Clermont's elite families between the late eighteenth century and the present. Thus the Maistre family ran Villenouvette from 1803 until it closed in 1954 and the last director of the concern, Jean Maistre, continues to live in the manufacture.
62. See pp. 263–4.
63. Audiganne, *Les populations ouvrières*, II, 229; 'Le Languedoc a une specialité: la production à bon marché.'

wise, a permanent quality. And thus many Languedocian cloth-making concerns were never totally to conform to the new style of enterprise of the Industrial Revolution, sharing characteristics with industrial concerns in other parts of France which had experienced significant growth in the eighteenth century: for instance those of Normandy whose entrepreneurs, David Landes writes, were 'notorious for their penny-pinching and short-sighted avidity ... [and regarded by Alsatian competitors] as merchants and speculators rather than as industrialists'.[64]

Rather than stressing the study's significance for interpreting European economic development in the eighteenth century (and it clearly does hold some significance), we would emphasize its importance as an illustration of a type of pre-industrial or 'proto-industrial' development. As such it demonstrates various factors: the centrality of the entrepreneurial role, the existence of different types of industrial structure for different qualities of cloth, and of fluctuations in these structures according to market conditions, and the operation of a development cycle in individual cloth-making centres which might contribute to explaining the often-noted discrepancies in the industrial performances of different towns ostensibly operating under similar circumstances.[65] In addition the study throws light on a central question in the 'proto-industrialization' discussion, the nature of the links with industrialization proper. Our conclusions would provide support for other studies in which it has been shown that proto-industrial areas subjected to extensive state intervention rarely participated positively in the industrialization process.[66]

Before discussing the implications of Clermont's experiences for the interpretation of French economic and social history in the eighteenth century it is necessary to establish how representative they were. This, in fact, is not easily done, for detailed studies on entrepreneurial behaviour and of the consequences of administrative intervention have long been out of vogue and so necessary information in most cases does not exist. It is, however, on slightly stronger grounds than the observed tendency for

64. *The Unbound Prometheus*, p. 161. And see the quotation of Reybaud at the head of this chapter.
65. For instance the discrepancy between the performances of Lille and Roubaix, emphasized by Landes, and mentioned in the introduction (see p. 17) and between Aachen and neighbouring rural textile producers in the eighteenth century (H. Kisch, 'Growth deterrents of a medieval heritage: the Aachen area woollen trades before 1790', *J.E.H.* 24 (1964), 525–31).
66. On this see M. Barkhausen, 'Government control and free enterprise in Western Germany and the Low Countries in the eighteenth century' in P. Earle (ed.), *Essays in European Economic History, 1500–1800*, pp. 212–73, and J. Kocka, 'Entrepreneurs', pp. 501–11.

all 'pre-industrial industrial' activity to take a remarkably similar form that we would hold that Clermont's case is a representative one, and that it does contribute to explaining the experiences of some crucial areas of the French economy during the last years of the Ancien Régime.

First, there is the fact of the widespread coincidence in the timing of both the expansion and the decline of industrial centres in France during the eighteenth century. The simultaneity in the timing of the upturn in Clermont's industrial production in the late 1680s and 1690s with that observed at Amiens and other Norman textile centres we have commented on in the introduction.[67] The rapid industrial expansion at Clermont during the first half of the century was representative too. The especially favourable performance of the French economy during the first half of the eighteenth century, pre-occupied English observers – in contrast the English economy was merely marking time – and has been noted by historians: prosperity was such, Germain Martin writes, that streets and even whole quarters of towns were rebuilt.[68] Other historians have quantified the growth rates; trade, it has been shown, expanded at a rate of 4.1% *per annum* between 1716 and 1748, whilst it grew only at 1.0% *per annum* between 1749 and 1778, recovering to a rate of 1.4% *per annum* between 1778 and 1789; and whereas it was the growth in re-exports which accounted for the revival after 1778, it was the export of the products of traditional industries, and above all those of textile industries, which predominated in the early expansion.[69] The predominance of the cloth industry in the expansion is demonstrated by Markovitch's quantitative work. His calculations confirm the typicality of the growth pattern observed at Clermont for they reveal rapid early expansion at the end of the seventeenth century, a slowing down in growth rates until the 1720s, the most solid expansion of all from 1727 to the 1750s, and then a universal break in the rate of expansion from the mid-1750s.[70] In view of the universality of this post-1750s slowing-down it would seem likely that the widespread suspicion that the French economy was moving backwards in the second half of the century, although in part a consequence of a growing awareness of the obviously more favourable English performance during these years, was also contributed to by the evidence of growing difficulties encountered by leading French industrial centres whose progress had been relatively unchecked during the first half of the century, and above all by those luxury industries which

67. See p. 14.
68. *La grande industrie sous Louis XV*, p. 7.
69. Braudel and Labrousse, *Histoire économique*, II, 503–05, 698; Crouzet, 'Angleterre et France', pp. 263–4.
70. *Les industries lainières*, pp. 21–34.

had spearheaded the industrial advance. 'Voyez les pays de manufactures de luxe:', wrote Dupont de Nemours in 1769, 'ce sont ceux où l'on trouve le plus de pauvres.'[71] And the generality of the crisis is confirmed by recent historians. Crouzet writes of a crisis in 'les vieilles industries textiles' (he is referring to wool and linen) which ceased to expand and even declined in certain regions such as Normandy, Brittany and Languedoc. The crisis is also recorded in the new *Histoire économique et sociale*: Pierre Léon writes of 'un sérieux freinage' which occurred after the mid-century in the 'industries du passé', whose performance was in sharp contrast to that of 'des industries "neuves" degagées de toute tradition, pourvue de gros capitaux, [qui] manifestent des cadences plus vigoureuses'. The crisis he links to that 'crise de l'Ancien Régime qui, sous des apparences de prospérité, atteindra si fortement l'économie du royaume'.[72] Certainly the contrast with the first half of the century was sharp and this Heckscher illustrated by signalling the contrasting attitudes revealed at the treaty of Utrecht of 1713 and the Eden treaty of 1786. In the case of the former a commercial clause was not ratified by the English for fear of French competition, whereas it was French industrialists who took a negative and fearful reaction to the threat of competition created by the latter.[73] The tables had been turned.

Local studies provide further confirmation of this conformity in the development patterns of France's traditional industries. An article by C. Brisson on Elbeuf and Louviers, for example, shows the stages of these towns' development until the mid-century to have been virtually identical to that observed at Clermont,[74] and Labrousse's calculations illustrate that Elbeuf's production, like Clermont's, experienced a sharp decline in the 1750s, from an index figure of 118 in 1757, to one of seventy-five in 1760.[75] And finally J. Kaplow's study on the same town reveals not only that, as at Clermont, there was an abrupt decline in the quality of production after the 1750s, but also that a gradual process of general impoverishment occurred in the town, which revealed itself in a rapid decline in brandy consumption, amongst other things.[76] The same decadence was apparent at Lyons. A priest from the Dauphiné observed in 1777 that when young he had witnessed the trade of the town 'très florissant' but that 'Aujourd'hui, il s'est bien ralenti ... Depuis trente ans, il y a beaucoup de misère dans cette ville. Tous les ouvriers ne

---

71. Cited by G. Weulersee, *Le mouvement physiocratique en France*, II, 544.
72. 'Angleterre et France', p. 269; Braudel and Labrousse, *Histoire économique*, II, 517–19.
73. *Mercantilism*, I, 193–6.
74. 'Origines et développement', pp. 215–19.
75. *Esquisse*, II, 546–50.
76. *Elbeuf during the Revolutionary Period: History and Social Structure*, pp. 44–7, 54–5.

peuvent travailler.'[77] Finally Dornic, in his study on the region of Le
Mans, reveals a similar 'crise profonde', which originated 'aux approches
de la guerre de Sept Ans', and, in a section entitled 'Le déclin fut-il
seulement régional?', states his belief that this local crisis was a reflection
of a general crisis in France's woollen industries. 'Ces fabriques n'avaient
guère cessé de progresser en France depuis Colbert', Dornic writes, 'et
surtout pendant les trente ans de paix, à peine troublés par quelques
rides, qui avaient suivi la mort de Louis XIV. Sauf exceptions, elles
seront en crise après la guerre de Sept Ans, crise longue, lente et
progressive.'[78]

So the stages of Clermont's development which we have documented
were representative and this supports our contentions about the town's
experiences. Universal, too, was the policy exercised towards guilds in all
those industrial centres which shared this rhythm of growth. This fact
will already have emerged in earlier chapters. The actual wording of the
guild regulations recorded by Clermont's clothiers in 1708 was probably
copied from similar regulations devised elsewhere, and the growing
restrictiveness of guilds in the 1720s and 1730s was, also, we have noted,
a general phenomenon. Both at Elbeuf and Louviers there developed a
situation of oligopoly similar to that observed at Clermont. Brisson
describes how 'quelques familles, apparentées entre elles ... tenaient en
main l'industrie locale'.[79] The phenomenon was a general one and its
serious consequences were once much emphasized by historians: 'le
moindre inconvénient de semblables prescriptions', wrote Pierre
Clément, referring to limitations on access to mastership, 'était
d'immobiliser l'industrie dans les mêmes familles et de restreindre le
nombre de concurrents',[80] and Martin-St-Léon connected the proliferation of the new guild system with the corruption which led to the fall of
the Ancien Régime. The mediaeval corporative system, with its lack of
distinctions of rank and fortune, he compared with the open naves and
vast doorways of Gothic cathedrals, the new guilds to the Bastille 'où se
retranche une oligarchie jalouse et avare qui ne voit pas grossir autour
d'elle le flot des assiégants'.[81]

The regulative policy, and the growing severity of that policy, applied,
likewise, to other areas of France and the practice of connivance with the
system, which we have observed at Clermont, was widespread. As Brisson
notes, again with reference to Elbeuf and Louviers, 'les drapiers se

77. L. Trénard, *Lyon de l'Encyclopédie au préromantisme*, I, 26–7, 29.
78. *L'industrie dans la Maine*, pp. 49, 229.
79. 'Origines et développement', p. 218.
80. *Colbert*, p. 222.
81. *Histoire des corporations*, I, 520.

faisaient eux-mêmes les auxiliaires d'un dirigisme dont les excès se manifestaient à tous les degrés'.[82] The significance of administrative intervention with French industry has been played down by modern economic historians. 'Le contraste entre le "dirigisme" français et le libéralisme anglais ne doit donc pas être surestimé, et l'incidence du cadre institutionnel apparaît réelle, mais limitée', writes Crouzet,[83] and whilst Heckscher's view that the existence of inspectors in France 'was one of the main reasons why French industrial development diverges from the English'[84] can be judged as extreme, it does seem that the importance of the phenomenon is in need of some reassessment. Much of French industrial activity was unregulated – in the Languedocian region the massive production of the remoter areas of the Pyrenees and Massif Central was beyond the reach of inspectors, for example[85] – but those industrial areas which played an important part in the industrial expansion in the first half of the century were, almost without exception, submitted to the discipline of the regulative system. The role of administrative intervention was, thus, important in what might be described as the leading sectors of French industrial growth in the first half of the century.

If the rhythm of Clermont's expansion and the incidence of both guild and regulative systems on its industry were representative, what of the causes of the town's crisis? Were these representative too? To establish this definitely, detailed local studies, over a long time scale, would need to be carried out but there are some scraps of evidence available already which suggest the possibility that industrial problems in other regions were occasioned by similar factors. First, there was throughout France a confusion similar to that which we have witnessed in Languedoc as a consequence both of the survival of elements of the regulative system into the second half of the century and of the fluctuations in the industrial policies of the Government.[86] Secondly, it is evident that, as Martin-St-Léon records, the guild and interventionist system had indeed gained the reputation, merited or not, of having become corrupt and of having been abused. The prominence given to demands for industrial freedom in the cahiers des doléances of many areas attests to this. Thirdly, and this time the evidence is of a more precise nature, there are signs that there occurred a general retirement of rich clothiers and merchants from

---

82. 'Origines et développement', p. 218.
83. 'Angleterre et France', p. 274.
84. *Mercantilism*, I, 154.
85. See on this production Markovitch, 'L'industrie lainière', p. 1626.
86. E.g. L. Trénard, 'The social crisis in Lyons on the eve of the French Revolution' in J. Kaplow (ed.), *New Perspectives on the French Revolution*, pp. 72–7.

commercial activity in parts of France other than Languedoc. At Elbeuf, for example, in the second half of the century there was a similar contrast to that observed at Clermont between the poverty of cloth-workers and the wealth of a small number of retired clothiers. The capitation there was calculated on the basis of the amount of wool imported into the town by each clothier. This had proved a satisfactory method of assessment when the town's wealthy citizens were clothiers, but by the end of the Ancien Régime this was clearly no longer the case and frequent complaints resulted. Similarly a tax on items consumed in the town was no longer equitable because of the new expenditure patterns of rich retired merchants and clothiers. It was explained in a memoir that injustice existed because 'le luxe qui s'est introduit depuis quelques années dans Elbeuf ayant fait perdre aux gens opulents l'usage des matières communes qui sont presque les seuls articles imposés au tarif et auxquels l'opulence a substitué la soierie, la porcelaine, les glaces, le sucre, le café et autres articles non imposés au tarif'.[87] Similarly, Arthur Young explained the distress which he found at Lyons (20,000 unemployed) in terms of the desertion of richer merchants: 'The chief cause of the evil felt here', he wrote, 'is the stagnation of trade occasioned by the emigrations of the rich from the kingdom . . .'[88] This evidence is patchy and indirect, but the hypothesis that France's industrial stability was damaged by a general retirement of enriched industrialists is a plausible one. The factors which favoured such a general retirement at Clermont and in other Languedocian centres applied elsewhere: the reversal in industrial policy in the 1750s was universal (freedom to manufacture any type of cloth was granted at Elbeuf in 1758, for example) and thus profitability declined everywhere; the level of enrichment in other industrial centres had been parallel to that observed in Clermont and so the possibility of a general retirement existed elsewhere; and finally, as in Languedoc, the advantages of rentier-type investments were increasing because of the increasing demographic pressure on land supply which was contributing to a rise in rents.[89] An additional piece of evidence, again of an indirect kind, was the fact of the increased demand in the last years of the Ancien Régime for all types of office and privileged position. Historians of the French Revolution have emphasized this and it does not seem unreasonable to connect it with the widespread desire for social advancement of the offspring of the commercial and industrial elites

87. Kaplow, *Elbeuf*, p. 56.
88. *Travels in France*, p. 306.
89. On the relationship between movements in rents, wages and prices see the useful summary of G. Lefebvre, 'The movement of prices and the origins of the French Revolution' in J. Kaplow (ed.), *New Perspectives on the French Revolution*, pp. 125–31.

which had been enriched by France's rapid economic growth in the first half of the eighteenth century.[90]

A claim having been made for Clermont's typicality we are now in a position to point to the general significance of a few aspects of the town's experiences.

In our earlier chapters we dwelt at some length on the nature of the crisis in Clermont's and Languedoc's industry in the seventeenth century, on the Colbertian remedies for this crisis, and on the influence of the Colbertian reforms on the industrial recovery whose origins we have traced to the late 1680s and 1690s. Our investigations, in addition to highlighting the importance of these early beginnings to the 'eighteenth-century' expansion in the French economy, throw light on several hotly debated issues in French economic history. Colbert's diagnosis of French industrial problems, and needs (in a European economic system characterized by the trading in high-quality products above all, for restricted, undynamic markets), we have seen was essentially correct, his reforms apt. These reforms were not, we have argued, responsible in themselves for the reviving demand situation in the last years of the seventeenth century, which was a European, and not purely a French phenomenon, but they contributed to the French ability to profit from this revival. We have also seen that the extension of both the regulative and the guild systems had the consequence that the right to respond to some of the most favourable market opportunities was limited first to certain towns, and then to selected individuals in these towns. The drawbacks of this policy, however, did not emerge in the short term. On the contrary the Colbertian contribution, and additions to it by his successors, equipped France remarkably well (as Heckscher demonstrated) for success in that European economy whose major characteristics remained substantially unchanged for the first half of the eighteenth century. The impressive French growth was certainly linked to the wealth, application and technical skills of its clothiers, the thoroughness with which regulations had been devised, and the control exercised by inspectors – all factors which clearly formed part of the Colbertian recovery plan. But what might be termed the 'Colbertian model' was beginning to show signs of wear by the 1740s and 1750s. This for two major reasons. The first, which we have amply documented in Clermont's case, was that it had become corrupt and its restrictiveness was having negative effects on the quality of entrepreneurship. The

90. See for example C. Lucas, 'Nobles, bourgeois and the origins of the French Revolution', *P. & P.* 60 (1973), 100–19.

second was that it was becoming out-dated. Emerging by the mid-eighteenth century was a world very different from that for which Colbert had originally devised the model. It was one in which the pace of economic change was accelerating, demand for lower-quality goods was increasing more rapidly than for luxury ones, and the keys to economic success were changing. Cheapness and the ability to respond rapidly to market trends were becoming more crucial than uniformity and regularity of quality and high production standards. And to succeed in this new world an economic change far more fundamental than the superficial tinkering carried out by Colbert and his successors was required. Greater, not lesser, competitiveness between entrepreneurs was necessary and, in that the major impulsion for this new style of economic growth came from the domestic economy, a generalized economic expansion, increase in well-being, and conversion to the consumer economy was required. The success of the first half of the century, rather than facilitating the process of adaptation to such a new economic system, may well have made it more difficult. It had created structural problems; it had given the labour force an unpleasant first experience of industrial employment; it had led to an exceptional concentration of capital, which had been one of the keys to the early success but which also provided entrepreneurs with the possibility of sidestepping the problem of adjustment by leaving industry; and finally it had left confusing legacies, the surviving institutions of the guild and regulative systems and an enduring and mistaken belief that economic success depended on the concoction of a new industrial policy. Awareness of these sorts of structural problems is implied, it would seem, by the two remarks of Pierre Léon cited earlier. By connecting the problems encountered by the traditional industries with that 'crise d'Ancien Régime' which occurred despite the long eighteenth-century prosperity he implies that, like the French political and social systems, the traditional industries appeared increasingly antiquated and anachronistic in the last years before the Revolution. By referring to other industries as 'neuves' and 'dégagées de toute tradition' he implies, too, the necessity for a qualitative distinction between different types of industry, and of economic growth, in eighteenth century France.

As has been shown in several studies, there was by no means invariable continuity between industrial and commercial development in the pre-industrial period and that which occurred during the industrialization process. This has been one of the major grounds for re-evaluating the importance of the links between the 'commercial revolution' and the 'industrial revolution'. Fortunes generated in commerce rarely found their way into industrial investment and were frequently squandered on conspicious consumption.[91] Acceptance of this idea contributes to emphasizing both the abruptness and the novelty of the industrial expansion which began in England in the late eighteenth century and was later to be labelled the Industrial Revolution. It was not automatically precipitated by commercial expansion, nor, as E. A. Wrigley has shown, by the 'modernization' process, which could lead to a stagnant situation such as that which developed in Holland, then the most 'modernized' country in Europe, in the second half of the eighteenth century,[92] nor by capital accumulation. As François Crouzet writes, 'the whole notion of enrichment *per se* as a precursor of the industrial revolution ought to be dimissed as a myth, in as much as the new techniques were pioneered mainly by small men, with comparatively little capital of their own'.[93] It seems probable, indeed, that certain variants of pre-industrial development, rather than being a positive influence on the process of industrialization, were actually a negative one. This is Domenico Sella's interesting argument in his new book on the economy of Lombardy in the seventeenth century. The decline of the Italian cities in the seventeenth century, he argues, far from having been a negative phenomenon was a necessary preliminary to modernization and industrialization proper, for their prosperity had been artificial, and they had exercised a colonial-type dominion over the countryside which had prevented any widely based economic expansion.[94] It was Italian and Dutch economic supremacy of a monopolistic kind which was to some extent supplanted by the French economic expansion in the first half of the eighteenth century and although, as we have seen, the success of the French industrial centres which participated in this expansion was initially based on genuine entrepreneurial and economic advantages, it was prolonged by the granting of privileges and monopolies which eventually made these centres, like the trading cities which they had replaced, barriers to a more general economic advance. Their failure, therefore, in the second half of the century might be judged as a positive phenomenon for French industrialization even if in the short term it contributed to a slowing-down in the pace of economic growth as well as to that general crisis which preceded the French Revolution.[95]

91. See for example M. W. Flinn, *The Origins of the Industrial Revolution*, pp. 56–68.
92. E. A. Wrigley, 'Modernization and the Industrial Revolution in England', *Journal of Interdisciplinary History* 3 (1972–3), 225–59.
93. In F. Crouzet (ed.), *Capital Formation in the Industrial Revolution*, p. 59.
94. *Crisis and Continuity*, pp. 135–46.
95. Several historians have emphasized that the possession of a significant industrial sector *before* industrialization proper can have its disadvantages. It is quite possible thus that the extent of the French success in traditional industries had a distinct retarding effect on the process of industrialization. To H. J. Habakkuk's statement, 'French industrial

In recent years the tendency among economic historians has been to play down the significance of the social and institutional contrasts between English and French society in the eighteenth century and to stress, instead, the similarity in the two countries' economic performances. The strongest grounds for doing this have been provided by quantitative evidence which does, indeed, suggest a parallel process of enrichment.[96] It would seem to be necessary, however, the conclusions drawn from this study would suggest, for the quantitative evidence to be subjected to criticism of a qualitative kind and, to use vocabulary already adopted by some French historians, to distinguish between 'industries neuves' and 'industries du passé'.

structure had got set in an oligopolistic pattern *before* the building of French railways and was strong enough to resist pressures set up by falling transport costs' ('The historical experience on the basic conditions of economic progress' in B. E. Supple (ed.), *The Experience of Economic Growth*, p. 121), can be added the quantitative work of F. Crouzet which shows that traditional industries, and above all textile industries, acted as a 'brake' on the process of industrialization in the nineteenth century. ('An annual index of French industrial production in the nineteenth century' in R. Cameron (ed.), *Essays in French Economic History*, pp. 260–5, 272–3.)

96. Crouzet was the first to emphasize the similarity ('Angleterre et France', especially pp. 260–2, 268–71). He has since been followed by W. W. Rostow, *How It All Began*, pp. 167–73; P. O'Brien and C. Keyder, *Economic Growth in Britain and France 1780–1914: Two Paths to the Twentieth Century*, p. 194: 'Over the eighteenth century France presumably caught up with Britain'; N. F. R. Crafts, 'Industrial Revolution in England and France: some thoughts on the question "why was England first?"', *Ec.H.R.* 30 (1977), 438–41; R. Roehl, 'French industrialization: a reconsideration', *Explorations in Economic History* 12 (1976), 238, 243, and N.B. p. 272: 'The reinterpretation of French industrialization has depended upon the behaviour of certain statistical trends, on a per-capita basis'; R. Davis, *The Rise of the Atlantic Economies*, pp. 301–13; A. S. Milward and S. B. Saul, *The Economic Development of Continental Europe*, pp. 32–3.

APPENDIX I

Languedoc's intendants

d'Aguesseau, Henri, 1673–85
Basville, Nicolas de Lamoignon de, 1685–1718
Bernage, Louis de, 1718–24
Bernage, Louis Bazile de, 1725–43
Le Nain, Jean d'Asfeld, 1743–50
St-Priest, Jean-Emmanuel de Guignard, 1751–85
(St-Priest, Marie-Joseph-Emmanuel de Guignard, intendant-adjoint, 1764–85)
Ballainvilliers, Charles-Bernard de, 1785–9

APPENDIX 2

Clermont's inspectors, 1727–91

Pierre Delagenière, 1727–39. Native of Paris. Served previously in Navarre, Laval and Carcassonne. Paralysed in August 1739.

Jean-Pierre Delagenière, 1739–40. Oldest son of Pierre Delagenière. Replaced his father until July 1740 when he was summoned to Paris, examined by members of the Bureau de Commerce, and appointed as inspector to Bayonne and Oleron.

Pierre-Marie Delagenière, 1740–44. Took over as inspector from brother. Official commission as inspector registered at Clermont by the conseil de ville on 17 April 1742. Transferred to Castres in 1744.

Dominique Tricou, 1744–56. Originally a négociant of Montpellier. Worked for eighteen years in Constantinople. Made inspector at Lodève in 1740. Moved to Castres, 1743, and to Clermont in 1744. Retired in 1756. Granted a pension of 800 *livres per annum*.

Jean-Baptiste Tricou, 1756–9. Worked as 'élève des manufactures' in 1740s. Appointments: Lodève, 1749; St-Pons, 1750; Clermont *and* Lodève, 1756; St-Chinian, 1759 (where he remained until retirement in the 1780s).

Barbot, 'de Vieux Moulin', 1759–63. Son of inspector of Alençon. Appointments: Alençon, Montauban, Limoux and Clermont in 1759. Recalled in 1763 on account of incompetence. Awarded pension which was paid irregularly.

Roland de la Platière, Jean-Marie, 1764–6. From an impoverished Robe family of Burgundy. Elève des manufactures in Rouen in 1755. Appointed to Clermont in 1764. Transferred to Amiens in 1766. Worked in Lyons between 1784 and 1789. Met Arthur Young there. Became minister of the interior in the Girondin government in 1792. Resigned January 1793. Committed suicide in November 1793 after hearing of the execution of his wife.

Vaugelade, Olivier Jean, 1766–74. Former élève des manufactures, appointed in September 1766.

Taillardat de St-James, Guillaume-Jean, 1774–80. Son of inspector for the Berry. Worked as élève des manufactures at Rouen, Elbeuf, Louviers, Andelys and Picardy. Commissioned as inspector for Clermont in September 1774. Transferred to Nîmes in 1780.

Bruté, 1780–6. Son of inspector for Montauban. Appointed to Clermont in 1780.

Tricou fils, 1786–91. Son of Jean-Baptiste. Elève des manufactures at Nîmes in 1782, sous-inspecteur at Moulins in 1783, appointed inspector for Carcassonne *and* Clermont-de-Lodève in 1786. With disappearance of inspectoral system during the revolution becomes involved in cloth-making on a commercial basis.

Glossary of cloth types, textile and administrative terms, weights and measures

Affineur	cloth-dresser
Assortisseur	wool-sorter
Aune	measure of 1.188 metres
Balle	bale of cloth: in the case of Languedoc's Levant industry bales were composed of 20 ½-pieces of cloth of 16 aunes
Ballot	small bale of cloth of 10 ½-pieces
Batteur	wool-beater
Billet de congé	note giving worker right to change employer
Cadis	narrow, light, woollen cloth, similar to serge, and produced by artisanal production unit in mountainous areas of Languedoc mainly; produced in villages of Lodévois before the expansion in the area's exports for the Levant
Canne	a variable measure: 1.987 metres at Montpellier, 1.796 metres at Toulouse
Canoneuse	operator of reeling machine for yarn
Cardeur	carder
Cardier	maker of cards
Chaîne	warp
Charge	load of 3 quintals and, in Clermont area, measure of 169.68 litres of oil
Commis	managerial assistant to merchant or clothier; in addition early inspectors were known as 'commis à l'inspection'
Communauté	smallest administrative unit, below diocese
Compoix	cadaster or detailed land register
Confrérie	type of guild, or corporation, in which religious and social functions were generally given precedence over the purely professional
Conseil de ville	elected town council of twelve
Conseil général	summoned for discussion of major issues; theoretically composed of all (male) inhabitants, in fact attended by principal tax-payers
Consuls	three elected annually to preside over affairs of communauté, but see Maire, Lieutenant-de-maire; first consul of Clermont had right to attend provincial Etats
Contraints	name of a range of broad-cloths produced at Carcassonne during the first half of the 17th century, and which included contraints-communs, -vingtquatrains, -façon d'Espagne and -vingthuitains larges

Contribution patriotique	voluntary tax raised in 1789
Cordelats	low-quality, woollen cloth of unstandardized type made mainly in mountainous areas of Languedoc; also produced irregularly in Clermont in the second half of the 17th century with odd lots of wool
Diocese	in Languedoc both religious and administrative unit
Drapier	term which denoted both clothier and cloth merchant; prefix of marchand generally added
Draps	woollen cloth: different qualities either described by number of threads to warp – e.g. vingtsixains had 2,600 warp threads – or by names listed below
Draps de Berry	high-quality broad-cloth, made with the best-quality, national wools from the Berry region; such cloth produced at Carcassonne in the first half of the seventeenth century
Draps façon d'Angleterre	imitations of English medley: high-quality broad-cloth in production of which Spanish wools were used; in contrast to most Languedocian cloth, wools were dyed before spinning; 3,000–4,200 threads to warp; breadth $1\frac{1}{2}$ aunes
Draps façon d'Elbeuf	high-quality broad-cloth, made with Spanish wools of middling quality on a pattern devised in Elbeuf; 2,800–3,000 threads to the warp
Draps façon d'Espagne	very fine cloth, made with highest-quality Spanish wools; 3,600+ threads to the warp; breadth $1\frac{1}{2}$ aunes
Draps façon d'Hollande	fine broad-cloth, made with Spanish wools according to the Dutch method (see p. 94); 3,000–4,200 threads to the warp; breadth 1 aune
Draps façon de Seau, or sceau	medium-quality broad-cloth, first made at Rouen and Beauvais and produced in Languedoc with wools from the dioceses of Narbonne and Béziers; 2,000 threads to the warp; breadth 1 aune
Draps fins mêlés	another name for draps façon d'Angleterre
Draps forts	heavy cloth, made of coarse wools for military and institutional uses primarily; Lodève's speciality but produced at Clermont in the 1690s
Draps larges	broad-cloth, but as in England came to denote, invariably, broad-cloth of high quality
Draps larges refins, suprafins, ségovie, écarlates, etc.	a variety of names all of which denote broad-cloth of high quality
Droguets	low-quality, light, narrow cloth made either entirely of wool, or of linen or cotton warp and woollen weft; made irregularly in Clermont in the second half of the 17th century, destined principally for women's skirts; breadth c. $\frac{1}{2}$ aune
Droguets façon d'Hollande et d'Angleterre	higher-quality versions of droguets, made entirely of wool, and destined for distant sale; produced at Carcassonne at end of 17th century

Embriseuse	dresser of wool (with oil)
Epotoyeuse	burler
Escardassage	preliminary carding process
Estamets	type of cloth being made at Limoux for distant markets in the 12th century
Fabricant	habitual term for clothier from *c.* 1720s; prefix of marchand generally added
Facteur	managerial assistant to clothier
Facturier	habitual term for clothier until *c.* 1720s; prefix of marchand generally added
Fixation	the quota system enforced on Languedoc's production for the Levant between 1741 and 1756
Foulonnier	fuller
Garde-juré, or juré-garde	elected officer of jurande
Jurande	corporation or guild
Juré-auneur	officer of jurande entrusted with measuring cloth and paper work
Lainier	wool-mixer
Leipziks	high-quality German cloth which sucessfully competed in the Levant from the 1770s; similar to Languedoc's londrins-premiers
Lieutenant-de-maire	Venal municipal office created in 1702
Lisière	selvedge or border of cloth
Liteuse	sower of dye-resistant margin into cloth
Londres, londres-ordinaires	cloth destined for popular consumption in the Levant; national wools; 2,000 threads to the warp; breadth $1\frac{1}{6}$ aunes
Londres-larges	heavier cloth for popular use in the Levant; national or inferior Spanish wools; 2,400 threads to warp; breadth $1\frac{1}{4}$ aunes
Londrins-premiers	high-quality broad-cloth for sale in Levant; made with first-quality Spanish wools; 3,200 threads to the warp; breadth $1\frac{1}{4}$ aunes
Londrins-seconds	medium-quality broad-cloth which achieved most sales in the Levant; 2,600 threads to the warp; breadth $1\frac{1}{6}$ aunes
Mahous	the highest quality produced for the Levant: name derives from the selling-line that such cloth should be worn by those related to Mahomet; highest-quality Spanish wools; minimum of 3,600 threads to warp; breadth $1\frac{1}{3}$ aunes
Mahous-seconds	slightly lower-quality version of the above; 3,000 threads to warp; breadth $1\frac{1}{3}$ aunes
Maire	venal municipal office, first purchased in Clermont in 1733
Meuniers	cloth named after the Lemonnier family, clothiers of Elbeuf in the early 17th century (Brisson, 'Origines', 215): a heavy but high-quality broad-cloth of $1\frac{1}{4}$ aunes breadth in the production of which Dutch-style techniques were used
Naucade	meridional term denoting whole piece of cloth of 32 aunes

Nims-londrins	cloth type introduced in the 1740s in Languedoc, and between londres-larges and londrins-seconds in quality, with 2,500 threads to warp
Ourdisseur	warper
Pan	$\frac{1}{8}$ of canne
Pareur	cloth-finisher
Pelades	wool taken from the carcases of sheep dying from natural causes
Pic	Levantine measure of *c.* $\frac{4}{5}$ of an aune
Pinchinats	broad-cloth of low quality, generally with 1,600 threads to the warp
Pistole	coin of Spanish origin, worth approximately 10 livres
Planquet	meridional term for cloth-dresser
Quatreforts	coarse, heavy cloth of low quality, similar to draps forts described above, and produced at Clermont for military demand during the revolutionary period
Quintal	weight of 100 livres
Rame	tenter
Rentrayeur	cloth repairer
Retorseur	operator of twisting mill
Retorsoir	twisting mill for rectifying yarn and warping
Sayes	an imitation of a Venetian cloth, similar to meuniers, and also known as parangons; intended for overcoats and horse-cloths, it was a heavy material, with between 2,000 and 3,000 threads to the warp
Serges	light cloth with worsted warp and wool weft, destined for popular consumption
Sétérée	625 cannes carrées in the Lodévois (24.69 ares)
Setier	measure of liquids and dry products: 65.70 litres at Clermont
Shalloons	worsted fabric of medium quality, produced mainly in Halifax; competed successfully with lower qualities of Languedocian cloth in the Levant in the second half of the 18th century
Subdélégué	assistant to intendant; in Languedoc there was one for each diocese
Syndic-général	executive officer of Etats
Tableau	annually published list of those entitled to participate in quota system; see Fixation
Tondeur	shearer
Trame	weft of cloth
Trieuse	wool-picker

Sources for weights and measures: R. E. Zupko, *French Weights and Measures before the Revolution*, pp. 11, 127, 154; Appolis, *Lodève*, pp. 603–7, 619; AN F12 642, Memoir of Magy, 1671, which includes details on Levantine measures.

Bibliography

MANUSCRIPT SOURCES

Archives Départementales de l'Hérault

Série B (Judicial archives)
1 B 10310, Cour des Comptes, Aides et Finances: examination of accounts of Villenouvette, 1683
8 B 396–420, Juridiction consulaire of Montpellier: bankruptcies, 1736–77

Juridiction ordinaire of Clermont, the seigneurial court of Clermont: incomplete records exist for the period 1759–90. An inventory, on filing cards, has been made.

Série C (Intendancy archives)
This is vastly rich in material relating to the economy of the province. Listed here are the numbers of bundles containing documents actually made use of in writing this book. This, however, it should be stressed, is far from being a complete list of the bundles which contain information about the province's cloth industry. I have grouped the bundles under the headings which correspond approximately to the most significant part of their contents (from the point of view of this study). Numbers of bundles containing a variety of information I have listed under more than one heading.
Relating to the Lodévois (taxation, descriptions of diocese, communal politics): 47, 949, 1744, 2498, 6554
Royal manufactures: 1123–4, 1277–84, 2122–3, 2139, 2181, 2182, 2202–3, 5544
Production statistics: 2117, 2123, 2126–8, 2135, 2180, 2185–7, 2189, 2208, 2210, 2212, 2216–18, 2226, 2231–4, 2339, 2410, 2476, 2554, 5519, 5525, 5534, 5585, 5588
Corporative affairs: 2131, 2152–3, 2773–4, 2792, 2799, 2801
Relating to inspectors: 2131, 2477, 2498–9, 2502, 2516
Technological questions: 2129–30, 2134, 2158–9, 2381
Labour questions (including migration): 2090, 2132, 2153, 2156, 2227, 2394, 2424, 2427, 2431, 2497–8, 2554, 5587, 5595, 5601
Capital equipment: 2036, 5569
The cloth industry in general:
pre-1700: 2199–2200, 2513, 2773–4, 2799, 2801
1700–19: 2122, 4674
1720–39: 2034, 2036, 2123, 2125–32, 2134–5, 2139, 2200–01, 2498, 2508, 4676–7, 4924, 5479, 5495, 5522, 5917

1740–9: 2039–40, 2043, 2047–53, 2055, 2142, 2148, 2152–3, 2156, 2158–60, 2201, 2429, 2499, 2523, 5523–4, 5533, 5545
1750–9: 2057, 2065, 2080, 2086–9, 2170, 2176, 2210, 2380, 2502, 2514, 2520, 2535, 2537, 5512, 5523, 5539, 5545, 5552–3, 5582, 5585, 5596, 5600–01, 6600
1760–9: 2177–79, 2201, 2212–5, 2223, 2531, 5471, 5535, 5545, 5554, 5566
1770–9: 2180, 2223, 5037, 5519, 5533, 5536, 5555–6, 5590
1780–9: 2190, 2296, 2432, 2592, 4932, 5525, 5528, 5545, 5563, 5592
Plaintes et placets to the commander of the province: 6762–78
Procès-verbaux of Etats of Languedoc, 1681–3, 1689, 1693–1721: 7214, 7222, 7248, 7267, 7277, 7280, 7285, 7292, 7295, 7301, 7307, 7311, 7317–18, 7322, 7326, 7332, 7339, 7341, 7343, 7350, 7354, 7359, 7363, 7365, 7368, 7370, 7373, 7377, 7380, 7385, 7389, 7390

Série I E (Fonds privés)
Fonds Villeneuvette
This was deposited in the departmental archives after I had completed my research. It is enormously rich, particularly for the nineteenth century. It has now been classified. It contains few records for the period before 1750 and these, rather than being concerned with the old royal manufacture, are largely connected with the affairs of Denis Gayraud, who bought the manufacture in 1793. Denis Gayraud was succeeded as director by his nephew, Joseph Maistre, who established an industrial dynasty which ran the concern until its closure in 1954. The last director, Jean Maistre, continues to reside in the manufacture. He has in his possession a number of documents relating to the manufacture and he kindly allowed me to examine these. In the text I have referred to these documents as belonging to the 'Archive de la Manufacture'. The following is a list of the principal items held by Monsieur Maistre:
Papers connected with a legal case brought before the Cour des Comptes, Aides et Finances of Montpellier by Clermont's consuls in 1680 to oppose Villenouvette's separation into a separate community
Details of Villenouvette's cloth exports via Marseilles, 1676–80
Copy of Letters Patent of 20 July 1677 by which Villenouvette was raised to the status of royal manufacture
Details of the consecration of a chapel in the manufacture in 1678
Full description of the manufacture, its cost, and its profitability, sent to Pouget in Paris on 20 January 1681
List of all families living in the manufacture in 1745
A variety of maps, plans, cloth samples and documents about the estate of Villenouvette

Série II E (Notarial archives)
Clermont, 1633–1763; II E 25 43, 58–62, 63–4, 70, 84–109, 112–14, 117–19, 124–9, 132, 134–6, 153–65, 237; II E 26 42, 46–8, 61, 70–1, 87–108, 116–56, 164–88
Montpellier, 1673–99: II E 57 386; II E 60 88, 90–2, 103; II E 62 86
Pézenas, 1693: II E 68 73
St-Chinian, 1686–92: II E 79 102–5

Série III E (Etat civil)
Clermont, 1758–74: 3 E 81[1] – 81[3]
Mourèze and Villenouvette, 1670–1720: 3 E 181[1 bis]

Série G (Visites pastorales)
4436, 1060–2, visits of Bishop of Lodève, 1631, 1649, 1659, 1740

Séries L and S (post-1789 administrative and public works)
L1259, information on Clermont's trade and industry in the 1790s
11 S 122, plan of Clermont de Lodève

Archives Départementales de l'Aude

Série C
5 C 41, 9 C 11, 9 C 17, 9 C 19, 9 C 21, 9 C 23, a variety of material relating to
Languedoc's and Carcassonne's industry, 1642–1753

Archives Départementales du Rhône

Série B
Tribunal de la Conservation, Fonds Moulins

Archives of Chamber of Commerce, Marseilles

Série H
158, 159, 174, 176, 177, 181, 182, Languedoc's industry, 1688–1784

Fonds Roux
LIX, 281–4, correspondence with Clermontais clothiers, 1757–1821

Archives Communales, Clermont (held mainly at Archives départementales)

BB1–BB9, délibérations communales, 1673–1790
CC14, account book of Jalaguié, 1702; *milliaire* for 1710
Unclassified, material on industries during period 1789–1815

Archives Municipales, Toulouse

HH 48, July 1640, acts relating to cloth trade

Archives Communales, Conques (held in mairie of Conques)

Etat civil of Conques (including Saptes), 1650–69

Bibliothèque Municipale, Montpellier

MS 48, 2 vol. memoirs of Ballainvilliers, 1788

Bibliothèque Municipale, Toulouse

MS 603, Description of province for d'Aguesseau, 1674

Archives Nationales

Série F12 (industry, pre-1789)
55, 58, 63, 65, 71, 74, 556, 557, 565, 642, 645, 676A, 842, 1378–82, 1384,

1387, procès-verbaux Bureau de Commerce and a variety of information on Languedoc's cloth industry, *c.* 1670–1789

Série G7 (diplomatic, pre-1789)
1684–5, consular correspondence from Levant, 1680s and 1690s

Bibliothèque Nationale

Fonds français
8037, General industrial survey of 1708
62431, Memoir from Levant, 1682

PRINTED SOURCES AND PRE-1800 PUBLICATIONS

Anonymous. *An Account of the Theater of War in France being a Geographical and Historical Description of Languedoc in General; and of the Lower Languedoc, and the Principality of Orange in Particular by a Native of Languedoc.* London, 1703
Arnould, A. M. *De la Balance du commerce et des relations extérieures de la France dans toutes les parties du globe.* 2 vols. Paris, 1791
Boislisle, A. M. de. *Correspondance des contrôleurs généraux avec les intendants.* 3 vols. Paris, 1864–97
Boulainvilliers, H. de. *Etat de la France.* 3 vols. London, 1727
Britannia Languens, or a Discourse of Trade (1680), in J. R. McCulloch (ed.), *Early English Tracts on Commerce.* Cambridge, 1964
chroniques du Languedoc, Les. 5 vols. Montpellier, 1875–9
Clément, P. *Lettres, instructions et mémoires de Colbert.* 7 vols. Paris, 1863
Depping, G. B. *Correspondance administrative sous le règne de Louis XIV.* 3 vols. Paris, 1852
Encyclopédie méthodique, Manufactures, arts et métiers, I. Paris, 1785
Expilly, J. *Dictionnaire géographique, historique et politique des Gaules et de la France.* 6 vols. Paris, 1762–70
Guiffrey, J. *Comptes des bâtiments du roi sous le règne de Louis XIV.* 2 vols. Paris, 1881
Lough, J. (ed.). *Locke's Travels in France, 1675–1679.* Cambridge, 1953
Mahul, M. *Cartulaire et archives des communes de l'ancien diocèse et de l'arrondissement administratif de Carcassonne.* 6 vols. Paris, 1857–71
Martin, E. *Cartulaire de la ville de Lodève.* Montpellier, 1900
Mandeville, B. *The Fable of the Bees.* Oxford, 1924
Partridge, W. *A Practical Treatise on Dying of Woollen, Cotton and Skein Silk with the Manufacture of Broadcloth and Cassimere including the most improved methods in the West of England.* 2nd edn. Pasold Research Fund, Edington, Wiltshire, 1973
règlemens des manufactures et teintures des étoffes qui se fabriquent dans le royaume, Les. Paris, 1701
Savary, J. *Le parfait négociant.* Paris, 1674
Savary des Bruslons, J. *Dictionnaire universel du commerce.* 3 vols. Paris, 1723
Smith, A. *The Wealth of Nations.* 2 vols. New Oxford edn, 1976
Smith, J. *Chronicon Rusticum-Commerciale; or Memoirs of Wool.* 2nd edn. 2 vols. London, 1757

Tour du Pin, Marquise de la. *Journal d'une femme de cinquante ans, 1778–1815*. 2 vols. Paris, 1913
Tucker, J. *Instructions for Travellers*. London, 1757
   Four Tracts, together with two sermons on political and commercial subjects. Gloucester, 1774
   A Brief Essay on the Advantages and Disadvantages which respectively attend France and Great Britain with regard to Trade with some Proposals for Removing the Principal Disadvantages of Great Britain. 2nd edn. London, 1750
Turgot, A. R. *Eloge de Vincent de Gournay* in P.-J. Vigreux (ed.), *Textes choisies de Turgot*. Paris, 1947
Voltaire. *Le siècle de Louis XIV*, 2 vols. Paris, 1929
Young, A. *Travels in France and Italy*. Everyman Edn. London, 1976

SECONDARY WORKS

Agulhon, M. *La sociabilité méridionale: confréries et associations dans la vie collective en Provence orientale à la fin du 18e siècle*. 2 vols. Aix-en-Provence, 1966
Alberge, C. 'Villeneuvette: une manufacture en Bas-Languedoc', *Etudes sur Pézenas et sa Région* I (1970)
Almanach des artisans du grenier poétique de Clermont-l'Hérault pour l'année 1843. Clermont-l'Hérault, 1843
Amiel, P. 'Clermont-l'Hérault pendant la Révolution'. Diplôme d'études supérieures, Montpellier, 1964
Appolis, E. *Un pays languedocien au milieu du dix-huitième siècle: le diocèse civil de Lodève*. Albi, 1951
   'Les seigneurs du diocèse de Lodève', *Cahiers d'histoire et d'archéologie*. Nîmes, 1947
Audiganne, A. *Les populations ouvrières et les industries de la France: études comparatives*. 2 vols. Paris, 1860
Aymard, M. 'Production, commerce et consommation des draps de laine du XIIe au XVIIe siècle', *Revue Historique* 499 (1971)
Baehrel, R. *Une croissance: La Basse-Provence rurale*. 2 vols. Paris, 1961
Bairoch, P. 'Agriculture and the Industrial Revolution, 1700–1914' in C. M. Cipolla (ed.), *The Fontana Economic History of Europe*, III. London, 1973
   Sous-développement et industrialisation. Paris, 1969
Ballot, C. *L'introduction du machinisme dans l'industrie française*. Paris, 1923
Barkhausen, M. 'Government control and free enterprise in Western Germany and the Low Countries in the eighteenth century' in P. Earle (ed.), *Essays in European Economic History, 1500–1800*. Oxford, 1974
Barral, P. *Considérations sur le régime municipal de Clermont-en-Lodévois aux XIIIe et XIVe siècles*. Montpellier, 1918
Baudrillart, H. *Les populations agricoles de la France: les populations du Midi*. Paris, 1893
Bergasse, L. *Histoire du commerce de Marseille*, IV, *De 1599 à 1660*. Paris, 1954
Bernet, G. 'Jean Giscard, marchand drapier toulousain sous Louis XIV', *A. du M*. 91 (1979)
Birkbeck, M. *Notes on a journey through France, from Dieppe through Paris and Lyons, to the Pyrenees, and back through Toulouse, in July, August and September, 1814, etc*. London, 1815

Blanqui, M. *Des classes ouvrières en France pendant l'année 1848.* Paris, 1849
Bobo, J.-P. 'Une communauté languedocienne au XVIIIᵉ siècle, Clermont-l'Hérault'. Diplôme d'études supérieures, Montpellier, 1965
Boissonnade P. *Colbert et le triomphe de l'étatisme.* Paris 1932
'Colbert, son système et les entreprises industrielles d'Etat en Languedoc: 1661–1683', *A. du M. 14* (1902)
'La production et le commerce des céréales, des vins et des eaux-de-vie en Languedoc dans la seconde moitié du XVIIᵉ siècle', *A. du M. 17* (1905)
'L'Etat, l'organisation et la crise de l'industrie languedocienne pendant les soixante premières années du XVIIᵉ siècle', *A. du M. 21* (1909)
Bondois, P. M. 'Etat de l'industrie textile en France d'après l'enquête du contrôleur général Desmaretz (début du XVIIIᵉ siècle)', *Bibliothèque de l'Ecole des Chartes* 114 (1943)
Braudel, F. *The Mediterranean and the Mediterranean World in the Age of Philip II.* 2nd edn. 2 vols. London, 1972
Civilisation matérielle, économie et capitalisme, XVᵉ–XVIIIᵉ siècle. 3 vols. Paris, 1979
'Histoire et sciences sociales: la longue durée' in his *Ecrits sur l'histoire.* Paris, 1977
Braudel, F., Jeannin, P., Meuvret, J. and Romano, R. 'Le déclin de Venise au XVIIᵉ siècle' in *Civiltà Veneziana* 9 (1963)
Braudel, F. and Labrousse, C. E. (eds). *Histoire économique et sociale de la France,* II, *1660 à 1789.* Paris, 1970
Braudel, F. and Spooner, F. 'Prices in Europe from 1450 to 1750' in E. E. Rich and C. H. Wilson (eds), *Cambridge Economic History of Europe,* IV. Cambridge, 1967
Brisson, C. 'Origines et développement de l'industrie drapière à Elbeuf et à Louviers', *Etudes Normandes* 13 (1952)
Carrière, C. *Les négociants marseillais au XVIIIᵉ siècle.* 2 vols. Institute Historique de Provence, 1973
'La draperie languedocienne dans la seconde moitié du XVIIᵉ siècle: contribution à l'étude de la conjoncture levantine' in *Conjoncture économique, structures sociales: hommage à Ernest Labrousse.* Paris, 1974
'Le travail des hommes (XVIIᵉ–XVIIIᵉ siècles)' in E. Baratier (ed.), *Histoire de Marseille.* Toulouse, 1973
Carrière, C. and Morineau, M. 'Draps du Languedoc et commerce du Levant au XVIIIᵉ siècle', *R.H.E.S.* 56 (1968)
Castel, E. 'Le château de Saptes. Etude anecdotique et descriptive', *Bulletin de la Société d'Etudes Scientifiques de l'Aude* 38 (1934)
Chambers, J. D. *Population, Economy and Society in Pre-Industrial England.* Oxford, 1972
Chapman, S. D. 'Industrial capital before the Industrial Revolution: an analysis of the assets of a thousand textile entrepeneurs, *c.* 1730–50' in N. B. Harte and K. G. Ponting (eds), *Textile History and Economic History.* Manchester, 1973
Chaunu, P. *La civilisation de l'Europe classique.* Paris, 1960
Chaunu, P and Gascon, R. (eds). *Histoire économique et sociale de la France,* I, pt. 1, *De 1450 à 1660: L'état et la ville.* Paris, 1977
Chaussinand-Nogaret, G. *Les financiers de Languedoc au XVIIIᵉ siècle.* Paris, 1970

Cilleuls, A. des. *Histoire et régime de la grande industrie en France aux XVIIe et XVIIIe siècles.* 2nd edn. New York, 1970

Cipolla, C. M. *Before the Industrial Revolution: European Society and Economy, 1000–1700.* London, 1976

Clément, P. *Histoire de la vie et de l'administration de Colbert.* Paris, 1846

Cole, C. W. *Colbert and a Century of French Mercantilism.* 2 vols. New York, 1939

Coleman, D. C. 'An innovation and its diffusion: the new draperies', *Ec.H.R.* 21 (1968)

Collier, R. and Billioud, J. *Histoire du commerce de Marseille,* III, *De 1480 à 1599.* Paris, 1951

Combarnous, G. 'Le développement topographique de Clermont-l'Hérault', *A. du M.* 72 (1960)

Combes, J. 'Les foires en Languedoc au moyen âge', *Annales* 13 (1958)

Coornaert, E. *Un centre industriel d'autrefois: la draperie sayetterie d'Hondschoote, XIVe–XVIIe siècles.* Paris, 1941

Les corporations en France avant 1789. Paris, 1941

'Les "manufactures" de Colbert', *Information Historique* 11 (1949)

'Une capitale de la laine: Leyde', *Annales* 1 (1946)

Courtecuisse, M. *La manufacture de draps fins Van Robais aux XVIIe et XVIIIe siècles.* Paris, 1920

Crafts, N. F. R. 'Industrial Revolution in England and France: some thoughts on the question "why was England first?"', *Ec.H.R.* 30 (1977)

Crémieux, A. *La vie politique et économique à Clermont.* Montpellier, 1949

Crouzet, F. 'Les origines du sous-développement économique du Sud-Ouest', *A. du M.* 71 (1959)

'Angleterre et France au XVIIIe siècle: essai d'analyse comparée de deux croissances économiques', *Annales* 21 (1966). Translated in R. M. Hartwell (ed.), *Causes of the Industrial Revolution.* London, 1967

'An annual index of French industrial production in the nineteenth century' in R. Cameron (ed.), *Essays in French Economic History.* American Economic Association, 1970

'Western Europe and Great Britain: "catching up" in the first half of the nineteenth century' in A. J. Youngson (ed.), *Economic Development in the Long Run.* London, 1972

Crouzet, F. (ed.). *Capital Formation in the Industrial Revolution.* London, 1972

Davis, R. 'England and the Mediterranean, 1570–1670' in F. J. Fisher (ed.), *Essays in the Economic and Social History of Tudor and Stuart England.* Cambridge, 1961

Aleppo and Devonshire Square. London, 1967

The Rise of the Atlantic Economies. London, 1973

Delouvrier, A. *Histoire de St Chinian-de-la-Corne et de ses environs.* Montpellier, 1896

Delumeau, J. *L'alun de Rome, XVe–XIXe siècles.* Paris, 1962

Dermigny, L. *Naissance et croissance d'un port: Sète de 1666 à 1880.* Sète, 1955

'De Montpellier à La Rochelle: route du commerce, route de la médecine au XVIIIe siècle', *A. du M.* 67 (1955)

'Une concurrence au port franc de Marseille: armement languedocien et trafic du Levant et de Barbarie', *Provence Historique* 5–6 (1955–6)

'Les foires de Pézenas et de Montagnac au XVIIIe siècle', *Congrès Régional de la Fédération Historique du Languedoc* 26 (1952)

Cargaisons indiennes, Solier et Cie (1781–93). 2 vols. Paris, 1960

Descimon, R. 'Structures d'un marché de draperie dans le Languedoc au milieu du XVIᵉ siècle', *Annales* 30 (1975)

De Vic, Dom. C. and Vaissète, Dom. J. *Histoire générale du Languedoc*. 14 vols. Toulouse, 1872–92. (Work completed by E. Roschach)

Deyon, P. *Le mercantilisme*. Paris, 1967

Etude sur la société urbaine au XVIIᵉ siècle: Amiens capitale provinciale. Paris, 1967

'Variations de la production textile aux XVIᵉ et XVIIᵉ siècles', *Annales* 18 (1963)

'La production manufacturière en France au XVIIᵉ siècle et ses problèmes', *XVIIᵉ Siècle* 70–1 (1966)

'La concurrence internationale des manufactures lainières aux XVIIᵉ et XVIIIᵉ siècles', *Annales* 27 (1972)

Dornic, F. *L'industrie textile dans la Maine et ses débouchés internationaux (1650–1815)*. Le Mans, 1955

Dugrand, R. *Villes et campagnes en Bas-Languedoc: le réseau urbain du Bas-Languedoc méditerranéen*. Paris, 1963

Durand, A. *Biographie clermontaise: histoire des hommes remarquables de la ville de Clermont-l'Hérault: sous le rapport des talens, des services et des vertus*. Montpellier, 1859

Annales de la ville de Clermont-l'Hérault et de ses environs depuis les premiers temps jusqu'à nos jours. Montpellier, 1867

Dutil, L. *L'état économique du Languedoc à la fin de l'Ancien-Régime*. Paris, 1911

Fisher, F. J. 'London's export trade in the seventeenth century', *Ec.H.R.* 3 (1950)

'Commercial trends in sixteenth century England', *Ec.H.R.* 10 (1939–40)

Flinn, M. W. *The Origins of the Industrial Revolution*. London, 1966

Fohlen, C. 'En Languedoc: vigne contre draperie', *Annales* 4 (1949)

Fontvieille, L. 'Les premières enquêtes industrielles de la France: 1692 et 1703', *Cahiers de l'I.S.E.A.* 3 (1969)

Freudenberger, H. *The Waldstein Woollen Mill: Noble Entrepreneurship in Eighteenth Century Bohemia*. Boston, 1963

'A case study of the Government's role in economic development in the eighteenth century: the Brno Fine-Cloth Factory' (Ph.D., University of Columbia, New York, 1957)

Gachon, P. *Quelques préliminaires de la révocation de l'édit de Nantes en Languedoc, 1661–1685*. Toulouse, 1899

Germain, A. *Histoire du commerce dé Montpellier antérieurement à l'ouverture du port de Cette*. 2 vols. Montpellier, 1861

Gide, C. *Cours d'économie politique*. Paris, 1909

Goubert, P. *Beauvais et le Beauvaisis de 1600 à 1730*. Paris, 1960

Granat, O. 'L'industrie de la draperie à Castres au dix-septième siècle et les "ordonnances" de Colbert', *A. du M.* 30 (1898)

Grassby, R. B. 'Social status and commercial enterprise under Louis XIV', *Ec.H.R.* 13 (1960–1)

Gruder, V. R. *The Royal Provincial Intendants: A Governing Elite in Eighteenth-Century France*. Ithaca, 1968

Habakkuk, H. J. 'The historical experience on the basic conditions of economic progress' in B. E. Supple (ed.), *The Experience of Economic Growth*. New York, 1963

Harris, J. R. *Industry and Technology in the Eighteenth Century: Britain and France.* Birmingham, 1972

'Skills, coal and British industry in the eighteenth century', *History* 61 (1976)

'Saint-Gobain and Ravenshead' in B. M. Ratcliffe (ed.), *Great Britain and her World, 1750–1914: Essays in Honour of W. O. Henderson.* Manchester, 1975

Heaton, H. *The Yorkshire Woollen and Worsted Industry from the Earliest Times to the Industrial Revolution.* Oxford, 1965

Heckscher, E. F. *Mercantilism.* 2 vols. London, 1935

Heyd, W. *Histoire du commerce de Levant au moyen âge.* 2 vols. Amsterdam, 1959

Hicks, J. R. *A Theory of Economic History.* Oxford, 1969

Hunt, L. A. 'Local élites at the end of the Old Régime: Troyes and Reims, 1780–89', *French Historical Studies* 9 (1976)

Jaupart, F. 'L'industrie drapière et le commerce des draps dans le diocèse de Carcassonne au XVIIIᵉ siècle', *Bulletin de la Société d'Etudes Scientifiques de l'Aude* 61 (1960)

Jones, C. D. H. 'Prostitution and the ruling class in eighteenth century Montpellier', *History Workshop: A Journal of Socialist Historians* 6 (1978)

'Poverty, vagrancy and society in the Montpellier region, 1740–1815' (Ph.D., University of Oxford, 1978)

Jones, E. L. 'Agricultural origins of industry', *P. & P.* 40 (1968)

'Environment, agriculture and industrialization in Europe', *Agricultural History* 51 (1977)

Jones, P. M. 'The rural bourgeoisie of the southern Massif-Central: a contribution to the study of the social structure of *ancien-régime* France', *Social History* 4 (1979)

Kaplow, J. *Elbeuf during the Revolutionary Period: History and Social Structure.* Baltimore, 1964

Kellenbenz, H. *The Rise of the European Economy: Economic History of Continental Europe, 1500–1750.* London, 1976

Kisch, H. 'Growth deterrents of a medieval heritage: the Aachen area woollen trades before 1790', *J.E.H.* 24 (1964)

Kocka, J. 'Entrepreneurs and managers in German industrialization' in P. Mathias and M. M. Postan (eds), *Cambridge Economic History of Europe,* VII, pt. 1. Cambridge, 1978

Koulischer, J. 'La grande industrie aux XVIIᵉ et XVIIIᵉ siècles: France, Allemagne et Russie', *Annales d'Histoire Economique et Sociale* 3 (1931)

Labrousse, C. E. *Esquisse du mouvement des prix et des revenus en France au XVIIIᵉ siècle.* 2 vols. Paris, 1932

La crise de l'économie française à la fin de l'ancien régime et au début de la révolution. Paris, 1944

Lafont, R. *Clefs pour l'Occitanie.* Paris, 1971

Landes, D. S. 'French entrepreneurship and industrial growth in the nineteenth century', *J.E.H.* 9 (1949)

The Unbound Prometheus. Cambridge, 1972

'Religion and enterprise: the case of the French textile industry' in E.C. Carter, R. Forster and J. N. Moody (eds), *Enterprise and Entrepreneurs in Nineteenth and Twentieth Century France.* Baltimore, 1976

Laurent, R. 'Propos sur l'histoire de Lodève', *Congrès Régional de la Fédération Historique du Languedoc* 36 (1963)

Lavergne, L. de. *Economie rurale de la France depuis 1789.* 3rd edn. Paris, 1866

Lavisse, E. *Histoire générale du IVe siècle à nos jours*, VII. Paris 1905
Lefebvre, G. 'The movement of prices and the origins of the French Revolution' in J. Kaplow (ed.), *New Perspectives on the French Revolution: Readings in Historical Sociology*. New York, 1975
Léon, P. 'La crise de l'économie française à la fin du règne de Louis XIV (1685–1715)', *Information Historique* 18 (1956)
Léon, P. (ed). *Papiers d'industriels et de commerçants lyonnais: Lyon et le grand commerce au XVIIIe siècle*. Lyons, undated
Le Roy Ladurie, E. *Les paysans de Languedoc*. 2 vols. Paris 1966
Histoire du Languedoc. 2nd edn. Paris, 1967
'L'histoire immobile', *Annales* 29 (1974)
'Les paysans français au XVIe siècle' in *Conjoncture économique, structures sociales: hommage à Ernest Labrousse*. Paris, 1974
'Family structures and inheritance customs in sixteenth century France' in J. Goody, J. Thirsk and E. P. Thompson (eds), *Family and Inheritance in Western Europe, 1700–1800*. Cambridge, 1976
Levasseur, E. *Histoire des classes ouvrières et de l'industrie en France avant 1789*. 2 vols. Paris, 1901
Lévy, C.-F. *Capitalistes et pouvoir au siècle des lumières*, II, *La révolution libérale*. Paris, 1979
Lévy-Leboyer, M. *Les banques européennes et l'industrialisation internationale dans la première moitié du XIXe siècle*. Paris, 1964
Lodge, E. C. *Sully, Colbert and Turgot, a Chapter in French Economic History*. New York, 1931
Lucas, C. 'Nobles, bourgeois and the origins of the French Revolution', *P. & P.* 60 (1973)
Mandrou, R. *Louis XIV en son temps, 1661–1715*. Paris, 1973
Mann, J. de L. *The Cloth Industry in the West of England from 1640 to 1880*. Oxford, 1971
Markovitch, T. J. 'L'industrie lainière à la fin du règne de Louis XIV et sous la Régence', *Cahiers de l'I.S.E.A.* 2 (1968)
'Le triple tricentenaire de Colbert: l'enquête, les règlements, les inspecteurs', *R.H.E.S.* 49 (1971)
Histoire des industries françaises, I, *Les industries lainières de Colbert à la Révolution*. Geneva, 1976
Martin, G. *La grande industrie en France sous le règne de Louis XIV*. Paris 1898
La grande industrie en France sous le règne de Louis XV. Paris 1900
Martin-St-Léon, E. *Histoire des corporations de métiers depuis leurs origines jusqu'à leur suppression en 1791*. Paris, 1922
Masson, P. *Histoire du commerce français dans le Levant au XVIIe siècle*. Paris, 1896
Histoire du commerce français dans le Levant au XVIIIe siècle. Paris, 1911
Mendels, F. F. 'Proto-industrialization: first stage of the industrialization process', *J.E.H.* 32 (1972)
Meuvret, J. 'Circulation monétaire et utilisation économique de la monnaie dans la France du XVIe et du XVIIe siècle', *Etudes d'Histoire Moderne et Contemporaine* 1 (1947)
'Agronomie et jardinage aux XVIe et XVIIe siècles' in *Eventail de l'histoire: hommage à Lucien Febvre*, II. Paris, 1953
'Les prix des céréales dans la France méditerranéenne au XVIIe siècle' in his

Etudes d'histoire économique. Paris, 1971

Milward, A. S. and Saul, S. B. *The Economic Development of Continental Europe,* *1780–1870.* London, 1973

Miskimin, H. A. *The Economy of Later Renaissance Europe, 1460–1600.* Cambridge, 1977

Moir, E. A. L. 'Gentlemen clothiers: a study of the organization of the Gloucestershire cloth industry, 1730–1835' in H.P.R. Finberg (ed.), *Gloucestershire Studies.* Leicester, 1957

Morineau, M. 'Marseille et Europe', *R.H.E.S.* 56 (1968)
  'Flottes de commerce et trafics français en Méditerranée au xviie siècle', *XVIIe siècle* 86–7 (1970)

Morineau, M. and Carrière, C. 'Draps de Languedoc et commerce du Levant au xviiie siècle', *R.H.E.S.* 56 (1968)

Mousnier, R. *Les hiérarchies sociales de 1450 à nos jours.* Paris, 1969

Nadal, J. *La población española.* 4th edn. Barcelona, 1976
  'Spain, 1830–1914' in C. M. Cipolla (ed.), *Fontana Economic History of Europe,* IV, pt. 2. London, 1973

O'Brien, P. and Keyder, C. *Economic Growth in Britain and France, 1780–1914: Two Paths to the Twentieth Century.* London, 1978

Paris, R. *Histoire du commerce de Marseille,* V, *De 1660 à 1789, le Levant.* Paris, 1957

Pirenne, H. 'The stages in the social history of capitalism', *American Historical Review* 19 (1914)

Pollard, S. *The Genesis of Modern Management.* Pelican edn. London, 1968

Port, C. *Essai sur l'histoire du commerce maritime de Narbonne.* Paris, 1854

Posthumus, N. W. *Inquiry into the History of Prices in Holland.* 2 vols. Leyden, 1946–65

Prégnon, Abbé. *Histoire du pays et de la ville de Sedan.* 3 vols. 1856

Priestley, M. 'Anglo-French trade and the unfavourable balance controversy, 1660–1685', *Ec.H.R.* 4 (1951–2)

Puech-Millau, M.-L. 'Un marchand castrais au xviie siècle d'après ses archives, Pierre Albert 1633–1708', *Revue du Tarn* 5 (1936)

Pullan, B. (ed.). *Crisis and Change in the Venetian Economy in the Sixteenth and Seventeenth Centuries.* London, 1968

Rambert, G. *Histoire du commerce de Marseille,* VI, *De 1660 à 1789, les colonies.* Paris, 1959
  Histoire du commerce de Marseille, VII, *De 1660 à 1789, l'Europe moins les trois péninsules méditerranées, les Etats-Unis.* Paris, 1966

Ramsay, G. D. *English Overseas Trade during the Centuries of Emergence.* London, 1957

Rapp, R. T. 'The unmaking of the Mediterranean trade hegemony: international trade rivalry and the commercial revolution', *J.E.H.* 35 (1975)

Rébuffat, F. and Courdurié, M. *Marseille et le négoce monétaire international (1785–90).* Marseilles, 1966

Reybaud, L. *La laine, nouvelle série des études sur le régime des manufactures.* Paris, 1867

Ringrose, D. R. 'Comments on papers by Reed, de Vries and Bean', *J.E.H.* 31 (1973)

Roehl, R. 'French industrialization: a reconsideration', *Explorations in Economic History* 12 (1976)

Roque, M. L. de la. *Armorial de la noblesse de Languedoc: généralité de Montpellier*. 2 vols. Montpellier, 1860
Rostow, W. W. *How It All Began*. London, 1975
Roure, C. 'La règlementation du commerce français au Levant sous l'ambassade du marquis de Villeneuve (1728–1741)' in J.-P. Filippini *et al*. (eds), *Dossiers sur le commerce français en Méditerranée*. Paris, 1976
Sagnac, P. *La formation de la société française moderne*. 2 vols. Paris, 1945–6
Saumade, G. 'Cambon et sa famille acquéreurs de biens nationaux, 1791 et 1793', *Annales Historiques de la Révolution Française* 16 (1939)
Sawyer, J. E. 'Strains in the social structure of modern France' in E. M. Earle (ed.), *Modern France, Problems of the Third and Fourth Republics*. Princeton, 1951
Sée, H. *Histoire économique de la France: le moyen âge et l'Ancien Régime*. 2 vols. Paris, 1939
Sella, D. *Crisis and Continuity: The Economy of Spanish Lombardy in the Seventeenth Century*. Cambridge, Massachussetts, 1979
'The rise and fall of the Venetian woollen industry' in B. Pullan (ed.), *Crisis and Change in the Venetian Economy in the Sixteenth and Seventeenth Centuries*. London, 1968
Sion, J. *La France méditerranéenne*. Paris, 1934
Soboul, A. *Les campagnes montpelliéraines à la fin de l'Ancien Régime*. Paris, 1938
Stendhal. *Mémoires d'un touriste*. Paris, 1953
Stone, L. 'Social mobility in England, 1500–1700', *P. & P.* 33 (1966)
Supple, B. E. *Commercial Crisis and Change in England, 1600–1642*. Cambridge, 1959
Svoronos, N.–G. *Le commerce de Salonique au XVIIIe siècle*. Paris, 1956
Teisserenc, F. *L'industrie lainière dans l'Hérault*. Montpellier, 1908
Teisseyre, L. 'L'industrie lainière à Nîmes au XVIIe siècle: crise conjoncturelle ou structurelle?', *A. du M.* 88 (1976)
Thirsk, J. 'Industries in the countryside' in F. J. Fisher (ed.), *Essays in the Economic and Social History of Tudor and Stuart England*. Cambridge, 1961
Thomas, L. J. *Montpellier, ville marchande*. Montpellier, 1908
Tirat, J.–Y. 'Circulation et commerce intérieur de la France au XVIIe siècle', *XVIIe Siècle* 70–1 (1966)
Trénard, L. *Lyon de l'Encyclopédie au préromantisme*. 2 vols. Paris, 1958
'The social crisis in Lyons on the eve of the French Revolution' in J. Kaplow (ed.), *New Perspectives on the French Revolution: Readings in Historical Sociology*. New York, 1975
Trouvé, Baron. *Description générale et statistique du département de l'Aude*. Paris, 1818
Vicens-Vives, J. *Manual de la historia economica de España*. 9th edn. Barcelona, 1972
Vilar, P. *La Catalogne dans l'Espagne moderne*. 3 vols. Paris, 1962
Or et monnaie dans l'histoire. Paris, 1974
Vries, J. de. *The Economy of Europe in an Age of Crisis, 1600–1750*. Cambridge, 1976
Wallerstein, I. *The Modern World-System: Capitalist Agriculture and the Origins of the European World-Economy in the Sixteenth Century*. New York, 1974
Weber, M. *Economy and Society* in H.H. Gerth and C. Wright Mills (eds), *From Max Weber: Essays in Sociology*. London, 1948

Weulersee, G. *Le mouvement physiocratique en France.* 2 vols. Paris, 1910

Wilson, C. H. 'The economic decline of the Netherlands', *Ec. H.R.* 9 (1939) 'Cloth production and international competition in the seventeenth century', *Ec.H.R.* 13 (1960)

Wilson R. G. 'The supremacy of the Yorkshire cloth industry in the eighteenth century' in N. B. Harte and K. G. Ponting (eds), *Textile History and Economic History: Essays in Honour of J. de L. Mann.* Manchester, 1973

Wolff, P. 'Esquisse d'une histoire de la draperie en Languedoc du XIIᵉ au début du XVIIIᵉ siècle' in *Produzione, commercio e consumo dei panni di lana. Atti della seconda settimana di studio (10–16 April 1970).* Florence, 1976

Wolff, P. (ed.). *Histoire du Languedoc.* Toulouse, 1967

Wood, A. C. *A History of the Levant Company.* Oxford, 1935

Wrigley, E. A. 'The process of modernization and the Industrial Revolution in England', *Journal of Interdisciplinary History* 3 (1972–3)

Zupko, R. E. *French Weights and Measures before the Revolution.* Indiana University Press, Bloomington, 1978

Index

(Names of Clermont-born have been italicized. Professional and geographical mobility have been signified as follows: Villet, Jean Roustan, merchant/clothier, Marseilles/Villenouvette/Clermont. The dioceses in which smaller villages and towns were situated have been indicated.)

Aachen, cloth production at, 451 n
Abbeville, 136, 173, 204
absolutism, 64
Agogné, Marie Louise Adélaïde, lady in waiting, Versailles, marriage of, 402
Agret, Guillaume, merchant, 66
agriculture: buildings for, 73–4; character- istics of small and large properties in, 73, 120; crises and turning-points in, 103, 219; fluctuations in, 7, 17–18, 72–3; growth in after industrial failure, 435, 436, 438, 439–40, 448; in Langue- doc, 21, 25–6, 46; peculiarities of in Mediterranean area, 43–4, 70; rating of land for tax, 70–1, 73; shortage of labour in because of industrial ex- pansion, 308–10; *see also* Clermont- de-Lodève, Lodève, Mediterranean economy
d'Aguesseau, Henri, intendant (1673–85), 103, 153, 216; arguments of about advantages of industry disproved, 439; correspondence of with Colbert, 156, 162, 163, 164, 170; intervenes at Estates to gain support for Colbertian schemes, 165–8, 177–8
Aigues-Mortes (Nîmes), 33
Albert (technical adviser on cloth indus- try), 332
Albi, 30, 31
Aleppo, 211, 250
Alès, diocese of, 200, 205, 240, 342
Alet, diocese of, 198, 199, 200, 238, 240
Allarde Law (1791), 442
Almeras, Guillaume, apprentice-clothier, Villenouvette, 192 n

Almes, Pierre, clothier, 109 n
Altayrac, Françoise, daughter of Jean, merchant, marriage of, 333
Altayrac, Jean, hat-maker, 291 n
Altayrac, Jean, merchant, Clermont/ Lyons/Clermont, 60 n, 63, 79, 265, 333; family links of, 290; finances cloth-making, 278; marriage of, 291 n property of attacked, 355; purchases mayoralty, 295
Altayrac, Marie, daughter of Jean, hat- maker, marriage of, 291
Altayrac, Marie, daughter of Jean, mer- chant, marriage of, 333
alum, 90–1
Amiens, 70, cloth industry at, 14, 92 n, 116, 126, 221, 243, 253, 452
Amsterdam, 118, 384
André (Carcassonnais clothier), 146
Angerly, Mathieu, merchant, Clermont/ Lyons, 60 n
Anterrieu, Jean, apprentice-clothier, Villenouvette, 192 n
Antwerp, 384
Appolis, Emile, historian, 40, 47, 73, 80, 90, 153, 333, 340
apprenticeship: fees, 96, 106–7, 116, 192, 205 n, 257, 279; function of, 197, 302, 361–2; labour migration and, 241, 260; life-style during, 59–64, 68, 194–5; numbers, and origins, of ap- prentices, 205–6, 220, 223–4, 230–1, 240, 242, 244
Archimbaud, Jean Baptiste, merchant, Lyons, 127
Archimbaud, Mathieu, merchant, Lyons, 63, 130

Printed in the United States
By Bookmasters